WHOSE BIRD?

Common Bird Names and the People They Commemorate

Bo Beolens
and
Michael Watkins

YALE UNIVERSITY PRESS
NEW HAVEN AND LONDON

PHOTOGRAPHIC CREDITS

Adan E. Treganza Anthropology Museum 20; Bridgeman Archive 210; The Condor (images reproduced with express permission of the Cooper Ornithological Society) 21, 35, 43, 44, 46, 49, 67, 111, 134, 140, 151, 184, 239, 244, 250, 250, 259, 268, 299, 322, 334, 348, 363, 373; Congregation de la Mission – the Vincentians, Paris 100; Cumming, Charles Atherton 255; Delaware Valley Ornithological Club 158; Diller, Dr Juliane 191; Florida State Museum 157; Graphics File, National Portrait Gallery, Smithsonian Institution, Washington DC 84; H. S. Gladstone collection 50, 91, 296, 313; Imaginario – Doctor Maria e Lourdes Beldi de Alcantara 356; Independence National Historical Park Collection, Philadelphia, Pennsylvania 85, 206; Library of Congress, Washington DC 61, 204, 226, 228, 292; Library of the Academy of Sciences of the U.S.S.R. 303; Library of the Natural History Museum, Tring 32, 35, 38, 41, 52, 57, 59. 63, 65, 69, 70, 78, 88, 92, 94, 96, 99, 131, 146, 159, 174, 198, 202, 205, 224, 238, 261, 287, 294, 297, 303, 305, 327, 332, 336, 357, 364, 369; Linnaean Society of London 66; Mearns, B. and R. 255; Mearns, Richard 315; Meinhertzhagen Esq., R.R. (courtesy of the Bodleian Library, Oxford) 230; Musée National du Chateau de Malmaison, Rueil-Malmaison 377; Museo Civico di Storia Naturale, Bra 93; Museum Heineanum, Halberstadt 161; National Botanic Gardens of Belgium 90; National Library of Australia 48; National Portrait Gallery, London 132, 164, 330; Olsen, Storrs L. 258; Ottenheimer Library Archives and Special Collections, University of Arkansas at Little Rock, Arkansas 227; Photographie Musée Pasteur 315; The Royal Entomological Society 342; Ruthven Deane Collection, Library of Congress, Washington DC 18, 328; Royal Society, London 298; Ruthven Deane Collection, Library of Congress, Washington DC 24, 65, 152; Smithsonian Institution 374; Snow Esq., David W 39; Staatlisches Museum fur Naturkunde, Stuttgart 44, 56, 56, 73, 74, 94, 116, 121, 128, 162, 172, 188, 190, 214, 261, 278, 280, 282, 283, 294, 301, 311, 311, 314, 327, 354; Tate, Peter 370; The Trustees of the Ilfracombe Museum 376; Theodor-Heuglin-Schule, Germany 166; Trustees of the National Library of Scotland, Edinburgh 276; Übersee-Museum, Bremen 127, 159; Università di Sassari, Sardinia 80; Università di Torino, Dipartimento di Biologia Animale 59; US Army Military History Institute, Carlisle Barracks, Pennsylvania 47

The publishers and authors have made every attempt to contact the copyright holders of the illustrations. In the few instances where they have been unsuccessful, they invite the copyright holders to contact them.

Cover illustration by Nik Borrow

Published 2003 in the United Kingdom by Christopher Helm, an imprint of A & C Black Publishers Ltd. and in the United States by Yale University Press.

ISBN 0-300-10359-X
Library of Congress Control Number: 2003113608

A catalogue record for this book is available from the British Library.

Paper produced with elemental chlorine-free pulp, harvested from managed sustainable forests.

The paper in this book meets the guidelines for permanence and durability of the Committee on Production Guidelines for Book Longevity of the Council on Library Resources.

Printed and bound in Great Britain by Cromwell Press Ltd, Trowbridge

Produced and designed by Fluke Art, Cornwall

10 9 8 7 6 5 4 3 2 1

FOREWORD
by
Ben Schott

Whose Bird? undertakes the impressive task of cataloguing those who have, in turn, catalogued the birds of the world. Yet while the scope and ambition of the book are almost Victorian, its style and humour are utterly modern. *Whose Bird?* will be as interesting and accessible to the general reader as to the serious ornithologist. (I should declare to the latter that I am one of the former.) Every bird's name tells a story, and the authors of *Whose Bird?* are story-tellers with a passion.

As T.S. Eliot might have said (had he not been so preoccupied with cats), 'the naming of birds is a difficult matter'. And he would have been right. As far as anyone can tell, few have died in the process of naming cats. In contrast, *Whose Bird?* identifies the staggering number of adventurous individuals who have died while naming birds. I won't spoil the fun which awaits within, but suffice to say if you can survive malaria, dysentery, shipwreck, 'accidental' shootings, oncoming trains, and hungry cannibals, then be sure to keep an eye out for the elephants.

At its heart, *Whose Bird?* is a book about remarkable people. Some, like Darwin or Livingstone, will be familiar to most. Others, like Gould or Cabanis, will be known to ornithologists and dedicated birders. The vast majority, I suspect, will be strangers to all of us. In a series of delightful vignettes we are introduced to a cast of intriguing characters: heroic adventurers, library-bound boffins, aristocratic patrons, mysterious lovers, fortunate schoolboys, respectable scientists, and caddish charlatans, to name but a few – each one of whom has achieved immortality through having a bird named after them.

In documenting the exploits of these characters *Whose Bird?* celebrates two eternal forces of human nature: the unquenchable thirst for knowledge, and the insatiable hunger for fame.

Ben Schott, May 2003

ACKNOWLEDGMENTS

Our particular thanks go to the following, all of whom have given us a great deal of help with bird names and their origins and with portraits of those commemorated: John McAllister of Wakkerstroom, Republic of South Africa, Owner Operator of "Beautiful Just Birding"; Ian Paulsen of Bainbridge Island, WA, American freelance wildlife biologist and Cofounder of the Washington (State) Ornithological Society; Paul Van Gasse of Kruibeke, Belgium; Manfred Warth, Archivist, Staatlisches Museum für Naturkunde, Stuttgart, Germany,

We would also like to thank the following institutions, which have been of great help – especially in filling the most recalcitrant gaps: Adan E. Treganza Anthropology Museum, San Francisco (Yoshiko Yamamoto); American Museum of Natural History, New York (Francois Vuilleumier, Curator Ornithology); American Ornithologists' Union (M. Ross Lein, Secretary); Archbold Biological Station, Lake Placid, Florida (Fred E Lohrer, Librarian); Artis Library, University of Amsterdam (Jaap De Visser & Jip Binsbergen); Bibliothèque centrale du Muséum national d'Histoire naturelle, Paris (Véronique Van de Ponseele, Service Iconographique); Biologiezentrum/Oberoesterreichisches Landesmuseum, Linz, Austria (Gerhard Aubrecht); British Natural History Museum (Peter Colston); California Academy of Sciences, San Francisco (Michele Wellck); Cambridge University Museum of Zoology (Anne Charlton); Canadian Museum of Nature, Ottawa (Chantal Dussault & Richard Martin); Carnegie Museum of Natural History, Pittsburg (Bernadette G Callery, Museum Librarian); Durban Natural Science Museum (David Allan, Curator of Birds); Estacao Biologia Marinham Ruschi, Brazil (André Ruschi); Field Museum of Natural History, Chicago (Thomas Schulenberg); Florida Museum of Natural History (Tom Webber); Institute of Geological and Nuclear Sciences Lower Hutt, New Zealand (Craig Jones, Fossil Collections Manager); Institute of Information Transmission Problems of the Russian Academy of Sciences, Russia (Dr Lev Rubanov); Liverpool Museum (Dr Malcolm Largen, Curator of Amphibians & Reptiles, Zoology Section); Museo Goeldi, Brazil (David C. Oren); Museum Heineanum, Halberstadt, Germany (Rüdiger Holz); National Botanic Gardens of Belgium (Raymond Clarysse, Librarian); National Museums of Kenya (Leon Bennun, Ornithology Department); Natural History Museum, Tring, UK (Dr Robert Prys-Jones, Head, Bird Group and Mrs Effie Warr, sometime ornithological curator); Northern State University, Aberdeen, South Dakota, USA (Professor Dan & Doctor Erika Tallman); Royal British Columbia Museum (Grant W. Hughes, Director, Curatorial Services Branch); Staatliches Naturhistorisches Museum Braunschweig, Braunschweig, Germany (S.Polel); Tanzania Bird Atlas (Liz & Neil Baker); Te Papa National Museum, Canterbury, New Zealand (Alan Tennyson, Ornithology Department); The Transvaal Museum, Pretoria, South Africa (Tamar Cassidy, Collection Manager); The Royal Society, London (Rupert Baker, Library Manager); Übersee Museum Bremen, Germany (Dr Peter-Rene Becker, Head of Department of Natural History); Western Australian Museum, Perth (Ron Johnstone, Curator, Ornithology); Zoological Institute & Museum, Hamburg, Germany (Cordula Bracker); Zoological Institute of the Russian Academy of Sciences, St Petersburg (Vadim Vysotsky, Department of Ornithology); Zoonomen (Alan Peterson).

We also wish to thank the following individuals for their invaluable help: Dr Peter Ballmann of Rösrath; Maria Butler; Stan Casto; Jonathan Stephenson Clarke; Luke Cole; Peter Colston; David Ervin Cummins; Casimir de Rham; Richard Dybowski; Karin Fricker; Joerg Froescher; Theodor-Heuglin-Schule; Dr Jack Grant-Mackie; John Hornbuckle; Christian Jouanin; Peter Kaestner; Adam Kent; Belinda McKay; Frank O'Connor; Malcolm Ogilvie; Narina Olliver; John O'Neill; Shaun Peters; Anthony Pittman; Storrs L. Olson; Robin K Panza; Kees Roselaar; Dr Paul Sabonadiere; Chris Sharpe; David Snow; Koen van Musschenbroek; Nicholas Watkins; Mrs Suzanne Watkins; Dr. Edwin O'Neill Willis; Alan Witherby; Dr F Zino.

Finally we would like to thank our editor Ernest Garcia, for his invaluable contribution, and Mike Unwin and Nigel Redman at A & C Black for steering the book to publication.

CONTENTS

INTRODUCTION

IN THE BEGINNING

The project that led to the compilation of this book started off as a bit of fun. It is worth telling just how it developed as an example of the terrible consequences which may arise from seemingly innocent beginnings.

Mike Watkins was the first of us to become curious and ask the question 'Whose bird?' He was intrigued by the number of birds named after people and had already compiled a list of about 150 when he put out an enquiry on UKBirdNet asking others for their contributions. He had some very useful responses from a number of different people, too numerous to mention individually. If you were one of them, please accept our most sincere thanks. One person who deserves a special mention is John McAllister, from Wakkerstroom (South Africa). He became very enthusiastic and came up with some quite comprehensive biographical details on some of the people behind the names as well as alternative (or more current) names for many of the birds.

Between them, Mike and John got the list up to about 1,000 entries and discussed what to do with it. Should they publish? Should they just put it up on the Internet? In the end they decided that it could be a good way to raise money for an organisation of which they are both members – the Disabled Birders Association (dba). Bo Crombet-Beolens (also known as the Fat Birder), who founded the dba, took a good look at the list and quickly turned the project from an amusing diversion into hard, but enjoyable, work. He suggested that we could publish it as a book, including not just the accumulated list but also biographical details of all those people mentioned – if it proved possible to find them. Furthermore, he suggested that we should research alternative names and illustrate the book with portraits of the people concerned. It was at this point that John decided to wish the project luck and withdraw, as his professional commitments meant he had not enough time. Mike and Bo then decided to go ahead themselves.

In the end, writing this book proved to be both a labour of love and extremely enlightening. We both learnt very much more about ornithology, as well amassing a lot of quite useless, but amusing, historical information; we are now fully qualified to enter 'Mastermind', or to be phoned as a friend on 'Who wants to be a Millionaire' (as long as we negotiate a share of the prize money in advance!). We had absolutely no idea how many individuals and birds we would eventually find. It seems that birding has always attracted eccentrics, and we have unearthed some fascinating accounts of the individual ornithologists, collectors and characters – some unconnected with birds – after whom birds have been named. Many are, of course, already very well known and we have simply summarised their biographies. Others are more obscure and in many cases only the sketchiest information was available. We greatly welcome hearing of any additions, corrections and further anecdotes about the people in this book. We regret the lack of even some very basic information such as dates of birth etc. and would be grateful for the supply of such information. Who knows, someday we may even get a second edition published! Meanwhile, we hope you have as much fun using it as we had writing it and, like us, learn from it too.

WHO IS IT FOR?

It occurred to us that birders often come across bird names that include a person (such names are properly called 'eponyms'), and their curiosity will be aroused just as ours was. You will know of some of these birds in your home area. You are certain to come across others on a foreign trip or whilst reading the books we birders seem to accumulate in such great numbers. You may even hear of a familiar bird given an unfamiliar person's name and want to know why. If so, then this book is for you. We hope that it will help satisfy your curiosity and answer your questions. Serious listers may even find that this book offers a new opportunity for a specialised worldwide list! However, you will never be able to see all of the birds mentioned here as, unfortunately, a number of them are as dead as the Dodo. Nevertheless, we included these extinct birds since illustrations of some of them exist and you might well find references to them in birding literature.

HOW TO USE THIS BOOK

This book is arranged alphabetically by names of people. Generally, the easiest way to find your bird is to look it up under the name of the person that is apparently embedded in the bird's common name. We say 'apparently', as things are not always as simple as they seem: in some bird names, for example, the apostrophe implying ownership is a transcription error; other birds' names may have been named after places and not people. We have included any names where we think confusion might arise, but do not promise to have been completely comprehensive in that respect. You should also beware of spelling. Surf the net and you may well find birds' names spelt in a number of different ways. We have tried to include entries on those alternatives, if we have ourselves come across them.

Each biography follows a standard format: first, you will find the name of the person honoured; next, there follows a list of birds named after that person, arranged in alphabetical order of English names. (This list gives eponymous English names, scientific names, names of the people who first described each species and the date of the original descriptions – in that sequence. Alternative English names follow in parentheses and are each preceded by the abbreviation Alt.); finally, there is a brief biography of that individual.

To assist you in your search, we have cross-referenced the entries by highlighting (in bold) the names of those who also appear elsewhere in the book. Some birds are named in different ways after the same person and we have also tried to marry these up using cross-references. So, for example, a species named after Queen Victoria might be called Queen Victoria's Bird or Victoria's Bird, or Queen's Bird or even Empress's Bird. Interestingly, this is most often the case where aristocratic titles are concerned. For example, the Earl of Derby, whose family name is Stanley, has birds named after him in at least three different ways.

We have provided an appendix of scientific names at the back. These often provided the only way in which we could cross-reference the various personal names which had, at various times, been given to the same bird. For example, if you look up *Lagopus mutus* in the appendix, you will find that the Rock Ptarmigan has at various times been named after 10 different people! The example of this particular species is discussed in more detail below.

Whilst we have done our best to make the information in this book accurate, we also want it to be an enjoyable read. During the writing of this book we were struck by certain similarities often shared by the individuals concerned; for example, the fact that so many were medical men, or that some have died in the strangest of circumstances. For your information and amusement we have analysed and collated some of these facts. You can read about them in the next chapter, 'How to get a bird named after you', and in a series of text boxes scattered throughout the book.

WHAT'S IN A NAME?

Tracking down the provenance of eponymous bird names, and finding out about the individuals responsible for them, proved to be fraught with difficulties. Our final list contains 2,368 entries. However, this may be misleading, since these entries actually cover only 2,246 birds. The names honour 1,124 individual people, but there are also 47 which sound like people's names but in fact are not, a few 'Gould only' entries (see below on these points), two which are almost certainly misspellings of Cabanis, two where we cannot decide whether they refer to a person or a place, and one which is almost certainly a wrong initial recorded by Gould – thus causing confusion with a well-established name (Louis Fraser). There are also five birds for which we have not been able to find scientific names. We wonder if they really exist, or ever existed, but they are included in case we discover the scientific name in the future or in the event that evidence one way or the other regarding their existence turns up. Most annoying of all, there are entries for eight people whom we have been unable to identify at all!

Describers and namers

New species are first brought to the notice of the scientific community in a formal, published description of a type specimen, essentially a dead example of the species which will eventually be lodged in a scientific collection. The person who describes the species will give it its scientific name, usually in Latin but sometimes in latinised ancient Greek! Sometimes the 'new' bird is later reclassified and then the scientific name may be changed. This frequently applies to generic names (the first part of a binomial name), but specific scientific names (the second part of a binomial name), once proposed, usually cannot be amended or replaced – there are precise and complicated rules governing any such name changes. Conventionally, a changed name is indicated by putting parentheses around the describer's name. For example, the Grey Heron was named *Ardea cinerea* by Linnaeus in 1758 and, since that name remains recognised to this day, the bird is officially named *Ardea cinerea* Linnaeus 1758. Linnaeus also described the Great Bittern as *Ardea stellaris* in the same year. However, Bitterns have since been awarded their own genus and we now officially call the bird *Botaurus stellaris* (Linnaeus 1758), the brackets showing that the name was not the namer's original choice. The scientific names used in this book are largely those in current use (we may have missed a few recently published taxonomic changes), but we have put the name of the original describer in parentheses after every entry; hence the normal convention regarding such brackets does NOT apply here.

Although we have used current scientific names as far as possible, these are not always as universal as the casual birder might suppose. In addition to some birds having been reclassified since they were first discovered and described, there are other cases where various authorities and text books do not agree on which name to use – this invariably applies to generic names, where there may be disagreement on a bird's taxonomic affinities.

There are no agreed conventions for English names and indeed the choice of vernacular names is often controversial. Very often the person who coined the scientific name will also have given it a vernacular name, which may not be an English name if the describer was not himself or herself an English-speaker. On the other hand, vernacular names – including English ones – have often been added afterwards, frequently by people other than the describers. In this book, therefore, when we refer to a bird having been NAMED by someone, we mean that that person gave it the ENGLISH name in question. We refer to someone as a DESCRIBER when they were responsible for the original description of the species and hence for its scientific or 'Latin' name. As we have said above, it is the describer's name which is given after the scientific name in the biographies.

The problem of John Gould and Richard Bowdler Sharpe

We came across a real problem in deciding whether some of the more puzzling birds on the list were purely imaginary inventions or genuine mistakes. For example, we know of several hummingbirds and waders which turned out to be hybrids and not new species. Gould published a considerable corpus of plates and, after his death, Sharpe put out many more, some of which were of images that Gould had either not published or not even finished. We suspect that either or both of these gentlemen may well have been deceived on occasion by skins they examined, especially if the specimen was in poor condition or incomplete. Modern scientific techniques now allow much more precise comparisons.

A good example of this problem was revealed by our efforts to identify the Conrad of Conrad's Inca. Gould calls the bird *Bourceria conradi*. Bourcier described a bird in 1847 that he named *Trochilus conradii*. He bought this bird from Parzudaki who collected it near Caracas. The bird was processed by Leadbeater (the taxidermist) and was part of the Loddiges Collection of hummingbirds and allies. Gould named another bird, Parzudaki's Starfrontlet, after Parzudaki. Unfortunately Parzudaki's first name was not Conrad and Gould seems to have stuck with the binomial (*conradii*) given to it by Bourcier, not noting, and possibly not even knowing, the identity of Conrad. We are no closer to having a definitive answer – as you will see in the entry.

Alas, it is very hard to discover how much Sharpe altered Gould's nomenclature when he took over Gould's work after the latter's death. Whatever happened is lost in the mists of time so any conjecture that Sharpe might have been tempted to make some embellishments to such a lucrative series of prints would be pure speculation. We are certain that a few of Gould's specimens were unique hybrids and not new species, as he believed. In similar vein, not every bird named by Lesson existed, both because he is known to have had a vivid imagination and because he is rumoured to have put bits of skins together to create 'new' birds.

As much of Gould's and Sharpe's work is undoubtedly perfectly valid, we have not eliminated anything we considered (however remotely) to be dubious as, again, you may come across reproductions of the plates or references to them elsewhere. We have, however, put an asterisk against the names of those species about which we have any serious doubts.

Birds named after peoples' titles

A number of birds are named in such a way that it would be very hard to find the relevant biography without a note against the name. An example of this is Rajah's Scops Owl (*Otus brookii*). Next to the name Rajah's Scops Owl in brackets you will see (v. Brooke). This directs you to the entry for Brooke, as this bird is named after Sir Charles Brooke, second Rajah of Sarawak. His uncle was Sir James Brooke, better known to history as the first 'White Rajah of Sarawak'.

Birds named after more than one person

Throughout the text you may come across several different names for the same species. In some cases these names are honorifics; for example, Dixon's Rock Ptarmigan is the same species as Reinhardt's Rock Ptarmigan. This peculiarity has sometimes come about through simple mistakes or misunderstandings – such as believing juveniles or females to be a different species from the adult male. In some cases, the same bird was found at about the same time in two different places and only later has it emerged that this is the same bird named twice. A good example is Cabanis's Tiger-Heron, which Heine named *Tigrisoma cabanisi* in 1859. It later emerged that Swainson had already named this bird *Tigrisoma mexicanum* – *the* scientific name by which it is now known – in 1834. Some of these duplications persist even today, with the same bird being called something different in different places or by different people.

The problem with trinomials

In some cases we found it impossible to deal with the problem of subspecies in a simple and clear manner. We therefore originally decided only to show the scientific binomials and list the various races by common name. Later we decided to add trinomials wherever possible and only the synonyms for the general species. However, where we could not track down the trinomial, the bird in question has a lot of entries under 'syn' – some of which will also be honorifics. For example, Montin originally described the Rock Ptarmigan (*Lagopus mutus*) in 1781. Its races (or supposed races or separate species) have been variously named after the following people: Chamberlain, Dixon, Eversmann, Nelson, Reinhardt, Sanford, Townsend, Turner, Kellogg and Welch. Not all of these are still regarded as distinct races and some may be clines or even aberrations. You will appreciate what we were up against!

We do not claim to have found all of the many named subspecies of birds – far from it! But if you are interested to see how many eponymous names have been given to the various forms of a particular species in the past (for example, see Rock Ptarmigan above), the Appendix of Scientific Names will guide you to them.

Unidentified persons

Unfortunately we have not been able to identify everyone whose name appears in that of a bird. There are, as we observed above, eight names on our list which are just not traceable. For example, who was the Lerch of Lerch's Sapphire (*Timolia lerchii*) and Lerch's Woodnymph (*Thalurania lerchi*)? Some Victorians seem to have had the sentimental notion of naming birds after female relatives or mistresses. In some cases we know the author has named the bird after a woman, but he has deliberately (gallantly?) withheld her full name; for example, Harry Church Oberholser did not identify the Alma he had in mind for Alma's Thrush (*Catharus ustulatus*). Such individuals clearly had no regard for those of us doing this kind of research!

Male or female?

In some cases we know that a bird is named after a man, even though its scientific name is in the feminine. This only seems to occur when a name ends in the letter 'a'. Presumably, the reason for this is that singular Latin nouns ending in 'a' are feminine – for example, 'mensa' means 'table' (nothing very feminine about that), and the possessive/genitive case is 'mensae', not 'mensai'. Thus the convention is that the feminine form is adopted in such cases. For example, Costa's Hummingbird is named after Louis Marie Panteleon Costa, Marquis de Beau-Regard, but the scientific name is *Calypte costae*. There are exceptions, to prove the rule. For instance, two birds named after Cervera (a wren and a rail) both have the binomial *cerverai*.

Red herrings

Further confusion arises from a number of birds which appear to be named after people, but – upon closer examination – turn out to be named after a place, such as an island, that was itself named after a person. We have included these with an appropriate note, as other sources of reference will not necessarily help the enquirer.

Interestingly this volume contains a couple of examples where, because the common local name has been incorrectly assumed to be a person, a misleading possessive apostrophe has been added.

Weighing the evidence

Ultimately, our decisions on what to include in this book depended upon the weight of available evidence. Wherever there is any doubt, we have made this clear. In some cases we have had to reject a possible attribution when the evidence is just too slim. For example, we might have attributed 'Buckley's Forest Falcon' to a man who was quite unusual and famous in his day.

> William Buckley (1780-1856). *Transported to Australia in 1802 for his part in a conspiracy to shoot the Duke of Kent. Escaped from Port Phillip penal colony and lived with the Aborigines for 32 years. Pardoned and employed by the authorities as an interpreter. Later settled in Tasmania where he died. Life of him by J. Morgan 1852.*

However the bird in question is South American and we could not imagine why anyone would name it after a man whose fame was associated with another continent! So we decided it would have to be left unassigned, which proved just as well since we finally identified the real Buckley.

HOW TO GET A BIRD NAMED AFTER YOU

Whilst the people after whom birds have been named are as unique and diverse as the birds themselves, it is also clear that certain people are more likely than others to achieve this honour. This chapter suggests who you need to be and what route you ought to follow if you wish to chart your own course towards scientific immortality.

DISCOVERY

In some ways it is relatively easy to get your name – or at least a Latinised version of it – into a scientific binomial. If you go out and discover a new bird, the person who writes its scientific description may well offer you that honour. Picking this person yourself will, of course, give you an added advantage. Discovering a new bird is also a very good way to get your name into its vernacular name. Go out into the depths of a neotropical forest and find a new antwren and it will be hard not to call it 'Your Antwren' – as well as having *youri* (or *yourae* if you are female) as the second part of its binomial name.

In the field

If you are willing to brave the wettest, hottest, steepest and thorniest wilderness, climb unscaled peaks, cast yourself away on remote atolls, risk frostbite in the frozen wastes or heatstroke in the desert dunes – and do all this for years on end – then you are in with a shout. En route you must shoot at least one of any type of bird you see, strip out the perishable parts, tie a label around its leg, then pack it with hundreds of its fellows into watertight trunks and send them all back home to the most well known birdman of your day. Your nationality will determine to whom you send your specimens. Those most generous to their 'collectors' – i.e., those most likely to name trophies after them – were Audubon in the United States, Gould in Britain, Bonaparte in France and so on.

Do not be fooled into thinking that discoverers and collectors of specimens were all motivated by a desire to expand scientific knowledge. Some were part of imperialist expansion and others were driven by economics. A great many collectors were there to make money by selling their specimens to rich amateur naturalists. Some even collected to create stuffed specimens or tableaux for the salons of Europe. Although many of these became very knowledgeable in their own right, they were also men of their times who collected dead birds in the way we might take photographs today. The worst excesses were motivated by the feather trade and many birds that were unknown to science became known only because their beautiful plumage had been collected to adorn the fashionable. Some of these desecrators of nature are honoured in the names of birds.

In a collection

Discovery, of course, is not always confined to the great outdoors. It is equally possible to find new birds amongst the skins in private or museum collections. Look through these annals and you will find a good number of ornithologists who hardly ever went abroad but are still celebrated in a common name because of their forensic skills back home. 'Discovery', in their case, meant realising that some former scientist had overlooked a subtle difference between specimens, or that some underling had put the wrong labels on them.

So, spending ten years up to your neck in leeches or assailed by malarial mosquitoes is not the only way to achieve your ambition. Many of our fellows have suffered nothing worse than bookworms while sorting through bird skins in musty museums. Their chances usually came courtesy of a collector who had been a little short-sighted or, at least, tired of the formaldehyde fumes and biting insects while cataloguing his collection in the gloom of a rainforest hammock. Dismissing his specimen as just another Smith's Ant-Bunting, this weary collector may have missed the subtle curve of the upper mandible and the almost imperceptible extension of the supercilium back from the eye. Years later, back in the museum, the triumphant scientist waves the bird aloft and writes up his detailed paper describing it as a new species. His motivation may be the noble desire to add to the sum of human knowledge, but his fingers are also crossed for glory. Will someone's DNA study show that there is not only Smith's Ant-Bunting but, in recognition of his meticulous library work, also a Watkins' Ant-Bunting? (Beware: even the cosy cocoon of academia has its dangers; at least one of the people named in this book died as a result of over-exposure to their secret preservative ingredient – arsenic!)

These days it need not be a full species either. Races of birds have often been distinguished by the discoverer's name being embodied in the last part of a trinomial name. So should you discover the dark race of the Forest Antwren, it is possible that the trinomial tag *youri* will be added to distinguish it from any other race. At some stage, birdwatchers as well as ornithologists may start using this tag to refer to the race they are seeing. Rather than calling it 'the Forest Antwren of the race *youri*', they are far more likely to use the simpler "Your Forest Antwren". Should a split occur, this common name is likely to stick and your trinomial tag may rise from bronze to silver medal position. Some people have even made it all the way to the top of the rostrum – gaining a gold medal when the scientific community decides that the bird actually represents a separate genus or family.

In the fossil record

Long-extinct birds are more likely to go through the reclassification process far more often than their extant fellows. There are clearly many more extinct species awaiting 'discovery', but you have to guess what their plumage might have looked like; fossil bones cannot help with this. So get out and start searching for fossils if you are desperate for immortality.

IDENTITY

So, you have decided that discovering a new bird is your best bet of achieving immortality – your name forever embodied in a species' name. But what sort of a person do you need to be to make it?

Victorians

The first answer to the above question is: 'a dead one'. Today, we have all rather missed the boat, since the heyday for such discovery has passed. It is not impossible to find new birds in the field nowadays; several have already been discovered in this millennium. However, the great leap forward took place around 150 years ago. Until the middle of the eighteenth century most well known birds had a variety of vernacular names. There are entire books written on the alternative regional names of, for example, birds that are found in Great Britain. One man's 'Windhover' was another man's 'Windkisser', and another's 'Cresshawk'. One of the earliest nomenclatural endeavours was to standardise these names whilst sorting out their place in systematic order. Although the scientific binomial naming system created by Linnaeus would have contained honorifics, very, very few common names did. Where common names were concerned, the use of one name in written accounts gave that name ascendancy over all other names. Hence the 'Windhover' became the Kestrel for the rest of time – until it got its prefix of 'Common' Kestrel to distinguish it from other kestrels.

However, as the scientists and travellers of the western world expanded their areas of study, a great number of new species were discovered by individuals which were named by them and after them. By the middle of the nineteenth century, countless expeditions intent on discovery had been sent to the far corners of the world. Hundreds of men (and they mostly were males) discovered thousands of undescribed species and took them back to museums and universities for cataloguing and formal scientific description. So it was the scientists and explorers of the Victorian era who managed the route to immortality more than most.

A similar but truncated process occurred as the United States expanded. The first settlers often based their names for local species on the birds of their country of origin.

The American Robin was so named purely because its red chest reminded people of the robin redbreast of England. Some local names were adopted and very familiar birds were named for characteristics such as mimicry (mockingbird), behaviour (sapsucker) or calls (whippoorwill). As the interior was explored and more new species became known, many were named for their discoverers, expedition leaders or sponsors.

Westerners

Being Victorian was not enough in itself. You really had to belong to a rich and imperial nation. Of the list of names of people whose nationality we have been able to discover, only 42 nationalities are represented. Of these, only seven nations have more than 20 people embodied in birds' common names: Britain, the United States and four other European countries. In total, 331 Britons, 201 Americans, 161 French, 137 Germans, 45 Dutch, 29 Italians and 21 Australians are celebrated, which perfectly reflects the balance of power in the world at the time. In the second division are 16 Russians, 16 New Zealanders, 15 Swedes, 14 Austrians, and 12 South Africans. Indeed, the nationality of those who have discovered birds consistently reflects those nations that were economically strongest at any moment in history. So, if you want to become immortalised in this way it helps to be born in the right place at the right time. Incidentally, it might seem unsurprising that the majority of the eponymous English names should come from Britain and America – the major English-speaking countries. However, the fact is that it was people from these countries who discovered the most birds in the first place. That is why so many of them are honoured in the species' vernacular and scientific names.

Scientists and gentlemen

Being born at the right time and in the right place was crucial in the naming of many birds. But success also seems to require money and a good scientific education. Of course, education was rare amongst the poor, while the better-off and educated often had no need to work for a living, and were free to pursue their whims and interests. The Victorians explored and collected like no-one else before or since. In the course of both exploring and obtaining specimens, many new species were collected and catalogued. A great number of these people were qualified zoologists, botanists and medical men. Indeed, medicine was one of the best routes into our lists for those with less than independent wealth. The practice of medicine not only opened scientific doors, but could also earn you a decent living and create valuable leisure time. Many medical men were amateur naturalists and some travelled the world with the military or as members of exploration teams where they were the most scientifically-trained people present when discoveries were made. On voyages of discovery the medical officer was usually responsible for overseeing the collection of specimens of flora and fauna.

So, it seems that the best way to have a bird named after you is to discover it. You would be best placed to achieve this as a Victorian British gentleman with leisure time to spend in quiet study or world exploration, or a Victorian British doctor – either devoting your spare time to natural history or taking paid employment as a ship's surgeon.

DESCRIPTION

Actually discovering a bird for yourself might be the best route to secure an eponym but it is not the only one. Many men have got there by describing or studying the discoveries of others. For a new species to be recognised by the scientific community, two things have to happen: firstly a specimen has to be collected; secondly it must be described. In most countries, that description must be published in a recognised scientific journal to have credence.

While some discoverers and collectors have written-up their own type descriptions, it is more usual for new specimens to be sent to a museum scientist for verification and formal description. Therefore, the number of people writing descriptions of new species was much smaller than those who were actually finding them. When a bottleneck of pending descriptions built up, those who relieved it often managed to get their own names ascribed to the scientific names of the species in question. If 40 people send 60 specimens to three scientists, it is highly likely that these scientists may also end up honoured in the common names. If their reputations live on, and their contemporaries did not honour them, history may.

OTHER PATHS TO GLORY

Fame and power

You may, at this point, be giving up on the idea of having a bird named after you. Perhaps you are allergic to mosquito spray and book dust and cannot see your way along any of these routes to glory. *Courage mon brave*! There is another route that requires neither field skills nor scientific slog: just marry into royalty! Those of noble birth or high social standing often do well in the bird-naming stakes without knowing (or even caring) a blind thing about feathered dinosaurs. Given that discoverers often waved the flags of their respective imperial powers, being the embodiment of the state would not harm your cause: many common names honour the Kings, Queens, Emperors, heroes and leaders of powerful nations. Your chances will be further enhanced by having a flamboyant personality or leading a colourful life.

Alternatively, if you are a famous scientist, particularly a zoologist or ornithologist admired by subsequent generations, then you stand a good chance of having a bird named after you in recognition of that heritage. If you taught the discoverer or your academic works influenced him, then you might well find yourself commemorated in the name of one of his discoveries.

Money and influence

You may not even need fame or fortune. Money may suffice: just enough to subsidise the likes of John James Audubon when he is down on his luck. If you have plenty of cash, then you could invest in an expedition or two: a number of people who have paid for collecting trips or supported individual scientists have been commemorated by their protégés. (Would-be sponsors may wish to have a quiet word beforehand to ensure that they achieve immortality basking in the glory of, say, John Doe's Pitta, rather than the ignominy of John Doe's tapeworm or dung beetle.) A few, like Rothschild, combined patronage with scientific endeavour of their own. Others, like Lady Amherst, kept live collections, zoos or museums of the results of such expeditions. The Rothschild model is a great example of multiple routes being best. He was a rich and famous aristocrat, a brilliant scientist and collector and a patron of many other fine scientists and artists. This man seemed to cover all bases!

If you cannot marry a prince, or be born into wealth and leisure, marry an ornithologist or try to be the fruit of one's loins. A number of the people appearing in this book were the wives, lovers, sons or daughters of the discoverer or describer of the species. Even being a servant can get you into the book. However, this route may well confine your fame to your forename only and leave posterity asking "Muriel who?". If you are an ambitious junior museum curator working under a great man of science, then marrying the boss's daughter can also be a good idea – you wouldn't be the first!

Being the sibling or parent of an ornithologist is not always as good as it might seem. Many who appear to have been honoured in this way have actually been used by their relative to get his own name in through the back door. It is strictly off-limits to name a bird after yourself – Mr John P Smith cannot decently call that bird 'Smith's Lark' after himself – but what's wrong with honouring his wonderful father or deserving older brother who just happen to share his surname? Sneaky, huh?

Bird qualities

It can also help to be famed for certain qualities that birds share. If you had a beautiful voice or were famed for flight or colour then you enhanced your chance of having birds named after you. A number of figures have been celebrated because the bird named after them is thought to share their qualities. In this respect it helps to be a deity, like Horus.

Picking the right birds

Certain bird families have more than their fair share of eponymous tags – the humming-birds *Trochilidae* and antbirds *Thamnophilidae* are the front-runners. These are very large families, which have resulted from the large-scale speciation that is a feature of the multiple ecological niches offered by tropical habitats. Furthermore, many of these species live close enough to each other for one explorer to have found several of them, and so to have increased the chances of his name becoming permanently associated with at least one of them. It is undoubtedly significant that the names-rich families are concentrated in remote tropical regions – parts of the world which had to be 'discovered' by European and American explorers. The avifaunas of these regions represented enormous pools of species just waiting to be named – a situation quite different from that in Europe, especially, where birds' vernacular names evolved in tandem with the local culture. The message is clear: make a close study of which places and families have been most productive. Forget trying to discover a new ibisbill or plains wanderer; stick to hummers and the like! A word of caution too: make sure that 'your' new bird is a genuine species. Getting your name associated with a sport or hybrid will mean the ignominy of having it consigned to history's trash heap instead of gracing the pages of the *Handbook of the Birds of the World*!

Forgery and theft

As in life generally, not everyone pursues their ambition along the moral high ground. Some people have stolen specimens, forged records of discovery or stolen other people's hard work by publishing first. A number of people have got away with this in their lifetimes but they are generally discovered and discredited later. However, being unmasked and discredited does not necessarily result in being expunged from the records: their names are still being used to this day and immortality is theirs. Whilst those who make a study of these things will know the cheats for what they were, most people will just see the name and not know the story behind it. This could therefore be a promising route for those without ethical qualms. Furthermore, to be discredited you have to be found out. Who knows, there may well be other charlatans still lurking undiscovered in these very pages.

Back-scratching

Another less than morally-upright route available is via the ornithological cartel. A coterie of scientists may well make deals amongst themselves, so aspiring birdmen should perhaps consider joining such a cabal. Mike says to Bo "That's a nice looking new weaver you've got there. Who are you going to name it after? By the way, as we are such old friends and colleagues, I was thinking of naming this entirely new lark after you." Bo replies "Thanks for the honour", and "You might be surprised by this, but I thought of naming the weaver after you!"

WHAT'S LEFT?

The tried and tested routes of the past are, for the most part, no longer open to any of us. Extinctions probably now outstrip discoveries and only a few people are able to find new species. The routes to discovery through field, fossil record or collection still exist, but very few new species are now being discovered. Of these, even fewer are likely to result in a common name embodying your own. These days, species tend to be named for their characteristics rather than their discoverer.

There will inevitably be some growth in the number of bird subspecies elevated to full-species status, and where the trinomial (race name) is named after a person it is more than likely that some of these will result in a common name honour. However, a great many of these scientific race names are already in place, and your chances of discovering a new subspecies are diminishing rapidly. The terrific growth in DNA study has resulted in a number of new species and subspecies being named. Indeed the whole avian family tree is increasingly being challenged and it is conceivable that this will produce a few new names. Perhaps, therefore, the DNA route is today's best bet for anyone aiming for nomenclatural immortality.

There is one other possibility: newly discovered species may now be offered for auction, with the scientific name going to the highest bidder and the money going to conservation to help secure the bird's threatened habitat. In one case the successful individual bought the specific scientific name only. However, it is not inconceivable that eponymous English names may also be on sale at some time in the future. In previous eras, it was 'expected' that wealthy sponsors of expeditions would be commemorated. Perhaps in the future we may dispense with such coy pretence and simply buy the right on the open market to have a new species named after us.

ABBOT

Abbot's Tanager *Thraupis abbas* (Deppe 1830)
(Alt. Yellow-winged Tanager)

Possibly named to honour J Abbot (1751–1840), an American philologist, according to Jobling. However, we favour Abbot Lawrence (1792–1855), a merchant, manufacturer, diplomat, statesman and philanthropist who may have had some links with the Deppe brothers, including Wilhelm Deppe who first described the Tanager. Abbot Lawrence supported the natural sciences in general and the work of Louis Agassiz in particular. Abbot Lawrence could easily have met or known about Ferdinand Deppe (1794–1861), Wilhelm Deppe's younger brother, who collected for the Museum of Berlin in Mexico from 1824 to 1827 with Count von Sack (who trained Deppe in the preparation of skins) and William Bullock. From 1828 to 1829 Ferdinand Deppe returned to Mexico with a botanist friend and collected still more botanical and zoological specimens, as well as native artefacts. He collected a little in California and also in Hawaii, on his journey home in 1830. Ferdinand Deppe was also an artist and gardener; he has a rose named after him, he discovered a species of begonia in Mexico and he is honoured in several plant names such as *Euphorbia deppeana*. The majority of his bird specimens was studied and catalogued by **Lichtenstein**, although very poorly and with little acknowledgement of Deppe. Most of Deppe's collections were only studied much later by the likes of **Cabanis**, Johann **Wagler** (1828), John **Gould** (1833, 1843), **Brehm** (1851), **Bonaparte** (1850), **Reichenbach**, **Schlegel** and P L **Sclater** (1868), all of whom studied some of Deppe's Mexican birds when they visited Berlin and who published descriptions of new species. Wilhelm Deppe was the accountant of the Zoological department at the Berlin Museum and first described the tanager in 1830, although he did no more than copy Lichtenstein's notes and it was Lichtenstein who assigned the name in 1928.

ABBOTT, W

Abbott's [Jungle] Babbler *Malacocincla abbotti* (**Blyth** 1957)
Abbott's Booby *Papasula (Sula) abbotti* (**Ridgway** 1893)
Abbott's Cuckoo-shrike *Coracina abbotti* (Riley 1918)
(Alt. Pygmy/Celebes Cuckoo-shrike, Celebes Mountain Greybird)
Abbott's Lesser Sulphur-crested Cockatoo *Cacatua sulphurea abbotti*
(**Oberholser** 1917)
Abbott's Starling *Cinnyricinclus femoralis* (Richmond 1897)

Dr William Louis Abbott (1860–1936) was a student, naturalist and collector. He studied the wildlife of the Indo-Malayan region, using his Singapore-based ship *Terrapin*, and made large collections of mammals from central and southeast Asia for the National Museum of Natural History (Smithsonian) in Washington D.C. He provided much of the Kenya material in the Smithsonian and was the author of *Ethnological Collections in the United States National Museum from Kilima-Njaro, East Africa* in their report of 1890/91. Sims described the babbler from a specimen taken in 1927.

ABDIM

Abdim's Stork *Ciconia abdimii* (**Lichtenstein** 1823)
(Alt. White-bellied Stork)

Bey El-Arnaut Abdim (1780–1827) was a Turkish governor of Dongola in Sudan from 1821 until 1827. He was of great assistance to **Rüppell** on his North African expedition. The type specimen of the stork was collected in the Sudan in 1823.

ABEILLE

Abeille's Grosbeak *Hesperiphona abeillei* (**Lesson**)
(Alt. Hooded Grosbeak)
Abeille's Hummingbird *Abeillia abeillei* (Lesson & **Delattre** 1839)
(Alt. Emerald-chinned Hummingbird)
Abeille's Oriole *Icterus galbula abeillei* (Lesson 1839)
(Syn.Baltimore/Northern Oriole)

Monsieur Abeille and his wife Felice were French naturalists and collectors. The subspecies of Baltimore Oriole was originally considered a full species. There is an illustration by **Gould** of a hummingbird called Abeille's Flutterer *Myiabeillia typica* which appears nowhere else and is possibly the same bird as Abeille's Hummingbird. We have no direct proof that the flutterer was named for either or both of them but it seems very likely. **Bonaparte** named a genus of hummingbirds *Abeillia* in 1850. Monsieur Abeille may have been Paul Emmanuel Abeille de Perrin (1798–1868), who we think was the father of Elzear Emmanuel Arene Abeille de Perrin (1843–1910), an entomologist of great standing who described many insects, in particular beetles.

ABERT

Abert's Towhee *Pipilo aberti* (**Baird** 1852)

James William Abert (1820–1897) was a Major in the United States Army and an ornithologist. He graduated from Princeton University in 1838 and entered the United States Military Academy at West Point that year. He transferred to the Corps of Topographical Engineers in 1843. In 1845 he was with Frémont's third expedition whose assignment was '*to make reconnaissance southward and eastward along the Canadian River through the country of Kiowa and Comanche*'. Frémont, however, chose to take his main party on to California and gave command of the Canadian River mission to Abert. The expedition followed the headwaters of the Canadian through the breaks in eastern New Mexico and into the Texas Panhandle. In his report Abert described in detail the geology, flora and fauna of the Canadian Valley and mapped the area. In 1846 he accompanied General Kearny's Army of the West to New Mexico while continuing his studies of natural science. Afterwards he visited each of the Rio Grande pueblos and he then went to Washington to submit his report to Congress. In the Civil War he served in the Shenandoah Valley from 1861 to 1862. In 1863 he was promoted to major and assigned to the United States Army Corps of Engineers. He was later severely injured by a fall from his horse, which led to his resignation from the army in 1864. He taught English literature at the University of Missouri from 1877 to 1879. Despite their value, his western frontier journals lay almost forgotten in government files until 1941, when Carroll first published the 1845 report in the Panhandle-Plains Historical Review. Keleher published Abert's New Mexico report in 1962. In 1967 and 1970 John Galvin, a Californian historian, edited special publications of the journals under the title *Through the Country of the Comanche Indians in 1845*. They featured illustrations of Abert's watercolours, many of which were obtained from his descendants. Abert also collected birds for **Baird**, including the towhee which Baird named after him.

ADALBERT

Adalbert's Eagle *Aquila adalberti* (**Brehm** 1861)
(Alt. Spanish Imperial Eagle)

Admiral Prince Heinrich Wilhelm Adalbert of Prussia (1811–1873) was a great traveller. He kept a diary of his *Royal Expedition to the Amazon, Maranhão, Recife, and Bahia 1842 & 1843*. This he published privately; only 100 copies were printed for distribution to his friends. Later Adalbert was closely associated with Bismarck and Raeder in the development of the Imperial German Navy and of land-based artillery. Both Adalbert and **Brehm**, who described the eagle, were Masons and so may well have been friends.

ADAMS

Adams' Snowfinch *Montifringilla adamsi* (Adams 1859)
(Alt. Tibetan/Black-winged Snowfinch)

Andrew Leith Adams (1826–1882) was a physician, naturalist and geologist. He served as an army surgeon in India around 1848 with the 22nd Foot (Cheshire Regiment). He wrote an influential report on the cholera epidemic in Malta, where the regiment was stationed at the time, in about 1865. Adams became an academic after retiring from the army, being variously Professor of Zoology at the Royal College of Science in Ireland and Professor of Natural History at Trinity College, Dublin. He published *Wanderings of a Naturalist in India, the Western Himalaya and Cashmere* in 1867 and *Notes of a Naturalist in the Nile Valley and Malta* in 1871. Adams himself wrote the snowfinch description in 1859 and accidentally named it after himself by making reference in print to a previously un-published description by Frederick Moore of the East India Company's London Museum.

ADELA

Adela's Hillstar *Oreotrochilus adelae* (**Gould**)*
(Alt. Wedge-tailed Hillstar *Oreotrochilus adela*)

Only in Gould do we find this common and scientific name. It is so similar to *Oreotrochilus adela* (Wedge-tailed Hillstar) that we think Gould may just have made a mistake in the spelling and so *adelae* was assumed to be named after a woman when in fact it is just a description of the plain colour of the bird!

ADELAIDE

Adelaide's Warbler *Dendroica adelaidae adelaidae* (**Baird** 1865)

Adelaide Swift was the daughter of Robert Swift, an American financier who was patron of a number of collecting trips and obtained the first specimen of the warbler. He collected for the Smithsonian in Puerto Rico, the type locality, in 1865 during a visit there with George Latimer. Three closely related island forms are now regarded as separate species: Adelaide's Warbler of Puerta Rico; St Lucia Warbler (*D. delicata*) and Barbuda Warbler (*D. subita*).

ADELBERT

Adelbert's Bowerbird *Sericulus bakeri* (**Chapin** 1929)
(Alt. Baker's/Beck's/Fire-maned/Macloud Bowerbird)

The bowerbird is confined to the Adelbert Mountains in New Guinea and so it is most likely to have been named for the area rather than directly after a man. We believe that the mountains were named after Adelbert von Chamisso (1781–1838), who is also known as Louis Charles Adelaide de Chamisso. Chamisso was the botanist aboard the *Rurik*, captained by Otto Von **Kotzabue**, which explored the South Seas from 1816 until 1823. The crew also conducted the first-ever hydrographical, botanical, and ethnological studies on the nearby Marshall Islands. He kept a diary, *Reise um die Welt mit der Romanzoffischen Entdeckungs-Expedition* (1836; 'Voyage Around the World with the Romanzov Discovery Expedition'), which became a classic of its kind. Adelbert von Chamisso was a German poet and naturalist, who was born in France at the Château de Boncourt. He served as a page at the court of William II of Prussia and, after army service and travels, he became keeper of the Royal Botanical Gardens. He edited the *Musenalmanach* between 1804 and 1806. His sentimental poetic cycle *Frauenliebe und Leben* (1830) was set to music by Schumann. *Peter Schlemihls wundersame Geschichte* (1814), his tale of a man who sold his shadow to the devil, has become legendary. He also wrote plays, an account of his travels in the Pacific (1836) and a work on linguistics (1837). Chamisso was also a noted scientist, involved in the discovery of the metagenesis of certain molluscs, and a philologist known for his studies of Australasian languages.

ADÉLIE

Adélie Penguin *Pygoscelis adeliae* (Hombron & Jacquinot 1841)

Adélie Dumont d'Urville (1798–1842) was the wife of Admiral Jules-Sebastien-César **Dumont d'Urville** the French explorer, who first found the penguin. He also named the Adélie coast of Antarctica after her. Various other places in and around Antarctica, where he explored in the *Astrolabe* in the mid-1820s, are named after him as well. The New Zealand islands, the Noises, are named following his remark about their shape. "*Voilà*," exclaimed d'Urville when he first saw the clumpy little group of islands. "*C'est noisettes*" (which is French for lamb chops!)

ADOLPH

Adolph's Hermit *Phaethornis (longeumareus) adolphi* (**Gould** 1857)
(Alt. Little Hermit)

Probably named for Adolphe **Barrot** (1801–1870), a French diplomat in Colombia, after whom **Bourcier** named a hummingbird. **Gould** described Adolph's Hermit from a specimen collected by Auguste Sallé in Cordova, Mexico but he used the name given by Bourcier, to whom the skin had originally been sent. Alternatively, the bird could conceivably have been named for Adolph(e) **De Lattre** who, together with his brother Henri, was a French collector and naturalist. De Lattre worked in Mexico from 1838 to 1843 and in Colombia in 1847. He first described a related species, the Long-tailed Hermit *Phaethornis superciliosus*, in 1843 in Mexico. Adolph's Hermit may have been an individual of a subspecies of the Little Hermit *P. longuemareus adolphi*.

ADOLPHINA

Adolphina's Myzomela *Myzomela adolphinae* (**Salvadori** 1876)
(Alt. Mountain/Elfin Myzomela, Mountain Red-headed Honeyeater)

Adolfina Bruijn was the wife of J Bruijn the Dutch botanist, explorer, and zoologist, according to Jobling. However, Salvadori described birds supplied by A A **Bruijn** and we can find nothing on a 'J' Bruijn. It could be that he was the brother of A A Bruijn but this is pure speculation. Our opinion is that this New Guinea endemic was named after A A Bruijn's wife, who would have been **Duyvenbode**'s daughter, but we can find no direct evidence for either.

AHARONI

Aharoni's Eagle Owl *Bubo bubo interpositus* (**Rothschild** & **Hartert** 1910)

Dr Israel Aharoni was born in Lithuania. He was professor of zoology at the University of Jerusalem in the 1930s and later a professor in the United States. According to one source, Israel Aharoni was a colourful character. '*He was born in Widzi on the Russian/ Polish border and then educated in Prague. He is known as the first Hebrew zoologist because he rediscovered or at least assigned Hebrew names to the animals of the Holy Land. At the time of his early life and expeditions in Jerusalem the region was still under the strict rule of the Turks. Aharoni, a Jew, in a Moslem world was only able to travel freely under the protection of the local Turkish Sultan and he received this because he obtained specimens for the Sultan's butterfly collection. On these collecting trips he appears to have collected just about every animal he came across, always assisted by local guides; the initial preparation of the specimens was done in the field and then they were sent to Berlin.*' He is most famous for finding the Golden Hamster *Mesocricetus auratus* in Syria, a mother with a litter. He kept them as pets and later took their progeny to the United States where they became the ancestors of all pet hamsters around the world. No specimens have since been found in the wild. He published his memoirs, *Memories of a Hebrew Zoologist*, in 1943. These had previously appeared in Hebrew. In 1930 he wrote *Die Saeugetiere Palaestinas Zeit Saeugetierk* and in 1932 *Die Muriden von Palaestina und Syrien* with his wife (B Aharoni) who seems to have assisted him in his work. He also contributed to the recent project to produce an *Atlas of the Breeding Birds of Arabia*. His fauna collection, including stuffed birds, is still preserved in a church museum in the Old City of Jerusalem as they are animals described in the Bible. Whilst we cannot link the owl directly to him, or find any other biographical information on either of the Aharonis, we do know that the owl is a resident of Syria.

AIKEN

Aiken's Screech Owl *Otus kennicottii aikeni* (**Brewster** 1891)
(Alt. Western Screech Owl)

Charles Edward Howard Aiken (1850–1936) was born in Vermont. He went to Colorado Springs in 1871 to his father's ranch in Turkey Creek. There he began to study and collect birds. He wrote descriptions of the nests of the Western Scrub-jay *Aphelocoma californica* and Virginia's Warbler *Vermivora virginiae*. In 1872 his work was edited by Dr Thomas M **Brewer** and published in the proceedings of the Boston Society of Natural History. For example, in 1875 a description of a nest of the Grey-headed Junco *Junco (hyemalis) caniceps* found by Aiken was published. In 1874 Aiken opened a taxidermy shop. Much of his time was spent in pursuit of birds. Aiken was described as a man of keen hearing and sight. He could recognise notes and imitate them by whistling. He also had a sharp eye for plumage. He identified a smaller, darker-marked race of the screech owl which was later named for him. Aiken also secured the first specimen known to science of the White-winged Junco *Junco (hyemalis) aikeni*. These two birds reflect Aiken's name in their scientific names, not so much for his contribution to ornithology but because he paid for the skins. In 1907 Colorado College purchased Aiken's collection of 4,700 specimens. Many items had already been sent to the Smithsonian. Other specimens were continually turned over to the college as he mounted them. Aiken joined the American Ornithologists' Union in 1898 and was made an Honorary Life Associate in 1926. Western Screech Owls live in Western North America and have at least eight subspecies. A number, including the one above, are named after people.

ALBERT

Prince Albert's Curassow *Crax alberti* (**Fraser** 1852)
(Alt. Blue-billed/Blue-knobbed/Colombian Curassow)
Albert's Lyrebird *Menura alberti* (**Bonaparte** 1850)
(Alt. Prince Albert's Lyrebird)
Prince Albert's Riflebird *Craspedophora alberti* (Gould)

Prince Albert, the Prince Consort (1819–1861), husband of Queen Victoria. Albert was a keen innovator, seeker of knowledge and interested in all of the sciences. Hence, although the birds were named in his honour, this may not have been purely an acknowledgement of his social standing. The riflebird is a **Gould** illustration and is, we feel, a confusion between two species, Victoria's Riflebird *Ptiloris victoriae* described by Gould in 1849 and D'Alberti's Bird-of-Paradise *Drepanornis albertisi* described by P L **Sclater** in 1883.

ALEXANDER, B

Alexander's Akalat *Sheppardia poensis* (Alexander 1903)
Alexander's Swift *Apus alexandri* (**Hartert** 1901)

Captain Boyd Alexander (1873–1910) was an African traveller and ornithologist. He was educated at Radley College from 1887 until 1891, joined the army in 1893 and was at Kumasi in 1900. Alexander studied birdlife in West Africa. He explored Lake Chad from 1904 until 1905 and made a geographical survey of West Africa between 1905 and 1906. He spent some time on the island of Fernando Pó (now Bioko) and many of the birds which he described have *poensis* in their binomial, referring to that island. He was a Royal Geographical Society medallist in 1908. He continued his African explorations from 1908 until 1910, when he was murdered by local people in Kenya. He published *From the Niger to the Nile* in two volumes in 1907. **Hartert** named the swift in his honour.

ALEXANDER, W

Alexander's Ptarmigan *Lagopus lagopus alexandrae* (**Grinnell** 1909)
(Alt. Willow Ptarmigan)

Wilfred Backhouse Alexander (1885–1965) was an English zoologist. He was educated at the University of Cambridge and became Assistant Superintendent of the Cambridge Museum of Zoology in 1910, also acting at this time as an Assistant Demonstrator in Zoology and Comparative Anatomy. He was an Assistant Naturalist to the Board of Agriculture and Fisheries in 1911. He then left for Australia, where he was Assistant at the Western Australian Museum from 1912 until 1915. He accompanied Professor W J Dakin on the first Percy Sladen Trust Expedition to the Abrolhos Islands in November 1913. During the British Association for the Advancement of Science meeting in 1914 he travelled throughout Australia on the presidential train. He was Keeper of Biology at the Western Australian Museum from 1915 until 1920 and was seconded to the Council for Scientific and Industrial Research (CSIR) as science abstractor between 1916 and 1919. He was biologist at the Commonwealth Prickly Pear Board in Brisbane from 1920 until 1924 and officer-in-charge from 1924 until 1925. He edited *The Emu* between 1924 and 1925. He then worked at the American Museum of Natural History in 1926, writing his best-known work *Birds of the Ocean,* which was first published in New York in 1928. This work is generally recognised to be the first ornithological field guide. Alexander was superintendent of the Tees Estuary survey from 1929 to 1930. He became director of the Oxford Bird Census (later to be constituted as the Edward Grey Institute of Field Ornithology, the EGI) in 1930 and stayed on until 1945. He then became librarian at the EGI from 1945 for 10 years. The Alexander Library at the EGI was named after him in 1947. He was elected as a Corresponding Fellow of the American Ornithologists' Union in 1921 and as a Fellow of the Royal Australasian Ornithologists' Union in 1939. He was awarded the Tucker Medal of the British Trust for Ornithology in 1955 and the Union Medal of the British Ornithologists' Union in 1959. The bird may have been named for him or his wife Annie Montague Alexander (1867–1950)

ALEXANDRA

Alexandra's Parrot *Polytelis alexandrae* (**Gould** 1863)
(Alt. Queen Alexandra's Parrot)

Alexandra, Princess of Wales, later Queen Alexandra (1844–1925). The parrot was named in 1863 by John **Gould** to celebrate the marriage of Alexandra to Edward VII. Considered by many to be one of the most exquisitely coloured and well-proportioned of all birds, the Alexandra's Parrot or Princess Parrot (Parakeet) was described by Baldwin Spencer as the most fitting of the Australian birds to bear the name of this illustrious lady. Alexandra's Parrot is a rare and elusive inhabitant of the desert regions of inland Australia.

ALEXANDRE

Alexandre's Hummingbird *Archilochus alexandri* (**Boucier** & **Mulsant** 1846)
(Alt. Black-chinned Hummingbird)

Dr M Alexandre discovered the species in the Sierra Madre of Mexico and sent it to Mexico City. He was a practising physician who also collected zoological specimens and sent them back to France.

ALFARO

Alfaro's Hummingbird *Saucerottia alfaroana* (Underwood 1896) [Extinct]

Anastasio (González) Alfaro (1865–1951) was a Costa Rican zoologist who was educated at the University of Santo Tomás. He was Director of the National Museum of Costa Rica.

ALICE

Alice's Emerald *Chlorostilbon alice* (**Bourcier** & **Mulsant** 1848)
(Alt. Green-tailed Emerald)

We can find no source for the name and it is odd that the scientific name is just 'Alice', and is not in anyway Latinised.

ALLEN, C

Allen's Hummingbird *Selasphorus sasin* (**Lesson** 1829)

Charles Andrew Allen (1841–1930) was a collector and taxidermist, who was born and raised in Massachusetts and later moved to California. After serving in the Union Army during the Civil War he returned home and worked at various jobs, including taxidermy. At one time he worked on fishing boats out of Newfoundland to learn more about the Atlantic seabirds. The heavily wooded hills are still just across the road from Allen's old homestead in California. It was somewhere near here that Allen shot the small birds

which he sent east to William **Brewster** with a note saying that they seemed to be a new species. He was also the inventor of the *Allen Hummer,* a birdcall device and was an authority on bird lore. Allen could hardly be called an ornithologist but he had not had much opportunity for education. He was not a student but an excellent collector, who became well versed in the habits of the birds and other animals with which he came in contact. Many years later Allen's account of the hummingbird which was named for him appeared in **Bent**'s *Life Histories Of North American Birds.* Brewster, C Hart **Merriam** and Major Charles **Bendire** (of thrasher fame) were among the many eastern-based scientists who bought bird and mammal skins from this Californian collector. Allen obtained the hummingbird in 1877 for **Henshaw**, who named it for him in appreciation. Ornithologists later determined that the bird had been discovered almost 50 years earlier by **Lesson** but the common name was retained.

ALLEN, REAR-ADMIRAL W

>Allen's Gallinule *Porphyrio alleni* (Thomson 1842)

Rear-Admiral William Allen (1793–1864) was an English naval officer who was involved in fighting the African slave trade. He led three expeditions to Africa; two in 1832 and, in 1841, to the Niger. Allen collected the type specimen at Idda, near the River Niger.

ALLEN, W

>Allen's Ptarmigan *Lagopus lagopus alleni* (**Stejneger** 1884)
>(Alt. Willow Ptarmigan)

William Allen (1770–1843) was a British Quaker, scientist and philanthropist. He entered Bevan's chemical establishment at Plough Court and carried on the business himself from 1795. He was made a fellow of the Linnean Society in 1801 and a Fellow of the Royal Society in 1807. He became a lecturer at Guy's Hospital from 1802 until 1826. Allen was an active opponent of slavery and an intimate of Clarkson, Wilberforce and James Mill, and also of Elizabeth Fry, the famous prison reformer.

ALMA

>Alma's Thrush *Catharus ustulatus almae* (**Oberholser** 1898)
>(Alt. Swainson's Thrush)

Harry Church **Oberholser** (1870–1963) wrote *Birds of Mt. Kilimanjaro* in 1905, *Birds of the Anamba Islands* in 1917 and *The Bird Life of Louisiana* in 1938. *The Bird Life of Texas* was published 11 years after his death. Oberholser did not identify the Alma he chose to honour in describing the subspecies, and we are not aware that her identity has ever been made known.

AMIES

>Amies' Penguin *Platydyptes amiesi* (**Oliver** 1931) [Extinct]

A C Amies (?–1949) was a student at Otago University, New Zealand when he found the first bone of this penguin in 1946. He was later a member of the Geological Survey of Malaya. He was killed on 25 July 1949 whilst travelling by river in Malaya, when communist guerrillas ambushed his boat. **Marples** named the extinct penguin after him.

ANABEL

Anabel's Bluebird *Sialia mexicanus anabelae* (Anthony 1889)
(Alt. Western San Pedro Bluebird)

Anabel Klinck Anthony (1867–1949) was the wife of Alfred Webster **Anthony** (1865–1939), who first described this distinct race of the Western Bluebird and named it after her.

ANCHIETA

Anchieta's Barbet *Stactolaema anchietae* (**Bocage** 1869)
Anchieta's Sunbird *Anthreptes anchietae* (Bocage 1878)
(Alt. Red-and-blue Sunbird)
Anchieta's Tchagra *Tchagra minuta anchietae* (Bocage 1870)
(Alt. Marsh Tchagra)

José de Anchieta (?–1897) was an independent Portuguese naturalist and collector in Africa, in particular in Angola and Mozambique. He collected many types of mammals and reptiles. A bat, a cobra, a chameleon, a python and a frog, among others, all share the vernacular name 'Anchieta's'.

ANDERSON

Anderson's Bamboo Partridge *Bambusicola fytchii* (Anderson 1869)
(Alt. Mountain Bamboo Partridge)
Anderson's Bulbul *Pycnonotus xanthorrhous andersoni* (Anderson 1871)
(Alt. Brown-breasted Bulbul)

John Anderson (1833–1900) was a qualified physician who became Professor of Comparative Anatomy at the Medical School in Calcutta and Director of the Indian Museum in Calcutta in 1865. In 1868 he joined an expedition to Burma and Yunnan in southwest China as naturalist. A second expedition in 1875 only collected in Burma. He wrote a zoological account of the two expeditions; the section on birds covers 233 species. R Bowdler **Sharpe** gave assistance in the report's preparation by verifying the identifications. He also wrote monographs of two whale genera. Anderson was elected a Fellow of the Royal Society in 1879.

ANDRÉ

André's Swift *Chaetura andrei* (**Berlepsch** & **Hartert** 1902)
(Alt. Ashy-tailed Swift)

Eugène André (1861–1922) was a French writer and naturalist. He collected in Venezuela between 1897 and 1900. He may have been in Trinidad around 1915. His book, *A Naturalist in the Guianas*, was published in 1904 in New York.

ANDREWS

Andrew's Frigatebird *Fregata andrewsi* (**Mathews** 1914)
(Alt. Christmas Frigatebird)

Dr C W Andrews (1866–1924) was a British geologist. He was very interested in dinosaurs and between 1895 and 1922 he published many articles on dinosaur fossils in the *Geological Magazine* and other publications. The fossilised remains of an ancestral cormorant from the Upper Cretaceous of Transylvania have been named *Elopteryx andrewsi* in his honour. He collected on Christmas Island between 1897 and 1908, when employed by the British Museum and whilst commissioned by the Christmas Island Phosphate Company to survey the natural history of the Islands. He was the first person to collect **Abbott**'s Booby *Sula abbotti* there. He wrote *A Monograph of Christmas Island (Indian Ocean)* in 1900.

ANDROMEDA

Andromeda Thrush *Zoothera andromedae* (**Temminck** 1826)
(Alt. Sunda/Ground Thrush)

Andromeda, in Greek mythology, was the daughter of Cepheus and Cassiopeia.

ANGELA

Angela Starthroat *Heliomaster angelae*
(Alt. Blue-tufted Starthroat *H.furcifer* [Shaw 1812])

Angela Kay Kepler is Australian born but a New Zealander by naturalisation. She is married to the American biologist Cameron B Kepler. The two often write together, both being specialists on Hawaii and its birds and flora. She wrote a *Comparative Study of Todies (Todidae), with Emphasis on the Puerto Rican Tody, Todus mexicanus* in 1977 and has also written guidebooks about Hawaii. The Elfin Woods Warbler *Dendroica angelae* is named after her in the binomial.

ANGELINA

Angelina's Scops Owl *Otus angelinae* (**Finsch** 1912)
(Alt. Javan Scops Owl)

Angeline Bartels was the wife of the author and zoologist Max Bartels, whose many works included *Medizin der Naturvölker, Urgeschichte der Medizin* in 1893 and *Das weib in der natur- und völkerkund: anthropologische studien* in 1905. Max Bartels worked in Java from the 1900s to the 1920s. Finsch spent a year on the Marshall Islands and Dr Otto Bartels was a government doctor there. We can only speculate on their relationships, if any.

ANNA D'ESSLING

Anna's Hummingbird *Calypte anna* (**Lesson** 1829)
(Alt. Columbian Hummingbird)

Princess Anna d' Essling, Duchess of Rivoli (1802–1887), was the wife of Prince Victor Masséna, the son of one of Napoleon's marshals. French naturalist René Primevere **Lesson** named the bird for her after having discovered the first specimen among several birds collected for Prince Victor's private collection. Lesson also named the Blue-throated Hummingbird *Lampornis clemenciae* after his own wife Clemence.

ANNA WEBER

Anna's Flowerpecker *Dicaeum annae* (**Büttikofer** 1894)
(Alt. Golden-rumped/Sunda/Flores Flowerpecker)

Anna A Weber van Bosse (1852–1942) was a Dutch Botanist. With her husband M C W Weber, she collected in the East Indies between 1888 and 1890 and again from 1899 and 1900. M C W Weber died in 1937. When Anna died their estate at Eerbeek was bequeathed to the *Het Gelders landschap* foundation. Their house is now an adult education centre. Their library and scientific correspondence were bequeathed to the library of the Royal Zoological Society *Natura Artis Magistra* (now the Artis Library, University of Amsterdam) and to the Zoological Museum of the University of Amsterdam (now called the Institute of Taxonomic Zoology [Zoological Museum]).

ANSORGE

Ansorge's Crombec *Sylvietta rufescens ansorgei* (**Hartert** 1907)
Ansorge's Greenbul *Andropadus ansorgei* (Hartert 1907)

Ansorge's Robin-Chat *Xenocopsychus ansorgei* (Hartert 1907)
(Alt. Angola Cave Chat)

Dr William John Ansorge (1850–1913) was an English explorer and collector who was active in Africa in the second half of the 19th century. He wrote *Under the African Sun* in 1899. He also collected a number of new species of fish from the Niger delta. His son, Sir Eric Cecil Ansorge (1887–1977), continued the family tradition of interest in natural history; he was a lepidopterist and was also interested in beetles. **Hartert** described the greenbul and the robin-chat in 1907.

ANTHONY

Anthony's Flowerpecker *Dicaeum anthonyi* (**McGregor** 1914)
(Alt. Yellow-crowned/Flame-crowned Flowerpecker)
Anthony's Green Heron *Butorides striatus anthonyi* (**Mearns** 1895)
(Striated/Green-backed Heron)
Anthony's Nightjar *Caprimulgus anthonyi* (**Chapman** 1923)
(Scrub Nightjar)
Anthony's Towhee *Pipilo fuscus* (**Swainson** 1827)
(Alt. Canyon Towhee)
Anthony's Vireo *Vireo huttoni obscurus* (Anthony 1890)
(Alt. Hutton's Vireo)

Alfred Webster Anthony (1865–1939) was an American collector and ornithologist. In 1886 he published *Field notes on the birds of Washington County, Oregon*. He was president of the Audubon Society in Portland in 1904. He collected birds for years in the Tualatin Valley, his specimens now being in the Carnegie Museum in Pittsburgh, Pennsylvania. Anthony was the first to publish a list of birds of Portland and the vicinity. Anthony's list was used by Florence Merriam **Bailey** in her *Handbook to the Birds of the Western United States* (1902). **Mearns** took the type specimen of the Striated Heron subspecies in Baja California.

ANTONIA

Antonia's Cotinga *Carpodectes antoniae* (**Ridgway** 1884)
(Alt. Yellow-billed Cotinga)

Antonia Zeledon was the sister of Jose **Zeledon** (1846–1923).

APOLINAR

Apolinar's Marsh Wren *Cistothorus apolinari* (**Chapman** 1914)

Brother Apolinar María (1877–1949) was a missionary Colombian monk and ornithologist.

APPERT

Appert's Greenbul *Phyllastrephus apperti* (**Colston** 1972)
(Alt. Appert's Tetraka)

The Reverend Otto Appert is a German missionary and amateur naturalist in Madagascar who collected this very localised greenbul there in 1962. He has written books and articles such as *Beobachtungen an Monias benschi in Südwest-Madagaskar* and *La répartition geographique des vangides dans la région du Mangoky et la question de leur présence aux différentes époques de l'année*, in 1968, *Zur Biologie der Mesitornithiformes (Nakas oder 'Stelzenrallen') Madagaskars und erste fotografische Dokumente von Vertretern der Ordnung*, in 1995 and *Distribution and biology of the Newtonias (Newtonia, Sylviidae) in the Mangoky region, Southwest Madagascar*, in 1997.

ARCÉ

Arce's Tanager *Buthraupis arcaei* (**Sclater** & **Salvin** 1869)
(Alt. Blue-and-gold Tanager)

Enrique Arcé was a collector in Costa Rica who obtained the specimen at Cordillera del Chucu, Veraguas. Arcé also appears in the scientific names of a number of Central American moths and butterflies e.g. *Hypocrita arcaei* and *Hypanartia arcaei*.

ARCHBOLD

Archbold's Bowerbird *Archboldia papuensis* (**Rand** 1940)
Archbold's Mountain Owlet-nightjar *Aegotheles archboldi* (Rand 1941)
(Alt. Eastern Mountain Owlet-nightjar)
Archbold's Newtonia *Newtonia archboldi* (**Delacour** & **Berlioz** 1931)
(Alt. Tabity Newtonia)
Archbold's Nightjar *Eurostopodus archboldi* (**Mayr** & Rand 1937)
(Alt. Archbold's/Mountain Eared Nightjar)

Richard Archbold (1907–1976) was an American 'Patron of Science' who became a zoologist at the American Museum of Natural History. He financed and led expeditions, particularly to Australasia. He set up a permanent research station at Lake Placid in Florida. Seven bird species from the early expeditions to New Guinea and Madagascar are named in his honour in their scientific names, as well as 18 insects, three spiders and a mammal, the shrew *Archboldomys luzonensis*.

ARISTOCRATS

As with royalty some birds were named after aristocrats because they were famous or admired, others because of aristocratic patronage but also many because the aristocrats were themselves naturalists or had an ornithologist as a relative.

The famous include Count Pierre Paul Francois Camille Savorgnan de **Brazza**, Count Otto Von **Kotzebue**, Graf Bela **Szechenyi** and Baron Carl Claus **von der Decken** who were famed explorers [and Lady Ann **Ross** was married to one], Baron G W W C van **Hoevell** who was a colonial governor and Marie Joseph Paul Yves Roch Gilbert du Mothier Marquis de **Lafayette** was a prominent politician. Henrietta **Frances**, Lady Cole, Sarah Countess **Amherst** and Baroness **Stella** Erggelet were patrons of expeditions or of naturalists.

Hieronim Florian Radziwill Konstanty Graf von **Branicki**, **Count Georges Louis Leclerc de Buffon**, Leonardo **Fea**, Masauyi Uji 18th Marquis **Hachisuka**, Hon. Edward Smith **Stanley** 13th Earl of Derby and Arthur Hay, the ninth Marquis of **Tweeddale**, Viscount Walden, were zoologists. Francis de la Porte, Comte de **Castelnau**, Marchese Francesco **Raggi**, Leopold Chretien Frederic Dagobert Baron **Cuvier**, Baron Friedrich Wilhelm Heinrich Alexander von **Humboldt**, Baron George Heinrich von **Langsdorff**, Baron Carl Friedrich von **Ludwig**, Baron **Popelaire** de Terloo, Lord Lionel Walter **Rothschild**, Baron Dr Johann Jacob von **Tschudi** and Conte Ercole **Turati** were naturalists. Louis Marie Panteleon **Costa**, Marquis de Beau-Regard, Friedrich Heinrich Freiherr von **Kittlitz**, Baron Noel Frederic Armand Andre de **LaFresnaye** and Conte Adelardo Tommaso Paleotti **Salvadori** were ornithologists. Lady Elizabeth **Gould** was, of course, married to an ornithologist and Lady Mary **MacGregor** was married to a naturalist. Count Joseph Napoleon **Primoli** had a grandfather who was an ornithologist.

ARCHER

Archer's Buzzard *Buteo (augur) archeri* W L **Sclater** 1918
Archer's Grey-winged Francolin *Francolinus levaillantoides archeri*
W L Sclater 1927
(Alt. Orange River/Smith's Francolin)
Archer's Lark *Heteromirafra archeri* (Clarke 1920)
Archer's Robin-Chat *Cossypha archeri* Sharpe 1902
(Alt. Archer's Ground Robin)

Sir Geoffrey Francis Archer (1882–1964) was an explorer who became Governor and Commander-in-Chief of British Somaliland from 1919 until 1922 and Governor-General of the Sudan from 1924 until 1926. He wrote *The Birds of British Somaliland and the Gulf of Aden: their life histories, breeding habits and eggs* with E M Godman, in four volumes published from 1937 to 1961. **Sharpe** described the robin-chat from a specimen collected by F J **Jackson** in Uganda in that year. **Sclater** described the francolin from a specimen which Archer collected. Colonel Robert Stephenson **Clarke** described the lark from a specimen which Archer collected in Somaliland in 1918.

ARMSTRONG

Armstrong's Sandpiper *Tringa guttifer* (**Nordmann** 1835)
(Alt. Nordmann's/Spotted Greenshank)

Frank Bradley Armstrong (1863–1915) was a Canadian ornithologist and taxidermist. He was the son of an amateur naturalist who collected in Massachusetts, in Mexico and, from 1890, in Texas. He wrote essays on ornithology, mammalogy and oology. He sent thousands of specimens to museums in Europe and the United States, including the Field Museum in Chicago and the Smithsonian Institution. He also kept a collection of 800 birds at his home in Brownsville.

ARNOTT

Arnott's Chat *Myrmecocichla arnotti* (**Tristram** 1869)
(Alt. Arnot's/White-headed Black-chat)

David Arnott (1822–1894) was a renowned, unscrupulous South African attorney. He lived at Colesberg, and contributed fossil reptiles, mammals, birds and insects to the South African Museum between 1858 and 1868.

ARTISTS

The following are recognised as outstanding artists as opposed to the very many naturalists who were also very fine draughtsmen and left a heritage of brilliant illustrations. Jacques **Barraband** was so famous for his art that he was commissioned by Napoleon Bonaparte to create wonderful watercolours. Ferdinand **Bauer** was originally a botanical illustrator as were Henry John **Elwes**, Jean Gabriel **Pretre** and Florent **Prevost** who all worked on museum collections. Henri **De Lattre** was more famous for his paintings of horses whilst John William **Lewin** scratched a living as a portrait artist. Despite his illustrious forename, Titian Ramsay **Peale** was actually best known for his pen and ink drawings of native Americans whereas George Dawson **Rowley** and his son were famed for their posters. Expense prevented William **MacGillivray** from using his watercolours to illustrate his books and he made do with less-esteemed engravings. Gyula von **Maderasz** had his landscapes hung in his country's national gallery. In more modern times Rex

Brasher painted almost twice as many North American birds as **Audubon** and was described as 'America's greatest bird painter', a phrase previously used to describe Andrew Jackson **Grayson**. Similarly, Isaac S **Sprague** was called America's best-known botanical illustrator. John **Gould** was known throughout the world as *the* bird artist but many of his 3,000 remarkably accurate illustrations were created by a team of artists which he headed, including his wife.

William **Ellis** is typical of many men honoured for their art as much as for any other attribute. He was a 'surgeon's mate' on a voyage of discovery. Sydney **Parkinson** was also trying to paint aboard ship whilst his paint was being eaten from the canvas by flies! For Leonardo **Fea** illustration was almost incidental as it also seems to have been for Alexandre **Prigogine** and George Miksch **Sutton**. Today the general public remembers Edward **Lear** for his limericks, and birders remember him for Lear's Macaw *Anodorhynchus leari*, but during his life he was considered one of the most talented illustrators of birds of the 19th century.

ASH

Ash's [Bush] Lark *Mirafra ashi* **Colston** 1982

Dr John Sidney Ash (1925–) is an Englishman and a leading expert on African ornithology, with a special interest in the Horn of Africa. He was co-author of *Birds of Somalia* in 1998, with John E Miskell. Ash and Miskell lived in Somalia and its environs over many years and they travelled to its remotest areas. They added over 50 first-time records and found one new species (above) and four new subspecies of birds. Ash was at one time the Research Director of the Game Research Association. From 1969 until 1977 he was head of the Medical Ecology Division of the United States Medical Research Unit in Ethiopia. Thereafter he worked as an ornithologist for the Food and Agriculture Organisation and other United Nations agencies in Somalia, Uganda, South Yemen and the Maldives. In 1967 he was awarded the Bernard Tucker Medal of the British Trust for Ornithology and in 1997 the Union Medal of the British Ornithologists' Union. For 23 years he was an honorary research associate of the Smithsonian Institute. He has written over 350 articles and reports. Peter **Colston**, a specialist on African birds in the bird section of the British Natural History Museum at Tring, named the lark after him from a specimen which Ash collected in southern Somalia in 1981.

ASTLEY

Astley's Leiothrix *Leiothrix lutea* (**Scopoli** 1786)
(Alt. Red-billed/Doubtful Leiothrix, Peking Robin)

Thomas Astley was a geographer, cartographer, publisher, bookseller and artist who did a series of engravings called *Voyages and Travels* in the 1740s. Between 1745 and 1747 he published in four volumes *A new General Collection of Voyages and Travels; consisting of the most esteemed relations, which have been hitherto published in any language; comprehending everything remarkable in its kind, in Europe, Asia, Africa, and America.* This publication brought together travel writings from various sources and languages and is generally recognised as one of the best sources of African travel writing of its era.

ATALA

Atala's Emerald *Chlorostilbon atala* (**Gould**)*

Another bird found only in **Gould**. We are of the opinion, particularly in the light of the scientific name *atala*, that this is another transcription error, i.e. it should be the Atala

Emerald rather than Atala's Emerald. Atala has the same root as Atlantis, a name for paradise and the land of the sun (which sinks in the west as, reputedly, did Atlantis). There is a genus of butterflies called *Atala* too and many hummingbirds are named after insects with which they share characteristics.

ATTWATER

Attwater's Prairie Chicken *Tympanuchus cupido attwateri* (**Bendire** 1893)
(Alt. Greater Prairie Chicken)

Henry Philemon Attwater (1854–1931) was a naturalist and conservationist. He was born in Brighton, England, and emigrated in 1873 to Ontario, Canada, where he farmed and kept bees. He became interested in natural history and, together with John A Morden, he prepared and exhibited natural history specimens in 1883. During 1884 the two men collected specimens in Bexar County, Texas. During the latter part of 1884 and early 1885 Attwater and Toudouze were employed to prepare and exhibit natural history specimens in the Texas pavilion at the New Orleans World's Fair. Attwater's major contributions to natural history were in the areas of ornithology and conservation. His three ornithological papers deal with the nesting habits of 50 species of birds in Bexar County, Texas, the occurrence of 242 species of birds near San Antonio and the deaths of thousands of warblers in 1892. He also contributed specimens to the Smithsonian, collected birds for George B **Sennett** and provided notes for W W Cooke's *Bird Migration in the Mississippi Valley*, which was published in 1888. He was elected a director of the National Audubon Society in about 1900 and again in 1905. Through his influence with farmers, by 1910 the Texas Audubon Society had gained affiliation with the Texas Farmers' Congress, the Texas Cotton Growers' Association and the Texas Corn Growers' Association. He was also active in the promotion of legislation to protect the Mourning Dove *Zenaida macroura*, which was rapidly declining during the early 1900s. His most important conservation works include *Boll Weevils and Birds*, in 1903, *Use and Value of Wild Birds to Texas Farmers and Stockmen and Fruit and Truck Growers* in 1914 and *The Disappearance of Wild Life*, in 1917. Attwater's White-footed Mouse *Peromyscus attwateri* and Attwater's Pocket Gopher *Geomys breviceps* are among several mammals named in his honour.

AUDEBERT

Audebert's Hummingbird *Chlorestes notatus* (Reich 1793)
(Alt. Blue-chinned Saphire)

Jean Baptiste Audebert (1759–1800) was a noted miniaturist and nature artist. He produced *Oiseaux dorés, où à reflets métalliques* with Francois **Vieillot** in 1800, which was issued in 32 parts over 26 months. He invented his own colour printing process for the 190 engraved plates, some of which are heightened in gold. He also issued a book in 1797 on monkeys drawn from life entitled *Histoire Naturelle des Singes*. In 1801, Vieillot described the Long-billed Starthroat *Heliomaster longirostris* and shared the authorship with Audebert, presumably as a posthumous tribute.

AUDOUIN

Audouin's Gull *Larus audouinii* (Payraudeau 1826)

Jean Victoire Audouin (1797–1841) was a French naturalist, born in Paris, where he studied medicine, natural history and pharmacy. Audouin was appointed assistant at the Musée National d'Histoire Naturelle in Paris in 1825 and in 1833 became professor of entomology there. He also published a work on the natural history of French coastal waters; *Récherches pour servir à l'histoire naturelle du littoral de la France*.

AUDUBON

Audubon's Caracara *Caracara (Polyborus) cheriway audubonii* (**Cassin** 1865)
    (Alt. Crested or Southern Caracara)
Audubon's Oriole *Icterus graduacauda* (**Lesson** 1839)
    (Alt. Black-headed Oriole)
Audubon's Shearwater *Puffinus lherminieri* (Lesson 1839)
    (Alt. Dusky-backed Shearwater)
Audubon's Warbler *Dendroica coronata auduboni* (J K **Townsend** 1837)
    (Alt. Yellow-rumped Warbler)
Audubon's Woodpecker *Picoides (Dendrocopus) villosus audubonii*
    (Swainson 1832)
    (Alt. Hairy Woodpecker)

John James Audubon (1785–1851) is remembered as the father of American ornithology and as a notable artist, collector and author. He gave several different accounts of his birth, but he was the illegitimate son of a French naval captain and a French girl who worked at his sugar plantation in San Domingo, Haiti. Audubon's mother died within a short time of his birth so Audubon's father took him back to France as a young child where he was adopted by Captain Audubon and his legal wife. When he was a teenager, Captain Audubon sent him to manage his plantation near Philadelphia. It was here that Audubon met and married his wife Lucy, whose support proved critical in achieving his success. He succeeded only because he went to England, where his work was appreciated and subscribers made possible the publication of his monumental *Birds of America* in four volumes between 1827 and 1838. *Birds of America* was literally an immense work. All the birds were life size so the 435 hand-coloured plates measured 76 x 69 cm and even then some of the larger species had to be bent into the unnatural poses which are something of a hallmark of his. A set of his plates sold for nearly US$ 3 million when last on the market. In the 1830s Audubon also wrote his *Ornithological Biography*, which describes the habits of the birds he drew. Audubon made a trip to the western regions in the 1840s, his last great adventure prior to his death in 1851. He spent weeks in the woods studying birds and other animals; and his spectacular drawings, although criticised as over-imaginative by some, were scenes he actually witnessed. **Cassin** described the caracara from a specimen shot by one of Audubon's assistants, Lehman or Ward, after Audubon himself had unsuccessfully hunted a single bird for several days.

AURELIA

Aurelia's Puffleg *Haplophaedia aureliae* (Bourcier & Mulsant 1846)
    (Alt. Greenish Puffleg)

Aurélie Henon was the wife of the French agronomist J L Henon, according to Jobling. Whilst we can find no supporting evidence, the fact that **Bourcier** and **Mulsant** described the hummingbird in the French journal *Annals of Science, Physics and Nature, of Agriculture and Industry* does support that possibility. **Gould** illustrated the bird and so may have obtained a specimen from Bourcier, as he did with many other hummingbirds. The name Aurelia has a long history deriving from a Roman martyr in Valerian's era who was beaten to death *c.*256 AD and later given sainthood. Other plants and animals, for example the ciliate protozoan *Paramecium aurelia*, the fungus *Phlyctochytrium aureliae* and the jellyfish genus *Aurelia*, commemorate the same name but not necessarily the same person.

AUSTEN

(see also **Godwin**-Austen)

> Austen's Spotted Babbler *Stachyris oglei* (Austen 1877)
> (Alt. Ogle's Spotted/Snowy-throated Babbler, Austen's Spotted Tree Babbler)
> Austen's Barwing *Actinodura waldeni* (Austen 1874)
> (Alt. Walden's/White-throated Barwing/Streak-throated Barwing)
> Austen's Brown Hornbill *Anorrhinus (tickelli) austeni* (**Jerdon** 1872)
> (Alt. Austen's Brown-backed Hornbill)
> Austen's Laughing-thrush *Garrulax (galbanus) austeni* (Austen 1871)
> (Alt. Yellow-throated Laughing-thrush)

Lieutenant-Colonel Henry Haversham Godwin-Austen (1834–1923) was a British army topographer, geologist and surveyor. As an officer from 1851 until 1877, he was assigned to several government surveys in northern India, especially in the Himalayas. He explored and surveyed the region of the Karakorum around K2. This Himalayan peak was also named Mount Godwin-Austen in his honour. He wrote *Birds of Assam* from 1870 until 1878. He was also an ornithologist and named and described quite a few birds himself, among which were the three at one time accorded his name. He also named the laughing-thrush *Garrulax austeni* after himself, an egocentric practice which is not considered good form among ornithologists. The type-localities of most of these birds are in Assam, where he collected, but he collected the barwing in Bengal, in 1874. The babbler was described from a specimen collected by M J **Ogle**.

AYRES

> Ayres' Cisticola *Cisticola ayresii* (**Bates** 1926)
> (Alt. Wing-snapping Cisticola)
> Ayres' Hawk-Eagle *Hieraaetus ayresii (dubius)* (**Gurney** 1862)
> (Alt. Ayres' Eagle)

Thomas Ayres (1828–1913) was a British-born collector and naturalist. He went to Pinetown in Natal, South Africa in 1850 and set about collecting birds. These he sent to Gurney in Norwich, England. Gurney published a series of 11 papers in *Ibis* between 1859 and 1873, describing the species which Ayres collected. He visited Australia and tried his luck in the goldfields there in 1852, but then returned to South Africa to settle in Potchefstroom as a hunter and trader. He was obviously eager to make his fortune out of gold, as in the early 1870s he was prospecting on the Lydenburg goldfields. He collected birds, beetles, butterflies and moths. At least 60 species, which were collected around Potch, are now very rare. His house was named the Ark as it was '*long, low and stuffed with animals and birds*'. He was a mentor to the young Roberts' boys (Austin **Roberts**) and accompanied a lot of the legendary hunters on expeditions, for example to Mashonaland. One of these was James **Jameson**. The collection of birds made on such expeditions was documented in a paper by **Shelley** in *Ibis* in 1882. After he returned to South Africa, he even operated a brewery for a couple of years making Ayres XX Pale Ale. Many people spoke highly of this beer including, it is rumoured, Captain William Cloudsley Lucas of the Bengal Yeomanry Cavalry, which was stationed at Rustenberg. Lucas wrote to Ayres saying that the beer had cured him of '*...nightly sweatings, terrible affections in the lumbar regions, and a chronic costiveness that had lasted eighteen years.*' Most unfortunately, Ayres had to close down the brewery when the government changed the law and it became illegal for private people to brew beer on a commercial basis.

AZARA

Azara's Bittern *Ixobrychus involucris* (**Viellot** 1823)
  (Alt. Stripe-backed/Pygmy/Little Red/Variegated Bittern)
Azara's Conure *Pyrrhura frontalis chiripepe* (Viellot 1818)
  (Alt. Maroon-bellied/Blaze-winged/Scaly-breasted Conure)
Azara's Sandplover *Charadrius collaris* (Viellot 1818)
  (Alt. Collared Plover)
Azara's Spinetail *Synallaxis azarae* (**d'Orbigny** 1835)

Félix Manuel de Azara (1746–1811) was born at Barbunales in Aragon, Spain. He was a military officer but also a naturalist and an engineer, who distinguished himself in various expeditions. He was appointed a member of the Spanish Commission and sent to South America in 1781, to settle the question of borders between the Portuguese and Spanish colonies. He attained the rank of Brigadier General when in command of the Paraguayan frontier from 1781 to 1801. Azara remained in South America until 1801. While there he turned his attention to the study of mammals, as an observer of the life and habits of quadrupeds in general. The agouti *Dasyprocta azarae is* named after him too. His observations, to which he added a large number of statements obtained by hearsay, were not always favourably received but today his perspicacity as a student of the life of South American mammals is generally acknowledged. He also extended his investigations to birds. Before leaving South America, he sent many notes and observations of a zoological nature to his brother, who was then Spanish Ambassador in Paris. These were published in 1801 by Moreau de Saint-Méry under the title of *Essai sur l'histoire naturelle des quadrupèdes du Paraguay*. In 1802 his *Apuntamientos para la Historia natural de los cuadrúpedos del Paraguay y Río de la Plata* was published in Madrid. In 1809 his *Voyage dans l'Amérique méridionale depuis 1781 jusqu'en 1801* was published, also in Madrid.

BACHMAN

Bachman's Sparrow *Aimophila aestivalis* (**Lichtenstein** 1823)
Bachman's Warbler *Vermivora bachmanii* (**Audubon** 1833) [Extinct]

Dr John Bachman (1790–1874) was a close friend of **Audubon**, who was greatly aided by this Lutheran minister of Charleston, South Carolina. His daughters were the first wives of Audubon's two sons. Audubon named both species after him. He wrote '*My friend Bachman has the merit of having discovered this pretty little warbler…*'. Audubon also immortalised his friend in the scientific name of the American Black Oystercatcher *Haematopus bachmani*.

BAER

Baer's Foliage-gleaner *Philydor dimidiatus baeri* **Hellmayr** 1911
Baer's Pochard *Aythya baeri* (**Radde** 1863)

Karl Ernst von Baer (Karl Maksimovich, 1792–1876) was a versatile Baltic-German (Estonian) naturalist as well as an explorer of Siberia. He is known as the father of Estonian science and world embryology. He was a contemporary of **Darwin**, with whom he corresponded.

BAILEY

Bailey's Chickadee *Parus gambeli baileyae* Grinnell 1908
(Alt. Mountain Chickadee)

Mrs Florence Augusta Bailey née Merriam (1863–1948) was an early proponent of the use of binoculars rather than the shotgun in ornithology! Her first book, *Birds Through an Opera Glass*, was published in 1889. She was vehemently opposed to the fashion of decorating women's hats with feathers or even whole birds. She was a younger sister of Clinton Hart **Merriam**, first chief of the United States Biological Survey. In 1899 she married Vernon Bailey, a pioneering naturalist in his own right, who worked for her brother with whom she was living at the time. She also wrote *A-birding on a Bronco* and then *Birds of Village and Field* in 1898. Her *Handbook of Birds of the Western United States*, published in 1902, was favourably described in the journal The Condor as '*the most complete text-book of regional ornithology which has ever been published*'. Bailey was the first woman to become a fellow of the American Ornithologists' Union in 1929 and was also the first woman recipient of its Brewster Medal in 1931, awarded for her comprehensive book *Birds of New Mexico* in 1928. Her last book was *Among the Birds in the Grand Canyon National Park*, published by the National Park Service in 1939. The chickadee was named in her honour in 1908.

BAILLON

Baillon's Crake *Porzana pusilla* (**Pallas** 1776)

Jean François Emmanuel Baillon (1744–1802) was a lawyer as well as a collector and naturalist from Abbeville, France. His son Louis Antoine François Baillon (1778–1851) was also a naturalist and collector.

BAIRD

Baird's Cormorant *Phalacrocorax pelagicus resplendens* (**Audubon** 1838)
(Alt. Pelagic Cormorant)
Baird's Creeper *Oreomystis bairdi* (**Stejneger** 1887)
(Alt. Kauai Creeper)
Baird's Flycatcher *Myiodynastes bairdii* (**Gambel** 1847)
Baird's Junco *Junco phaeonotus bairdi* **Ridgway** 1883
(Alt. Yellow-eyed Junco)

Baird's Sandpiper *Calidris bairdii* (Coues 1861)
Baird's Sparrow *Ammodramus bairdii* (Audubon 1844)
Baird's Trogon *Trogon bairdii* (**Lawrence** 1868)
Baird's Wren *Thryomanes bewickii eremophilus* (**Oberholser** 1898)

Spencer Fullerton Baird (1823–1887) was an American zoologist who became a giant of American ornithology. He organized expeditions with the *Albatross*. Baird was Assistant Secretary (until 1878) and then Secretary of the United States National Museum, the Smithsonian Institution. He wrote a *Catalogue of North American Birds* in 1858. The young Baird became a friend of John James **Audubon** and sent him collected specimens. Audubon named the sparrow after him and **Coues** the sandpiper and junco.

BAKER, E C S

Baker's Yuhina *Yuhina bakeri* (**Rothschild** 1926)
(Alt. Blyth's/Chestnut-headed Yuhina, White-naped Ixulus)

Edward Charles Stuart Baker (1864–1944) was a policeman in India in the colonial period, between 1883 and 1912. He was also an amateur ornithologist, oologist and collector. Baker was a productive author, writing *The Indian Ducks and their Allies* in 1908, *Game Birds of India, Burmah and Ceylon* in 1921, *Fauna of British India: Birds* in 1922, *Mishni the Man-eater* in 1928, *The Nidification of the Birds of the Indian Empire* in 1932 and *Cuckoo Problems* in 1942.

BAKER, G

Baker's Bowerbird *Sericulus bakeri* (**Chapin** 1929)
(Alt. Adelbert's/Beck's/Fire-maned/Macloud Bowerbird)

George Fisher Baker Jr (1878–1937) was an American banker who became a Trustee of the Museum of Natural History. The Critically Endangered San Cristobal Moorhen *Gallinula sylvestris* was originally named *Edithornis sylvestris* by **Mayr** in 1933 after Baker's wife, Edith.

BAKER, J

Baker's Pigeon *Ducula bakeri* (Kinnear 1928)
(Alt. Vanuatu Imperial-pigeon)

John Randal Baker (1900–1984) was a British zoologist who collected in the New Hebrides between 1922 and 1924. His works include *The seasons in a tropical rain-forest (New Hebrides)*.

BALLMANN

Ballmann's Malimbe *Malimbus ballmanni* (Wolters 1974)
(Alt. Tai/Gola Malimbe)

Dr Peter Ballmann (1941–) is a German geoscientist who is studying fossil birds and avian osteology. He studied geology in Germany and at Leiden, writing his dissertation on fossil birds. He collected a few birds, some of which he could not identify, whilst he was working in 1971 as a field pedologist in the Ivory Coast. These he took to the König Museum in Bonn. Among the collection was the malimbe which is now named after him. Ballmann presented the specimen to the König Museum. He later worked in Costa Rica from 1973 to 1974, in Saudi Arabia from 1981 to 1984 and in Swaziland in 1985. He clearly regards himself as an amateur, as he wrote to us '*I have met real ornithologists and bird watchers and it impressed me most that the good ones could identify the birds just by sight and did not have to shoot them first.*' Ballman published extensively on paleo-ornithology in the 1960s and 1970s. His works include *Die Vögel aus der altburdigalen Spaltenfüllung von Wintershof (West) bei Eichstätt in Bayern* in 1969, *Fossile Vögel aus dem Neogen der Halbinsel Gargano (Italien)* Parts 1 and 2, in 1973 and 1976 respectively, *Les Oiseaux Miocènes de Grive-Saint Alban (Isère)* in 1969 and *Fossile Glareolidae aus dem Miozäm des Nördliinger Reis* in 1979. In 1983 he published, in the Journal of Vertebrate Palaeontology, *A new species of fossil barbet (Aves: Piciformes) from the Middle Miocene of the Noerdlinger Ries (southern Germany)*. He has described several newly discovered fossil birds including barbets, owls and others.

BANCROFT

Bancroft's Night Heron *Nycticorax violaceus bancrofti* (Huey 1927)
(Alt. Yellow-crowned Night Heron)
Bancroft's Screech Owl *Otus kennicottii* (**Elliot** 1867)
(Alt. Western Screech Owl)

Griffing Bancroft Jr (?–1998) was an ornithologist and journalist who wrote *The Flight of the Least Petrel* in 1932. He was also an accomplished egg collector who donated 30,000 birds' eggs to the United States Natural History Museum in 1941. He was instrumental in setting up the Sanival reserve in Florida. Bancroft is also noteworthy as one of the first people to be awarded the Medal of Freedom, the highest honour for a civilian in the United States, for his work in the field of psychological warfare. His third wife, Jane Eads Bancroft, said of him in an interview in 1998: '*He's a very interesting person. He's really an ornithologist and he's written several books about birds. When he was very young, he went on all these birding expeditions with his father, Griffing Bancroft, Sr., in California, and they went around in Baja California and around various mountainous regions. They collected birds' eggs – in those days, it was all right to do it – for the San Diego Museum. At one point, before World War II, they had one of the largest private collections of bird eggs in the country. They have two birds named after them. That was his main interest at first. Now since then, he has worked on a newspaper in San Diego*'. Jane Eads Bancroft collected a snake which her friend Klauber named *Sonora bancroftae* in her honour in 1943. Bancroft's grandfather (Hubert Howe Bancroft, 1832–1918) is renowned for his 65-volume history of the United States, which he sold in 1905 to the University of California for $150,000 in three equal annual payments. Hubert Bancroft later donated his collection to the University of California and the library there is named for him; he was killed by a street car.

BANGS

Bangs' Black Parrot *Coracopsis nigra libs* (Bangs 1927)
Bangs' Sparrow *Amphispiza bilineata bangsi* Grinnell 1927
(Alt. Black-throated Sparrow)

Outram Bangs (1862–1932) was an American zoologist who was born in Watertown, Massachusetts. The family spent a year in England in 1873. Bangs attended Harvard from 1880 to 1884. In 1890 he began a systematic study of the mammals of eastern North America. He wrote over 70 books and articles, 55 of them on mammals, including an article on *The Florida Puma* which was published in the Proceedings of the Biological Society of Washington in 1899. His collection of over 10,000 mammalian skins and skulls, including over 100 type specimens, was presented to Harvard College in 1899. Bangs was appointed Assistant in Mammalogy at Harvard and became Curator of Mammals at the Harvard Museum of Comparative Zoology in 1900. Bangs also collected bird specimens. He visited Jamaica in 1906 and collected over 100 birds there but his trip was cut short by dengue fever. In 1908 his collection of over 24,000 bird skins was presented to the Museum of Comparative Zoology and he went on to increase it. In 1925 he went to Europe, visiting museums, ornithologists and arranging scientific exchanges. He was a member of the American Ornithologists' Union and wrote articles for its journal, *The Auk*. Bangs is commemorated in a number of binomials, including the Santa Marta Antpitta *Grallaria bangsi*, and in the tanager genus *Bangsia*.

BANKS

Banks' Dove Petrel *Pachyptila desolata banksii* (**Smith** 1840)
(Alt. Antarctic Prion)
Banksian Cockatoo *Calyptorhynchus banksii* (**Latham** 1790)
(Alt. Latham's/Red-tailed/Great-billed Cockatoo)

Sir Joseph Banks (1743–1820) was a highly influential English botanist and explorer. He was born in London and studied at Oxford. He made a voyage to Newfoundland in 1776 collecting plants. Banks accompanied James **Cook**'s expedition round the world in the *Endeavour* (1768–1771). He is perhaps best-known for founding and stocking Kew Gardens – the foremost botanical collection and research institution in the world. He was an important patron of science and in 1778 he was elected president of the Royal Society, an office he held for 41 years. Banks founded the African Association and the Australian colony of New South Wales owes its origin mainly to him.

BANNERMAN

Bannerman's Paradise-flycatcher *Terpsiphone rufocinerea bannermani* **Chapin** 1948
Bannerman's Pipit *Anthus similis bannermani* (**Bates** 1930) (Alt. Long-billed Pipit)
Bannerman's Shearwater *Puffinus* (*lherminieri*) *bannermani* (**Mathews** & Iredale 1915)
Bannerman's Sunbird *Nectarinia bannermani* (**Grant** & Mackworth-Praed 1943) (Alt. Blue-headed Sunbird)
Bannerman's Turaco *Tauraco bannermani* (Bates 1923)
Bannerman's Weaver *Ploceus bannermani* (Chapin 1932)

Dr David Armitage Bannerman (1886–1979) was a British ornithologist on the staff of the British Museum. He was Chairman of the British Ornithologists' Club from 1932 until 1935 and became Honorary President of the Scottish Ornithologists' Club in 1959. He was an early leader in the conservation movement. His numerous publications included the standard multi-volume works *The Birds of Tropical West Africa* and *The Birds of the Atlantic Islands*. Malcolm Ogilvie, a leading British ornithologist, told us: '*I met him a number of times before he died. He was Scottish and retired here* (to Scotland) *after a long and very productive life, producing books on West Africa, the Canaries, the Azores, the British Isles, Cyprus, etc., etc., all lavishly produced, with specially commissioned paintings by George Lodge and David Reid-Henry paid for by Bannerman himself who had a private income.*'

BARAU

Barau's Petrel *Pterodroma baraui* (**Jouanin** 1964)

Armand Barau (1921–1989) was co-author in 1982 with Nicolas Barré and Christian H **Jouanin** of *Oiseaux de la Réunion*, the first serious study of the birds of that island. He was an agronomist, landowner and amateur ornithologist in Réunion, and from 1962 to 1989 was President of the Centre d'Essai de Recherche et de Formation (CERF), an organisation concerned with sugar production. Jouanin encouraged him to look for the Mascarene Black Petrel *Pterodroma aterrima*, which had not been collected since the 19th century. That species was rediscovered in 1970 but Barau first identified the petrel that is now named after him in 1963.

BARLOW, C B

Barlow's Chickadee *Parus rufescens barlowi* (**Grinnell** 1900) (Alt. Chestnut-sided Chickadee)

Chester Barlow (1874–1902) was the assistant cashier at the Santa Clara Valley Bank and

an amateur ornithologist and oologist. He was the first secretary of the Cooper Ornithological Society and held the post for nearly 10 years despite his youth. He was the author of many articles from 1892 until 1902 in The Naturalist, the Oologist and especially in The Nidologist and Condor. These included a *Paper on the Pileolated and Yellow Warblers* published in The Nidologist in 1893 and *Some additions to Van Denburgh's list of land birds of Santa Clara Co., California,* published in The Condor in 1900. This race of the chickadee is confined to the Central California coast.

BARLOW, C S

Barlow's Lark *Certhilauda barlowi* (**Roberts** 1937)
(Alt. Karoo Lark)

Charles Sydney 'Punch' Barlow (1905–1979) was a distinguished South African Businessman. The fifth edition of Roberts' *Birds of South Africa* carries this dedication to Barlow: '*C.S. 'Punch' Barlow, best known as one of South Africa's foremost businessmen, was an ardent conservationist and one of the founder members of the John Voelcker Bird Book Fund that initially raised the money for the publication of The Birds of Southern Africa. He was a friend of the original author, the late Dr Austin Roberts, with whom he went on bird discovery expeditions and there are several subspecies named after him. Among his major interests were his collection of ornithological books, concern for the expansion of knowledge and conservation of habitats. He is remembered as a great entrepreneur, philanthropist, sportsman and lover of nature. Barlow was also Chairman of the Barlow Rand Group (now defunct), which was one of South Africa's largest Mining Houses. He remained chairman of the John Voelcker Bird Book Fund until his death in 1979.*' The bird is sometimes regarded as a race of the Karoo Lark *C. albescens barlowi*.

BARNARD

Barnard's Parakeet *Barnardius barnardi* (**Vigors** & **Horsfield** 1827)
(Alt. Mallee Ringneck)
Barnard's Purple Brush Turkey *Alectura lathami* J E Gray 1831
(Alt. Australian Brush Turkey)

Edward Barnard FRS, FLS, FRHS, FZS (1786–1861) was a zoologist, botanist and horticulturalist who also became Agent-General for the Crown Colonies. **J E Gray** described the brush turkey from a specimen collected by A Cunningham.

BARNES

Barnes' Wheatear *Oenanthe finschii barnesi* (Oates 1890)
(Alt. Finsch's/White-backed/Arabian Wheatear, Barnes' Chat)

Henry Edward Barnes was a professional British soldier. He was originally apprenticed to his father, a cabinet maker, but he ran away to join the army as a private. He rose through the ranks and was eventually commissioned. At one point he was posted to Aden, where he arrived in 1866. He wrote on Indian and Arabian birds including such articles as *On the birds of Aden* in Ibis and *List of birds noted at Aden and its vicinity* in the Journal of the Bombay Natural History Society in 1893 and also the *Handbook to the Birds of the Bombay Presidency*, which was published by Calcutta Central Press in 1885. This race, which was described in the 1940s, is larger than the nominate and is found in the Caucasus. **Heuglin** described the species in 1869 in *Ornithologie Nordost-Afrika*. **Meinertzhagen** described a bird in 1949 as *Oenanthe lugens vauriei* which has since been treated as a synonym of with Barnes' Wheatear.

BARON

Baron's Spinetail *Cranioleuca baroni* (**Salvin** 1895)

O T Baron (1847–1926) was a German engineer in Peru and Ecuador, and an amateur ornithologist and collector. In 1897 he wrote a paper entitled *Notes on the localities visited by O T Baron in Northern Peru and on the Trochilidae found there.* Osbert **Salvin** named the spinetail after him.

BARON ROTHSCHILD

Baron Rothschild Hermit *Phaethornis syrmatophorus* (**Gould** 1851)
(Alt. Tawny-bellied Hermit)

See **Rothschild**.

BARRABAND

Barraband's Parrot *Pionopsitta barrabandi* (**Kuhl** 1820)
(Alt. Orange-cheeked Parrot)

Jacques Barraband (1767–1809) has been called the '*Audubon of France*'. His watercolours of flowers and birds, engraved by Langlois, were created between 1801 and 1804 by direct commission of Napoleon Bonaparte. François **Levaillant**, an adventurer and natural historian, who was one of the first to record sightings of Australian parrots, wrote *Histoire Naturelle Des Perroquets*. He employed Barraband whose skill was greatly esteemed and his name lent prestige to Levaillant's sumptuous work. Barraband's brilliantly coloured engravings of exotic birds coupled with Levaillant's precise descriptions represent the height of realistic bird art of the time.

BARRATT

Barratt's Warbler *Bradypterus barratti* (**Sharpe** 1876)
(Alt. African Scrub Warbler)

F A Barratt (*c.*1847–1875) was a collector in the Transvaal. **Sharpe** described the warbler from a specimen collected in the Transvaal and sent to the British Museum by Barratt in 1875.

BARROT

Barrot's Fairy *Heliothryx barroti* (**Bourcier** 1843)
(Alt. Purple-crowned Fairy)

Theodore Adolphe Barrot (1801–1870) was a French diplomat who served in Colombia from 1831 until 1835 and in the Philippines from 1835 until 1838. In 1864 he became a Senator under Napoleon III in the Second Empire. He wrote *Unless Haste is Made: A French Sceptic's Account of the Sandwich Islands* in 1836. He had the distinction that, although not of noble blood, he became a Knight of the Royal Illustrious Order of St Januarius, which was founded in Naples in the 16th century by the Habsburg King of the Kingdom of the two Sicilies.

BARROW

Barrow's Bustard *Eupodotis* (*senegalensis*) *barrowii* (J E **Gray** 1829)
(Alt. White-bellied Bustard)
Barrow's Goldeneye *Bucephala islandica* (Gmelin 1789)

Sir John Barrow (1764–1848) was Secretary to the Admiralty and a founder of the Royal Geographical Society. He was a great advocate of arctic exploration. **Swainson** named the Barrow's Goldeneye after him. His name also lives on through several geographical features in the North West Passage to the Pacific Ocean, such as Barrow Point in Alaska and the Barrow Strait of northern Canada. Although Barrow visited Greenland as a boy, he never actually visited the places named after him. He laid the foundation stone for the Monument in his honour, a tower 100-feet high at The Hoad at Ulverston, in Cumbria, which was completed in 1850. He was created a baronet.

BARTELS

Bartels' Wood Owl *Strix (leptogrammica) bartelsi* (**Finsch** 1906)
(Alt. Brown Wood Owl)

Max E G Bartels (1871–1936) was a Dutch plantation owner and naturalist who lived in Java from 1896 until his death. He is also commemorated in the scientific name of the Javan Hawk-Eagle *Spizaetus bartelsi* and a number of mammals are named after him including Bartels' Flying Squirrel *Hylopectes bartelsi* and Bartels' Rat *Maxomys bartelsi*.

BARTLETT

Bartlett's Bleeding-heart *Gallicolumba criniger* (**Pucheran** 1853)
(Alt. Mindanao Bleeding-heart)
Bartlett's Emerald *Amazilia lactea bartletti* (**Gould** 1866)
(Alt. Sapphire-spangled Emerald)
Bartlett's Tinamou *Crypturellus bartletti* (**Sclater** & **Salvin** 1873)

Abraham Dee Bartlett (1812–1897) was a taxidermist and zoologist who was the superintendent of the Gardens of the Zoological Society in Regent's Park, London, between 1859 and 1897. '*I am informed by Mr. Bartlett that in the Zoological Gardens…*' wrote Charles Darwin in *The Origin of Species*. He mentions him again in *The Descent of Man and Selection in Relation to Sex*, in 1896, where he wrote '*I asked Mr. Bartlett, of the Zoological Gardens, who has had very large experience with birds, whether the male tragopan… was polygamous, and I was struck by his answering, I do not know, but should think so from his splendid colours.*' Bartlett published many articles on his work and experiences at the London Zoo, including, for example, *Notes on the breeding of several species of birds in the Society's Gardens during the year 1867*, published in 1868 in the Proceedings of the Zoological Society.

BARTRAM

Bartram's Sandpiper *Bartramia longicauda* (**Bechstein** 1812)
(Alt. Upland Sandpiper, Bartramian Tattler)

William Bartram (1739–1823) was an American naturalist, explorer and botanist who has been called the Grandfather of American Ornithology, perhaps because he was the protector of Alexander **Wilson**, who was known as the Father of American Ornithology in his time. He accompanied his father John Bartram (America's 'first' botanist) on a number of expeditions; to the Catskill Mountains in 1753 to 1754, to New York and Connecticut in 1755 and to Florida in 1765. William remained in the South drawing flora, collecting botanical specimens, becoming an accomplished ornithologist and befriending both colonial planters and Native American tribes. With the advent of the American War of Independence, he joined the Georgia Militia and served with them in 1776. He returned to his home in Pennsylvania in 1777 and wrote about his travels. In 1782 he was offered the position of Professor of Botany at the University of Pennsylvania, but it appears that he never lectured there. As well as befriending Alexander Wilson he took his nephew, Thomas **Say** under his wing. Bartram put together a *Catalogue of Birds of North America.*

BATCHELDER

Batchelder's Woodpecker *Picoides pubescens gairdnerii* (Batchelder 1900)
(Alt. Downy/Gairdner's Woodpecker)

Charles Foster Batchelder (1856–1954) was an American artist and amateur ornithologist, and a leading light in the Nuttall Ornithological Club. He wrote *An Account of the Nuttall Ornithological Club 1873 to 1919* and *A Bibliography of the Published Writings of William **Brewster**,* as well as information on the nesting habits of the Yellow-breasted Chat *Icteria virens* and the Bald Eagle *Haliaeetus leucocephalus.*

BATES

Bates' [Black] Swift *Apus batesi* (**Sharpe** 1904)
Bates' Nightjar *Caprimulgus batesi* (Sharpe 1906)
Bates' Paradise-flycatcher *Terpsiphone batesi* (Sharpe 1886)
Bates' [Olive] Sunbird *Nectarinia batesi* (**Ogilvie-Grant** 1908)
Bates' Weaver *Ploceus batesi* (Sharpe 1908)

George Latimer Bates (1863–1940) was born in Illinois, and travelled in West Africa between 1895 and 1931. He wrote a *Handbook of the Birds of West Africa* in 1930 and a number of articles which were published in *Ibis* notably *Birds of the Southern Sahara and adjoining countries* in 1933. He also left unpublished manuscripts of the *Birds of Arabia,* whihc were subsequently utilised by **Meinertzhagen** for his 1950s work on the subject. An African member of the nettle family, *Pouzolzia batesii,* is also named after him.

BAUDIN

Baudin's Cockatoo *Calyptorhynchus baudinii* (**Lear** 1832)
(Alt. Long-billed/White-tailed Black-Cockatoo)

Nicolas Thomas Baudin (1754–1803). On 18 Oct 1800, Captain Baudin set out from Le Havre with two corvettes, the *Géographe* and the *Naturaliste,* carrying five zoologists, 17 other scientists, three artists and two astronomers among others. In March 1804 the *Géographe* crawled back to Le Havre with a living cargo of 72 birds and other animals but no captain, the unfortunate Baudin having died of tuberculosis in Mauritius. However, he did leave an artistic legacy, 46 watercolours and drawings amassed on the expedition to Australia. After the expedition's official artists decamped en route, it was his decision to replace them with assistant gunners Petit and Lesueur. '*It will be seen from the work of these two young men whether my choice was good or bad,*' wrote Baudin in his log. The results were stunning.

BAUER

Bauer's Parakeet *Barnardius zonarius* (Shaw 1905)
(Alt. Port Lincoln Ringneck)

Ferdinand Bauer (1760–1826) was an Austrian illustrator who sailed with the *Investigator* to Australia at the turn of the 19th century, after being recommended by Joseph **Banks**. Bauer had previously worked as a botanical illustrator at the University of Vienna. He made a botanical trip to Greece, where he spent 18 months, and then moved to England where he converted his sketches, which numbered over 1,500, to paintings. The genus is named after Edward **Barnard.**

BAUMANN

Baumann's [Olive] Greenbul *Phyllastrephus baumanni* (**Reichenow** 1895)

Oskar Baumann (1864–1899) was an Austrian (German) explorer and geographer who explored widely in Africa; the Congo in 1885; Fernando Pó in 1886, Usambara (modern-day Tanzania) in 1888 and German East Africa and other regions from 1890 to 1995. He also ascertained the source of the Kagera River and was the first European to see the Serengeti.

BEAL

Beal's Storm Petrel *Oceanodroma leucorhoa beali* (Emerson 1906)
(Alt. Leach's Storm Petrel)

Professor Foster Ellenborough Lascelles Beal (1840–1916) was employed by the Biological Survey of the United States Department of Agriculture. He worked on birds common to agricultural and horticultural areas and was described as an 'economic ornithologist' by 'Condor'. For example he investigated the diet of the Cedar Waxwing *Bombycilla cedrorum* and found that they had very little impact on horticulture, no doubt saving them from the farmers' wrath! He was a very hard worker and was described as '*having kept his eyes to the microscope more hours per day, and more days, than anyone*' which must have been the case since he studied the stomach contents of 37,000 birds! His favourite saying was 'ignorance is better than error'. He wrote a great many articles on bird diets in great detail. Otto Emerson, who supplied the above photographic portrait to The Condor, described this now synonymised race of the storm petrel.

BEAUDOUIN

Beaudouin's Snake-eagle *Circaetus beaudouini* (**Verreaux** & **Des Murs** 1862)
(Alt. Beaudouin's Harrier Eagle)

M Beaudouin was a professional collector employed by **Verreaux**. In about 1862 he was collecting in Portuguese Guinea (now Guinea-Bissau).

BEAUFORT

Beaufort's Black-capped Lory *Lorius lory viridicrissalis* (De Beaufort 1909)
(Alt. Black-capped/Western Black-capped/Tricoloured Lory)

Professor Lieven Ferdinand De Beaufort (1879–1968) was a Dutch zoologist whose main interests were birds and fish. He was one of the founders of the Nederlandse Ornithologische Vereeniging and its president from 1924 to 1956. He undertook his first expedition to the Indo-Australian Archipelago in 1900. He collected extensively with M **Weber** in New Guinea from 1907 until 1922, obtaining specimens of 474 birds. In 1922 he succeeded Weber as Director of the Zoological Museum in Amsterdam and stayed in that post until 1949. From 1911 until 1964 he published with Weber *The Fishes of the Indo-Australian Archipelago* in six volumes.

BEAVAN

Beavan's Bullfinch *Pyrrhula erythaca* (**Blyth** 1862)
(Alt. Grey-headed Bullfinch)
Beavan's Wren-Warbler *Prinia rufescens* (Blyth 1847)
(Alt. Rufous/Rufescent/Lesser-brown/Dark-crowned Prinia, Lesser-brown Wren-Warbler)

Captain Robert C Beavan (1841–1870) wrote the *List of India Birds* in 1868. He served with **Tytler** in the Andaman Islands. His health was poor and he was twice invalided home to England, on the second occasion dying at sea at the age of only 29. He has several birds and at least one fish, all from the same part of the world, named after him in their scientific names, including *Prinia beavani* (now probably *P. rufescens*) and *Parus (rubidiventris) beavani* (Sikkim Black Tit).

BECCARI

Beccari's Ground Dove *Gallicolumba beccarii* (**Salvadori** 1876)
Beccari's Pygmy Parrot *Micropsitta pusio beccarii* (**Sclater** 1866)
Beccari's Scops Owl *Otus beccarii* (Salvadori 1876)
Beccari's Scrubwren *Sericornis beccarii* (Salvadori 1874)
    (Alt. Tropical Scrubwren, Little Sericornis)

Dr Odoardo Beccari (1843–1920) was an Italian botanist. He explored the Arfak Mountains during extensive zoological exploration with d'**Albertis** in 1872–1873, recorded in *Wanderings in the Great Forests of Borneo*. He also explored and collected in the Celebes and New Guinea, as well as in Sumatra, where he found the Titan Arum or Corpse Flower *Amorphophallus titanum*, the world's largest flower. Seeds of it were sent to the Royal Botanic Gardens at Kew and were successfully grown, flowering for the first time in cultivation in 1889. At some stage of his career he also collected in Ethiopia.

BECHSTEIN

Bechstein's Violet-necked Lory *Eos squamata riciniata* (Bechstein 1811)
    (Alt. Wallace's Violet-necked/Moluccan Red Lory)

Johann Mathaus Bechstein (1757–1822) was a German scientist. From 1810 until 1818 he was director of the Herzoglichen Academy of Forestry. In 1810 he adopted Ludwig Bechstein, who became famous for writing fairy tales. He himself wrote *Gemeinnutzige Naturgeschichte Deutschlands* in 1789 and *The natural history of cage birds: their management, habits, food, diseases, treatment, breeding, and the methods of catching them* which was published posthumously in 1837. Bechstein's Bat *Myotis bechsteinii* is also named after him.

BECK

Beck's Bowerbird *Sericulus bakeri* (**Chapin** 1929)
    (Alt. Baker's/Fire-maned/Macloud Bowerbird)
Beck's Petrel *Pterodroma (rostrata) becki* (**Murphy** 1928)
    (Alt. Tahiti/Solomon Islands/Peale's Petrel, Peale's Fulmar)

Rollo Howard Beck (1870–1950) was an American collector. Mearns & Mearns in *The Bird Collectors* (Academic Press, 1998) says of him '*among bird collectors (he) stands pre-eminent as the supreme seabird specialist*'. He collected for the Museum of the California Academy of Sciences and then for the American Museum of Natural History and was well known to Murphy who '*held him in high regard*' and named the petrel after him. He spent time in the Galápagos from 1897 to 1898, Alaska in 1911 and New Guinea in 1928. On many of his trips he was accompanied by his wife Ida. One trip lasted five years, whilst they explored the South American coast, and another in the South Seas lasted nearly ten, when they were part of the Sanford-Whitney Expedition.

BEDFORD

Bedford's Paradise-flycatcher *Terpsiphone bedfordi* (**Ogilvie-Grant** 1907)
(Alt. Red-bellied Paradise-flycatcher)

Herbrand Arthur Russell, 11th Duke of Bedford (1858–1940), was a president of the Zoological Society of London from 1899 until 1936. He was also a trustee of the British Museum. **Ogilvie-Grant** originally described the flycatcher as *Trochocercus bedfordi* from a specimen from the eastern Congo. He also originally named another three birds after Bedford in their binomials; a brush warbler *Bradypterus bedfordi*, the Tit-Hylia *Pholidornis (rushiae) bedfordi* and a form of the Eurasian Nuthatch *Sitta (europaea) bedfordi*.

BEECHEY

Beechey's Jay *Cyanocorax beecheii* (**Vigors** 1829)
(Alt. Purplish-backed Jay)

Captain Frederick William Beechey (1796–1856) was a noted geographer and mapmaker. He led an expedition to the Pacific and the Bering Strait in *HMS Blossom* 1825 to 1828, which made significant discoveries in the Arctic, California and in the Pacific islands. During that voyage Beechey took a formal pardon to Adams, the last survivor of the Mutiny on the *Bounty*, on Pitcairn Island. *The Zoology of Captain Beechey's Voyage* was published in 1839 with the section on ornithology by Nicholas with coloured plates by George B Sowerby. A further book, *The Botany of Captain Beechey's Voyage*, was published in 1841. **Collie** collected many specimens that were not in good condition when they got back to England but he had made coloured drawings. Very many specimens were collected on that voyage so it is unsurprising that one would be named for the captain. During the voyage, in 1825, he named Point Barrow after Sir John **Barrow** of the British Admiralty. He made further voyages such as that on *HMS Sulphur* in 1836.

BEHN

Behn's Parakeet *Brotogeris chiriri behni* (**Neumann** 1931)
(Alt. Yellow-chevroned/Yellow-winged/Orange-winged/Parakeet)
Behn's Thrush *Turdus subalaris* (**Seebohm** 1877)
(Alt. Eastern Slaty/Slaty-capped Thrush)

William Friedrich Georg Behn (1808–1878) was a German explorer, who is famed for his crossing of South America in 1847. He was the Director of the Zoological Museum of the Christian Albrechts University of Kiel from 1836 until 1868.

BEICK

Beick's Blood Pheasant *Ithaginis cruentus beicki* (**Mayr** & Birkhead 1937)

Walter Beick (1883–1933) was a Russian of Baltic-German origin who was educated at St Petersburg, Berlin and Munich and was wounded in World War I while serving in the Russian Imperial army. In 1920, fearful of Bolshevik persecution, he fled to China, where he collected and studied natural history in Kansu province. In 1927 he joined the Swiss explorer Wilhelm Filchner (1877–1957) on his expedition to Central Asia. Several attempts were made on Beick's life whilst in China, where the authorities suspected him of being a spy for Turkestan. He eventually sent all his work to the Zoological Museum in Berlin and, severely depressed and convinced that he was surrounded by enemies, shot himself. About a dozen subspecies of Asian birds have *beicki* as the trinomial, including Greater Spotted Woodpecker *Dendrocops major beicki*, Sinai Rosefinch *Carpodacus synoicus beicki* and Lesser Short-toed Lark *Calandrella rufescens beicki*.

BEL

Bel's Silver Pheasant *Lophura nycthemera beli* (**Oustalet** 1898)

Bel was a collector in central Vietnam, the only area where the bird occurs. He bought the first specimen to Europe in 1897 and it was described by **Oustalet** in 1898. The second specimen was bought to Europe by **Delacour** in 1924.

BELCHER

Belcher's Gull *Larus belcheri* (**Vigors** 1829)
(Alt. Band-tailed/Simeon's Gull)

Admiral Sir Edward Belcher CB (1799–1877) was a British explorer. He explored the Pacific coast of America from 1825 until 1828. He was then in command of the *Samarang* and surveyed the coast of Borneo, the Philippine Islands and Formosa (Taiwan) from 1843 until 1846. He also explored the Arctic from 1852 until 1854, searching for Franklin. He was court-martialled, but acquitted, in 1854 for abandoning three ships during this search. Sir John **Barrow** wrote to Captain James Clark **Ross** of his surprise at the charges against Sir Edward. Belcher was the author of *The Last of the Arctic Voyages; Being a Narrative of the Expedition in HMS Assistance, under the Command of... in Search of Sir John Franklin, During the Years 1852–53–54 with Notes on the Natural History by Sir John Richardson* in 1855. He became an admiral in 1872.

BELDING

Belding's Plover *Charadrius wilsonia beldingi* (**Ridgway** 1919)
(Alt. Wilson's Plover)
Belding's Rail *Rallus longirostris beldingi* (Ridgway 1882)
(Alt. Clapper Rail)
Belding's Scrub-jay *Aphelocoma coerulescens* (Bosc 1798)
(Alt. Florida Scrub-jay)
Belding's Sparrow *Passerculus sandwichensis beldingi* (**Dickey** 1915)
(Alt. Savannah Sparrow)
Belding's Yellowthroat *Geothlypis beldingi* (Ridgway 1882)
(Alt. Peninsular Yellowthroat)

Lyman Belding (1829–1917) was a professional bird collector who wrote a series of articles: *Collecting in the Cape Region of Lower California, West* in 1877; *Catalogue of a collection of birds made near the southern extremity of the Peninsula of Lower California* in 1882; *Second catalogue of a collection of birds made near the southern extremity of Lower California* in 1883; *List of birds found at Guaymas, Sonora* in December 1882 and April 1883, *Land birds of the Pacific district* in 1890 and *A part of my experience in collecting* in 1900. The birds were named after him because he collected the early specimens.

BELFORD

Belford's Melidectes *Melidectes belfordi* (**De Vis** 1890)
(Alt. Belford's Honeyeater)

George Belford (?–1906) was the son of a Samoan chief, who collected for Sir William McGregor, presumably the Sir William McGregor who was Administrator and Lieutenant Governor of British New Guinea (around 1891) and also Governor of Queensland (1909–1914). **De Vis** first described the honeyeater in the Annual Report on British New Guinea, which was published in Queensland.

BELGIANS

Who said there are no famous Belgians apart from the surrealist painter Rene Magritte, Hercule Poirot and Jean-Claude Van Damme ('the muscles from Brussels')? There are a number who have attained scientific immortality by having birds named after them. Princess **Stephanie** of Belgium managed it through her fame not so much as a Belgian but as the wife of the heir to the Austro-Hungarian Empire. Charles Frédéric **Dubois** and his son Alphonse Joseph Charles Dubois were both ornithologists and managed it as did Commandant P F **Nahan**, by virtue of his prowess as an explorer. Both Henri Eugene Alphonse Hubert **Schouteden** and Lieutenant Colonel A F G **Weyns**, managed it by discovering animals in the Congo and Baron **Popelaire** de Terloo's collecting in Peru not only attracted fame and a bird name but that of a giant snail too! Nor is it just historic figures; Professor J C **Ruwet** has managed the same feat in the last couple of years. Alexandre **Prigogine** may have been Russian born but he was a Belgian citizen.

BELL

> Bell's Sparrow *Amphispiza belli* (**Cassin** 1850)
> (Alt. Sage Sparrow)
> Bell's Vireo *Vireo bellii* (**Audubon** 1844)
> Bell's Warbler *Basileuterus belli* (**Giraud** 1841)
> (Alt. Golden-browed Warbler)

John Graham Bell (1812–1899) was an American taxidermist who went with **Audubon** on his Missouri River Trip of 1843. He also taught taxidermy to the young Theodore Roosevelt. Bell visited California on a collecting expedition from 1849 to 1850 and discovered four new species, all described by John **Cassin**: **Lawrence**'s Goldfinch *Carduelis lawrencei*, White-headed Woodpecker *Picoides albolarvatus*, **Williamson**'s Sapsucker and Sage Sparrow. Bell shot his first Sage Sparrow near Sonoma and Cassin gave the little bird the Latin name *Emberiza belli* in his honour.

BENDIRE

> Bendire's Crossbill *Loxia curvirostra bendirei* Ridgway 1884
> (Alt. Red Crossbill)
> Bendire's Summer Sparrow *Aimophila carpalis* (Coues 1873)
> (Alt. Rufous-winged Sparrow)
> Bendire's Thrasher *Toxostoma bendirei* (Coues 1873)

Major Charles Emil Bendire (1836–1897) was an oologist, zoologist and army surgeon who was born in Germany and emigrated to the United States. He collected birds' eggs in the 1860s and 1870s while stationed at frontier posts throughout the Department of Columbia and was famous for the copious notes which he made of everything he observed. Fellow officers sent Bendire feathers and eggs from other posts in the West. He became honorary Curator of Oology at the Smithsonian Institution in 1883 and compiled two volumes entitled *Life Histories of North American Birds*. He personally oversaw the watercolour illustrations to ensure accuracy. This work was curtailed when he died at the age of 60 of Bright's Disease. A lake and a mountain in Oregon are named for Bendire. His remarkable collection of 8,000 eggs remains an exhibit at the American Natural History Museum in Washington. Fans of Westerns might like to know that he also once argued Chief Cochise into a truce. **Coues** named the Thrasher after him.

BENNETT, E

Bennett's Woodpecker *Campethera bennetti* (A **Smith** 1836)

Edward Turner Bennett (1797–1836) was a British naturalist. In 1822 he promoted the setting up of a London entomological club. This was developed in association with the Linnean Society into a zoological club which was the starting point for the establishment of the Zoological Society of London in 1826, of which he became the first vice-secretary. In 1831 he became secretary and held this post until his premature death in 1836, aged just 39 years. Andrew **Smith**, one of the most outstanding collectors and travellers of his era, named the woodpecker after him.

BENNETT, G

Bennett's Bird-of-Paradise *Drepanornis albertisi cervinicauda* (P L **Sclater** 1883)
Bennett's Cassowary *Casuarius bennetti* (**Gould** 1858)
(Alt. Australian/Dwarf Cassowary)

Dr George Bennett (1804–1893) was a British surgeon, botanist and zoologist. He settled permanently in Australia in 1836. He wrote *A recent visit to several of the Polynesian islands*, a scientific paper, in 1830 as well as *Wanderings in New South Wales, Batavia* in 1834 and *Gatherings of a Naturalist in Australia – Being Observations Principally on the Animal and Vegetable Productions of New South Wales, New Zealand, and some of the Austral Islands* in 1860. He was the first curator and secretary of the Australian Museum (from 1835) and an early conservationist. In 1860 he wrote: '*Many of the Australian quadrupeds and birds are not only peculiar to that country, but are, even there, of comparatively rare occurrence: and such has been the war of extermination recklessly waged against, that they are in a fair way of becoming extinct. Even in our own time, several have been exterminated; and unless the hand of man be stayed from their destruction, the Ornithorhynchus and the Echidna, the Emeu and the Megapodius, like the Dodo, Moa and Notornis, will shortly exist only in the pages of the naturalist. The Author hopes that what he has been induced to say with reference to this important subject will not be without weight to every thoughtful colonist.*' The fact that all four survive today in good numbers may well owe a great deal to his timely campaign. He spent 50 years unsuccessfully trying to understand monotreme and marsupial biology fully.

BENSBACH

Bensbach's Bird-of-Paradise *Ianthothorex bensbachii* (**Gould***)

J Bensbach was living at the end of the 19th century on Ternate in the Molucca. **Gould** illustrated the bird but we can find no other reference to it. However, there is a Bensbach River in Papua New Guinea and it is an area renowned for birds of paradise, so this may be a transcription error and the bird may have been named for the geographical area and not for the man. Alternatively, both the bird and the river may be named for our otherwise unidentified fellow.

BENSCH

Bensch's Monia *Monias benschi* (**Oustalet** & Grandidier 1903)
(Alt. Subdesert Mesite/Bensch's Mesite/Rail)

Jean Henri Émile Bensch (1868–1944) was an administrator in the French colonial regime in Madagascar. Between 1921 and 1923 he was Administrator of the islands of Saint Pierre and Miquelon, and was Governor there from 1923 to 1928. In 1899 he was recorded as having sent bird specimens to Paris and there is a later reference (1912) to his collection of insects being examined by a fellow enthusiast.

BENSON

Benson's Rock Thrush *Pseudocossyphus bensoni* (Farkas 1971)
(Alt. Farkas' Rock Thrush/Robin-Chat)

Constantine Walter Benson (1909–1982), known as 'Con', was born and educated in England. He studied at Cambridge, where achieved the distinction of an athletics blue before he embarked on a career in the colonial service. He spent 20 years in Nyasaland (now Malawi) and was awarded the OBE on his retirement in 1965. He was a major figure in central African ornithology and an ultra-meticulous systematist. He collected in central Africa for over 30 years, aided throughout by Jali Makawa. His numerous publications included several books notably *Birds of Zambia* in 1971 (with R K Brooke *et al.*) and *Birds of Malawi,* in 1977 (with his wife Mary). He was editor of the Bulletin of the British Ornithologists' Club from 1969 to 1974 and catalogued the bird collections in the University Museum at Cambridge. **Farkas** described the rock thrush in 1971 but Kinnear had described the Benson specimen in 1938, assigning it to a different genus. It may be an apocryphal tale but Con is said to have *tasted* all the specimens he collected – apparently owls taste the worst and turacos the best.

BENT

Bent's Crossbill *Loxia curvirostra benti* (Griscon 1937)
(Alt. Red Crossbill)

Arthur Cleveland Bent (1866–1954) was a successful businessman and a renowned amateur Massachusetts ornithologist. He wrote *Life Histories of North American Birds.* Until recently, this massive work of 26 volumes, comprising over 10,000 pages of information, represented perhaps the single most comprehensive resource on the natural history of North American birds.

BEREZOWSKI

Berezowski's Blood Pheasant *Ithaginis cruentus berezowskii* (**Bianchi** 1908)
(Alt. Mrs Sage's Blood Pheasant)

M Berezovski was a Russian zoologist and an associate of **Bianchi**. Together they discovered and described the Black-throated Robin *Erithacus obscurus*, in 1891. The Forest Musk Deer *Moschus berezovski* is also named after him.

BERLA

Berla's Golden-tailed Parrotlet *Touit surda ruficauda* (Berla 1954)

Herbert Franzioni Berla (1912–1985) was a Brazilian ornithologist and expert on mites who worked for the National Museum in Rio de Janeiro. He made a collecting trip to Pernambucao in 1946 collecting and cataloguing 160 plus bird species. Berla himself described this potential race of the parrotlet although most authorities consider that Swainson (1820) has priority if the subspecies is recognised.

BERLEPSCH

Berlepsch's Canastero *Asthenes berlepschi* (Hellmayr 1917)
Berlepsch's Emerald *Chlorostilbon poortmani* (**Bourcier** 1843)
   (Alt. Cabini's/Poortman's/Short-tailed Emerald)
Berlepsch's Gnatcatcher *Polioptila dumicola* (**Viellot** 1817)
   (Alt. Masked Gnatcatcher)
Berlepsch's Parakeet *Pyrrhura melanura berlepschi* (**Salvadori** 1891)
   (Alt. Maroon-tailed Parakeet)
Berlepsch's Pigeon *Columba subvinacea* (**Lawrence** 1868)
   (Alt. Ruddy Pigeon)
Berlepsch's Tinamou *Crypturellus berlepschi* (**Rothschild** 1897)
Berlepsch's Spotted Woodcreeper *Xiphorhynchus erythropygius aequatorialis* (Berlepsch & Taczanowski 1884)
   (Alt. Spot-throated Woodcreeper)

Hans Karl Hermann Ludwig Graf von Berlepsch (1850–1915) was a German ornithologist and author, who collected in Latin America. Jointly with **Hellmayr**, he revised the catalogue of **Tschudi**'s collection in the Natural History Museum at Neuchâtel. He named a number of birds in their binomials after his wife, Emm,a with the Latinised *emmae*.

BERLIOZ

Berlioz's Black Flycatcher *Melaenornis ardesiacus* (Berlioz 1936)
   (Alt. Yellow-eyed Black Flycatcher)
Berlioz's Pheasant *Lophura nycthemera berliozi* (**Delacour** & Jabouille 1928)
   (Alt. Silver Pheasant)
Berlioz's Sunbird *Anthreptes rectirostris* (Shaw 1912)
   (Alt. Yellow-chinned/Grey-chinned/Green-backed/Green/Western Sunbird)
Berlioz's Swift *Apus berliozi* (**Ripley** 1965)
   (Alt. Forbes-Watson's Swift)
Berlioz's Tyrant *Knipolegus subflammulatus* (Berlioz 1959)
   (Alt. Andean Tyrant)
Berlioz's Woodnymph *Augasma cyaneo-beryllina* (Berlioz 1965)

Jacques Berlioz (1891–1975) was a French ornithologist and author who was in charge of the bird department at the Paris museum in the mid-20th century. His publications included *Étude d'une Collection d'Oiseaux du Tchad* in 1938 and *Le Développement de l'Ornithologie et l'industrie Plumassière* in 1959. The woodnymph is now considered to be a hybrid.

BERNIER

Bernier's Teal *Anas bernieri* (**Hartlaub** 1860)
   (Alt. Madagascar Teal)

Bernier's Vanga *Oriolia bernieri* (**Delacour** 1854)

Chevalier J A Bernier was a French naval surgeon. He was also a botanist and collector who spent some time between 1831 and 1834 in Madagascar. He took 198 specimens back to France, where they were catalogued in 1835.

BERNSTEIN

Bernstein's Black Lory *Chalcopsitta atra bernsteini* (**Rosenberg** 1861)
(Alt. Bernstein's Black/Glossy Lory)
Bernstein's Coucal *Centropus bernsteini* (**Schlegel** 1866)
(Alt. Lesser Black Coucal)
Bernstein's Red Lory *Eos bornea bernsteini* (Rosenberg 1863)
(Alt. Greater/Rothschild's Red Lory)

Heinrich Agathon Bernstein (1828–1865) was a German zoologist and collector. He left a diary of his last journey (1864–1865) from Ternate to New Guinea. Confusion might arise as the name Berstein, latinised *bersteini,* also appears but we are satisfied that Berstein is just a misspelling of Bernstein.

BERTAM

Bertam's Weaver *Ploceus bertrandi* (Shelley 1893)
(Alt. Bertram's Weaver)

See **Bertram**.

BERTHELOT

Berthelot's Pipit *Anthus berthelotii* (**Bolle** 1862)
(Alt. Canary Island Pipit)

Sabin Berthelot (1794–1880) was the French consul in Tenerife. He wrote *Histoire naturelle des Îles Canaries* in 1835. He also wrote a book on *The Exploration of the Southern Coast of Spain* in 1867.

BERTONI

Bertoni's Antbird *Drymophila rubricollis* (Bertoni 1901)

Arnoldo de Winkelried Bertoni (1857–1929) was an ornithologist. In 1879 he wrote *A Guide to the Birds of South America*. He was also the author of the *New Birds of Paraguay* and *Paraguay Fauna*.

BERTRAM

Bertram's Weaver *Ploceus bertrandi* (**Shelley** 1893)
(Alt. Bertrands Weaver)

Bertram Lutley Sclater (1866–1897) was a captain in the British army, having previously been a lieutenant in the Royal Engineers. He served in Uganda and other parts of Africa and explored and mapped in Nyasaland (now Malawi) in the 1880s and 1890s. A sub-species of the Rose-breasted Bush Shrike *Malaconotus olivaceus bertrandi* is also named after him. **Shelley** described the weaver, which was collected in Nyasaland. Shelley had been a grenadier in 1860s and was employed by the South African government as a surveyor so their shared occupations may account for the association between them. Shelley also named a shrike (a boubou) from Nyasaland *Laniarius bertrandi* in its original description of 1894.

BERTRAND

Bertrand's Weaver *Ploceus bertrandi* (Shelley 1893)
(Alt. Bertram's/Bertam's Weaver)

See **Bertram**.

BEWICK

Bewick's Swan *Cygnus bewickii* (**Yarrell** 1830)
Bewick's Wren *Thryomanes bewickii* (**Audubon** 1827)

Thomas Bewick (1753–1828) was an English ornithologist and engraver; the best-known English illustrator of his generation. His fine woodcuts of birds, mammals and rural scenes made woodcutting an art form. He never saw America but most natural history students, including **Audubon**, knew Bewick's works. Audubon met the elderly Bewick on his first trip to England in 1827 and honoured Bewick in naming after him a new wren, which he'd shot in Louisiana 16 years before. Audubon wrote: '*A complete Englishman, full of life and energy though now seventy-four, very witty and clever, better acquainted with America than most of his countrymen, and an honor to England.*' And '*...Thomas Bewick is a son of Nature. Nature alone reared him under her peaceful care, and he in gratitude of heart has copied one department of her works that must stand unrivalled forever*'
This latter reference is of course to Bewick's woodcuts of British birds. Shortly before he died, Bewick paid a final visit to Audubon and encountered another visitor, William **Swainson**. It was an informal gathering of the three greatest natural history artists of their age.

BIANCHI

Bianchi's Blood Pheasant *Ithacinus cruentus michaelis* (Bianchi 1903)
Bianchi's Pheasant *Phasianus colchicus bianchii* (Buturlin 1904)
Bianchi's Warbler *Seicercus (burkii) valentini* (**Hartert** 1907)
(Alt. Golden-spectacled Warbler)

Valentin L Bianchi (1857–1920) was a Russian zoologist and ornithologist who was an associate of **Berezovski**. Together they discovered and described the Black-throated Robin *Erithacus obscurus* in 1891. He was Curator of the Ornithological Department of the Imperial Academy of Sciences at St Petersburg. Writing with GG Jacobson, he published *Orthoptera and Pseudoneuroptera of the Russian Empire and adjacent countries* in 1905 in St Petersburg. He was also the author of *Colymbiformes et Procellariiformes*, which is the first volume of *Faune de la Russie et des Pays Limitrophes,* which was published in 1911 in St Petersburg. His son V V Bianki is a well-known writer on nature and ornithology in present day Russia.

BICHENO

Bicheno's Finch *Stizoptera (Poephila) bichenovii* (**Vigors** & **Horsfield** 1927)
(Alt. Double-barred/Banded/Owl-faced/White/Black-rumped/Owl-finch)

James Ebenezer Bicheno (1785–1851) was the British Colonial Secretary for Van Diemen's Land (now Tasmania) from 1843–1851. He was a keen amateur botanist and experimented with plants on his farm on the banks of the New Town rivulet. Bicheno was famous for his girth; it being said that '*he could fit three full bags of wheat into his trousers*'. He made economic and scientific studies, was called to the Bar in 1822 and was secretary of the Linnean Society from 1825 to 1832 as well as being a partner in a Glamorganshire iron-works from 1832 until 1842. He had a number of papers on botany and natural history published in the Linnean Society's journal, the Transactions. He also assisted Sir William **Jardine** in preparing the two volumes of *Illustrations of Ornithology* published in 1830. Bicheno lectured on botany to the Mechanics Institute and had papers published in the Transactions of the Royal Society of Tasmania. Furthermore, he was an early vice-president of the Royal Society of Tasmania. He also wrote *Observations on the Philosophy of Criminal Jurisprudence with remarks on Penitentiary Prisons* in 1819. Bicheno died in Hobart in 1851 and bequeathed his substantial library to Tasmania. It was incorporated into the first Tasmanian Library. A Tasmanian town was named after him the year he died, in recognition of his involvement in its development.

BICKNELL

Bicknell's Thrush *Catharus bicknelli* (**Ridgway** 1882)

Eugene P Bicknell (1859–1927) was a founder of the American Ornithologists' Union. The then 21-year-old amateur ornithologist climbed the summit of Slide Mountain in the Catskills, not far from New York City on 15 June 1881. After he arrived near the top he heard Swainson's Thrushes *Catharus ustulatus* singing and calling. Then he heard an unfamiliar song that was more reminiscent of a Veery *C. fuscescens*. A thrush-sized bird flew across the opening enabling him a clean shot to collect it. He believed it to be a Grey-cheeked Thrush *C. minimus* but sent the specimen to Dr Robert **Ridgway** at the American Museum of Natural History, who classified it as a new subspecies of the Grey-cheeked Thrush, and gave it the name Bicknell's Thrush in 1882. It was elevated to full-species status in 1995 based on DNA studies and differences in size, song and zoo-geography, after work by Dr Henri Ouellet in 1993.

BIDDULPH

Biddulph's Ground Jay *Podoces biddulphi* (**Hume** 1874)
(Alt. Xinjang Ground Jay)

Sir John Biddulph (1840–1921) was an army colonel and a member of the Yarkand Mission to areas around northern India in 1873. In 1907 he published *The Pirates of Malabar* and *An Englishwoman in India Two Hundred Years Ago.*

BIET

Biet's Laughing-thrush *Garrulax bieti* (**Oustalet** 1897)
(Alt. White-speckled Laughing-thrush)

Monsignor Felix Biet (1838–1904) was a French missionary on the Burmese/Chinese border. He was posted to Bhamo in 1873 and became Bishop of Diana. His name is also commemorated in the scientific name of the Chinese Desert Cat *Felis bieti*.

BINGHAM

Bingham's Bulbul *Hypsipetes thompsoni* (Bingham 1900)

Colonel Charles Thomas Bingham (1848–1908) was an entomologist. He wrote, among other works, *The Fauna of British India, including Ceylon and Burma*. The scientific honorific is for Henry Nilus Thompson (?–1938), who was a forestry officer in Burma.

BISHOP

Bishop's Oo *Moho bishopi* (**Rothschild** 1893)
(Alt. Molokai Oo)

Charles Reed Bishop (1822–1915) was an American businessman who lived in Hawaii.

The Bishop's O-o was endemic to Molokai and was discovered by H C Palmer, a collector for Lord **Rothschild,** in 1892. He founded the Bishop Museum on Oahu, the largest museum dedicated to the study of the Pacific. The museum was erected as a tribute to his wife, Princess Bernice Pauahi Bishop (1831–1884), a member of Hawaii's royal family. Rothschild named the bird after him in 1889 and wrote the description in 1893.

BISMARCK

Bismarck's Hanging Parrot *Loriculus aurantiifrons tener* (P L **Sclater** 1877)

Whilst there might be an outside chance that this parrot is named after the German Chancellor we believe it to be after the Bismarck Archipelago as the bird is found in Northern New Guinea and some of the islands of that archipelago.

BLACKBURN

Blackburnian Warbler *Dendroica fusca* (Müller 1776)

Mrs Anna Blackburn(e) (1740–1793) was a botanist who owned a museum at Fairfield in Lancashire, England. She was a correspondent of Linnaeus and a patron of ornithology in London. Her brother, Ashton Blackburn, collected a specimen of the warbler. She never married, but preferred to be called Mrs Blackburn as it gave her more standing and authority.

BLAKE

Blake's Spinetail *Synallaxis courseni* (Blake 1971)
(Alt. Apurímac/Coursen's Spinetail)

Emmet Reid Blake (1908–1997) was an American ornithologist who was Emeritus Curator of Birds at the Field Museum of Natural History in Chicago. He was actively collecting in Mexico in the 1940s and 1950s. He wrote *Birds of Mexico* in 1953 and *Manual of Neotropical Birds* in 1977.

BLAKISTON

Blakiston's Fish Owl *Ketupa blakistoni* (**Seebohm** 1884)

Thomas Wright Blakiston (1832–1891) was born in Lymington, Hampshire, England. In 1851 he was commissioned and later fought in the Crimean War. From 1857 until 1859 he explored western Canada with the **Palliser** Expedition and three years later was in China, where he organised an expedition up the Yangtze River, going 900 miles further than any Westerner before him. Most of the next 23 years was spent on business in Japan but he compiled a catalogue of the birds of northern Japan and is today renowned as one of that country's outstanding naturalists. Blakiston lavished money on his hobby, the study of birds, and he became world-famous in ornithology. He preserved many bird specimens, 1,331 of which are now in the museum attached to the Agricultural Department of Hokkaido University. In 1886 he moved to the United States. While visiting San Diego he caught pneumonia and died. He published various essays on birds in Japan and some accounts of his explorations in the Tohoku district, besides the accounts of his expedition along the Yangtze River and his essays on birds in Canada. Blakiston was the first person to establish that animals in Hokkaido, Japan's northern island, have northern Asian affinities and differ in appearance from those in Honshu. As a result of Blakiston's work, the Tsugaru Strait, which divide Hokkaido from Honshu, became known as an important zoogeographical boundary: the 'Blakiston Line'. **Seebohm** described the owl from a specimen that Blakiston collected in Hakodadi, Yezo, Japan, in 1883.

BLANDFORD

See **Blanford**.

BLANDING

Blanding's Finch *Chlorura chlorura* (**Audubon** 1839)
(Alt. Green-tailed Towhee)

Dr William Blanding (1772–1857) was an American physician and chemist, who had a collection of birds. He was an active member of the Philadelphia Academy of Natural Sciences and once presented a paper there entitled *Fecundity of the Bass*. He had many interests, including archaeology and native culture, and it was he who found a site, known as Mulberry, which was once a capital city of Cofitachequi, a chiefdom on the Wateree river in central South Carolina from *c.*1100 to 1700. He was also a numismatist who manufactured 'ancient' coins as a hobby. He was a friend and patron of **Gambel**, who named the bird after him. Gambel originally called it the Green-tailed Towhee *Fringilla blandingiana* but although the scientific name has changed, Blanding is still often honoured in the common name. He was a keen amateur herpetologist too and Blanding's Turtle *Emydoidea blandingii*, which he discovered in 1830, was also named after him by Holbrook in 1838 who wrote '*This animal was first observed by Dr William Blanding, of Philadelphia, an accurate Naturalist, whose name I have given to the species.*'

BLANFORD

Blanford's Lark *Calandrella blanfordi* (**Shelley** 1902)
Blanford's Olive Bulbul *Pycnonotus blanfordi* (**Jerdon** 1872)
(Alt. Streak-eared Bulbul)
Blanford's Rosefinch *Carpodacus rubescens* (Blanford 1871)
(Alt. Crimson Rosefinch)
Blanford's Saw-wing *Psalidoprocne pristoptera blanfordi* (Blundell & Lovat 1899)
(Alt. Black Rough-winged Swallow)
Blanford's Snowfinch *Pyrgilauda blanfordi* (**Hume** 1876)
(Alt. Plain-backed Snowfinch)
Blanford's Warbler *Sylvia leucomelaena* (**Ehrenberg** 1833)
(Alt. Arabian/Red Sea Warbler)

William Thomas Blanford (1832–1905) was a geologist and zoologist. He studied at the Royal School of Mines between 1852 and 1854 and at Freiberg in Saxony before obtaining a post in the Indian Geological Survey in 1854, where he investigated coal mines at Talchir from 1854 until 1857. He then undertook a geological survey of Burma in 1860 and was appointed deputy superintendent. He surveyed in Bombay from 1862 until 1866. He was then attached to the Abyssinian expedition in 1867. Blanford published works on the geology of Abyssinia (now Ethiopia) in 1870 and of India in 1879, before settling in London in 1881. He edited works for the government on Indian fauna, contributing two volumes on mammals in 1888 and 1891. He was elected to Fellowships of the Royal Society and the Royal Geographical Society in 1874 and was president of the latter from 1888 until 1890. The Indian government published *The Scientific Results of the Second Yarkand Mission: Mammalia* by Blanford in 1879. Blanford's name is sometimes incorrectly spelt as Blandford.

BLASIUS

Blasius' Wren-Babbler *Ptilocichla mindanensis* (Blasius 1890)
(Alt. Striated/Streaked Ground Babbler/Wren-Babbler)

Dr Wilhelm August Heinrich Blasius MD PhD (1845–1912) was a German ornithologist,

as were both his brother, Rudolf Blasius (1842–1907) and his father, Johann Heinrich Blasius (1809–1870). In 1870 he was the Director of the Brunswick Museum, which boasted two specimens of the Great Auk. He became Professor of Zoology and Botany in the Herzogliche Technische Hochschule in Brunswick in 1871. He is also famed for having used the *Braunschwiegisches Anzigen*, a daily newspaper, to publish descriptions quickly, thus acquiring priority for names which he suggested over those proposed in the more ponderous and mainly English scientific journals. Apparently, this practice was one motivation for the founding of the British Ornithologists' Club and its Bulletin.

BLEWITT

> Blewitt's Owl *Athene blewitti* (**Hume** 1881)
> (Alt. Forest Owlet)

William Turnbull Blewitt (1816–1889) was born in India, where his father was serving in the British army, and eventually died there of heart disease. He worked in the Civil Service in the Punjab as a customs official. Blewitt and his associates Ball and James Davidson were amateurs who collected together. Davidson sent a specimen of the owl to **Hume**, who was the first to describe it.

BLIGH

> Bligh's Whistling Thrush *Myophonus blighi* (Holdsworth 1872)
> (Alt. Sri Lankan/Ceylon Whistling Thrush)

Samuel Bligh was a British coffee planter in Ceylon from 1872 until 1887, in which year he wrote notes on every bird species there. He discovered the whistling thrush in 1868 and it was the last endemic bird species found on the island until Deepal Warakagoda discovered a new species of owl in 2001.

BLISSETT

> Blissett's Wattle-eye *Platysteira blissetti* (**Sharpe** 1872)
> (Alt. Red-cheeked Wattle-eye)

H F Blissett (1847–1916) was a British Colonial Administrator in West Africa from 1869 until 1885. He was an amateur naturalist and collected there. **Sharpe** described the wattle-eye from a specimen, collected by A Swanzy, in the Gold Coast (now Ghana).

BLUMENBACH

> Blumenbach's Curassow *Crax blumenbachii* (**Spix** 1825)
> (Alt. Red-billed/Red-wattled Curassow)

Johann Friedrich Blumenbach (1752–1841) was a German anatomist, physician, anthropologist, naturalist, physiologist, historian and bibliographer who many regarded as Linnaeus' natural successor. He is also considered to be the founder of modern anthropology and his system for the classification of human races, devised in 1775, is still of considerable relevance today. He coined the word Caucasian as a description of the white race and, indeed, was the first to use the term 'race' to distinguish between different morphs of humanity. His many publications included *On the Natural Varieties of Mankind*, in 1775, and *Handbuch der Naturgeschichte* in 1779. He also taught both **Wied** and **Humboldt**. Blumenbach never travelled outside Europe but people sent him specimens and objects from all over the world.

BLYTH

Blyth's Cuckoo *Cuculus saturatus* (Blyth 1843)
 (Alt. Oriental/Himalayan/Sunda/Indonesian Cuckoo)
Blyth's Frogmouth *Batrachostomus affinis* (Blyth 1847)
Blyth's Hawk-Eagle *Spizaetus alboniger* (Blyth 1845)
Blyth's Hornbill *Aceros subruficollis* (Blyth 1843)
 (Alt. Plain-pouched Hornbill)
Blyth's Jungle Babbler *Trichastoma rostratum* (Blyth 1842)
 (Alt. Mangrove Brown Babbler, White-chested [Jungle] Babbler)
Blyth's Kingfisher *Alcedo hercules* (Laubmann 1917)
Blyth's Leaf Warbler *Phylloscopus reguloides* (Blyth 1842)
 (Alt. Blyth's Crowned Willow Warbler)
Blyth's Long-tailed Tit *Aegithalos iouschistos* (Blyth 1845)
 (Alt. Rufous-fronted Tit)
Blyth's Olive Bulbul *Iole* (*Hypsipetes*) *virescens* (**Temminck** 1825)
 (Alt. Olive Bulbul)
Blyth's Parakeet *Psittacula caniceps* (Blyth 1846)
 (Alt. Nicobar Parakeet)
Blyth's Parrotbill *Paradoxornis nipalensis* (**Hodgson** 1838)
 (Alt. Black-throated Parrotbill)
Blyth's Pipit *Anthus godlewskii* (**Taczanowski** 1876)
 (Alt. Godlewski's Pipit)
Blyth's Rosefinch *Carpodacus rhodochlamys* (**Brandt** 1843)
 (Alt. Pink-backed Rosefinch/Red-mantled Rosefinch)
Blyth's Reed Warbler *Acrocephalus dumetorum* (Blyth 1849)
Blyth's Tragopan *Tragopan blythii* (**Jerdon** 1870)
Blyth's Yuhina *Yuhina bakeri* (**Rothschild** 1926)
 (Alt. White-naped/Baker's /Chestnut-headed Yuhina)

Edward Blyth (1810–1873) was an English zoologist and author. He was Curator of the Museum of the Asiatic Society of Bengal from 1842 to 1864 and author of its catalogue. He wrote *The Natural History of Cranes* in 1881. **Hume** said of him: '*Neither neglect nor harshness could drive, nor wealth nor worldly advantages tempt him, from what he deemed the nobler path. [He was] ill paid and subjected ... to ceaseless humiliations*'. In a similar tribute Arthur Grote wrote: '*Had he been a less imaginative and more practical man, he must have been a prosperous one... All that he knew was at the service of everybody. No one asking him for information asked in vain*'.

BOCAGE

Bocage's Akalat *Sheppardia bocagei* (**Finsch** & **Hartlaub** 1870)
 (Alt. Bocage's Ground Robin, Rufous-cheeked Robin-Chat)
Bocage's Bush Shrike *Malaconotus bocagei*
 (Alt. Grey-green/Grey Bush Shrike)
Bocage's Longbill *Amaurocichla bocagei* (**Sharpe** 1892)
Bocage's Sunbird *Nectarinia bocagei* (**Shelley** 1879)

Bocage's [Golden] Weaver *Ploceus temporalis* (Bocage 1880)
Bocage's Waxbill *Estrilda melanotis bocagei*
(Alt. Swee/Yellow-bellied Waxbill)

José Vicente Barboza du Bocage (1823–1907) was Director of the National Zoological Museum of Lisbon, Portugal, which is now named in his honour. He became known as the father of Angolan ornithology and wrote *Ornithologie d'Angola*. He also collected sponges and other specimens.

BODIN

Bodin's Amazon *Amazona festiva bodini* (**Finsch** 1873)
(Alt. Festive Parrot, Red-backed Amazon)

Dr Karl-August Heinrich Bodinus (1814–1884) was a recognised restorer, as well as Director of the Zoological Garden of Berlin. **Finsch** named and described this race of the parrot.

BODINUS

See **Bodin**.

BOEHM

Boehm's Bee-eater *Merops boehmi* (**Reichenow** 1882)
Boehm's Flufftail *Sarothrura boehmi* (Reichenow 1900)
(Alt. Boehm's Crake, Streaky-breasted Flufftail)
Boehm's Flycatcher *Myiornis boehmi* (Reichenow 1884)
Boehm's Spine-tailed Swift *Neafrapus boehmi* (**Schalow** 1882)
(Alt. Boehm's /Bat-like Spinetail)

Dr Richard Böhm (1854–1884) was a German traveller and zoologist who worked in Tanzania and Zaïre during the late 1800s until his premature death from malaria. He wrote *Von Sansibar zum Tanganjika*, which was published in 1888.

BOLLE

Bolle's Pigeon *Columba bollii* (**Godman** 1872)
(Alt. Bolle's Laurel Pigeon)

Carl August Bolle (1821–1909) was a German collector, naturalist and botanist. He wrote *Meiner zweiter Beitrage zur Vogelkunde der Canarischen Insein* in 1857.

BONAPARTE

Bonaparte's Barbet *Gymnobucco bonapartei* (**Hartlaub** 1854)
(Alt. Grey-throated Barbet)
Bonaparte's Blackbird *Sturnella superciliaris* (Bonaparte 1851)
(Alt. White-browed Blackbird)
Bonaparte's Euphonia *Euphonia hirundinacea* (Bonaparte 1838)
(Alt. Yellow-throated Euphonia)
Bonaparte's Friarbird *Melitograis gilolensis* (Strong 1850)
(Alt. White-streaked/Striated/Gilolo Friarbird)
Bonaparte's Hanging Parrot *Loriculus philippensis bonapartei* (Souancé 1856)
(Alt. Black-billed Hanging Parrot)
Bonaparte's Gull *Larus philadelphia* (Ord 1815)
Bonaparte's Nightjar *Caprimulgus concretus* (Bonaparte 1850)
Bonaparte's Sandpiper *Calidris fuscicollis* (**Vieillot** 1819)
(Alt. White-rumped Sandpiper)

Bonaparte's Starfrontlet *Coeligena bonapartei* (Boissoneau 1840)
(Alt. Golden-bellied Starfrontlet)
Bonaparte's Tinamou *Nothocercus bonapartei* (G R **Gray** 1867)
(Alt. Highland Tinamou)

Prince Charles Lucien Bonaparte [originally Jules Laurent Lucien] (1803–1857) was a nephew of the famous statesman, the Emperor Napoleon Bonaparte. He was a renowned ornithologist, both in Europe and the United States. Bonaparte was much travelled but he spent many years in the United States cataloguing birds, and he has been described as the 'father of systematic ornithology'. He eventually settled in Paris and commenced his *Conspectus Generum Avium*, a catalogue of every bird species in the world. He died before finishing it, but its publication was heralded as a major step forward in accomplishing one of the most important goals of ornithology: a complete list of the world's birds. He also wrote *American Ornithology*, in 1825, and *Iconografia della Fauna Italica – uccelli*, in 1832. **Swainson** described Bonaparte as '*destined by nature to confer unperishable benefits on this noble science*'.

BONELLI

Bonelli's Eagle *Hieraaetus fasciatus* (**Vieillot** 1822)
Bonelli's Warbler *Phylloscopus bonelli* (Vieillot 1819)
(Alt. Western Bonelli's Warbler)

Franco Andrea Bonelli (1784–1830) was an ornithologist and collector. In 1809 he began to teach at the university of Turin. Two years later he became the curator of the museum there and totally re-catalogued the collection according to scientific principles. During this time he described the birds which were later to carry his name. The collection grew and became one of Europe's greatest assemblages of ornithological specimens during his lifetime. He wrote *Catalogue des Oiseaux du Piémont* in 1811.

BORRERO

Borrero's Cinnamon Teal *Anas cyanoptera borreroi* (Snyder & Lumsden 1951)

Jose Ignacio Borrero has studied Colombian birds since the 1940s. He has written such books as *Avifauna de la Región de Soatá, Departamento de Boyacá, Colombia* in 1955 and articles including *Notes on the breeding behaviour of Reiffer's Hummingbird/Amazilia Tzacatl*. He first described this race of the Cinnamon Teal, which is the rarest one (there appears to be no recent records) and lives only in Colombia.

BOTANISTS

A surprisingly high number of eponymous botanists appear in these pages. That is quite apart from general naturalists and all-rounders such as Frank **Ludlow**, Dr George **Thurber**, Captain Francis Kingdon-**Ward** and Alice **Northrop** who dabbled in many disciplines. **Anna** A Weber van Bosse was a botanist but was married to an ornithologist, which always helps, and Jens Wilken **Hornemann** was a friend of

Holboell. Philip Barker **Webb** was great friends with Sabin **Berthelot** and Johannes Elias **Teijsmann** was probably a friend of **Büttikofer**.

Being with James Cook's voyage no doubt made Sir Joseph **Banks** even more prominent that he would have been and these expeditions, with a range of naturalists on board, led to many such cross-over honorifics. Banks' librarian Robert **Brown** was, figuratively, in the same boat. Certainly this is true of Jean **Baptiste**, Louis Claude Theodore **Leschenault** de la Tour and Friedrich Wilhelm **Sieber** too. Carl **Lauterbach** actually led such an expedition. Dr Odoardo **Beccari**'s explorations with d'**Albertis** explain the former's honouring. L J K **Brace** was among collectors of plants not averse to taking other kinds of specimens whilst they were at it. It remains a mystery why certain other botanists, such as Pieter Willem **Korthals**, **Warszewiscz** or Franz **Neumayer** were given such an honour but the sheer fame of some, such as Elmer Drew **Merrill** and Dr Guido Frederico João **Pabst**, are explanation enough. Georg **Zenker** probably owned the land that 'his' birds lived on.

BOTHA

Botha's Lark *Spizocorys* (*Botha*) *fringillaris* (Sundevall 1850)

General Louis Botha (1862–1919) was a soldier, who was the first Prime Minister of the Union of South Africa, from 1910 until 1919, having previously been the Prime Minister of the Transvaal in 1907. **Shelley** named the lark in his honour.

BOTTA

Botta's Wheatear *Oenanthe bottae* (**Bonaparte** 1854)
(Alt. Red-breasted Wheatear)

Paul-Emile Botta (1802–1879) was a traveller and a doctor. Early in his career he spent a year on board the French ship *Héros* as ship's surgeon and naturalist. Around 1827 the vessel traded on the Californian coast under the command of Captain Auguste Duhaut-Cilly, who recorded expeditions ashore with Botta. He wrote *Notes on a Journey in Arabia* and *Account of a Journey in Yemen* in 1841. He was in Arabia from 1832 until 1846, excavating near Nineveh, the ancient capital of Assyria, from 1842 until 1845.

BOTTERI

Botteri's Sparrow *Aimophila botterii* (P L **Sclater** 1858)

Matteo Botteri (1808–1877) was an ornithologist and collector. He was born in what later became Yugoslavia and lived in Mexico, where he founded a museum at Orizaba. In 1854 he collected a specimen of the sparrow.

BOUCARD

Boucard's Antwren *Microrhopias quixensis boucardi* (P L **Sclater** 1858)
(Alt. Dot-winged Antwren)
Boucard's Hermit *Phaethornis adolphi* (**Gould** 1857)
Boucard's Hummingbird *Amazilia boucardi* (**Mulsant** 1877)
(Alt. Mangrove Hummingbird)
Boucard's Summer Sparrow *Aimophila ruficeps* (**Cassin** 1852)
(Alt. Rufous-crowned Sparrow)
Boucard's Tinamou *Crypturellus boucardi* (P L Sclater 1859)
(Alt. Slaty-breasted Tinamou)

Boucard's Wren *Campylorhynchus jocosus* (P L Sclater 1860)
(Alt. Spotted Wren)

Adolphe Boucard (1839–1905) was a French naturalist who collected in Mexico and spent more than 40 years killing hummingbirds for science and for the fashion trade. He moved to London in 1890. He passed the latter years of his life in his villa near Ryde on the Isle of Wight. He was author of *The Hummingbird* in 1891. In 1894 he wrote that '*Now-a-days the mania of collecting is spread among all classes of society, and that everyone possess, either a gallery of pictures, aquarels, drawings, or a fine library, an album of postage stamps, a collection of embroideries, laces, fans, shoes, sticks, pipes, ethnological curios, arms, prints, handbills, watches, bronzes, buttons, and such like, a collection of humming-birds should be the one selected by ladies. It is as beautiful and much more varied than a collection of precious stones and costs much less...*'

BOULTON

Boulton's Hill Partridge *Arborophila rufipectus* (Boulton 1932)
(Alt. Sichuan [Hill] Partridge)
Boulton's Puff-back Flycatcher *Batis margaritae* (Boulton 1934)
(Alt. Margaret's/Boulton's Batis)

Wilfrid Rudyerd Boulton (1901–1983) was the Curator of Birds at The Field Museum, Chicago. From 1931 until 1946 he collected in West Africa, Angola and the Kalahari Desert. Boulton himself collected the hill partridge in southern Sichuan, China.

BOURCIER

Bourcier's Hermit *Phaethornis bourcieri* (**Lesson** 1832)
Bourcier's Quail-Dove *Geotrygon frenata* (**Tschudi** 1843)
(Alt. White-throated/Pink-faced/Alamor/Peruvian Quail-Dove)

Jules Bourcier (1797–1873) was French Consul to Ecuador between 1849 and 1850, and was a collector and naturalist who specialised in hummingbirds, writing a great many descriptions of new species. He named several *franciae* in their scientific binomials after his daughter Francia.

BOURKE

Bourke's Parrot *Neophema (Neopsephotus) bourkii* (**Gould** 1841)

General Sir Richard Bourke KCB (1777–1855) was Governor of New South Wales from 1831 until 1837. The parrot was discovered in 1835 and was described and named by **Gould** in 1841. It may not have been named *directly* after Sir Richard, as it was found on the banks of the river Bogan near Fort Bourke, which had already been named after him. Hence it may really be named for a place rather than a person. Bourke was a relative of the great Parliamentarian Edmund Burke, with whom he stayed when in London.

BOURNS

Bourns' Hanging Parrot *Lorisculus philippensis bournsi* (**McGregor** 1905)
(Alt. Colasisi/Philippine/Luzon Hanging Parrot)

Major Frank Swift Bourns was a veteran of the American Civil War, who became chief surgeon and president of the Manila Board of Health in the Philippines and was responsible for starting a vaccination programme against the smallpox that was decimating the local population, around 1902. He set up a farm, using the cows to produce the vaccine. He first came to the Philippines with the Steere Expedition of 1887 to 1889, along with Dean C **Worcester**, after whom another race of the parrot is named.

BOUVIER

Bouvier's Fishing Owl *Scotopelia bouvieri* (**Sharpe** 1875)
(Alt. Vermiculated Fishing Owl)
Bouvier's Sunbird *Nectarinia bouvieri* (**Shelley** 1877)
(Alt. [Southern] Orange-tufted Sunbird)

Aimé Bouvier was a French collector and zoologist who appears to have been active around 1870. He is also remembered in the scientific names of many other animals; insects, fishes etc. as well as birds. He made two trips to Australia to collect birds, the first to Cairns between 1884 and 1885 and the second, with the taxidermist Walter Burton, to northwestern Australia in 1886. Thereafter he collected on Thursday Island, off Cape York, and at Palmerston in Northern Territory in 1886. Many of the skins were presented to the British Museum in 1887 and the remainder given to G M **Mathews**. **Sharpe** described the owl in 1875 and E P **Ramsay** named it in the same year.

BOWER

Bower's Shrike-thrush *Colluricincla boweri* (**Ramsay** 1885)
(Alt. Stripe-breasted Shrike-thrush)

Captain Thomas Henry Bowyer-Bower (1862–1886) was the English-born curator of ornithology at the Western Australian Museum, *c*.1886. He was a naturalist and collector, especially of the avifauna of Australia, and sent many specimens of rare and new forms to the British Museum and the Royal Zoological Society. He collected in Queensland in 1884 and 1885. In 1886 he went to northwestern Australia and Northern territory with the taxidermist Walter Burton, where he died, very young, of typhoid. A total of 192 species from the 1886 trip was nonetheless sent to the British Museum. After his death his mother sent his collection to G M **Mathews**, who catalogued it. Mathews named the (defunct) shrike-thrush genus *Boweryia* after him, along with a number of species and races including the Double-eyed Fig Parrot *Opopsitta diophthalma boweri*, the Green Figbird *Sphecotheres vieilloti boweri*, the Fernwren *Oreoscopus gutturalis boweri* and the Yellow Chat *Leachena (Ephthianura) crocea boweri*. **Ramsay** described the shrike-thrush and named it after Bowyer-Bower, in 1885, together with a race of the Red-backed Fairy-wren *Malurus cruentatus (melanocephalus) boweri*.

BOYER

Boyer's Cuckoo-shrike *Coracina boyeri* (G R **Gray** 1846)
(Alt. White-lored Cuckoo-shrike)

Joseph Emmanuel P Boyer (1815–?) was a French sea captain who explored in the Pacific with Dumont **d'Urville**. In 1840, when he was a young officer, they visited New Zealand and he assisted with survey work there and during the rest of the voyage. He is also commemorated in the binomial of a plant from the Philippines, *Convoluta boyeri*, but is not the Boyer commemorated in the names of a number of fish and shellfish from European and North African coastal waters; that was an earlier Boyer. However, we feel it likely that the gastropod *Megalacron boyeri* was named in his honour, as it was described at around the same period as the cuckoo-shrike and also occurs in New Guinea.

BRACE

Brace's Emerald *Chlorostilbon bracei* (**Lawrence** 1877) [Extinct]
(Alt. Brace's Hummingbird)

L J K Brace (1852–1938) was a botanist and collector from the Bahamas. As well as collecting birds, he also sent botanical specimens to the New York Botanical Gardens. Brace's Emerald is now extinct and is known only from a single specimen taken by Brace, on New Providence Island, in the Bahamas group, on 13 July 1877, and described by **Lawrence** in the same year. Lawrence assigned it to the no longer recognised genus *Sporadinus*. It was formerly treated as a subspecies of the Cuban Emerald *C.ricordii*, but has been considered a full species since 1987.

BRADFIELD

Bradfield's Hornbill *Tockus bradfieldi* (**Roberts** 1930)
Bradfield's Lark *Mirafra naevia* (**Strickland** 1853)
(Alt. Large-billed Sabota Lark)
Bradfield's Swift *Apus bradfieldi* (Roberts 1926)

R D Bradfield (1882–1949) was a South African farmer, naturalist and collector, who lived in Namibia for most of his life with his wife, M Bradfield. Austin **Roberts** named the Hornbill after Bradfield and his wife, who collected the first specimen near their farm Quickborn at the Waterberg, near Okahandja, Namibia, and sent them to him at the Transvaal Museum. R D Bradfield had the swift, a southwest African endemic, named for his wife.

BRANDT

Brandt's Cormorant *Phalacrocorax penicillatus* (Brandt 1837)
Brandt's Jay *Garrulus glandarius brandtii* (**Eversmann** 1842)
Brandt's Rosy Finch *Leucosticte brandti* (**Bonaparte** 1850)
(Alt. Black-headed Mountain Finch)

Johann Friedrich von Brandt (1802–1879) was a German zoologist who explored Siberia. He became head of the Zoological Museum in St Petersburg, and described several birds from the western United States, including the cormorant which is named for him. Brandt also wrote the first descriptions of the Red-legged Kittiwake *Rissa brevirostris* and the Spectacled Eider *Somateria fischeri*. His book *Descriptiones et cons animalium rossicorum novorum vel minus rite cognitorum, and C.aves*, dealing in particular with Russia, was published in St Petersburg in 1836. He is also commemorated in Brandt's Bat *Myotis brandtii* and other animals as diverse as a woodlouse and a piranha.

BRANICKI

Branicki's Conure *Leptosittaca branickii* (**Berlepsch** & **Stolzmann** 1894)
(Alt. Golden-plumed Parakeet/Conure)
Branicki's Hummingbird *Heliodoxa branickii* (**Taczanowski** 1874)
(Alt. Rufous-webbed Brilliant)
Branicki's Ibis *Theristicus* (*melanopis*) *branickii* (Berlepsch & Stolzmann 1894)
(Alt. Andean/Puna Buff-necked Ibis)

Hieronim Florian Radziwill Konstanty Graf von Branicki (1824–1884) was a Polish zoologist who co-founded the Branicki Museum of Warsaw with his brother Wladyslaw (1848–1914).

BRASHER

Brasher's Warbler *Basileuterus culicivorus brasherii* (**Giraud** 1841)
(Alt. Golden-crowned Warbler)

Rex Brasher (1869–1960) has been described as America's greatest bird painter. He painted almost twice as many North American birds as Louis Aggasiz **Fuertes** or John James **Audubon,** a total of 875 watercolours of 1,200 species or subspecies of birds in their natural habitats, based on the American Ornithologists' Union *Checklist of North American Birds.* The University of Connecticut is preserving the collection. All 875 were painted between 1911 and 1924 at his farm, Chickadee Valley, in Kent, Connecticut. Prior to 1911, Brasher destroyed 500 bird paintings after he became despondent because he considered his work to be inadequate. He painted all his birds from life and many people consider them more accurate than Audubon's. John Burroughs called Brasher '*the greatest bird painter of all time*'.

BRASS

Brass's Friarbird *Philemon brassi* (**Rand** 1940)

Dr Leonard J Brass (1900–1971) collected plant specimens for the Queensland Herbarium from the 1930s to the 1960s. He was collector for several of the **Archbold** Expeditions to Papua New Guinea. He succeeded Rand, who was the first Resident Biologist of the Archbold Biological Station, which was established in 1941, and remained in that post until his retirement in 1967.

BRAUN

Braun's Bush Shrike *Laniarius brauni* (**Bannerman** 1939)
(Alt. Orange-breasted Bush Shrike)

R H Braun (1908–?) was a German collector who was active in Angola and southern Africa. The minnow, *Varicorhinus brauni,* an African toad, *Bufo brauni,* and a reptile, Braun's Mabuya *Mabuya brauni,* may be named after him too. A collection which he made of botanical specimens is still held in Swaziland. **Bannerman** described the bush shrike as a race of Lühder's Bush Shrike *Laniarius luehderi.*

BRAZZA

Brazza's Martin *Phedina brazzae* (**Oustalet** 1886)
(Alt. Brazza's Swallow, Congo Martin)

Count Pierre Paul François Camille Savorgnan de Brazza (1852–1905) was a distinguished French explorer, born of Italian descent in Rio de Janeiro. He entered the French navy in 1870, served in the Gabon and explored to Ogowe from 1876 until 1878. In 1878 the French government gave him 100,000 francs for exploring the country north of the Congo, where he secured vast grants of land for France and founded stations including that of Brazzaville on the north shore of Stanley Pool. He returned in 1883, largely unsubsidised by the French government and by 1886 had established 26 stations. His explorations continued until 1897. From 1890 to 1891 he was Governor of the French Congo.

BREHM

Brehm's Parrot *Psittacella brehmii* (**Schlegel** 1871)
(Alt. Brehm's Tiger Parrot)

Alfred Edmund Brehm (1829–1884) was a German traveller, collector and zoologist. He

collected in Egypt and the Sudan in 1852, in Spain in 1856 and in Norway in 1860. He wrote *Das leben der vogel* in 1861. The Emperor of Austria honoured him by granting him a peerage in 1878. His elder brother, Oskar, joined him in Africa but was drowned in 1850, having got out of his depth whilst bathing in a river.

BREWER

Brewer's Blackbird *Euphagus cyanocephalus* (**Wagler** 1829)
Brewer's Duck *Anas breweri*
  (Alt. Hybrid Mallard *A.platyrhynchos* x Gadwall *A.strepera*)
Brewer's Sparrow *Spizella breweri* (Cassin 1856)

Dr Thomas Mayo Brewer (1814–1880) was an American naturalist and ornithologist who co-wrote the *History of North American Birds* with **Baird** and **Ridgway**. He was also the author of *North American Oology* in 1857. He was very involved in politics, a family trait as his father had actually taken part in the Boston Tea Party. He had contempt for those studying birds in the field, preferring to study their skins in museum collections! He also defended the House Sparrow *Passer domesticus* against moves to eliminate this introduced species from the United States. **Audubon** named the blackbird, which **Wagler** first described, and **Cassin** described and named thesparrow. The duck was named by **Audubon** who wrote '*I have named this Duck after my friend Thomas M Brewer of Boston, as a mark of the estimation in which I hold him as an accomplished ornithologist*'. Brewer's only daughter, **Lucy**, was named after Audubon's wife. In turn a hummingbird, the Honduran Emerald *Amazilia luciae,* was named for Lucy by her father's friend, George **Lawrence**.

BREWSTER

Brewster's Booby *Sula leucogaster* (Boddaert 1783)
  (Alt. Brown Booby)
Brewster's Egret *Egretta thula* (Molina 1782)
  (Alt. Snowy Egret)
Brewster's Green Conure *Aratinga holochlora brewsteri* (**Nelson** 1928)
  (Alt. Green/Orange-throated/Mexican/Pacific/Nicaraguan Parakeet/Conure)
Brewster's Screech Owl *Otus kennicottii bendirei* (Brewster 1882)
  (Alt. Western Screech Owl)
Brewster's Warbler *Vermivora chrysoptera x V. pinus*
  (Alt. Brewster's Hybrid Vermivora, Lawrence's Warbler)
Brewster's Woodpecker *Melanerpes uropygialis* (**Baird** 1854)
  (Alt. Gila Woodpecker)

William Brewster (1851–1919) was an ornithologist. He was born in South Reading (now Wakefield), Massachusetts. He graduated from the Cambridge High School in 1869 but was prevented by a difficulty with his eyes from entering Harvard. Subsequently he devoted his attention exclusively to the study of ornithology, becoming assistant in charge of the

collection of birds and mammals in the Boston Society of Natural History in 1880 and Curator of Ornithology at the Museum of Comparative Zoology, Cambridge in 1885. He wrote *Birds of the Cape Regions of Lower California* in 1902 and *Birds of the Cambridge Region of Massachusetts* in 1906. The eminent ornithologist Ludlow **Griscom** of Harvard wrote, '*Having now spent some thirteen years in studying Brewster's field work and records, it is my humble opinion that he was one of the greatest and most naturally gifted field ornithologists that America has ever produced.*' Brewster's Warbler proved to be a hybrid of the Blue-winged Warbler and the Golden-winged Warbler. Brewster described this Californian race of the screech owl in 1882 and three other races in 1888, 1891 and 1902. Western Screech Owls live in western North America and have at least eight subspecies, a number of which are named after people.

BRIDGES

Bridges' Antshrike *Thamnophilus bridgesi* (P L **Sclater** 1856)
(Alt. Black-hooded Antshrike)
Bridges' Gull *Larus bridgersi* (**Fraser** 1845)
Bridges' Woodhewer *Drymornis bridgesii* (**Eyton** 1850)
(Alt. Scimitar-billed Woodhewer/Woodcreeper)

Thomas C Bridges (1807–1865) was a traveller and collector in tropical America from 1822 until 1865. There are mammals from Chile named for him, such as the Brushtail Rat or Bridges' Degu *Octodon bridgesi*, as well as birds from Central America. **Eyton** (some sources say Richmond) described the woodhewer, from a specimen collected by Bridges in Bolivia, and **P L Sclater** described the antshrike from a specimen which Bridges collected in Panama. In 1889, P L Sclater also described an antbird *Upucerthia bridgesi* which Bridges collected in Bolivia in 1846, and which commemorates the collector in its binomial. G R **Gray** described a form of the Dusky-legged Guan *Penelope* (*obscura*) *bridgesi* in 1860 which Bridges collected in the same place at the same time. L **Fraser** described *Larus bridgesi* from a specimen collected by Bridges in 1843 in Valparaiso, Chile. The name is defunct and we are unclear to which species it now refers. There are another three dozen specimens of birds in the British Museum collected by Bridges in Chile, Bolivia and Guatemala and bought by, or sent to, a number of ornithologists.

BRIGIDA

Brigida's Woodcreeper *Hylexetastes brigidai* (Cardoso, Novaes & Oren 1995)

Manoel Santa Brigida is a Brazilian ornithologist who collected the holotype. He worked as senior taxidermist in the ornithology section of the Museu Paraense Emilio Goeldi in the last two decades of the 20th century. According to the Bulletin of the British Ornithologists' Club '*During this time, he contributed tirelessly to the expansion of Museu Goeldi's bird collections and, consequently, to our knowledge of the systematics and distribution of Amazonian birds*'. The woodcreeper was only named in 1995. It was first described by José M Cardoso da Silva, Fernando C **Novaes** and David C Oren.

BROOK

Brook's Lorikeet *Trichoglossus haematodus brooki* (**Ogilvie-Grant** 1907)
(Alt. Brook's Lory, Rainbow Lorikeet)

E J Brook was an aviculturalist and evidently a very keen parrot breeder as a member of the Parrot Society recently wrote, of the Black Lory *Chalcopsitta atra* '*This was the first time the species had been bred in England since E J Brook was successful in 1909*'. Brook's Lorikeet was collected by W **Goodfellow** and presented to the British Museum by Brook (as were other bird specimens collected by Goodfellow in Ecuador), in whose possession the bird died. Goodfellow also collected for another aviculturalist, Mrs Marion **Johnstone** who, like Brook, was a successful breeder (of parrots). **Ogilvie-Grant** originally described the lorikeet as a full species.

BROOKE

Brooke's Scops Owl *Otus brookii* (**Sharpe** 1892)
(Alt. Rajah's Scops Owl)

Sir Charles Johnson Brooke (1829–1917) was originally plain Charles Johnson but took the name Brooke when he became the second 'White Rajah' of Sarawak (from 1868 to 1917), on the death of his uncle, James Brooke, the original 'White Rajah' (See also **Rajah**). Rajah James invited Wallace to collect in Sarawak but it isn't clear if Wallace went. Rajah Charles was a notable eccentric who lost an eye in a riding accident and replaced it with a false one which had originally been destined for a stuffed albatross.

BROOKS, A

Brooks's Niltava *Cyornis poliogenys* (W E **Brooks** 1879)
(Alt. Pale-chinned [Blue-] Flycatcher)
Brooks's Willow Warbler *Phylloscopus subviridis* (W E Brooks 1872)
(Alt. Brook's Leaf Warbler)

Allan Cyril Brooks (1869–1946) was born at Etawa, India where his father, William **Brooks**, was a civil engineer. At the age of four, Allan was sent home to England and remained there until 1881, when his father emigrated to Canada to farm at Milton, Ontario. Even as a small boy Allan was interested in natural history and was encouraged by his father's ornithologist friends. In England, the taxidermist John Hancock taught him how to blow eggs, collect butterflies and recognise plants. In 1885 Allan was taught to prepare skins by Thomas McIlwraith, the veteran birdman of eastern Canada. By the time he was 18 he was an excellent marksman and skinner. In 1887, W E Brooks moved to British Columbia and Allan devoted every hour he could spare from farm work to searching for, and observing, wildlife. He spent the whole of 1887 hunting for and preparing specimens for museums and private collectors. In 1906, Brooks received his first major contract, to illustrate Dawson and Bowles' *Birds of Washington*. Allan Brooks also conserved songbirds near his home by shooting predators including many birds of prey!

BROOKS, W

Brooks's Nuthatch *Sitta cashmirensis* (A Brooks 1871)
(Alt. Kashmir Nuthatch)

William Edwin Brooks (1829–1899) worked as assistant to his father, W A Brooks of Newcastle-on-Tyne, who was the chief engineer on the Tyne docks. In 1856 he went to India as civil engineer on the East India Railway. Subsequently, in 1881, he moved to Canada where he collected specimens for the British Museum. He was the father of Allan **Brooks**.

BROWN, G

Brown's Long-tailed Pigeon *Reinwardtoena browni* (**Sclater** 1877)
(Alt. Pied Cuckoo-Dove)
Brown's Monarch *Monarcha browni* (**Ramsay** 1883)
(Alt. Kulambangra Monarch)

The Reverend George Brown DD (1835–1917) was a missionary to Melanesia. He was a Methodist and in 1875 he seems to have been the first Christian Missionary to have landed in New Ireland, the islands to the east of the mainland of Papua New Guinea and part of the present-day country. He spent much time exploring in the company of **Cockerell**. He published *George Brown, D.D., Pioneer Missionary and Explorer. An Autobiography* in 1905.

BROWN, R

Brown's Parakeet *Platycercus brownii* (**Kuhl** 1820)
(Alt. Northern Rosella)
Brown's Tern *Sterna antillarum* (**Lesson** 1847)
(Alt. Least Tern)

Robert Brown (1773–1858) was a botanist, who was educated at Aberdeen and Edinburgh and began studying the flora of Scotland in 1791. He was an army official in Ireland in 1795 and naturalist to Captain Flinders' Australasian expedition from 1801 until 1805. He was librarian to the Linnean Society and to Sir Joseph **Banks** and published *Prodromus Florae Novae Hollandiae et insula Van-Diemen* in 1810. He was eminent for his investigations into the impregnation of plants.

BRUCE

Bruce's Green Pigeon *Treron waalia* (**Meyer** 1793)
Bruce's Scops Owl *Otus brucei* (**Hume** 1872)
(Alt. Striated Scops Owl)

The Reverend Henry James Bruce (1835–1909) was an American missionary in India from 1862 until his death. He was born at Hardwick, Massachusetts and died at Panchgani (India). He published several books in the Marathi language.

BRUIJN

Bruijn's Bird-of-Paradise *Drepanornis bruijnii* (**Oustalet** 1880)
(Alt. Pale-billed Sicklebill)
Bruijn's Pygmy Parrot *Micropsitta bruijnii* (**Salvadori** 1875)
(Alt. Red-breasted/Mountain/Red-headed Pygmy Parrot)
Bruijn's Brush Turkey *Aepypodius bruijnii* (Oustalet 1880)

Anton August Bruijn (?–1885) was a Dutch plumassier or feather merchant, who was the son-in-law of **Duyvenbode.** He exhibited many natural history specimens during the large international Colonial Trade Exhibition in Amsterdam, in the summer of 1883. Others have described him as a botanist, explorer and zoologist and use a different initial, which might mean there were two men of the same name, perhaps brothers, who were operating in the same area. Hunters employed by Bruijn in 1880 collected 22 of the 24 known specimens of the brush turkey. Recently the head and bones of a specimen were given to an ornithologist on the Indonesian island of Waigeo; the remainder having been caught, cooked and eaten. In May 2002, after many years of doubt as to its survival, the bird was observed in the wild and subsequently its nest mounds were discovered. The New Guinea Echidna *Proechidna bruijnii,* discovered in 1877, is also named after him.

BRÜNNICH

Brünnich's Guillemot *Uria lomvia* (Linnaeus 1764)
(Alt. Brünnich's/Thick-billed Murre)

Morten Thrane Brünnich (1737–1827) was bird curator in Copenhagen and worked on Guillemots. He is described by the Danish bibliographer Jean Anker as the '*founder of Danish faunistic zoology*' and was a highly praised systematist. He wrote: *Ornithologia borealis* in 1764, which was a description of a private collection of birds of Denmark, Iceland and other parts of northern Europe.

BRYANT

Bryant's Grassquit *Tiaris olivacea bryanti* (**Ridgway** 1894)
(Alt. Yellow-faced Grassquit)
Bryant's Sparrow *Passerculus sandwichensis* (Gmelin 1789)
(Alt. Savannah Sparrow)

Dr Henry Bryant (1820–1867) of Boston, Massachusetts, was a physician and naturalist who trained in Paris and served a year in the French army in North Africa before returning to Boston. As he was in poor health, he did not practice as a doctor but spent his time bird collecting instead, travelling widely in North America and the Caribbean. During the American Civil War he was the surgeon of the 20th Massachusetts Regiment. In 1866 **LaFresnaye**'s collection was put up for sale by his widow and Bryant bought the lot and donated it to the Boston Natural History Society.

BUCHANAN

Buchanan's Bunting *Emberiza buchanani* (**Blyth** 1845)
(Alt. Grey-necked/Grey-hooded Bunting)

Dr Francis Hamilton Buchanan (1762–1829) was a Scottish physician. He was an assistant-surgeon on board a man-of-war but had to retire through ill health. His health stayed poor for some years, but in 1794 he took a job as surgeon for the East India Company in Bengal. The voyage to India seemed to restore his health fully and, once there, he started collecting plants in Pegu, Ava and the Andaman Islands. These specimens, with drawings, he presented to Sir Joseph **Banks**. He also studied fish. In 1798 he worked for the Board of Trade in Calcutta. From 1800, until his return to Britain in 1807, he continued to study plants and animals in Mysore. Buchanan collected in both India and Nepal. He returned to Calcutta to become superintendent of the botanical gardens there, and later became surgeon to the Governor-General of India. In 1815 he returned to Britain following the death of his elder brother, leaving him heir to the family seat at Leney in Perthshire. Following this inheritance he changed his name to Hamilton, his mother's maiden name. He spent the rest of his life at Leney, improving the gardens by planting many exotics there. He wrote *Travels in the Mysore* and *A History of Nepal*.

BUCKLEY

Buckley's Cotinga *Laniisoma* (*elegans*) *buckleyi* (**Sclater** & **Salvin** 1880)
(Alt. Elegant Mourner/Shrike-like Cotinga)

Buckley's Forest Falcon *Micrastur buckleyi* (Swann 1919)
   (Alt. Traylor's Forest Falcon)
Buckley's Ground Dove *Columbina buckleyi* (Sclater & Salvin 1877)
   (Alt. Ecuadorian Ground Dove)
Buckley's Lark *Mirafra rufocinnamomea buckleyi*

Colonel Charles Buckley was an entomologist working for the Smithsonian expedition, which was sponsored by the Western Union Telegraph in 1866, who collected in Bolivia and Ecuador and a little in Suriname between 1875 and 1889. The British Museum houses a large fish collection made by him at the same time, including several species that commemorate him in their binomials, such as *Parodon buckleyi* and *Pimelodella buckley*. There are also over 80 species of birds collected by him in the British Museum. Buckley collected for a number of artists and ornithologists, including **Gould**, who commemorated him in the binomial of a Bolivian hummingbird *Pinarolaema buckleyi* in 1880. **Sclater** and **Salvin** originally named the ground dove *Chamaepelia buckleyi*. They also honoured him in the binomial of a cotinga *Ptilochloris buckleyi* in 1880 as did **Godman** in the same year with the Black-crowned Tityra *Tityra (inquisitor) buckleyi*.

BUERGERS

Bürgers's Hawk *Erythrotriorchis (Accipiter) buergersi* (**Reichenow** 1914)
   (Alt. Chestnut-shouldered Hawk, Bürger's Sparrowhawk/Goshawk;
   Chestnut-mantled/Chestnut-shouldered Goshawk;)
Bürgers's Blue-collared Parrot *Geoffroyus simplex buergersi* (**Neumann** 1922)
   (Alt. Lilac-collared Parrot)

T J Bürgers (1881–1954) was a German zoologist who was employed in New Guinea. He is also commemorated in the scientific names of the Long-winged Parrot *Geoffroyus simplex buergersi*, a snake *Toxicocalamus buergersi*, a stilt fly *Nestima buergersi*, a beetle *Aegus buergersi*, a race of **Goodfellow**'s Tree-kangaroo *Dendrolagus goodfellowi buergersi* and a Ringtail Possum *Pseudocheirus corinnae buergersi*. These animals are all from the same area of New Guinea, a location which also has a Bürgers Mountain.

BÜTTIKOFER

Büttikofer's Babbler *Trichastoma buettikoferi* (**Blyth** 1859)
   (Alt. Tickell's/Buff-breasted/Mountain Brown Babbler)
Büttikofer's Warbler *Buettikoferella bivittata* (**Stresemann** 1928)
   (Alt. Buff-banded Grassbird)

Johan Büttikofer (1850–1929) was a Swiss zoologist. Büttikofer's Epauletted Bat *Epomops buettikoferi* is named after him. He seems to have had a special interest in ichthyology, and a number of fishes that were described by him have *buettikoferei* in the scientific name.

BUFFON

Buffon's Macaw *Ara ambigua* (**Bechstein** 1811)
   (Alt. Great Green Macaw)
Buffon's Plumeleteer *Chalybura buffoni* (**Lesson** 1832)
   (Alt. White-vented Plumeleteer, Buffon's Humming-
   bird)
Buffon's Skua *Stercorarius longicaudus* (**Viellot** 1819)
   (Alt. Long-tailed Skua/Jaeger)

Count Georges Louis Leclerc de Buffon (1707–1788) was famous for having developed the species concept. His *Histoire naturelle des oiseaux* published between 1770 and

1785 formed volumes 16–24 of his *Histoire Naturelle Générale et Particulière*, the entire work being published between 1749 and 1804.

BULLER

Buller's Albatross *Diomedea bulleri* (**Rothschild** 1893)
Buller's Gull *Larus bulleri* (**Hutton** 1871)
   (Black-billed Gull)
Buller's Shearwater *Puffinus bulleri* (Salvin 1881)
   (Alt. Grey-backed/New Zealand Shearwater)

Sir Walter Lawry Buller (1838–1906) was a New Zealand lawyer and ornithologist, and author of *A History of the Birds of New Zealand*. He was a government minister in New Zealand from 1896 to 1899. Although born in New Zealand, he achieved his ambition to go 'home' and so he died in England, a country gentleman. He tried to sell Rothschild a specimen of a Laughing Owl for a large sum of money. Rothschild examined the bird and realised that it was a fake, particularly as its tail came from another bird of a different genus! Rothschild pointed all this out publicly and loudly, and Buller was humiliated. Buller himself collected the type specimen of the shearwater, and was honoured by **Salvin** who named it after him.

BULLOCK

Bullock's Oriole *Icterus bullockii* (**Swainson** 1827)

William Bullock (1773–1849) was an English traveller and amateur naturalist and a former goldsmith. He established a travelling museum in London, with 3,000 skins and 32,000 other curiosities that he had collected. These he auctioned off in 1819. He travelled with his son, who also collected, and Ferdinand Deppe in the southern United States and Mexico where he bought up abandoned silver and gold mines. He collected a number of specimens new to science. His friend **Swainson**, to whom he sold many specimens, named the oriole in his honour from a bird which Bullock collected whilst visiting one of his mines near Mexico City.

BULWER, H

Bulwer's Pheasant *Lophura bulweri* (**Sharpe** 1874)

Sir Henry Ernest Gascoyne Bulwer (1836–1914) was a career diplomat who became Governor of Labuan, Borneo between 1871 and 1875. He was Lieutenant-Governor of Natal between 1875 and 1880, at which time his secretary was Henry Rider Haggard, the famous author of *King Solomon's Mines* and *She*, among other novels. From 1886 to 1892 he was High Commissioner in Cyprus. He was related to Sir Henry Bulwer-Lytton, the Victorian novelist.

BULWER, J

Bulwer's Petrel *Bulweria bulwerii* (**Jardine** & Selby 1828)
St Helena Bulwer's Petrel *Bulweria bifax* (Olson 1975) [Extinct]

The Reverend James Bulwer (1794–1879) was a Scots collector, naturalist and conchologist. He was a member of the Linnean Society. Bulwer collected the petrel in Madeira in 1827. The petrel genus *Bulweria* and its derivative genus *Pseudobulweria* are also named for him.

BUQUET

Buquet's Puffleg *Eriocnemis luciani* (**Bourcier** 1847)
(Alt. Sapphire-vented Puffleg)

J Lucian Buquet (1807–1889) was a French entomologist. The beetle family Lucanidae is named for him. His entomological collection was purchased, as part of a wider holding, by the British Museum. In 1854 he published *Lettre de M. G. de Mniszech* in the *Annales de la Société Entomologique de France*. He may have published other people's works on entomology in Paris. **Bourcier** first described the hummingbird in 1847 and **Gould** painted it shortly afterwards.

BURBIDGE

Burbidge's Blue-backed Parrot *Tanygnathus sumatranus burbidgii* (**Sharpe** 1879)
(Alt. Blue-backed/Azure-rumped/Müller's Parrot)

Frederick William Burbidge (1847–1905) was an English explorer, discoverer, botanist, artist and lithographer of plants. He was gardener at Kew Gardens from 1868 to 1870. He was sent to Borneo by James Veitch & Sons, and is well known for his exploration of the Kinabalu region, where he collected many orchids, from 1877 to 1879. He wrote *Gardens of the Sun: A Naturalist's Journal of Borneo and the Sulu Archipelago* in 1880. He later became Director of the Botanical Gardens at Trinity College, Dublin. He named a number of plants to honour his wife.

BURCHELL

Burchell's' Bustard *Neotis denhami burchellii*
(Alt. Denham's Bustard)
Burchell's Coucal *Centropus* (*superciliosus*) *burchelli* (**Swainson** 1838)
Burchell's Courser *Cursorius rufus* (**Gould** 1837)
Burchell's Gonolek *Laniarius atrococcineus* (Burchell 1822)

(Alt. Crimson-breasted Shrike)
Burchell's Sandgrouse *Pterocles burchelli* (W L **Sclater** 1922)
Burchell's Starling *Lamprotornis australis* (A **Smith** 1836)

William John Burchell (1781–1863) was an English explorer-naturalist who went to the Cape of Good Hope in 1810 and undertook a major exploration of interior South Africa between 1811 and 1815, during which he travelled more than 7,000 km through largely unexplored country. He published his two-volume work, *Travels in the Interior of Southern Africa*, in 1822 and 1824. Burchell was the first person to describe the White Rhinoceros *Ceratotherium simum*. He was renowned as a meticulous collector, botanist and artist. Among the species named in his honour are Burchell's Zebra *Equus burchellii* and a small forest tree *Burchellia bubalina*. He returned to London in 1815 to work on his collections. In 1825 he spent two months in Lisbon and then proceeded to Brazil where he collected extensively, not returning again to England until 1830. He became increasingly reclusive and in the last two years of his life became seriously ill, eventually taking his own life. The status of Burchell's Bustard is very uncertain as it is only known from the type specimen taken in east Sudan.

BURMEISTER

Burmeister's Seriema *Chunga burmeisteri* (**Hartlaub** 1860)
(Alt. Black-legged/Lesser Seriema)

Karl Hermann Konrad Burmeister (1807–1892) was a German ornithologist who was a

Professor and Director of the Institute of Zoology of Martin Luther University at Halle Wittenberg, Germany, from 1837 to 1861. He sent many specimens to the zoological collections at the institute. These were largely collected during his two expeditions to South America; to Brazil (1850–1852) and to the La Plata region of Argentina (1857–1860). Subsequently, he was resident in Argentina from 1861 until his death. He founded the Institute at the Museo Nacional in Buenos Aires and became its first director, remaining in post until his retirement in 1880. He wrote *Reise nach Brasilien* in 1853.

BUSINESSMEN

Charles Sydney 'Punch' **Barlow** was Chairman of the Barlow Rand Group, a giant South African mining and manufacturing group, and had Barlow's Lark named after him through his sponsorship of collecting expeditions, as did the Dutch-born South African Bernhard **Carp**. On the other hand, Arthur Cleveland **Bent** used his business to achieve the wealth necessary for him to pursue his first love of ornithology, as did Henry **Seebohm** and Quaker John **Cassin**, whom George Newbold **Lawrence**, who himself had made a fortune in pharmaceuticals, accompanied on collecting expeditions. George Burritt **Sennett** used his iron foundry wealth to gain the free time to collect and then to pay others to take over when the demands of business prevented him from collecting for himself. Charles Reed **Bishop** used his wealth to create a museum in Hawaii dedicated to his wife's memory. John Spedan **Lewis**, who founded the John Lewis Partnership, and Anthony **Kuser**, who owned utilities in New Jersey, were both primarily businessmen. Quite why British businessman H Berkeley **James** was honoured remains obscure.

CABANI

We are of the opinion that this is a misspelling of Cabanis (see below). Similarly there are entries below for Cabini and Caboni, which we also consider to be misspellings. In our view the birds are all named after Jean Louis Cabanis, whether the name is given as Cabani's, Cabanis's, Cabini's or Caboni's.

CABANIS

Cabanis's Bunting *Emberiza cabanisi* (**Reichenow** 1875)
  (Alt. Cabanis's Yellow Bunting, Three-streaked Bunting)
Cabanis's Greenbul *Phyllastrephus fischeri cabanisi* (**Sharpe** 1882)
Cabanis's Ground Sparrow *Melozone biarcuatum* (**Prevost** & **Des Murs** 1846)
  (Alt. Prevost's/Rusty-crowned/Chiapas/White-faced Ground Sparrow)

Cabanis's Spinetail *Synallaxis cabanisi* (**Berlepsch** & Leverkuhn 1890)
Cabanis's Tanager *Tangara cabanisi* (P L **Sclater** 1868)
  (Alt. Azure-rumped Tanager)
Cabanis's Thrush *Turdus plebejus* (Cabanis 1861)
  (Alt. [American] Mountain Thrush/Robin)
Cabanis's Tiger-Heron *Tigrisoma mexicanum* (**Swainson** 1834)
  (Alt. Bare-throated/Caboni's/Mexican Tiger-heron/Tiger-bittern)
Cabanis's Woodpecker *Picoides villosus hyloscopus* (Cabanis & **Heine** 1863)
  (Alt. Hairy Woodpecker)

Jean Louis Cabanis (1816–1906) was the most influential European ornithologist of his day. He founded the Journal für Ornithologie and edited it for over 40 years. Although he never visited Africa himself, various collectors sent skins to him at the Berlin Museum. **Reichenow**, who succeeded him at the museum and described the bunting, was his son-in-law. **Heine** named the heron *Tigrisoma cabanisi* in 1859 but it was later found to have been named earlier by **Swainson** as *Tigrisoma mexicanum*.

CABINI

Cabini's Emerald *Chlorostilbon poortmani* (**Bourcier** 1843)
  (Alt. Short-tailed/ Poortman's/Berlepsch's Emerald)

We are of the opinion that this too is a misspelling of **Cabanis** (see his entry above) but have left the bird under the (probably) wrong name in case any reader also comes across the misspelling.

CABONI

Caboni's Tiger-heron *Tigrisoma mexicanum* (**Swainson** 1834)
  (Alt. Bare-throated/Cabanis's/Mexican Tiger-heron/Tiger-bittern)

We are of the opinion that this is yet another misspelling of **Cabanis** (see his entry above) but have left the bird under the wrong name, in case any reader also comes across the misspelling.

CABOT

Cabot's Tern *Sterna sandvicensis acuflavidus* (Cabot 1848)
  (Alt. Sandwich Tern)
Cabot's Tragopan *Tragopan caboti* (**Gould** 1857)
  (Alt. Chinese Tragopan)

Dr Samuel Cabot (1815–1885), a physician and ornithologist, was the Curator of the Department of Ornithology at Boston's Society of Natural History. In the 1840s he made an important expedition to the Yucátan Peninsula, where he discovered several new species. He described the tern subspecies which bears his name. His collection of 3,000 mounted birds is now at the Museum of Comparative Zoology, Harvard.

CAIRNS

Cairns' Warbler *Dendroica caerulescens cairnsi* (**Coues** 1897)
  (Alt. Black-throated Blue Warbler)

John Simpson Cairns (1862–1895) was an American ornithologist who conducted field studies in the late 19th century near what is now the Craggy Gardens Recreation Area in North Carolina. He corresponded with William Brewster and his letters, written between 1887 and 1895, were published in the North Carolina Historical Review. Brewster and Cairns were instrumental in proving the palaeontologist Edward Cope's hypothesis that much of the fauna in the Black Mountains was identical to that occurring 1,600 km further north. A local travel guide relates '*Within five years after the Civil War, however, a number of zoologists visited the Appalachians to do survey work. These included Edward Drinker Cope (he was famous for his work in palaeozoology), William **Brewster** after whom the hybrid Brewster's Warbler is named, and John Simpson Cairns, a local ornithologist who accidentally shot and killed himself while collecting birds north of Balsam Gap. The Parkway provides easy access to many excellent bird-watching sites, and Craggy Gardens holds an esteemed reputation for birds. This is due in part to the work of John S. Cairns who late in the nineteenth century conducted field studies nearby.*' (McDaniel 1998).

CALLIOPE

Calliope Hummingbird *Stellula calliope* (**Gould** 1847)

Named for Calliope, the Muse of Epic Poetry in Greek mythology. Calliope (Calliopeia), the *Fair Voiced* and the eldest Muse, is shown crowned in gold and holding a writing tablet, sometimes a roll of paper or a book. Calliope is known for taking a fancy to Achilles and for having taught him how to cheer his friends by singing at banquets. Zeus called her to mediate between Aphrodite and Persephone in their quarrel over the possession of Adonis. She settled the dispute by giving them equal access, providing Adonis with some badly needed free time to himself. By Apollo, she bore Linus, who was slain by Hercules, and Orpheus.

CAMPBELL

Campbell's Fairy-wren *Malurus campbelli* Schodde 1982
Campbell's Hill Partridge *Arborophila* (*orientalis*) *campbelli* (**Robinson** 1904)
  (Alt. Grey-breasted/ Sumatran/ Sunda/ Horsfield's/ Bare-throated [Tree] Hill Partridge)

The fairy-wren was only discovered in 1980 when netted by bird-ringer Robert Watt Campbell in southeastern New Guinea. This bird was first named as a new species, Campbell's Fairy-wren *Malurus campbelli*. However, it is treated as a subspecies of the Broad-billed Fairy-wren *M. grayi* by most relevant publications (e.g. Coates 1990 and Clements 1991), although not by all (e.g. Sibley & Monroe 1990 & Wells 1998). The partridge is likely to receive full species status as the Malayan Partridge *Arborophila campbelli*.

CANDE

Cande's Manakin *Manacus candei* (**Parzudaki** 1841)
  (Alt. White-collared Manakin *Pipra candei*)

Admiral A Maussion Ferdinand de Cande (1801–1867) was a French explorer of South America. **D'Orbigny** commemorated him in the binomials of several gastropods including *Gibbula candei* in 1838 and *Patella candei* in 1840, both from the Canaries, and *Antillophos candei* from the Caribbean in 1853. Another gastropod, *Epitonium candeanum*, described by d'Orbigny in 1842 is known as Cande's Wentletrap in the vernacular. D'Orbigny also described the White-whiskered Spinetail *Synallaxis candei* in 1838.

CANFIELD

Canfield's Quail *Callipepla californica canfieldae* (**Van Rossem** 1939)
  (Alt. California Quail)

May Canfield (1879–1938) lived on the Californian side of the Colorado River, in Bard, Imperial County, and collected birds. She was the aunt of Lawrence M Huey, who was the curator of birds at the San Diego Natural History Museum in the early to mid 1900s. She is recorded as having donated specimens to the museum.

CANIVET

Canivet's Emerald *Chlorostilbon canivetii* (**Lesson** 1832)
(Alt. [Canivetti's] Fork-tailed Emerald)

Emmanuel Canivet de Carentan was a French collector and ornithologist. Some time before 1828 he wrote a manual on the preparation of animal, plant and other specimens, together with the botanist and geologist Pierre Botard (1789–1859). This was published in 1832 as the *Manual de Naturalista Dissector*, which is one of the classic works on taxidermy. Canivet also wrote *Catalogue des Oiseaux du Département de la Manche* in 1843. Elsewhere, Canivet is described simply as a 'curiosity dealer' rather than as a man of science.

CARMIOL

Carmiol's Tanager *Chlorothraupis carmioli* (**Lawrence** 1868)
(Alt. Olive/Yellow-lored Tanager)
Carmiol's Vireo *Vireo carmioli* (**Baird** 1866)
(Alt. Yellow-winged Vireo)

Julian Carmiol was a Swiss scientist and was amongst those recruited by the Costa Rican government at the beginning of the 20th century to improve the country's education system. He explored in Costa Rica in 1863 under the aegis of the Smithsonian Institution, and also went with the Smithsonian on their Alaskan expedition of 1863. Specimens of molluscs and other invertebrates, which he collected independently, were sent to European institutions. He is also celebrated in the scientific name of *Phaedranassa carmioli*, a flower of the Amaryllis family. The vireo is named after him and the tanager after his son F Carmiol, who was also a collector.

CARNABY

Carnaby's Black Cockatoo *Calyptorhynchus latirostris* (Carnaby 1948)
(Alt. White-tailed/Slender-billed/Short-billed Black Cockatoo)
Carnaby's White-tailed Black Cockatoo *Calyptorhynchus funereus latirostris*

Keith Carnaby was an entomologist whose collection is housed by the British Natural History Museum. He published *Jewel Beetles of Western Australia* in 1986. The town Boyup Brook in Western Australia has a butterfly collection, officially known as the Carnaby Collection of Beetles and Butterflies, which is regarded as second in excellence only to that of the British Museum.

CAROLA

Carola Parotia *Parotia carolae* (**A.B.Meyer** 1894)
(Alt. Queen Carola's Parotia, Queen Carola's Six-wired Bird-of-Paradise)

See **Queen Carola**.

CAROLINE

Caroline's Shortwing *Brachypteryx leucophrys carolinae*
(Alt. Lesser Shortwing)

Caroline Ash is the daughter of the British ornithologist Dr John Sidney **Ash**. The bird was described in 1981 and is a native of southern Asia.

CARP

Carp's Black Tit *Parus carpi* (Macdonald & B P **Hall** 1957)

Bernhard Carp (1901–1966) was a Dutch-born South African businessman and Cape Town naturalist, who sponsored many collecting expeditions, particularly to Namibia, by the Zoological Museum of Amsterdam University. The businessman and hunter bought important mammal collections in South Africa and donated them to the museum. Political considerations made it difficult but after some time the board of the university decided to accept the very important collection, which included rare Lagomorph skins and skulls. Carp wrote an autobiography entitled *Why I Chose Africa*. The tit was collected in 1951 and was originally described as a subspecies of the Southern Black Tit *Parus niger carpi*.

CARRIKER

Carriker's Conure *Aratinga wagleri minor* (Carriker 1933)
 (Alt. Red-fronted/Cordilleras Conure, Scarlet-fronted/Cordilleras Parakeet)
Carriker's Mountain Tanager *Dubusia taeniata carrikeri* (**Wetmore** 1946)
 (Alt. Buff-breasted Mountain Tanager)

Melbourne Armstrong Carriker Jr (1879–1965) was one of the great early naturalists of Central and northern South America, particularly Colombia. As well as his interest in ornithology, he was one of the great experts on Mallophaga. In 1910, his was the first modern systematic publication of the birds of Costa Rica, in which he listed 713 species for the country. He greatly enhanced the bird collections of the Carnegie Museum and the Smithsonian Institution. He is the subject of a biography written by his grandson, Professor Melbourne R Carriker.

CARRUTHERS

Carruthers's Cisticola *Cisticola carruthersi* (**Ogilvie-Grant** 1909)

Alexander Douglas Mitchell Carruthers (1882–1962) was an explorer and naturalist. He was educated at Haileybury and Trinity College, Cambridge and then trained in land survey and taxidermy. He went with the British Museum expedition to Ruwenzori from 1905 to 1906 and travelled in Russian Turkestan and the borders of Afghanistan from 1907 until 1908. There he did research on wild sheep. He also explored the deserts of Outer Mongolia and the upper Yenisey River in 1910, with John H Miller and Morgan Philips Price. Carruthers was honorary secretary of the Royal Geographical Society between 1916 and 1921. His publications include *Unknown Mongolia*, in 1913, *Arabian Adventure*, in 1935 and *Beyond the Caspian, A Naturalist in Central Asia*, in 1949.

CARTER

Carter's Albatross *Thalassarche [chlororhynchos] carteri* (**Mathews** 1912)
 (Alt. Indian Yellow-nosed Albatross/Mollymawk)
Carter's Desertbird *Eremiornis carteri* (**North** 1900)
 (Alt. Spinifexbird)

Thomas Carter (1863–1931) was an English ornithologist who collected and published extensively on birds in Western Australia, but was born and died in Yorkshire. Four species and fourteen subspecies of bird were named after him. He worked in his father's business and made several ornithological trips, including one to Iceland, but mostly to Australia; Western Australia in 1887, Jackeroo, Boolathanna Station from 1887 to 1889 and Point Cloates from 1889 to 1902. During these journeys he identified 180 bird species and collected 170. He returned to England in 1903 with 500 bird skins, which are now in the American Museum of Natural History, New York. He settled in Western Australia from 1904 to 1913, making ornithological observations which later appeared in *The Emu*. Thereafter, he moved back to England in 1914 but made several visits to Western Australia to look for birds between 1916 and 1928. On his 1916 visit he researched the birds of Shark Bay and Dirk Hartog Island, and discovered two new species; the Desertbird and the Rufous-crowned Emu-wren *Stipiturus ruficeps*. He was a founding member of the Royal Australasian Ornithologists' Union. The albatross is given full-species status by some as the Indian Yellow-nosed Albatross *Thalassarche carteri*.

CASSIN

Cassin's Auklet *Ptychoramphus aleuticus* (**Pallas** 1811)
Cassin's Bullfinch *Pyrrhula pyrrhula cassini* (**Baird** 1869)
   (Alt. Eurasian Bullfinch)
Cassin's Dove *Leptotila cassini* (Lawrence 1867)
   (Alt. Grey-chested Dove)
Cassin's Finch *Carpodacus cassinii* (Baird 1854)
   (Alt. Cassin's Purple Finch)
Cassin's Hawk-Eagle *Hieraaetus* (*Spizaetus*) *africanus* (Cassin 1865)
Cassin's Grey Flycatcher *Muscicapa cassini* (**Heine** 1860)
   (Alt. Cassin's Flycatcher)
Cassin's Jay *Gymnorhinus cyanocephalus* (**Wied-Neuwied** 1841)
   (Alt. Pinyon Jay, Maximilian's Jay, Maximilian's Nutcracker)
Cassin's Kingbird *Tyrannus vociferans* (Swainson 1826)
Cassin's Malimbe *Malimbus cassini* (**Elliott** 1859)
   (Alt. Black-throated Malimbe)
Cassin's Sharp-billed Honeyguide *Prodotiscus insignis* (Cassin 1856)
   (Alt. Cassin's Honeyguide)
Cassin's Sparrow *Aimophila cassinii* (**Woodhouse** 1852)
Cassin's Spinetail *Neafrapus cassini* (**Sclater** 1863)
Cassin's Tern *Sterna hirundinacea* (**Lesson** 1831)
   (Alt. South American Tern)
Cassin's Vireo *Vireo* (*solitarius*) *cassinii* (**Xanthus** 1858)
   (Alt. Solitary Vireo)

John Cassin (1813–1869) was a Quaker businessman and the unpaid Curator of Ornithology at the Academy of Natural Sciences of Philadelphia for over a quarter of a century. He is regarded as one of the giants of American ornithology. He described 198 species of birds, many from his expeditions around the world including one to Japan. Cassin accompanied Admiral Perry on this latter historic voyage, serving as the official ornithologist. Among his written works are *Illustrations of the Birds of California, Texas, Oregon, British and Russian America*, in 1865 and *Birds of Chile*, in 1855. He was employed on a railway survey in the late 1850s. The lithographer J T Bowen, who died during the production of the railroad surveys, made his drawings into lithographs. Cassin married Bowen's widow **Lavinia**, at the same time assuming the presidency of the Bowen Company. **Swainson** named Cassin's Kingbird and **Baird** named and described Cassin's Finch and the bullfinch race. **Gambel** gave Cassin's Auklet its common name but **Pallas** described it. **Lawrence** described and named the dove after him.

CASTELNAU

Castelnau's Antshrike *Thamnophilus cryptoleucus* (Menegaux & **Hellmayr** 1906)

Francis Louis Nompar de Caumont, Comte de Laporte de Castelnau [in brief – Comte de Castelnau] (1810–1880) was a career diplomat and naturalist, who was born in London, studied natural science in Paris and then led a French scientific expedition to study the lakes of Canada, the United States and Mexico between 1837 and 1841. From 1843 to 1847 an expedition led by him was the first to cross South America from Peru to Brazil, following the watershed between the Amazon and the Río de la Plata systems, collecting specimens all the way. Following this he assumed several diplomatic posts including Consul-General in Melbourne in 1862 and then as the French Consul there from 1864 until 1877. Soon after his return to France he undertook another long voyage of exploration together with two botanists and a taxidermist. He retired in 1877 and died in Melbourne in 1880. The genus *Laportea* (a tropical stinging tree) was named after him as were many insects and fishes. He is also commemorated in the scientific name of the Plain-breasted Piculet *Picumnus castelnau*.

CAVE

Cave's Lark *Mirafra barlowi cavei* (**Macdonald** 1953)
(Alt. Barlow's Lark)

Colonel Francis O Cave wrote, with James D **Macdonald**, the classic *Birds of the Sudan – Their Identification and Distribution* in 1955. He also published *Unusual behaviour of a tigress with live bait* in the Journal of the Bombay Natural History Society in 1927. The same Macdonald first described the lark in 1953. Cave also collected in the Sudan, as evidenced by a number of holotypes in the British Museum of Natural History. In 1974 he published *Notes on birds from the southern Sudan* in the Bulletin of the British Ornithologists' Club. Cave became a Catholic missionary in Sudan in the late 1960s and abandoned serious ornithology. The lark is found on the inland red sands near the mouth of the Orange River, in the Northern Cape Province of South Africa and southern Namibia. Cave's Lark was only temporarily considered a species while the systematics of this group were being elucidated. The South African ornithologist, Callan Cohen, has studied these birds and their hybridisation in some detail, and *cavei* is now regarded as a subspecies of Barlow's Lark.

CECILIA

Cecilia's Dove *Metriopelia ceciliae* (**Lesson** 1845)
(Alt. Bare-faced Ground/Bare-eyed Ground/Yellow-eyed/Spectacled Dove)
Cecilia's Rosella *Platycercus eximius ceciliae* (**Mathews** 1911)
(Alt. Eastern/Common/Red/Red-headed/Golden-mantled Rosella)

Cecile Gautrau was the daughter of the French naturalist René Primavere **Lesson**.

CERVERA

Cervera's Wren *Ferminia cerverai* (Barbour 1926)
(Alt. Zapata Wren, Cuban Marsh Wren)
Cervera's Rail *Cyanolimnas cerverai* (Barbour & **J.L.Peters** 1927)
(Alt. Zapata Rail, Santo Tomás Gallinule)

Fermín Zanón Cervera (1875–1944) was a Spanish soldier and naturalist. He fought in the Cuban war of independence in 1898 on the Spanish side and then returned to Spain in their Civil Guard. He came back to Cuba in 1904 and married there. He also visited Mexico. He spent a number of years working for the American naturalist, Dr Thomas Barbour, who recommended he visited the Zapata Swamp collecting. Fermín Cervera discovered the wren, a Cuban endemic, in 1926 and the rail in 1927, in the locality of Santo Tomás. He not only knew all the calls of birds but could imitate them, and he recognised that there were unnamed species in the swamp simply because he heard calls that were new to him. He was also an entomologist and there are several species of antlion named after him. Barbour named the birds after Cervera in his descriptions in The Auk. The wren was thought to be extinct due to excessive 'collecting' but was rediscovered in 1980.

CETTI

Cetti's Warbler *Cettia cetti* (**Temminck** 1820)

Fr Francesco Cetti (1726–1778) was an Italian Jesuit priest, zoologist and mathematician who wrote the *Storia Naturale di Sardegna*. The second volume (1776) deals with birds in Sardinia. The warbler genus *Cettia*, of 15 principally-Asiatic species, is named for him.

Cetti and G G Moris, it is thought that Cetti is the man on the right.

CHABERT

Chabert's Vanga *Leptopterus chabert* (S **Müller** 1776)

This is not a person at all but derives from the local (Malagasy) name for the bird: *tcha-chert-be*.

CHALLENGER

Challenger's Lory *Eos histrio challengeri* (**Salvadori** 1891)
(Alt. Red and Blue Lory/Blue-tailed[Diademed] Lory)

We believe that this race of parrot was not named after a person but after *HMS Challenger*, the lead ship in an oceanographic expedition to the Pacific, from 1860 to 1868, which explored the area of Nenusa Island where the bird is found.

CHAMBERLAIN

Chamberlain's Ptarmigan *Lagopus mutus chamberlaini* (**Clark** 1907)
(Alt. Rock Ptarmigan)

Montague Chamberlain (1844–1924) was a Canadian ornithologist who was born in St John, New Brunswick. While at Harvard, he began a revision of **Nuttall**'s 1832 publication, *Ornithology*, which was published in 1891. In 1892 he edited and published *The Birds of Greenland,* based on the research of Andreas Hagerup. He also presented papers on *The Song Birds of New England* and *The Eastern Birds of Prey* to the Harvard Natural History Society. His last work on birds was *Some Canadian Birds*, published in 1895.

CHAPIN

Chapin's Apalis *Apalis sharpii chapini* (**Friedmann** 1928)
(Alt. Sharpe's Apalis)
Chapin's Crombec *Sylvietta* (*leucophrys*) *chapini* (**Schouteden** 1947)
(Alt. White-browed Crombec)
Chapin's Flycatcher *Muscicapa lendu* (Chapin 1932)
Chapin's Puff-backed Flycatcher *Batis* (*minima*) *ituriensis* (Chapin 1932)
(Alt. Ituri Batis)
Chapin's Flycatcher-babbler *Lioptilus chapini* (Schouteden 1949)
(Alt. Chapin's Mountain Babbler)
Chapin's Least Honeyguide *Indicator exilis* (**Cassin** 1856)
(Alt. Least Honeyguide)

Chapin's Spinetail *Telacanthura melanopygia* (Chapin 1915)
(Alt. Black/Ituri Mottle-throated Spinetail)

Dr James Paul Chapin (1889–1964) was an American ornithologist. He was joint leader of the Lang-Chapin Expedition, which made the first comprehensive biological survey of what was then the Belgian Congo, from 1909 until 1915. He was ornithology curator for the American Museum of Natural History and president of the Explorers' Club from 1949 to 1950. He wrote *Birds of the Belgian Congo* in 1932, which largely earned him the award of the Daniel Giraud Elliot Gold Medal that year.

CHAPLIN

Chaplin's Barbet *Lybius chaplini* (**Clarke** 1920)
Chaplin's Pipit *Anthus nyassae* (**Neumann** 1906)
(Alt. Woodland/Brachystegia Pipit)

Sir Francis Drummond Percy Chaplin (1866–1933) was a civil servant who was Administrator in Rhodesia (now Zimbabwe) and Nyasaland (now Malawi) from 1914 until 1923.

CHAPMAN

Chapman's Antshrike *Thamnophilus zarumae* (Chapman 1921)
Chapman's Cacique *Amblycercus holosericeus australis* (Chapman 1919)
(Alt. Yellow-billed Cacique)
Chapman's Conure *Pyrrhura melanura chapmani* (Bond & Meyer de Schauensee 1940)
(Alt. Maroon-tailed Parakeet)
Chapman's Grosbeak *Pheucticus aureoventris terminalis* (Chapman 1919)
(Alt. Black-backed Grosbeak)
Chapman's Ground Cuckoo *Neomorphus rufipennis* (G R **Gray** 1849)
(Alt. Rufous-winged Ground Cuckoo)
Chapman's Mitred Conure *Aratinga mitrata alticola* (Chapman 1921)
(Alt. Mitred Parakeet)
Chapman's Petrel *Oceanodroma leucorhoa chapmani* (**Berlepsch** 1906)
(Alt. Leach's Petrel)
Chapman's Swift *Chaetura chapmani* (**Hellmayr** 1907)
Chapman's Tyrannulet *Phylloscartes chapmani* (**Gilliard** 1940)
Chapman's Warbler *Xenoligea montana* (Chapman 1917)
(Alt. White-winged [Ground] Warbler)
Chapman's Mealy Amazon *Amazona farinosa chapmani* (**Traylor** 1948)
Chapman's Sapphire-rumped Parrotlet *Touit purpurata viridiceps* (Chapman 1921)
Chapman's Trogon *Trogon massena australis* (Chapman 1915)
(Alt. Slaty-tailed Trogon)

Frank Michler Chapman (1864–1945) was Curator of Ornithology for the American Museum of Natural History, New York, from 1908 until 1942. He photographed and collected data on North American birds for over 50 years and did much to popularise birdwatching in the United States in the 20th century. In 1899 he began publishing *Bird Lore* magazine, which became a unifying national forum for the Audubon movement. Chapman sponsored the first national Christmas Bird Count in 1900. He wrote *Handbook of birds of eastern North America, with keys to the species and descriptions of their plumages, nests, and eggs* in 1903, *The Distribution of Bird Life in Columbia* in 1917 and *The Distribution of Bird Life in Ecuador* in 1926.

CHARLATANS AND CHEATS

There are some odd characters among the ranks of our 'birdmen'. Some may have invented birds, some lied about having collected specimens that they actually stole (see Kleptomaniacs and Unscrupulous Birdmen) and a few led double lives or lived in fantasy worlds. Not all have been fine upstanding fellows.

For example, **Hume** described John **Xantus** as '*a most unusual man, a mixture of real scientific ability and general unreliability.*' He was a charlatan of great note but apparently never falsified any of his data, and was a notable collector and field ornithologist. Xantus fled Hungary in 1848, having been part of an unsuccessful revolt against the Austrian Empire. Poor but well educated he wrote grandiose accounts of his exploits in America, always with him in charge of expeditions. These tales were published in Hungary, where he became famous. He once publishing a photo of himself as a US Navy captain although he had never served in the navy at all. As the Smithsonian says: '*Despite the fact that he plagiarised other travel accounts of the American West, lied about his status and achievements, and always claimed to be superior to those around him, Xantus did great work for Baird and the Smithsonian*'.

Despite his undoubted stature as a great scientist not every bird named by **Lesson** actually existed. He is known to have had a vivid imagination and it was rumoured that he may have put bits of skins together to create entirely 'new' birds. This may have been prompted by circumstances of his time when the clamour for the new may have pressured him to satisfy demand when supply was short. **Gould** cannot be directly accused of any such skulduggery but his agents and executors could have ruined his reputation. Half-finished work and portraits of immature and aberrant examples, which were posthumously published as full species, led to much confusion (well, at least it confused us a lot!).

Even apparently honourable men like Sir W L **Buller** strayed into such falsehood. He sent Rothschild a completely spurious stuffed owl.

CHARLES

>Charles's Mockingbird *Nesomimus trifasciatus* (**Gould** 1837)
>Charles's Tree Finch *Camarhynchus pauper* (Gould 1837)
>   (Alt. Charles' Insectivorous/Santa Maria/Floreana Tree Finch)

See **Darwin**.

CHARLIE

>Charlie's Comet *Cometes caroli* (**Gould***)
>   (Alt. Bronze-tailed Comet)

This is another 'Gould' bird to which we can find no reference elsewhere. However, it has been suggested that it was named by the French ornithologist Prince Charles **Bonaparte** for his daughter, Charlotte Honorine Josephine Pauline Contessa **Primoli** di Foglia (1832–1891). If this is correct, we are at a loss to explain use of the masculine *caroli* instead of the feminine equivalent *carolae*.

CHARLOTTE

>Charlotte's Bulbul *Hypsipetes charlottae* (**Blyth** 1844)
>   (Alt. Buff-vented Bulbul, Crested/Finsch's Olive[-brown] Bulbul)

Queen Charlotte (1744–1818) was the wife of King George III of Great Britain. Most sources agree that the bulbul was named after this Queen. **Finsch** coined the scientific honorific *charlottae* in 1867. The bird seems to have been rediscovered and renamed as the Buff-vented Bulbul *Iole olivacea*, but he present name has been resurrested in some lists.

CHERRIE

Cherrie's Antwren *Myrmotherula cherriei* (**Berlepsch** & **Hartert** 1902)
Cherrie's Nighthawk *Chordeiles minor aserriensis* (Cherrie 1896)
(Alt. Common Nighthawk)
Cherrie's Swift *Cypseloides cherriei* (**Ridgway** 1893)
(Alt. Spot-fronted Swift)
Cherrie's Tanager *Ramphocelus* (*passerinii*) *costaricensis* (Cherrie 1891)
(Alt. Scarlet-rumped Tanager)

George Kruck Cherrie (1865–1948) was a naturalist and ornithologist who accompanied Theodore Roosevelt on a trip in Brazil, in 1913, to find the source of one of the tributaries of the Amazon. He was Assistant Curator to the Department of Ornithology at The Field Museum, Chicago, in the 1890s. He also collected extensively in Costa Rica between 1894 and 1897 and, with his wife Stella M Cherrie, in Colombia in 1898. In *Through the Brazilian Wilderness* published in 1914, Roosevelt described him thus '…*efficient and fearless man; and willy-nilly he had been forced at times to vary his career by taking part in insurrections. Twice he had been behind the bars in consequence, on one occasion spending three months in a prison of a certain South American state, expecting each day to be taken out and shot. In another state he had, as an interlude to his ornithological pursuits, followed the career of a gun-runner, acting as such off and on for two and a half years. The particular revolutionary chief whose fortunes he was following finally came into power, and Cherrie immortalized his name by naming a new species of ant-thrush after him — a delightful touch, in its practical combination of those not normally kindred pursuits, ornithology and gun-running.*' Cherrie published *Ornithology Orinoco* in 1916. He also published *Dark Trails* in 1930, as well as *Adventures of a Naturalist*.

CHRISTINA

Christina's Barbthroat *Threnetes niger christinae* (Grantsau 1969)
(Alt. Bronze/Pale/White-tailed Barbthroat)

Christina Swinhoe was the wife of Robert **Swinhoe**. See also Mrs Swinhoe's Sunbird *Aethopyga christinae*. The proposed race *christinae* is a synonym of *loehkeni*.

CHUBB

Chubb's Cisticola *Cisticola chubbi* (**Sharpe** 1892)
Chubb's Twinspot *Mandingoa nitidula chubbi* (**Ogilvie**-**Grant** 1912)

Ernest Charles Chubb (1884–1972) was an ornithologist who became curator of the Museum in Durban, South Africa. His father Charles, a fellow ornithologist, had been a curator at the British Museum but was knocked down and killed by a car as he left the premises, in 1924. Chubb senior wrote *The Birds of British Guiana*, based on the collection of Frederick Vavasour McConnell and, with Lord Brabourne, *The Birds of South America*. In 1945 Ernest became president of the Southern Africa Association for Advancement of Science. Two years earlier, he wrote a paper *Record of nesting of skimmer at St Lucia* (Ostrich 14:111–112). It is probable that he named the twinspot for his father as most sources, vouchsafe that it is the father for whom the bird is named, but the scientific name is definitely for Ernest, not Charles.

CHUCK WILL

Chuck-will's-widow *Caprimulgus rufus* (Gmelin 1789)
(Alt. Ruddy Nightjar)

This is not named for a person but after the bird's call.

CIRCE

Circe Hummingbird *Cynanthus latirostris* (**Swainson** 1827)
(Alt. Broad-billed Hummingbird)

The Circe of Greek legend wove delicate and dazzling fabrics while singing beautifully. The name might be a reference to the bird's song, nest-making or dazzling colours. Circe also turned Picus into a woodpecker.

CLAPPERTON

Clapperton's Francolin *Francolinus* (*Pternistis*) *clappertoni* Children 1826

Hugh Clapperton (1788–1827) was an explorer who was born in Annan, Dumfries and Galloway, Scotland. He served in both the merchant navy and the Royal Navy, travelling to India and Canada. He took part in an expedition that sought the source of the River Niger. Clapperton reached Lake Chad in 1823, which is the source of one of the Niger's major tributaries. On a second expedition to the same area, he died of fever near Sokoto (Nigeria). His travelling companion Major **Denham** returned with records of the expedition, which were published as the *Journal of a Second Expedition into the Interior of Africa* in 1829.

CLARKE, G

Clarke's Blood Pheasant *Ithaginis cruentus clarkei* (**Rothschild** 1920)
Clarke's Weaver *Ploceus golandi* (Clarke 1913)

Brigadier-General Goland Vanholt Clarke (1875–1944) was an ornithologist and collector in Africa and the Middle East. He actually spelt his name Clarke with an 'e' but it is misspelt 'Clark' in some references. He collected the weaver and sent it to his elder brother, Colonel Stephenson Robert Clarke (1862–1948), who wrote the description in 1913. Again a misprint has reached the literature and he is often referred to erroneously as Colonel Robert Stephenson Clarke. One of the colonel's great-grandsons provided us full details about the brothers, and Louis C G Clarke (see **Ludovic**). We can assume that the colonel named the bird after his brother rather than himself. The colonel too was a naturalist, a great traveller and a keen hunter of big game. He was also very interested in botany. He wrote descriptions of a great number of birds. We suspect that the Blood Pheasant and also Clarke's Gazelle (*Ammodorcas clarkei*) are both named after a member of the family, but we confess that we don't know which! In 1893 he bought Borde Hill House and created the very famous garden there, which remains in the care of his descendants.

CLARK, J

Clark's Grebe *Aechmophorus* (*occidentalis*) *clarkii* (**Lawrence** 1858)

John Henry Clark (1830–1885) was an American surveyor, naturalist and collector. Under the auspices of the Smithsonian Institution, he conducted the Texas Boundary Survey in 1860. He collected the type specimen of a ground snake *Sonora semiannulata* in 1851, while engaged in the United States and Mexican Boundary Survey.

CLARK, W

Clark's Nutcracker *Nucifraga columbiana* (**Wilson** 1811)

Captain William Clark (1770–1838) was a military man and explorer, who later became Governor of Missouri Territory. The **Lewis** & Clark expedition of 1804 to 1806 crossed the American continent to the Pacific. On 22 August 1805, William Clark was struggling down the canyon of the Salmon River, testing out the Indians' warning that it could not be navigated. Although his attention was mainly directed towards the topography, and the Indians he met at the North Fork of the Salmon, he noticed a new bird. Pioneer ornithologist Thomas Jefferson sent the first specimen to **Alexander Wilson** for description. Wilson, a contemporary of Lewis and Clark, later named it *Nucifraga columbiana* Columbia (River) Nut-breaker. He also gave it its common name, Clark's Nutcracker in 1811.

CLOT BEY

Clot Bey's (Thick-billed) Lark *Ramphocoris clotbey* (**Bonaparte** 1850)

Antoine-Barthélmy Clot (1793–1868) was a French physician who became the head of the Egyptian army medical corps. He established the first hospital there in 1827. Indeed he is considered to be the founder of modern medicine in Egypt and has streets named after him in Cairo. He was resident in Egypt and was awarded the honorary title of 'Bey' by Mohammed Ali Pasha (who called him Klute Bey), for his services to Egyptian medicine, in 1832.

COBB

Cobb's Wren *Troglodytes cobbi* (**Chubb** 1909)

Arthur F Cobb was a farmer in the Falkland Islands. He was the manager of Bleaker Island farm in 1910, when he wrote *Wild Life in the Falklands,* which includes a note on the decline in numbers of the Striated Caracara *Phalcoboenus australis.* He wrote *Birds of the Falkland Islands – A record of Observation With the Camera* in 1933. The wren is a Falkland Islands endemic, and Cobb collected it in 1909. Cobb could write evocatively; he once described the sound of massed Rockhopper Penguins *Eudyptes chrysocome* being '*as if thousands of wheelbarrows, all badly in need of greasing, are being pushed at full speed.*'

COCKERELL

Cockerell's Fantail *Rhipidura cockerelli* (**Ramsay** 1879)
(Alt. White-winged Fantail)

James T Cockerell (1847–1895) was an Australian collector who worked in the field between 1865 and 1891. He visited both Samoa in 1874 and the Bismarck Archipelago in 1876, in the company of the Reverend George **Brown**. He collected entomological specimens, particularly those of Australian stingless bees.

CODRINGTON

Codrington's Indigobird *Vidua codringtoni* (Neave 1907)
(Alt. Green Indigobird)

Robert Edward Codrington (1869–1908) was the colonial Administrator in Northern

Rhodesia (now Zambia) from 1898 until 1907. He wrote several articles for the Geographical Journal, such as *A journey from Fort Jameson, to Old Chitambo and the Tanganyika Plateau* in 1900 and *A voyage on Lake Tanganyika* in 1902.

COE

Coe's Honeyguide *Melignomon eisentrauti* Louette 1981
(Alt. Yellow-footed/Eisentraut's Honeyguide)

Malcolm Coe (?1930–) is a tropical ecologist and naturalist. He worked at the University of Nairobi from 1956 until 1968 and then at the Animal Ecology Research Group, Department of Zoology, University of Oxford, from 1968 until his retirement in 1995. For a while he was very heavily into herbivore nutrition, at times travelling through Heathrow with suitcases full of elephant dung; we can only imagine the scene had he ever had to open his bags for customs! His fieldwork experience (both faunal and floral) includes East, central and southern Africa, as well as India, and he has travelled in Sabah, China, Thailand and Panama. He has also taken part in a number of expeditions; to Mount Kenya in 1957; Liberia in 1964 and 1966; the South Turkana Expedition, Kenya, in 1968–1970; the Royal Society Aldabra Expeditions to the Indian Ocean between 1970 until 1982; the Kora Research Project, Kenya, 1982–1985 and the Mkomazi Ecological Research Programme, Tanzania, 1990–1997. He was awarded the Royal Geographical Society Busk Medal, in 1988, as well as the Zoological Society of Southern Africa Gold Medal, in 1989. Serle collected the first specimen in 1956 but considered it to be an immature **Zenker**'s Honeyguide *Melignomon zenkeri*. The initial collector was thus not **Eisentraut**, as claimed by Louette, who collected one in 1957. Coe saw the bird in the Nimba research compound in 1964. He said: "*It flew from the forest edge where it appeared to be searching amongst the leaves and branches of a large climbing Combretum then started on the wire. I watched it several times during the day and felt sure it was a honeyguide but one that was quite unknown to me*". Coe wrote this up but did not seek publication. **Colston** wrote a description in 1980, submitting it to Bulletin of the British Ornithologists' Club, when he took responsibility for the Nimba collection at the British Natural History Museum. Shortly afterwards, Louette asked to borrow the specimen for comparison with a bird he had seen near Nimba (although the staff at Nimba were unaware of his visit there) and Colston sent him a copy of his own unpublished description. Without informing anyone Louette published a description, naming the bird *Melignomon eisentrauti* in 1981, pre-empting Colston, whose own paper was in press and was published soon after. As Coe had so much to do with the discovery his name was proposed for the common name.

COLLIE

Collie's Magpie-jay *Calocitta colliei* (**Vigors** 1829)
(Alt. Black-throated Magpie-jay)

Lieutenant Dr Alexander Collie (1793–1835) was the naval surgeon and naturalist on an expedition from 1825 until 1828 led by Captain Frederick Beechey on *HMS Blossom*, which made some significant ornithological findings during the voyage from Chile to Alaska. Collie collected many specimens that did not survive the return journey to England in good condition but he made some coloured drawings of birds he thought were new and also took extensive notes. From these, the British ornithologist Nicholas A **Vigors** included a chapter on ornithology in his *Zoology of Captain Beechey's Voyage, 1839*. Vigors named several species new to science, including a number from California: the Black Turnstone *Arenaria melanocephala*, Pygmy Nuthatch *Sitta pygmaea*, **Bewick**'s Wren *Thryomanes bewickii*, California Towhee *Pipilo crissalis*, Band-tailed Pigeon *Columba fasciata*, Western Bluebird *Sialia mexicana*, Black Phoebe *Sayornis nigricans* and American Avocet *Recurvirostra americana*. Vigors noted that Collie collected some birds in San Francisco: Red-winged Blackbird *Agelaius phoeniceus*, Belted Kingfisher *Ceryle alcyon*, American Avocet and a Least Bittern

Ixobrychus exilis 'shot on the margin of a streamlet of water surrounded by low shrubs'. Collie also collected live specimens of Band-tailed Pigeons, Northern Flickers *Colaptes auratus*, Pygmy Nuthatches, American Robins *Turdus migratorius*, Semipalmated Plovers *Charadrius semipalmatus*, Scrub Jays *Aphelocoma californica*, Hairy Woodpeckers *Picoides villosus* and California Quails *Callipepla californica* that went on to be exhibited live in London Zoo. Off Alaska they took the type specimen of **Kittlitz**'s Murrelet *Brachyramphus brevirostris*. In Mexico, Collie collected a new long-tailed corvid, the Black-throated Magpie-jay *Calocitta colliei*, which Vigors named after Collie. Dr Collie went to Perth as a colonial administrator where he died before Vigors' work was published. When aboard *HMS Sulphur* he discovered what is now the Collie River in Western Australia. A town in Australia was also named after him.

COLLS

Colls' Forest Robin *Cercotrichas leucosticta collsi* (**Alexander** 1907)
(Alt. Forest/Western/Northern Bearded Scrub Robin)

Howard Colls seems to have been collecting in West Africa around 1906 to 1907. Boyd **Alexander** described the robin from a specimen which Colls collected in the northern Belgian Congo.

COLSTON

Colston's Bulbul *Phyllastrephus apperti* (Colston 1972)
(Alt. Appert's Tetraka, Appert's Greenbul)

Peter R Colston (1935–) is a field ornithologist who was Senior Curator at the British Natural History Museum (in London and Tring) until his retirement in 1995. There he was responsible for the largest and best-maintained scientific collections of bird skins in the world, comprising over one million specimens. Before joining the museum bird room staff in 1961 he had worked in insurance and had also served two years in the Royal Air Force. As a keen amateur he had contributed to and assisted in the production of the *London Bird Report*. He was also a regular visitor to the museum at South Kensington. Shortly after joining he was despatched to Andalucia where he learnt to collect and prepare his first study skins with full supporting data. This was to set him in good stead for a series of museum expeditions to Australia, sponsored by Major Harold **Hall**, an Australian philanthropist interested in natural history. On the first expedition (November 1962–June 1963) he collected extensively in eastern Australia and was responsible for finding and obtaining the first specimens of an undescribed Australo-Papuan babbler in southern Queensland, now known as Hall's Babbler *Pomatostomus halli*. In 1966 he collected in southwest Australia. On his second visit to Africa, in 1970, he joined the Royal Geographical Society's expedition to northern Turkana, Kenya. Subsequently he became the museum's specialist on African birds. He published descriptions of four new species: Appert's (or Colston's) Greenbul, Ash's Lark *Mirafra ashi*, Coe's Honeyguide *Melignomon eisentrauti* and Mangrove Reed Warbler *Acrocephalus avicenniae*. He also described a further seven new subspecies and he has two races named *colstoni* in his honour. He contributed to *An Atlas of Speciation in African Birds* (**Hall** & **Moreau** 1970) and, with K Curry-Lindahl co-wrote *The Birds of the Mount Nimba, Liberia*. He served as a member of the British Ornithologists' Union Records Committee and subsequently co-authored *A Field Guide to the Rare Birds of Britain & Europe*, with Ian Lewington and Per Alström. Always a wader enthusiast, he also published *The Waders of Britain and Europe, North Africa and the Middle East*, with Philip Burton. Colston was a contributor to later volumes of *The Birds of Africa* and *The Birds of the Western Palearctic*. Between 1989 and 1995 he made private trips to China, together with Per Alström and Urban Olsson, which resulted in the discovery of three previously unknown *Phylloscopus* leaf warblers whose descriptions have subsequently been published. Father **Appert** collected two specimens of the bulbul from southwestern Madagascar. They were preserved in alcohol, which often causes delicate colours to fade. Colston described the new species in Ibis 114:89–92 and Michael Walters, of the NHM (Tring) gave it the name Colston's Bulbul in his *Complete Birds of the World* (1980).

COMMERSON

Commerson's Scops Owl *Otus commersoni* [Extinct]

Philibert Commerson (1727–1773) was known as 'doctor, botanist and naturalist of the King'. He accompanied the French explorer Louis Antoine de Bougainville on his round-the-world expedition of 1766–1769 on *La Boudeuse* and *L'Etoile*. Commerson was primarily a botanist but he has a wide diversity of animal species also named after him, including Commerson's Dolphin *Cephalorhynchus commersinii*, which he first observed in 1787, Commerson's Frogfish *Antennarius commersoni* and Commerson's Cornetfish *Fistularia commersonii*. He also discovered the vine Bougainvillea in the 1760s, naming it for the expedition leader. The owl, which was a native of Mauritius, became extinct in 1837.

COMTE DE PARIS

See **Conte de Paris**.

CONNAUGHT

Duchess of Connaught's Parakeet *Charmosyna margaritae* (Tristram 1879)
(Alt. Duchess Parakeet)

Louise Margaret of Prussia, Her Royal Highness the Princess of Connaught (1860–1917). Canon **Tristram** named the parakeet in honour of the Princess. It was discovered by Lieutenant **Richards** RN in the Solomon Islands.

CONOVER

Conover's Dove *Leptotila conoveri* (Bond & Meyer de Schauensee 1943)
(Alt. Tolima Dove)

Henry Boardman Conover (1892–1950) was a soldier and amateur ornithologist. He served in the United States Army in the First World War. All through his life he was an enthusiast for field sports. Around 1920 he became interested in scientific ornithology, particularly in relation to gamebirds. He was a Trustee of The Field Museum of Chicago, to which donated his collection of ornithological texts. He made significant contributions to **Hellmayr**'s *The Catalogue of Birds of the Americas*. Conover published articles in The Auk; *Game birds of the Hooper Bay region, Alaska* in 1926 and *A new species of rail from Paraguay*, in 1934.

CONRAD

Conrad's Inca *Bourceria conradi* (**Gould***)

This is another of 'Gould's birds' and only mentioned in his engravings. The entry below is, therefore, speculative. The hummingbird could possibly have been named after

Thomas Conrad von Baldenstein (1784–1878), a well-known natural scientist who made a name for himself as an entomologist and apiarist. However, was chiefly famous as an ornithologist, whose scientific works on the birdlife of the Alps were recognised by various societies in Switzerland and abroad, who variously made him an honorary member. Alternatively, the name might have been for Timothy Abbott Conrad (1803–1877), an American geologist at the New York State Survey, Smithsonian Institution and the North Carolina Geological Survey, among others. His papers at Stanton have letters describing an expedition, which discovered fossils and new species of Cretaceous shells, many from Texas. As the bird is South American, one might assume that T A Conrad is the more likely but as it is a 'Gould' bird and he was in Europe, the attribution to T Conrad von Baldenstein is just as likely. Gould calls the bird *Bourceria conradi*. **Bourcier** described a bird in 1847 which he named *Trochilus conradi*. This bird was bought from the collector **Parzudaki** (after whom Gould named another bird), who had collected it near Caracas. It was acquired by the taxidermist **Leadbeater** and was part of the **Loddiges** collection of hummingbirds and allies

CONSTANT

Constant's Starthroat *Heliomaster constantii* (**De Lattre** 1843)
(Alt. Plain-capped Starthroat)

C Constant (1820–1905) was a French collector and taxidermist. He is also commemorated in the fossil ammonite *Peltoceratoides williamsoni constantii*.

CONTE DE PARIS

Conte de Paris' Starfrontlet *Coeligena lutetiae* (**Delattre** & **Bourcier** 1846)
(Alt. Buff-winged/Comte de Paris' Starfrontlet)

The title Comte de Paris is a title enjoyed by many members of the French royal houses, including Henri Prince d'Orléans (1867–1901). However, in view of the describers and the date of the description, we feel it most likely to have been named after the titleholder of the time. This was Louis-Philippe of Orléans (1773–1850), King of France from 1830 to 1848, when he abdicated and fled to England.

CONVERS

Convers' Thorntail *Popelairia conversii* (**Bourcier** & **Mulsant** 1846)
(Alt. Green Thorntail)

M Convers was a French naturalist who collected in Colombia in the middle of the 19th century. The thorntail was illustrated by Gould, who called it *Gouldia conversi*.

COOK

Cook's Petrel *Pterodroma cookii* (G R **Gray** 1843) [Extinct]

James Cook (1728–1779) was, of course, one of the most famed explorers of all time, so there are many biographies to consult. Cook commanded *HMS Endeavour* on its expeditions, whose achievements included the discovery of eastern Australia, in 1770, and much of New Zealand. He was killed in a skirmish with natives in Hawaii.

COOPER

Cooper's Buzzard *Buteo jamaicensis* (Gmelin 1788)
(Alt. Red-tailed Hawk)
Cooper's Flycatcher *Muscicapa cooperi* (**Nuttall** 1831)
(Alt. Olive-sided Flycatcher)
Cooper's Hawk *Accipiter cooperii* (**Bonaparte** 1820)
Cooper's Sandpiper *Pisobia* (*Tringa*) *cooperii*
Cooper's Tanager *Piranga rubra cooperi* (**Ridgway** 1869)
(Alt. Summer Tanager)

William C Cooper (1798–1864) was a New York conchologist and collector. He was one of the founders of the American Museum of Natural History in New York. He was also the father of Dr James G Cooper (1830–1902), who worked for the Pacific Railroad Survey in California and for whom the Cooper Ornithological Society is named, as well as a number of birds in their scientific names. He was the first to describe the Evening Grosbeak *Coccothraustes vespertinus*. **Bonaparte** described and named Cooper's Hawk. **Nuttall** described the flycatcher but the name was superseded by a later description of the bird by **Swainson**. Cooper's Sandpiper is believed to have been a hybrid between a Curlew Sandpiper *Calidris ferruginea* and a Sharp-tailed Sandpiper *C.acuminata.*

COQUEREL

Coquerel's Coua *Coua coquereli* (Grandidier 1867)
(Alt. Coquerel's Madagascar Coucal)

Dr Charles Coquerel (1822–1867) was a surgeon in the French Imperial Navy and an entomologist who was involved in collecting expeditions to Madagascar and neighbouring islands. He was the first to identify the screw-worm fly in 1858 and gave it the name *hominivorax*, which literally means 'man-eater'. Many of the specimens which he collected, mostly of insects, were only studied after his death. He was author of many scientific papers such as *Orthoptères de Bourbon et de Madagascar* and *Sur les Monandroptères et Raphiderus.*

COQUI

Coqui Francolin *Francolinus coqui* (A **Smith** 1836)

This is not named for a person but for the sound of the bird's call 'Ko Kwee'. It has been suggested that it might be after a Mr Coqui, a friend of Sir Andrew **Smith**, who described the bird in 1836, but we prefer the first explanation.

CORA

Cora's Sheartail *Thaumastura cora* (**Lesson** & Gamot 1827)
(Alt. Peruvian Sheartail)

Cora was a mythological Inca princess of the sun. She appears in a novel, *Les Incas, ou la destruction de l'Empire du Pérou*, which was published by Jean Francois Marmontel in 1777, and which is the subject of an opera libretto written by Gudmund Göran Adlerbeth called *Cora och Alonzo*. This was the first opera to be staged and sung in Swedish at the Royal Opera in Stockholm, when it opened in 1782. The bird is a Peruvian endemic.

CORNELIA

Cornelia's Eclectus Parrot *Eclectus roratus cornelia* (**Bonaparte** 1850)
(Alt. Kalanga, Grand Eclectus/King Parrot)

We believe that this bird was not named after a person since the trinomial is not accorded the appropriate Latin gender. However, it is possible that the Cornelia in question was Madame Laetitia Bonaparte (1750–1836), the mother of Napoleon I. It seems that 'Cornelia' was a family nickname for her. The Emperor, in his writings from St Helena, refers to her as a '*rural Cornelia*' and describes her as behaving and acting '*as a Cornelia*'. She was very definitely a great matriarch, being known by all the family as 'Madame Mère'. **Bonaparte**, who described the bird, may well have had his grandmother in mind when he did so. He also had a daughter called Laetitia, presumably named after her grandmother. See also the entries for **Letitia** and **Zénaide** for some of the ramifications of the Bonaparte family.

CORY

Cory's Shearwater *Calonectris diomedea* (**Scopoli** 1769)
Cory's Bittern *Ixobrychus neoxenus*
(Alt. Chory's Bittern)

Charles Barney Cory (1857–1921) was an American ornithologist. He donated his collection of 19,000 bird specimens to The Field Museum, in Chicago, in exchange for departmental status for ornithology and his appointment as lifetime curator without residence obligations. The Department of Ornithology, with Curator Cory and Assistant Curators, G K **Cherrie** and N Dearborn, remained separate for six years. He wrote *The Birds of Haiti and San Domingo* in 1885, *The Birds of the West Indies* in 1889 and *The Birds of Illinois and Wisconsin* in 1909. Cory was the first person to describe the shearwater as a species, and he named the Atlantic subspecies, *C. d. borealis*, in 1881. **Scopoli** originally described the species in 1769 but thought it to be a race of another shearwater. The Bittern proved to be a rare erythristic morph of the Least Bittern *I.exilis* and not a separate species. We believe Chory is a mistaken rendering of Cory.

COSTA

Costa's Hummingbird *Calypte costae* (**Bourcier** 1839)

Louis Marie Panteleon Costa, Marquis de Beau-Regard (1806–1864), was a Sardinian aristocrat and collector who was also an accomplished amateur ornithologist, archaeologist and historian. He specialised in hummingbirds and had a notable collection. In recognition of this, **Bourcier** named this species in his honour.

COUCH

Couch's Jay *Aphelocoma ultramarina couchii* (**Baird**)
(Alt. Grey-breasted/Arizona/Mexican/Sieber's Jay)
Couch's Kingbird *Tyrannus couchii* (Baird 1858)
(Alt. Olive-backed Kingbird)

General Darius Nash Couch (1822–1897) was a United States Army officer and a general during the Civil War. He was also an explorer, who took leave of absence to lead a zoological expedition in Mexico.

COUES

Coues' Flycatcher *Contopus pertinax* (**Cabanis** & **Heine** 1859)
  (Alt. Greater Pewee)
Coues' Gadwall *Anas strepera couesi* [Extinct]
Coue's Redpoll *Carduelis hornemanni exilipes* (Coues 1862)
  (Alt. Arctic/Hoary Redpoll)

Dr Elliott B Coues [pronounced Cows] (1842–1899) was a United States Army Surgeon and one of the founders of the American Ornithologists' Union. Coues collected a warbler and asked **Baird** to name it in honour of his sister, **Grace** Darlington Coues (1847–1939), hence Grace's Warbler *Dendroica graciae*. He is also the person who named the sandpiper *Calidris bairdii* after Baird, as he was one of Baird's collectors. Amongst other works he wrote *Handbook of Field and General Ornithology* in 1890, *A Checklist of North American Birds* in 1873 and the *Key to North American Birds*, the latter published in five editions in two volumes between 1872 and 1903.

COULON

Coulon's Macaw *Propyrrhura couloni* (P L **Sclater** 1876)
  (Alt. Blue-headed Macaw)

Paul Louis de Coulon (1804–1894) was a Swiss naturalist. He was a joint founder, with Louis Agassiz, of the Natural History Museum of Neuchâtel and left money to it upon his death.

COUNT RAGGI

Count Raggi's Bird-of-Paradise *Paradisaea raggiana* P L **Sclater** 1873
  (Alt. Marquis Raggi's Bird-of-Paradise)

Marchese Francesco Raggi was an Italian naturalist who explored and collected in Peru in the mid-19th century. **Sclater** named the Red-plumed Paradise Bird *Paradisea raggiana* from skins sent to him by **D'Alberti**.

COURSEN

Coursen's Spinetail *Synallaxis courseni* (**Blake** 1971)
  (Alt. Apurímac/Blake's Spinetail)

C Blair Coursen was an American field ornithologist. With Edward E Ford and Colin C Sanborn he wrote *Birds of the Chicago Region* in 1934. In 1962 he published an article in Turtox News on *Kitchen Botany*, aimed at encouraging schoolchildren to become interested in vegetables.

COURTOIS

Courtois' Laughing-thrush *Garrulax galbanus* (**Godwin-Austen** 1874)
  (Alt. Austen's/Yellow-throated Laughing-thrush)

The Reverend Fréderic Courtois (1860–1928) was a French missionary to China from 1901 until his death. He was an amateur naturalist and in 1903 he was appointed Director of the Natural History Museum in Sikawei, near Shanghai. He wrote *Les Oiseaux du Musée de Zi-Ka-Wei* in 1912.

COX

Cox's Sandpiper *Calidris paramelanotos* Parker 1982

John B Cox is a British-born Australian ornithologist, resident in Adelaide, who collected two specimens of this bird in South Australia in 1973. They were first described by S A Parker in 1982. Another birder came forward claiming priority and there was much argument and debate regarding this at the time. Based on genetic evidence, it is now thought that Cox's Sandpiper is not a species but a hybrid, probably between Curlew Sandpiper *Calidris ferruginea* and Pectoral Sandpiper *C.melanotos*. Cox, himself also came to this conclusion. With N C H Reid he wrote *An Annotated Checklist of the Birds of South Australia*, in 1979.

COXEN

Coxen's Double-eyed Fig Parrot *Cyclopsitta diophthalma coxeni* **Gould** 1867
(Alt. Double-eyed Fig Parrot/Lorilet)

Charles Coxen (1809–1876) was one of the founders of the Queensland Philosophical Society and a principal founder of the Queensland Museum. He was honorary curator of the museum from 1871 until 1876. **Gould** described the parrot in 1867 from a specimen that was sent to him by **Waller** after the appearance of the original description, which was based on a drawing by Coxen based on specimens in his possession. Waller also collected a nightjar species in Port Albany, Cape York, Queensland. Gould was married to Coxen's sister, Elizabeth, who travelled with him to Australia where the bird is found, along with Henry Coxen, their nephew, and her brother. Both Elizabeth and her brother were themselves amateur artists.

CRANCH

Cranch's Francolin *Francolinus afer cranchii* (Leach 1818)
(Alt. Red-necked Francolin)

John Cranch (1758–1816) was a British explorer of tropical Africa and also an accomplished natural historian. He took part in an expedition in 1816 led by Captain J K Tuckey, R N to discover the source of the Congo river. **Wagler** described the race, probably following Tuckey's name but reduced it to subspecies status.

CRAVERI

Craveri's Murrelet *Brachyramphus* [*Synthliboramphus*] *craveri* (**Salvadori** 1865)
(Alt. Xanthus's Murrelet)

Frederico Craveri (1815–1890) was an Italian scientist, a chemist and a pioneer in the field of meteorology. He was also an explorer, teacher and scholar, who spent 20 years in Mexico, from 1840 until 1859, travelling and collecting. He obtained the murrelet, which was named after himself and his brother 20 years later by **Sclater**, although **Salvadori** wrote the description in 1865. The 'F Craveri' Museum of Natural History in Bra, Italy, was founded by Craveri in the brothers' former house and now houses their collections. Strictly speaking, the name should be 'Craveris' Murrelet' because the bird was named for the two brothers. The less-celebrated brother was named Ettore.

CRAWFURD

Crawfurd's Kalij *Lophura nycthemera crawfurdi* (J E **Gray** 1829)
(Alt. Kalij Pheasant)

Dr John Crawfurd (1783–1868) was a British physician, scholar, administrator and diplomat. He joined the Honourable East India Company and, in 1810, was with Lord Minto's expedition to capture Java from the Dutch. Subsequently he was in Penang and in Singapore with **Raffles**. He has been described as the '*Scotsman who made Singapore British*'. After several years, and a journey back to London, he returned to India and was employed as a diplomat, heading missions to Thailand, Burma (now Myanmar) and Cochin China (now part of southern Vietnam). In 1820, he published *History of the Indian Archipelago*. **Darwin** in his writings refers to a Mr Crawfurd who had advised him on hybrid fowls that he had observed in Indonesia. The same Crawfurd read a paper at Oxford, in 1860, *On the relation of the Domesticated Animals to Civilisation*.

CRETZSCHMAR

Cretzschmar's Babbler *Turdoides leucocephalus* (Cretzschmar 1827)
(Alt. White-headed Babbler)

Cretzschmar's Bunting *Emberiza caesia*
(Cretzschmar 1827)

Dr Philipp Jakob Cretzschmar (1786–1845) was a German physician who taught anatomy at the Senckenberg Institute in Frankfurt. He was the founder and second director of Die Senckenbergische Naturforschende Gesellschaft, which was a natural history society and also a founder of the Senckenberg Natural History Museum.

CROOKSHANK

Crookshank's White-eye *Zosterops fuscicapillus crookshanki* **Mayr** & Rand 1935
(Alt. Capped White-eye)

Probably named after Arthur Crookshank (1824–1891) who was a British colonial officer. He rose through the ranks, as he was formerly junior mate and then second mate of the *Ariel*, which sailed to Sarawak. He became a colonial officer from 1843 to 1873 under Sir Charles Johnson **Brooke**, rising to Resident in 1870. There are a number of other candidates, which is hardly surprising given that J H Walker wrote *A Confusion of Crookshanks (sic): Personalities and Power in the Lives of the Early Brookes*, in 1997. **Salvadori** described the nominate form in 1876. This race of the white-eye is confined to Goodenough Island, which is part of Papua New Guinea.

CROSSLEY

Crossley's Babbler *Mystacornis crossleyi* (Grandidier 1870)
(Alt. Crossley's Timalia)
Crossley's Ground Roller *Atelornis crossleyi* (**Sharpe** 1875)
(Alt. Rufous-headed Roller)
Crossley's Ground Thrush *Zoothera crossleyi* (Sharpe 1871)

A Crossley collected in Africa (Madagascar and Cameroon) in the 1870s. There are specimens of six non-passerine collected by him in the British Museum (Natural History); the Shining-blue Kingfisher *Alcedo guentheri*, the Rufous-headed Ground Roller *Atelornis crossleyi*, the Collared Nightjar *Caprimulgus enarratus*, the crake *Corethrura insularis*, the Madagascar Serpent-eagle *Eutriochis astur* and the Swift *Cypselus gracilis* (the latter is recorded as E Crossley, although as it was collected at the same place and time as the others, it is not clear if this is a transcription error or whether there were two members of the family collecting). There are also eight passerines, which he collected, in the museum: Short-billed Greenbul *Bernieria zosterops*, *Ceblepyris major*, Sharpe's Robin-Chat *Cossypha sharpei*, Sunbird Asity *Neodrepanis coruscans*, Yellow-browed Tetraka *Oxylabes xanthophrys*, Ward's Flycatcher *Pseudobias wardi*, *Turdus crossleyi* and *Vanga griseipectus*. Not all of these names are still current. By virtue of the other fauna commemorating him it is clear he did not confine his efforts to collecting birds. For example there is the Furry-eared Dwarf Lemur *Cheirogaleus crossleyi*, and butterflies and moths such as Crossley's Forest Queen *Euxanthe crossleyi* and *Godartia crossleyi*.

CUMING

Cuming's Scrubfowl *Megapodius cumingii* (Dillwyn 1853)
(Alt. Philippine/Tabon Scrubfowl, Philippine Megapode)

Hugh Cuming (1791–1865) was an English naturalist and conchologist, who has been described as the 'Prince of Collectors'. He collected in the Neotropics from 1822 until 1826 and again from 1828 to 1830. He also collected in Polynesia between 1827 and 1828, and in the East Indies from 1836 until 1840. He preceded **Darwin** in having collected in the Galápagos in 1829. His shell collection is housed in the Linnean Library in London.

CURATORS

Being a museum curator very much enhances one's chances of having a bird named after you. Firstly, you are likely to be sent on collecting expeditions where you (or your helpers) may discover a bird you can name. [It can happen the other way around, where collecting leads to appointment as a curator]. Examples of such well-placed curators include: John **Anderson**, José Vicente Barboza du **Bocage**, Wolfrid Rudyerd **Boulton**, Thomas Henry Bowyer-**Bower**, Karl Hermann Konrad **Burmeister**, Dr James Paul **Chapin**, Joseph Scattergood **Dixon**, Herbert **Friedman**, Carl A **Gibson**-Hill, Juan Cristóbal **Gundlach**, Robert **Hall**, Hermann **von Ihering**, Sir William **Jardine**, Louis C G **Clarke**, Gerlof Fokko **Mees**, Professor Dr Edgardo **Moltoni**, Olivério Mario de Oliveira de **Pinto**, Othmar **Reiser**, Robert **Ridgway**, Herbert Christopher **Robinson**, Professor Dr Joseph Beal **Steere**, Professor Erwin Friedrich Theodor **Stresemann**, Wladyslaw **Taczanowski** and Nicolai **Zarudny**. As a curator you will also be sent specimens and asked to write the formal descriptions. Whilst it is poor form to name something after yourself in a description which you yourself write, the fact that you are asked to write such a description may well lead to a reciprocal arrangement with the person who asked, or even an invitation by the discoverer to call the bird your own. In this position you can, of course, always name a bird after your father, which seems to have been the case with Ernest Charles **Chubb**.

Many curators have been fortunate enough to name or re-name birds within their museum collections, which have not been catalogued, or that have been mis-identified. Later ornithologists may honour others, due to the excellence of their work. Examples of curators who most probably fit this latter category are: William **Brewster**, Morten Thrane **Brünnich**, Daniel Giraud **Elliot**, John Edward **Gray**, Joseph **Grinnell**, William Robert **Ogilvie-Grant**, August von **Pelzeln**, and Richard Bowdler **Sharpe**. Not even the quoted examples necessarily neatly fit into one category or another. Some people found new birds on expeditions and discovered misidentified birds in collections, and were also honoured by others. Peter **Colston**, an outstanding source of information for this volume, certainly discovered birds in the field and some which were misidentified in museums, and he has been honoured by others for both his scholarship and fieldcraft. Another example was Austen L **Rand**. Lord Lionel Walter **Rothschild** could be slotted into some of the categories above or in a special one for men who established museums, along with the likes of **Bishop**, but he probably deserves unique treatment.

CUVIER

Cuvier's Kinglet *Regulus cuvieri* (**Audubon** 1812)
(Alt. Cuvier's Crested Wren, Cuvier's Regulus)
Cuvier's Rail *Dryolimnas cuvieri* (**Pucheran** 1845)
Cuvier's Sabrewing *Phaeochroa cuvierii* (**DeLattre** & **Bourcier** 1846)
(Alt. Cuvier's [Scaly-breasted] Hummingbird)
Cuvier's Toucan *Ramphastos tucanus cuvieri* (**Wagler** 1827)
(Alt. White-throated Toucan)

Leopold Chretien Frederic Dagobert Baron Cuvier (1769–1832) – better known by his pen name Georges Cuvier – was a French naturalist. He believed that palaeontological discontinuities were evidence of sudden and widespread catastrophes, that is, that extinctions do happen. He is also famed for having stayed in a top government post, as permanent secretary of the Academy of Sciences, through three regimes including Napoleon's! It may be that some of the birds were named for his brother Fréderick (1773–1838), who was director of the Paris Zoological and Botanical Gardens. Audubon said of the kinglet he collected in June 1812 '*I named this pretty and rare species after Baron Cuvier, not merely by way of acknowledgment for the kind attentions which I received at the hands of that deservedly celebrated naturalist, but as a homage due by every student of nature to one unrivalled in the knowledge of General Zoology*'.

Cuvier wrote *Tableau élémentaire de l'histoire naturelle des animaux* in 1798, *Mémoires sur les espèces d'éléphants vivants et fossils* in 1800, *Leçons d'anatomie comparée* between 1801 and 1805, *Récherches sur les ossements fossiles des quadrupeds* in 1812 and *Le Règne animal destribué d'après son organisation* in 1817. Cuvier's Kinglet probably never existed as a species at all but was a misclassified aberrant individual Ruby-crowned Kinglet *Regulus calendula*!

CYCLOPS

Cyclops Lorikeet *Charmosyna josefinae cyclopum* (**Hartert** 1930)
(Alt. Josephine's Lory)

This race of Josephine's Lory is not strictly named for a person. It can appear to have one eye in the middle of its head, recalling the Cyclops, the one-eyed giant in Homer's Odyssey.

DABBENE

Dabbene's Guan *Penelope dabbenei* (**Hellmayr** & **Conover** 1942)
(Alt. Red-faced Guan)

Roberto Dabbene (1864–1938) was an Argentinian ornithologist. He was the first president of the Asociación Ornitológica del Plata, in 1916. Among his publications are, in 1917; *Especies y subespecies aparentemente nuevas de Geositta y Cinclodes de la República Argentina y del sur de Chile* in Physis, *Los vencejos (Cypselidae) de la República Argentina* in El Hornero and *Miscelánea ornitológica. La perdiz de California en Chile; la perdiz Nothoprocta perdicaria* also in El Hornero, in 1921 *Notas sobre el petrel plateado Pricoella antarctica* (Stephens) in the Revista Chilena de Historia Natural, and in 1930 *Los Picaflores de Chile.*

D'ALBERTIS

D'Albertis' Bird-of-Paradise *Drepanornis albertisi* (P L **Sclater** 1883)
(Alt. Black-billed Sicklebill)
D'Albertis' Grassbird *Megalurus albolimbatus* (D'Albertis & **Salvadori** 1879)
(Alt. Fly River Grassbird/Grass Warbler)
D'Albertis' Mountain Pigeon *Gymnophaps albertisii* (Salvadori 1854)
(Alt. Papuan Bare-eyed [Mountain] Pigeon)
D'Albertis' Orange-breasted Fig Parrot *Cyclopsitta gulielmiterti suavissima*
(P L Sclater 1876)

Cavaglieri Luigo M D'Albertis (1841–1901) was an Italian botanist, ethnologist and zoologist. He was in New Guinea from 1871 to 1877, where he ventured further than any European, using a steamboat furnished by the New South Wales government, so that he could explore and chart the Fly River. He obviously had a very adventurous time of it, being attacked by natives who fired arrows at him. He is reported to have taken a number of human skulls and even a recently severed head of an elderly woman. His behaviour towards the local people probably contributed considerably to their hostility to later European explorers. Presumably, he also collected natural history specimens as he is commemorated in the names of a number of mammals and the snake D'Albertis's Python *Leiopython albertisii.*

DAMMERMAN

Dammerman's Moustached Parakeet *Psittacula alexandri dammermani*
(Chasen & Kloss 1932)
(Alt. Red-breasted/Moustached/Banded/Bearded/Rose-breasted Parakeet,
Java Moustached Parakeet)

Dr Karel Willem Dammerman (1888–1951) was a Dutch field zoologist, botanist and collector, who worked in the East Indies from the beginning of the 20th century. He wrote *Preservation of Wildlife and Nature Reserves in the Netherlands Indies,* in 1929, and also wrote an article the same year on *The Orang Pendek or Ape-man of Sumatra.*

DANISH

Denmark is a small nation with a long history of ornithological pursuit and many birders today. A few Danes have managed to join the ranks of our 'birdmen' over and above Princess **Alexandra,** who is honoured through fame rather than ornithological acumen. Morten Thrane **Brünnich** has already been mentioned in these notes as a museum curator and excellent ornithologist deserving of the honour, but is one of just six other Danes making it on merit. Jens Wilken **Hornemann** was a brilliant botanist earning the honour conferred upon him by an ornithologist friend **Holboell**, who was also a naval Captain and after whom birds were named by, guess who, Hornemann! The other famed Dane Dr Nathaniel **Wallich**, became well known for establishing a museum in Calcutta and, more important for this botanist, the botanical gardens that still thrive there. **Waterstradt** was another all-round naturalist who found new birds. A more recent example is Finn **Salomonsen**, who was both an ornithologist and an artist.

DANJOU

Danjou's Babbler *Jabouilleia danjoui* (**Robinson** & Kloss 1919)
(Alt. Short-tailed Scimitar Babbler)

André Danjou was the French consul in Singapore in 1919.

D'ARNAUD

D'Arnaud's Barbet *Trachyphonus darnaudii* (**Prevost** & **Des Murs** 1847)

A (or J) D'Arnaud was an explorer and big-game hunter who left France for the Sudan in 1839. His first trip was an Egyptian expedition looking for the source of the White Nile and penetrated further than any other previous expedition. He explored in the Sudan from 1841 to 1842 under the leadership of a Turkish officer, Selim Bimbashi, and in the company of Thibaut, a French Muslim who was the French consular agent at Khartoum for nearly 40 years, and Sabatier. He also explored in Ethiopia until 1843. The barbet may be conspecific with the Red-and-yellow Barbet *T. erythrocephalus*.

DARWIN

Darwin's Cactus Ground Finch *Geospiza scandens* (**Gould** 1837)
Darwin's Caracara *Phalcoboenus albogularis* (Gould 1837)
(Alt. White-throated Caracara)
Darwin's Cocos Island Finch *Pinaroloxias inornata* (Gould 1843)
Darwin's Large Cactus Ground Finch *Geospiza conirostris* (**Ridgway** 1890)
Darwin's Large Ground Finch *Geospiza magnirostris* (Gould 1837)
Darwin's Large Tree Finch *Camarhynchus psittacula* (Gould 1837)
Darwin's Mangrove Finch *Camarhynchus heliobates* (Snodgrass & Heller 1901)
Darwin's Medium Ground Finch *Geospiza fortis* (Ridgway 1890)
Darwin's Medium Tree Finch *Camarhynchus pauper* (Gould 1837)
Darwin's Nothura *Nothura darwinii* (**Salvadori** 1895)
(Alt. Darwin's Tynamou)
Darwin's [Pucras] Pheasant *Pucrasia macrolopha darwinii* (**Swinhoe** 1872)
(Alt. Koklass Pheasant)
Darwin's Rail *Coturnicops notatus* (Gould 1841)
(Alt. Speckled Rail or Speckled Crake)
Darwin's Rhea *Pterocnemia pennata* (**d'Orbigny** 1834)
(Alt. Lesser Rhea)
Darwin's Sharp-beaked Ground Finch *Geospiza difficilis* (**Sharpe** 1888)

Darwin's Small Ground Finch *Geospiza fuliginosa* (Gould 1837)
Darwin's Small Tree Finch *Camarhynchus parvulus* (Gould 1837)
Darwin's Tanager *Thraupis bonariensis darwinii*
  (Alt. Blue-and-yellow Tanager)
Darwin's Vegetarian Finch *Camarhynchus crassirostris* (Gould 1837)
Darwin's Warbler Finch *Certhidea olivacea* (Gould 1837)
Darwin's Woodpecker Finch *Camarhynchus pallidus* (P L **Sclater** & **Salvin** 1870)

Charles Darwin (1809–1892) was the prime advocate, together with **Wallace**, of Natural Selection as the way in which speciation occurs. To quote from his most famous work *On the Origin of Species by Means of Natural Selection*, first published in 1859, '*I have called this principle, by which each slight variation, if useful, is preserved, by the term Natural Selection.*'
From 1831 to 1836 Darwin was the naturalist on *HMS Beagle* on her scientific expedition round the world. In South America he found fossils of extinct animals that were similar to extant species. On the Galápagos Islands he noticed many variations among plants and animals of the same general type as those in South America. Darwin collected specimens for further study everywhere he went. On his return to London he conducted thorough research of his notes and specimens. Out of this study grew several related theories; evolution did occur; evolutionary change was gradual, taking thousands or even millions of years; the primary mechanism for evolution was a process called Natural Selection; and the millions of species alive today arose from a single original life form through a branching process called 'specialisation'. However, Darwin held back on publication for many years through not wanting to offend Christians, especially his wife.

Swinhoe wrote this description of a new Chinese pheasant, which he obtained in December, 1871: '*The same mountains have also yielded a Pucras Pheasant remarkable for the absence of the golden neck-spot which adorns the Pucrasia xanthospila of Northern and Western China… It is of the same model as the other two closely allied species, Pucrasia macrolopha of the Himalayas and the above-mentioned, but differs sufficiently from either to be recognized as a third race of this curious type. I propose to dedicate this discovery to Mr. Charles Darwin.*' In addition to birds styled 'Darwin's', Charles's Mockingbird *Nesomimus trifasciatus* and Charles's Tree Finch *Camarhynchus pauper* are also named after Darwin. He studied the mockingbird himself whilst he was in the Galápagos Islands.

DAUBENTON

Daubenton's Curassow *Crax daubentoni* (G R **Gray** 1867)
  (Alt. Yellow-knobbed Curassow)
Daubenton's Parakeet *Psittacula eques* (Boddaert 1783) [Extinct]
  (Alt. Réunion Parakeet)

Almost certainly Dr Louis Jean-Marie d'Aubenton (1716–1800); some sources say 1799 as he died on 1st Jan 1800). Daubenton, as his name is more commonly spelt, was a French naturalist. His work covered many fields including comparative anatomy, plant physiology, palaeontology, mineralogy and experimental agriculture. He was professor of mineralogy at the 'Jardin des Plantes' and of natural history at the School of Medicine in Paris. In 1793 he became the first director of the Museum of Natural History in Paris. He wrote *Les Planches Elumineez d'Histoire Naturelle*, in 1765, and collaborated with **Buffon** on the many volumes constituting '*Histoire Naturelle des Oiseaux*'. He completed a great number of zoological descriptions (including 182 species of quadrupeds) for the first section of Georges Buffon's work *Histoire Naturelle Générale et Particulière,* which was published between 1794 and 1804. Daubenton was a strange man. He was unusual for his day in being a vegetarian, once saying: '*It is to be presumed that man, while he lives in a* *natural state and a graded climate, where the earth spontaneously produces every type of fruit, he feeds himself with these and does not eat animals.'* Less unusual for his time, he was a racist, believing in the superiority of Europeans. He once said that Europeans were: *'the model for beauty'* and that *'Africans were not born with noses that flat, and lips that thick'*, but that *'African parents, after judging their children to be lacking in beauty, would crush their noses and squeeze their lips so that they swell and thus believe they have beautified nature while disfiguring it'*. He is perhaps more famed for the Daubenton's Bat *Myotis daubentonii*. He is also credited with introducing Merino sheep into France. G R **Gray** described the curassow from a specimen bought from **Leadbeater** some years earlier. One source says the birds are named after Edme Louis d'Aubenton (1732–1788), who was also French naturalist.

DAVID, A

> David's Tree-partridge *Arborophila davidi* (**Delacour** & Jabouille 1931)
> (Alt. Orange-necked/breasted [Hill] Partridge, David's Hill Partridge)

André D David-Beaulieu (1896–19?) was a naturalist who was a civil servant in French Indochina in the 1940s. He wrote *Les Oiseaux de la Région de Honquan* in 1932, *Les Oiseaux de la Province de Savannakhet* in 1949 and *Les Oiseaux du Tranninh* in 1944. **Delacour** collected the partridge in 1927.

DAVID, PÈRE

> (Père) David's Blood Pheasant *Ithaginis cruentus sinensis* (David 1873)
> (Père) David's Bush Warbler *Bradypterus davidi* (**La Touche** 1907)
> (Père) David's Hill Warbler *Prinia criniger* (**Hodgson** 1836)
> (Alt. Striated/Hill/Brown Hill/Prinia, Brown Hill Warbler)
> (Père) David's Laughing-thrush *Garrulax davidi* (**Swinhoe** 1868)
> (Alt. Plain Laughing-thrush)
> (Père) David's Niltava *Niltava davidi* (La Touche 1907)
> (Alt. Fukien/Fujian Niltava)
> (Père) David's (Wood) Owl *Strix davidi* (**Sharpe** 1875)
> (Alt. Ural Owl)
> (Père) David's Parrotbill *Paradoxornis davidianus* (**Slater** 1897)
> (Alt. Short-tailed Parrotbill, David's Crowtit)
> (Père) David's Rubythroat *Luscinia* (*Erithacus*) *pectardens* (David 1877)
> (Alt. Firethroat)
> (Père) David's Snowfinch *Montifringilla davidiana* (J **Verreaux** 1871)
> (Alt. Small Snowfinch)
> David's Swan *Cygnus davidi* (Swinhoe 1870) [Extinct]
> (Père) David's Tit *Parus davidi* (Berezowski & **Bianchi** 1891)
> (Alt. Rusty-breasted Tit)

Fr Jean Pierre Armand David (1826–1900) was a French Lazarist priest as well as a fine zoologist, who taught in Savona, where both **Doria** and **d'Albertis** were among his pupils. He went as a missionary to China and was the first to observe many animals, including birds, as well as the deer *Elaphurus davidianus* named for him and the Giant Panda *Ailuropoda melanoleuca*. He did not arrive in China until 1862 and only started collecting a year later. The French naturalist Alphonse **Milne-Edwards** classified many specimens collected by Père David. This remarkable man collected thousands of specimens and had many plants and other animals named after him as well as birds. He co-authored, with **Oustalet**, *Les Oiseaux de Chine*, which they finished in 1877. **Swinhoe** described the swan from the sole known specimen, which has since been lost.

DAVISON

Davison's Ibis *Pseudibis davisoni* (**Hume** 1875)
(Alt. White-shouldered/Davidson's Ibis)

William Ruxton Davison (?–1893) was curator of Raffles Museum, in Singapore, between 1887 and 1893. Hume & Davison published *A Revised List of the Birds of Tenasserim* in 1878. Davison also wrote articles such as *Notes on the nidification of some Burmese birds*. There are a number of bird names commemorating the man in their binomials that only appear on some Indian lists, and may have been superseded, or are not now recognised as species; *Geronticus davisoni*, *Megalaima davisoni*, *Ixus davisoni*, *Leioptila davisoni* and *Hemixus davisoni*. He wrote descriptions of six birds which are now held in the British Museum, four of which he collected himself in India or the Malay peninsular: Indian Jungle Mynah *Acridotheres* (*fuscus*) *torquatus*, *Campophaga minor*, *Gerygone pectoralis*, *Merula erythrotis*, *Ptilocichla leucogastra* and *Trochalopterum cinnamomeum*. Once again, not all of these names are in current usage.

DECKEN

See **Von Decken**.

DEFILLIPI

Defillipi's Petrel *Pterodroma* (*cookii*) *defilippiana* (Giglioli & **Salvadori** 1869).
(Alt. Defilippe's Petrel)

Filippo de' Filippi (1814-1867) was an Italian doctor, traveller and zoologist. He visited, among other places, Alaska, Mongolia and Turkestan. He succeeded Bonelli as professor of zoology at the Museum of Natural History in Turin. His efforts to disseminate knowledge of Darwin's evolutionary theory included the presentation of a seminal lecture in 1864 – L'uomo e le scimmie (Man and the Apes). Filippi was the scientist who accompanied the Duke of the Abruzzi's expedition to Alaska, and he also led an expediton in 1863 to explore Persia (now Iran). He died of cholera in Hong Kong. See also Philippi.

DEGLAND

Degland's Scoter *Melanitta* (*fusca*) *deglandi* (**Bonaparte** 1850)
(Alt. White-winged Velvet Scoter)

Dr Côme Damien Degland (1787–1856) was senior physician at the Saint Sauveur Hospital in Lille and also director of the natural history museum there. He published *Ornithologie Européenne* in 1849. He assembled a collection of 1,800 specimens of European birds and these are still on display in the museum. **Bonaparte** named the scoter after him.

DEIGNAN

Deignan's Babbler *Stachyris rodolphei* (Deignan 1939)

Herbert Girton Deignan (1906–?) was a fellow of the John Simon Guggenheim Memorial Foundation in 1952 and worked for the United States National Migration Museum. He was an associate of Alexander Wetmore, who wrote *The Birds of the Republic of Panamá*. Deignan travelled in the Far East including Thailand in the 1930s. Deignan corresponded with Wetmore over the latter's expedition to Panama of 1957. He wrote *The Birds of Northern Thailand*, in 1945, *Type Specimens of Birds in the United States National Museum*, in 1961 and *Checklist of the Birds of Thailand*, in 1963. The western race of Grey-eyed Bulbul *Iole propinqua lekhakuni* was named by Deignan after his friend Dr Boonsong Lekagul in 1953, as was a race of the Hill Blue Flycatcher *Cyornis banyumas lekhakuni* in 1930. Deignan himself described the babbler in 1939, along with two other new babblers, in *Three new birds of the genus Stachyris*, published in the Zoology Series Field Museum Natural History.

DELACOUR

Delacour's Crested Fireback *Lophura ignita macartneyi* (**Temminck** 1813)
Delacour's Broadbill *Smithornis capensis delacouri* **Bannerman** 1923
(Alt. African Broadbill)
Delacour's Little Grebe *Tachybaptus rufolavatus* (Delacour 1932)
(Alt. Alaotra Grebe)

Dr Jean Theodore Delacour (1890–1985) was a French-American ornithologist renowned not only for discovering but also for rearing some of the rarest birds in the world. He was born in Paris and died in Los Angeles. In France, in the years 1919 and 1920, he created the zoological gardens at Clères and donated them to the French Natural History Museum, in Paris, in 1967. He wrote *Birds of Malaysia* in 1947 and *Birds of the Philippines*, with Ernst **Mayr** in 1946, as well as many other ornithological books, including his memoirs *The Living Air: The Memoirs of an Ornithologist* . He undertook a number of expeditions to Indochina, in particular Vietnam, and collected there, especially pheasants. He is commemorated in the scientific names of a number of animal species from catfish to langurs.

DELALANDE

Delalande's Antpipit *Corythopis delalandi* (**Lesson** 1830)
(Alt. Southern Antpipit)
Delalande's Coua *Coua delalandi* (**Temminck** 1827) [Extinct]
Delalande's Plovercrest *Stephanoxis lalandi* (**Vieillot** 1818)
(Alt. Black-breasted Plovercrest)

Pierre Antoine Delalande (1787–1823) worked for the Paris museum. He collected with Auguste de Sainte-Hilaire in the region around Rio de Janeiro in 1816 and, with his nephew **Verreaux** and Andrew **Smith**, in the African Cape in 1818. Later **Geoffrey de Sainte-Hilaire** employed him as a taxidermist.

DE LAUTOUR

De Lautour's Duck *Beziura delautouri* (Forbes 1892) [Extinct]

Dr H de Lautour of Oamaru, New Zealand. **Forbes**, who described the duck, said of de Lautour… '*This gentleman…is well known through his papers on the diatomaceous deposits discovered by him in his district…*' and '*…I have proposed the name of Biziura de Lautouri, after the gentleman to whom I am indebted for the acquisition of these bones.*' De Lautour had been told about moa bones that had been uncovered. The duck became extinct in 1742.

DE LATTRE'S

(See also **Henry**)

De Lattre's Coquette *Lophornis delattrei* (**Lesson** 1839)
(Alt. Rufous-crested Coquette)
De Lattre's Sabrewing *Campylopterus hemileucurus* (**Lichtenstein** 1830)
(Alt. Violet Sabrewing)

Henri De Lattre (1801–1867), like his brother Adolph, was a French collector, naturalist and artist; he specialised in painting animals in general and horses in particular. Around 1840 he painted a portrait of Boston, a famous American thoroughbred. In 1838 he collected in Mexico with his brother. Both brothers have birds' scientific names named after them but only Henri seems to have ever had common names in his honour. There are certainly birds which incorporate *delattrei* (for Henri) and *delatrii* (for Adolphe) in their scientific names. *Henrici* is usually employed for either A H Henrici (?–1836), a Dutch army officer in the East Indies, or Henri Prince D'Orleans (1867–1901), a French explorer who collected in Tibet and China around 1890.

DELEGORGUE

Delegorgue's Pigeon *Columba delegorguei* (Delegorgue 1847)
(Alt. Eastern Bronze-naped Pigeon)

Louis Adolphe Joseph Delegorgue (1814–1850) was a French hunter and naturalist who bequeathed the collections he made in southern Africa between 1830 and 1839 to the British Natural History Museum. He describes his adventures in a book – *Travels in Southern Africa* – published in 1847. He also collected with **Wahlberg**. He may actually have named the pigeon after himself, which would of course have been very bad form, but we could give him the benefit of the doubt and assume it to have been named after a close relative.

DENHAM

Denham's Bustard *Neotis denhami* (Children 1826)
(Alt. Stanley's/Jackson's Bustard)

Dixon Denham FRS (1786–1828) was an English soldier, a lieutenant-colonel, who explored very extensively in many parts of Africa. His exploits included a crossing of the Sahara from Tripoli to Lake Chad with **Clapperton**. He was also a fine illustrator. Denham became Governor-General of Sierra Leone, where he died of fever. The tree *Meryta denhami* in New Caledonia is named in his honour. He wrote *Narrative of Travels and Discoveries in Northern and Central Africa* in 1826.

DEPLANCHE

Deplanche's Lorikeet *Trichoglossus haematodus deplanchii* (**Verreaux** & **Des Murs** 1860)
(Alt. Rainbow Lorikeet/Parakeet)

Emile Deplanche was a surgeon in the French Navy. He co-wrote with Eugène Vieillard *Essais sur la Nouvelle Calédonie* in 1863. The Rainbow Lorikeet appears in these pages several times, as many of the 19 races are named after particular people. Almost every race is confined to particular islands; in this case to New Caledonia and the Loyalty Islands.

DERBY

Derby's Flycatcher *Pitangus sulphuratus* (Linnaeus 1766)
(Alt. Great Kiskadee)
Derby's Guan *Oreophasis derbianus* (G R **Gray** 1844)
(Alt. Horned Guan, Lord Derby's Mountain Pheasant)
Derby's Puffleg *Eriocnemis derbyi* (**Bourcier** & **Delattre** 1846)
(Black-winged Puffleg)

Edward Smith Stanley (1775–1851) was 13th Earl of Derby. See **Stanley**.

DE RHAM

De Rham's Garnet *Lamprolaima rhami* (**Lesson** 1839)
(Alt. Garnet-throated Hummingbird)

Henri Casimir de Rham (1785–1873) was a Swiss diplomat and amateur naturalist who collected in the United States. In 1803 he emigrated to New York, where he started a successful business in the cotton trade. He was the Swiss Consul there until 1846. In 1832 he founded the Swiss Benevolent Society of New York, the oldest Swiss benevolent organisation in the United States.

DESMAREST

Desmarest's Fig Parrot *Psittaculirostris desmarestii* (Desmarest 1826)
(Alt. Orange-breasted Fig Parrot)

Anselme Gaetan Desmarest (1784–1838) was a French palaeontologist. In 1805 he wrote *Histoire Naturelle des Tangaras, des Manakins et des Todiers*. In 1825 he published *Considérations générales sur la classe des crustacés – et description des espèces de ces animaux, qui vivent dans la mer, sur les côtes, ou dans les eaux douces de la France*. He was also the author, with André-Marie Dumeril, of the *Dictionnaire des Sciences Naturelles* (Insects and Crustaceans) which was published in Paris by F G Levrault, between 1816 and 1830.

DES MURS

Des Murs' Antbird *Hylophylax punctulata* (Des Murs 1856)
(Alt. Dot-backed Antbird)
Des Murs' Wiretail *Sylviorthorhynchus desmursii* (Des Murs 1847)
(Alt. Des Murs' Spinetail)

Marc Antoine Parfait Oeillet Des Murs (1804–1878) was a French naturalist who published *Iconographie Ornithologique* in 1849.

DEVILLE

Deville's Conure *Pyrrhura frontalis devillei* (Massena & Souancé 1854)
(Alt. Maroon-bellied/Brown-eared/Scaly-breasted/Blaze-winged Conure)
Deville's Parakeet *Brotogeris cyanoptera cyanoptera* (**Pelzeln** 1870)
(Alt. Cobalt-winged Parakeet)

Emile Deville (1824–1853) was a French naturalist who collected in Latin America from 1843 to 1847. By order of King Louis-Philippe, **Castelnau** accompanied the botanist H A **Weddell**, the geologist E **d'Osery** and Deville to Brazil and Peru during this period. A South American fossil horse from the Pleistocene *Hippidion devillei*, an insect of the order Odonata *Mnesarete devillei* and the Ecuadorian Striated Antbird *Drymophila devilleii devilleii* all appear to be named after Deville in their binomials. The suggestions that the birds may be named after Charles Joseph Sainte-Claire Deville (1814–1876), a geologist and meteorologist, or his brother Etienne (1818–1881), strike us as tenuous as, although Charles Deville may have been born in St Thomas in the West Indies, where his father was the French Consul, we cannot trace any connection with the South American mainland and he appears to have spent his professional life in France. Etienne was a chemist with no links to natural history; he experimented with turpentine and balsam and discovered the hydrocarbon toluene.

DE VIS

De Vis' Bird-of-Paradise *Paradisea* (*raggiana*) *intermedia* (**De Vis** 1894)
(Alt. Raggiana Crested Bird-of-Paradise)
De Vis' Tree Warbler *Acanthiza murina* (De Vis 1897)
(Alt. Papuan Thornbill)

Charles Walter De Vis (1829–1915) was a British born cleric who gave up the Church to concentrate on being an ornithologist. He was the first director, between 1882 and 1905, of the Queensland museum. Before joining the museum, De Vis published many popular articles under the pen name of 'Thickthorn'. He was a founder member of the Royal Society of Queensland in 1884 and their president from 1888 until 1889. He was also a founder member of the Australasian Ornithologists' Union, in 1901, and its first vice-president. He described 551 new fossil and living species, including the Bird-of-Paradise, a New Guinean endemic, **Guise**'s Honeyeater *Ptiloprora guisei*, in 1890, and the thornbill. He is also commemorated in the Australian species, De Vis' Banded Snake *Denisonia devisi*.

DIAMOND

Diamond's Paradise-Crow *Phonygammus keraudrenii* (Cracraft 1992)
(Alt. Trumpet Manucode)

Dr Jared M Diamond (1937–) is an American physiologist, who is a Professor at the Medical School of University College Los Angeles, in California. Since 1985 he has also been a Research Associate in Ornithology and Mammalogy at the Los Angeles County Museum of Natural History. He is interested in nutrition and in ornithology. He has published extensively, including detailed studies of the avifauna of Papua New Guinea, where the manucode is found, and the Philippines. Dr Diamond's studies on bird diversity in New Guinea tropical rainforests have made fundamental contributions to our understanding of species' coexistence, altitudinal segregation of montane species, speciation in rainforest environments and bowerbird evolution. In 2001 he won the Tyler Prize for Environmental Achievement for pioneering work in conservation biology – he also has a MacArthur Foundation award and in 1998 won the Pulitzer prize for his book *Guns, Germs and Steel.*

DIARD

Diard's Fireback *Lophura diardi* (**Bonaparte** 1856)
(Alt. Siamese Fireback)
Diard's Trogon *Harpactes diardii* (**Temminck** 1832)

Pierre Medard Diard (1795–1863) was a French explorer, who collected in the East Indies between 1827 and 1848. Temminck reports that Diard's specimens from Borneo arrived at Leiden in 1828. He is also honoured in the binomial of a cuckoo, the Black-bellied Malkoha *Phenicophaeus diardi*, as well as in those of the spider *Hyllus diardi*, the beetle *Macronota diardi*, the snake *Typhlops diardi* and a subspecies of the Clouded Leopard *Neofelis nebulosa diardi*, all from his former haunts in southeast Asia. He also collected the first specimen of a crocodile *Crocodylus raninus* from Brunei.

DICKEY

Dickey's Egret *Egretta rufescens dickeyi* (**Van Rossem** 1926)
(Alt. Reddish Egret)
Dickey's Jay *Cyanocorax dickeyi* (Moore 1935)
(Alt. Tufted Jay)

Donald Ryder Dickey (1887–1932) was an American ornithologist, collector and photographer. He was born in Iowa but lived most of his life in California. Between 1908 and 1923 he took 7,000 black-and-white photographs and collected 50,000 specimens of birds and mammals. These form the Donald Ryder Dickey Collection, which his widow presented to University College Los Angeles. His publications were many, the most notable on birds being *The Birds of El Salvador*, 1938, written jointly with A J **van Rossem**. Ten other American birds and mammals include *dickeyi* in their scientific names.

DICKINSON

Dickinson's Kestrel *Falco dickinsoni* (P L **Sclater** 1864)

Dr John Dickinson (1832–1863) was an English physician and missionary. He joined **Livingstone** but died of blackwater fever in Nyasaland (now Malawi). He collected the type specimen of the kestrel himself.

DIGGLES

Diggles's Finch *Poephila cincta atropygialis* (Diggles 1876)
(Alt. Parson Finch)
Diggles's Chocolate Parson Finch *Poephila cincta nigrotecta* (Diggles 1876)

Silvester Diggles (1845–1922) was an Australian ornithologist. He wrote *The Ornithology of Australia*, which was published between 1866 and 1870, and illustrated it with the help of his niece, Rowena Birkett. There is a published volume of his correspondence with E P **Ramsay**.

DIEFFENBACH

Dieffenbach's Rail *Gallirallus dieffenbachii* (G R **Gray** 1843) [Extinct]

Johann Karl Ernst Dieffenbach (1811–1855) was a German naturalist. He travelled widely in New Zealand and published *Travels in New Zealand*, in 1843, in which the descriptions of the birds, including the rail, were by G R **Gray**. Dieffenbach made the first translation into German of Darwin's *The Voyage of the Beagle*, in 1844; itself the first translation of any book by Darwin into a foreign language. Several tropical American plants have the genus name *Dieffenbachia* in his honour. In 1839, Dieffenbach and James Heberley became the first Europeans to climb Mount Taranaki. He died of typhus.

DINELLI

Dinelli's Doradito *Pseudocolopteryx dinellianus* (**Lillo** 1905)

In 1918 Luis Dinelli published *Notas biológicas sobre las aves del noroeste de la República Argentina*, the principal area where the bird is found. He is also commemorated in the trinomial of the bat *Myotis levis dinelli*. The botanist and ornithologist Miguel Lillo (1862–1931) described the doradito.

DIPLOMATS

A number of professions are ideal for birders – close to top of that list must be diplomat – you get lots of foreign travel and access wherever you go, and you will probably have plenty of free time to pursue your hobby at the government's expense! Among those so blessed were Frenchmen Sabin **Berthelot**, who was the French consul in Tenerife, Jules **Bourcier**, consul to Ecuador, Francis de la Porte, Comte de **Castelnau**, who had many posts around the world, André **Danjou** who was consul in Singapore, and M **Soumagne** was consul in Madagascar. Among English diplomats were Sir Henry Ernest Gascoyne **Bulwer**, a career diplomat who became Governor of Labuan, Borneo, The Hon Mountstuart **Elphinstone** and John **Crawfurd**, both of whom served in India, Sir Godfrey Yeatman **Lagden** who served in several African countries, William Thomas **Pritchard** who was British Consular Agent in Samoa, Sir Alfred **Sharpe** who was H. M. Commissioner and Consul-General in British Central Africa, Robert **Swinhoe** a diplomat in China and Thomas **Waters** who was in the British Consular Service in East Africa. Other nationals include Carl Hieronymus **Euler**, the Swiss consul in Rio de Janeiro in Brazil, Dr Hendrik Antoon **Lorentz** a Dutch diplomat in Indonesia and P L **Jouy** an American diplomat in Japan and Korea.

DIXON

Dixon's Ptarmigan *Lagopus mutus dixoni* (Grinnell 1909)
(Alt. Rock Ptarmigan)

Joseph Scattergood Dixon (1884–1952) was an ornithologist who accompanied Miss Annie Alexander on the expeditions which she financed and led to Alaska, in 1907 and 1908, to collect birds. He was employed by the Museum of Vertebrate Zoology at Berkeley as Assistant Curator of Mammals and Economic Ornithology before leaving to work for the National Park Service in 1931. Many of the numerous races of the Rock Ptarmigan are named after people.

DODSON

Dodson's Bulbul *Pycnonotus* (*barbatus*) *dodsoni* (**Sharpe** 1895)
(Alt. Common Bulbul)

W Dodson was a taxidermist who collected in the Middle East and Morocco at the end of the 19th century. With the ornithologist, Arthur Blayney **Percival**, he took part in a Royal Society expedition to Arabia in 1899, which collected many specimens. He is also commemorated in the *dodsoni* race of the Southern Grey Shrike *Lanius meridionalis* and in the binomial of the Spotted Thick-knee *Oedicnemus dodsoni*, now *Burhinus capensis dodsoni*. Of the eight specimens of the bulbul held in the British Museum, two are recorded as having been collected in North Africa by E Dodson in the early 1900s and we are of the opinion that this is the same man. The bulbul is now generally regarded as a subspecies of the Common Bulbul *P. barbatus*.

DOHERTY

Doherty's Bush Shrike *Telophorus* (*Malaconotus*) *dohertyi* (**Rothschild** 1901)
Doherty's Fruit Dove *Ptilinopus dohertyi* (Rothschild 1896)
(Alt. Purple-tailed/Red-naped Fruit Dove)
Doherty's Greybird *Coracina dohertyi* (**Hartert** 1896)
(Alt. Sumba Greybird/Cicadabird/Cuckoo-shrike, Black-barred Cuckoo-shrike)
Doherty's Hanging Parrot *Loriculus philippensis dohertyi* (Hartert 1906)
(Alt. Colasisi/Philippine/Luzon Hanging Parrot)
Doherty's White-eye *Lophozosterops dohertyi* (Hartert 1896)
(Alt. Crested/Dark-crowned White-eye, Crested Darkeye)

William Doherty (1857–1901) was an American collector regarded by **Rothschild** as the best he had ever employed. Before becoming a collector, he travelled from 1877 through Europe, Turkey and into Palestine and Egypt and thence to Persia (now Iran) in 1881. From 1882 he started collecting entomological specimens seriously, if only to bolster his finances, and from 1882 until 1883 he roamed through India, Burma (now Myanmar) and the Malay Archipelago ,and he was in the far reaches of Indonesia by 1887. He went to England, to visit **Hartert** at Tring, in 1895, and it was there that he met Lord Rothschild, who recruited him into the ranks of bird collectors. An article by B Verdcourt, in The Conchologists' Newsletter in 1992, mentions him collecting molluscs in East Africa, where he died of dysentery in Nairobi.

DOHRN, H

Dohrn's Flycatcher *Horizorhinus dohrni* (**Hartlaub** 1866)
(Alt. Dohrn's Thrush-Babbler)
Dohrn's Warbler *Acrocephalus brevipennis* (Keulemans 1866)
(Alt. Cape Verde [Islands] Cane/Swamp Warbler)

Heinrich Wolfgang Ludwig Dohrn (1838–1913) was a German politician and entomologist. His family came from Pommern, part of which is now in Poland. He studied entomology at Szczecin (Stettin) and graduated in 1858. He collected on Príncipe in 1865. His father was Dr Karl Augustus Dohrn (see below) and his younger brother was Felix Anton Dohrn (1840–1909), the founder of the Stazione Zoologica di Messina 'Anton Dohrn'. Felix Anton's godfather was Felix Mendelssohn, the composer.

DOHRN, K

Dohrn's Hermit *Glaucis [Ramphodon] dohrnii* (**Bourcier** & **Mulsant** 1852)
(Alt. Hawk-billed Hermit)

The German Dr Karl Augustus Dohrn (1806–1892) inherited a fortune from his grandfather, who was a sugar, spice and wine entrepreneur in Stettin. He was well able to afford to follow his hobbies, which also included entomology. He had at least two sons; Heinrich Wolfgang Ludwig Dohrn (see above) and Felix Anton Dohrn (also mentioned above).

DOLAN

Dolan's Eared Pheasant *Crossoptilon crossoptilon dolani* (Meyer de Schauensee 1938)
(Alt. White Eared Pheasant)

Brooke Dolan II (1908–1945) was an American naturalist who studied at Princeton and Harvard. His early adult years were spent as an Asian explorer, making several expeditions to Siberia, Sichuan, in China, and Tibet. His first Tibetan expedition was from 1931 to 1932 with Ernst Schäfer and he returned to the Tibetan borderlands from 1934 to 1935. In 1938 he published *Zoological results of the second Dolan expedition to western China and eastern Tibet, 1934–1936* in the Proceedings of the Academy of Natural Science Philadelphia. He joined the Army air force after the Japanese bombing of Pearl Harbor. His expedition to Lhasa, Tibet, from India, between 1942 and 1943, was as a captain and was funded by the Office of Strategic Services (OSS), since Franklin D Roosevelt wanted to explore the possibility of moving military supplies to Chiang Kai-shek's Republican Chinese government via Tibet. Lieutenant Colonel Ilya Tolstoy, grandson of the Russian author Leo Tolstoy, accompanied him. Dolan took a signed photograph of FDR as a gift for the young Fourteenth Dalai Lama. After this he joined the United States Military Observer Group in Yunnan. '*He was killed while attempting the rescue of Allied bomber crews downed behind enemy lines in Chongking while on a mission for the OSS*' (Hoffman 1983). He may also be commemorated in the scientific name of the Blackwater Sandfiltering Mayfly *Homoeoneuria dolani,* which occurs in the eastern United States.

DONALDSON-SMITH

Donaldson-Smith's Nightjar *Caprimulgus donaldsoni* (**Sharpe** 1895)
Donaldson-Smith's Sparrow-weaver *Plocepasser donaldsoni* (Sharpe 1895)

Arthur Donaldson-Smith (1864–1939) was a traveller and big-game hunter of American birth who seems to have spent a great deal of time in East Africa. He was probably in Ethiopia in 1896 and may have been present at the Ethiopian victory over the Italians at the Battle of Adwa. He published *Through Unknown African Countries* in 1897. He was elected a Fellow of the Royal Geographical Society.

D'ORBIGNY

D'Orbigny's Chat-tyrant *Ochthoeca oenanthoides* (d'Orbigny & **Lefresnaire** 1837)
D'Orbigny's Puffleg *Eriocnemis d'orbignyi* (**Gould***)
D'Orbigny's Seedsnipe *Thinocorus orbignyianus* (**Saint-Hilaire** & **Lesson** 1831)
(Alt. Grey-breasted Seedsnipe)
D'Orbigny's Woodcreeper *Dendrocincla fuliginosa atrirostris* (d'Orbigny & Lefresnaire 1838)

Alcide Dessalines d'Orbigny (1802–1857) was a traveller, collector, illustrator and naturalist. He was the author of *Dictionnaire Universel d'Histoire Naturelle*. His father Charles-Marie Dessalines d'Orbigny (1770–1856) was a ship's surgeon. He and Alcide studied shells. Alcide went to the Academy of Science in Paris to pursue his methodical paintings and classification of natural history specimens. The Muséum National d'Histoire Naturelle, in Paris, sent to him to South America in July 1826. There, the Spanish briefly imprisoned him, mistaking his compass and barometer, which had been supplied by **Humboldt**, for 'instruments of espionage'. After he left prison, he lived for a year with the Guaranis Indians learning their language. He spent five years in Argentina and then travelled north along the Chilean and Peruvian coasts, before moving into Bolivia, returning to France, in 1834. Once home he donated thousands of specimens of animals: birds, fish, reptiles, insects, mammals as well as plants, samples of rocks, fossils, land surveys, pre-Colombian pottery etc. to the Muséum National d'Histoire Naturelle. His fossil collection led him to determine that there were many geological layers, revealing that they must have been laid down over millions of years. This was the first time such an idea was put forward. We can only identify the puffleg as a **Gould** engraving.

DORIA

Doria's Hawk *Accipiter* (*Megatriorchis*) *doriae* (**Salvadori** & **Albertis** 1875)
(Alt. Doria's Goshawk)

Marchese Giacomo Doria (1840–1913) was an Italian ornithologist who collected in Persia (Iran) with **de Filippi**, between 1862 and 1863, and in Borneo with **Beccari**, between 1865 and 1866. He was the first Director of the Museo Civico di Storia Naturale in Turin from 1867 until his death. Doria's Tree Kangaroo *Dendrolagus dorianus* is also named after him.

DOROTHY

Dorothy's Grasswren *Amytornis dorotheae* (**Mathews** 1914)
(Alt. Carpenter/Carpentarian/Red-winged Grasswren)

Dorothy White was the daughter of the Australian naturalist, surveyor and rancher Henry Luke White (1860–1927). His collection of over 13,000 specimens of birds and their eggs from throughout Australia, donated to the Victoria Museum in 1917, is one of the top three such collections in the world. The egg collection is the most important of all Australian birds egg collections.

DORST

Dorst's Cisticola *Cisticola dorsti* (Chappuis & **Érard** 1991)

Professor Dr Jean Dorst (1924–2001) was a French ornithologist and Secretary General of the Charles Darwin Foundation. He was administrator of the Oceanographic Institute, a former member of the Council of the Société Nationale de Protection de la Nature (SNPN), a member of the Association of the Scientific Writers of France and honorary president of the French browsers and travellers. He was also an honorary member of the American Ornithologists' Union, the Deutsche Ornithologische Gesellschaft, the British Ornithologists' Union, the Zoological Society of London, the Sociedad Portuguesa de Ornitologia and the Academy of Alsace, as well as a Corresponding Member of the Academy of Science of Montpellier. He was a Membre de l'Institut, the French Académie des Sciences and Director of the Muséum National d'Histoire Naturelle. He headed the Laboratoire de Zoologie (Mammifères et Oiseaux) of the French Natural History Museum for almost 30 years. He published *Les migrations des oiseaux* in 1956, *Les Oiseaux* in 1959, and the *La Vie des Oiseaux* in 1972, among many others. Chappuis and Érard, who described the cisticola, separated it from the Red-pate Cisticola *Cisticola ruficeps* by song and tail length.

D'OSERY

D'Osery's Hermit *Phaethornis oseryi* (**Gould***)

Eugene Comte D'Osery (1818–1846) was a French traveller and collector. The bird was named after this member of **Castelnau**'s collecting expedition to the source of the Amazon, who was killed by Indians. '*Between 1843 and 1847 Castelnau and his party sailed to Rio de Janeiro on board the French brig 'Petit-Thouards', and began his meteorological, magnetic, botanical, and zoological observations there. The expedition resolved to cross South America from Rio via Minas Gerais. Goiás, and Mato Grosso. They explored the north of Mato Grosso, the Paraguay River as far as Asunción, and from Vila Bela they travelled to Bolivia through Potosí, finally reaching La Paz. From there they journeyed to Lima, where they spent some time, then proceeded to the source of the Amazon from whence they sailed to Pará. Owing to the death of a member of the expedition, d' Osery, who was killed by Indians, a large part of the records were lost... However, the minutes were saved, which made the writing of this history of the expedition possible.*' We can only find the bird as a Gould engraving, although the man certainly has birds named after him in binomials, such as the Casqued Oropendola *Psarocolius oseryi*, and also fish such as *Xiphostoma oseryi*, as well as plants, insects and others.

DOUBLEDAY

Doubleday's Hummingbird *Cyanophaia doubledayi* (**Swainson** 1827)
(Alt. Broad-billed hummingbird)

Henry Doubleday (1808–1875), an entomologist and ornithologist, was known as 'Henry Doubleday, the Epping Naturalist'. He was a member of the Entomological Society by 1833 and introduced the practice of 'sugaring' to capture moths. He published *A Nomenclature of British Birds* in 1838 and tried to establish uniformity in entomological nomenclature through his *Synonymic List of British Lepidoptera*, which appeared between 1847 and 1850. His family also founded the publishing company, Doubleday.

DOUGALL

Dougall's Tern *Sterna dougallii* (**Montagu** 1813)
(Alt. Roseate Tern)

Dr Peter McDougall (1777–1814) was a Scots physician and amateur naturalist from Glasgow. **Montagu** described the tern from some birds collected by McDougall in the Firth of Clyde. When McDougall sent the specimens to Montagu he drew the latter's attention to the difference between these birds and all the other terns that '*swarmed in their company on the same rocky islands*'.

DOW

Dow Tanager *Tangara dowii* (**Salvin** 1863)
(Alt. Spangle-cheeked Tanager)

Captain J M Dow (1827–1894) was an American naturalist and explorer. He collected plants and animals in South and Central America, notably in Costa Rica. There is a London Zoological Society paper written by A Günther, in 1869, entitled *An account of the fishes of the states of Central America, based on collections made by Capt. J. M. Dow, F. Godman, Esq., and O. Salvin, Esq.* From 1892 to 1894 Dow was in command of the schooner *Starbuck*. He worked for the American Packet Service and sent plants to Britain. There are a number of plants (particularly orchids) named for him and, judging by the binomials, after his wife or some other female relative.

DROWNE

Drowne's Fantail *Rhipidura drownei* (**Mayr** 1931)
(Alt. Brown/Mountain Fantail)

Frederick P Drowne was an American traveller and collector. He was active in the Galápagos from 1897 to 1898, and in the Solomon Islands in 1930. He kept a diary which was incorporated in *Review of the Ornithology of the Galápagos Islands, with notes on the Webster-Harris Expedition* in 1899 by **Hartert** & **Rothschild**. He wrote a monograph, *The Reptiles and Batrachians of Rhode Island*, in 1905.

DUBOIS

Dubois' Leaf Warbler *Phylloscopus cebuensis*
(A Dubois 1900)
(Alt. Lemon-throated [Leaf] Warbler, Cebu Warbler)
Dubois' Seedeater *Sporophila ardesiaca* (A Dubois 1894)

Charles Fréderic Dubois (1804–1867) was a Belgian naturalist, as was his son Alphonse Joseph Charles Dubois (1839–1921), after whom the birds *might* have been named instead. They published many works together including *Les Oiseaux de l'Europe*, whihc appeared between 1868 and 1872. The book was completed by Alphonse and published after C F Dubois' death.

DU CHAILLU

Duchaillu's Yellow-spotted Barbet *Buccanodon duchaillui* (**Cassin** 1855)
(Alt. Yellow-spotted Barbet)

Paul Belloni Du Chaillu (*c.*1831–1903) was a French-born American explorer and anthropologist. Whilst he was born in Paris, he spent his childhood in Gabon, in West Africa, where his father was a trader. He learned the local languages and became interested in exploring further inland. He went to the United States in 1852 and became a citizen. With the support of the Philadelphia Academy of Natural Sciences he put together an expedition to explore Gabon from 1855 until 1859. He collected widely, the specimens including many live birds and other animals, some of them previously unknown to science. He took back gorillas to the USA where they had never been seen before. His published account of the expedition *Explorations in Equatorial Africa* (1861). He also virtually redrew the map of the region's geography. Du Chaillu made a second expedition from 1863 to 1865, during which he visited hitherto unknown areas and verified previous reports of Pygmy people. His account of the latter expedition was published, in 1867, as *A Journey to Ashango-Land*. He also wrote *Stories of the Gorilla Country* in 1867, *Wild Life under the Equator* in 1868, *My Apingi Kingdom* in 1870 and *The Country of the Dwarfs* in 1871. He also travelled in Scandinavia from 1871 to 1878 and wrote about it in *The Land of the Midnight Sun* in 1881 and *The Viking Age* in 1889.

DUCHASSAIN

Duchassain's Hummingbird *Lepidopyga coeruleogularis* (**Gould** 1850)
(Alt. Sapphire-throated Hummingbird)

We believe this to be another transcription error and that the bird was named for Placide Duchassaing de Fonbressin (1819–1873), a zoologist who was active at the right time and in the right place. There are records of specimens of marine corals and sponges collected by him on the Panama coast around 1850. Duchassaing was born on Guadeloupe, to a French-Creole family of planters. He was sent to school in France and went to the university in Paris, achieving a doctorate in medicine, geology and zoology. He returned to Guadeloupe as a physician. He travelled widely in the Caribbean to neighbouring islands; Nevis, St Eustatius, St Martin, St Barthélemy, St Croix, Cuba and also Panama, treating people during cholera outbreaks. In 1867 he returned to France where he eventually died. Duchassaing was a natural history collector who sent many specimens to Europe. He wrote *Mémoire sur les Coralliaires des Antilles* in 1860 and co-wrote, with Michelotti an Italian lawyer, *Spongiaires de la Mer Caraibe* in 1864. His treatment of sick people in Panama may have led to the naming of the hummingbird in his honour. **Gould** first described the hummingbird from a bird collected by M **Warszewicz** in Chiriquí, Panama.

DUCORPS

Ducorps' Corella *Cacatua ducorpsii* (**Pucheran** 1853)
(Alt. Ducorps' Cockatoo)

L J Ducorps was an explorer for the French navy.

DUFRESNE

Dufresne's Amazon *Amazona dufresniana* (Shaw 1812)
(Alt. Blue-cheeked Amazon)
Dufresne's Waxbill *Estrilda melanotis* (**Temminck** 1823)
(Alt. Swee/Yellow-billed/Green Waxbill)

Louis Dufresne (1752–1832) was a French conchologist and an all-round zoologist. The Gray or Dufresne's Langur *Semnopithecus entellus*, which he described in 1797, is also named after him.

DUGAND

Dugand's Antwren *Herpsilochmus dugandi* (Meyer de Schauensee 1945)

Armando Dugand (1906–1971) was a Colombian naturalist and Director of the Institute of Natural Sciences of the National University of Colombia from 1940 until 1953. He was one of the founders in 1940 of the magazine Caldasia. During the 1940s he headed several bird collecting expeditions for the institute into the Colombian interior.

DUMONT

Dumont's Myna *Mino dumontii* (**Lesson** 1827)
(Alt. Papuan/Yellow-faced Myna)

Admiral Jules Sebastien César, Vicompte Dumont d'Urville (1790–1842), the famous French explorer is most likely to be the Dumont in question. His wife was the **Adélie** after whom the penguin is named. The admiral was a brilliant sailor who captained two great voyages to the Pacific and the Antarctic. He was second officer aboard *La Coquille* in a voyage around the world from 1822 to 1825, and took on the botany and entomology for the voyage reporting to Lesson, who was chief medical officer and director of natural history research. As captain, his first voyage from 1826 to 1829, solved the mystery of the disappearance of the *Pérouse*. During his second voyage, from 1837 to 1840, he was the first to establish that Antarctica was a continent. He charted, and made a risky landing on, the coast that he named 'Terre Adélie' for his wife. Dumont was also the man who transported the statue of the 'Venus de Milo' from the island of Milos, where it was found, to France, in 1820. He, his wife and child were burned to death in a railway accident near Paris in 1842. The myna could just possibly have been named after Charles Henri Fréderic Dumont de Saint-Croix (?–1830), who was a French ornithologist and Lesson's father-in-law.

DUNN

Dunn's Lark *Eremalauda dunni* (**Shelley** 1904)

Colonel Henry Nason Dunn (1864–1952) was a British army surgeon who became a big-game hunter. He left diaries relating to his time, from 1897 to 1906, in Sudan and Somaliland, to the National Army Museum. Dunn himself collected the lark. (Henry Dunn should not to be confused with Emmet R Dunn who has many animals, from salamanders to rodents, named after him in their scientific binomials.)

DU PONT, J E

Du Pont's Blue-backed Parrot *Tanygnathus sumatranus duponti* (Parkes 1971)
(Alt. Azure-rumped Parrot)

John Eleuthere du Pont (1938–) is an American ornithologist. He wrote *South Pacific Birds* in 1976, *Philippine Birds* in 1971 and, with C S Weaver, *Recent Volutidae of the World* in 1970. He has also published articles, such as *Notes on Philippine birds* with Rodolphe Meyer de Schauensee, in 1959, and *Notes from Western Samoa, including the description of a new Parrot-finch (Erythrura),* in The Wilson Bulletin, in 1972. He has described over 20 new species of birds. Du Pont founded the Delaware Museum of Natural History in 1957, and its collection of molluscs, birds and bird books very much reflects the his interests.

DUPONT, L

Dupont's Lark *Chersophilus dupontii* (**Vieillot** 1820)

Léonard Puech Dupont (1795–1828) was a French naturalist and collector in the early 19th century. **Vieillot** named the lark after him when Dupont showed it to him, having collected it in Provence, according to Vieillot's label, although this may be in error. Dupont went on the Joseph Ritchie expedition to Africa but left following a dispute, taking 200 specimens with him back to Paris. This was just a year before the lark was named, so it could actually have been collected in Africa, which is more likely, although a Provence record cannot be entirely discounted.

DUPONT, M

Dupont's Hummingbird *Tilmatura dupontii* (**Lesson** 1832)
(Alt. Sparkling-tailed Hummingbird)

Monsieur Dupont (?–1873) was a French dealer in natural history.

DUTCH

There are at least 45 Dutch nationals celebrated in the 'English' or common names of birds, as one might expect from this most enthusiastic of birding nations. The vast majority were professional or amateur naturalists or collectors, the only real exception being a King!

DUYVENBODE

Duyvenbode's Lory *Chalcopsitta duivenbodei* (**Dubois** 1884)
(Alt. Brown Lory)
Duyvenbode's Sunbird *Aethopyga duyvenbodei* (**Schlegel** 1871)
(Alt. Elegant/Sanghir Yellow-backed Sunbird)

Maarten Dirk van Renesse van Duyvenbode was a Dutch merchant, and father-in-law of Anton August **Bruijn**, who ran a plantation in the Moluccas, where the lory is found. He styled himself the 'King of Ternate'. Interestingly the name means pigeon-post messenger and was an honorific conferred when the family used carrier pigeons to keep in touch with William of Orange during the siege of Leiden. **Wallace** said of him that he was '*a native of Ternate, of an ancient Dutch family, but who was educated in England, and speaks our language perfectly. He was a very rich man, owned half the town, possessed many ships, and above a hundred slaves. He was moreover, well educated, and fond of literature and science—a phenomenon in these regions*'. Like Bruijn he was heavily involved in the feather trade. He exhibited many natural history specimens during the large international Colonial Trade Exhibition in Amsterdam, in the summer of 1883. The scientific name of the lory seems to have been misspelled and subsequently wrongly transcribed many years ago. Some sources claim the lory was named for C W K van Duyvenbode, who may be the same person.

DYBOWSKI

Dybowski's Dusky Twinspot *Euschistospiza dybowskii* (**Oustalet** 1892)
(Alt. Dusky Twinspot)

Jan (Jean-Thadée) Dybowski (1856–1928) was a botanist and an explorer of Africa, especially equatorial regions. He led a Congo expedition in 1891 and wrote accounts of his travels, to Chad, in 1893 (*La route du Tchad*) and to the Congo, in 1912 (*Le Congo Meconnu*). Dybowski established new gardens and plantations in Tunisia and organised schools of agriculture. Later (*c.*1908) he became French Inspector-General of colonial agriculture. There are a number of fish honouring Dybowski in their scientific names, such as *Comephorus dybowskii*, *Ladislavia dybowski* and *Squalidus dybowski*, and there is also Dybowski's Deer *Cervus nippon dybowskii*. However, the Dybowski family included many scientists, including an outstanding arachnologist, so it is very difficult to track down quite what is named after whom. (See also **Xavier** Dybowski who might have been Jan's brother or even, according to one source, the same person). Dybowski was largely responsible for the isolation and introduction of the psychotropic drug ibogaïne. The first botanical description of the Iboga plant dates from 1889 in the Congo. In 1901, Dybowski and Landrin isolated the alkaloid which they named ibogaïne from the bark of the root, and showed it to have the same psychoactive properties as the root itself.

EARLE

Earle's Babbler *Turdoides* (*Argya*) *earlei* (**Blyth** 1844)
(Alt. Striated Babbler)

Willis Earle was an English merchant in India in 1844. He *might* have been the same person as the Willis Earle who was a wealthy coal merchant living near Liverpool in 1810, and who also seems to have been involved in the slave trade.

EARL OF DERBY

Earl of Derby's Parakeet *Platycercus icterotis* (**Kuhl** 1820)
(Alt. Western/Yellow-cheeked Rosella, Stanley Parakeet)

See **Stanley**.

EAST INDIA COMPANY – A STATE WITHIN A STATE

A Royal Charter granted by Queen Elizabeth I established the East India Company in 1600. Its original objective was to break the Dutch monopoly of the spice trade, but after the massacre of British merchants at Amboina, in 1625, it turned its attentions to India. It controlled its own armed forces and, as it became increasingly involved in the politics and affairs of the Indian princes, took control of land in order to protect its commercial activities. In the 18th century it faced serious competition from the French East India Company, and fought wars against forces that supported the French under their able leader, Dupleix. In Robert Clive (1725–1774) the company found an extremely able military leader and his brilliant seizure of Arcot in 1751 and other significant victories, culminating in the battle of Plassey in 1757, effectively broke French influence in India. Clive returned to England but was attacked by political opponents and eventually committed suicide.

The effect of Clive's victories and administration was that the company ruled virtually the whole country for the next 100 years, although the government in Westminster took more interest and exercised increasing control over the company's interests. As a result, regular units of the British army were stationed in India in support of the company's own armed forces. In 1857 the Indian Mutiny broke out. After it was finally crushed in 1858, the British government took complete control of Indian affairs and the East India Company was dissolved the same year. The armed forces of the company were either disbanded or reformed into Indian regiments of the British army. The resulting force was known as the Indian army, until the independence of India and Pakistan in 1947.

The company really was a state within a state; it maintained its own armed forces on land and at sea; it controlled an enormous amount of money and a huge armed merchant fleet, and it even had its own Honours system.

Moreover, its employees collected many scientific specimens and the company maintained its own museum. After dissolution, most of its exhibits were donated to the various sections of the British Museum, with the bird skins being sent to the Natural History Collection at Tring.

Many of the people in this book spent some of their time in British India, which we can define as the present-day countries of India, Pakistan, Bangladesh, Sri Lanka (then Ceylon) and Myanmar (then Burma). They are often, but not always, referred to as having a military rank. We think a considerable number were either employed by the company or were closely associated with it. However, because there was a period in which both the company's and the regular army's units were in India, we cannot always be sure which of the two a particular person worked for.

The following people, who appear here, were all associated with the company: Dr Francis Hamilton **Buchanan**, Dr John **Crawfurd**, The Hon Mountstuart **Elphinstone**, Major-General Thomas **Hardwicke**, Brian Houghton **Hodgson**, Dr Thomas **Horsfield**, Thomas Claverhill **Jerdon**, General Th R **Macqueen**, Sir Clements Robert **Markham**, Colonel William Henry **Sykes**, George Percy **Badger** and Dr Nathaniel **Wallich**.

EATON

Eaton's Pintail *Anas* (*acuta*) *eatoni* (**Sharpe** 1875)
(Alt. Kerguelen/Southern Pintail)

Reverend Alfred Edmund Eaton (1845–1929) was an English explorer, entomologist and naturalist who published many scientific papers between the 1860s and 1920. He collected on Spitzbergen, and in Madeira and Tenerife in spring 1902.

EDWARD

Edward's Hummingbird *Amazilia* (*Saucerottia*) *edward* (**Delattre** & **Bourcier** 1846)
(Alt. Snowy-breasted/White-bellied/Snowy-bellied Hummingbird)

Dr Edward T Wilson was a British naturalist and collector who founded the Cheltenham Camera Club, the seventh-oldest camera club in Britain, in 1865. He was the father of Dr Edward A Wilson (1872–1912), the author of *The Birds of Antarctica*, who died with Captain Robert Falcon Scott during their return from the South Pole.

EDWARDS

Edwards' Fig Parrot *Psittaculirostris edwardsii* (**Oustalet** 1885)
Edwards' Lorikeet *Trichoglossus haematodus capistratus* (**Bechstein** 1811)
(Alt. Rainbow Lorikeet)
Edwards' Pheasant *Lophura edwardsi* (Oustalet 1896)
Edwards' Rosefinch *Carpodacus edwardsii* (**Verreaux** 1871)
(Alt. Dark-rumped/Large/Pink-throated/Ruddy Rosefinch)

Alphonse Milne-Edwards (1835–1900) – see **Milne-Edwards**. Many of the races of the Rainbow Lorikeet are named after particular people. Almost every race is isolated on particular islands; in this case Timor.

EICHHORN

Eichhorn's Friarbird *Philemon eichhorni* (**Rothschild** & **Hartert** 1924)
(Alt. New Ireland Friarbird)

Albert F Eichhorn (?–1933) was an Australian farmer. He collected in New Guinea in 1900, in the Solomon Islands in 1903 and 1907 and in New Ireland and New Britain in the 1920s. He is also commemorated in the scientific name of another honeyeater, the Yellow-vented Myzomela *Myzomela eichhorni*.

EISENTRAUT

Eisentraut's Honeyguide *Melignomon eisentrauti* (Louette 1981)
(Alt. Yellow-footed/Coe's Honeyguide)

Professor Dr Martin Eisentraut (1902–1994) was a German zoologist and collector. He was on the staff of the Berlin Zoological Museum, working on bat migration and on the physiology of hibernation, when he went on his first overseas trip, to West Africa in 1938. He left Berlin in 1950 to become curator of mammals at the Stuttgart Museum, remaining there until 1957. He then became director of the Alexander Koenig Museum in Bonn, where he lived for the rest of his life. Between 1954 and 1973 he made six trips to Bioko and Cameroon. Much of the material collected on these trips is still being studied. He has several mammals named after him, including a bat *Pipistrellus eisentrauti*, two mice, *Lophuromys eisentrauti* and *Colomys* (*goslingi*) *eisentrauti*, and a shrew *Myosorex eisentrauti*. Eisentraut published many scientific papers and three books, including *Notes on the Birds of Fernando Pó Island, Spanish Equatorial Africa*, in 1968. He also published a slim volume of poems. Louette described the honeyguide in 1981 in a Belgian publication, long after Peter **Colston** had submitted a description to the Bulletin of the British Ornithologists' Club, which they had not yet published. Had Colston's description taken precedence the bird would be known, quite rightly, as **Coe**'s Honeyguide. Louette assumed, incorrectly, that Eisentraut had collected the first specimen when, in fact, it was Dr W Serle who obtained an immature bird at Bakebe, Cameroon in August 1956).

ELEONORA

Eleonora's Falcon *Falco eleonorae* (Gené 1839)

Eleonora of Arborea (*c.*1350–1404) was the warrior-princess national heroine of Sardinia who passed enlightened legislation to protect birds of prey (although cynics might say that this was to keep them for the aristocracy alone). She died in 1404 '*during an epidemic of the pest* (plague)'. The Falcon was first observed in Sardinia in 1830. Alberto Ferrero Della **Marmora** named it in her honour and Gené described it.

ELEONORA

Eleonora's Cockatoo *Cacatua galerita eleonora* (**Finsch** 1863)
(Alt. Sulphur-crested Cockatoo)

Given the non-Latinised trinomial we doubt whether this bird is named after a person. However, **Finsch**, who described this race, did name birds after his daughter so Eleanor might have been another woman in his life.

ELEPHANTS' REVENGE

What are the chances of being killed by an elephant? It must be many millions to one. Notwithstanding this, the remarkable fact is that in our survey of little over 1,000 people who have had birds named after them, no fewer than three, Frank Linsly **James**, Eugenio Prince **Ruspoli** and Johan August **Wahlberg** were killed by elephants!

In 1856 Wahlberg was exploring the headwaters of the Limpopo River when a wounded elephant killed him. In 1890 the same fate befell James; again it was a wounded animal. Then, just three years later, Prince Ruspoli met an identical end in what was described as 'an encounter with an elephant' in Ethiopia; one that he himself had wounded. All of the beasts were of the African species *Loxodonta africana*.

ELICIA

Elicia's Goldentail *Hylocharis eliciae* (**Bourcier** & **Mulsant** 1846)
(Alt. Blue-throated Goldentail)

Named for Elicia Alain, by **Bourcier** & **Mulsant**, who wrote the description. We have been unable to discover anything about her.

ELLIOT

Elliot's Laughing-thrush *Garrulax elliotii* (J **Verreaux** 1870)
Elliot's Pheasant *Syrmaticus elliotii* (**Swinhoe** 1872)
Elliot's Pitta *Pitta elliotii* (**Oustalet** 1874)
(Alt. Bar-bellied Pitta)
Elliot's Storm Petrel *Oceanites gracilis* (Elliot 1859)
(Alt. White-vented Storm Petrel)
Elliot's Woodpecker *Dendropicos elliotii* (**Cassin** 1863)

Daniel Giraud Elliot (1835–1915) was Curator of Zoology at The Field Museum in Chicago and was one of the founders of the American Ornithologists' Union. He had a great interest in ornithology and was independently wealthy and that enabled him to produce a series of bird books illustrated by magnificent colour plates, including his own excellent work, long after most publishers employed smaller formats and cheaper techniques. Elliot could also afford to commission the best bird artists of the day, including Josef Wolf and Josef Smit, both formerly employed by John **Gould**. The lithograph series include works on pittas, pheasants, hornbills and birds of prey.

ELLIS

Ellis' Sandpiper *Prosobonia ellisi* (**Sharpe** 1906) [Extinct]

William Webb Ellis (?–1786) was a surgeon's mate, artist and collector on Cook's third voyage. Against the orders of the Admiralty, he published a two-volume version of the **Cook** expedition in 1782, which contained engravings made from his own drawings. He also corresponded with Sir Joseph **Banks**. We assume him to be a relative (the grandfather perhaps) of the famous William Webb Ellis, who invented Rugby football in 1823 by picking up and running with the ball during a game of soccer; however, we have no direct evidence of such relationship. **Sharpe** prepared the description from fossil material.

ELPHINSTONE

Elphinstone's Pigeon *Columba elphinstonii* (**Sykes** 1832)
(Alt. Nilgiri/Spotted-necked[Wood-]Pigeon)

The Hon Mountstuart Elphinstone (1779–1859) went to India in 1795 as an employee of the East India Company, but became a diplomat in Poona and other Indian 'Residencies', and was British Governor of Bombay from 1819 until 1827. Although a diplomat, he gained a reputation for courage in various military actions. In 1827 he returned to England and was twice offered the post of Governor-General of India but he declined it on both occasions for reasons of poor health. In retirement he wrote a history of India.

ELWES

Elwes' Crake *Amaurornis bicolor* (**Walden** 1872)
(Alt. Black-tailed Crake)
Elwes' Eared Pheasant *Crossoptilon harmani* (Elwes 1881)
(Alt. Tibetan/Harman's Eared Pheasant)

Henry John Elwes FRS (1846–1922) was a wealthy English collector and illustrator, mainly of plants but he also collected birds, butterflies and moths. He was interested in natural history in general as evidenced by his *Memoirs of Travel, Sport and Natural History*. He also wrote an article on *The Geographic Distribution of Asiatic Birds* in 1873. Most of his writing was on birds but he also wrote *The Trees of Great Britain and Ireland*, a work in seven volumes, published from 1906 to 1913. He wrote a number of other monographs such as one on lilies in 1880. After five years in the Guards he travelled very widely, visiting every country in Europe, Asia Minor, India, Tibet, Mexico, North America, Chile, Russia, Siberia, Formosa, China and Japan. Elwes discovered many plants, including *Pleione hookeriana, Satyrium nepalense, Arisaema nepenthoides, A. utile* and *A. griffithii*. There are also a number of species named after him, such as *Eremurus elwesii, Porpax elwesii* and *Fritillaria elwesii*. At his home at Colesbourne Park, where he lived for the 47 years until his death, he created a collection of about 140 different varieties of snowdrops, including the one named after him, *Galanthus elwesii*. His great-grandson and his wife now live in the house whose gardens are open to the public. **Walden** described the Crake but **Hume** named it (as *Porzana elwesi*), in 1875, from a specimen collected by Elwes; this may be a case of an earlier description taking precedence but the vernacular name of a later supposed type specimen enduring. H J Elwes himself described the pheasant in 1881. It was '*collected by a native surveyor of Lieut. **Harman**'s*'.

EMIN

Emin's Shrike *Lanius gubernator* (**Hartlaub** 1882)
Emin's Weaver *Ploceus baglafecht* (Daudin 1799)
(Alt. Baglafecht/Reichenow's/Stuhlmann's Weaver)

Emin Pasha (1840–1892), whose real name was Eduard Schnitzer, was a German explorer and administrator in Africa who made important contributions to the geographical knowledge of the Sudan and central Africa. He became a physician in Albania, which was then a part of the Ottaman Empire. The people there called him *Emin*, meaning *faithful one*. In 1876, he was appointed as medical officer to the staff of General Charles G Gordon, British Governor-General and Administrator of the Sudan. Gordon, who became world famous by being killed by the Mahdi at Khartoum in 1885, appointed Emin, with the title of Bey, to be the *Pasha* (governor) of the southern Sudanese province of Equatoria in 1878. Emin then began his explorations, as well as being active as a naturalist and collector. As a ruler, Emin's claim to fame was that he abolished slavery in the territories which he commanded. A Sudanese uprising in 1885 forced him to retreat into what is now Uganda. In 1888, a search party, led by Henry Morton Stanley, on what was to be his last African expedition, reached Emin. In 1890, Emin joined the German East Africa Company, which controlled what is now Tanzania. He led an expedition to the upper Congo River region but was beheaded by slave traders in the region of Lake Tanganyika.

EMIN BEY

Emin Bey's Sparrow *Passer eminibey* (**Hartlaub** 1880)
(Alt. Chestnut Sparrow)

See **Emin** above.

EMMA

Emma's White-eared Conure *Pyrrhura leucotis emma* (**Salvadori** 1891)
(Alt. White-eared/Grey-breasted/Blue-naped Conure, Maroon-faced Parakeet)

Emma Gräfin von Berlepsch was the wife of the German ornithologist Hans Graf von **Berlepsch**, who collected in South America where this species is found.

EMPEROR

Emperor-of-Germany Bird of Paradise *Paradisaea guilielmi* (**Cabanis** 1888)
(Alt. Emperor Bird of Paradise)

Kaiser Wilhelm I (1797–1888). As John **Gould** produced a plate of this bird before his own death in 1881, we assume that the German Emperor referred to was Kaiser Wilhelm I. He was born Friedrich Wilhelm Ludwig of Hohenzollern and ascended the Prussian throne in 1861, being proclaimed German Emperor in 1871. In the latter part of the 19th century the northern half of what is now Papua New Guinea, where the bird occurs, was a German colony.

EMPRESS

Empress Hummingbird *Heliodoxa imperatrix* (**Gould** 1856)
(Alt. Empress Brilliant)

Marie Luise Augusta Katharina, Princess of Saxe-Weimar and Eisenach (1811–1890). For the same reason as above (see **Emperor**), we consider that this hummingbird is named after the wife of Kaiser Wilhelm I.

ENGELBACH

Engelbach's Silver Pheasant *Lophura nycthemera engelbachi* (**Delacour** 1948)

Dr P Engelbach was an amateur French ornithologist, who was a resident of Kampot, a town in Cambodia, in the 1930s. He accompanied **Delacour** on his sixth expedition to Indochina (Laos) in 1931 to 1932. He was also one of the earliest people to encounter the Chestnut-headed Partridge *Arborophila cambodiana* in Bokor, an area close to his home in Kampot, which he visited in 1935 and 1936. He carried out a limited ornithological survey of the Cardamom Mountains in Cambodia in 1944, which he published in 1952 as *Notes de voyage dans les monts des Cardamomes (Cambodge)*. Earlier, in 1938, he wrote a *Note sur quelques oiseaux du Cambodge* but this was apparently never published. He is also commemorated in the trinomial of a race of the Little Cuckoo-Dove *Macropygia ruficeps engelbachi*, which was described by Delacour in 1928.

ÉRARD

Erard's Lark *Mirafra degodiensis erardi* (Érard 1975)
(Alt. Degodi/Ergard's Lark)

Christian Érard is a Professor and Assistant Director at the Laboratoire de Zoologie (Mammifères & Oiseaux) of the Paris Natural History Museum. He is a specialist in birds of tropical wet forests. From 1968 to 1990 he spent much of his time in the field, in various countries of Africa and South America. Indeed, between 1968 and 1987, he spent a total of 53 months in the field, making five visits to French Guiana and no fewer than 17 trips to various African countries, which included over two years in Gabon. He has published many scientific papers, several books and most recently an online paper in March 2002. His most notable publications included a collaborative work *Oiseaux de Guyane* in 1992. He is also a president of the Société Ornithologique de France and editor of *Revue d'Ecologie: La Terre et la Vie*, which is published by the Societé Nationale de Protection de la Nature.

ERCKEL

Erckel's Francolin *Francolinus erckelii* (**Rüppell** 1835)

Theodor Erckel (1811–1897) was a German taxidermist who became a servant and helper to **Rüppell** in 1825, and accompanied him on his second journey to Ethiopia in 1830. They returned to Europe in 1834 and Erckel worked as Rüppell's assistant at the institute at Frankfurt University. The institute's director, **Cretzschmar** and Rüppell quarrelled to such an extent that Rüppell withdrew in 1844, and Erckel then took over as curator of the collections. He remained *in situ* until his retirement in 1880. In 1891 he was elected a life member of Die Senckenbergische Naturforschende Gesellschaft, the natural history society in Frankfurt, which Cretzschmar had founded. Rüppell described the francolin and named it after Erckel in recognition of his loyal service.

ERGARD

Ergard's Lark *Mirafra degodiensis* (Érard 1975)
(Alt. Erard's/Degodi Lark)

We are convinced that this is a transcription error and refers to Erard's Lark. [See **Érard**].

ERLANGER

Erlanger's Lark *Calandrella cinerea erlangeri*
   (**Neumann** 1906)
   (Alt. Greater Short-toed/Red-capped Lark)

Baron Carlo von Erlanger (1872–1904) was a German collector from Ingelheim, in the Rhineland. He travelled in Tunisia and Ethiopia in 1893 and 1897 and wrote two trip reports.

ESTELLA

Estella's Hillstar *Oreotrochilus estella* (**d'Orbigny** & Lafresnaye 1838)
   (Alt. Andean Hillstar)

Estelle-Marie d'Orbigny (1801–1893) was the elder (by just one year) sister of the describer, Alcide Dessalines **d'Orbigny**. However, as the scientific name is not in the genitive, it may be meant to convey the quality of the bird and that Estella's Hillstar actually means something like 'Starlike Hillstar'. It is only in **Gould** that we find 'Estella's'; everywhere else it is just 'Estella'. d'Orbigny & Lafresnaye also described **Adela**'s (Wedge-tailed) Hillstar (q.v. for a another possible Gould misunderstanding) and so they may have persisted with the idea of a name to imply a quality rather than a person. Of course, d'Orbigny may have implied both and so, as we English say, he 'killed two birds with one stone'!

EUGENIE

Eugenie's Fruit Dove *Ptilinopus eugeniae* (**Gould** 1856)
   (Alt. White-headed Fruit Dove)

The Empress Eugénie (1826–1920) was a Spanish countess who became the wife of Napoleon III and reigned in France from 1853 until 1870. Interestingly, she was the first person to have an asteroid named after her. She also has a very large diamond named in her honour, appropriately, since she was renowned for her lavish and stylish lifestyle.

EULER

Euler's Flycatcher *Lathrotriccus euleri* (**Cabanis** 1870)

Carl Hieronymus Euler (1834–1901) was the Swiss consul in Rio de Janeiro, Brazil, from 1897 until his death. Our ornithological knowledge of the region of the north Paraíba valley and its 369 species is largely due to a survey undertaken by this Swiss amateur ornithologist and farmer, between 1867 and 1900, and through his studies on the breeding behaviour of Brazilian birds. He deposited his collections in the Berlin Museum. Together with his comments on nests and eggs, they largely derive from the 'Good Farm Valley, Cantagalo' which was his property. Unfortunately, about 40% of the avifauna described by Carl Euler can no longer be found there. **Cabanis** first described the flycatcher from a specimen which Euler sent him.

EVERETT

Everett's Blue-backed Parrot *Tanygnathus sumatranus everetti* (**Tweeddale** 1887)
Everett's Bulbul *Ixos everetti* (Tweeddale 1887)
   (Alt. Yellowish/Yellow-washed/Plain-throated Bulbul)
Everett's Buttonquail *Turnix everetti* (**Hartert** 1898)
   (Alt. Sumba Buttonquail)
Everett's Flowerpecker *Dicaeum everetti* (**Sharpe** 1877)
   (Alt. Brown-backed Flowerpecker)

Everett's Ground Thrush *Zoothera everetti* (Sharpe 1892)
  (Alt. Everett's Thrush)
Everett's Hornbill *Aceros everetti* (**Rothschild** 1897)
  (Alt. Sumba Hornbill)
Everett's Monarch *Monarcha everetti* (Hartert 1896)
  (Alt. White-tipped/Djampea Monarch)
Everett's Spiderhunter *Arachnothera everetti* (Sharpe 1893)
  (Alt. Bornean Spiderhunter)
Everett's White-eye *Zosterops everetti* (Tweeddale 1878)

Alfred Hart Everett (1848–1898) was a British civil servant who worked as an administrator in the East Indies. He collected widely and it is believed that a jawbone of an Orang-Utan *Pongo pygmaeus* which he found in a cave may have been used in the 'Piltdown Man' hoax. He seems to have been an 'all-rounder' who was interested in all aspects of natural history and anthropology. His death made the front page of the Sarawak Gazette.

EVERSMANN

Eversmann's Booted Warbler *Hippolais caligata* (**Lichtenstein** 1823)
  (Alt. Booted Warbler)
Eversmann's Ptarmigan *Lagopus mutus eversmanni* (**Elliot** 1896)
  (Alt. Rock Ptarmigan)
Eversmann's Pigeon *Columba eversmanni* (**Bonaparte** 1856)
  (Alt. Pale-backed Pigeon, Yellow-eyed Stock Dove)
Eversmann's Redstart *Phoenicurus erythronotus* (Eversmann 1841)
Eversmann's Warbler *Phylloscopus borealis* (**Blasius** 1858)
  (Alt. Arctic [Leaf/Willow] Warbler)

Alexander Eduard Friedrich Eversmann (1794–1860) [in the Russian style, Eduard Aleksandrovich Eversmann] was a pioneer Russian entomologist and Professor of Zoology at Kazan in Russia. His travels and publications involved remote areas of the Russian Empire. He seems to have concentrated on Lepidoptera and a number of butterflies are named after him, for instance, Evermann's Parnassian *Parnassius eversmanni*. The Rock Ptarmigan has many aliases appearing in this volume, as most of its many races are named after someone.

EWING

Ewing's Fruit Pigeon *Ptilinopus regina* (**Swainson** 1825)
  (Alt. Red-crowned/Rose-crowned/Grey-capped/Pink-capped/Red-capped/
  Red-headed/Blue-spotted Fruit Dove)

Reverend Thomas J Ewing (?–1876) was an Australian teacher, amateur naturalist and collector who lived in Tasmania. E T Emmett, in *Tasmania by Road and Track* wrote '*In 1874 the Rev. T J Ewing saw over 100 Peppermint trees Eucalyptus amygdalina – the tallest trees in the world, 40ft in circumference, and measured one which was 60ft* [in girth] *at 4ft from the ground*'. He wrote *List of Birds of Tasmania*.

EXPLORERS

Exploration is another great pursuit for 'birdmen'. Explorers have had birds named after them simply because of their fame as explorers. They include: William Friedrich Georg **Behn**, François **Leguat**, Harry St John Bridger **Philby**, Antonio **Raimondi** and J **Rouget** and, of course, Meriwether **Lewis** and William **Clark**, who crossed America and reached the Pacific.

It was more usual was for birds to be named after the leader or organiser of the expedition (sometimes posthumously) as in the cases of Jan **Dybowski**, Alfred A

Marche, Eugenio Prince **Ruspoli**, William **Scoresby**, Graf Bela **Szechenyi** and Baron Carl Claus **von der Decken**.

However, the vast majority of those honoured in this connection are people who themselves went exploring and discovered more than new lands and cultures; they discovered many new fauna and flora. Amongst those who discovered the birds named for them are: Hugh **Clapperton** (probably), William **Bartram**, Oskar **Baumann**, William John **Burchell**, Alexander Douglas Mitchell **Carruthers**, J **D'Arnaud** (probably), Dr Gustav Adolf **Fischer**, Henry Ogg **Forbes**, John **Gilbert**, Walter **Goodfellow**, James Sligo **Jameson**, Friedrich Heinrich Freiherr von **Kittlitz**, Jan S **Kubary**, François **Le Vaillant**, **Maximilian** Alexander Philip Prince zu **Wied-Neuwied**, Albert S **Meek**, Francisco Josue Pascasio **Moreno**, Commandant P F **Nahan**, Henri **Prince** d'Orleans (probably), Henry Cushier **Raven**, Captain Vladimir **Roborovski**, Lieutenant Colonel A F G **Weyns**, John **Whitehead** and **Xavier** Dybowski.

EYLES

Eyles' Harrier *Circus eylesi* (**Scarlett** 1953) [Extinct]

James [Jim] R Eyles was an amateur archaeologist and the major excavator of the Wairau Bar site in New Zealand. In 1939, when still a schoolboy, he discovered a Moa hunter's burial site near Blenheim, which included a Moa's egg from which the contents had been extracted. Scarlett assisted by Eyles, excavated the site in 1942. Articles mentioning him are scattered in records of the Canterbury Museum and the Royal Society of New Zealand library. **Scarlett** named the harrier from fossil material.

EYTON

Eyton's Hill Partridge *Arborophila charltonii* (Eyton 1845)
  (Alt. Chestnut-necklaced/breasted[Tree]Hill Partridge, Scaly-breasted Partridge)
Eyton's Whistling-duck *Dendrocygna eytoni* (Eyton 1838)
  (Alt. Plumed Whistling [Tree]-duck)

Thomas Campbell Eyton (1809–1880) was an English naturalist. He matriculated from St John's College, Cambridge, in 1828, and was a correspondent of **Agassiz** and **Darwin**, although he was an opponent of Darwinism. He published *History of the Rarer British Birds* in 1836, *A Monograph on the Anatidae, Or Duck Tribe* in 1838, *A History of Oyster and Oyster Fisheries* in 1858 and *Osteologia Avium* between 1871 and 1878. He described both birds as well as 20 other species.

FALKENSTEIN

Falkenstein's Greenbul *Chlorocichla falkensteini* (**Reichenow** 1874)
  (Alt. Yellow-necked Greenbul)

Johann Falkenstein (1842–1917) was a German surgeon who collected in Africa between 1873 and 1876.

FAMOUS FEMALE ORNITHOLOGISTS

Most of the women whose names appear in these pages were not ornithologists in their own right. Some sponsored expeditions and one had a large collection of fowl. Most were honoured either because they were famous for reasons not associated with birds or because they were the wives, the daughters and, we believe in a number of cases, the mistresses of ornithologists. Nine exceptions stand out as female ornithologists. Felice **Abeille** worked with her husband and it is not clear whom the birds were named by or after; it may have been either or both but it matters little as they were both experts. Alice (Rich) **Northrop** was also originally part of a husband-and-wife team but her husband died tragically young and Alice went on for many years establishing a formidable reputation and body of work. Beryl Patricia **Hall** was a respected ornithologist who worked at the British Natural History Museum. May **Canfield** was a real character and collected widely in the United States. Maria Emilie **Snethlage** was a German ornithologist; a Doctor of Natural Philosophy and an assistant in zoology at the Berlin Museum, who collected in the Amazon forests and elsewhere in her adopted Brazil from 1905 until her death. Angela Kay **Kepler** often writes jointly with her husband. Dr Erika **Tallman** and her husband are both ornithologists. Theresa **Clay** was an ornithologist as well as a parasitologist. Finally, Maria **Koepcke** was, perhaps, the most famous woman ornithologist ever, and she came to be known as the Mother of Peruvian Ornithology. Approximately 275 new species have been described since 1950, but women have described fewer than 20 of these! Even then, almost all of these women have described the species in collaboration with one or several men, the only exceptions being Maria Koepcke in the 1950s and more recently Pamela Rasmussen.

FANNIN

Fannin's Heron *Ardea herodias fannini* (**Chapman** 1901)
(Alt. Great Blue Heron)

John [Jack] Fannin (1837–?) was an Ontario-born Canadian naturalist and taxidermist. He was the first curator, in 1886, of the Provincial Museum of Natural History and Anthropology, which is now the Royal British Columbia Museum. He started the museum's collection of birds, other animals, plants and historical artefacts from British Columbia. He retired from the museum in 1904. He was collecting and preserving specimens as early as 1870. He published the first checklist of birds for British Columbia in 1891, covering 307 species. In 1898 he updated it as *A Preliminary Catalogue of the Collections of Natural History and Ethnology in the Provincial Museum, Victoria B.C. In 1894 he noted 'Mr. Charles deB. Green, who spends a good deal of his spare time in making collections for the Museum, writes me from Kettle River, Okanogan district, British Columbia, to the effect that while climbing to an osprey's nest he was surprised to find his actions resented by not only the ospreys but also by a pair of Canada geese* (Branta canadensis)*, the latter birds making quite a fuss all the time Mr. Green was in the tree.'* As the Fannin Sheep, a colour variation of Stone's Sheep *Ovis dalli stonei*, is found in the same area, we assume that it too has been named in his honour.

FANNY

Fanny's Woodstar *Myrtis fanny* (**Lesson** 1838)
(Alt. Purple-collared Woodstar)

This hummingbird is probably named after Mrs Frances 'Fanny' Wilson, who is known to have been alive in 1846. Her husband was the British collector, Edward Wilson.

FARKAS

Farkas' Rock Thrush *Pseudocossyphus bensoni* (Farkas 1971)
(Alt. Benson's Rock Thrush or Farkas' Robin-Chat)

Dr Tibor B Farkas is a South African ornithologist. He led the Ornithology Department of the National Museum of Bloemfontein from 1971 to 1987 and has published a number of works including *Notes on the biology and ethnology of the Natal Robin Cossypha natalensis*, in 1969, and a number of papers on the Barberspan Nature Reserve in the early 1960s. He was still writing in the late 1980s with publications such as *Occurrence of the Barred Warbler in the Orange Free State*, in 1986, and *The birds of Korannaberg, eastern Orange Free State, South Africa*, in 1988. He has worked in southern Africa and also Japan.

FARMERS

Farmers are luckier than most in being able to promote the welfare of birds upon their own lands and some of those recorded here had considerable estates. R D **Bradfield** was a South African farmer who, together with his wife, collected birds on his farm in Namibia. Arthur F **Cobb** also collected on his farm in the Falkland Islands; we are not clear whether the wren named after him was collected there; although he certainly secured the type specimen. Edward **Harris** was a New Jersey farmer friend of **Audubon**'s but he was also a keen ornithologist. John Porter **McCown** had collected birds before he took up farming. Thomas **Lincoln** was also a friend of Audubon's and collected with him, before returning to farming in Maine. Johann Andreas **Naumann** was a German farmer and ornithologist who wrote about the birds of his country, and so may well have observed much on his own land.

FEA

Fea's Petrel *Pterodroma feae* (**Salvadori** 1899)
(Alt. Cape Verde Petrel or Gongon)
Fea's Thrush *Turdus feae* (Salvadori 1887)
(Alt. Grey-sided Thrush)

Leonardo Fea (1852–1903) was an Italian explorer, zoologist, painter and naturalist. Fea, who was then Assistant at the Natural History Museum in Genoa, liked exploring far off and little-known countries. He visited the Cape Verde Islands in 1898. The islands, at about 600 km from Senegal, were not as challenging to visit as some of his other destinations. He had already made an expedition to Burma (now Myanmar). He was a friend of **Salvadori**, who first described the petrel from a specimen collected by Fea on the Cape Verdes.

FEATHER MERCHANT

In our view the person who least deserved to be honoured in the name of a bird was Anton August **Bruijn**. He was a feather merchant and from the middle to the end of the 19th century was responsible for the death of thousands of birds. Ironically, one species, Bruijn's Brush Turkey is only known from 24 specimens, 22 of them brought in by his paid collectors. In the last few years it was proven to still be extant only when some local people gave the remains of one which they had just eaten to a visiting ornithologist, and it was seen in the wild in May 2002.

FERNANDEZ

Juan Fernández Firecrown *Sephanoides fernandensis* (King 1831)
Juan Fernández Petrel *Pterodroma externa* (**Salvin** 1875)
Juan Fernández Tit-Tyrant *Anairetes fernandezianus* (**Philippi** 1857)

These birds are not named directly after a person but after the three Juan Fernández Islands off the coast of Chile, to which they are all endemic. The islands were named after Juan Fernández de Quiros, Portuguese navigator in the employ of the Spanish crown, who discovered them in the 1570s. The major island's claim to fame is that it was where Alexander Selkirk was marooned in 1704 and became the real-life Robinson Crusoe. It is now more often known as Isla Robinson Crusoe. Fernández also established a Christian settlement at Espiritu Santo, Vanuatu.

FERNANDINA

Fernandina's Flicker *Colaptes fernandinae* (**Vigors** 1827)
(Alt. Cuban Flicker)

Fernandina was once another name for Cuba. We think that the name is just another way of saying Cuban Flicker.

FIELDEN

Fielden's Falconet *Polihierax insignis* (Tweeddale 1871)
(Alt. White-rumped Falcon)

Colonel Henry Wemyss Fielden CB [sometimes spelt Feilden] (1838–1921) was a noted British natural historian and explorer, who nonetheless fought in the American Civil War, for the Confederate side. He was a member of the Zoological Society. In 1872 he visited the Faeroe Islands to look for a reported Great Auk *Pinguinus impennis*, despite it having been presumed extinct since 1844. He was a contributor of various notes and regional lists, which appeared in early issues of The Ibis, such as *Ornithological notes from Natal* by Majors E A Butler, H W Feilden and Captain S G Reid, in 1882, who '*found [them]selves condemned to a life of comparative idleness for months at Newcastle, owing to the unexpectedly peaceful results of the operations against the Boers…*' and, by Fielden alone *On the birds of Barbados*, in 1889. In 1899 *Two summer voyages to Novaja Zemlja and the island of Barents Sea. With Appendices on the Botany and Geology by Colonel HW Feilden* was published in London; as was, on another occasion, *Narrative of a Voyage to the Polar Sea During 1875– 6 in HM Ships 'Alert' and 'Discovery' – With Notes on the Natural History edited by HW Feilden*. He also published a number of articles in The Zoologist, such as *The nest of the alligator*, in 1870. **Tweeddale** described the falconet from a specimen, collected by **Lloyd** at Tonghoo, Burma.

FINN

Finn's Weaver *Ploceus megarhynchus* (**Hume** 1866)
(Alt. Finn's Baya Weaver, [Indian] Yellow Weaver)

Frank Finn was the author of many books on the birds of India in the first half of the 20th century; *Lists of Birds in the Indian Museum, Garden and Aviary Birds of India, Game Birds of India and Asia, How to Know the Indian Ducks, The Birds of Calcutta, How to Know The Indian Waders, Indian Sporting Birds* and *The Water Fowl of India and Asia* among others. **Hume** first described the weaver from a specimen which Finn collected at Kaladoongi in India, and **Oates** gave it its vernacular name in 1889 or 1890. Frank Finn used over 100 of the illustrations from Hume's *The Game Birds of India* in his *Indian Sporting Birds*, 35 years later.

FINSCH

Finsch's Amazon *Amazona finschii* (**P L Sclater** 1864)
  (Alt. Lilac-crowned Amazon)
Finsch's Bearded Bulbul *Alophoixus finschii* (**Salvadori** 1871)
Finsch's [Olive-]Brown Bulbul *Iole olivacea* (**Blyth** 1844)
  (Alt. Buff-vented Bulbul)
Finsch's Conure *Aratinga finschi* (**Salvin** 1871)
  (Alt. Crimson-fronted Parakeet)
Finsch's Duck *Euryanas finschii* (Van Beneden 1875) [Extinct]
Finsch's Euphonia *Euphagus cyanocephalus* (**Wagler** 1829)
Finsch's Flycatcher-Thrush *Neocossyphus finschii* (**Sharpe** 1870)
  (Alt. Finsch's Broad-billed Ant-thrush, Finsch's Rusty Flycatcher)
Finsch's Francolin *Francolinus* (*Scleroptila*) *finschi* (**Bocage** 1881)
Finsch's Honeyeater *Lichmera notabilis* (Finsch 1898)
  (Alt. Black-chested/-necklaced/White-bellied/Wetlar Honeyeater)
Finsch's Parrot *Psittacula finschii* (**Hume** 1874)
  (Alt. Hume's/Grey-headed Parakeet, Eastern/Finsch's Slaty-headed Parakeet)
Finsch's Pygmy Parrot *Micropsitta finschii* (**E P Ramsay** 1881**)**
Finsch's Reed Warbler *Acrocephalus rehsei* (Finsch 1883)
  (Alt. Nauru Reed Warbler, Nauru Warbler)
Finsch's Rufous-bellied Fruit Pigeon *Ducula finschii* (E P Ramsay 1882)
  (Alt. Finsch's Imperial Pigeon)
Finsch's Wheatear *Oenanthe finschii* (**Heuglin** 1869)
Finsch's White-eye *Zosterops finschii* (**Hartlaub** 1868)
  (Alt. Dusky White-eye)

Friedrich Hermann Otto Finsch (1839–1917) was a German ethnographer, naturalist and traveller. He visited the Balkans, North America, Lapland, Turkestan and northwestern China (with Alfred **Brehm**) and also the South Seas, spending nearly a year (1879/80) on the Marshall Islands. In 1884 Bismarck appointed him Imperial Commissioner for the German Colony of 'Kaiser-Wilhelm-Land', in what is now Papua New Guinea. He founded the town of Finschhafen there in 1885, which remained the seat of German administration until 1918. He was the director of a number of museums at various times including Bremen (where he succeeded Hartlaub as curator in 1884) and Brunswick. Among many other publications he co-wrote *Die Vogel Ost Afrika* with **Hartlaub**. He named a number of birds in their scientific binomials with the Latinised version of his daughter Esther's name '*estherae*'. The duck was a New Zealand bird which became extinct at some time between the Polynesian and European colonisations.

FISCHER, GEORG

Fischer's Fruit Dove *Ptilinopus fischeri* (Bruggeman 1876)
  (Alt. Red-eared Fruit Dove)

Georg Fischer was a Dutch surgeon who collected in the East Indies in the 1890s.

FISCHER, GUSTAV

Fischer's Finch-lark *Eremopterix leucopareia* (Fischer & **Reichenow** 1884)
  (Alt. Fischer's Sparrow-lark)

Fischer's Greenbul *Phyllastrephus fischeri* (Reichenow 1879)
Fischer's Lovebird *Agapornis fischeri* (Reichenow 1887)
Fischer's Starling *Spreo fischeri* (Reichenow 1884)
Fischer's Turaco *Tauraco fischeri* (Reichenow 1878)
Fischer's Whydah *Vidua fischeri* (Reichenow 1882)
(Alt. Straw-tailed Whydah)

Dr Gustav Adolf Fischer (1848–1886) was a German explorer of East and Central Africa.
Fischer and **Reichenow** were obviously very close friends, as the latter described all six birds.

FISCHER, J

Fischer's Eider *Somateria fischeri* (**Brandt** 1847)
(Alt. Spectacled Eider)
Fischer's Petrel *Pterodroma inexpectata* (Forster 1844)
(Alt. Mottled Petrel)

Johann Gotthelf Fischer von Waldheim (1771–1853) is often regarded as a Russian, but he was a German anatomist, entomologist and palaeontologist. He appears to have been sent to Moscow by the Emperor Napoleon, presumably in one of the periods before 1812, when Napoleon was on good terms with the Tsar Alexander I, and he remained in Russia for the rest of his life. Fischer's major contributions in virtually every field of natural history made him one of the intellectual giants of his age. His other particular areas of expertise included the study of molluscs and other marine invertebrates.

FITZROY

Fitzroy's Cockatoo *Cacatua galerita fitzroyi* (**Mathews** 1912)
(Alt. Mathew's/Sulphur-crested Cockatoo)

We do not think that this bird was named directly after a person as *fitzroyi* is a Latinised name of the Fitzroy River, in the north of Western Australia, where this subspecies of the Sulphur-crested Cockatoo was first seen. However, the river was named after Captain Fitzroy, who commanded *HMS Beagle* on Darwin's voyage and who later founded the Meteorological Office in London.

FLECK

Fleck's Coucal *Centropus senegalensis flecki* (**Reichenow** 1893)
(Alt. Senegal Coucal)

Dr Eduard Fleck (1843–after 1911) was a German ornithologist who explored and collected in German South-West Africa (now Namibia) between 1889 and 1892. He sent his specimens to **Reichenow** in Berlin. In 1894 he was elected a member of the Deutsche Ornithologische Gesellschaft (German Ornithological Society) and published extensively. However, after a few years the flow of publications abruptly ceased when, in about 1895, he moved to the village of Azuga in the Transylvanian Alps, an area that in his day was part of the Austro-Hungarian Empire, and is now in Romania. There, with a friend from his youth, he set up a factory to make Portland cement and in 1911 he was described as being '*a private scholar and director of a cement factory*'.

FLEMING

Fleming's Grouse *Dendragapus obscurus richardsoni* (Douglas 1829)
(Alt. Richardson's/Blue Grouse)

Probably named after John Fleming DD (1785–1857), a Scottish clergyman, zoologist and geologist, who published *The Philosophy of Zoology* in 1822 (which impressed Charles Darwin who agreed with many of his theories) and *A History of British Animals* in 1828. He became professor of Natural Philosophy at King's College, Aberdeen, and then Professor of Natural History at the Free Church College, Edinburgh, where he built up the museum's collections. He was the first to delineate the pheasant genus *Lophura*. **Say** first described the Blue Grouse in 1823. Douglas described the race *richardsoni* in 1829 and it appears that the proposed subspecies *flemingi* was absorbed within *richardsoni*. Fleming may have been partly responsible for changing the vernacular name from Richardson's Grouse to Fleming's Grouse, or it just may be that it was named to honour his academic standing.

FLORESI

Floresi's Flamebearer *Selasphorus floresii* (**Gould** 1861)

Don Floresi d'Areais collected in Mexico and supplied specimens to **Gould**. He appears to have been mainly a botanical collector and is commemorated in the binomials of a number of Central and South American plants e.g. an Ecuadorian orchid, *Lepanthes floresii* and two Mexican cacti, *Echinocereus floresii* and *Mammillaria floresii*. Gould described the Hummingbird from a bird collected by Floresi in Mexico in 1845. It is now regarded as a hybrid of **Allen**'s Hummingbird *Selasphorus sasin* and **Anna**'s Hummingbird *Calypte anna*. (The adjective *floresii* also refers to the Flores island group in the Lesser Sundas, Indonesia, so beware assuming that everything named *floresii* refers to this man!)

FOERSTER

Foerster's Melidectes *Melidectes foersteri* (**Rothschild** & **Hartert** 1911)
(Alt. Huon Wattled Honeyeater)

See **Förster**.

FORBES, H

Forbes' Forest Rail *Rallina forbesi* (**Sharpe** 1887)
(Alt. Forbes's Chestnut Rail)
Forbes' Mannikin *Lonchura hunsteini* (**Finsch** 1886)
(Alt. New Ireland Finch/Munia/Mannikin, Buff-breasted Mannikin)
Forbes's Parakeet *Cyanoramphus* (*auriceps*) *forbesi* (**Rothschild** 1893)

Henry Ogg Forbes (1851–1932) was a Scottish explorer and natural history collector, who retraced **Wallace**'s footsteps in the Moluccas on one of his expeditions and published *A Naturalist's Wanderings in the Eastern Archipelago* in 1885. After a number of ill-fated expeditions in New Guinea, Forbes was appointed meteorological observer in Port Moresby. He was later Director of the Canterbury Museum, New Zealand, from 1890 until 1893 and consulting director on museums in Liverpool, from 1911 until 1932. The rail was illustrated in **Gould**'s *The birds of New Guinea and the Adjacent Papuan Islands, Including Many New Species Recently Discovered in Australia*.

FORBES, W

Forbes's Blackbird *Curaeus forbesi* (P L **Sclater** 1886)
Forbes' [Banded] Plover *Charadrius* (*tricollaris*) *forbesi* (G E **Shelley** 1883)

William Alexander Forbes (1855–1883) was a British anatomist, collector and zoologist. He became a Member of the Zoological Society in London. He collected in the Americas, particularly in Brazil, where he conducted a survey of the birds of Pernambuco in 1881. He also collected in West Africa in 1882, where he died on the Upper Niger River. He published valuable papers on bird anatomy: *Report on the anatomy of the petrels (Tubinares), collected during the voyage of HMS Challenger, Zoology of the Challenger Expedition*, in 1882, and *Contributions to the anatomy of passerine birds, On the structure of the stomach in certain genera of tanagers*, in Proceedings of the Zoological Society, in 1880.

FORBES-WATSON

Forbes-Watson's Swift *Apus berliozi* (**Ripley** 1965)

Alec D Forbes-Watson wrote extensively on African birds, mostly in collaboration with R J Dowsett. He has written many articles including *Eggs of the Arabian Ostrich* and *Observations at a nest of the Cuckoo-Roller Leptosomus discolor*, in 1967 and *Notes on birds observed in the Comoros on behalf of the Smithsonian Institution*, in 1969, as well as being co-author of the *Checklist of Birds of the Afrotropical and Malagasy Regions* in 1993. He also wrote the description, in 1970, of a type specimen which he collected in Liberia, the Liberian Black Flycatcher *Melaenornis annamarulae*. Whilst the swift is not endemic to the Socotra, where he observed it, it is one of its few strongholds and home to one of the two races. **Ash** published a study of Forbes-Watson's Swift in 1981.

FORBUSH

Forbush's Sparrow *Melospiza lincolnii* (**Audubon** 1834)
(Alt. Lincoln's Sparrow)

Edward Howe Forbush (1858–1929) was the American ornithologist after whom the Forbush Bird Club was named. He had very little formal education but began learning about ornithology and taxidermy as a child. He was made ornithologist to the Massachusetts Board of Agriculture in 1903, then State Ornithologist in 1908 and became the first director of the Massachusetts Department of Agriculture's Division of Ornithology in 1920. Among his published works are *Useful Birds and their Protection*, published in 1905, and *Birds of Massachusetts and other New England states*, written in 1925. The latter was illustrated by Louis **Agassiz Fuertes**. He took part in collecting expeditions to Florida, the Pacific Northwest, Western Canada and Alaska. He was a co-founder of the Naturalists' Exchange; now the Naturalists Club at the Museum of Science in Springfield, Massachusetts. **Audubon**, who described the sparrow, named it after **Lincoln**.

FORSTEN

Forsten's Lorikeet *Trichoglossus haematodus forsteni* (**Bonaparte** 1850)
(Alt. Rainbow Lorikeet, Rainbow Lory)
Forsten's Oriole *Oriolus forsteni* (Bonaparte 1850)
Forsten's Scrubfowl *Megapodius forsteni* (G R **Gray** 1847)
(Alt. Forsten's Megapode)

Eltio Alegondas Forsten (1811–1843) collected in the East Indies between 1838 and his death. He was primarily a botanist and was interested in the pharmaceutical properties of plants, on which he wrote at least one scientific paper *Dissertatio botanico-pharmaceutico-medica inauguralis de cedrela febrifuga*, in 1836. As he published this at the Lugduno Batavorum (which appears to be the Latin for Leiden), we assume that he was Dutch, despite the most unusual first names! The Rainbow Lorikeet appears in these pages several times, as many of the 19 races are named after particular people. Almost every race is endemic to an island or group of islands; in this case Sumbawa.

FORSTER, G

Forster's Dove of Tanna *Gallicolumba ferruginea* (**Wagler** 1829) [Extinct]
(Alt. Tanna Ground Dove)

Johann George Adam Forster (1754–1794), known as George, sailed with his father **Johann R Forster** aboard the *Resolution*. He was elected a Fellow of the Royal Society in 1775 for his share in the description of the flora of the South Seas. Later in his life, he became Professor of Natural History at Wilna and Librarian at Mainz. **Wagler** described the dove, but the specimen has long since been lost. The only other record of it is a crude painting by Forster himself. Tanna is one of the islands of Vanuatu.

FORSTER, J

Forster's Caracara *Phalcoboenus australis* (Gmelin 1788)
(Alt. Striated Caracara)
Forster's Petrel/Shearwater *Puffinus gavia* (J R Forster 1844)
(Alt. Fluttering Shearwater, Brown-beaked Petrel/Shearwater)
Forster's Tern *Sterna forsteri* (**Nuttall** 1834)

 Johann Reinhold Forster (1729–1798) was originally a clergyman in Danzig. He became a naturalist and accompanied James **Cook**, the famous British explorer of the Pacific Ocean, on his second voyage around the world from 1772 until 1773. This voyage extended further into Antarctic waters than anyone had previously reached. Forster discovered five new species of penguin. However, he gained a reputation as a constant complainer and troublemaker. His complaints of Cook continued after his return and became public, destroying Forster's career in England. He went to Germany and became a Professor of History and Mineralogy. Unpleasant and troublesome to the end, Forster refused to relinquish his notes of the voyage. They were not found and published until almost 50 years after his death. His son Johann George Adam (known as George) (1754–1794) was also on Cook's voyage as an artist and has a number of birds' scientific names named for him.

FÖRSTER

Förster's Honeyeater *Melidectes foersteri* (Rothschild & **Hartert** 1911)
(Alt. Huon [Wattled] Melidectes/Honeyeater)

F Förster (1865–1918) was a German botanist and collector. He described two new birds-of-paradise with **Rothschild** in 1906.

FOX

Fox's Weaver *Ploceus spekeoides* (**Grant** & Mackworth-Praed 1947)

Harold Munro Fox FRS [born Fuchs] (1889–1967) was an English zoologist who was born in London and educated in Cambridge. From 1911 to 1912 he worked at the Plymouth Laboratory and in 1912 in Naples, before becoming a lecturer in Zoology at the Royal College of Science (now Imperial College), London, in 1913. After the First World War he worked as a Lecturer in Biology in Cairo, between 1919 and 1923. He returned to Cambridge between 1924 and 1927 but also led an expedition to Egypt to study the fauna of the Suez Canal between 1924 and 1925. He became Professor of Zoology at the University of Birmingham, from 1927 until 1941, and then Professor of Zoology at Bedford College, London, between 1941 and 1954.

FRANCES

Frances's Goshawk *Accipiter francesii* (A **Smith** 1834)
(Alt. Frances's Sparrowhawk)

Henrietta Frances, Lady Cole (*c*.1785–1848) was a patroness of science. Sir Andrew **Smith** named the goshawk after her and wrote '*To Lady Frances Cole I am indebted for the only specimen I possess of this apparently undescribed species, – and the name it bears in the South African Museum is an indication of the high respect entertained for Her Ladyship as a well known and zealous Patroness of Science.*' She apparently had the holotype collected for her in Madagascar.

FRANCIA

Francia's Azure Crown *Amazilia* (*Agyrtria*) *franciae* (**Bourcier** & **Mulsant** 1846)
(Alt. Andean Emerald)

Francia Bourcier was the daughter of Jules **Bourcier** (1797–1873), who was an amateur naturalist and the French Consul to Ecuador between 1849 and 1850. Bourcier and **Mulsant** described the bird in 1846, naming it after the former's daughter.

FRANKLIN

Franklin's Grouse *Falcipennis canadensis franklini* (Douglas 1829)
(Alt. Spruce Grouse)
Franklin's Gull *Larus pipixcan* (**Wagler** 1832)
Franklin's Nightjar *Caprimulgus monticolus* (**Horsfield** 1821)
Franklin's Prinia *Prinia hodgsoni* (**Blyth** 1844)
(Alt. Ashy-grey/Hodgson's/Franklin's/Grey-breasted Prinia/Wren-warbler)

Sir John Franklin (1786–1847) was an officer in the Royal Navy and is best known as an explorer of the Northwest Passage. The youngest of 12 boys, Franklin joined the navy in his youth and spent the rest of his life in its service. He undertook his first arctic voyage in 1818, commanding a vessel trying to reach the North Pole. In 1819 he led his first attempt to find the Northwest Passage, the sea route across the Arctic to the Pacific Ocean. He returned empty-handed after two years amid rumours of starvation, murder and cannibalism. Franklin was involved in several more voyages to the north, before disappearing in 1845 in another attempt to cross the arctic by sea. A search was undertaken under the command of Sir Clements Robert **Markham**. **Vieillot** named the gull which **Wagler** described.

FRANTZIUS

Frantzius' Nightingale-Thrush *Catharus frantzii* **Cabanis** 1861
(Alt. Ruddy-capped Nightingale-Thrush)

Alexander von Frantzius (1821–1877) was a German doctor. He and fellow physician Carl **Hoffmann** went to Costa Rica in 1853 and began to explore the country and collect mainly botanical specimens. Frantzius became a successful businessman and the eventual owner of a drugstore known popularly as 'Botica Francesa', which is currently one of the largest private organizations in Costa Rica. Advertisements in the press of the time said that the drugstore was '*managed by naturalists Frantzius and Zeledón*'. An extinct volcano in Costa Rica is also named after him.

FRASER, L

Fraser's Ant-thrush *Neocossyphus fraseri* (**Strickland** 1844)
(Alt. Rufous Broad-billed Ant-thrush, Rufous/Rusty Flycatcher-Thrush)
Fraser's Eagle Owl *Bubo poensis* (Fraser 1854)
(Alt. Nduk Eagle Owl)
Fraser's Flycatcher *Fraseria ocreata* (Strickland 1844)
(Alt. African Forest Flycatcher)
Fraser's Rusty Thrush *Neocossyphus rufus* (**Fischer** & **Reichenow** 1884)
(Alt. Red-tailed Ant-thrush)
Fraser's Spinetail *Cranioleuca antisiensis* (P L **Sclater** 1859)
(Alt. Line-cheeked Spinetail)
Fraser's Sunbird *Anthreptes fraseri* (**Jardine** & Selby 1843)
(Alt. Scarlet-tufted Sunbird)
Fraser's Warbler *Basileuterus fraseri* (P L Sclater 1884)
(Alt. Grey-and-gold Warbler)

Louis Fraser (1810–1866) was a British zoologist and collector. He was also variously a curator, explorer, zookeeper, consul, author, dealer and taxidermist. He collected in Nigeria between 1841 and 1842, in Ecuador in 1859 and in California in 1860. He published *Zoologica Typica* in 1860. Fraser was Consul of the Bight of Benin (Nigeria) from 1852 until 1853. At some stage of his life, he was Curator to the Museum of the Zoological Society of London and took charge of Lord Derby's zoological collections at Knowsley. He was also a natural history dealer.

FRASER, T

Fraser's Hermit *Glaucis fraseri* (**Gould** 1861)

Gould described this hummingbird in 1861 stating that a T Fraser had collected it in Esmeraldas, Ecuador. Since Louis Fraser, who like Gould worked for the London Zoological Society Museum at one time, was collecting in Ecuador for Philip **Sclater** in 1860, we believe that Gould made a mistake in the transcription of the initial in his description. We consider, therefore, that he named the bird after Louis Fraser. The name is not current and we are unsure to which species it refers.

FRAZAR

Frazar's Green Heron *Butorides striatus frazari* (**Brewster** 1888)
(Alt. Striated Heron)
Frazar's Oystercatcher *Haematopus palliatus frazari* (**Temminck** 1820)
(Alt. American Oystercatcher)
Frazar's Vireo *Vireo huttoni* (**Cassin** 1851)
(Alt. Hutton's/Anthony's/Stephen's Vireo)

Marston Abbott Frazar was a paid collector for **Sennett** in the 1880s. He wrote *An Ornithologist's Summer in Labrador* in 1887. The oystercatcher is sometimes treated as a valid subspecies but it is more often thought to represent a hybrid between the American Oystercatcher *H.palliatus* and the American Black Oystercatcher *H.bachmani*. The heron is a Mexican race of the Striated Heron.

FREER

Freer's Blue-backed Parrot *Tanygnathus sumatranus freeri* (**McGregor** 1910)
(Alt. Blue-backed/Azure-rumped Parrot)

Paul Caspar Freer MD PhD (1862–1912) was Professor of Chemistry at the University of

Michigan and later director of the Government Scientific Laboratories, Manila and Dean of the Philippine Islands Medical School. He also edited the Philippine Journal of Science, in which **McGregor** published his description of this race of the parrot.

FRICK

Frick's Sombre Greenbul *Andropadus importunus fricki* (Mearns)

Childs Frick (1883–1965) was the son of Henry Clay Frick, co-founder of the United States Steel Corporation and whose mansion overlooking Central Park in Manhattan now houses the world-renowned Frick Collection of paintings, sculpture and decorative art. He did not follow his father into industry but became a brilliant scientist in his own right. He was honorary curator of the Department of Vertebrate Palaeontology at the Princeton Museum of Natural History, which he often supported with his own funds. He excavated for fossils in North America and also undertook an expedition to Ethiopia and Kenya, and catalogued the birds recorded there in a book, in 1937. Frick is also commemorated by an extinct Sabre-toothed Cat *Barbourofelis fricki* and a fossil gastropod *Otollonia fricki* amongst others. On his death, in 1965, he bequeathed the world's largest collection of mammalian fossils, more than 250,000 specimens, to the American Museum of Natural History in New York City. It was his efforts, more than anyone else's, that were responsible for our knowledge of prehistoric North American camels, rhinoceroses, antelope-like animals, deer and carnivores. The greenbul was among the birds collected on the 1930s expedition, but is now generally considered to be a juvenile *A. importunus insularis.*

FRIEDMANN

Friedmann's Bushlark *Mirafra pulpa* (Friedmann 1930)
(Alt. Sagon Bushlark)

Herbert Friedmann (1900–1987) was an American ornithologist. In 1929 he published a classic monograph *The Cowbirds: A Study of the Biology of Social Parasitism.* He contributed to the ornithological collection at Cornell University and became Curator of Birds at the Department of Zoology of the United States National Museum of Natural History in 1929, and remained in that post until 1961. He was President of the American Ornithologists' Union from 1938 to 1939. He died of cancer in 1987.

FUERTES

Fuertes' Hawk *Buteo jamaicensis fuertesi* (**Sutton** & Van Tyne 1935)
(Alt. Krider's Hawk)
Fuertes' Oriole *Icterus spurius fuertesi* (**Chapman** 1911)
(Alt. Orchard Oriole)
Fuertes' Parrot *Hapalopsittaca fuertesi* (Chapman 1912)
(Alt. Indigo-winged Parrot)

Louis Agassiz Fuertes (1874–1927) was an ornithologist and a painter of birds. He showed great interest and skill from a very early age. He met Elliott **Coues** in 1894 and showed him some of his paintings. He was greatly encouraged by Coues' comments on his work and they seem to have finally decided him to concentrate on painting birds as a career. He went on collecting trips to Florida in 1898, Alaska in 1899 and Texas and New Mexico in 1901. In addition to his travels within the USA, he also visited the Bahamas, the Canadian prairies and Rockies, the Yucatán, eastern Mexico, and Jamaica, all before the outbreak of the First World War. He also travelled to Abyssinia (Ethiopia) in 1926 with W H **Osgood**. He lectured on ornithology at Cornell University from 1923 until his death, in a road accident, in 1927.

FÜLLEBORN

Fülleborn's Alethe *Alethe fuelleborni* (**Reichenow** 1900)
Fülleborn's Boubou *Laniarius fuelleborni* (Reichenow 1900)
  (Alt. Fülleborn's Black Boubou)
Fülleborn's Longclaw *Macronyx fuelleborni* (Reichenow 1900)
  (Alt. [Indian] Yellow Weaver)

Dr Friederich Fülleborn (1866–1933) was a German physician who worked in Tanganyika (now Tanzania) between 1896 and 1900. He later he became a Professor at Hamburg University and was an expert on tropical diseases, being a member of the Institute of Ship and Tropical Diseases in Hamburg. An East African fish, Fülleborn's Cichlid, appears to be have been named after him, as well as the above birds.

GADOW

Gadow's Sunbird *Nectarinia kilimensis gadowi* **Bocage** 1892
  (Alt. Bronzy Sunbird)

Dr Hans Friedrich Gadow (1855–1928) was a German zoologist. His main contribution to ornithology was to devise a method of taxonomy based on comparisons of 40 characteristics, which he first set out in a paper to the Zoological Society of London, *On the classification of birds* in 1892. His most important work comprised the two volumes on bird classification within Dr H G Bronn's monumental work on recent and fossil zoology, *Die Klassen und Ordnungen des Thier-Reich*. He wrote a number of descriptions of type specimens held by the British Museum. He is also commemorated in the scientific name of the feather louse *Rallicola gadowi*. Gadow wrote *A Dictionary of Birds* with Alfred **Newton** between 1893 and 1896. He also contributed the article *Bird* to the Encyclopaedia Britannica.

GAIMARD

Gaimard's Cormorant *Phalacrocorax gaimardi* (**Lesson** & Garnot 1828)
  (Alt. Red-legged[-footed] Shag/Cormorant)

Joseph (or Jean, according to other sources) Paul Gaimard (1793–1858) was a French naval surgeon, explorer and naturalist. He made a voyage to Australia and the Pacific, from 1817 to 1819, aboard the *Uranie*, during which time he kept a journal, *Journal Du Voyage de Circumnavigation, tenu par Mr Gaimard, Chirurgien à Bord de la Corvette L'Uranie*. Whilst he continued with his journal further entries were lost when the ship was wrecked off the Falklands. He was aboard the *Astrolabe*, under the command of **Dumont D'Urville**, when it visited New Zealand in 1826. Here he collected birds, including two previously unknown species, the South Island Fernbird *Megalurus punctatus* and the Grey Warbler *Gerygone igata*. From 1838 until 1840 he led an expedition aboard the *Récherche* to northern

Europe, visiting Iceland, the Faeroe Islands, northern Norway, Archangel and Spitsbergen. His contemporary, the zoologist Henrik Krøyer, who went with Gaimard to Spitsbergen, in 1838, described him thus; '*he was of medium build, with curly black hair and a rather unattractive face, but with a charming and agreeable manner*'. He was something of a dandy and, when visiting Iceland, gave out many sketches of himself! He is also commemorated in both the common and scientific names of a number of fish species from several different oceans.

GAIRDNER

Gairdner's Woodpecker *Picoides pubescens gairdnerii* (Batchelder 1900)
(Alt. Downy/Batchelder's Woodpecker)

Dr Meredith Gairdner (?–1837) was a naturalist from Edinburgh, Scotland. He left for Canada in 1832, in the employ of the Hudson's Bay Company, and was stationed at a post on the Columbia River for about two years. During that time he studied and investigated natural history, and collected materials to prepare a monograph of the vast district bordering the river. He also witnessed an eruption of Mt St Helens. Unfortunately his strength was sapped by attacks of tuberculosis, which he contracted when he was sent to treat an outbreak, a disease which ultimately proved fatal. An odd claim to fame is that, in his last year of life, he exhumed the body of a local Indian chief, severed the skull and sent it to England to a friend who was a phrenologist. He believed in the native American's inherent inferiority and hoped to learn why this particular native had managed to become so powerful. The skull was part of a display at the Haler Royal Naval Hospital Museum in Gosport, England, for many years. He left for Hawaii hoping it would assist his health but died there, leaving bequests to help poor Hawaiian children. In 1834 he published *Observations During a Voyage from England to Fort Vancouver, on the North-west Coast of America*. **James Audubon** wrote '…*a specimen of a Woodpecker sent from the Columbia river by Dr Meredith Gairdner to Professor Jameson of Edinburgh, who kindly lent it to me for the purpose of being described, I found to be the Picus linealus of Linnaeus, a species which appears to be very extensively distributed, being, according to various authors, plentiful in Cayenne, Guiana, Brazil, and even Paraguay. The specimen, which was shot near Fort Vancouver, is an adult male, but has been injured in the wings. Along with it were specimens of Picus harrisii and Picus ruber, shot in the same neighbourhood. I hope to be able to give a figure of this species at the end of the present work.*' The Steelhead Rainbow Trout *Salmo gairdneri* was also named in his honour in the binomial.

GAMBEL

Gambel's Chickadee *Parus gambeli* (**Ridgway** 1886)
(Alt. Mountain Chickadee)
Gambel's Quail *Callipepla gambelii* (Gambel 1843)
Gambel's Shrike *Lanius ludovicianus gambeli* (**Dickey** 1915)
(Alt. Loggerhead Shrike)
Gambel's Sparrow *Zonotrichia leucophrys gambeli* (**Nuttall** 1856)
(Alt. White-crowned Sparrow)

William Gambel (1821–1849) was an American naturalist and collector, and the first ornithologist to spend any time in California collecting birds. He travelling following his qualification as a physician, in Philadelphia. He soon broke the first rule of natural history nomenclatural etiquette; that is, you do not name a bird you discover after yourself. While riding along the Santa Fe Trail in 1842, Gambel collected a specimen and sent it to a museum, labelled 'Gambel's Quail', apparently believing his friend Thomas **Nuttall** had already named it so. Gambel was mistaken, but the name became official nonetheless. According to John **Cassin** it was he who named it in Gambel's honour, so the above tale may be apocryphal. Gambel in turn named Nuttall's Woodpecker *Picoides nuttallii* for his friend. Gambel was also an assistant curator at the Natural (now National) Academy of Sciences. He died of typhoid at the age of 30 while attempting to cross the Sierra Nevada Mountains in midwinter, with a party on its way to the goldfields of California; the famous 49ers of the California Goldrush. Gambel's Oak *Quercus gambelii* is also named for him.

GAME WARDENS

We find it surprising that only two game wardens have been commemorated in the common names of birds. Such a profession leads to much exposure in areas where new birds may well come to notice and conservation professionals should be well placed to discover or describe such species. Roden E **Symons** was a warden in South Africa and *did* discover and name a bird on the reserve where he worked (Symons' Siskin). Major Ian R **Grimwood** was a warden in Kenya and is largely responsible for rescuing the Oryx *Oryx gazella* from the edge of oblivion.

GARBE

Garbe's Antwren *Myrmotherula longipennis garbei* (H von Ihering 1905)
(Alt. Long-winged Antwren)

P Ernest W Garbe (1853–1925) was a naturalist collecting in Brazil at the turn of the 19th century. He became zoologist for the Paulista Museum. He also collected the first specimen of the rare and threatened bat *Lichonycteris obscura*. **Pelzeln** described the nominate race of Long-winged Antwren.

GARDENER

Gardener's Bowerbird *Amblyornis macgregoriae* (**De Vis** 1890)
(Alt. MacGregor's Bowerbird)

This name is in error; it is not Gardener's Bowerbird but *a* 'Gardener Bowerbird' – which is a subgroup of the family.

GARLEPP

Garlepp's Tinamou *Crypturellus* (*atrocapillus*) *garleppi* (**Berlepsch** 1892)

Gustav Garlepp (1862–1907) was a German who collected in Latin America between 1883 and 1897, including in Bolivia around 1896. He is also commemorated in the trinomial of another bird, a highland race of the Greater Rhea *Pterocnemia tarapacensis garleppi*.

GAUDICHAUD

Gaudichaud's Kingfisher *Dacelo guadichaudi* (**Gaimard** 1824)
(Alt. Rufous-bellied Kookaburra)

Charles Gaudichaud-Beaupré (1789–1854) was born in Angoulème, France. He studied pharmacy and became a dispenser in the French navy in 1810. Later he took part in several large expeditions as a naturalist; around the world aboard, the *Uranie* and *Physicienne*, from 1817 until 1820, to eastern and western South America with the *Herminie*, from 1831 until 1833 and again around the world on *Bonite*, in 1836 to 1837. After the *Bonite* expedition, Gaudichaud was appointed professor in pharmacy, in Paris. He was attached to the Paris museum and worked on the botanical collections from his expeditions.

GEISLER

Geisler's Catbird *Ailuroedus geislerorum* (**Gould***)
(Alt. Stone's Catbird)

Bruno Geisler (1857–1945) and his brother H G Geisler were German taxidermists who collected together in New Guinea between 1884 and 1892. The bird is apparently named after both brothers. It seems to be another name only ascribed by **Gould**.

GEOFFROY

Geoffroy's Blood Pheasant *Ithaginis cruentus geoffroyi* (**J Verreaux** 1867)
Geoffroy's Dotterel *Charadrius leschenaultii* (**Lesson** 1826)
(Alt. Greater/Large/Large-billed Sand Plover)
Geoffroy's Dove *Claravis godefrida* (**Temminck** 1811)
(Alt. Purple-winged Ground Dove)
Geoffroy's Parrot *Geoffroyus geoffroyi* (**Bechstein** 1811)
(Red-cheeked Parrot)
Geoffroy's Wedgebill *Augastes geoffroyi* (**Bourcier** 1843)
(Alt. Wedge-billed Hummingbird)

Étienne Geoffroy Saint-Hilaire (1772–1844) was a French naturalist. He originally trained for the Church but abandoned it to become professor of zoology at the age of 21, when the Jardin du Roi was renamed Le Musée National d'Histoire Naturelle. In his *Philosophie Anatomique* (1818–1822), and other works, he expounded the theory that all animals conform to a single plan of structure. This was strongly opposed by **Cuvier**, who had been his friend, and in 1830 a widely publicised debate between the two took place. Despite their differences, the two men did not become enemies; they respected each other's research, and in 1832 Geoffroy gave one of the orations at Cuvier's funeral. Modern developmental biologists have confirmed some of Geoffroy Saint-Hilaire's ideas. His son, Isidore Geoffroy Saint-Hilaire (1805–1861), was also a zoologist, and was an authority on deviation from normal structure. He succeeded to his father's professorships.

GERMAIN

Germain's Peacock-Pheasant *Polyplectron germaini* (**Elliot** 1866)
Germain's Swiftlet *Collocalia germani* (**Oustalet** 1876)
(Alt. Oustalet's Swiftlet)

Louis Rodolphe Germain (1827–1917) was a veterinary surgeon in the French colonial army, serving in Indochina (Vietnam) from 1862 until 1867. In 1875 he went to New Caledonia, until 1878. He made considerable zoological collections in his spare time, donating them to the Paris museum. They included the first specimen of the pheasant, which **Elliot** named for him.

GERMAN

German's Swiftlet *Collocalia germani* (**Oustalet** 1876)

This appears to be an error in nomenclature and really refers to **Germain** above.

GERMANS

A total of 137 Germans have had birds named after them in the vernacular or 'English' names, putting them in fourth place, after Great Britain, the United States and France. They are far too many to list here.

GESTRO

Gestro's Fruit Dove *Ptilinopus ornatus* (**Schlegel** 1871)
(Alt. Ornate Fruit Dove)

Raffaello Gestro (1845–1936) was an Italian zoologist and a noted entomologist. He was Deputy Director and then Director of the Museo Civico di Storia Naturale, of Genova, and President of the Societa Entomologica Italiana. He has been described as one of the most important Italian coleopterists, having published no fewer than 147 papers on the taxonomy of Coleoptera (beetles). He described 936 new insect species, many based on specimens from other Italian collectors, including **Fea**, **D'Albertis**, and **Beccari**. He also has many insects and some mammals named after him.

GHIGI

Ghigi's Grey Peacock-Pheasant *Polyplectron bicalcaratum ghigii* (**Delacour** & Jabouille 1924)

Professor Alessandro Ghigi (1875–1970) was Chancellor of Bologna University, from 1931 to 1943, and seems to have been more interested in breeding hybrids than anything else. He is probably best described as a geneticist. He was a friend of **Delacour,** who gave him specimens he had collected on his various expeditions to Vietnam. Ghigi developed pheasant hybrids in captivity, including one known as Ghigi's Golden Pheasant (*Chrysolophus pictus* mut. *Luteus*). He also developed a 'Salmon Golden' variety of pheasant. He also was involved in the study and breeding of doves.

GIBSON

Gibson's Albatross *Diomedea gibsoni* Robertson & Warham 1992
(Alt. Auckland Wandering Albatross)

J Doug Gibson (?–1984) was an Australian ornithologist with a deep interest in seabirds, their ecology and distribution, and was a pioneer of albatross studies. He was a founder member of the Illawarra Bird Observers Club, which published his *The Birds of the County of Camden (Including the Illawarra Region)*. He also wrote numerous articles from the 1950s until the late 1970s, which were published in Australasian journals including Corella, Emu, Australian Bird Watcher, Gould League Notes, Australian Bird Bander, Notornis and Australian Birds. Together with members of the New South Wales Albatross Study Group, Gibson suggested a unified system for describing the plumage of the great albatrosses. Known as the 'Gibson Plumage Index' (GPI) or 'Gibson Code', the system gives numerical values to particular degrees of coloration on the back, head, inner wing and tail. This was set out in 1967 in an article published in 'Notornis'; *The Wandering Albatross (Diomedea exulans): results of banding and observations in New South Wales coastal waters and Tasman Sea*. Robertson and Nunn elevated this former race of the Wandering Albatross *D. exulans* to species status, although the taxonomy remains controversial.

GIEROW

Gierow's Bishop *Euplectes gierowii* (**Cabanis** 1880)
(Alt. Black Bishop)

H Gierow was a Swedish naturalist who was collecting in Angola in the 1880s.

GILBERT NKWOCHA

Gilbert's Mountain Babbler *Kupeornis gilberti* (**Serle** 1949)
(Alt. White-throated Mountain Babbler)

See **Nkwocha**.

GILBERT, J

Gilbert's Whistler *Pachycephala inornata* (**Gould** 1841)

John Gilbert (1812–1845) was a naturalist and explorer. He was born in London and was trained as a taxidermist by the Zoological Society of London, who employed him in that role. He became Curator of the Shropshire and North Wales Natural History Society in Shrewsbury but, as the society was short of funds, his contract was terminated in 1837. The next year he left for Australia where he was speared to death on 28 June 1845 by Aborigines at the Gulf of Carpentaria. This unfortunate event happened while he was taking part in Ludwig Leichhardt's expedition to Port Essington, between 1844 and 1845, on which he was the naturalist. Previously, between 1840 and 1842, he was Gould's principal (and assiduous) collector of birds and other animals in southwestern Western Australia. He also collected plants. A small, rabbit-sized marsupial, called Gilbert's Potoroo (*Potorous gilbertii*), is also named for him. Following this discovery, the species was lost for *c.* 100 years and officially proclaimed as extinct. It was rediscovered in 1994.

GILLETT

Gillett's Lark *Mirafra gilletti* (**Sharpe** 1895)

Major F A Gillett (1872–1944) was a big-game hunter in Somalia around 1894.

GILLIARD

Gilliard's Honeyeater *Melidectes whitemanensis* (Gilliard 1960)
(Alt. Bismarck Honeyeater)

Ernest Thomas Gilliard (1912–1965) was an American ornithologist who was closely associated with the American Museum of Natural History in New York. He wrote chiefly on birds of New Guinea, his books including *Birds of Paradise and Bower Birds* and *Living Birds of the World*, in 1959. His *Handbook of New Guinea Birds*, written with A L Rand, seems to have first been published in 1968. A book including ethnographic photographs, which he took in 1953 and 1954, of Kanganam village, on the Middle Sepik River, has also been published. Between 1958 and 1959 Gilliard took part in the New Britain Expedition and an exploration of the Whiteman Mountains, which explains the scientific name of the above species.

GILMAN

Gilman's Screech Owl *Otus* (*kennicottii/asio*) *gilmani* (**Dickey** 1916)
(Alt. Saguaro/Saguard/Western Screech Owl)

M French Gilman (1871–1944) was a well-respected, all-round naturalist from California who studied the wildlife of a number of sites, including Death Valley, where he was caretaker in the 1930s. He also has a number of plants named after him in their scientific names, including at least one genus, *Gilmania*, and also the species *Astragalus gilmanii*, *Cymopterus gilmanii*, *Ericameria gilmanii*, *Eriogonum gilmanii* and *Petalonyx gilmanii*. He was a member of the Cooper Ornithological Society from 1901 until his death. Both Western and Eastern Screech Owls live in North America, and possess at least 22 largely allopatric subspecies between them. A number, including the one below, are named after people. In this case, it is variously described as a race of the eastern or western species! *Gilmani* is often lumped with the race *aikeni*.

GODIN

Godin's Puffleg *Eriocnemis godini* (**Bourcier** 1851)
(Alt. Turquoise-throated/Isaacson's/Long-billed Puffleg)

Jean Godin des Odonais (1712–1792) was a French naturalist who was a professor in Quito. He also studied Amerindian languages and the flora of Ecuador. When he married an heiress in 1743 he resigned his chair and gave his time to natural science and Indian languages. He explored in Ecuador and northern Peru, and collected a herbarium containing more than 4,000 species of plants. He also made drawings of over 800 species of animals. Later he spent 15 years exploring Cayenne and Brazilian Guiana, north of the Amazon. He donated his botanical collections to the Paris Natural History Museum, where they are still preserved. He published widely on both the plants and animals of northern South America, and also wrote dictionaries of South American languages. His wife was also a remarkable woman; setting off to join her husband she attempted, with others, to row 450 miles upriver and then cross a desert. Her Indian guides abandoned them, and the rest of her party perished, but she emerged alone after many weeks. Prince Charles **Bonaparte**, "*has given Madame Godin's name to a remarkable species of South American birds, the Chamaepelia Oodinae, consecrated,*" he said, "*to the memory, which can never be too much honoured, of Isabel Godin des Odonais, who, alone and abandoned, travelled across the American continent in its greatest width, sustained by her greatness of soul and her martyrdom to duty.*" (Alternatively Jobling thinks the bird is named for Louis Godin (1704–1760) a French scientist who worked in Peru in 1735.) There is confusion between Godin's Puffleg and **Soederstrom**'s Puffleg *E.soederstromi*, which too has been called *Eriocnemis godini* at times!

GODLEWSKI

Godlewski's Bunting *Emberiza godlewskii* (**Taczanowski** 1874)
Godlewski's Pipit *Anthus godlewskii* (Taczanowski 1876)
(Alt. Blyth's Pipit)

Wiktor Ignacy Godlewski (1831–1900) was a Polish zoologist. He was exiled to Siberia after the failed Polish uprising, and the bunting is found in that area. Polish naturalists who were political exiles in Siberia, including Benedykt **Dybowski**, Godlewski and Michal **Jankowski**, could study the fauna of the Lake Baikal and other regions of eastern Siberia, largely thanks to the help of the Zoological Cabinet of the Branickis Museum in Warsaw. They sent their materials to the cabinet and **Taczanowski** mediated the sale of a part of these collections to the museums of Western Europe. The funds obtained in this way, together with donations from the Branicki brothers, made it possible for the exiles to survive and continue their studies.

GODMAN

Godman's Fig Parrot *Psittaculirostris desmarestii godmani* (**Ogilvie-Grant** 1911)
(Alt. Large Fig Parrot)

Doctor Frederick du Cane Godman FRS (1834–1919) was a British naturalist who, with his friend Osbert **Salvin**, compiled the massive *Biologia Centrali Americana*, which was issued in parts from 1888 until 1904. Godman and Salvin also presented their joint collection to the British Museum of Natural History over a 15-year period, starting in 1885. Godman qualified as a lawyer but was wealthy and had no need to earn a living, so he devoted his life to ornithology. He visited Norway, Russia, the Azores, Madeira, the Canary Islands, India, Egypt, South Africa, Guatemala, British Honduras (now Belize) and Jamaica. Some of his travels were made with Salvin. The Godman-Salvin Medal, a prestigious award of the British Ornithologists' Union, is named after the two men.

GODWIN-AUSTEN

Godwin-Austen's Wren-Babbler *Spelaeornis chocolatinus* (Godwin-Austen & **Walden** 1875)
(Alt. Long-tailed Wren-Babbler)
Godwin-Austen's Laughing-thrush *Garrulax austeni* (Godwin-Austen 1870)

See **Austen**.

GOELDI

Goeldi's Antbird *Myrmeciza goeldii* (**Snethlage** 1908)
(Alt. Goldi's Antbird)

Emil August Goeldi (1859–1917) was a Swiss zoologist who was born in Zurich. He went to Brazil in 1880, where at first he worked at the Museu Nacional. Later he reorganised the Pará Museum of Natural History and Ethnography, which was founded in 1866. The institution today bears his name: Museu Paraense Emílio Goeldi. He became well known for his studies of Brazilian birds and mammals. Goeldi returned to Switzerland in 1907 to teach biology and physical geography at the University of Bern until his death ten years later. He wrote *Aves do Brasil*, in 1894, and *Die Vogelwelt des Amazonensstromes* in 1901. He was also a racist who did not like Brazilians and worked in a Swiss enclave!

GOETHALS

Goethals' Hummingbird *Goethalsia bella* **Nelson** 1912
(Alt. Pirre Hummingbird)

George Washington Goethals (1858–1928) was a United States Army Colonel. He was the Chairman and Chief Engineer of the Panama Canal from 1907 until 1914, and personally directed the construction of the canal. He completed the project six months ahead of schedule and $23 million below budget. A crane operator on the canal said of him '*Few men could have stood the amount of work he put on himself. Men broke down; men went crazy; men took to drink. The colonel kept as keen as a brier*'. Goethals was also the Governor of the Panama Canal Zone from 1914 until 1916.

GOFFIN

Goffin's Cockatoo *Cacatua goffini* (**Finsch** 1863)
(Alt. Tanimbar Cockatoo, Tanimbar Corella)

Lieutenant Andreas Leopold Goffin (1837–1863) was an officer in the Dutch navy. Other sources say that he was a German, Andrea Goffin, who worked as a scientist in a Dutch museum in Leiden, and that **Finsch**, who first described the cockatoo, was his friend and honoured him following his untimely death.

GOLDI

See **Goeldi**.

GOLDIE

Goldie's Bird of Paradise *Paradisaea decora* (**Salvin** & **Godman** 1883)
Goldie's Lorikeet *Psitteuteles goldiei* (**Sharpe** 1882)

Andrew Goldie (1840–1891) was born in Scotland and died in Port Moresby, Papua New Guinea. He emigrated to New Zealand in 1862 and worked there as a nurseryman until around 1873. He then travelled to Britain in 1874 and Melbourne in 1875, and then began exploration in New Guinea in 1876. Whilst collecting in New Guinea, in 1877, he discovered and named the Goldie River and discovered traces of gold. He then explored the south coast of New Papua Guinea in 1878, naming the Blunden River, Milport Harbour and Glasgow Harbour. Goldie returned to Sydney in 1878 to have gold samples assayed. He bought land near Hanubada, New Guinea, and established a trading store in 1878. He named the Redlick group of islands and discovered Teste Island in Freshwater Bay in 1879. He was given £400 as compensation by the government in 1886, when they decided to remove European settlement from the Hanubada area, and he used it to purchase 50 suburban acres and three town allotments on which he built Port Moresby's first store in January 1897. When he procured the first mutilated skins of one of the birds of paradise from the natives, he wrote as follows: '*The feathers from the tail have been frequently obtained along the coast. The natives said that the bird was only to be obtained at a considerable distance from Morocco inland on the mountains*'.

GOLDMAN

Goldman's Hummingbird *Goldmania violiceps* (**Nelson** 1911)
  (Alt. Violet-capped Hummingbird)
Goldman's Quail-Dove *Geotrygon goldmani* (Nelson 1912)
  (Alt. Russet-crowned Quail-Dove)
Goldman's Warbler *Dendroica coronata goldmani* Nelson 1897
  (Alt. Yellow-rumped Warbler)
Goldman's Yellowthroat *Geothlypis trichas* (**Ridgway** 1882)
  (Alt. Belding's Yellowthroat)

Major Edward Alphonso Goldman (1873–1946) was a field naturalist and mammalogist who was born in Mount Carroll, Illinois. **Nelson** hired him in January 1892 to assist his biological investigations of California and Mexico, and then employed him as Field Naturalist and eventually Senior Biologist with the United States Bureau of Biological Survey. He spent nearly 14 years collecting in every region of Mexico. The biological explorations and collecting expeditions made by Edward William Nelson and Edward Alphonso Goldman, in Mexico, from 1892 to 1906, are said to have been '*among the most important ever achieved by two workers for any single country*'. They conducted investigations in every state in Mexico, collecting 17,400 mammals and 12,400 birds, as well as amassing an enormous fund of information on the natural history of the country. The best account of their work is Goldman's *Biological Investigations in Mexico*, Smithsonian Miscellaneous Collections, vol. 115, 1951. Goldman also had an honorary position with the Smithsonian Institution, as an Associate in Zoology, from 1928 to 1946. From 1911 to 1912, he was part of the Biological Survey of Panama, during the construction of the canal. His results were published in *The Mammals of Panama* in 1920. In 1936 he assisted the United States government in negotiating with Mexico to protect migratory birds. Goldman's bibliography includes more than 200 titles. He named over 300 forms of mammals, most of them subspecies. About 50 mammals, birds, reptiles, molluscs and plants bear his name, for example Goldman's Woodrat *Neotoma goldmani*. Goldman Peak in Baja California was also named in his honour. He was President of the Biological Society of Washington, from 1927 until 1929, and of the American Society of Mammalogists, in 1946.

GOLIATH

Goliath Heron *Ardea goliath* (**Cretzschmar** 1827)
Goliath Coucal *Centropus goliath* (**Bonaparte** 1850)

Goliath of Gath (about 1,030 BC) was a Philistine warrior of giant size, who was killed with a sling shot by David, later King of the Jews. (See 1 Samuel 17.4, Old Testament of the Bible.)

GOODFELLOW

Goodfellow's Jungle Flycatcher *Rhinomyias goodfellowi* (**Ogilvie-Grant** 1905)
(Alt. Slaty-backed/Mindanao Jungle Flycatcher)
Goodfellow's Kingfisher *Ceyx goodfellowi* (Ogilvie-Grant 1905)
Goodfellow's Lory *Eos bornea goodfellowi* (Ogilvie-Grant 1907)
(Alt. [Buru] Red Lory)
Goodfellow's White-eye *Lophozosterops goodfellowi* (**Hartert** 1903)
(Alt. Black-masked White-eye)

Walter Goodfellow (1866–1953) was a British ornithologist and explorer. He discovered the Mikado Pheasant in Formosa and led the British Ornithologists' Union's Expedition to New Guinea. He collected live birds for Mrs **Johnstone**, a well-known aviculturist, who received an award for breeding the lorikeet named after her. Goodfellow's Tree Kangaroo *Dendrolagus goodfellowi* is also named after him. Goodfellow's collection was later acquired by the British Museum. He was awarded the British Ornithologists' Union Medal in 1912. **Ogilvie-Grant** described the the kingfisher from a specimen collected by Goodfellow in Mindanao.

GOODSON

Goodson's Pigeon *Columba goodsoni* (**Hartert** 1902)
(Alt. Dusky Pigeon)
Goodson's Pipit *Anthus leucophrys goodsoni* R **Meinertzhagen** 1920
(Alt. Plain-backed Pipit)

Arthur T Goodson (1873–1931) was an assistant ornithologist at the **Rothschild** Museum, which is now incorporated in the Natural History Museum, Tring. His father may have been Thomas Goodson, a smith in Tring who was dependent on the Rothschild family for custom. A butterfly, Goodson's Hairstreak *Cyanophrys goodson*, which is found in the USA, was probably named after him, by Clench in 1946.

GOSLING

Gosling's Apalis *Apalis goslingi* (**Alexander** 1908)

Captain G B Gosling (1872–1906) was an explorer and zoologist. He followed the Uele River, exploring and collecting from the Niger to the Nile, in 1904, on Boyd **Alexander**'s expedition.

GOSSE

Gosse's Macaw *Ara gossei* (**Rothschild** 1905)
(Alt. Yellow-headed Macaw)

Philip Henry Gosse (1810–1888) was an English naturalist, a Plymouth Brethren missionary and a science populariser, who is now best known for his attempt to reconcile biblical literalism with uniformitarianism. He tried to reconcile biblical ideas on creation with the growing evidence of geological eras of millions of years duration in his work *Omphalos: An Attempt to Untie the Geological Knot*, in which he advanced the theory that fossils had never lived but that God had inserted them into rocks during the Creation as a way of making the world appear older than it was!. His son, his only child, famously wrote *Father and Son*, and his birth was noted by Gosse in his diary as '*Received green swallow from Jamaica. E delivered of a son*'; he was clearly a man engrossed in his work! Gosse made a career of writing textbooks on a wide range of subjects, from Jamaican natural history to marine biology.

GOUDOT

Goudot's Guan *Chamaepetes goudotii* (**Lesson** 1828)
(Alt. Sickle-winged Guan)

Justin-Marie Goudot was a French zoologist who worked in Colombia from 1822 until

1843, being described by some as a '*furious collector of birds*'. He was the first head of the zoology department of the Colombian National Museum having been asked by **Cuvier** and **Humbolt**, on behalf of the new Vice-President, Francisco Antonio Zea, to create the department, in 1822. He was a noted collector of invertebrates and took many type specimens of, for example, millipedes. He wrote a paper on the Mountain Tapir *Tapirus pinchaque* in 1843; *Nouvelles observations sur le Tapir Pinchaque.*

GOULD

Gould's Albatross *Thalassarche chrysostoma* (Gould 1841)
(Alt. Grey-headed Albatross)
Gould's Broadbill *Serilophus lunatus* (Gould 1834)
(Alt. Silver-breasted/Hodgson's/Collared Broadbill)
Gould's Bronze Cuckoo *Chrysococcyx lucidus* (Gould 1859)
(Alt. Shining Bronze Cuckoo)
Gould's Coquette *Lophornis gouldii* (**Lesson** 1832)
(Alt. Dot-eared Coquette)
Gould's Dusky Plumeleteer *Chalybura urochrysia* (Gould 1861)
(Alt. Bronze-tailed/Black-vented Plumeleteer)
Gould's Emerald *Chlorostilbon elegans* (Gould 1860) [Extinct]
Gould's Euphonia *Euphonia gouldi* (P L **Sclater** 1857)
(Alt. Olive-backed Euphonia)
Gouldian Finch *Erythrura gouldiae* (Gould 1844)
Gould's Frogmouth *Batrachostomus stellatus* (Gould 1837)
Gould's Fulvetta *Alcippe brunnea* (Gould 1863)
(Alt. Gould's/Rufous-headed/Rufous-backed/Rufous-capped Tit-Babbler,
Dusky Fulvetta)
Gould's Harrier *Circus approximans gouldi* (**Peale** 1848)
(Alt. Australasian Swamp/Pacific Marsh Harrier)
Gould's Hermit *Phaethornis griseogularis* (Gould 1851)
(Alt. Grey-chinned Hermit)
Gould's Inca *Coeligena inca* (Gould 1852)
Gould's Jewelfront *Heliodoxa aurescens* (Gould 1846)
Gould's Parrotbill *Paradoxornis flavirostris* (Gould 1836)
(Alt. Black-breasted/Yellow-billed Parrotbill)
Gould's Petrel *Pterodroma leucoptera* (Gould 1844)
(Alt. White-winged/Sooty-capped/White-throated Petrel)
Gould's Red-tailed Black Cockatoo *Calyptorhynchus* (*banksii*) *macrorhynchus*
(Gould 1836)
Gould's Shortwing *Brachypteryx stellata* (Gould 1868)
Gould's Sunangel *Heliangelus micraster* Gould 1872
(Alt. Little Sunangel)
Gould's Sunbird *Aethopyga gouldiae* (**Vigors** 1831)
(Alt. Mrs Gould's/Blue-throated/Simla Yellow-backed Sunbird)
Gould's Toucanet *Selenidera gouldii* (**Natterer** 1837)
Gould's Turkey *Meleagris gallopavo mexicana* (Gould 1856)
(Alt. Wild Turkey)
Gould's Violet-ear *Colibri coruscans* (Gould 1846)
(Alt. Sparkling/Chequered/Columbina Violet-ear)
Gould's Zebra Dove *Geopelia placida* (Gould 1844)
(Alt. Peaceful Dove)

John Gould (1804–1881) was the son of a gardener at Windsor Castle who became an ilustrious British ornithologist, artist and taxidermist. Gould was born in Dorset, England, in 1804 and went on during his 76-year lifespan to be acknowledged around the world as

The Bird Man'. He was employed as a taxidermist by the newly formed Zoological Society of London and travelled widely in Europe, Asia, and Australia. He was arguably the greatest and certainly the most prolific publisher and original author of ornithological works in the world. From 1830 to 1881 in excess of 46 volumes of reference work were produced by him in colour. He published 41 works on birds, with 2,999 remarkably accurate illustrations by a team of artists, including his wife. His first book, on Himalayan birds, was based on skins shipped to London but later in his career he travelled to see birds in their natural habitats. In 1838 Gould and his wife, Elizabeth, arrived in Australia to spend 19 months studying and recording the natural history of the continent. By the time they left Gould had not only recorded most of Australia's known birds, and collected information on nearly 200 new species, but he had also gathered data for a major contribution to the study of Australian mammals. His best known works include: *The Birds of Europe, The Birds of Great Britain, The Birds of New Guinea* and *The Birds of Asia*. He also wrote monographs on the Macropodidae, Odontophorinae, Trochilidae and Pittidae. Gould was a commercial man and Victorian England was fascinated by the exotic, including those exquisite jewels the hummingbirds, a group with which his name is particularly associated. His superb paintings, and prints of these and other birds were greatly sought after, so much so that he probably had trouble keeping up with the demand. The large corpus of unpublished and unfinished work which he left at his death supports this. We touch on his relationship with **Sharpe** a great deal in this volume. Gould's Sunbird is more properly known as Mrs Gould's Sunbird (see **Mrs Gould** in section M). The Gouldian Finch so impressed him with its gorgeous plumage when he discovered it that he named it after his late wife, a name by which it is no longer known (See **Lady Gould**).

GRACE

Grace's Warbler *Dendroica graciae* (**Baird** 1865)

Grace Darlington Page [Née Coues] (1847–1925), was the sister of Dr Eliot **Coues.** She married Charles Albert Page, the United States Ambassador to Switzerland, in 1868. After his death she married Dana Estes, a publisher, in 1884. S F **Baird** described the warbler, which was collected by Coues, who asked him to name it after his sister who was just 18 at the time.

GRANT

Grant's Bluebill *Spermophaga poliogenys* (**Ogilvie-Grant** 1906)
  (Alt. Grant's Forest Weaver, Grant's Red-headed Bluebill)
Grant's Leaf Warbler *Phylloscopus subaffinis* (Ogilvie-Grant 1900)
  (Alt. Buff-throated Warbler)
Grant's Niltava *Cyornis hainanus* (Ogilvie-Grant 1900)
  (Alt. Hainan Blue Flycatcher)
Grant's Starling *Aplonis mystacea* (Ogilvie-Grant 1911)
  (Alt. Yellow-eyed Starling)
Grant's Wood Hoopoe *Phoeniculus damarensis* (Ogilvie-Grant 1901)
  (Alt. Violet Wood Hoopoe)

Captain Claude Henry Baxter Grant (1878–1958) was a British ornithologist and collector. He collected **Rudd**'s Lark and named it after the man who financed his collecting trips. He was Editor of the Bulletin of the British Ornithologists' Club from 1935 to 1940.

Grant was co-author of *Birds of Eastern and North Eastern Africa* and also wrote the *African Handbook of Birds* in 1952. **Ogilvie-Grant** described all the birds; we wonder whether he might have been a relative.

GRANT-MACKIE

Grant-Mackie's Wren *Pachyplichas jagmi* (Millener 1988) [Extinct]

Dr Jack A Grant-Mackie (1932–) is a palaeontologist. He teaches at the University of Auckland, New Zealand in the department of geology where his principal research interest concerns the Triassic-Jurassic marine macro-faunas of the southwest Pacific, especially molluscs, and their biogeography and correlation. His secondary research interest is New Zealand fossil birds, especially those of the Quaternary. He wrote (with eight other authors) the *Jurassic palaeo-biogeography of Australasia* in Memoirs of the Australasian Association of Palaeontologists, in 2000. He also wrote *Late Triassic-Jurassic palynofloral assemblages from Murihiku strata of New Zealand, and comparisons with China* with W-P Zhang, in the Journal of the Royal Society of New Zealand, in 2001. The scientific honorific is a 'joke' based on Grant-Mackie's initials, perpetrated by Millener, one of his PhD students, who wrote the description – but it is nonetheless valid.

GRAUER

Grauer's Green Broadbill *Pseudocalyptomena graueri* (**Rothschild** 1909)
(Alt. African Green/Grauer's Broadbill)
Grauer's Cuckoo-shrike *Coracina graueri* (**Neumann** 1908)
Grauer's Ground Thrush *Zoothera cameronensis graueri* Sassi 1908
(Alt. Black-eared Ground Thrush)
Grauer's Rush Warbler *Bradypterus gruaeri* (Neumann 1908)
(Alt. Grauer's Swamp/Scrub/Bush Warbler, Grauer's Warbler)
Grauer's Warbler *Graueria vittata* (**Hartert** 1908)

Rudolf Grauer (1870–1927) was a zoologist who collected extensively during an expedition to the Belgian Congo in 1909. He also has a gorilla named after him.

GRAY, G

Gray's Piping Guan *Pipile cumanensis grayi* (**Pelzeln** 1870)
(Alt. Blue-throated Piping Guan)
Gray's Robin *Turdus grayi* (**Bonaparte** 1838)
(Alt. Clay-coloured Robin, Clay-coloured Thrush, Gray's Thrush)
Gray's Shag *Phalacrocorax chalconotus* (G R Gray 1845)
(Alt. Bronze/Stewart Island Shag/Cormorant)
Gray's Tanager *Piranga rubriceps* (G R Gray 1844)
(Alt. Red-hooded Tanager)
Gray's Warbler *Locustella fasciolata* (G R Gray 1861)
(Alt. Gray's/Large Grasshopper Warbler)

George Robert Gray (1808–1872) was the younger brother of **John Edward Gray**. He was an assistant keeper ornithologist at the British Museum's Department of Zoology. He wrote *Genera of Birds* in 1844. He also wrote *A Fasciculus of the Birds of China* in 1871, which had illustrations by **Swainson**. Together with his brother he published a *Catalogue of the Mammalia and Birds of New Guinea in the Collection of the British Museum*, in 1859.

Although we have assigned most of the 'Gray' birds under the entry for J E Gray, many of the descriptions were written by his brother G R Gray. Some were named after one brother by the other brother, and some have later been named Gray's 'whatever' in recognition of the describer. In short, it is very difficult to separate the two so, when you see Gray's 'bird', it could commemorate either brother. We suggest you honour both!

GRAY, J

Gray's Brush Turkey *Macrocephalon maleo* (S **Müller** 1846)
(Alt. Maleo/Maleofowl])
Gray's Goshawk *Accipiter henicogrammus* (G R **Gray 1861**)
(Alt. Moluccan Goshawk)
Gray's Greybird *Coracina schisticeps* (G R Gray 1846)
(Alt. Grey-headed Cuckoo-shrike, White-winged/Philippine Greybird)
Gray's Honeyeater *Xanthotis polygramma* (G R Gray 1862)
(Alt. [Many-]Spotted Honeyeater)
Gray's Lark *Ammomanes grayi* (**Wahlberg** 1855)
(Gray's Sandlark)
Gray's Malimbe *Malimbus nitens* (J E Gray 1831)
Gray's Oriole *Oriolus phaeochromus* (**G R Gray 1861**)
(Alt. Dusky(Brown)/Halmahera/Moluccan Oriole)
Gray's Sapphire *Hylocharis grayi* (**DeLattre** & **Bourcier** 1846)
(Alt. Blue-headed/Puritan Sapphire)

John Edward Gray (1800–1875) was a British ornithologist and entomologist. He started work at the British Museum in 1824, with a temporary appointment at 15 shillings a day, but between 1840 and 1874 he was Curator of Birds and then head of the Department of Zoology. Gray published descriptions of a large number of animal species, including many Australian reptiles and mammals. He was the leading authority on many reptiles, including turtles. Gray was also an ardent philatelist and claimed that he was the world's first stamp collector. He worked at the museum with his brother **George Robert Gray** (see above) and together they published a *Catalogue of the Mammalia and Birds of New Guinea in the Collection of the British Museum* in 1859. He wrote *Gleanings from the Menagerie and Aviary at Knowsley Hall*, published between 1846 and 1850, which was illustrated by **Lear**. Gray suffered a severe stroke which paralysed his right side, including his writing hand, in 1869. Yet he continued to publish to the end of his life by dictating to his wife, Maria Emma; she had always worked with him as an artist and occasional co-author.

GRAYSON

Grayson's Parrotlet *Forpus cyanopygius insularis* (**Ridgway** 1888)
(Alt. Mexican/Tres-Marias Parrotlet)
Grayson's Robin *Turdus rufopalliatus* (**Lafresnaye** 1840)
(Alt. Rufous-backed Robin)
Grayson's Thrush *Turdus graysoni* (Ridgway 1882)

Andrew Jackson Grayson (1819–1869) was an American ornithologist and artist. Appropriately for a birdman, his father's middle name was Wren. He was considered to be the most accomplished bird painter in North America of his time, and was often referred to as 'the Audubon of the West'. When Grayson began to paint the birds of western America in 1853 there was no systematic avifaunal record from the Sierra Nevada to the Pacific Ocean. Grayson regarded his *Birds of the Pacific Slope* as a completion of Audubon's *Birds of America*, which did not include all the birds of the West. The Smithsonian Institution recruited Grayson as a field ornithologist and he became one of their principal collectors for California, Mexico and its offshore islands. He discovered many new species, some of which were named after him. He also wrote species accounts, recorded scientific data and published articles on travel and natural history. However, his greatest achievement was his paintings of birds, which are virtually colour-perfect and depict their subjects in natural settings and activities. Over 16 years he painted more than 175 bird portraits, of which 156 survive, preserved in a single collection. Ill-luck often beset Grayson in his latter years. He was shipwrecked; his son was mysteriously murdered; he was bankrupted; and he contracted yellow fever on a field expedition, from which he died. The robin and the thrush may be the same species. They have been split by some and lumped by others, and their taxonomic status is still uncertain.

GREENWAY

Greenway's Blood Pheasant *Ithaginis cruentus holoptilus* (**Riley** 1925)
(Alt. Rock's Blood Pheasant)

Dr James Cowan Greenway Jr (1903–1989) was an American collector and ornithologist. He was a close friend of **Delacour**, whom he accompanied on expeditions to Vietnam in 1929 to 1930 and 1938 to 1939. A major objective of these expeditions was to search for pheasants in general, and Edwards' Pheasants in particular, and together they wrote *VIIe Expedition Ornithologique en Indochine française*, published in 1940. Greenway was one of the authors/editors (with **Peters**, **Mayr** and others) of *Check-list of Birds of the* World, published in 1931 and, with Mayr, he produced the second edition. He worked with Mayr and **Griscom** and in 1959 was Curator of Birds at the Museum of Comparative Zoology, at Harvard.

GREY

Grey's Fruit Dove *Ptilinopus greyii* (**Bonaparte** 1857)
(Alt. Red-bellied Fruit Dove)

Sir George Grey (1812–1898) was a soldier, explorer, colonial governor, premier and scholar. He explored Western Australia on government-financed expeditions, to Hanover Bay and to Shark Bay, between 1837 to 1839. On the first expedition Grey was speared by an Aborigine, whom he shot, but he nevertheless championed the cause of assimilation. In 1845 he was appointed Governor of New Zealand, where he faced even greater difficulties than in South Australia. Grey's greatest success was his management of Maori affairs. He scrupulously observed the terms of the Treaty of Waitangi and assured Maoris that their rights to land were fully recognised. In 1853 he became Governor of the Cape Colony and High Commissioner for South Africa. Grey's problem there, again, was race relations. He sought to convert the frontier tribes to Christianity; to 'civilise' them. Grey supported mission schools and built a hospital for African patients. He returned to New Zealand where he was elected to its parliament. While politics left him little time to devote to scholarship, he was a keen naturalist and botanist, and he established extensive collections and important libraries at Cape Town and Auckland. He wrote books on Australian Aboriginal vocabularies and on his Western Australian explorations, as well as taking a scholarly interest in the Maori language and culture.

GRIMWOOD

Grimwood's Longclaw *Macronyx grimwoodi* (**Benson** 1955)

Major Ian R Grimwood (1912–?) was the Chief Game Warden of Kenya for many years in the mid-20th century (1959–1964) and he had a great hand in rescuing the Oryx *Oryx gazella* from the edge of extinction. He acted as guide in Africa to Colonel Charles A Lindbergh, the famous airman who made the first solo transatlantic flight in *The Spirit of St Louis*. In 1972 he was awarded the World Wildlife Fund gold medal. The citation was '...*for his dedication to the conservation of wildlife in Africa, Asia and Latin America; his contribution to the establishment of national parks and game reserves in Kenya, Pakistan and Peru, and to the survival of endangered species such as oryx and vicuña.*'

GRINNELL, G

Grinnell's Chickadee *Parus gambeli abbreviatus* (**Ridgway** 1886)
   (Alt. Mountain Chickadee)
Grinnell's Jay *Cyanocitta stelleri carbonacea* (Grinnell 1900)
   (Alt. Steller's/Osgood's/Queen Charlotte's Jay)
Grinnell's Screech Owl *Otus kennicottii* (**Elliot** 1867)
   (Alt. Western Screech Owl)
Grinnell's Waterthrush *Seiurus noveboracensis notabilis* (Ridgway 1886)
   (Alt. Northern Waterthrush)

George Bird Grinnell (1848–1938) was an American ornithologist, publisher, and conservationist. He went to the school in John James Audubon's mansion in Assigning, New York, which was near the Grinnell family home. George and his brothers and sisters knew the Audubon family well and played in the grounds and the buildings of the estate, including the barn that housed collections of Audubon's bird skins and specimens. Despite a poor degree, he talked his way on to a fossil collecting expedition, in 1870, and then served as the naturalist on Custer's expedition to the Black Hills in 1874. He returned to study and gained a doctorate in palaeontology in 1880. He was very interested in Native Americans and got on so well with them that many tribes had names for him. The Pawnee called him 'White Wolf' and eventually adopted him into their tribe. The Gros Ventre called him 'Gray Clothes', the Black Feet 'Fisher Hat' and the Cheyenne called him 'Wikis', which means 'bird', observing that he came and went with the seasons. He wrote 26 books including *The Cheyenne Indians – Their History and Ways of Life*, in 1923. He was also editor of *Forest and Stream*, the leading natural history magazine in North America. He was the founder of the Audubon Society in 1886 and began publication of its *Audubon Magazine* the next year. In only three months more than 38,000 people joined the society. Overwhelmed by the response, Grinnell had to disband the group in 1888 (although it was subsequently reconstituted). He was also an early member of the American Ornithologists' Union from shortly after its foundation in 1883. He became an advisor to Theodore Roosevelt and Glacier National Park was established through his efforts. He was photographer on the Harriman Expedition.

The National Wildlife Confederation Hall of Fame citation reads: '*To accomplish his goal of ensuring effective enforcement of game laws, Grinnell advocated a game warden system to be financed by small fees from all hunters. The notion that the traditionally free and unstructured activity of hunting must be financially supported by sportsmen themselves and regulated on the state level was a revolutionary concept that would become a cornerstone of game management. Realizing that the enforcement of game laws was the solution to only half a problem, Grinnell turned his attention to habitat conservation. In 1882, he began an editorial effort to persuade America to manage timberlands efficiently to yield a sustained 'crop.' He was also drawn to the plight of Yellowstone National Park, launching a campaign to expose Federal neglect and ensure the park against commercialisation. Grinnell's efforts attracted the admiration and support of Theodore Roosevelt, an avid reader of Forest and Stream. Before he ascended to the presidency, Roosevelt launched his career as a conservationist by joining Grinnell's battle for Yellowstone. When Roosevelt became president in 1901, the conservation philosophy first formulated by George Bird Grinnell became the basis of the American conservation program.*'

GRINNELL, J

Grinnell's Crossbill *Loxia curvirostra grinnelli* Griscom 1937
   (Alt. Red Crossbill)
Grinnell's Shrike *Lanius ludovicianus grinnelli* (Grinnell & Miller 1944)
   (Alt. Loggerhead/Nelson's Shrike)

Joseph Grinnell (1877–1939) was instrumental in shaping the philosophy of the United States National Park System. He was director of the Museum of Vertebrate Zoology from

1908 until his death in 1939 and an '*incomparable authority on the birds and mammals of the West Coast*'. When he died in 1939 his post was taken by **Miller**, with whom he had often published. It was he who coined the expression 'niche' in the context of 'competitive exclusion' and the expression is now used universally for almost any situation where species (including people) have established an exclusive position. 'Niche marketing' is an example of how the term has been over-used. Grinnell was also editor of The Condor and co-author with A H Miller of *The Distribution of the Birds of California*.

GRISCOM

Griscom's Antwren *Myrmotherula brachyura ignota* Griscom 1929
(Alt. Pygmy Antwren)

Ludlow Griscom (1890–1959) was an American ornithologist. He kept notes on the birds he observed on field trips throughout the state of Massachusetts during the 1930s, the 1940s and the 1950s. He was an early advocate of identifying birds through binoculars by field marks, rather than by shooting them and 'collecting specimens'. He was a pioneer of conservation and in many ways born before his time. For example, while he was in Guatemala collecting birds for the American Museum of Natural History in the early 1930s, he noted that coffee growers left much of the natural forest to shade their plants and that '*in such growth, the avifauna was little, if any, different from its original condition*', something that went otherwise unnoticed for decades. The Conventions of the American Birding Association have bestowed since 1980 an award named the 'Ludlow Griscom Distinguished Birder Award'. Griscom's Antwren has been recently proven to be conspecific with Short-billed Antwren *M. obscura*, but the name *ignota* has priority.

GRUBER

Gruber's Hawk *Buteo solitarius* (**Peale** 1848)
(Alt. Hawaiian Hawk)

August Gruber (1853–1938) was primarily, a protozoologist, and a Professor of Zoology at the University of Freiburg.

GUERIN

Guerin's Helmetcrest *Oxypogon guerinii* (A Boissonneau 1840)
(Alt. Bearded Helmetcrest)

Felix Edouard Guerin-Meneville (1799–1874) was an entomologist. He is most well known for his illustrated work *Iconographie du Règne Animal de G. Cuvier 1829–44*, a complement to **Cuvier**'s and Latreille's work (which lacked illustrations), and also for introducing silkworm breeding to France. There is a Felix-Edouard Guerin-Meneville Collection of Crustacea at The Academy of Natural Sciences, Philadelphia. He made the first description of Rouget's Rail *Rougetius rougetii*. He seems to have been something of an all-rounder, with scientific papers on plants, insects and others to his name.

GUILDING

Guilding's Amazon *Amazona guildingii* (**Vigors** 1837)
(Alt. St Vincent Parrot)

The Reverend Lansdown Guilding BA (1797–1831) was an amateur naturalist. He was educated at Oxford in England but was born and died on St Vincent, in the West Indies.

Guilding left his collection to the British Natural History Museum. In an article, in 1835 Edward **Blyth** quotes him as saying '*Domestic birds, from flying little, have their muscles relaxed, or, perhaps, they never acquire their natural strength, for want of exercise. I have observed the geese in Worcestershire, in harvest time, to take very long flights; but, though they went on boldly, they never ascended very far into the air.*'

GUIMET

Guimet's Flutterer *Klais guimeti* (**Bourcier** 1843)
(Alt. Violet-headed Hummingbird)

Jean Baptiste Guimet (1795–1871) was a French chemist whose fortune was based on the invention of a blue dye, which made him extremely famous in his time. His son travelled the world collecting art, artefacts and natural exhibits for their own museum.

GUISE

Guise's Honeyeater *Ptiloprora guisei* (**De Vis** 1894)
(Syn.Green-eyed/Striated/Brown-backed/Rufous-backed/Red-backed Honeyeater)

GÜLDENSTÄDT

Güldenstädt's Redstart *Phoenicurus erythrogastrus* (Guldenstädt 1775)
(Alt. White-winged Redstart)

Professor Johann Anton Güldenstädt (1745–1781) was a Baltic-German, who was born in Riga in Latvia, at that time part of the Russian Empire. He was a physician and natural scientist who became a professor at the Academy of Sciences in St Petersburg. His *Reisen durch Russland und im caucasischen Gebürge* was published posthumously, in St Petersburg, between 1787 and 1791. He was the first to describe a number of birds, including the Ferruginous Duck *Aythya nyroca*. The redstart may have been collected by Güldenstädt, as he certainly travelled extensively, everywhere from Georgia to Finland, and he is known to have made expeditions to the Caucasus and Transcaucasus regions, where the bird occurs, between 1768 and 1773.

GUNDLACH

Gundlach's Hawk *Accipiter gundlachii* (**Lawrence** 1860)
Gundlach's Mockingbird *Mimus gundlachii* (**Cabanis** 1855)
(Alt. Bahama Mockingbird)

Juan Cristóbal Gundlach [originally Johannes Christoff] (1810–1896) was a German-born, naturalised Cuban ornithologist and collector. He began to learn the art of dissection and taxidermy by watching his older brother, who was a zoology student. An event that nearly cost him his life ironically allowed him to follow his chosen profession with impunity. During a hunting accident, he discharged a small gun so close to his nose that he lost his sense of smell. Following this, he could calmly dissect, macerate and clean skeletons without discomfort. He was a curator at the University of Marburg and later at the Senckenberg Museum of Frankfurt. In 1839 he took part in a collecting expedition to Cuba and stayed on and collected there, and in Puerto Rico. He wrote the first major work on the island's birds, *Ornitología Cubana*, in 1876, and is commemorated in the scientific and common names of several species, including the hawk, Antillean Nighthawk *Chordeiles gundlachii*, and Cuban Vireo *Vireo gundlachii*. He was zealous and single-minded and tended to keep what he collected- and to prepare it and describe it for science himself.

GUNNING

Gunning's Robin *Sheppardia gunningi* (Haagner 1909)
(Alt. East Coast Akalat)

Dr Jan Willem Bowdewyn Gunning (1860–1913) was a Dutch physician. He went to South Africa in 1884 and was appointed Director at the (now) Transvaal Museum, in Pretoria, in 1896 a post which he held until shortly before his death. He founded the Pretoria National Zoo, which he seems to have started in his garden. Gunning was co-founder of the African Ornithologists' Union. Austin **Roberts** worked under him. (The generic name honours Peter **Sheppard**, a fellow South African ornithologist.)

GUNNISON

Gunnison's Sage Grouse *Centrocercus minimus* (Young, Braun, Oyler-Mccance, Huff & Quinn, 2000)
(Alt. Gunnison Sage Grouse)

This bird is named after Gunnison County in Colorado, USA, and not after a person. The species has recently been separated from the Sage Grouse *C. urophasianus*. It is endemic to a few counties in Colorado and Utah. A rodent, Gunnison's Prairie Dog *Cynomys gunnisoni* is also named after the region.

GURNEY

Gurney's Buzzard *Buteo poecilochrous* (Gurney 1879)
(Alt. Puna Hawk)
Gurney's Eagle *Aquila gurneyi* (G R **Gray** 1861)
Gurney's Ground Thrush *Zoothera gurneyi* (**Hartlaub** 1864)
(Alt. Orange [Ground] Thrush)
Gurney's Pitta *Pitta gurneyi* Hume 1875
(Alt. Black-breasted Pitta)
Gurney's Sugarbird *Promerops gurneyi* (**J Verreaux** 1871)

John Henry Gurney (1819–1890) was a banker in Norwich, England, and an amateur ornithologist who worked at the British Natural History Museum. Most of his writing was on the birds of his own county. However, he also wrote on collections of African birds, as well as editing the works of others. His son, who shared the same name, (1848–1922), was also an ornithologist. **Hume** named the Pitta as a tribute to his ornithological colleague J H Gurney (the elder).

GUSTAV

Gustav's Parakeet *Brotogeris cyanoptera gustavi* (**Berlepsch** 1889)
(Alt. Cobalt-winged Parakeet)

Gustaaf Schlegel (1840–1903) was a Dutch ornithologist and sinologist. He was the first to describe the recently rediscovered Chinese Crested Tern *Sterna bernsteini*, in 1863.

GUY

Guy 's [White-tailed] Hermit *Phaethornis guy* (**Lesson** 1883)
(Alt. Green Hermit)

J Guy was a French naturalist. Both **Lesson** in 1833 and, later, **Gould** described and illustrated this hummingbird.

HAAST

Haast's Eagle *Harpagornis moorei* (Haast 1872) [Extinct]

Dr Sir Johann Franz Julius von Haast, KCMG (1822–1887), a geologist, was born in Bonn and died in Christchurch, New Zealand. He became a naturalised New Zealander when he decided to remain in that country, where he worked for the Canterbury provincial government. He was instrumental in founding the Canterbury Museum and became its first director. He described the eagle in 1872 from bones discovered a few years earlier. The binomial honours George Moore, who owned the Glenmark Station, where many subfossil bird bones were excavated. The Haast Pass in the Southern Alps, the Haast River and the town of Haast, all in New Zealand, are named after him, and the Franz Josef Glacier was named by Haast to honour the Austro-Hungarian Emperor.

HACHISUKA

Hachisuka's Sunbird *Aethopyga primigenius* (Hachisuka 1941)
(Alt. Grey-hooded Sunbird)

Masauyi Uji Hachisuka, 18th Marquis Hachisuka (1903–1953), was a Japanese ornithologist who studied biology at Cambridge. In 1929 he led an expedition of 50 men to the top of Mount Apo on Mindanao, in the Philippines, and he established a bird collecting centre at Galong. He published *Birds of the Philippine Islands*, from 1931 to 1935, and *A Handbook of the Birds of Iceland*, in 1927. He worked and wrote a great deal in the early 1950s. He collected the sunbird which he described himself.

HAHN

Hahn's Macaw *Diopsittaca nobilis nobilis* (**Ridgway** 1912)
(Alt. Red-shouldered Macaw)

Dr Carl Wilhelm Hahn (1786–1835) was a German (Bavarian) zoologist. He was the son of a palace gardener, who was originally from Hungary. He called himself a 'nature researcher' and he was very proficient at drawing, but did not or could not colour his illustrations himself. He moved from Fürth to Nürnberg (Nuremberg) in 1816, as there were no competent illustrators/colourists to be found in Fürth. Many of his drawings were of insects and spiders, as well as fishes, as he was primarily an entomologist, but most of his writings seemed to have been on spiders, including his *Monagraphie der Spinnen* in 1820. Hahn published an ornithological atlas in 1834 and he was the author of *Die Vögel aus Asien, Afrika. America und Neuholland,* which appeared in various parts between 1819 and 1836. He complained to the Bavarian Public Natural History Society that he had spent all his money in the pursuit of science and his art. He died in Nürnberg of a pulmonary infection. The old scientific name for the northern Brazilian Macaw population was *Ara* (now *Diopsittaca*) *nobilis hahni* (Souancé, 1856). **Ridgway**, who recorded and named the bird, transferred the superseded subspecies name to the vernacular to honour the original scientist, Hahn.

HALL, H

Hall's Babbler *Pomatostomus halli* (Cowles 1964)
(Alt. Hall's White-throated Babbler)

Major Harold Wesley Hall (1888–?) was an Australian zoologist, collector, explorer and philanthropist as well as an entrepreneur, who promoted 'Hall's fortified wines'. Harold Hall was interested in supporting research in natural history, having made considerable money through the Mt Morgan gold fields. In 1961, he was approached by James D MacDonald, who headed the Bird Room at the British Museum (Natural History) from the 1930s until his retirement in 1968. MacDonald secured sponsorship of £25,000 (£5,000 p/a for 5 years) to undertake the museum's 'Harold Hall Expeditions'. In 1963 MacDonald led the first of five 'Harold Hall bird collecting expeditions' to Australia to rebuild the Australian bird collections, which had been lost because of the sale of the **Mathews** and **Rothschild** collections to American institutions. Other Bird Room staff led the other expeditions, including Mrs Pat **Hall** (see next entry), who subsequently edited a book on the findings of all five expeditions. Peter **Colston** also took part in several of the expeditions.

HALL, P

Hall's Greenbul *Andropadus hallae* (**Prigogine** 1972)
(Alt. Mrs Hall's Greenbul)

[Beryl] Patricia Hall (1917–) is an ornithologist and was a voluntary assistant – and later an Honorary Associate – of the British Natural History Museum, who worked in the Bird Room from 1947 until 1971. She took part in museum expeditions to South West Africa (now Namibia) in 1949/50 with J D Macdonald and Colonel **Cave**, to Bechuanaland (now Botswana) in 1950, 1957 and 1962, and to Angola in 1957. She also led the third **Harold Hall** expedition to Australia, in 1965. She was the author (with R E **Moreau**) of *An Atlas of Speciation in African Passerine Birds*, in 1970, and she edited *Birds of the Harold Hall Australian Expeditions 1962–1970*, in 1974. She has written two autobiographical books; *What a Way to Win a War*, in 1978 and *A Hawk from a Handsaw*, in 1993. Pat Hall now lives in Hampshire, England. She was awarded the Union Medal of the British Ornithologists' Union in 1973. There are three or four bird subspecies that bear her name in their scientific forms. The greenbul was originally thought to be an aberrant melanistic individual of the Little Green Bulbul *Pycnonotus virens*.

HALL, R

Hall's Giant Petrel *Macronectes halli* (**Mathews** 1912)
(Alt. Northern Giant Petrel)

Robert Hall (1867–1949) was an Australian naturalist and ornithologist. He was a founder member of the Royal Australian Ornithologists' Union and its president from 1912 to 1913, as well as curator of the Tasmanian Museum and Botanical Gardens from 1908 until 1912, and thereafter an orchard grower in Tasmania. Hall was a keen collector and parts of his private bird and egg collections are in the Tasmanian Museum and the Australian National Museum, Melbourne. His Siberian collection is held at the Natural History Museum, at Tring, England, and was obtained in 1903 with a certain Ernie Trebilcock. He wrote a number of papers including *Notes on a collection of bird skins from the Fitzroy River, northwestern Australia*, around 1900. **Mathews** initially described the petrel as a race of (Southern) Giant Petrel *Macronectes giganteus*, from a specimen collected by Dr R **McCormick** on the Antarctic expedition led by Sir James **Ross**.

HALLSTROM

Hallstrom's Parrot *Psittacella madaraszi hallstromi* (**Mayr** & **Gilliard** 1951)
(Alt. Madarasz's Tiger [Ground]Parrot, Plain-breasted Little Parrot)

Sir Edward John Lees Hallstrom (1886–1970) was born in Coonamble, New South Wales, Australia. He was a pioneer of refrigeration, a philanthropist and leading aviculturist. He began work in a furniture factory at the age of 13, but he later opened his own factory to make ice-chests and then wooden cabinets for refrigerators. He eventually designed and manufactured the first popular domestic Australian refrigerator. Hallstrom made generous donations to medical research, children's hospitals and the Taronga Zoo in Sydney, becoming an honorary life director of the zoo. In 1940 he commissioned the artist Cayley to paint all of the Australian parrots. Twenty-nine large watercolours were produced and presented to the Royal Zoological Society of New South Wales. He visited New Guinea (home of the parrot named after him) in 1950. There is a fine research collection of 1,600 rare books on Asia and the Pacific known as the Hallstrom Pacific Collection. It was purchased with funds given to the Commonwealth government, in 1948, by Hallstrom for the purpose of establishing a library of Pacific affairs and colonial administration. The National Library transferred the collection to the University of New South Wales Library, on permanent loan. Among the rare books in the collection is John Gould's *Birds of New Guinea*. In the 1950s he established a centre in the southern highlands of Papua New Guinea from which, ostensibly, to introduce local sheep farming but his real reason was to have a base from which a well-known collector, Fred W Shaw Mayer (after whom *Astrapia mayeri* is named) could devote all his time to collecting birds of paradise specimens for him and the Sydney Zoo. He is credited with enabling the rapid breeding of captive Golden-shouldered Parrots *Psephotus chrysopterygius* at Taronga Zoo in Sydney in the 1950s. However, there was corruption, which involved trafficking in rare and endangered species during his time as director there and he stands accused of giving in to pressure to appoint the corrupt officials who carried out this trade. The rare New Guinea Singing Dog *Canis hallstromi* commemorates him in the binomial.

HAMMOND, W A

Hammond's Flycatcher *Empidonax hammondii*
(**Xantus** 1858)

Dr William Alexander Hammond (1828–1900) was Surgeon-General of the United States army. He collected birds for **Baird**. Through him **Xantus** got to work with Baird and so named the flycatcher after him in gratitude.

HAMMOND, W O

Hammond's Petrel *Puffinus mauretanicus* (**Lowe** 1921)
(Alt. Balearic Shearwater)

W O Hammond was a banker who lived and worked in Canterbury, Kent, England. He is noted for his watercolour portraits of 360 British birds. They were never exhibited publicly yet were particularly admired by Edward Wilson of the Antarctic, another accomplished bird artist, who commented on their '*refinement, truth and exactness*'. As a wealthy gentleman he was a hobbyist rather than a professional artist. His descendants recently sold the portraits to the Canterbury Museum. They are all quite small – almost miniatures – and are bound into several volumes.

HARCOURT

Harcourt's Storm Petrel *Oceanodroma* (*Hydrobates*) *castro* (Harcourt 1851)
(Alt. Madeiran Storm Petrel, Band-rumped Storm Petrel)

Edwin Vernon Harcourt (1825–1891) was an English naturalist. He was author of *Sketch of Madeira Containing Information for the Traveller or Invalid Visitor*, in which he describes the petrel. **Darwin**, in *The Origin of Species*, refers to him as a man who was '*very knowledgeable about Madeira*'.

HARDY

Hardy's Pygmy Owl *Glaucidium hardyi* Vielliard 1989
(Alt. Amazonian Pygmy Owl)

John William (Bill) Hardy (1930–) is an American ornithologist and author. After graduating from the Southern Illinois University he completed an MA at Michigan State University and a PhD at the University of Kansas. Thereafter he was Professor of Biology at Occidental College, Los Angeles, from 1961 to 1973. He went on to be Curator (now Curator Emeritus) of Ornithology and Bioacoustics at the Florida Museum of Natural History, at the University of Florida, from 1973 until 1995. Hardy was a pioneer of studies of vocal and social behaviour in jays and parrots, but he is best known for his series of more than two dozen 'sound monographs' issued on audio cassette, including *Sounds of Florida Birds*, in 1998, and the most recent edition *Voices of the New World Owls*, in 1999, as well as *Voices of the Tinamous* among others. He was the founder of the Florida Museum of Natural History Bioacoustic Laboratory and Archive, which has grown to become the second largest (in number of bird species represented) in the Western Hemisphere. A subspecies of Red-bellied Woodpecker *Melanerpes* (*Centurus*) *carolinus harpaceus* is partly named after him (*harpaceus* is a compound of pieces of three people's names: J W Hardy, E C Pielou and George J Wallace).

HARDWICKE

Hardwicke's Leafbird *Chloropsis hardwickii* (**Jardine** & Selby 1830)
(Alt. Orange-bellied Leafbird)

Major-General Thomas Hardwicke (1756–1835) served with the Bengal Artillery, which in his day was a regiment in the Bengal Army of the Honourable East India Company. He was an amateur naturalist, who is credited with being the first to make the Red Panda *Ailurus fulgens* widely known, through a paper which he presented to the Linnean Society of London in 1821; *Description of a new genus...from the Himalaya chain of hills between Nepaul [sic] and the Snowy Mountains*. **Cuvier** stole a march on Hardwicke in naming the Red Panda because Hardwicke's return to England was delayed.

HARINGTON

Harington's Babbler *Stachyris* (*rufifrons*) *ambigua* (Harington 1915)

Col Herbert Hasting Harington (1868–1916) was an English soldier and amateur naturalist. He wrote *Harington's Birds of Burma*, which was published in 1909.

HARLAN

Harlan's Hawk *Buteo jamaicaensis harlani* (**Audubon** 1830)
(Alt. Red-tailed Hawk)

Dr Richard Harlan (1796–1843) was a physician. **Audubon** named this distinctive dark subspecies of the common Red-tailed Hawk in honour of his friend. He said upon bestowing the honour, "*This I might have done sooner, had not I waited until a species should occur, which in size and importance should bear some proportion to my gratitude toward that learned and accomplished friend.*" Harlan, a young Quaker doctor, was a supporter of Audubon in the bitter feud that developed among members of the Philadelphia Academy of Natural Sciences, in 1823, between followers of the deceased Alexander **Wilson**, including George **Ord**, who had taken on the task of finishing Wilson's bird volumes, and Audubon's supporters, who favoured his more 'artistic' style of bird of painting. Ord's campaign against Audubon succeeded in denying him membership of the academy for many years. Harlan was also an amateur palaeontologist and helped discover the first American plesiosaur. He also published *Fauna Americana*.

HARMAN

Harman's Eared Pheasant *Crossoptilon harmani* (**Elwes** 1881)
(Alt. Tibetan/Elwes's Eared Pheasant)

Lieutenant H J Harman (1850–1883) was a surveyor and an officer in the British Indian army.

HARRIS, E

Harris's Hawk *Parabuteo unicinctus harrisi* (**Audubon** 1837)
Harris's Sparrow *Zonotrichia querula* (**Nuttall** 1840)
Harris's Woodpecker *Picoides villosus harrisi* (Audubon 1838)
(Alt. Hairy Woodpecker)

Edward Harris (1799–1863) was a New Jersey farmer and amateur ornithologist. The hawk was named by **Audubon** to honour his friend, who had helped him financially in 1823 during the preparation of his *Birds of America* when Audubon, in his own words had been reduced '*to the lowest degree of indigence.*' Audubon had then just experienced a humiliating departure from Philadelphia, where supporters of the deceased Alexander **Wilson** had succeeded in denying him membership into the Academy of Natural Science (see **Harlan** above). Harris bought several of Audubon's paintings and gave him an extra $100 in appreciation of his talent. Audubon called Harris '*one of the best friends I have in the world,*' and in his honour he also dedicated the sparrow (described by **Nuttall**) and the subspecies of the Hairy Woodpecker.

HARRIS, J

Harris' Penguin *Marplesornis novaezealandiae* (**Marples** 1960) [Extinct]

John Williams Harris (1808–1872) was English born and was variously a farmer, a trader and a whaler. He was one of the first Europeans to settle in Poverty Bay, New Zealand. He established the first whaling station there and travelled to Sydney to buy equipment for it. He took with him on that voyage a bone from a large bird, and Richard Owen used it, in 1838, to verify the previous existence of the Moa in New Zealand. We believe he was honoured in the name of the penguin because of this. His collection of specimens, mostly birds, is housed in the Tullie House Museum, in Cumbria, England.

HARTERT

Hartert's Camaroptera *Camaroptera brachyura harterti* (Zedlitz 1911)
   (Alt. Green-backed Camaroptera)
Hartert's Double-eyed Fig Parrot *Cyclopsitta diophthalma virago* (Hartert 1895)
Hartert's Fairy Lorikeet *Charmosyna pulchella rothschildi* (Hartert 1930)
Hartert's Flycatcher *Ficedula harterti* (**Sieber** 1928)
   (Alt. Sumba Flycatcher)
Hartert's Orange-fronted Hanging Parrot *Loriculus aurantifrons meeki*
   (Hartert 1895)
Hartert's Pygmy Parrot *Micropsitta bruijnii necopinata* Hartert 1925
   (Alt. Red-breasted Pygmy Parrot)
Hartert's White-eye *Zosterops luteirostris* (Hartert 1904)
   (Alt. Splendid/Gizo White-eye)
Hartert's Woodstar *Acestrura harterti* (Hartert, 1897)

Ernst Johann Otto Hartert (1859–1933) was a German ornithologist and oologist. He wrote *Die Vögel der paläarktischen Fauna* and collaborated with many others in writings from the 1890s through to the 1920s. He travelled extensively, often on behalf of his employer Walter **Rothschild** (later Lord Rothschild). He was the ornithological curator of Rothchild's private museum at Tring, which later became an annexe to the British Museum (Natural History), housing all of the bird skins. The woodstar is known only from the type specimen from Colombia and is a hybrid.

HARTLAUB

Hartlaub's Babbler *Turdoides hartlaubii* (**Bocage** 1868)
   (Alt. Angola Babbler)
Hartlaub's Bustard *Lissotis hartlaubii* (**Heuglin** 1863)
Hartlaub's Duck *Pteronetta hartlaubi* (**Cassin** 1860)
   (Alt. Hartlaub's Goose/Teal)
Hartlaub's Francolin *Francolinus* (*Pternistis*) *hartlaubi* (Bocage 1870)
Hartlaub's Gull *Larus* (*novaehollandiae*) *hartlaubii* (Bruch 1853)
   (Alt. King Gull)
Hartlaub's Jay *Cissilopha melanocyaneus* (**Fischer** & **Reichenow** 1884)
   (Alt. Bushy-crested Jay)
Hartlaub's Marsh Widow *Euplectes hartlaubi* (Bocage 1878)
   (Alt. Marsh Widowbird)
Hartlaub's Sheathbill *Chionis minor* (Fischer & Reichenow 1904)
   (Alt. Black-faced/Kerguelen/Lesser Sheathbill)
Hartlaub's Sunbird *Nectarinia hartlaubi* (Hartlaub 1857)
   (Alt. Príncipe Sunbird)

Hartlaub's Turaco *Tauraco hartlaubi* (Fischer & Reichenow 1884)
Hartlaub's Warbler *Parula superciliosa* (Hartlaub 1844)
   (Alt. Crescent-chested Warbler)

Karel Johan Gustav Hartlaub (1814–1900) was an academic and explorer. He was Professor of Zoology at Bremen and collected in East Africa in 1857. He trained as a medical doctor but his hobby was 'exotic' ornithology and he published a number of papers on African birds, including checklists. He collaborated with **Finsch** on a book on the birds of Polynesia. He also founded the *Journal für Ornithologie* with **Cabanis**. Many people sent him specimens, which he eventually donated to the Hamburg Museum. He wrote the first descriptions of over 30 southern African birds.

HARWOOD

Harwood's Francolin *Francolinus harwoodi* (Blundell & Lovat 1899)

Leonard Harwood was an English naturalist and taxidermist. As well as the bird, he has a mayfly *Cheumatopsyche harwoodi*, a Kenyan gerbil *Gerbillus harwoodi*, a beetle *Atheta harwoodi* and another arthropod *Physatocheila harwoodi* named in his honour. The francolin was originally thought to be an Ethiopian endemic, but it is actually very widely distributed.

HASBROUCK

Hasbrouck's Screech Owl *Otus asio hasbroucki* (**Ridgway** 1914)
(Alt. Eastern Screech Owl)

Dr Edwin Marble Hasbrouck (1866–1956) was an ornithologist and physician, who was active in Texas in the 1880s. He graduated from Georgetown Medical School in 1895 and began his medical practice in 1897. He was a doctor for some years, attached to a survey team in Texas running telegraph and powerlines. He became a captain in the United States army medical corps in the First World War after which he was in the Veterans Administration as an 'examining surgeon'. He wrote several papers; *Summer birds of Eastland County, Texas* in The Auk in 1889, *Evolution and dichromatism in the genus Megascops* in The American Naturalist in 1893 and others on the Carolina Parakeet *Conuropsis carolinensis* and the Ivory-billed Woodpecker *Campephilus principalis*. David Ervin Cummins of Sarasota Florida, USA, E M Hasbrouck's grandson told us '*I remember, in about nineteen thirty-something, my grandfather taking me down to the Natural History Museum (I think) and showing me his work site and thousands and thousands of drawers of bird skins. He was taking each skin, checking for ID, noting condition and tagging all written by hand. He spent many years in his retirement doing this kind of volunteer work*'. Eastern Screech Owls live in eastern North America and have at least six allopatric subspecies. A number, including the one above, are named for people.

HAUXWELL

Hauxwell's Thrush *Turdus hauxwelli* (**Lawrence** 1869)

J Hauxwell was an English bird collector mentioned by Henry Walter Bates in *The Naturalist on the River Amazon*, first published in 1864. At one point Bates writes of being shown how to use '*a blow-gun, by Julio, a Juri Indian, then in the employ of Mr. Hauxwell, an English bird-collector*'. We can surmise that Hauxwell's Thrush was first collected by this method, probably much better than shooting as it would not damage the bird skin. Hauxwell is also commemorated in the scientific names of other birds, such as the Plain-throated Antwren *Myrmotherula hauxwelli* and other animals, including the dragonfly *Mnesarete hauxwelli*.

HEERMANN

Heermann's Gull *Larus heermanni* (**Cassin** 1852)

Dr Adolpus Lewis Heermann (1827–1865) was an army physician and naturalist. He was one of many naturalists who came to the attention of Spencer **Baird** at the Smithsonian Institution, and he was assigned to a surveying party for the Pacific Railroad line. Heermann was especially interested in collecting birds' eggs and he is credited with coining the term 'oology' for the practice. He retired from the army early due to illness and died two years later in a hunting accident; he stumbled and his rifle discharged and killed him. He appears to have looked many years older than he was – the effect, among other things, of syphilis.

HEILPRIN

Heilprin's Jay *Cyanocorax heilprini* (Gentry 1885)
(Alt. Azure-naped Jay)

Professor Angelo Heilprin (1853–1907) was a Hungarian-born American geographer, scientist and explorer. He was Professor of Invertebrate Palaeontology at the Academy of Natural Sciences in Philadelphia. He wrote *A Complete Pronouncing Gazetteer or Geographical Dictionary of the World*, with his son Louis, and *The Geographical and Geological Distribution of Animals*, in 1907. In an article in the proceedings of the Academy of Natural Sciences Philadelphia, in 1882, entitled *On the Value of the 'Neoarctic' as One of the Primary Zoological Regions,* he tried to show that the Nearctic and Palæarctic should form one region – the Triarctic (now Holarctic). He went with Peary on his arctic expedition of 1891 to 1892. In 1902 he examined an erupting volcano, Mount Pelee on the island of Martinique, at close range. He also founded the *American Alpine Club*. He died in 1907, shortly before he was due to give the presidential address to the Association of American Geographers.

HEINE

Heine's Ground Thrush *Zoothera heinei* (**Cabanis** 1850)
(Alt. Scaly/ Russet-tailed/Heine's/Olive-tailed Thrush, Australian Ground Thrush)
Heine's Kingbird *Tyrannus apolites* (Cabanis & Heine, 1859)

Ferdinand Heine (1809–1894) was a German collector whose massive collection is housed by the Naturkunde-museum (Museum of Natural Science), a part of the Heineanum Halberstadt Museum in Halberstadt, Saxony. His was recognised as the largest private collection of birds in the mid 19th century. It has 15,000 books and 27,000 specimens. **Cabanis**, who described the ground thrush, also wrote about Heine in Museum Heineanum, *Verzeichniss de Ornithologischensammlung des Oberamtmann Ferdinand Heine auf Gut St. Burchard vor Halberstadt.* The kingbird is now considered to be a hybrid and not a valid species.

HEINRICH

Heinrich's Brush Cuckoo *Cacomantis heinrichi* (**Stresemann** 1931)
(Alt. Moluccan Cuckoo)
Heinrich's Eared Nightjar *Eurostopodus diabolicus* (Stresemann 1931)
(Alt. Sulawesi/Satanic/Celebes/Devilish/Diabolical/Kalabat[Eared]Nightjar)
Heinrich's Robin[chat] *Cossypha heinrichi* (**Rand** 1955)
(Alt. White-headed/Rand's/Angola Robin-Chat)
Heinrich's [Whistling] Thrush *Geomalia heinrichi* (Stresemann 1931)
(Alt. Celebes/Sulawesi Mountain [Ground]Thrush)

Gerd Heinrich (1896–19) was a German ornithologist in the East Indies, as was his wife Hildegard. He wrote *Der Vogel Schnarch* in 1932.

HEINROTH

Heinroth's Fantail *Rhipidura matthiae* (Heinroth 1902)
  (Alt. [St] Matthias Fantail)
Heinroth's Reed Warbler *Acrocephalus stentoreus celebensis* (Heinroth 1903)
  (Alt. Clamorous Reed Warbler)
Heinroth's Shearwater *Puffinus heinrothi* (**Reichenow** 1919)

Oskar August Heinroth (1871–1945) was very interested in natural history even as a child. He qualified as a medical doctor, but after just one year in practice he turned his full-time attention to zoology. He worked as an unpaid assistant at Berlin Zoo, supporting himself by writing scientific papers. He only began to be paid after his two-year expedition to the South Seas, where we may presume he saw the shearwater named after him, which probably breeds somewhere around the Solomon Isles. He wrote *The Birds of Central Europe* with his first wife Magdalena Wiebe. His second wife Katharina (1897–1989), was a director of the zoo, and wrote *The Birds* with him (published 1958).

HELENA

Helena's Calypte *Mellisuga helenae* (Lembeye 1850)
  (Alt. Bee Hummingbird)

Helen Booth was the wife of the German-born Cuban ornithologist Juan Cristóbal **Gundlach** (1810–1896), who wrote the catalogue of the Cuban birds. Gundlach first found the hummingbird, whose male is the smallest known bird, in 1844, but he decided not to send it to **Cassells** and instead kept it in his own collection.

HELIODORE

Heliodore's Woodstar *Calothorax heliodori* (**Gould***)

Another name only found in a **Gould** painting. In any event it is unlikely that it was ever intended to have the apostrophe; heliodor is a yellow, semi-precious gemstone otherwise known as Golden Beryl. We assume that the bird was a shining colourful gem! The Gorgeted Woodstar is *Acestrura heliodor*, which might be the source of confusion.

HELLMAYR

Hellmayr's Pipit *Anthus hellmayri* (**Hartert** 1909)
Hellmayr's Rusty-faced Parrot *Hapalopsittaca amazonina theresae* (Hellmayr 1915)
Hellmayr's Woodcreeper *Xiphorhynchus spixii* (*elegans*) *insignis* (Hellmayr 1905)

Charles Eduard Hellmayr (1878–1944) was a German zoologist who worked in the United States. In 1922 he was the first associate-level Curator in Zoology at The Field Museum in Chicago. Hellmayr's speciality in Neotropical birds was a major impetus to the development of what has now become a major international resource in that area of the world at the museum. His publications, from the 1920s to the 1960s, included a *Catalogue of Birds of the Americas and the Adjacent Islands*, with **Conover**, and *The Birds of Chile*.

HELOISE

Heloise's Hummingbird *Atthis heloisa* (**Lesson** & **Delattre** 1839)
  (Alt. Morcom's Hummingbird)

Heloise (1101–1164) was the niece of Canon Fulbert of Notre Dame. She is famous for her tragic love affair with Abelard. Abelard and Heloise were secretly married but tried to maintain the fiction that they were single. They had a son called Astrolabe. It all turned out badly; Abelard became a Dominican monk and Heloise a nun.

HEMPRICH

Hemprich's Gull *Larus hemprichii* (Bruch 1853)
(Alt. Sooty Gull)
Hemprich's Hornbill *Tockus hemprichii* (Ehrenberg 1833)

Wilhelm Friedrich Hemprich (1796-1825), the son of a physician, became a lecturer in natural science and physiology, following a brief career as a medical officer. He was also a traveller and collector, principally of marine animals, but he also discovered many new birds. In 1828 he wrote *Natural historical journeys in Egypt and Arabia*, with Ehrenberg. He also collected on a trip which retraced Humbolt's journey in Asia. Hemprich died whilst on a collecting expedition of Massawa fever, in northeast Africa, thereby bringing to an end the rich partnership he had enjoyed with Christian Ehrenberg.

HENDERSON, G

Henderson's Ground Jay *Podoces hendersoni* (**Hume** 1871)
(Alt. Mongolian Ground Jay)

Lieutenant-Colonel Dr George Henderson (1837–1929) was an English traveller. He collected the first specimen of the ground jay on the first Yarkand Mission to Central Asia. Disguised as a merchant and calling himself Ismail Khan, Henderson reached Leh in 1864. '*The ornithological collections from here and from the second mission were first treated by Allan Hume, but his manuscript was stolen and sold as waste paper. Altogether 350 forms are described, with extracts of notes from the diary of Dr Stoliczka and notes given by Colonel Biddulph in manuscript to Hume. The report also includes all the species obtained by Dr Henderson and Dr Soully and previously treated in publication by them. The work does therefore deal with the whole of material secured by the British expeditions into Central Asia*'. He wrote *Lahore to Yarkand: Incidents of the Route and Natural History of the Countries Traversed by yhe Expedition of 1870*, with Allan Hume, published in 1873.

HENDERSON

Henderson Fruit Dove *Ptilinopus insularis* (**North** 1908)
Henderson Petrel *Pterodroma atrata* (**Mathews** 1912)

This is a place and not a person. The two birds are named after their breeding place, Henderson Island, in the Pitcairn group. (Henderson Island was rediscovered by Captain James Henderson of the British East India merchant ship *Hercules*, in 1819, and is named after the venerable captain.)

HENKE

Henke's Sunbird *Leptocoma sperata henkei* (**A B Meyer** 1884)
(Alt. Purple-throated/Van Hasselt's Sunbird)

Possibly named for Thaddaeus (Tadeá) Peregrinus Xaverius Haenke (1761–1816), a Czech who became very interested in botany at an early age. He gained the degree of Doctor of Philosophy in 1782, and in 1789 was offered a position as botanist on the Malaspina Expedition. He had a most adventurous time; he missed his ship twice and had to swim ashore when it capsized whilst approaching Montevideo, losing all his possessions except his credentials from King Carlos IV of Spain. He eventually crossed the continent to Santiago de Chile where he rejoined the expedition. He collected over 2,500 botanical specimens whilst crossing South America. The Malaspina Expedition explored North and South America, Guam in the Mariana Islands, and the Philippines, and eventually returned to Peru via the Botany Bay convict settlement in Australia, New Zealand and Tonga. He left the ship at Callao in 1793. He was meant to return to Europe but was delayed through injuries caused by falling off a horse and then was imprisoned as he was regarded as a dangerous pro-revolutionary radical. He became on very good terms with the local governor who enabled him to stay in what is now Peru and Bolivia until his death. Haenke travelled and researched widely and discovered the giant water lily *Victoria amazonia*, the leaves of which can reach 2.5 metres in diameter, in 1801. It is not known what caused his death but poison is suspected, being administered either accidentally by his maid, who thought it was medicine, or deliberately to dispose of him. The specimens which he collected on the Malaspina Expedition were taken to Spain but his private collection was sent to Europe by a firm of Bohemian glass merchants and, after various vicissitudes, was eventually acquired for the National Museum in Prague. The sunbird is a native of Luzon in the Philippines, which Haenke is known to have visited. The bird is the Philippines race of the Purple-throated Sunbird.

HENRY DE LATTRE

Henry de Lattre's Cacique *Delattria henrici* (**Gould***)

Henri de Lattre (1801–1867) See **De Lattre;** the only reference we can find for the bird is amongst the **Gould** engravings, where one can also find *Delattria clemenciae* which Gould also called the Blue-throated Cacique.

HENRY

Henry's Laughing-thrush *Garrulax henrici* (**Oustalet** 1892)
(Alt. Brown-cheeked/Prince d'Orleans Laughing-thrush)

See **Prince Henry**.

HENSLOW

Henslow's Sparrow *Ammodramus henslowii* (**Audubon** 1829)

The Reverend John Stevens Henslow (1796–1861) was an English botanist and geologist. **Audubon** named the sparrow in honour of this professor of botany at Cambridge University, who had advised him on booksellers in England when publishing *Birds of America*. In 1831 Henslow was asked by Captain Fitzroy of the *Beagle* to recommend a young naturalist to join an expedition around the world without pay. Henslow picked a promising young student of his named Charles **Darwin**. It was to Henslow that Darwin shipped all of the specimens he collected throughout his journey and to whom he first told his theory of evolution. A devout cleric, in addition to his academic duties, Henslow always remained a sceptic, but he was pleased by the impact made by his former student.

HENST

Henst's Goshawk *Accipiter henstii* (**Schlegel** 1873)

G (Possibly Gilihelmus) Van Der Henst was a collector in Madagascar. He is mentioned as being with a D C **Van Dam** when they killed and collected a lemur, the Crowned Sifaka

Propithecus coronatus, near Bombotek on the Northeast coast of Madagascar, which is interesting since the goshawk is a predator of lemurs.

HEPBURN

Hepburn's Finch *Leucosticte* (*tephrocotis*) *littoralis* (**Baird** 1869)
(Alt. Grey-cheeked/Grey-crowned Rosy Finch)

James Edward Hepburn (1810–1869) qualified as a lawyer in London and immigrated to California in 1852. He travelled very widely, between San Francisco and Vancouver, and once went as far north as Sitka. He did not confine himself to coastal regions and made a number forays to the Rockies. His skins and specimens went to various places and people; Sir William **Jardine** and **Tristram** both had some, and others went to Baird at the Smithsonian. His relatives presented what is now known as the Hepburn Collection to the University of Cambridge Zoological Museum, in 1870. It consists mostly of material from western North America but also includes specimens from the Atlantic coast of the United States, from Chile and from some Pacific islands. **Swanson** described the Grey-crowned Rosy Finch *Leucosticte tephrocotis* in 1832, but the race *littoralis* which is sometimes elevated to species status was described and named after Hepburn by Baird, in 1869.

HERALD

Herald's Petrel *Pterodroma arminjoniana* (Giglioli & **Salvadori** 1869*)*
(Alt. Herald Petrel)

We do not think that this bird was named after a person, not even a member of that class of people who paraded around in tabards blowing the King's trumpet! Rather we believe it is named after the British ship *HMS Herald*, which conducted surveys in the Pacific from 1845 to 1851. A number of birds have the Latinised *heraldica* in their scientific names through being discovered during these voyages. The Herald Petrel was thought to have two subspecies; one race with *heraldica* as the trinomial, but it is now considered monotypic. Captain H Kellet RN, Lieutenant Wood RN, Dr F M Rayner or J **Macgillivray** collected most of the different species named during the *Herald*'s voyages, and **Salvadori** described a number of them.

HERBERT

Herbert's Babbler *Stachyris herberti* (E C S **Baker** 1920)
(Alt. Sooty (Tree) Babbler, Spotted Tree Babbler)
Herbert's Woodland Warbler *Phylloscopus herberti* (**Boyd Alexander** 1903)
(Alt. Black-capped Woodland Warbler)

E G Herbert (1870–1951) was an English collector and naturalist. He wrote an article on *Nests and eggs of birds in Central Siam* in the Journal of the Natural History Society of Siam, in 1926.

HERPETOLOGISTS

Whilst some lizards and snakes do live in trees and a couple are even to be spotted gliding, one would think that herpetologists would not be well placed to spot new birds. Why Arthur **Loveridge**, an American herpetologist, was honoured we do not know. However, it is clear that Johann Georg **Wagler**, a German herpetologist became immortalised in a bird name. He was **Spix**'s assistant and upon the former's death became Director of the Zoological Museum of the University of Munich, and worked there to continue the treatment of the extensive collections from Brazil. Of course, as we know, birds are the direct descendants of dinosaurs and so are not without herpetological credentials.

HERRAN

Herran's Thornbill *Chalcostigma herrani* (**De Lattre** & **Bourcier** 1846)
(Alt. Rainbow-bearded Thornbill)

Pedro Alcantara Herran (1800–1872) was a Colombian general, politician and President of New Granada (now Colombia) from 1841 until 1844.

HEUDE

Heude's Parrotbill *Paradoxornis heudei* (**David** 1872)
(Alt. Reed/Eye-browed/Yangtze Parrotbill)

Pierre Marie Heude (1836–1902) was a French conchologist and Jesuit missionary, who collected and described specimens whilst living in China at the end of the 1800s. Whilst his records were preserved and used by others, his collection was thought lost for over 100 years. However, Australian scientists working Beijing recently rediscovered it, still with labels in his handwriting. He wrote, *Mémoires concernant l'Histoire Naturelle de l'Empire Chinois, par des Pères de la Compagnie de Jésus,* which was published in a series of instalments bound in different volumes printed in Shanghai. His best-known work is said to be *Conchyliologie fluviatile de la province de Nanking (et la Chine Centrale).* He died at Zi-ka-wei in China.

HEUGLIN

Heuglin's Bustard *Neotis heuglini* (**Hartlaub** 1859)
Heuglin's Courser *Rhinoptilus cinctus cinctus* (Heuglin 1863)
(Alt. Three-banded Courser)
Heuglin's Francolin *Francolinus icterorhynchus* (Heuglin 1863)
Heuglin's Gull *Larus (argentatus) heuglini* (Bree 1876)
Heuglin's Masked Weaver *Ploceus heuglini* (**Reichenow** 1886)
Heuglin's Robin-Chat *Cossypha heuglini* (Hartlaub 1866)
(Alt. White-browed Robin-Chat, Heuglin's Robin)
Heuglin's Wheatear *Oenanthe heuglini* (**Finsch** & Hartlaub 1870)
Heuglin's White-eye *Zosterops poliogaster* (Heuglin 1861)
(Alt. Montane/African/Highland/Kikuyu/Kulal/Taita/South Pare/Mountain/
Broad-ringed White-eye)

Theodor von Heuglin (1824–1876) was born in Ditzingen, Germany, where the local school is named after him. He became a mining engineer and ornithologist. He is recorded as exploring Central Africa and Abyssinia (Ethiopia) in 1861. He also explored in eastern Africa and he published an account of its birds, *Ornithologie Nordost-Afrika,* in 1869. Heuglin was a vocal opponent of evolutionary theories, perhaps since he was the son of the local priest in Ditzingen. He died of pneumonia and is buried in the Prague Cemetery in Stuttgart.

HILDEBRAND

See **Hildebrandt**.

HILDEBRANDT

Hildebrandt's Francolin *Francolinus hildebrandti* (**Cabanis** 1878)
    (Alt. Hildebrand's Francolin, Hildebrandt's Spurfowl)
Hildebrandt's Starling *Lamprotornis hildebrandti* (Cabanis 1878)

Johann Maria Hildebrandt (1847–1881) was a German who collected in East Africa, Madagascar and the Comoro Islands from 1872 until his death. He was also interested in languages and in 1876 published *Zeitschrift für Ethiopia*.

HINDE

Hinde's Pied Babbler *Turdoides hindei* (**Sharpe** 1900)

Dr Sidney Langford Hinde (1863–1931) was Medical Officer of the Interior in British East Africa and a Captain in the Congo Free State Forces, as well as a naturalist and collector. He was also a Provincial Commissioner in Kenya and collected there too. A viper which he collected is named in his honour. He wrote *The Fall of The Congo Arabs*, in 1897 and *The Last of the Masai*, with Hildegarde in 1901.

HODGSON

Hodgson's Partridge *Perdix hodgsoniae* (Hodgson 1857)
    (Alt. Tibetan Partridge)

Anne Hodgson (?–1868) was the wife of the British naturalist Brian **Hodgson** (see below), who described the bird and named it after her.

HODGSON

Hodgson's Broadbill *Serilophus lunatus* (**Gould** 1834)
    (Alt. Silver-breasted/Gould's/Collared Broadbill)
Hodgson's Bushchat *Saxicola insignis* (G R **Gray** 1846)
    (Alt. Hodgson's Stonechat, White-throated Bushchat)
Hodgson's Frogmouth *Batrachostomus hodgsoni* (G R Gray 1859)
Hodgson's Fulvetta *Alcippe vinipectus* (Hodgson 1838)
    (Alt. White-browed Fulvetta/Tit-Babbler)
Hodgson's Grandala *Grandala coelicolor* (Hodgson 1843)
Hodgson's Hawk-Cuckoo *Cuculus fugax* (**Horsfield** 1843)
    (Alt. Fugitive Hawk-Cuckoo)
Hodgson's Hawk-Eagle *Spizaetus nipalensis orientalis* (Hodgson 1836)
    (Alt. Mountain Hawk-Eagle)
Hodgson's Imperial Pigeon *Ducula badia* (**Raffles** 1822)
    (Alt. Pied/Spice/Nutmeg/Torresian/Australian/White/White Fruit/Black
    [Imperial] Pigeon)
Hodgson's Long-tailed Warbler *Prinia cinereocapilla* (Hodgson 1854)
    (Alt. Grey-crowned Prinia)
Hodgson's Munia *Lonchura striata* (Linnaeus 1766)
    (Alt. White-rumped/White-backed/Sharp-tailed Munia/Mannikin, Society/
    Bengalese Finch)
Hodgson's Pied Wagtail *Motacilla alba alboides* Hodgson 1836
Hodgson's Pigeon *Columba hodgsonii* (**Vigors** 1832)
    (Alt. Speckled Wood Pigeon)
Hodgson's Pipit *Anthus roseatus* (**Blyth** 1847)
    (Alt. Rosy Pipit)
Hodgson's Redstart *Phoenicurus hodgsoni* (Moore 1854)
    (Alt. Hodgson's/Chinese Shortwing, White-bellied Redstart)

Hodgson's Rosy Finch *Leucosticte nemoricola* (Hodgson 1836)
(Alt. Plain Mountain Finch)

Brian Houghton Hodgson FRC (1800–1894) was an official of the East India Company and Assistant Resident in Nepal, from 1825 until 1843, and in Darjeeling between 1845 and 1859. He was very interested in Buddhism and was among those who introduced the idea to Britain in the 19th century. He also took an interest in the languages of Nepal and northern India. Hodgson wrote books on Indian birds with **Hume** and others. He amassed a collection of 9,512 specimens of birds, belonging to 672 species, of which 124 had never been described previously. He got the credit for describing 79 of these but failed to describe the rest before others did. A fiercely patriotic man, he once said that **Cuvier** (who had stolen a march on Hardwicke by naming the Red Panda *Ailurus fulgens* because **Hardwicke**'s return to England was delayed) would '*prevent England reaping the zoological harvest of her own domains*'. He described no fewer than 138 different passerines and lodged many specimens with the British Museum (Natural History). He named some birds for his wife Anne (see above). Hodgson also described a wagtail which he collected in Nepal, in 1836, as a new species *Motacilla alboides*, but it is now regarded as a subspecies of *M. alba*.

HOEVELL

Hoevell's Flycatcher *Cyornis hoevelli* (**A B Meyer** 1903)
(Alt. Blue-fronted/Celebes Niltava/Flycatcher)

Baron G W W C van Hoevell (1848–?) was the Dutch colonial Governor of Celebes (now Sulawesi) in 1902. In 1875 he published *Ambon en meer bepaaldelijk de Oeliasers.*

HOFFMANN

Hoffmann's Ant-thrush *Formicarius analis hoffmanni* (**Cabanis** 1861)
(Black-faced Ant-thrush)
Hoffmann's Conure *Pyrrhura hoffmanni* (Cabanis 1861)
(Alt. Sulphur-winged Parakeet)
Hoffmann's Woodpecker *Melanerpes hoffmannii* (Cabanis 1862)

Carl Hoffmann (1823–1859) was a German physician. He went to Costa Rica in 1853 with Alexander von **Frantzius** and began to explore the country and collect specimens, mainly botanical ones. He was later a physician to the Costa Rican army.

HOFFMANNS

Hoffmanns's Woodcreeper *Dendrocolaptes hoffmannsi* **Hellmayr** 1909

W Hoffmanns (1865–1909) was a German naturalist who collected in Peru and Brazil between 1903 and 1908. A Brazilian monkey *Callicebus hoffmannsi* was described and named after him by Thomas, in 1908.

HOGDEN

Hogden's Rail *Gallinula hogdeni* (**Scarlett** 1955) [Extinct]

J & R Hogden. Hodgen is the name of the family which owns the swamp where the bones of Hodgen's Rail were first found in Pyramid Valley, North Canterbury, New Zealand, by Ron Scarlett.

HOLBOELL

Holboell's Grebe *Podiceps grisegena holboelli* (**Reinhardt** 1854)
(Alt. Red-necked Grebe)

Holboell's Redpoll *Carduelis flammea holboelli* (Holboell)
(Alt. Common Redpoll)

Carl Peter Holboell (1795–1856) was a captain in the Danish Royal Navy who served in Greenland and became interested in natural history there. Holboell's Rock Cress *Arabis holboellii* was named after him by Jens Wilken **Hornemann**, in 1828, as a *quid pro quo* for Holboell naming a redpoll after Hornemann, which, however, is no longer recognised as a valid taxon.

HOLUB

Holub's Golden Weaver *Ploceus xanthops* (**Hartlaub** 1862)
(Alt. (Large) Golden Weaver)

Emil Holub (1847–1902) was a Bohemian (Czech) naturalist who also studied South African fossils. Like his father he trained as a physician but was always fascinated by wildlife and foreign lands, and his compelling ambition was to follow in the footsteps of David **Livingstone**. He has been described as '*a doctor of medicine, a zoologist, a botanist, a hunter, a taxidermist, an artist and cartographer, an avid collector of specimens and, above all, a keen observer*'. His first trip to Africa was in 1872 and he practiced as a doctor to pay his way. He travelled extensively in south-central Africa gathering varied and valuable natural history material, including over 30,000 specimens! On his return from his first trip he wrote *Seven Years in Africa*. In 1883 he took another trip to Africa, which ended in disaster after ten weeks when a number of the party died from malaria and all the equipment was lost. When he returned to Europe he fell upon hard times and was forced to sell much of his collection. He, too, eventually died from malaria, which he had contracted on his second trip.

HOMBRON

Hombron's Kingfisher *Actenoides hombroni* (**Bonaparte** 1850)
(Alt. Blue-capped/Hombron's [Wood] Kingfisher)

Dr Jacques Bernard Hombron (1798–1852) was a French naval surgeon and naturalist. He was in the Pacific aboard the *Astrolabe* and *Zelée* from 1837 until 1840, and wrote *Adventures les plus Curieuses des Voyageurs* in 1847. He described a number of mammals and plants with Jaquinot.

HOOGERWERF

Hoogerwerf's Pheasant *Lophura* (*inornata*) *hoogerwerfi* (Chasen 1939)
(Alt. Sumatran Pheasant)

Andries Hoogerwerf (1907–1977) wrote much on Indonesian birds, particularly Java, from late the 1940s through to the 1970s. His works include *The birds of Cibodas* (Java) in 1949 and *Udjung Kulon: The Land of the Last Javan Rhinoceros* in 1970, but most works have been on birds. He is believed to have been the only person to photograph the now-extinct Javan Tiger *Panthera tigris* (ssp.), in 1938. The taxonomic status of the pheasant is unclear, since it is known only from one female specimen. Males have not been described fully, other than as being 'dark'. It may be conspecific with **Salvadori**'s Pheasant *Lophura inornata*.

HOPKE

Hopke's Cotinga *Carpodectes hopkei* (**Berlepsch** 1897)
(Alt. Black-tipped Cotinga)

Gustav Hopke was a 19th century German field collector who specialised in South American mammals, *Mustelidae* in general but Coypu *Myocastor coypus* in particular. He collected mostly in Paraguay and Chile around 1897, but he was also collecting in Colombia in the 1870s, where the cotinga occurs.

HORNBY

Hornby's Storm Petrel *Oceanodroma hornbyi* (G R .**Gray** 1854)
(Alt. Ringed Storm Petrel)

Admiral Sir Geoffrey Phipps Hornby (1785–1867) was the British commander-in-chief in the Pacific between 1847 and 1850. Around 1850, when still a Rear-Admiral, he was off the coast of British Columbia and collections of specimens were taken from there. He also has a lighthouse, the Hornby Light, named after him in New South Wales, indirectly since it was named after his daughter who married the governor. (Captain Geoffrey Phipps Hornby – his son we think – became famous in the so-called 'Pig War', a territorial dispute between the United States and Canada, in 1859, which was a stand off with no shots fired.)

HORNEMANN

Hornemann's Redpoll *Carduelis hornemanni* (Holboell 1843)
(Alt. Coue's/Hoary Redpoll)

Jens Wilken Hornemann (1770–1841) was a Danish botanist, a professor at the University of Copenhagen, who wrote *Flora Danica* in 1806. He and Holboell were friends and **Holboell** described and named the redpoll. In turn Hornemann honoured Holboell by naming Holboell's Rock Cress *Arabis holboelli* after him.

HORSFIELD

Horsfield's Babbler *Trichastoma sepiarium* (Horsfield 1821)
(Alt. Horsfield's Jungle Babbler)
Horsfield's Bronze Cuckoo/Hawk-Cuckoo *Chrysococcyx basalis* (Horsfield 1821)
(Alt. Meyer's/White-eared/Narrow-billed Bronze Cuckoo)
Horsfield's Goshawk/Sparrowhawk *Accipiter soloensis* (Horsfield 1821)
(Alt. Chinese/Grey Goshawk/Sparrowhawk, Grey Froghawk)
Horsfield's Hill Partridge *Arborophila orientalis* (Horsfield 1821)
(Alt. Grey-breasted/Sumatran/Sunda/Grey-bellied/Bare-throated/
Campbell's [Hill/Tree] Partridge)
Horsfield's Kalij *Lophura leucomelaena moffitti* (**Latham** 1790)
(Alt. Black-breasted Kalij, Horsfield's Pheasant)
Horsfield's Lark *Mirafra javanica* (Horsfield 1821)
(Alt. Eastern Singing/Australian/Javan/Cinnamon [Bush]Lark)
Horsfield's Scimitar Babbler *Pomatorhinus ochraceiceps* (**Walden** 1873)
(Alt. Lloyd's/Ochraceous Scimitar Babbler)
Horsfield's Thrush *Zoothera horsfieldi* (**Bonaparte** 1857)
(Alt. Spot[ted]-winged Thrush)
Horsfield's Woodcock *Scolopax saturata* (Horsfield 1821)
(Alt. Dusky/Rufous/Javanese/East Indian/Indonesian/Rosenberg's
Woodcock)

Dr Thomas Horsfield (1773–1859) was an American naturalist. He was trained as a doctor but became an explorer and prolific collector of plants and animals. He began his career in Java while it was under Dutch rule, but then Napoleon Bonaparte annexed Holland. This enabled the British East India Company to take control over the island in 1811. In 1819 Horsfield's poor health made him seek other employment and he was moved by the company to continue his research under their direction, in London, as Curator and then Keeper of the India House Museum. Whilst in Java he became a good friend of Sir Thomas Stamford **Raffles**. He wrote *Zoological Researches in Java and the Neighbouring Islands* in 1824. **Latham** described the Kalij, and later named it after Horsfield.

HORUS

Horus Swift *Apus horus* (**Heuglin** 1869)

Horus, son of Ra (also known as Osiris), was one of the Gods of ancient Egypt, a falcon deity representing the sky.

HOSE

Hose's Broadbill *Calyptomena hosii* (**Sharpe** 1892)

Sir Charles Hose (1863–1929) was a naturalist who lived in Sarawak and Malaysia from 1884 to 1907. He was 'Resident of Baram' in 1902. Hose successfully investigated the principle cause of the disease beri-beri. He was also a good cartographer who produced the first reliable map of Sarawak. Fort Hose in Sarawak (now a museum) was named after him. '*Naturalist Charles Hose noted that he had seen an owlet so deceived by Kalimantan people imitating the bird that it flew right into the house the sound had come from, looking for its potential mate.*' He wrote *Fifty Years of Romance and Research* in 1927 and *The Field Book of a Jungle Wallah* in 1929. A number of birds have *emiliae* in their scientific names, after his wife Emilie and Black Oriole *Oriolus hosii* also commemorates Hose.

HOSKINS

Hoskins' Pygmy Owl *Glaucidium* (*gnoma*) *hoskinsii* (**Brewster** 1888)
(Alt. Cape/Baja Pygmy Owl – probably conspecific with Northern Pygmy Owl *G. gnoma*)

Francis Hoskins was an assistant to M A **Frazar**, who was a paid bird collector for **Sennett**. Frazar collected the first specimen of this owl and of many other birds in Baja California.

HOTTENTOT

Hottentot is the former name for the indigenous Khoi Khoi people of southern Africa. It is most unusual for indigenous peoples to have birds named after them, especially during the colonial period. It shows an admirable liberalism on the part of **Le Vaillant,** the person who named the birds in both cases. Elsewhere in this volume, one sadly finds that some ornithologists have been passionate racists, so it was refreshing to find one who showed respect for the locals. Levaillant named **Klaas**' Cuckoo *Chrysococcyx klaas* after his Khoi Khoi servant who, it is thought, found the bird in 1784. No more is known about him, but he may have been related to the other Khoi Khoi so honoured. **Narina** (meaning flower) was said to be a beautiful girl and the Narina Trogon *Apaloderma narina* was named after her in 1806. According to **Lesson**, she was probably Le Vaillant's mistress.

HOWARD

Howard's Grouse *Dendragapus obscurus howardi* (**Dickey** & **Van Rossem** 1923)
(Alt. Mount Pinos Blue/Sooty Grouse)

O W Howard was a member of the Cooper Ornithological Club (now Society) in Los Angeles, California. He personalised his stationery with: '*O W Howard, Field Work a Speciality in Ornithology, Oology and Entomology*'. He published a number of articles in The Condor from 1899 to 1906, including *Nesting of Belding's Sparrow,* in 1899 and *The English Sparrow in the Southwest,* in 1906. **Dickey** and **van Rossem** described this race of the Blue Grouse following an original description of the bird in The Condor, in recognition of his '*many years of enthusiastic ornithological work in southern California and Arizona*' and for his local knowledge of the area and his assistance when they collected the bird at Mt Pinos.

HOWELL

> Howell's Nighthawk *Chordeiles minor howelli* (**Oberholser** 1914)
> (Alt. Common Nighthawk)

Arthur Holmes Howell (1872–1940) was an American ornithologist. He joined The Bureau of Biological Survey of the United States Department of Agriculture in 1895; ten years later Harry C Oberholser joined him there. His periodical field service took him to many western States but his most notable work was done in the south. Howell published on the birds and life zones of Arkansas (and other regions), where the subspecies concerned is found. He wrote the 579-page *Florida Bird Life* in 1932.

HOY

> Hoy's Screech Owl *Otus hoyi* König & Straneck 1989
> (Alt. Montane-forest Screech Owl)

 Gunnar Arthur Hoy (1901–1997) was a Norwegian-born ornithologist of German extraction; his father was German and his mother Swedish. As such, he was required to join the German army after their occupation of Norway during the Second World War. As a result, after the war he was accused of being a collaborator and was imprisoned. In 1951 he emigrated to Argentina with his wife and six-year old son, and by 1954 he was a curator at the Natural History Museum of the University of Salta. Hoy kept in touch with many of the world's leading ornithologists and became the 'Grand Old Man of Argentinean Ornithology'. He published a number of articles, mostly in the Argentine journal Historia Natural, such as *Un ave nueva para la Argentina Contopus virens*, in 1981, *Hydropsalis climacocerca (Chudy) (Caprimulgidae), nuevo para la Argentina*, and an article on *Nothoprocta pentlandii patriciae*, in 1987. He is also commemorated in the trinomial of a race of Rufous-banded Miner *Geositta rufipennis hoyi*, described in 1980. König (who wrote Hoy's obituary) and Straneck described this South American owl.

HUDSON

> Hudson's Black Tyrant *Knipolegus hudsoni* (P L **Sclater** 1872)
> Hudson's Canastero *Asthenes hudsoni* (P L Sclater 1874)
> (Alt. Hudson's Soft-tail)

William Henry Hudson (1841–1922) was born in Buenos Aires of American parents. He spent his childhood on the pampas but developed a heart condition and had to emigrate to England in 1870. He is generally regarded as a British author, naturalist and ornithologist. However, he is best known for his exotic romances, especially *Green Mansions*, published in 1904, which is set in a South American jungle. His novel, *Far Away and Long Ago* in 1918, lovingly recalls his childhood. Hudson was a sensitive observer of nature, particularly birds. His books describe plants and animals in a highly personal manner with great force and beauty. Other works are *The Purple Land* in 1885, *Argentine Ornithology* in 1888, *The Naturalist in La Plata* in 1892, *A Shepherd's Life* in 1910 and *A Hind in Richmond Park* in 1922. The novelist John Galsworthy said of him: '*Hudson is...the finest living observer, and the greatest living lover of bird and animal life, and of Nature in her moods.*'

HUMBLOT

Humblot's Flycatcher *Humblotia flavirostris* (**Oustalet** & **Milne-Edwards** 1885)
  (Alt. Grand Comoro Flycatcher)
Humblot's Heron *Ardea humbloti* (Grandidier & Milne-Edwards 1885)
  (Alt. Madagascar Heron)
Humblot's Sunbird *Nectarinia humbloti* (Oustalet & Milne-Edwards 1885)

Henri Joseph Léon Humblot (1852–1914) seems to have been sent to the Comoros from Madagascar in 1884 to ensure that France was recognised as the 'protector' nation of the former. This was achieved and he became 'Resident' in 1886. Sometime later his formal power was removed but he remained the biggest landholder, using slaves to farm his land. He must have been an amateur naturalist as he is credited with the discovery in 1885 of the orchid *Angraecum leonis* as described by **Reichenbach**. He also sent various specimens, including orchids, to Sander & Co – orchid dealers.

HUMBOLDT

Humboldt Penguin *Spheniscus humboldti* (Meyen 1834)
Humboldt's Sapphire *Hylocharis humboldti* (**Bourcier** & **Mulsant** 1852)

Baron Friedrich Wilhelm Heinrich Alexander von Humboldt (1769–1859) was a Prussian naturalist, explorer and politician. He explored in South America from 1799 until around 1805, collecting thousands of specimens, mapping and studying natural phenomena. The trip took in parts of Venezuela, Peru, Ecuador, Colombia and Mexico. In 1829 he made a journey of similarly epic proportions ranging from the Urals east to Siberia. He was also a patron of Agassiz. Humboldt's *Personal Narrative* was inspirational to later travellers in the tropics, notably **Darwin** and **Wallace**. His most famous writing was the five-volume work *The Cosmos,* published between 1845 and 1862. Humboldt did research in many other fields, including astronomy, forestry and mineralogy. The Humboldt Current that runs south to north just west of the South American continent was named after him. The Sapphire was only split from the Blue-headed Sapphire *H. grayi* in 1998.

HUME

Hume's Babbler *Stachyris rufifrons* (Hume 1873)
  (Alt. Rufous-fronted Babbler)
Hume's Blue-throated Barbet *Megalaima incognita* (Hume 1874)
  (Alt. Moustached Barbet)
Hume's Ground Chough *Pseudopodoces humilis* (Hume 1871)
  (Alt. Ground Tit, Hume's Groundpecker, Tibetan Ground Jay)
Hume's Brown Hawk-Owl *Ninox scutulata obscura* (Hume 1873)
  (Alt. Hume's Hawk-Owl)
Hume's Leaf Warbler *Phylloscopus humei* (**W E Brooks** 1878)
  (Alt. Hume's Warbler)
Hume's Owl *Strix butleri* (Hume 1878)
  (Alt. Hume's Tawny Owl)
Hume's Parakeet *Psittacula finschii* (Hume 1874)
  (Alt. Finsch's Parrot, Grey-headed/Eastern Slaty-headed Parakeet)
Hume's [Large-billed] Reed Warbler *Acrocephalus orinus* (Hume 1867)
  (Alt. Large-billed Reed Warbler)
Hume's Short-toed Lark *Calandrella acutirostris* (Hume 1873)
  (Alt. Hume's Lark)
Hume's Swiftlet *Aerodramus maximus* (Hume 1878)

(Alt. Edible-nest/White-nest/Grey-rumped/Andaman Swiflet)
Hume's Wheatear *Oenanthe albonigra* (Hume 1872)
Hume's [Lesser] Whitethroat *Sylvia althaea* (Hume 1878)
Hume's Wren-Babbler *Sphenocichla humei* (**Mandelli** 1873)
(Alt. Wedge-billed Wren-[Babbler], Wedge-billed Tree Babbler)

Allan Octavian Hume CB (1829–1912) was a famous Theosophist and poet, and also a writer on Indian birds. He was born in London to a Radical Member of Parliament, Joseph Hume. A O Hume joined the Bengal Civil Service at the age of 20 and was appointed to the district of Etawah, Uttar Pradesh. Here, he introduced free primary education and founded a vernacular newspaper, Lokmitra (People's Friend). He wrote *Agricultural Reform of India* and the three-volume classic, *The Game Birds of India*. His other ornithological works included *Indian Oology and Ornithology* in 1869, *The Nests and Eggs of Indian Birds* in 1889 and *Stray Feathers*, published in ten volumes between 1873 and 1883. After his retirement, he was a co-founder of the Indian National Congress in 1885 and became its General Secretary until 1906. The Large-billed Reed Warbler *Acrocephalus orinus* is known only from the type specimen which Hume, collected in Himachal Pradesh, India.

HUNSTEIN

Hunstein's Bird of Paradise *Phonygama hunsteini* (**Sharpe** 1883)
(Alt. Hunstein's Manucode)
Hunstein's Mannikin *Lonchura hunsteini* (**Finsch** 1886)
(Alt. Mottled/Hunstein's Munia)

C Hunstein (1843–1888) was the German administrator of German New Guinea from 1885 until his death. He is commemorated in New Guinea by the Hunstein Mountains, the Hunstein Forest and also many trees and plants bearing his name. **Sharpe** described the manucode from a specimen collected by Hunstein.

HUNTER

Hunter's Cisticola *Cisticola hunteri* (**Shelley** 1889)
Hunter's Sunbird *Nectarinia hunteri* (Shelley 1889)

H C V Hunter (1861–1934) was (ironically) a big-game hunter and zoologist. Hunter's Hartebeest *Damaliscus hunteri*, first discovered in 1888, is named after him.

HUNTERS

Isn't it extraordinary that a bird should be named after a hunter, let alone a hunter called **Hunter** (see above)? This is not so remarkable since we know of at least four other hunters who are so honoured. Perhaps many hunters have turned conservationist, like poachers who turn to game-keeping. A L **Archer** is a good example of such a person; he was a hunter in Kenya who became involved in that country's conservation efforts. More often, hunters 'collected' specimens and there are many such collectors represented in this book. In the middle of the 19th century there was no seeming contradiction between hunting and natural history, and Louis Adolphe Joseph **Delegorgue** was an example of a man who shot a lot of what interested him! Arthur **Donaldson-Smith** pursued a career as a big-game hunter but he discovered a number of species and he was certainly a good natural historian. We don't know much about Major F A **Gillett**, except that he too was a hunter.

HUTCHINS

Hutchins' Goose *Branta canadensis* (**Richardson** 1831)
(now Canada Goose/Richardson's Goose)

Dr Thomas Hutchins (1730–1790) was an English naturalist and surgeon who worked for the Hudson's Bay Company as Chief Factor in Fort Albany from 1774 to 1782. His *Observations on Hudson's Bay* was published in about 1780.

HUTTON, F

Hutton's Shearwater *Puffinus huttoni* (**Kellogg** & **Chapman** 1899)
Hutton's Fruit Dove *Ptilinopus huttoni* (**Finsch** 1874)
(Alt. Rapa Island/Long-billed Fruit Dove)

Frederick Wollaston Hutton (1836–1905) was an English geologist and zoologist, who settled in New Zealand. He served in the Indian Mercantile Marine, and then in the army from 1855 until 1865. He saw service in both the Crimean War and the Indian Mutiny. Hutton wrote his *Catalogue of the Birds of New Zealand* in 1871. In memory of him, the Hutton Memorial Fund was established, in 1909, by the Royal Society of New Zealand, to support the award of the Hutton Medal and to provide grants for the encouragement of research into the zoology, botany and geology of New Zealand.

HUTTON, W

Hutton's Vireo *Vireo huttoni* (**Cassin** 1851)
(Alt. Anthony's/Frazar's/Stephen's Vireo)

William Rich Hutton (1826–1901) was an artist, a surveyor and a civil engineer. In 1847 he worked for a year in California as a clerk to his uncle, who was paymaster for the volunteers who formed part of the 1st New York Regiment. In 1849 he was chosen to assist Lieutenant Ord in the pueblo survey. He spent that summer helping with the survey, and sketched and drew scenes in the area in his spare time. Although he was on the move all the time, he supplied the Smithsonian with a number of specimens, including that of a vireo which he took near Monterrey and which was named after him. He returned to Washington DC in 1853. He married one of Francis Clopper's daughters and inherited the Clopper estate and woodlands, which now form part of Seneca Creek State Park. Among his engineering projects were the old Cabin John Bridge and the Washington Aqueduct, the Washington Bridge over the Harlem River and the Hudson River Tunnel in New York. He was embarrassed by the honour, which he thought had been given by **Baird**, and said in a letter to a relative '...*it goes against my principles to name after individuals unless for important scientific service.*' In fact **Cassin** described the vireo. There have been at least two books written about him.

IHERING

Ihering's Antwren *Myrmotherula iheringi* (**Snethlage** 1914)
Ihering's Tyrannulet *Phylloscartes difficilis* (H van Ihering & R von Ihering 1907)
   (Alt. Serra do Mar Tyrannulet)
Ihering's Woodcreeper *Xiphorhynchus spixii* (*elegans*) *juruanus*

Hermann von Ihering (1850–1930) was a German-Brazilian zoologist. He arrived in Brazil in 1880 and settled in Rio Grande do Sul. He founded the São Paulo museum in 1894 and spent 22 years as its first director. In 1907 he published *Catálogos da Fauna Brasileira. As Aves do Brazil*, with his son Rudolpho von Ihering (1883–1939) as his co-author. In 1924 he returned to Germany, where he died in 1930. Another Antwren, the rare Narrow-billed Antwren *Formicivora iheringi*, also commemorates this great ornithologist.

IJIMA

Ijima's Pheasant *Syrmaticus soemmerringii ijimae* (**Temminck** 1830)
Ijima's Willow Warbler *Phylloscopus ijimae* (**Stejneger** 1892)

I Ijima (1861–1921) was Professor of Zoology at Tokyo University and first President of the Ornithological Society of Japan. **Temminck**, who described the pheasant, also gave it a vernacular name that commemorated Professor Ijima.

ILLIGER

Illiger's Macaw *Primolius maracana* (**Vieillot** 1816)
   (Alt. Blue-winged Macaw)

'Carl' Johann Karl Wilhelm Illiger (1775–1813) was a German zoologist. He was the first Director of the Zoological Museum of the University of Berlin, which is now named after him, from 1811 until his premature death. It is interesting that the famous football stadium in Rio de Janeiro is also called Maracana, after a (heavily polluted) canalised stream which flows through the site. Illiger is credited with inventing the word 'Proboscidean' for the elephants, an order of mammals with a trunk!

INSECTIVORES AND ENTOMOLOGISTS

One might suppose that, if entomologists were ever honoured in the names of birds, they would be confined to insectivorous birds – but this is just not the case. For a start, there are many entomologists in this volume and their names are embodied in a range of bird families. Charles Thomas **Bingham** was the first to describe the omnivorous bulbul that carries his name. J Lucian **Buquet** is honoured in the name of a puffleg that also has quite catholic tastes. Keith **Carnaby**'s name is lent to a cockatoo, which is much more likely to eat fruit and seeds than insects. Heinrich Wolfgang Ludwig **Dohrn** is however, much more appropriately, associated with a flycatcher. Henry **Doubleday** was also an ornithologist and so may be forgiven for being associated with a nectar feeding hummingbird, as were John Edward **Gray**, who has many birds named after him, including honeyeaters and carnivorous hawks, and Bror Yngve **Sjostedt**, whose birds range from owls to greenbuls. Alexander Eduard Friedrich **Eversmann** was not just an insect man – he was a general zoologist and is celebrated in a number of species, including insect-eating warblers, but also vegetarian pigeons and ptarmigan. Felix Edouard **Guerin-Meneville** was an all-rounder too. C J **Swierstra** was a zoologist and curator, as well as an entomologist. Charles Francis Massy **Swynnerton** was also an all-rounder, but has an insect-eating robin named after him. There is a logic to naming a vulture after Hermann Julius **Kolbe** – after all, watching beetles and flies at a corpse must give one plenty of opportunities to see vultures. Theobald Johannes **Krüper** was probably honoured for his general scientific standing, but nuthatches are insect-eaters. Edward **Spalding** was in the employ of **MacCleay**, which explains why he was honoured. We are not clear why William **Spence** was commemorated in the name of a sunangel.

ISAACSON

Isaacson's Puffleg *Eriocnemis godini isaacsonii* (Bourcier 1851)
(Alt. Turquoise-throated/Godin's/Long-billed Puffleg)

Joseph P Isaacson was an English naturalist who was Curator of the Liverpool Zoological Gardens around 1838. **Gould** illustrated the puffleg which he obtained from **Bourcier**. There is confusion between this species and **Soederstrom**'s Puffleg *E. soederstomi*, which has been called *E. godini* too at times!

ISABELLA

Isabella's Oriole *Oriolus isabellae* (**Ogilvie-Grant** 1894)
(Alt. Green/Olive-lored/Isabela Oriole)

This Philippine oriole was discovered and described by **Ogilvie-Grant**, and it happens that his mother's name is Isabela, so it could have been named for her. However, the bird is an inhabitant of Isabela province, which was named in 1856 after Queen Isabella of Spain. As it is most often referred to as the Isabela Oriole we believe it was named for the province rather than directly for a person, although the province name was originally spelt Isabella as well.

ISIDOR(E)

Isidor's Eagle *Oroaetus isidori* (**Des Murs** 1845)
(Alt. Black-and-chestnut Eagle)
Isidors's Rufous Babbler *Pomatostomus isidorei* (**Lesson** 1827)
(Alt. New Guinea Babbler)

Isidore Geoffroy Saint Hilaire (1805–1861) was the son of Étienne **Geoffroy Saint Hilaire** and continued his father's professorial work. He was also author of *Histoire Générale et Particulière des Anomalies de l'organisation Chez l'homme et les Animaux* in 1857.

ITALIANS AND IRISH

No fewer than 27 Italians appear in these notes – a few are historic figures but most are ornithologists, including some giants of the profession such as **Bonelli** and the wonderfully named **Passerini**. Only five Irishmen are celebrated including one Irish American (**Lloyd**), who was a collector. The others were Andrew Leith **Adams** and J S **Jameson,** both well-travelled naturalists, Bernard Rogan **Ross**, the Hudson Bay Factor, and Nicholas Aylward **Vigors**, the most outstanding scientist among the Irish contingent.

JACKSON

Jackson's Akalat *Sheppardia aequatorialis* (Jackson 1906)
   (Alt. Equatorial Akalat)
Jackson's Bustard *Neotis denhami jacksoni* (**Bannerman** 1930)
   (Alt. Denham's/Stanley's Bustard)
Jackson's Crimsonwing *Cryptospiza jacksoni* (**Sharpe** 1902)
   (Alt. Dusky Crimsonwing, Jackson's Hill Finch)
Jackson's Francolin *Francolinus jacksoni* (**Ogilvie-Grant** 1891)
Jackson's Golden-backed Weaver *Ploceus jacksoni* (**Shelley** 1888)
   (Alt. Golden-backed Weaver)
Jackson's Hornbill *Tockus jacksoni* (Ogilvie-Grant 1891)
Jackson's Pipit *Anthus* (*cinnamomeus*) *latistriatus* (Jackson 1899)
Jackson's Widow *Euplectes jacksoni* (Sharpe 1891)
   (Alt. Jackson's Widowbird/Whydah)

Sir Frederick John Jackson (1859–1929) was an English administrator and explorer but also a naturalist and a keen ornithologist. He led a British expedition to make contact with Emin Pasha after the latter was isolated by the Mahdi's victory in the Sudan. In 1889 he led another expedition, financed by the British East Africa Company, to explore the new Kenya colony, and he later became its first governor. He was also Governor of Uganda from 1911 until 1918 and described the country as '*a hidden Eden, a wonderland for birds*'. He wrote *The Birds of Kenya Colony and the Uganda Protectorate* in 1928.

JAMES, F

James' Tchagra *Tchagra jamesi* (**Shelley** 1885)
   (Alt. Three-streaked Tchagra)

Frank Linsly James (1851–1890) was an explorer of the Sudan, Somalia, India and Mexico. He published *Experiences and Adventures During Three Winters Spent in the Sudan*, in 1883 and *The Unknown Horn of Africa; an Exploration from Berbera to the Leopard River*, which was edited by his widow and published in 1890. He was killed by a wounded elephant.

JAMES, H

James's Flamingo *Phoenicopterus* [*Phoenicoparrus*] *jamesi* (P L **Sclater** 1886)
   (Alt. Puna Flamingo)

Henry Berkeley James (1846–1892) was a British businessman who spent nearly 20 years in Chile. He employed a collector called Carlos, who obtained the specimen at Rahmer, in Tarapaca, north Chile. Mrs Berkeley James presented it to the British Natural History Museum.

JAMESON

Jameson's Antpecker *Parmoptila jamesoni jamesoni* (**Sharpe** & **Usher** 1872)
(Alt. Red-fronted Flowerpecker/Antpecker)
Jameson's Firefinch *Lagonosticta rhodopareia* (**Heuglin** 1868)
(Alt. Jameson's Hylia-finch, Pink-backed Firefinch)
Jameson's Wattle-eye *Platysteira jamesoni* (Sharpe 1890)

James Sligo Jameson (1856–1888) was an Irish hunter, explorer and naturalist. He collected in Borneo, South Africa, Spain, Algeria, the Rocky Mountains and, finally, in the Belgian Congo, where he died of haemorrhagic fever, at Bangala, whilst on an expedition with **Stanley** to rescue **Emin Pasha**. According to his obituary in The Times of 8 November 1890, he witnessed a cannibal banquet in the Upper Congo and was accused by Stanley of instigating it. He wrote *Story of the Rear Column of the Emin Pasha Relief Expedition,* which was published posthumously in 1890.

JAMESON

Jameson's Brilliant *Heliodoxa jamesoni* (**Gould***)
Jameson's Snipe *Gallinago jamesoni* (**Bonaparte** 1855)
(Alt. Andean Snipe)

Dr William Jameson (1796–1873) was a botanist and a professor at the University of Quito. Between 1864 and 1865 he prepared an account of the Ecuadorian flora, *Synopsis Plantarum Quitensium.* He was clearly an all-rounder since he collected a number of holotypes of birds as well as many plants. He was among the first to descend into the crater of Chimborazo, an extinct volcano in the Ecuadorian Andes. **Bonaparte** described the snipe from a specimen collected by Jameson in the Ecuadorian Andes. The brilliant appears in a **Gould** painting.

JANKOWSKI

Jankowski's Bunting *Emberiza jankowskii* (**Taczanowski** 1888**)**
(Alt. Rufous-backed Bunting)
Jankowski's Swan *Cygnus columbianus jankowskii* (Alphéraky 1904)
(Alt. [Eastern] Bewick's Swan)

Michel Jankowski (1840–1903) was a Polish zoologist who was exiled to Siberia with Wiktor **Godlewski** and others from 1863 until his death. There they were able to study the fauna of Lake Baikal and other regions of eastern Siberia largely because of the financial support of the Zoological Cabinet back in Poland.

JAPANESE

Few Japanese have had birds named after them which may seem surprising, given their relative wealth, history of exploration and tradition of scientific pursuit. However, it must be remembered that until Commodore Perry visited the country in the 1850s, and effectively brought about the Meiji Revolution, the country had been entirely cut off from the outside world and the real surprise is how quickly the Japanese nation moved from being a mediaeval society of samurai warriors to becoming a leading technological nation. Those celebrated in English common names are mostly ornithologists. Masauyi Uji **Hachisuka** was educated in England, explored in the Philippines and established a bird collecting centre there. I **Ijima** was Professor of Zoology at Tokyo University and first president of the Ornithological Society of Japan. Viscount Yorikatsu **Matsudaira** was a career ornithologist. T **Noguchi** was a Japanese collector.

JARDINE

Jardine's Babbler *Turdoides jardineii* (**A Smith** 1836)
(Alt. Arrow-marked Babbler)
Jardine's Harrier *Circus assimilis* (Jardine & Selby 1828)
(Alt. Spotted/Allied Harrier)
Jardine's Hummingbird *Boissonneaua jardini* (**Bourcier** 1851)
(Alt. Velvet-purple Coronet)
Jardine's Panoplites *Panoplites jardini* (**Gould***)
Jardine's Parrot *Poicephalus gulielmi* (Jardine 1849)
(Alt. Red-fronted/Red-headed Parrot)
Jardine's Pygmy Owl *Glaucidium jardinii* (**Bonaparte** 1855)
(Alt. Andean Pygmy Owl)

Sir William Jardine, Seventh Baronet of Applegarth (1800–1874) was a Scottish ornithologist who produced the *Naturalist's Library*, from 1833 to 1845. His private museum was said to be among the finest of his day. He wrote *Illustrations of Ornithology* in 1826 (with Prideaux Selby), *The Natural History of Hummingbirds* in 1833 and *The Natural History of the Nectariniidae* in 1834. The panoplites, a hummingbird, is only found as a **Gould** print.

JELSKI

Jelski's Bush Tyrant *Knipolegus signatus* (**Taczanowski** 1875)
(Alt. Andean Tyrant)
Jelski's Chat-Tyrant *Ochthoeca jelskii* Taczanowski 1883
Jelski's Coppertail *Metallura heterocerca* (**Gould***)
Jelski's Woodnymph *Thalurania jelskii* (Gould*)

Konstanty Jelski (1837–1896) was a Polish ornithologist who discovered about sixty new species of birds. His specimens are displayed in museums in Lima, where he was a curator between 1874 and 1878, and also in Paris, Warsaw and elsewhere. He returned to Poland in 1878 to become Curator of the Krakow Museum, a post he held until his death. The woodnymph and coppertail are '**Gould**' birds; the only references we can find relate to Gould's prints.

JERDON

Jerdon's Babbler *Chrysomma altirostre* (Jerdon 1862) [Extinct]
(Alt. Jerdon's Moupinia)
Jerdon's Baza *Aviceda jerdoni* (**Blyth** 1842)
Jerdon's Bushchat *Saxicola jerdoni* (Blyth 1867)
Jerdon's Bushlark *Mirafra affinis* (Blyth 1845)
Jerdon's Courser *Cursorius (Rhinoptilus) bitorquatus* (Blyth 1848)
Jerdon's Imperial Pigeon *Ducula badia* (**Raffles** 1822)
(Alt. Grey-headed/Band-tailed/Hodgson's/Bronze-backed/Maroon-backed/ Mountain Imperial Pigeon)

Jerdon's Laughing-thrush *Garrulax jerdoni* (Blyth 1851)
(Alt. Grey/White-breasted/Kerala Laughing-thrush)
Jerdon's Leafbird *Chloropsis cochinchinensis jerdoni* Blyth 1844
(Alt. Blue-winged/Yellow-headed/Golden-headed Leafbird, Golden-mantled Chloropsis)
Jerdon's Mannikin *Lonchura kelaarti jerdoni* (Jerdon 1863)
(Alt. Rufous-bellied/Rufous-breasted Munia, [Ceylon] Hill Munia)
Jerdon's Minivet *Pericrocotus erythropygius* (Jerdon 1840)
(Alt. White-bellied Minivet)
Jerdon's Nightjar *Caprimulgus atripennis* (Jerdon 1845)
Jerdon's Willow Warbler *Phylloscopus griseolus* (Blyth 1847)
(Alt. Sulphur-bellied Warbler)
Jerdon's Starling *Sturnus burmannicus* (Jerdon 1862)
(Alt. Vinous-breasted Starling)

Thomas Claverhill Jerdon (1811–1872) was a British physician who had both zoological and botanical interests. He was born in Durham and educated at the University of Edinburgh, in 1828. He studied medicine and became an assistant-surgeon in the East India Company. Jerdon published *Birds of India* between 1862 and 1864, which according to **Darwin** was *the* book on Indian birds. He also wrote *Illustrations of Indian Ornithology* and *The Game Birds and Wildfowl of India*, as well as *Mammals of India* and writings on ants among others.

JOHANNA

Johanna's Sunbird *Nectarinia johannae* (E & J Verreaux 1851)
(Alt. Madame Verreaux's Sunbird)

Johanna Verreaux was the wife of Jules P **Verreaux** (1807–1873). He and E Verreaux named the sunbird in her honour.

JOHANNIS

Johannes's Tody-Tyrant *Hemitriccus iohannis* (Snethlage 1907)

João Baptista de Sá was a collector on the Museu **Goeldi** expedition to the Rio Purús region of Brazil, in 1904. **Snethlage**, who described the tody-tyrant, may well have named it for the German translation of João, which is Johanne or Johannes. There is some speculation that he may have been an intimate friend of Ms Snethlage. Although we can find no confirmation of this, our source wrote '*Snethlage was no nun, nor saint for that matter and very advanced for her times. She seems to have had a number of paramours during her stint there*'. There has also been speculation that the name referred to Schönmann, the other collector on the trip, who prepared specimens, but this seems unlikely since his forename was, in fact, Joseph.

JOHNSTON

Johnston's Turaco *Musophaga johnstoni* (**Sharpe** 1901)
(Alt. Ruwenzori Turaco)

Sir Harry Hamilton Johnston (1858–1927) was a formidable English explorer and colonial administrator. He was a larger-than-life character and became known as the 'Tiny Giant' since as he was just five feet tall. Johnston was also an accomplished painter, photographer, cartographer, linguist, naturalist and writer. He started exploring tropical Africa in 1882 and the following year met up with Henry Morton Stanley in the Congo. He travelled in Cameroon, Nigeria, Liberia, Mozambique, Zanzibar, Nyasaland (now Malawi), Southern Rhodesia (now Zimbabwe), Angola, the Congo, South Africa, Tanzania, Kenya, Uganda and North Africa. In 1884 he was in East Africa and the following year joined the colonial service, serving in a number of posts in various African countries; Cameroon, Nigeria, Liberia, Mozambique, Tunisia, Zanzibar and Uganda. He also established a British Protectorate in Nyasaland. Johnston was Queen Victoria's first Commissioner and Consul-General to British Central Africa. He was a member of the Royal Academy of Art and his paintings of African wildlife are exceptional. He spoke over 30 African languages, as well as Arabic, Italian, Spanish, French and Portuguese. He was knighted in 1896 and retired in 1904, when he continued his pursuit of natural history. He discovered more than 100 new birds, reptiles, mammals and insects. Perhaps the most notable of all these is the Okapi *Okapia johnstoni*. He wrote more than 60 books including *The Story of My Life* in 1923, as well as more than 600 monographs and short articles. He made the very first Edison cylinder recordings in Africa, which have passed down his squeaky voice to posterity.

JOHNSTONE

Johnstone's Bush Robin *Luscinia johnstoniae* (**Ogilvie-Grant** 1906)
(Alt. Collared Bush Robin)
Johnstone's Lorikeet *Trichoglossus johnstoniae* (**Hartert** 1903)
(Alt. Mindanao/Mrs Johnstone's Lorikeet)

Mrs Marion Johnstone was a well-known aviculturist who received an award for breeding the lorikeet which is named after her. Goodfellow sent a bird to Mrs Johnstone in England in 1903, which was the first Johnstone's Lorikeet to be imported into Europe. Mrs Johnstone was the first to breed them successfully in captivity anywhere. This, and the robin, were discovered by Walter **Goodfellow**.

JONES

Jones's Silver Pheasant *Lophura nycthemera jonesi* (**Oates** 1903)

Probably named after Major Henry Jones who was an artist that specialised in painting pheasants and similar birds. Around the year 1900, he painted a series of pictures from the collection of the Zoological Society of London and nearly 90 years later Paul A Johnsgard used them as illustrations in his books *The Pheasants of the World* and *Bustards, Hemipodes, and Sandgrouse: Birds of Dry Places*.

JORET

Joret's Koklass *Pucrasia macrolopha joretiana* (**Heude** 1883)
(Alt. Koklass Pheasant)

We can find no evidence that Joret was a person and on balance we think this is a case of someone elses assuming that the bird must been named after a person and so inventing 'Joret's'. Our rationale for this is that *joretiana* is not in the genitive (*joreti* or *joretae*, as it should be if named after someone called Joret) but is an adjective, agreeing in the feminine nominative case with the Latin *pucrasia*. There is a subspecies of Dybowski's Sika Deer which has the scientific name *Cervus nippon joretianus* and, in this example, *joretianus* agrees with the Latin masculine of *Cervus*. Interestingly, **Heude**, who described the bird in 1883, also described a number of subspecies of Sika Deer, including the Hokkaido Sika Deer *Cervus nippon yesoensis*.

JOSEPHINE

Josephine's Lory *Charmosyna josefinae* (**Finsch** 1873)
(Alt. Josephine's Lorikeet)

Josephine Finsch was the wife of the German ornithologist Friedrich Hermann Otto **Finsch** (1839-1917).

JOUANIN

Jouanin's Petrel *Bulweria fallax* (Jouanin 1955)
(Alt. Jouanin's Gadfly Petrel)

Christian Jouanin (born 1925) is a French ornithologist who began his long association with the Paris museum at the age of 15. He was a pupil of Jacques **Berlioz**, who was in charge of the bird department there. His interests have been divided between humming-birds and petrels – an apparently strange association, but one shared with Osbert **Salvin** who was active in the 19th century. Jouanin's Petrel is one of the commonest oceanic birds in the Arabian Sea. Jouanin pointed out the differences between it and **Bonaparte**'s *Pterodoma aterrima*, the name until then given to the dark medium-sized petrel of the Arabian Sea, and described it as a new species. This event stimulated his interest in the Indian Ocean and he began to search for the breeding grounds of *P. aterrima*, a species which had not been collected since the preceding century. His quest led to the discovery of another unknown gadfly petrel, which he named Barau's Petrel *P baraui* for his friend and correspondent on Réunion Island, Armand **Barau**. Shortly afterwards he made the distinction between the Réunion and Seychelles populations of **Audubon**'s Shearwater *Puffinus lherminieri*, naming the Seychelles representatives *nicolae* after his wife (who he married when they were both 22 years old and with whom he has two daughters). In 1963 he participated with Francis Roux in an expedition to the Selvagems organised by G E Maul, the Director of the Funchal Museum in Madeira, and from this resulted a lasting friendship with the Zinos. Invited by Alec **Zino** to undetake ornithological studies in the Madeiran archipelago, he prepared a long study project on the biology and population dynamics of **Cory**'s Shearwater *Calonectris diomedea* and collaborated with Alec Zino in his conservation of the Selvagens. That project, which is ongoing, has resulted in over 80 publications authored by J-L Mougin, C Jouanin, F Roux, P A Zino and F Zino. Jouanin is co-author with Jean-Louis Mougin, of the chapter on the 'Procellarii-formes' in Peters' *Check-list of the Birds of the World*, Vol 1, second edition (1978). In 1997, in conjunction with Jean-François Voisin and Jean-Louis Mougin, he published, *Liste des types d'oiseaux des collections du Muséum national d'Histoire naturelle Procellariiformes (avec une note sur les catalogues du Laboratoire des Mammifères et Oiseaux)*. Jouanin is deeply involved in conservation activities. He was Founder and Director of the MAR Bureau (conservation of wetlands) in Paris, from 1965 to 1970, General Secretary of the French Societé Nationale de Protection de la Nature, from 1966 to 1981, and director of its publication *Le Courrier de la Nature* from 1967 to the present day. He was Vice-President of the International Union for the Conservation of Nature (IUCN) from 1970 to 1975, a Member of the International Ornithological Committee since 1954, and of its Permanent Executive Committee, from 1970 to 1978. He still found time to write most of the above for this publication!

JOURDAN

Jourdan's Woodstar *Chaetocercus jourdanii* (**Bourcier** 1839)
(Alt. Rufous-shafted Woodstar)

Jourdan was a collector in Trinidad.

JOUY

Jouyi's Wood Pigeon *Columba jouyi* (**Stejneger** 1887)
(Alt. Silver-banded Black/Silver-crescented/Riu-Kiu Black/Ryukyu Wood Pigeon)

Pierre Louis Jouy (1856–1894) was an American diplomat and amateur naturalist, and ethnographer. He wrote a *Hand-book of a Unique Collection of Ancient and Modern Korean and Chinese Works of Art, Procured in Korea During 1883* with Edward Grey in 1888. He was collecting in Japan in 1881 and Korea from 1885 to 1889, mostly with Dr F C Dale. Several species of fish, which he collected whilst in Hong Kong and Shanghai, in 1882 and 1883, are named after him in their scientific names. Later, around 1892, he collected in Arizona and New Mexico. There are a number of articles relating to his travels in the Smithsonian Institution annual reports of the 1880s.

JULIE

> Julie's Hummingbird *Damophila julie* (**Bourcier** 1842)
> (Alt. Violet-bellied Hummingbird)

Probably named after Julie **Mulsant**, wife of the French naturalist, or his granddaughter, also called Julie. Mulsant worked very closely with **Bourcier** and they jointly described many birds.

KAEDING

> Kaeding's Storm Petrel *Oceanodroma* (*leucorhoa*) *kaedingi* (Emerson 1906)
> (Alt. Leach's Storm Petrel, Leach's/Beal's/Gould's/White-winged/Socorro Petrel)

Henry Barroilhet 'HB' Kaeding (1877–1913) was a mineralogist and miner. He was also an amateur ornithologist who collected with his brother. He met Chester **Barlow** and joined the Cooper Ornithological Society through him. He visited Mexico, Korea and Nicaragua both through his work and on private expeditions. In 1897 he published *In Mexican waters* in The Nidologist, which included a description of the first collection of the eggs of the Black-vented Shearwater *Puffinus opisthomelas*. Kaeding also wrote *Bird life on the Farallone Islands* in The Condor in 1903 and *Birds from the West Coast of Lower California and Adjacent Islands* in 1905. The petrel occurs chiefly in Mexican Pacific waters.

KAEMPFER

> Kaempfer's Tody-Tyrant *Hemitriccus kaempferi* (**Zimmer** 1953)

Emil Kaempfer was a German collector who put together a large collection of South American fauna for the American Natural History Museum, between 1926 and 1931, when he collected birds in eastern Brazil. A catalogue of these species was published, in 1939, as *Studies of Birds from Eastern Brazil and Paraguay*, based on his collection. The bird was known only from one specimen collected by Kaempfer, in 1926, in southern Brazil, until its rediscovery in 1990 or 1991, as reported in World Birdwatch in December 1991 by M Pearman. Kaempfer collected a number of other birds which were known only from his specimens for many years. An example is the Caatinga Woodpecker, now generally regarded as a race (*obrieni*) of Rufous-headed Woodpecker *Celeus spectabilis* or perhaps, more likely, a separate species, which is known only from an adult female specimen collected by Kaempfer in 1926.

KAESTNER

Kaestner's Antpitta *Grallaria kaestneri* (Stiles 1992)
(Alt. Cundinamarca Antpitta)

Peter G Kaestner (1953–) is an American diplomat. He was born in Baltimore, Maryland and graduated in biology from Cornell University in 1976. He then served as a Peace Corps volunteer, teaching in a secondary school in Nyankunde Village in former Zaïre. He entered the Foreign Service in 1980 – the perfect career for a birder! He has served in India, Papua New Guinea, Colombia, Malaysia, Namibia, Guatemala and Brazil. As a birder, he is ranked in the top four world listers and he is recognised by the *Guinness Book of Records* as having been the first person ever to see a representative of each of the 159 bird families of the world. In 1989 he discovered the new antpitta in the mountains of eastern Colombia. The vernacular name proposed by the describer, Gary Stiles, was the 'Cundinamarca Antpitta'. However, there are those who have always called it 'Kaestner's Antpitta', not least because the bird may not be restricted to the Colombian state of Cundinamarca and the former name may be eventually abandoned in favour of the latter.

KALINOWSKI

Kalinowski's Tinamou *Nothoprocta kalinowskii* (**Berlepsch** & Stoltzman 1902)
(Alt. Taczanowski's Tinamou)

Jan Kalinowski (1860–1942) was a Polish zoologist who led an expedition to Peru from 1889 to 1902. The tinamou is endemic to Peru but until very recently it was only known from two old specimens, one of them collected by Kalinowski in 1894, apparently at altitude of 4,575 m just south of Cuzco. It was rediscovered by Gunnar Engblom, in 2000.

KANDT

Kandt's Waxbill *Estrilda kandti* (**Reichenow** 1902)
(Alt. Black-headed Waxbill)

Dr Richard Kandt (1867–1918) was a physician and the first German 'Resident' in Rwanda from 1907 until 1913. He was sent on an expedition by the Kaiser and Bismarck to find the source of the Nile in 1898.

KAWALL

Kawall's Parrot *Amazona kawalli* (Grantsau & Camargo 1989)
(Alt. White-cheeked/Blue-cheeked Amazon)

Nelson Kawall (1928–) was a leading Brazilian aviculturalist and exponent of captive breeding programmes. He kept and bred budgerigars as a child and received his first parrot, a Blue-fronted Amazon *Amazona aestiva*, as a present when he was 12 years old. He has been very interested in Brazilian parrots ever since. In 1968 he established himself as a commercial breeder, whose company AVEX was involved in the import and export of parrots. He became a friend and admirer of the ornithologist Rolf Grantsau and learned a lot about parrots by regularly examining Rolf's skin collection. It was this experience that increased his ability to detect differences between different species and races of parrots. He bred a number of species for the first time in captivity. He was the first Brazilian breeder to sex his birds; first by laparoscopy, later by karyotype and since

1992 by DNA. He has always collaborated with any university interested in studying parrots. At one time he had some 50 different species of parrots in the facilities he constructed in the yard of his house. Later he decided to specialise in rare and exotic species and their colour mutations. His collection included a pair of Spix's Macaws *Ara spixii* and he was a leading exponent of their conservation. He closed his establishment in 1978, mainly because of changes in Brazilian legislation with regard to the commercial exploitation of native fauna. At that time he transferred the Brazilian species to his house, where he continued his breeding activities privately. He published an article, in 1999, in Atualidades Ornitológicas about his struggle to save Spix's Macaw from extinction through the formation of the 'Permanent Committee for the Recovery of the Spix's Macaw'. In 1968 while visiting his friend and fellow bird lover José Xavier de Mendonça in Santarém, Pará, he had the opportunity to see for the first time an unusual specimen which displayed some of the characteristics of the Mealy Amazon *Amazona farinosa* but with some very evident differences. He brought this bird to São Paulo where he spotted another specimen with the same characteristics in the aviary of another breeder, Alcides Vertamatti. He gathered these two birds and two specimens of *Amazona farinosa* in his house and called a meeting of a group of breeders and Rolf Gransau, to convince them that this was a new species. This meeting was the determining factor leading to the description of *Amazona kawalli* in 1990 and the subsequent identification of its present distribution. The bird was described and named by Grantsau and Helio Camargo, the then curator of the avian skin collection at the Sao Paulo Natural History Museum. As far as Kawall was concerned, José Xavier de Mendonça was the true discoverer of *Amazona kawalli*. In 1997 Kawall discontinued his activities as a breeder of Brazilian parrots. He is still an important contributor and counsellor for many young ornithologists and breeders. There was also probably a live example of Kawall's Parrot in London Zoo, in 1975, as a photograph taken there appears to be of this species. The species may first have been detected as long ago as 1924 as a short article written by **Stresemann** in Ornithologische Mitteilungen described the characteristics of a skin giving it the name *rubricauda* (red-tailed). Streseman wrote that he believed it to be a '*curious mutation*' of the Mealy Amazon. The authenticity of the species was resolved by A J Pittman and N J Collar, who compared live specimens, photographs and skins from collections in London, Berlin and Brazil and recorded their findings in the Bulletin of the British Ornithologists' Club in 1996; *Amazona kawalli is a valid name for a valid species* (Bull. B.O.C 116:256–265).

KEAY

Keay's Bleeding-heart *Gallicolumba keayi* (W E Clarke 1900)
(Alt. Negros Bleeding-heart/Blood-breasted Pigeon)

W A Keay was a sugar planter on Negros (Philippines).

KELLEY

Kelley' s Tit-Babbler *Macronous kelleyi* (**Delacour** 1932)
(Alt. Grey-faced Tit-Babbler)

W V Kelley (1861–1932) was an American philanthropist and sponsor. There were a number of Kelley-Roosevelt Field Museum Expeditions in the late 1920s and 1930s, and there were also Delacour expeditions around this time. It is likely that they knew each other and that Kelley sponsored Delacour's work.

KELLOGG

Kellogg's Ptarmigan *Lagopus mutus kellogae* (**Grinnell** 1910)
(Alt. Rock Ptarmigan)

Clara Louise Kellogg (1879–1967) was an intrepid naturalist who explored the American

West from Alaska to the tip of Baja California for more than half a century, in conjunction with Annie M Alexander. These two women contributed more than 25,000 fossil, plant and animal specimens to the University of California's Natural History Museum. In 1910 Kellogg published the second-ever paper on mammalogy in the United States known to be authored by a woman. The Louise Kellogg research award of the Museum of Vertebrate Zoology at the University of California, Berkeley, is in her memory.

KEMP

Kemp's Longbill *Macrosphenus kempi* (**Sharpe** 1905)

Robin [Robert] Kemp (1871–?) was originally an accountant who worked for a company building a railway in Sierra Leone. However, he became a naturalist and professional collector and combined his collecting in Sierra Leone, between 1902 and 1904, with his day job. He collected in other parts of Africa around 1906–1908, in Australia from 1912 to 1914, and in Argentina from 1916 until 1917. (There is also a hybrid turtle named Kemp's Ridley Turtle *Lepidochelys kempi* but this is after a fisherman, Richard Kemp, who first sent a specimen to a museum.)

KENNICOTT

Kennicott's Screech Owl *Otus kennicottii* (**Elliot** 1867)
    (Alt. Western Screech Owl)
Kennicott's Willow Warbler *Phylloscopus borealis* (H **Blasius** 1858)
    (Alt. Arctic Warbler)

Robert Kennicott (1835–1866) was an American naturalist who founded the Chicago Academy of Sciences and who explored the American Northwest from 1857 to 1859. At 17 he was sent to study under Dr Jared Potter **Kirtland** in Cleveland. Kennicott worked for **Baird** at the Smithsonian, largely helping classify animals collected on the western frontier by army personnel involved in railroad surveys. Through Baird he went to Canada and met Hudson's Bay's chief trader, Bernard **Ross**, who became a close friend. Elliott **Coues** recognised a new sandpiper among the specimens which Kennicott sent to the Smithsonian and he named it Baird's Sandpiper *Calidris bairdii*. One of Baird's biographers described Kennicott thus: '*He became the consummate collector, and when more demanding responsibilities intruded upon his direct involvement in collecting and classifying, he became a collector of collectors. Under his training and guidance virtually all the major natural scientists of the nineteenth century developed their enthusiasms and their professional competence.*' After a period as a curator in Chicago he left to explore 'Russian America' and spent the rest of his life in Alaska where he collected a small owl near Sitka. He sent the specimen back to the Chicago Academy, where Daniel **Elliot** recognised it as a new species and named it *Otus kennicottii* in his honour. Kennicott suffered a second and fatal heart attack near Nulato, Alaska, at the age of just 30, in 1866. H **Blasius** described the warbler in 1858.

KENRICK

Kenrick's Starling *Poeoptera kenricki* (**Shelley** 1894)

Major R W E Kenrick was a British Army officer in Kenya. The type specimen in the British Natural History Museum was first discovered and apparently collected by Kenrick in the Usambara Mountains. Kenrick presented it to the museum in 1894. The museum also has a specimen of young female, which was collected in 1879, and it is not entirely clear which of the two birds is Kenrick's specimen.

KENYON

Kenyon's Shag *Phalacrocorax kenyoni* (Siegel-Causey 1991)

Karl W Kenyon is a wildlife biologist. He collected the type specimen of the shag on 22 February 1959 from a fish net. The shag was not described until 1991, by Siegel-Causey, but its taxonomic status remains in doubt. Rohwer, Filardi, Bostwick and Peterson in their *A critical evaluation of Kenyon's Shag* (*Phalacrocorax* [*stictocarbo*] *kenyoni*) in The Auk 117(2000): 308–320, virtually dismiss it and conclude that it is within the variation possible for the Pelagic Cormorant *Phalacrocorax pelagicus*. Kenyon also carried out a 4,000-mile aerial search for the Caribbean Monk Seal *Monachus tropicalis*, in 1973, concluding that it is extinct – as was feared.

KERAUDREN

Keraudren's Manucode *Manucodia keraudrenii* (**Lesson** & Garnot 1826)
(Alt. Trumpet Manucode)

Pierre F Keraudren was a French military physician. He was trained at the School of Naval Medicine, Brest, in 1782. In 1801 he was ship's surgeon aboard the *Géographe* under Nicolas-Thomas **Baudin** on trips to Mauritius, Australia and elsewhere. The bird must have been collected in Irian Jaya during one of these voyages. Baudin named Cape Keraudren in Western Australia, now a nature reserve, after him. In 1813, he was appointed by Napoleon to be the French Navy's Medical Corps Inspector-General, a position which he held for 32 years. He wrote a description of the cholera outbreak in India of 1831.

KESSLER

Kessler's Thrush *Turdus kessleri* (**Przewalski** 1876)
(Alt. White-backed Thrush)

Karl Theodorovich Kessler (1815–1881) was a Russian German zoologist and collector, who apparently took part in the 1874 Fedtschensko expedition to Turkestan and the Aral-Caspian Expedition of 1877. He wrote about fishes in the reports on the two expeditions. In 1880 he was Dean of St Petersburg University.

KING LOUIS (XVI)

King Louis (XVI)'s Starfront *Coeligena iris* (**Gould** 1854)
(Alt. Rainbow Starfrontlet)

Louis XVI (1754–1793) was King of France at the time of the French Revolution, which started with the storming of the Bastille on 14 July 1789 and which led him to the guillotine.

KING OF SAXONY

King of Saxony's Bird of Paradise *Pteridophora alberti* (Meyer 1894)
(Alt. King-of-Saxony Bird of Paradise)

Albert (1828–1902) was King of Saxony from 1873. Whilst he was a Catholic king of a country with a significant Protestant minority, he seems to have been a popular monarch among all parties. He was also a soldier who fought in the Seven Weeks' War of 1866. **Meyer**, who described the bird, was German, so presumably he named it for his own monarch.

KIRK

Kirk's Francolin *Francolinus sephaena rovuma* (G R **Gray** 1867)
(Alt. Crested Francolin)
Kirk's White-eye *Zosterops kirkii* (**Shelley** 1880)
(Alt. Grand Comoro White-eye)

Sir John Kirk, MD (1832–1922), was a Scottish administrator in Africa. He took part, as a physician and naturalist, on David Livingstone's second Zambezi expedition, from 1858 until 1863. Kirk contributed much to the eradication of the slave trade. He was Vice-Consul in Zanzibar in 1866, and then Consul-General in 1873. During his service he persuaded the sultan to abolish the slave trade in 1873 and to concede mainland territories to the British East Africa Company in 1887. He served on the Tsetse Fly Commission in 1886. Kirk was a polymath whose interests included botany, geography, history, geology, chemistry and photography, as well as the study of Swahili, Arabic, Spanish, Portuguese and French. He was a Fellow of the Royal Botanical Society, who collected and sent specimens to the Royal Botanical Gardens at Kew in London. He also collected the first fishes from Lake Nyasa to reach Western science and observed that they were almost all endemic. He received numerous honorary degrees and awards, including the Fellowships of the Royal Society of London and the Geographical Society of Marcella.

KIRTLAND

Kirtland's Saw-whet Owl *Aegolius acadicus* (J F Gmelin 1788)
(Alt. Northern Saw-whet Owl)
Kirtland's Warbler *Dendroica kirtlandii* (**Baird** 1852)

Dr Jared Potter Kirtland (1793–1877) was a naturalist, botanist, doctor, legislator, teacher and writer. He also founded the Cleveland Museum of Natural History and the Cleveland Medical College. He was a contemporary of **Agassiz**, **Audubon** and other notables who were documenting and classifying the plants and animals of North America at that time. Kirtland was named after his maternal grandfather, Jared Potter, who was himself a distinguished physician and amateur naturalist. He was an accomplished horticulturalist who managed a large plantation of white mulberry trees for the rearing of silkworms and who is credited with originating 26 varieties of cherries and six of pears. Kirtland made one important scientific discovery that brought him national attention. He asserted that the freshwater mussels (Unionacea) have distinct sexes which had been mistakenly classified previously as different species. The Assistant-Secretary of the Smithsonian Institution disputed this at first but, when Agassiz proved Kirtland right, he later made up for his early doubts by giving Kirtland's name to a specimen of a warbler, which the naturalist had been the first to collect and classify.

KITTLITZ

Kittlitz's Crake *Porzana monasa* (Kittlitz 1858) [Extinct]
(Alt. Kosrae/Kusai/Ponape Crake)
Kittlitz's Murrelet *Brachyramphus brevirostris* (**Vigors** 1829)
Kittlitz's Plover *Charadrius pecuarius* (**Temminck** 1823) [Extinct]
(Alt. Kittlitz's Sandplover)
Kittlitz's Starling *Aplonis corvina* (Kittlitz 1833)
(Alt. Kosrae/Kusai [Mountain]Starling)
Kittlitz's Thrush *Zoothera terrestris* (Kittlitz 1830) [Extinct]
(Alt. Bonin Thrush)
Kittlitz's Woodpigeon *Columba versicolor* (Kittlitz 1832)
(Alt. Bonin Woodpigeon/Shining Pigeon/Bonin Black Pigeon/Bonin Fruit Pigeon)

Friedrich Heinrich Freiherr von Kittlitz (1799–1874) was a Polish-born German artist, naval officer, explorer and ornithologist. He was a friend of Eduard **Rüppell** who encouraged his interest in natural history and he went with him to North Africa in 1831. Between 1826 and 1829 he undertook a round-the-world journey under Lutke, the 'Senjavin' Expedition, following which he published *Twenty-Four Views of the Vegetation of the Coasts and Islands of the Pacific*, in 1861. He was the first person to collect the murrelet.

KLAAS

Klaas' Cuckoo *Chrysococcyx klaas* (**Stephens** 1815)

Levaillant named Klaas' Cuckoo after his Khoi Khoi (Hottentot) servant, who presumably found the bird in 1784. No more is known about him.

KLAGES

Klages' Antwren *Myrmotherula klagesi* (**Todd** 1927)

Samuel M Klages (1875–1957) was an American collector. He left the United States for South America in 1891 and collected in a range of countries; in Venezuela from 1898 until 1913, Trinidad & Tobago from 1912 until 1913, Venezuela from 1913 to 1914 and again in 1919, French Guiana from 1917 to 1918 and in Brazil in 1919 and again from 1920 to 1926. Most of these trips were undertaken for the Bird Section of the Carnegie Museum of Natural History in Pittsburgh. He continued to make trips to South America until 1932. He then lived for a while with a niece, Alva Held, a high school counsellor, her mother and his sister Mary Amelia, in Knoxville. Apparently he annoyed Alva when his hair and moustache dye stained her bathroom sink and he left and set up home in an apartment. He must have made bad investments as he is listed in the 1943 Pittsburgh city directory as a writer at a Perrysville Avenue address and in receipt of the state dole. He wrote an unpublished romantic novel and offered a publisher an account of his travels, but his manuscripts were all burnt after he died of heart disease, having already been diagnosed as senile. He is commemorated in a number of moths such as *Amaxia klagesi*, *Tessella klagesi*, *Ordishia klagesi* and *Robinsonia klagesi* and other insects such as the Hymenoptera *Trybliographa klagesi* and *Belyta klagesi*. **Salvadori** first described the antwren in 1867, which is known only from a few localities in west Brazil on the lower Amazon in western Pará, from Óbidos to Santarém, as a subspecies of Salvadori's Antwren *Myrmotherula minor*. **Todd** redescribed the antwren in 1927, splitting it from Salvadori's, whihc is restricted to coastal southeast Brazil.

KLEINSCHMIDT

Kleinschmidt's Falcon *Falco kreyenborgi* (Kleinschmidt, 1929)
(Alt. Peregrine Falcon)

Theodor Kleinschmidt (1870–1954) was a German ornithologist who explored and collected in the Pacific. He published *Theodor Kleinschmidt's Notes on the Hill Tribes of Viti Levu*, 1877–1878. In 1925, a German traveller named Kreyenborg who was visiting southern Argentina trapped a white falcon there and sent it back to Germany. Kleinschmidt saw the bird in 1929 and named it as a new species, *Falco kreyenborgi*. Scientists observed only two more birds like this until 1980 when one was seen in a nest of Peregrine Falcons *Falco peregrinus*. In 1981 to 1982 the same scientists returned to Argentina and found many more white falcons, both as adults and as nestlings in the nests of Argentine Peregrine Falcons. Sometimes there were white falcon pulli in the nests of 'normal dark' Peregrine adults. In 1983 the scientific community officially accepted that the white falcon of Argentina is actually just a very rare colour morph of the Peregrine and is not another species at all.

KLEPTOMANIACS

One might assume, quite wrongly, that all ornithologists and bird collectors were honest and upright fellows. There are examples of people who have been anything but the soul of veracity (see Charlatans). However, one larger than life figure does stand out as a virtual kleptomaniac – his strongly-suspected theft of skins and stuffed specimens from museums is almost unprecedented. Richard **Meinertzhagen**, despite his many undoubted qualities, was eventually accused of mendacity and thievery. Despite long suspicion, documentary evidence of probable fraud only emerged in 1993, when the British ornithologist Alan Knox published an exposé; he had examined almost 100 redpolls that Meinertzhagen had donated to the British Natural History Museum and noted that, whilst most had been prepared to the 'average' taxidermy standards typical of Meinertzhagen, a few of the best-looking birds had been prepared with a variety of better techniques. Knox concluded that this proved that the latter had been appropriated by Meinertzhagen. This claim was reinforced when researchers looking for the Forest Owlet in India deduced that Meinertzhagen had stolen and claimed specimens as his own; this was only apparent because he had claimed to have found the bird in an area where it had never been seen and, which furthermore, his own records revealed that he had never visited! These allegations were made only after Meinertzhagen's death in 1967, although some had held similar suspcions during his lifetime.

KOCH

Koch's Pitta *Pitta kochi* (Bruggemann 1876)
  (Alt. Whiskered Pitta)

Gottlieb von Koch (1849–1914) was a German collector and taxidermist who was Director of the Hessian Federal State Museum at the turn of the 19th century. In 1887 he published *Die Gorgoniden des Golfes von Neapel und der angrenzenden Meeresabschnitte*. The pitta is endemic to the northern island of Luzon in the Philippines.

KOEPCKE

Koepcke's Cacique *Cacicus koepckeae* (O'Neill 1965)
  (Alt. Selva Cacique)
Koepcke's Hermit *Phaethornis koepckeae* (Weske & Terborgh 1977)
Koepcke's Owl *Otus koepckeae* (Hekstra 1982)
  (Alt. Maria Koepcke's Screech Owl)

Maria Koepcke (1924–1971) was born Maria Emilia Ana von Mikulicz-Radecki in Leipzig, Germany. She went to Peru in 1950, where she joined her husband Hans, an ecologist, at the Museum of Natural History in San Marcos, in 1960, as an ornithologist. She eventually came to be known as 'the Mother of Peruvian Ornithology'. Her study of a coastal biome of Peru was a seminal work. She also wrote *Corte Ecológico Transversal en los Andes del Peru Central* in 1954, *Die Vögel des Waldes von Zarate* in 1958 and *Las Aves del Departmento de Lima* in 1964. She was killed in an air crash in Amazonia on Christmas Eve 1971. The owl is a Peruvian endemic, which was first described by Gerrit Paulus Hekstra and named in her honour.

KOLBE

Kolbe's Vulture *Gyps coprotheres* (J R **Forster** 1798)
(Alt. Cape Griffon/Vulture)

Peter Kolbe (1675–1726) was a Dutch Boer who lived in the Cape region of South Africa from 1705 to 1713. English translations often refer to him mistakenly as P Kolben. He published several studies about the eagles and vultures of South Africa. He also wrote *The present state of the Cape of Good-Hope – A Particular Account of the Several Nations of the Hottentots,* the English translation of which was published in 1731. He also introduced the musical instrument, the goura, to the outside world. J R **Forster** first described the vulture in 1798 but we imagine that since many of Forster's notes were not published until 50 years after his death the vernacular name was assigned to Kolbe instead.

KORTHALS

Korthals's Green Pigeon *Treron sphenura korthalsi* (**Bonaparte** 1855)
(Alt. Wedge-tailed/Korthasi's/Singing/Kokla [Green]Pigeon)

Pieter Willem Korthals (1807–1892) was a German (some say Dutch) botanist who collected mostly in Sumatra in the 1830s and 1840s. His name is associated with a number of orchids but his work on pitcher plants was seminal; in 1839 he published the first monograph on Nepenthes (pitcher plants), naming nine species. He collected specimens of the Giant Pitcher Plant *Nepenthes rajah* in the highlands of Borneo. In the 1840s he was working on the Durian fruit *Durio zibethinus*. The pigeon is found in Sumatra.

KOSSLOW

See **Kozlov**.

KOZLOV

Kozlov's Accentor *Prunella koslowi* (**Przevalsky** 1887)
(Alt. Mongolian Accentor)
Koslow's Babax *Babax koslowi* (**Bianchi** 1906)
(Alt. Tibetan Babax)
Koslow's Bunting *Emberiza koslowi* (Bianchi 1904)
(Alt. Tibetan Bunting)

General Pyotr Kuzmich Kozlov (1863–1935) was a Russian who was one of **Przevalsky**'s companions on his fourth and last expedition, and who explored in central Asia around the turn of the century. He wrote *Mongoliya I Kam*. He was sent to Tibet to improve political relations there but he stopped on the Silk Road in 1908, when he discovered Khara-Khoto, the 'Black City', which had been described by Marco Polo. Khara-Khoto lies just inside the present-day Chinese border with Mongolia. It was '*the city of his dreams*' and he made excavations uncovering many scrolls, which he took back for study.

KOTZEBUE

Kotzebue's Kittiwake *Rissa tridactyla* (Linnaeus 1758)
(Alt. Black-legged Kittiwake)

Count Otto Von Kotzebue (1787–1846) was a Russian naval officer and Estonian explorer. He was born and died in Reval, now Tallinn in Estonia, which was part of Russia in his day. He travelled with von Krusenstern on his circumnavigation of the world, between 1803 and 1806, and he then commanded two further voyages around the world, from 1815 to 1818, and 1823 to 1826. He discovered around 400 islands in the South Seas, checked the location of others and gathered information on the Pacific coast of Siberia.

He also explored the northwest coast of Alaska, then a Russian possession, looking for a Northwest Passage. In 1816 he discovered and explored Kotzebue Sound. His expeditions made reports on ethnography and natural history. He wrote *A Voyage of Discovery* in 1821 and *A New Voyage round the World* in 1830. John Muir records '*Kotzebue's gull, the kittiwake, about the ship; no seals or walrus…*' in *The Cruise of the Corwin*, his journal of the Arctic Expedition of 1881. We think the bird is named after the area, which was named after the man, but it may have been collected on his voyage.

KRETSCHMER

Kretschmer's Longbill *Macrosphenus kretschmeri* (**Reichenow** & **Neumann** 1895)
(Alt. Kretschmer's Greenbul)

Dr Eugen Franz Kretschmer (1868–1894) was a German collector in Kenya. His youth was spent in Russian-occupied Poland. He studied medicine in Munich, Leipzig and Kiel. From 1891 to 1893 he was associated with the museum in Kiel and in 1894 he joined the Berlin Natural History Museum's expedition to British East Africa. As he was such a keen ornithologist the museum in Berlin, to which his small collection went after his death, had great hopes that he would become a major figure in the field. Their hopes were dashed as shortly after leaving the station at Marangu, he, his companion Dr Lent, and 13 native Kenyans were all murdered.

KRIDER

Krider's Hawk *Buteo jamaicensis krideri* (Hoopes 1873)
(Alt. Red-tailed Hawk)

John Krider (1819–?1896) was a Philadelphia taxidermist, gunsmith and professional collector who took two specimens of the hawk in Iowa in 1872. Unusually, Krider published his field notes in books and also in articles in *Forest and Stream* magazine. In 1848, he and **Heermann** made a bird collecting expedition to Florida. It was probably he and Milnor Klapp who were the authors of *Krider's Sporting Anecdotes, Illustrative of the Habits of Certain Varieties of American Game,* published in Philadelphia in 1853. Nathaniel H Bishop recorded that '*Monday, November 9, was a cold, wet day. Mr. Knight and the old, enthusiastic gunsmith-naturalist of the city, Mr. John Krider, assisted me to embark in my now decked, provisioned, and loaded canoe*' in his *Voyage of a Paper Canoe* in 1874.

KRÜPER

Krüper's Nuthatch *Sitta krueperi* (**Pelzeln** 1863)

Theobald Johannes Krüper (1829–1921) was a German ornithologist, entomologist, collector and natural history trader. He wrote *Ornithologische Notizen Uber Griechenland* in 1862 and *Beitrag zur Ornithologie Kleinasiens* in 1875. He became Director of the Museum of Athens University in 1872 and continued in that post until his death.

KUBARY

Kubary's Crow *Corvus kubaryi* (**Reichenow** 1885)
(Alt. Guam/Mariana Crow)

Jan S Kubary (1846–1896) was a Polish explorer and an involuntary emigrant from his native Poland. He collected in the Pacific from 1868 to 1879 and in New Guinea from 1885 until 1895, for Godeffroy & Son Co. Many of his specimens are in the Godeffroy Museum in Hamburg. He was part of the Branicki Zoological Cabinet and enriched them with valuable specimens. He had landholdings on Pohnpei in Micronesia. He wrote (in Polish and German) the three volume *Ethnographische Beitrage Zur Kenntnis des Karolinen*

Archipels in 1889 as well as a number of articles for the Journal Des Museum Godeffroy, mostly on ethnography with a particular interest in religious practices.

KUHL

Kuhl's Cape Parrot *Poicephalus robustus fuscicollis* (Kuhl 1820)
Kuhl's Ground Thrush *Zoothera interpres* (**Temminck** 1826)
(Alt. Chestnut-capped Thrush)
Kuhl's Parakeet *Vini kuhlii* (**Vigors** 1824)
(Alt. Kuhl's Lorikeet)
Kuhl's Sunbird *Aethopyga eximia* (**Horsfield** 1821)
(Alt. White-flanked Sunbird)

Dr Heinrich Kuhl (1796–1821) was a German ornithologist who was an assistant to Conrad Jacob Temminck. He also worked with Johan Conrad van Hasselt in Java for the Netherlands Committee for Natural Science. He wrote *Conspectus Psittacorum* in 1820 Kuhl died in Buitenzorg of a tropical disease.

KÜHN

Kühn's Myzomela *Myzomela kuehni* (**Rothschild** 1903)
(Alt. Crimson-hooded Myzomela)
Kühn's White-eye *Zosterops kuehni*
(Alt. Ambon/Amboina Yellow White-eye) (**Hartert** 1906)

Dr Heinrich Kühn (1860–1906) was a German naturalist who collected in Sulawesi between 1882 and 1885, and in the Kai Islands around 1898.

KUMLIEN

Kumlien's [Iceland] Gull *Larus glaucoides kumlieni* (**Brewster** 1883)

Thure Ludwig Theodor Kumlien (1819–1888) was a Swedish naturalist who later settled in America. He lived in Wisconsin and collected on his own land. He also acted as a collecting agent for various European museums, including the Natural History Museum in Stockholm. In 1867 he became Professor of Natural Science at Albion College and in 1883 Curator at the Milwaukie Museum in Wisconsin. He co-wrote *History of American Birds*. His son Ludwig (1853–1902) was also an American ornithologist who, with N Hollister, wrote *The birds of Wisconsin* which was published in 1903 in the Bulletin of the Wisconsin Natural History Society. Ludwig Kumlien joined the Howgates Arctic Expedition from 1877 to 1878 as a zoologist, and between 1879 and 1891 he worked for the United States Government in fisheries investigation and contributed to *North American Food Fishes*. From 1891 until his death, Ludwig Kumlien was professor of Natural Science and Physics at Milton College. This race of the Iceland Gull is a strong candidate for species status.

KUSER

Kuser's Blood Pheasant *Ithaginis cruentus kuseri* (Beebe 1912)

Colonel Anthony Rudolph Kuser of Trenton, New Jersey, was an American of Swiss descent, who was an avid pheasant fancier and a wealthy patron of the New York Zoological Park. 'Colonel' was an honorary title given for serving as a member of Governor Abbett's staff. He also served Governors Wertz and Griggs. He was President of the South Jersey Gas and Electric Lighting Company, which he took over in 1909 and he was also Vice-President of the Public Services Corporation of New Jersey. He had interests in a brewery and in an ice-making company, together with his four brothers. In 1909 he offered $60,000 for an expedition to conduct research on pheasants and to write an updated monograph on the family. His only condition was to have William Beebe, who later wrote the required monograph, as the expedition leader. Kuser declared himself willing to pay for all the best artists to do the colour plates, to meet all the printing, binding and marketing costs, and even to let the book be published in the name of the New York Zoological Society. Kuser bequeathed money to the New Jersey Audubon Society. Beebe is much more famous for his exploits in descending to the depths of the oceans in his bathysphere, but he also made exceptional contributions to ornithology.

LABAT

Labat's Conure *Aratinga labati* (Labat 1724) [Extinct]
(Alt. Guadeloupe Parakeet)

Jean Baptiste Labat (1663–1738) was a French Dominican missionary, although British 17th century biographers wrote of him as a pirate because he defended Guadeloupe against the English. He was sent to the West Indies and explored a number of islands. In 1703 he founded the city of Basse-Terre in Guadeloupe. He also performed valuable botanical research and wrote extensively about his travels. His account of a hunting expedition conducted on 14–15 March 1696 described how a party of six men captured more than 200 Black-capped Petrels *Pterodroma hasitata*, which they hauled from their burrows in Guadeloupe. Apparently he also decimated the flamingo colony on Aves Island in 1705. The conure became extinct in 1722.

LAFAYETTE

Lafayette's Junglefowl *Gallus lafayetii* (**Lesson** 1831)
(Alt. Ceylon Junglefowl)

Marie Joseph Paul Yves Roch Gilbert du Mothier, Marquis de Lafayette (1757–1834) was a French nobleman and cavalry officer. He inherited a large fortune but, coming from a long military line, he studied at the military academy in Versailles and became a cavalry captain at the age of 16. In 1777 he bought a ship and left for America to fight in the revolution against the British. He was appointed a major-general and was assigned to the staff of George Washington. He had several notable victories. After the British surrender he returned home, where he cooperated closely with Ambassadors Benjamin Franklin and then Thomas Jefferson on behalf of American interests. In France he worked toward establishing a constitutional monarchy in the period before the French Revolution of 1789. He tried unsuccessfully to help the reluctant King and Queen, was denounced as a traitor and had to flee the country. He returned in 1800 and found his fortune had been confiscated. In 1815 he was elected to the Chamber of Deputies. As one of its vice-presidents, he worked for Napoleon's abdication after the Battle of Waterloo. Lafayette became a focus of resistance to the Bourbon kings and in 1830 he led the Revolution dethroning them. He refused the presidency of the new republic and instead helped to make Louis Philippe the constitutional monarch of France, although by the time of his death he regretted having supported Philippe and preferred the republican option. The junglefowl was named in his honour by **Lesson** at the height of Lafayette's fame. The city of La Fayette in California is also named after him, as is Fayettevilly in North Carolina, and a number of other cities.

LA SAGRA

La Sagra's Flycatcher *Myiarchus sagrae* (**Gundlach** 1852)

Ramón de la Sagra (1801–1871) was a Spanish economist and botanist who lived and worked in Cuba, and died in Switzerland. He was appointed Director of the Havana Botanical Gardens in 1822, a post he retained until 1834. During this time he established a model farm and collected widely. In later life he returned to Spain and devoted himself to the study of political economy before joining the French revolution of 1854. He wrote *Principios de Botanica Agricola* in 1833 and the 13 volumes of *Historia Física, Política y Natural de la Isla de Cuba*, which appeared between 1839 and 1861.

LA SELLE

La Selle's Thrush *Turdus swalesi* (**Wetmore** 1927)
(Alt. La Selle Thrush)

This is another transcription error as the thrush was named after a geographical location and not a person; it was orginally thought to be confined to 'Massif de la Selle', Haiti, where it is now extirpated, although it survives elsewhere on the island of Hispaniola. However, its original name, Swales's Thrush, honoured Bradshaw H Swales, who co-authored the first comprehensive avifauna of Hispaniola with Alexander **Wetmore**, in 1931.

LA TOUCHE

La Touche's Shortwing *Luscinia obscura* (**Berezowski** & **Bianchi** 1891)
(Alt. Blackthroat, Black-throated [Blue] Robin)

John David Digues La Touche (1861–1935) was French born and English educated. He was Inspector of Customs in China from 1882 until 1921 and wrote *A Handbook of the Birds of Eastern China* in 1925. He intended to retire to Ireland but died at sea on the way home from Spain.

LADY AMHERST

Lady Amherst's Pheasant *Chrysolophus amherstiae* (**Leadbeater** 1829)

Sarah Countess Amherst (1762–1838) was married to William Pitt Amherst, who was the Governor General of Bengal from 1822 until 1828. Lord Amherst was responsible for sending the first specimen of the bird to London in 1828. It did not survive the journey but, nevertheless, the ornithologist **Leadbeater** used that specimen for his official description. In July 1869 the first live specimens successfully reached London. A plant, Lady Amherst's Grobya *Grobya amherstiae* is also named after her.

LADY GOULD

Lady Gouldian Finch *Chloebia gouldiae* (**Gould** 1844)
(Alt. Gouldian Finch)

Lady Elizabeth Gould (1804–1841). In 1841 the English ornithologist, John Gould, while on an Australian expedition, came across what most believe to be the most beautiful finch in the world. John **Gould** named this magnificent finch 'The Lady Gouldian', to honour his artist wife.

LADY MACGREGOR

Lady MacGregor Bowerbird *Amblyornis macgregoriae* (**De Vis** 1890)
(Alt. Crested/Macha-breasted Bowerbird)

Lady Mary MacGregor was the wife of Dr Sir William MacGregor (1846–1919) a British diplomat, physician and amateur naturalist. He was in the diplomatic corps and served as a medical officer in the Seychelles, as Fiji's chief medical officer from 1875 until 1888 and then as Administrator of British New Guinea. In 1899, MacGregor was appointed Governor of Lagos, then a separate colony in what is now Nigeria. He served there until 1904, when he became Governor of Newfoundland. His final appointment was as Governor of Queensland, Australia, in 1910 and he remained there until he retired in 1914 and returned to Aberdeen. The Bowerbird is a New Guinean species which was first described when MacGregor was Governor of its country of origin. Lady MacGregor also had a locomotive and a rhododendron named after her.

LADY ROSS

Lady Ross's Turaco *Musophaga rossae* (Gould 1852)
(Alt. Ross's or Lady Ross's Lourie, Violet Plantain-eater)

Lady Ann Ross (1817–1857) was the wife of Rear-Admiral Sir James Clark Ross (1802–1862) the discoverer of the Magnetic North Pole. While stationed on St Helena, she received a live specimen of the lourie from an unknown locality in West Africa and kept it in captivity for ten years. The description was based on a sketch and some moulted feathers which she sent to **Gould**, who named the turaco after her. Her husband discovered the Ross Sea and the Ross Ice Shelf. He discovered an island in January 1841 which Scott, on his first expedition, named Ross Island in his honour. Ross joined the Royal Navy at the age of 12. He was also a member of several important expeditions to the Arctic. He commanded *Erebus* and *Terror* during the Antarctic expedition of 1839–1843. It was while close to the Magnetic South Pole that he broke through a wide expanse of pack ice and into a large and clear sea that later bore his name.

LAETITIA

See **Letitia**.

LAFRESNAYE

Lafresnaye's Piculet *Picumnus lafresnayi* (**Malherbe** 1862)
Lafresnaye's Rail *Tricholimnas lafresnayanus* (**Verreaux** 1904)
(Alt. New Caledonian Rail)
Lafresnaye's Spinetail *Synallaxis hellmayri* (**Reiser** 1905)
(Alt. Reiser's/White-browed/Red-shouldered Spinetail)
Lafresnaye's Vanga *Xenopirostris xenopirostris* (Lafresnaye 1850)

Baron Nöel Fréderic Armand André de LaFresnaye (1783–1861) was a French ornithologist and collector. He wrote with **d'Orbigny** and described a number of species including parrots and macaws. Lafresnaye's Spinetail was named by **Bonaparte** and described by Reiser, and recorded as such in **Gould**'s monograph with the words '…*to convey a compliment to Madame la Baronne de Lafresnaye, the niece of Montbeillard…*'. The rail is often described as extinct but there are recent indications that it may yet survive.

LAGDEN

Lagden's Bush Shrike *Malaconotus lagdeni* (**Sharpe** 1884)

Sir Godfrey Yeatman Lagden (1851–1934) was an English diplomat. He first went to South Africa in 1878. Later he was Private Secretary to Sir Owen Lanyon. He was besieged for a time in Pretoria. Subsequently he became a war correspondent during the Egyptian campaign of 1882 to 1883. He served as a diplomat in Sierra Leone and the Gold Coast (now Ghana) and then in Basutoland (now Lesotho) in 1884, where he became Resident Commissioner in 1890. In 1892 he was appointed Commissioner in Swaziland, and again in Basutoland (now Lesotho) from 1893 to 1901. He served during the South African War and was repeatedly mentioned in despatches. He wrote a standard book on the Basutos in 1909; *The Basutos: the mountaineers and their country; being a narrative of events relating to the tribe from its formation early in the nineteenth century to the present day*, having been Chairman of the Inter-Colonial South African Native Affairs Commission from 1902 until 1904. He was also a distinguished hunter. Another claim to fame was that he played first-class cricket for the MCC (Marylebone Cricket Club). His family founded the Yeatman Hospital in Sherborne, Dorset, England, the town in which he was born.

LAGRANDIÈRE

Lagrandieri's Barbet *Megalaima lagrandieri* (**J Verreaux** 1868)
  (Alt. Red-vented Barbet)

Vice-Admiral Pierre P de Lagrandière (1807–1876) was the French Governor of Cochin-China (now southern Vietnam). He is best known for having occupied three Cambodian provinces, on instruction from France.

LAGRANDIERI

See **Lagrandière**.

LANGSDORFF

Langsdorff's Toucanet *Selenidera reinwardtii* (**Wagler** 1827)
  (Alt. Golden-collared Toucanet)
Langsdorff's Thorntail *Popelairia langsdorffi* (**Temminck** 1821)
  (Alt. Black-bellied/Black-breasted Thorntail)

Baron Georg Heinrich von Langsdorff (1774–1852) was a German physician, botanist, zoologist, traveller and naturalist. He wrote *Remarks and Observations on a Voyage Around the World from 1803–1807.* He led an expedition to Brazil in 1822 and later became Russian consul in that country and continued to collect there.

LATHAM

Latham's Cockatoo *Calyptorhynchus banksii* (Latham 1790)
  (Alt. Banksian/Leach's Red-tailed/Great-billed[Black] Cockatoo)
Latham's Forest Francolin *Francolinus lathami* (**Hartlaub** 1854)
Latham's Myna *Scissirostrum dubium* (Latham 1802)
  (Alt. Celebes/Finch-billed/Grosbeak/Scissorbill Myna or Starling)
Latham's Snipe *Gallinago hardwickii* (**J E Gray** 1831)
  (Alt. Japanese Snipe)

Dr John Latham (1740–1837) was a British physician, naturalist and author. He played a leading role in the formation of the Linnean Society of London, in 1788, and was a Fellow of the Royal Society. He was a practicing doctor in Kent, England, until his retirement in 1796. He wrote *General Synopsis of Birds* from 1781 to 1785, contributed the descriptions of birds in *The Voyage of Governor Phillip to Botany Bay*, in 1789, and wrote the *Index Ornithologicus*, in 1790 and the *General History of Birds* from 1821 to 1828, the last of which he started when he was 81 years old. He designed, sketched and coloured the illustrations himself. He knew all the important English naturalists and collectors of his day, and so he was able to examine practically all the specimens and drawings of Australian birds which reached England. In his later books he provided the first published descriptions and scientific names of many Australian birds, including the Emu *Dromaius novaehollandiae*, White Cockatoo *Cacatua galerita*, Wedge-tailed Eagle *Aquila audax*, Superb Lyrebird *Menura novaehollandiae* and Australian Magpie *Gymnorhina tibicen*. He has been called the 'grandfather' of Australian ornithology. He was also the first to describe the Hyacinth Macaw *Anodorhynchus hyacinthus*.

LAURA

Laura's Woodland Warbler *Phylloscopus laurae* (**Boulton** 1931)
(Alt. Mrs Boulton's Woodland Warbler, Laura's [Wood]Warbler)

Laura Boulton (1889–1980) was the wife of the American ornithologist Wolfrid Rudyerd **Boulton** (1901–1983), who wrote the first description of the warbler and named it to honour his wife, who had collected it.

LAUTERBACH

Lauterbach's Bowerbird *Chlamydera lauterbachi* (**Reichenow** 1897)
(Alt. Yellow-breasted Bowerbird)

Carl Lauterbach (1864–1937) was a German botanist who collected in northern New Guinea. He wrote widely on orchids and led a scientific expedition to New Guinea in 1890 to 1891.

LAVINIA

Lavinia's Tanager *Tangara lavinia* (**Cassin** 1858)
(Alt. Rufous-winged Tanager)

Lavinia Bowen was an American painter of lithographs and is famed for her natural history studies. Many of these were drawn by Titian R **Peale**, a noted natural scientist who collected specimens as a member of the government-sponsored United States Exploring expedition of 1838–1842, and coloured by her. Her husband John T Bowen (d. 1856) was the respected lithographer of Philadelphia, who printed many of John **Audubon**'s lithographs. The colouring of lithographs normally involved teams of colourists, usually women, each assigned to fill in one colour of the print only. However, it seems that Lavinia was often the sole colourist as she was expert in that art. When J T Bowen died, Lavinia operated the company, which changed its name from J T Bowen's to Bowen's & Co. She eventually took on John **Cassin** as a partner and later married him.

LAWES

Lawes' Parotia *Parotia lawesii* (**Ramsay** 1885)
(Alt. Lawes' Six-wired Bird of Paradise)

The Reverend William George Lawes (1839–1907) was a missionary in New Guinea. In 1875 Lawes, who was employed by the London Missionary Society, produced the first printed piece of paper in Papua New Guinea. He went on to write *Grammar & Vocabulary of Language Spoken by Motu Tribe (New Guinea)* in 1896 and he translated the Bible into Motu. He is also credited with collecting *Dendrobium lawesii*, one of the easiest New Guinean orchid species to cultivate in a greenhouse.

LAWRENCE

Lawrence's Crested Flycatcher *Myiarchus tuberculifer lawrencei*
(Alt. Dusky-capped Flycatcher)
Lawrence's Flycatcher *Lathrotriccus euleri lawrencei* (J A **Allen** 1889)
(Alt. Euler's Flycatcher)
Lawrence's Goldfinch *Carduelis lawrencei* (Cassin 1852)
Lawrence's Quail-Dove *Geotrygon lawrencii* (**Salvin** 1874)
(Alt. Purplish-backed Quail-Dove)
Lawrence's Thrush *Turdus lawrencii* (**Coues** 1880)
Lawrence's Tufted-cheek *Pseudocolaptes lawrencii* (**Ridgway** 1878)
(Alt. Buffy Tufted-cheek)
Lawrence's Warbler *Vermivora chrysoptera x V. pinus*
(Alt. Brewster's Warbler)

George Newbold Lawrence (1806–1895) was a businessman involved with wholesale pharmaceuticals. He was also an amateur ornithologist who helped on Pacific surveys for **Baird** and **Cassin**, reporting on waterbirds, and then worked at the Smithsonian as a volunteer, describing the birds collected on a number of the surveys. He left his collection of 8,000 skins to the American Museum of Natural History. Lawrence's Warbler proved to be a hybrid of the Blue-winged and Golden-winged Warblers. **Cassin** named the goldfinch after him when he described it.

LAWSON

Lawson's Batis *Batis* (*poensis*) *occulta* (Lawson 1984)
(Alt. Lawson's Puff-back Flycatcher, West African Batis, Bioko Batis)

W J Lawson is an amateur ornithologist who was based for some time at the Durban Natural Science Museum. His description of the new batis; *The West African mainland forest dwelling population of Batis; a new species* appeared in the Bulletin of the British Ornithologist's Club. He also wrote *Speciation in the forest-dwelling populations of the avian genus Batis* in 1986 in the Bulletin and *Systematics and evolution in the Savanna species of the genus Batis* in another journal in 1987. He has published a number of articles in the South African journal Ostrich, including *Variation in the South African populations of the Coucal Centropus superciliosus* in 1962 and a *Note on the breeding of the Lemon-breasted Canary in captivity*, in 1970.

LAWYERS

The law was a profession, certainly in Britain in the 19th century, which was home to many upper-class men and those who had time to pursue other interests. David **Arnott** was a renowned, unscrupulous South African attorney. Jean François Emmanuel **Baillon** was a French lawyer and amateur ornithologist, whose son followed him in his interests. Sir Walter Lawry **Buller** was a New Zealander who shared both interests, birds and the law, and retired to England as a country gentleman. Alfred **Malherbe** was a French magistrate and judge and a passionate botanist, zoologist and ornithologist which was inspired by his youth in the tropics. Dr Fernando Capocchi **Novaes** is a Brazilian who practiced law before his retirement. Dr Philip Lutley **Sclater** is perhaps the best example of a practising lawyer who managed to pursue his passion for birds to the extent that he became one of the ornithological giants of his generation.

LAYARD

Layard's Black-headed Weaver *Ploceus nigriceps* (Layard 1867)
(Alt. Layard's Weaver)

Layard's Chat *Cercomela tractrac* (**Wilkes** 1817)
  (Alt. Tractrac Chat)
Layard's Flycatcher *Muscicapa muttui* (Layard 1854)
  (Alt. Brown-breasted Flycatcher)
Layard's Parakeet *Psittacula calthorpae* (**Blyth** 1849)
  (Alt. Emerald-collared Parakeet)
Layard's Seedeater *Serinus leucopterus* (**Sharpe** 1871)
  (Alt. White-winged/Protea Seedeater, Protea Canary)
Layard's Tit-Babbler *Parisoma* (*Sylvia*) *layardi* (**Hartlaub** 1862)
  (Alt. Layard's Tit-Warbler)
Layard's White-eye *Zosterops explorator* (Layard 1875)

Edgar Leopold Layard (1824–1900) was born in Italy. He spent ten years in Ceylon (now Sri Lanka) before going to the Cape Colony of South Africa as a civil servant in 1854, on the staff of the Governor Sir George Grey. In 1855 he became Curator of the South African Museum in his spare time. He collected locally and obtained the tit-babbler in South Africa, although people sent him specimens from wider afield. Layard later worked in Brazil, Fiji and New Caledonia. He wrote *The Birds of South Africa*, in 1867, which was later updated by **Sharpe**. The parakeet's specific name is after his first wife, whose maiden surname was Calthorp.

LE CONTE, J

Le Conte's Sparrow *Ammodramus leconteii* (**Latham** 1790)

Dr John Le Conte (1818–1891) was a physician who operated a gunpowder factory for the Confederacy during the United States Civil War. He was an amateur naturalist who was President of the University of California, at Berkeley, between 1875 and 1881. He was the first cousin of John L **Le Conte** (below). **Audubon** named the sparrow after him in 1844.

LE CONTE, J L

Le Conte's Thrasher *Toxostoma lecontei* (Lawrence 1851)

Dr John Lawrence Le Conte (1825–1883) was an American entomologist and biologist. He was also a physician during the United States Civil War. His father John Eatton Le Conte (1784–1860) was also a naturalist, as a well a US army engineer, and some of his writings are addressed to his son who may also have contributed some illustrations. He was first cousin of Dr John L **Le Conte** (above). John **Lawrence** named the thrasher after him in his description.

LEACH

Leach's Red-tailed Cockatoo *Calyptorhynchus banksii* (**Gould** 1837)
  (Alt. Latham's/Great-billed[Black] Cockatoo)
Leach's Storm Petrel *Oceanodroma leucorhoa* (Vieillot 1818)
  (Alt. Leach's/Beal's/Gould's/Socorro Petrel, Kaeding's Storm Petrel)
Leach's Kingfisher *Dacelo leachii* (**Vigors** & **Horsefield** 1827)
  (Alt. Blue-winged Kookaburra)

William Elford Leach (1790–1836) was a British zoologist. He originally studied medicine but he did not practice and instead was employed at the British Museum, where he became a world-renowned expert on crustaceans and also worked on insects, mammals and birds. He wrote *The Zoological Miscellany* in 1814. **Vieillot** named the storm petrel after him when Leach found it in a collection of specimens which he purchased from the auction of the estate of William **Bullock** and sent it to Vieillot for description. Only in **Gould** is the kingfisher described as Leach's.

LEADBEATER

Leadbeater's Brilliant *Heliodoxa leadbeateri* (**Bourcier** 1843)
  (Alt. Violet-fronted Brilliant)
Leadbeater's Cockatoo *Cacatua leadbeateri* (**Vigors** 1831)
  (Alt. Major Mitchell's/Pink Cockatoo)

Benjamin Leadbeater (1760–1837) was a taxidermist and a dealer in natural objects in London, as well as a good ornithologist. He often supplied specimens to museums and, in particular, he sent many skins to **Gould**. The hummingbird was described by **Bourcier** but had previously been named by **Vigors**. The latter described the cockatoo from a specimen shown to him by Leadbeater. Many other creatures bear his name.

LEAR

Lear's Macaw *Anodorhynchus leari* (**Bonaparte** 1856)
  (Alt. Indigo Macaw)

Edward Lear (1812–1888) was a poet, traveller and artist. He is famous for his nonsense verse, limericks, stories and songs, such as *The Owl and the Pussycat*, but he was also one of the most talented illustrators of birds of the 19th century. He was involved from the age of 15 in preparing posters, leaflets and advertisements and was a largely self-taught artist. At 18 he began working on the *Illustrations of the family of the Psittacidae or Parrots*, which was finished in 1832. From 1832 to 1837 Lear worked for Lord **Stanley**, the 13th Earl of Derby, who was President of the Zoological Society of London. He worked as an illustrator for many of the book publishers of the time, particularly John **Gould**, with whom he contributed to *The Birds of Europe* between 1832 and 1837, the *Monograph of the Ramphistidae, or Family of Toucans* in 1834 and 1835, and finally the *Monograph of the Trogonidae, or Family of Trogons* in 1838. He is believed to be the first bird illustrator who preferred to draw from live specimens when possible, rather than using skins. After 1837 Lear spent most of the rest of his life in southern Europe where he died, aged 75, in Italy.

LECLANCHER

Lechlancher's Bunting *Passerina leclancherii* (**Lafresnaye** 1840)
  (Alt. Orange-breasted Bunting)
Lechlancher's Pigeon *Ptilinopus leclancheri* (**Bonaparte** 1855)
  (Alt. Black-chinned Fruit Dove)

C R A Leclancher (1804–1857) was a French ship's surgeon aboard the *Bayonnaise* from 1847 until 1850, whose work was the subject of *Étude du journal sanitaire du chirurgien navigant CRA Leclancher sur la corvette la Bayonnaise*. He also voyaged to Arabia and Japan around 1841.

LEGGE

Legge's Baza *Aviceda jerdoni ceylonensis* (Legge 1876)
  (Alt. Jerdon's/Blythe's/Brown Baza, Brown-crested Lizard Hawk)
Legge's Flowerpecker *Dicaeum vincens* (**Sclater** 1872)
  (Alt. White-throated Flowerpecker)

William Vincent Legge (1841–1918) was a professional soldier as well as a keen collector of bird skins. He was born in Van Diemen's Land (now Tasmania) but was educated in

England, France and Germany. He was commissioned in the Royal Artillery in 1862 and then served in Melbourne from 1867 until 1868. From there he went to Ceylon (now Sri Lanka) where, as Secretary of the Royal Asiatic Society, he reorganised the museum at Colombo and made a large collection of birds. He was the military commander in Tasmania from 1883 to 1890 and again from 1898 until 1904, when he retired from the army with the rank of Lieutenant-Colonel. Legge was also a founder of the (Royal) Australasian Ornithologists' Union in 1901 and was its first President. He was a member of the British Ornithologists' Union and an honorary fellow of the American Ornithologists' Union. He wrote *History of the Birds of Ceylon*, in 1880, and *Systematic List of Tasmanian Birds* in 1887. He also assisted in the compilation of the *List of Vernacular Names for Australian Birds*. The bird skins he collected in Ceylon were presented to the Hobart Museum in Tasmania in 1902.

LEGUAT

Leguat's Gelinote *Aphanapteryx leguati* (**Milne-Edwards** 1874) [Extinct]
(Alt. Rodriques Blue Rail)
Leguat's Owl *Bubo leguati* [Extinct]
Leguat's Starling *Necrospar rodericanus* (**Sclater** 1879) [Extinct]
(Alt. Rodriguez's Starling)

François Leguat of Bresse (1637–1735) was a French naturalist and explorer. He spent time on the island of Rodriguez as the First Resident and Historian there, between 1691 and 1693. He wrote *Voyage et Avantures en Deux Îles Desertes des Indies Orientales*, in 1708, which covered his travels to and within Rodriguez, Mauritius, Java and the Cape of Good Hope. It is recorded that he '*noted that vast herds of the* (now-extinct) *Rodrigues tortoise seemed to include certain individuals with the responsibility of sentinels, but he wryly commented that it wasn't clear what predator they were looking for, or how the alarm would be sounded, or what effective response the herd might take*'. It is also noted that, in 1693, he spent several months on Mauritius looking for Dodos *Raphus cucullatus* but did not find any.

LERCH

Lerch's Sapphire *Timolia lerchii* (**Gould***)
Lerch's Woodnymph *Thalurania lerchi* (Gould*)

The woodnymph is probably a hybrid and only one specimen is known from a trade skin. It may well be named after the trader who supplied it. Whoever Lerch was, he was apparently active in New Grenada (which was a republic in the northern part of South America) for about 20 years from 1847. Both the hummingbirds are only found as **Gould** engravings.

LESCHENAULT

Leschenault's Forktail *Enicurus leschenaulti* (**Vieillot** 1818)
(Alt. Black-breasted/White-crowned Forktail)

Jean Baptiste Louis Claude Theodore Leschenault de la Tour (1773–1826) was a French botanist who served as naturalist to two Kings of France, Louis XVIII (1814–1824) and Charles X (1824–1830). He wrote one of the first descriptions of coconuts and the extraction of their oil. He was botanist on the voyage of the *Casuarina*, *Géographe* and *Naturaliste*, between 1801 and 1803, and collected widely in Australia from 1801 to 1802. The ships visited the northwest, west and south coasts of Western Australia, coastal South Australia, Port Jackson, New South Wales and King Island in the Bass Strait. Bunbury in Western Australia was seen and named Port Leschenault after him by the French explorer Captain De Freycinet, from his ship the *Casuarina* in 1803. He collected in Java between 1803 and 1806 and in India between 1816 and 1822. He also visited the Cape Verde Islands, Cape of Good Hope, Ceylon (now Sri Lanka), Brazil and British Guiana (now Guyana).

LESSON

Lesson's Bird of Paradise *Diphyllodes saleucides* (**Gould***)
Lesson's Euphonia *Euphonia affinis* (Lesson 1842)
  (Alt. Scrub/Black-throated Euphonia)
Lesson's Motmot *Momotus momota lessonii* (Lesson 1842)
  (Alt. Blue-crowned Motmot)
Lesson's Oriole *Icterus chrysater* (Lesson 1844)
  (Alt. Yellow-backed Oriole)
Lesson's Seedeater *Sporophila bouvronides* (Lesson 1831)
  (Alt. Capped Seedeater)
Lesson's Peacock-Pheasant *Polyplectron chalcurum* (Lesson 1831)
  (Alt. Bronze-tailed Peacock-Pheasant)

René Primevère Lesson (1794–1849) was a French ornithologist and naturalist of enormous influence and importance. Whilst he was best known as a zoologist he was also a skilled botanist and Professor of Botany at Rochefort. He was employed on the *Coquille*, in 1822, as a botanist and then on the *Astrolabe*, between 1826 and 1829, as a naturalist and collector. The *Astrolabe's* surgeon and botanist was his brother, Pierre Adolphe Lesson (1805–1888) who later became professor of a school of naval medicine. Both voyages were in the Pacific and called at many islands including New Zealand. Lesson named **Anna**'s Hummingbird *Calypte anna*, **Rivoli**'s Hummingbird *Eugenes fulgens*, in honour of the Duke of Rivoli, and also the Blue-throated Hummingbird *Lampornis clemenciae* for his second wife Clémence. He published a considerable number of ornithological texts including *Manuel d'Ornithologie*, in 1828, *Histoire Naturelle des Oiseaux-Mouches*, in 1829, *Histoire Naturelle des Colibris*, in 1830, *Centurie Zoologique*, in 1830, *Traite d'Ornithologie*, in 1831, *Les Trochiides*, in 1831, *Illustrations d'Ornithologie*, in 1831, and *Histoire Naturelle des Oiseaux de Paradis et des Epimaques*, in 1834. The bird-of-paradise is only found in a **Gould** engraving.

LESUEUR

See **Sueur**.

LETITIA

Letitia's Hummingbird *Gouldia laetitiae* (**Gould***)

According to one source the bird is named after Laetitia del Gallo Roccagiovine (1850–?), who was the daughter of Princess Julie Charlotte Pauline Zénaïde Laetitia Désirée Bartholomée Bonaparte (1830–1900) and Marquese Alessandro Gaetano Carlo del Gallo Roccagiovine (1826–1892) and a grand-daughter of the French ornithologist Prince Charles **Bonaparte**. Of course, Napoleon Bonaparte also had a daughter Letitia. We can find no definitive evidence as to which Letitia the bird honours except that it is one of the Bonaparte family and probably arose through the relationship between **Gould** and Charles Bonaparte. (See also the entry for Cornelia, which shows yet another Bonaparte Laetitia, the lady known as Madame Mère, mother of Napoleon and grandmother of Charles.) The only references to the bird that we can find are Gould illustrations. The genus *Gouldia* was called *Popelairia* by others, indicating that much independent taxonomic work was in progress at the time, which may have led to one species name being superseded by another.

LEVAILLANT

Levaillant's Barbet *Trachyphonus vaillantii* (Ranzani 1821)
 (Alt. Crested Barbet)
Levaillant's Bush Shrike *Tchagra tchagra* (**Vieillot** 1816)
 (Alt. Southern Tchagra)
Levaillant's Cisticola *Cisticola tinniens* (**Lichtenstein** 1842)
 (Alt. Tinkling Cisticola)
Levaillant's Cuckoo *Clamator levaillantii* (**Swainson** 1829)
Levaillant's Green Woodpecker *Picus vaillantii* (**Malherbe** 1847)
 (Alt. Algerian Green Woodpecker, Levaillant's Woodpecker)
Levaillant's Parrot *Poicephalus robustus* (J F Gmelin 1788)
 (Alt. Brown-necked/Amatola/Pirie/Green Parrot/Knysna/Red-crowned/
 Red-shouldered/Cape Parrot)

François Le Vaillant (1753–1824) was a French traveller, explorer, collector and naturalist. He was born in Dutch Guiana (Suriname), the son of the French consul there. Birds attracted his interest from an early age and he spent a lot of his time collecting specimens. As a result, he became acquainted with many of Europe's private collectors. He went to the Cape Province of South Africa, in 1781, in the employ of the Dutch East India Company, the first real ornithologist to visit the area. There he both explored and collected specimens, eventually publishing a six-volume book, *Historie Naturelle des Oiseaux d'Africa*, which is a classic of African ornithology. This work was published between the years 1801 and 1806, in Paris, and contained 144 colour-printed engravings. The well-known artist, Jacques **Barraband**, drew the plates. Peree, Gremillier, and Bouquet engraved them and they were printed in colour and finished by hand by Langlois and Rousset. Le Vaillant also gave the common name to the Bateleur *Terathopius ecaudatus*. Over 2,000 skins were sent to Jacob Temminck, who financed his expedition. His son C J **Temminck** studied and categorised the specimens, and then incorporated them into the museum at Leiden. A large collection of his specimens is said to have been lost on one occasion when a Dutch ship was attacked and sunk by the English. However, it is rumoured he may also have invented a number of birds, even going as far as creating 'new' birds by putting together pieces from various specimens of other species!

LEWIN

Lewin's Honeyeater *Meliphaga lewinii* (**Swainson** 1837)
Lewin's Lesser Honeyeater *Meliphaga notata* (**MacGillivray** 1914)
 (Alt. Yellow-spotted Honeyeater)
Lewin's Rail *Lewinia pectoralis* (**Temminck** 1831)

John William Lewin (1770–1819) was an English naturalist and engraver. He was born in England and went to Sydney, Australia, in 1800 and collected widely there until his death. His father (some sources say his older brother), William Lewin, was the author of a seven-volume work, *Birds of Great Britain*. Lewin accompanied James Grant on his survey expeditions to the Bass Strait and then to the Hunter River. He lived his later life in Sydney earning a meagre living as a portrait artist. Governor Macquarie appointed Lewin to the position of city coroner in 1814. He also accompanied Macquarie and made drawings during the construction of the historic new road across the Blue Mountains. Macquarie commissioned Lewin to draw the plants collected by the Surveyor-General, Henry Oxley, in his explorations of the country beyond Bathurst, the Liverpool Plains and the New England District. As well as his natural history paintings, Lewin also painted landscapes and portraits of Aboriginals. He wrote *Prodromus Entomology, Natural History of Lepidopterous Insects of New South Wales* and *Birds of New Holland* in 1808. An 1813 edition of this latter publication was the first illustrated book to be engraved and printed in Australia. He also wrote *A Natural History of the Birds of New South Wales*, which was published in 1838.

LEWIS, J

Lewis's Silver Pheasant *Lophura nycthemera lewisi* (**Delacour** & Jabouille 1928)

John Spedan Lewis (1885–1963) was a British businessman who took over his father's shops and turned them into the now well-known, employee-owned, John Lewis Partnership. He owned important bird collections in Britain. In 1928 he financed and took part in an expedition to Vietnam with his friend **Delacour**. The expedition, which sought to collect Edwards' Pheasants *Lophura edwardsi*, was successful and, in 1929, Lewis bred chicks from birds obtained during this enterprise.

LEWIS, M

Lewis's Woodpecker *Melanerpes lewis* (**G R Gray** 1849)

Captain Meriwether Lewis (1774–1809) was one half of the 'Lewis and Clark' duo, whose famous expedition collected the woodpecker in 1805, near Helena, Montana. Incidentally, this may be the only bird specimen left from that expedition; it resides at Harvard. Lewis was chosen to lead the expedition by President Thomas Jefferson; he was the latter's private secretary at the time. Jefferson wrote, '*It was impossible to find a character who, to a complete science in botany, natural history, mineralogy & astronomy, joined the firmness of constitution & character, prudence, habits adapted to the woods, & a familiarity with the Indian manners & character, requisite for this undertaking. All the latter qualifications Capt. Lewis has.*' Before becoming Jefferson's secretary he had grown up in the country, managed the family plantation and spent time in the army both as an ordinary soldier and then as an officer. Lewis chose **Clark**, a friend he had made whilst in the army, to accompany him. The famous journey of exploration took a year and a half and covered more than 4,000 miles to the Pacific Ocean. Lewis was fascinated with the Native Americans, plants, animals, fossils, geological formations, topography and other facets of the trip, all of which he recorded in his journal entries. As a reward for his success he was appointed to the Governorship of the Louisiana Territory. In 1809 he undertook a journey to Washington in order to clear his name after having been publicly accused of misusing public money. En route he met his death from two gunshot wounds to the head and chest, and it still is not known whether this was murder or suicide. Alexander **Wilson** named the woodpecker after Lewis but G R **Gray** wrote the formal description.

LICHTENSTEIN

Lichtenstein's Desert Finch *Rhodopechys obsoleta* (Lichtenstein 1823)
(Alt. Desert/Black-billed Finch)
Lichtenstein's Foliage-gleaner *Philydor lichtensteini* (**Cabanis** & **Heine** 1859)
(Alt. Ochre-breasted Foliage-gleaner)

Lichtenstein's Foliage-gleaner *Philydor erythropterus* (P L **Sclater** 1856)
(Alt. Chestnut-winged Foliage-gleaner)
Lichtenstein's Kingbird *Tyrannus melancholicus* (**Vieillot** 1819)
(Alt. Tropical Kingbird)
Lichtenstein's Noble Macaw *Ara nobilis cumanensis* (Lichtenstein 1823)
(Alt. Noble Macaw)
Lichtenstein's Oriole *Icterus gularis* (**Wagler** 1829)
(Alt. Altamira Oriole)
Lichtenstein's Sandgrouse *Pterocles lichtensteinii* (**Temminck** 1825)

Martin Hinrich Carl Lichtenstein (1780–1857) was a German, physician, traveller and ornithologist who founded the Berlin Zoo in 1815. Between 1802 and 1806 he travelled widely in South Africa and whilst there he became the personal physician to the Dutch Governor of the Cape of Good Hope. He wrote *Reisen in Sudlichen Africa* in 1810. Lichtenstein studied many species sent to the Berlin Museum by others and, '*whilst he gave every species, or what he judged to be a species, a name, this was done without consulting the recent English and French literature. His only aim was to give the specimens in question a distinguishing mark for his personal needs. These names were used in Lichtenstein's registers and reappeared on the labels of the mounted specimens, but only exceptionally were they published by himself in connection with a scientific description*'. This caused much unnecessary confusion and trouble to others! A fellow German zoologist, Johann **Wagler**, named the oriole in his honour.

LIDTH

Lidth's Jay *Garrulus lidthi* (**Bonaparte** 1850)
(Alt. Purple Jay)

Theodor Gerard van Lidth de Jeude (1788–1863) was a Dutch zoologist. He published extensively in Holland, mainly on veterinary matters, including an account of the bone structure of horses' heads.

LILFORD

Lilford's Woodpecker *Dendrocopos leucotos lilfordi* (**Sharpe** & Dresser 1871)
(Alt. White-backed Woodpecker)

Lord Lilford or Thomas Littleton Powys, fourth Baron Lilford (1833–1896), was interested in animals from an early age. Whilst at school (Harrow) he kept a small menagerie and at university (Christ Church, Oxford) a larger one. He was plagued with gout throughout his life but, as far as his health allowed, he spent all his spare time travelling to study animals, especially birds. In 1853 he went to the Isles of Scilly, Wales and Ireland and after meeting Edward Clough Newcome, the best falconer of his day, he took up falconry himself. In 1854 he joined his county militia and served in Dublin and Devonport until the end of 1855. From 1856 to 1858 he cruised the Mediterranean with Hercules Rowley. He visited Spain and other parts of the Mediterranean frequently between 1864 and 1882 and rediscovered the rare Audouin's Gull *Larus audouinii*. He was elected a Fellow of the Zoological Society in 1852 and a Fellow of the Linnean Society in 1862. He was one of the founders of the British Ornithologists' Union in 1858 and its President from 1867. He was also the first President of the Northamptonshire Natural History Society. His aviaries at Lilford were noted for their birds of prey and indeed it was he who was responsible for the introduction of the Little Owl *Athene noctua* to Britain during the 1880s through a release scheme from his Northamptonshire home. He wrote the two-volume *Notes on the Birds of Northamptonshire and Neighbourhood* in 1895, and the seven-volume *Coloured Figures of the Birds of the British Islands*, which was finished by **Salvin** after Lilford died. He also wrote many papers on ornithology in the Journal of the Northamptonshire Natural History Society, Proceedings of the Zoological Society and

Ibis among others. **Sharpe** originally classified the woodpecker as a full species, *Picus lilfordi*, from a specimen taken by Lilford in Greece, in 1857, but it was later reclassified as a race of the White-backed Woodpecker. Sharpe also described a crane as *Grus lilfordi* in 1894 from an Indian specimen but this too is now regarded as a race of Common Crane, *Grus grus lilfordi*.

LILIAN

Lilian's Lovebird *Agapornis lilianae* (**Shelley** 1894)
(Alt. Nyasa Lovebird)

Lillian Elizabeth Lutley Sclater (*c.* 1870–1957) was a British naturalist who accompanied her brother, William Lutley **Sclater**, on an expedition to Nyasaland (now Malawi) where the lovebird was collected.

LILIAN

Lilian's Meadowlark *Sturnella magna lilianae* (**Oberholser** 1930)
(Alt. Eastern Meadowlark)

Lilian Hanna Baldwin was the wife of S Prentiss Baldwin, who was an American patron of natural history. She was thus honoured for presenting a collection of birds to the Cleveland museum which contained a specimen of this race of meadowlark. S P Baldwin was himself an amateur ornithologist who wrote a number of articles in the 1920s and 1930s including *The Marriage Relations of the House Wren* in The Auk, in 1921. **Oberholser** also named a race of the House Wren *Troglodytes aedon baldwini* after his friend. There is a 1931 paper entitled *Measurements of Birds* by S P Baldwin, H C Oberholser, and L G Worley published by the Cleveland Museum of Natural History.

LILLO

Lillo's Canastero *Asthenes sclateri lilloi* (**Oustalet** 1904)

Miguel Lillo (1862–1931) was an Argentine naturalist. He was primarily a botanist but had a wide knowledge of other sciences although he was largely self-taught. He actually was a real all-rounder with interests in classical literature and languages, as well as science, and he took meticulous meteorological notes throughout his life. Lillo had a career in teaching, research and the administration of scientific institutions. He retired from teaching in 1918 but remained as Honorary Director of the National Museum. Most of his natural history work was conducted in his home province of Tucumán although he undertook a study tour of Europe as a young man. In 1905 he wrote a book on Tucumán's animals, concentrating on birds, which contained descriptions of new species. He wrote widely on the botany of Tucumán and published a work on Argentina's trees in 1910. In 1914 he was given an honorary doctorate by the National Museum and he was awarded the Francisco P **Moreno** prize in 1928. Lillo is also commemorated in the binomials of a great number of plants and, in particular, trees.

LINA

Lina's Sunbird *Aethopyga linaraborae* (Kennedy, Gonzales & Miranda 1997)

Lina Rabor (?–1997) was the wife of Dioscoro (Joe) Rabor (1911–1996), a pre-eminent Phillipine zoologist and conservationist, and accompanied him on all his research trips. Robert S Kennedy, an ornithologist with the Cincinnati Museum of Natural History and Science, began an inventory of wildlife in the Philippines, in 1989, in conjunction with the National Museum of the Philippines. He and his co-workers named the species Lina's Sunbird in her honour, from a mislabelled specimen. Her husband first found the bird in 1965, but seems to have misindentified it as the Apo Sunbird *Aethopyga boltoni*, a species discovered in 1903. Eventually, the specimens, with mislabelled tags, made their way to the Smithsonian Institution's National Museum of Natural History, in Washington, D.C. and the Field Museum of Natural History in Chicago. Kennedy noted that the 'new' sunbird has iridescent patches of blues, purples and emerald on its forehead, tail, wings and ears, which the Apo lacks.

LINCOLN

Lincoln's Sparrow *Melospiza lincolnii* (**Audubon** 1834)
(Alt. Forbush's Sparrow)

Thomas Lincoln (1812–1883) was an American naturalist. At 21 years old he went on a trip with **Audubon** to Labrador, where he shot the bird that now bears his name. Audubon named it after him; he originally called it 'Tom's Finch' and it was the only new bird discovered on that expedition. Another expedition member described him as '*quiet, reserved, sensible, practical and reliable.*' Lincoln became a farmer, and a noted local abolitionist, back in his home state of Maine. He later said of Audubon '*a nice man, but as Frenchy as thunder.*'

LINDEN

Linden's Helmetcrest *Oxypogon guerinii lindenii* (**Gould** 1848)
(Alt. Bearded Helmetcrest)

Jean Jules Linden (1817–1898) was a Luxembourgian botanist who collected and dealt in exotic plants, of which he produced the rather beautiful *Catalogue du Plantes Exotiques*. He travelled extensively and collected plants in South America before he was 20, between 1835 and 1837. The Oxford University Herbarium holds much of his collection. He went on a second expedition, to Central America, between 1838 and 1841. In 1851 he was appointed the first scientific director of the Zoological Gardens of Brussels. A year later he gave up some of his duties and became Head of Botany. Four years after that his replacement was dismissed and Linden again became scientific director, a post which he held until 1861. He then went into commercial horticulture and kept a nursery where he cultivated many exotics which were sent to him. Linden is often regarded as the man who, in his day, introduced a passion for orchids into Belgium, France and beyond. The 17-volume *Lindenia: Iconographie des Orchidées* was edited by his son Lucien Linden (1853–1940) and Emile Rodigas. It was styled in his honour and was originally published as a periodical. A number of plants from the rainforests of Central and South America, such as *Xanthosoma lindenii, Aristolochia arborea linden* and a great number of orchids, were named in his honour, as is the dragonfly *Cercion lindeni.*

LIND

Lind's Sunbird *Aethopyga linaraborae* (Kennedy, Gonzales & Miranda 1997)

See **Lina**.

LIVINGSTONE

Livingstone's [Yellow] Flycatcher *Erythrocercus livingstonei* (G R **Gray** 1870)
(Alt. Livingstone's Monarch)
Livingstone's Lourie *Tauraco livingstonii* (G R Gray 1864)
(Alt. Livingstone's Turaco)

David Livingstone (1813–1873) was a Scottish doctor and missionary, and undoubtedly the most famous African explorer. Livingstone is remembered as the first European to have gone into the heart of Africa, and as someone who came to be regarded as a saint in his own lifetime. He worked in a cotton mill from the age of ten, earning extra income by selling tea from farm to farm. He studied Latin and Greek on his own, and elected to become a missionary when he was persuaded that science and theology were not in opposition, training at the London Missionary Society and, in medicine, in Glasgow. Livingstone left for South Africa in 1840. His many expeditions brought him fame as a surgeon and scientist over the next few years, but his missionary efforts were less successful. He sympathised with the lot of the indigenous people and so made enemies among white settlers. It annoyed many that he learned the languages and tribal customs of the people he tried to convert. Nevertheless, his indictment of the slave trade did much to make anti-slavery laws enforced. In 1853 his expedition into the interior of the continent lasted three years. He discovered the Victoria Falls during this trip, a find which sealed his fame on his return to Britain in 1856. His last expedition, begun in 1866, was to search for the source of the Nile. False reports of his death, and the public's 'need to know' where the lost explorer was, led to Stanley's equally famous mission to find him.

LLOYD

Lloyd's Bushtit *Psaltriparus lloydi* (*minimus*) (**Sennett** 1887)
    (Alt. Black-eared Bushtit)
Lloyd's Scimitar Babbler *Pomatorhinus ochraceiceps* (**Walden** 1873)
    (Alt. Red-billed Scimitar Babbler)

William Lloyd (1854–?) was born in Ireland and immigrated to Texas. He was employed as a collector and obtained the bushtit in 1887 in the Texan Trans-Pecos. He provided the specimen to **Sennett**, who described it.

LODDIGES

Loddiges' Plovercrest *Cephalepis loddigesia* (**Gould***)
Loddiges' Spatuletail *Loddigesia mirabilis* (**Bourcier** 1847)
    (Alt. Marvellous Spatuletail)

George Loddiges (1784–1846) was a British naturalist, dealer and taxidermist, who specialised in hummingbirds. He was also a botanical artist who made a major contributor to his father's publication, *The Botanical Cabinet* (1817–1833). The German traveller Richard Schomburgk, on a visit to London in 1840, said "*Amongst the many private collections which I had an opportunity of visiting, there was one that particularly engaged the whole of my attention: it was the beautiful, really fairy-like collection of humming-birds, the property of Loddiges, the market-gardener, containing all the species of this interesting family at present known, and considerably richer in them than is the British Museum. The perfectly natural and tasteful way of stuffing, and the charming method of grouping them on the part of Loddiges Jr., has made the room in which the collection is set up, a regular Wizard's Den. The comprehensive collection of Orchids and Palms belonging to these gentlemen likewise deserves the most praiseworthy mention.*'

LONGUEMARE, A

Longuemare's Hermit *Phaethornis longuemareus* (**Lesson** 1832)
    (Alt. Pretre's/Little Hermit)

Alphonse Pierre Françoise Le Touze de Longuemare (1803–1881) was a French amateur who collected a specimen of the Hermit in 1830 which now bears his name.

LONGUEMARE, G

> Longuemare's Sunangel *Heliangelus* [*amethysticollis*] *clarisse*
> (G Longuemare 1841)

Guoye de Longuemare described the type specimen, which he collected. (We have found it impossible to ascertain whether Guoye de Longuemare and Alphonse Pierre Françoise Le Touze de Longuemare were one and the same person, or even brothers who collected together in the same part of the world).

LÖNNBERG

> Lönnberg's Skua *Catharacta lonnbergi* (**Mathews** 1912)
> (Alt. Subantarctic/Brown Skua)

Professor Axel Johan Einar Lönnberg (1865–1942) was a Swedish zoologist who mainly worked at the Vertebrate Department of the Swedish Museum of Natural History, in Stockholm. Between 1925 and 1942 he was the last prefect of the Kristineberg Marine Zoological Station. He founded the biological journal *Fauna och Flora*.

LOPDELL

> Lopdell's Penguin *Archaeosphenicus lopdelli* (Marples 1952) [Extinct]

Dr J C Lopdell was a colleague of **Marples** when he described the Penguin. Dr and Mrs J C Lopdell assisted Marples with the finding and sorting of bones, so he named the bird after them both rather than an individual.

LOPEZ

> Lopez's Warbler *Bradypterus lopezi* (**Alexander** 1903)
> (Alt. Evergreen Forest Warbler)

José Lopez was a Portuguese collector in Africa. He collected for Boyd **Alexander** in 1897 as a boy and returned to England with him. Boyd then took him on all his trips to Africa, including to the island of Bioko (now part of Equatorial Guinea) in 1902. He was still with him when local people killed Alexander in 1910. Cap Lopez in Gabon, just across the water from Bioko, may also have been named after him.

LORD DERBY

> Lord Derby's Aracari *Aulacorhynchus derbianus* (**Gould** 1835)
> (Alt. Chestnut-tipped Toucanet)
> Lord Derby's Kiskadee *Pitangus sulphuratus derbianus* (Kaup 1952)
> (Alt. Great Kiskadee)
> Lord Derby's Mountain Pheasant *Oreophasis derbianus* (**G R Gray** 1884)
> (Alt. Horned Guan, Derby's Guan/Mountain Pheasant)
> Lord Derby's Parakeet *Platycercus icterotis* (**Kuhl** 1820)
> (Alt. Western/Yellow-cheeked Rosella, Stanley Parakeet)

See **Stanley**.

LORD HOWE

> Lord Howe's Rail *Gallirallus sylvestris* (**P L Sclater** 1869)
> (Alt. Lord Howe Woodhen, Lord Howe [Island] [Wood]Rail)

We believe this bird to be at one remove from being named after Lord Howe. It occurs on Lord Howe Island, off the east coast of Australia, and is named after that island rather than directly for the man. The island was discovered in 1788 and named after the then First Lord of the Admiralty by Lieutenant Ball RN, in *HMS Supply*, whilst sailing from Sydney to Norfolk Island.

LORENTZ

Lorentz's Bulbul *Phyllastrephus lorenzi* (**Sassi** 1914)
(Alt. Sassi's [Olive] Greenbul)
Lorentz's Painted Parrot *Psittacella picta lorentzi* (**Van Oort** 1910)
Lorentz's Whistler *Pachycephala lorentzi* (**Mayr** 1931)

Dr Hendrik Antoon Lorentz (1871–1943) was a Dutch diplomat who explored New Guinea from 1907 to 1909. There is a Lorentz Nature Reserve there in Irian Jaya named after him because, in 1909, he was the first-known explorer to make contact with the 'Dani' tribe during an expedition to Mt Trikora.

LORIA

Loria's Bird-of-Paradise *Cnemophilus loriae* (**Salvadori** 1894)

Dr Lamberto Loria (1855–1913) was an Italian ethnologist who collected in New Guinea in 1889 and 1890. He also founded the first Italian Museum of Ethnography, in 1906, in Florence. The museum was subsequently transferred to Rome, after he organised the first ethnography exhibition there in 1911. When the 5,000 objects in the Florence museum were transferred to the capital, over 30,000 objects collected by Loria and his assistants from throughout the country were added to the collections.

LOST AT SEA

Sir John **Franklin** disappeared in 1845 on one of his numerous attempts to cross the Arctic by sea. This is not only notable because Franklin had birds named for him but also because he was searched for several times and a number of new birds were discovered during the searches. One was named after Sir Clements Robert **Markham**, who commanded the first search, and another searcher, Admiral Sir Edward **Belcher** CB, also had a bird named after him.

LOTEN

Loten's Sunbird *Nectarinia lotenia* (Linnaeus 1766)
(Alt. Long-billed Sunbird)

Johan Gideon Loten (1710–1789) was the Dutch Governor of Makassar (now Celebes, Indonesia) from 1743 to 1749 and of Ceylon (now Sri Lanka) from 1752 until 1757. He was also an amateur naturalist who attempted the first systematic documentation of Ceylon's birdlife. He collected many specimens, especially of birds, but since they proved difficult to preserve, a young artist of mixed Singhalese-European descent, named Pieter Cornelis de Bevere, made coloured drawings of them. Loten's notes reveal that de Bevere drew from living or freshly dead specimens. The bulk of the illustrations, including 101 plates depicting birds, are in the British Museum in London. Loten himself lived in England for many years. He did not use binomial scientific names and this meant that the birds illustrated in his work remained unnamed and hence unknown to science until others identified them after his death.

LOVERIDGE

Loveridge's Sunbird *Nectarinia loveridgei* (**Hartert** 1922)

Arthur Loveridge (1891–1980) was an American herpetologist. He wrote *Many Happy Days I've Squandered*, in 1949, and *I Drank the Zambesi*, in 1954. He retired to St Helena.

LOWE

Lowe's Grey Peacock-Pheasant *Polyplectron bicalcaratum bailyi* (Lowe 1925)
Lowe's Penguin *Archaeosphenicus lowei* (**Marples** 1952) [Extinct]
Lowe's Swiftlet *Collocalia maxima* (**Hume** 1878)
  (Alt. Black-nest Swiftlet)

Percy Roycroft Lowe (1870–1948) was an ornithologist who was the President of the British Ornithologists' Union from 1933 until 1943.

LUCIFER

Lucifer's Hummingbird *Calothorax lucifer* (**Swainson** 1820)

We presume that this bird is named for the fallen angel Lucifer of the Judeo-Christian tradition, referred to in the fourteenth chapter of the Biblical book of Isaiah, at the twelfth verse: '*How art thou fallen from heaven, O Lucifer, son of the morning! How art thou cut down to the ground, which didst weaken the nations!*' Its deeply forked tail may have something to do with its name.

LUCY

Lucy's Warbler *Vermivora luciae* (J.G Cooper 1861)

Lucy Hunter Baird (1848–1913) was the only child of S F **Baird**; she was 13 when the warbler was named after her and described by J G Cooper.

LUCY

Lucy's Emerald *Amazilia luciae* (**Lawrence** 1868)
  (Alt. Honduran/Honduras Emerald)

Lucy Brewer was the only daughter of the American ornithologist Dr Thomas Mayo Brewer (1814–1880). Audubon and Brewer were friends, and she was named after **Audubon**'s wife. In turn her father's friend, George **Lawrence** who described the emerald, named it after Lucy.

LUDLOW

Ludlow's Fulvetta *Alcippe ludlowi* (Kinnear 1935)
  (Alt. Brown-throated Fulvetta)

Frank Ludlow (1885–1972) was a British educationist, botanist, ornithologist and explorer. He seems to have made the biggest impact as a botanist, being associated with the discovery of new species of peonies, primulas and rhododendrons. He collected widely in Bhutan, Chinese Turkestan and Tibet, often with other collectors such as George Sheriff, as well as with **Sillem**.

LUDOVIC

Ludovic's Nightjar *Caprimulgus inornatus ludovicianus* (Clarke 1913)
  (Alt. Plain Nightjar)

Louis C G Clarke (1881–1960) was the son of Goland Clarke and a nephew of Stephenson

Robert Clarke (see Clarke). He was a naturalist who collected in Somalia and the Curator of the Fitzwilliam Museum of Anthropology and Archaeology at Cambridge, England, from 1937 until 1946. We do not know which member of the family actually collected the bird, in 1912, in Abyssinia (now Ethiopia), but it was described in 1913 (the same year as Clarke's Weaver) by Colonel Stephenson Robert **Clarke** who described it and named it after his cousin, Ludovic (*ludovicianus*) being the Latin for Louis. In view of the proximity of dates there may be reason to think that at least two members of the Clarke family were travelling together in East Africa, and so who collected what is probably a matter for conjecture!

LUDWIG

Ludwig's Bustard *Neotis ludwigii* (**Rüppell** 1837)

Baron Carl Friedrich von Ludwig (1784–1847) went to Cape Town as a pharmacist in 1805. He married well and became a well-known collector who sent many specimens to German museums. **Rüppell** described and named the bustard after him.

LÜHDER

Lühder's Bush Shrike *Laniarius luehderi* (**Reichenow** 1874)

W Lühder (1847–1873) was a German naturalist who was collected in Cameroon in 1872. He wrote an article, *Notizen über den Bock*, in 1871.

LULU

Lulu's Tody-Tyrant *Poecilotriccus luluae* (Johnson & Jones 2001)

Lulu May Von Hagen was an avian geneticist. This new species was described in 2001 by N K Johnson and R E Jones in The Auk 118(2): 334–341. Its known range is a limited area of northern Peru, east of Bágua Grande and south of the Río Marañón. It was named in honour of the late Lulu May Von Hagen in recognition of '*her generous and dedicated support of research in avian genetics*'.

LYNES

Lynes' Pygmy Bustard *Lophotis savilei* (Lynes 1920)
(Alt. Savile's Bustard)
Lynes's Cisticola *Cisticola distinctus* (Lynes 1930)
Lynes's Flufftail *Sarothrura lugens lynesi* (**Grant** & Mackworth-Praed 1934)
(Alt. Chestnut-headed Flufftail)

Rear-Admiral Hubert Lynes (1874–1942) was an amateur ornithologist who collected in China from 1910 to 1913 and in Africa from 1926 to 1927. He wrote a *Review of the Genus Cisticola*, in 1930, which played a key part in revealing some order among this large assemblage of often confusingly similar species. He was awarded the Godman-Salvin Gold Medal by the British Ornithologists' Union in 1936.

MACCLOUNIE

MacClounie's Barbet *Lybius minor macclounii* (**Shelley** 1889)
  (Alt. Black-backed Barbet)
MacClounie's Robin-Chat *Cossypha anomala macclounii* (Shelley 1903)
  (Alt. Olive-flanked Robin-Chat)

John M MacClounie (sometimes spelt McClounie) was a British naturalist who collected in Nyasaland (now Malawi) between 1895 and 1906. He wrote a report in 1902 recommending that the Nyika Plateau, where he collected the type specimen of a parasitic plant *Loranthus nyikensis*, should be declared a protected area. His recommendation was not accepted then, although much of the plateau is now a national park. The barbet is often regarded as a separate species; **Shelley** described it as *Melanobucco macclounii*, from a specimen collected by MacClounie and presented to the British Museum (Natural History) by Lieutenant-Colonel W H Manning. Shelley also described the robin-chat.

MACCONNELL

McConnell's Flycatcher *Mionectes macconnelli* (**Chubb** 1919)
McConnell's Spinetail *Synallaxis macconnelli* (Chubb 1919)

See **McConnell**.

MACCORMICK

MacCormick's Skua *Catharacta maccormicki* (**Saunders** 1893)
  (Alt. South Polar/Antarctic Skua)

See **McCormick**.

MACFARLANE

MacFarlane's Screech Owl *Otus kennicottii macfarlanei* (**Brewster** 1882)
  (Alt. Western Screech Owl)

Roderick Ross MacFarlane (1833–1920) was a trader, collector and naturalist. He is usually remembered in relation to the collecting of specimens of the Eskimo Curlew *Numenius borealis*, which may now be extinct. MacFarlane joined the Hudson's Bay Company, in the Northwest Territories, as an assistant clerk in 1852. In 1857 he was sent to explore the possibilities of trade with the Inuit. At the same time, Robert **Kennicott**, sponsored by the Smithsonian Institution, visited various of the Hudson's Bay Company posts. After being exposed for three years to Kennicott's training and enthusiasm, MacFarlane became the most ardent collector for the Smithsonian Institution in the arctic. He went on one organised egg-collecting trip each year from 1862 to 1865, usually starting at the peak of the nesting (and mosquito) season, around 10 June, and returning about mid-July. Because of the unpredictable behaviour of the Inuit, his route varied. His party consisted of at least 21 Indian packers, hunters, collectors and canoe carriers, as well as pack dogs. He spent the long winters at Fort Anderson packing his material and writing notes by candlelight for each of his numbered specimens. In late winter or the following spring the collections were shipped out for forwarding to Spencer **Baird** at the Smithsonian. The process of dispatch was not without its vicissitudes however, as recorded in Mac-Farlane's own writings: '*For the reasons mentioned in my letters (1866) to Professor Baird, but a small portion of the 'Anderson Collection' 1865, was forwarded by the boats of 1866. Several cases and parcels were carried overland to Fort Good Hope during the Summer, while the remainder thereof, together with the whole of the Small Collection of 1866, and certain notes and memoranda connected with Collections '65 and preceding years, was secured near 'Lockhart' [Carnwath] river. Before these could, however, be sent from Good Hope, Wolverines and other animals broke into the cache, and destroyed all the bird skins, besides the rarest and finest eggs – in fact, everything that had been left there was destroyed irreparably, except one box containing a lot of Geese, Duck & other Eggs which shall be forwarded to Washington in 1869. The last of the cases of 1865 were sent off by the Boats of 1867, and have doubtless ere this reached their destination*'.

In 1865 scarlet fever literally wiped out the Indian hunters at the fort and measles was equally devastating to the Inuit. Much of what was collected thereafter was lost. That notwithstanding, his success is evident by the fact that his collection of 1862 consisted of 550 cases of specimens. He also wrote the *Birds and Mammals of Northern Canada*. **Brewster** described the owl subspecies, which is now regarded as a synonym of *O.k.bendirei*.

MACGILLIVRAY, J

MacGillivray's Petrel *Pseudobulweria macgillivrayi* (G R **Gray** 1860) Extinct
(Alt. Fiji Petrel)

John MacGillivray (1821–1867) was the son of William MacGillivray (see next entry). He emigrated and became one of Australia's leading naturalists. He was naturalist on the 1844 British Expedition to the Cape York Peninsular in Queensland, Australia. This expedition of four ships was led by the *Fly*. On this expedition he was retained to collect animal specimens for **Stanley**. He also was on the vessel *Rattlesnake* with Thomas Huxley on its 1846 to 1850 expedition to New Guinea and Australia. He was also on board HMS *Herald* as a naturalist and was one of the earliest scientists to visit Tristan da Cunha in 1852.

MACGILLIVRAY, W

MacGillivray's Warbler *Oporornis tolmiei* (**Townsend** 1839)

William MacGillivray (1796–1851) was a Scottish artist and professor who occupied the Regius Chair of Natural History at Marischal College in Aberdeen, in 1841. He grew up on the isle of Lewis and gained extensive knowledge of the fauna and flora of the Scottish highlands by engaging in field trips where he often walked hundreds of miles. He has been called 'the first ecologist'. In 1819 he wrote '*If I were to be a painter by profession my aim would be to copy nature with the scrupulous, yea, even servile attention; instead of displaying a genius that scorned control by a masterly dash, which would produce the likeness of nothing on earth*'. MacGillivray wrote *A History of British Birds* in five volumes, which he intended to illustrate with coloured plates based on his watercolours, but the great expense involved prevented him. His son, Paul Howard MacGillivray, presented the watercolours to The British Museum (Natural History) in 1892. He also worked as Curator of the Museum of the Royal College of Surgeons in Edinburgh. **Townsend** initially suggested naming the warbler after William Tolmie of the Hudson Bay Company, who co-wrote Audubon's *Ornithological Biography*. However **Audubon** himself decided to rename it after MacGillivray, which explains both the common and scientific names.

MACGILLIVRAY, W D

MacGillivray's Fairy-wren *Malurus coronatus macgillivrayi* (**Mathews** 1913)
(Alt. Purple-crowned Fairy-wren)

MacGillivray's Prion *Pachyptila salvini macgillivrayi* (Mathews 1912)

William David Kerr MacGillivray (1867–1933) was a naturalist, medical practitioner and ornithologist in Broken Hill, Australia, from 1901 to 1933, where he had a good reputation as a surgeon. He was a keen amateur ornithologist and wrote a number of articles and papers on birds. At the time of his death he was working on a book on Australian birds for use in schools. An Australian subspecies of the Eclectus Parrot *Eclectus roratus macgillivrayi* and the Palm Cockatoo *Probosciger aterrimus macgillivrayi* may also be named after him.

MACGREGOR

MacGregor's Bird-of-Paradise *Macgregoria pulchra* (**De Vis** 1897)
(Alt. Macgregor's Honeyeater)
MacGregor's Bowerbird *Amblyornis macgregoriae* (De Vis 1890)
(Alt. Gardener's Bowerbird)

Lady Mary Macgregor was the wife of Sir William MacGregor (1846–1919), a naturalist, collector and diplomat. He was Chief Medical Officer in Fiji, Administrator in New Guinea, later Governor of Lagos and then Newfoundland from 1904 to 1909, and finally Governor of Queensland from 1909 until 1914. Both birds are named for her. Recent DNA work suggests that the latter is not in fact a bird-of-paradise but is a honeyeater, hence the alternative name.

MACKINDER

MacKinder's Eagle Owl *Bubo capensis mackinderi* (**Sharpe** 1889)
(Alt. Cape Eagle Owl)

Sir Halford John MacKinder (1861–1947) was a mapmaker and traveller, and the first person recorded as having climbed to the top of Mt Kenya. He studied geography at Oxford and, although he wasn't a mountaineer, he thought that climbing Mount Kenya would establish him as an adventurer and explorer. He first trained in the Alps and hired Italian guides to help him climb the peak. In 1899, they managed to reach the mountain despite local hostilities and cut a way through the forests to the alpine zone. Several attempts on the summit failed, but on the 13 September they managed to find a way to the top. This race of the Eagle Owl is found on Mt Kenya and was originally described by **Sharpe** as *Bubo mackinderi*, from a specimen collected by MacKinder.

MACKINLAY

Mackinlay's Cuckoo-Dove *Macropygia mackinlayi* (E P **Ramsay** 1878)
(Alt. Spot-breasted Cuckoo-Dove)

Archibald Mackinlay (1850–1924) was a Scottish explorer and naturalist.

MACKINNON

Mackinnon's Grey Shrike *Lanius mackinnoni* (**Sharpe** 1891)
(Alt. Mackinnon's Fiscal/Shrike)

Archibald Donald Mackinnon CMG OBE (1864–1937) graduated from Aberdeen University in 1892 with a degree in medicine. He was a medical officer in Uganda from 1894 to 1897 and was Director of Transport there from 1898 to 1899. **Sharpe** described the shrike from a specimen collected in Kenya by F J Jackson.

MACKLOT

Macklot's Pitta *Pitta erythrogaster* (**Temminck** 1834)
(Alt. Red-bellied Pitta)

Macklot's Sunbird *Nectarinia calcostetha* (**Jardine** 1843)
(Alt. Copper-throated Sunbird)
Macklot's Trogon* *Harpactes* (*reinwardtii*) *mackloti* (Temminck 1832)

Heinrich C Macklot was a taxidermist who was appointed to assist members of the Dutch Natural Science Commission. He went on an expedition to New Guinea and Timor on the *Triton* from 1828 to 1830. Macklot's Python *Liasis mackloti* and the Panay Giant Fruit Bat *Acerodon mackloti* are also named after him. Macklot's Trogon is an original lithograph, with later hand colouring, by **Gould** and Richter for Gould's *A Monograph of the Trogonidae or Family of Trogons* 1836–38. The bat, python, pitta and sunbird come from Timor. There are no trogons in Timor so we assume that Macklot collected it in nearby Java earlier.

MACLEAY

Macleay's Honeyeater *Meliphaga macleayana* (**Ramsay** 1875)
(Alt. Yellow-streaked Honeyeater)
Macleay's Forest Kingfisher *Halcyon macleayii* (Jardine & Selby 1830)

William John Macleay (1820–1891) was a politician and naturalist who wrote widely on entomology, ichthyology and zoology and who took part in several collecting expeditions. The whole of the Macleay family were avid naturalists and collectors, so much so that the Macleay Museum University of Sydney was built in 1887 to house their vast natural history collection. They began collecting insects in the late 18th century, when Alexander Macleay (1767–1848), a diplomat and entomologist, went to Sydney as Colonial Secretary in 1826. He already had one of the largest privately owned insect collections in the world. It was added to by his son, William Sharp Macleay (1792–1865), and expanded to include all aspects of natural history by William's cousin, William John Macleay. He, in turn, donated the collections to Sydney University, in 1887, as soon as the museum building was ready.

MACQUEEN

MacQueen's Bustard *Chlamydotis* (*undulata*) *macqueenii* (J E **Gray** 1832)
(Alt. Houbara Bustard)

General Th R MacQueen (1792–1840) collected in the Himalayas and northwest India and presented the bustard to the British Museum (Natural History). At the time when he collected it, he was a major in the 45th Bengal Native Infantry, a regiment in the Bengal Army of the Honourable East India Company.

MADAME VERREAUX

Madame Verreaux's Sunbird *Nectarinia johannae* (E & J **Verreaux** 1851)

See **Johanna**.

MADARÁSZ

Madarász's Parrot *Psittacella Madaraszi* (A B **Meyer** 1886)
(Alt. Madarász's Tiger Parrot)

Gyula von Madarász [Gyula Madarász Gyulara] (1858–1931) was a Hungarian ornithologist and painter, whose landscapes and birds were exhibited in the National Salon. He illustrated his own work *Magyarorszag madarai* (Birds of Hungary), which was published in Hungarian and German. He was also a contributor to *Zeitschrift fur Ornithologie* and made a special study of the manakins (Pipridae). One remarkable fact is that his name 'Madarász' means 'birder'. His papers were held by the Royal Hungarian Museum, in Budapest, where he was Curator of Birds from 1881 to 1915, but unfortunately the museum was destroyed in 1956 during the fighting in the anti-Communist uprising.

MAES

Maes' Laughing-thrush *Garrulax maesi* (**Oustalet** 1890)
(Alt. Grey Laughing-thrush)

Albert Maes (?–1914) was a French aviculturalist.

MAGNOLIA

Magnolia Warbler *Dendroica magnolia* (A **Wilson** 1811)

Pierre Magnol (1638–1715) was a French physician and botanist, who came from a long line of apothecaries. The Magnolia tree and subsequently the warbler are named after him, the bird indirectly in relation to its supposed habitat, although it actually frequents conifers. Magnol renounced his Calvinist faith as this was preventing him from gaining public office. In his *Prodromus historiae generalis plantarum*, in 1689, he was among the first to classify plants in tables making possible quick identification. He was also the first person to use the term 'family' in the sense of a natural group. In another work, *Botanicum Monspeliense* in 1676, he described 1,354 species growing around the area where he lived. He gave their habitats and added notes on their medicinal or other uses. This work was the basis for the Linnaean dissertation on the Montpellier region in 1756. His other works included *Hortus regius Monspeliensis*, in 1697, which was a catalogue of his own garden and *Novus caracter plantarum*, published posthumously in 1720.

MAJOR MITCHELL

Major Mitchell's Cockatoo *Cacatua leadbeateri* (**Vigors** 1831)
(Alt. Pink Cocatoo)

See **Mitchell**.

MALCOLM

Malcolm's Babbler *Turdoides malcolmi* (**Sykes** 1832)
(Alt. Large Grey Babbler)

Major-General Sir John Malcolm (1760–1833) was the Governor of Bombay in 1827 and an amateur historian. He was a close friend and correspondent of the First Duke of Wellington. During his career he was an envoy in Persia with the Shah's army. He was also responsible for incorporating 'Holkars' into British India after he defeated the local ruler's troops at Mahidpur in 1818. He must have been enormously wealthy since he once lost £30,000 at a single sitting of cards (whist) at White's Club in London. He wrote a number of historical texts including *History of Persia, A Memoir of Central India including Malwa and Adjoining Provinces* and *Historical Account of the Rise and Progress of the Bengal Infantry, from its first formation in 1757 to 1796, when the present Regulations took place: together with a Detail of the Services on which the several Battalions have been employed during that period*. **Sykes** described the babbler as *Timalia malcolmi*, from a specimen which Malcolm collected from the plains of the Deccan, India.

MALHERBE

Malherbe's Flicker *Colaptes auratus* (Linnaeus 1758)
(Alt. Northern/Mearn's Flicker)
Malherbe's Golden-backed Woodpecker *Chrysocolaptes indicus* (**Scopoli** 1886)
(Alt. Greater Golden-backed Woodpecker)
Malherbe's Parakeet *Cyanoramphus malherbii* (**Souancé** 1857)

Alfred Malherbe (1804–1866) was a French magistrate and judge and a passionate botanist, zoologist and ornithologist. His interest in nature was inspired by his childhood in the tropics. He produced a major study of the woodpeckers, the four-volume *Monographie des picidées*, published between 1861 and 1862, which describes every known species of woodpecker, with hand-colored lithographs accompanying the detailed review. He also wrote extensively on the birds of Algeria and Sicily. At one time he was Administrator of the Museum of Metz.

MANDELLI

Mandelli's Snowfinch *Montifringilla taczanowskii* (**Przevalsky** 1876)
(Alt. White-rumped Snowfinch)

Louis Mandelli (1833–1880) was a tea planter in Assam in India, who was the subject of a book, *L. Mandelli, Darjeeling Tea Planter & Ornithologist* by Fred Pinn. This account contains several pages of birds identified and named by Mandelli, but does not mention the Snowfinch although it refers to his excursions into 'the snow' seeking birds. His collections are now in the Natural History Museum, Tring.

MANDT

Mandt's Guillemot *Cepphus grylle mandtii* (Mandt 1822)
(Alt. Black Guillemot)

Martin Wilhelm Mandt (1800–1858) was a German zoologist and physician at the Russian Imperial court of Tsar Nicholas I. He wrote *Observationes in historiam naturalem et anatomiam comparatam in itinere Groenlandico factæ*, in 1822.

MAPPIN

Mappin's Moa *Pachyornis* [*elephantopus*] *mappini* (Owen 1946) [Extinct]

Sir Frank Crossley Mappin Bt, (1884–1975) was born in England but, even after he inherited a considerable estate in England in 1920, he decided that New Zealand was where he wanted to live. He had first gone there in 1908, when he was variously a farmer, a flax cutter, a land negotiator and a politician. He was also noted for his charitable donations. Mappin went on several trips to the King Country and Lake Waikaremoana searching caves for moa bones, and clearly he was successful at it! There is much confusion about just how many different moas there were with estimates ranging from 12–40 species – 'Mappin's Moa' was probably a race of *Pachyornis elephantopus*.

MARCHE

Marche's Fruit Dove *Ptilinopus marchei* (**Oustalet** 1880)
(Alt. Flame-breasted Fruit Dove)

Alfred A Marche (1844–1898) was a French explorer. He wrote *Trois Voyages dans l'Afrique Occidentale*, in 1879, and *Lucon et Palaouan*, in 1887. After his visit to the Philippines, from 1879 to 1883, he wrote *Voyage aux Philippines*, which included a number of local recipes for cooking wild boar and venison. He also conducted archaeological exploration and removed a vast number of artefacts, all of which were sent to the Musée de l'Homme, in Paris.

MARGARET

Margaret's Batis *Batis margaritae* (**Boulton** 1934)
(Alt. Boulton's Batis, Boulton's Puffback Flycatcher)
Margaret's Hummingbird *Lampornis margaritae* (**Salvin** & **Godman** 1889)
(Alt. Amethyst-throated Hummingbird)

Margaret Lander Holt was the wife of the American ornithologist E G Holt. In 1921 and

1922 the National Museum of Rio de Janeiro organised two expeditions in the Itatiaia National Park, Brazil, where Holt, who worked for the American Museum of Natural History, New York, identified 187 species. The hummingbird is often treated as a subspecies of the Amethyst-throated Hummingbird *Lampornis amethystinus*.

MARGARETTA

Margaretta's Hermit *Phaethornis (superciliosus) margarettae* (Ruschi 1972)
(Alt. Great-billed/Margaretha Hermit)

Margaretta Lammot Du Pont Greenwalt (?–1991) was married to Crawford H Greenwalt (1902–1993), the President of the Dupont Corporation from 1948 to 1962, who financed many studies undertaken by his friend, the Brazilian ornithologist Dr Augusto Ruschi (1916–1986). In 1973 Ruschi photographed orchids with Greenwalt. A well-known conservationist, Greenwalt photographed hummingbirds in Brazil and Ecuador and designed equipment to photograph them in flight. He also wrote award-winning books and articles based on his avian researches. He published *Hummingbirds*, in 1960, and *Bird Song: Acoustics and Physiology*, in 1968. Ruschi named the new bird for his friend's wife.

MARGARIT

Margarit's Parakeet *Bolborhynchus aurifrons margaritae* (**Berlioz** & **Dorst** 1956)
(Alt. Mountain Parakeet)

See **Margaret** Holt above.

MARIA KOEPCKE

Maria Koepcke's Screech Owl *Otus koepckeae* (Hekstra 1982)
(Alt. Maria Koepcke's Owl)

See **Koepcke**.

MARKHAM

Markham's Storm Petrel *Oceanodroma markhami* (**Salvin** 1883)
(Alt. Sooty Storm Petrel)

Sir Clements Robert Markham (1830–1916) was an English explorer. Whilst serving in the navy he was sent on an expedition to the Arctic to search for the explorer Sir John Franklin, between 1850 and 1851. After he left the service, in 1852, he travelled to Peru and explored the eastern slopes of the Andes. He became an acknowledged expert on the Inca civilization, and wrote *The Incas of Peru* in 1910. For ten years, from 1867 to 1877, he supervised geographical work in India where he also explored. Among his interests was promoting the the importance of quinine as a cure for malaria, and he encouraged the East India Company to set up plantations in India. He was President of the Royal Geographical Society from 1893 until 1905. Markham published 50 works, including accounts of his own travels as well as biographies of other explorers and travellers, such as *The Voyages of Pedro Fernandez de Quiros, 1595 to 1606*, which he both translated and edited. He was a promoter of Antarctic exploration and helped to raise money to finance Scott's 1901 expedition. He had met Scott when the latter was just 18 and announced at the time: '*My final conclusion was that Scott was the destined man to command the Antarctic expedition.* The storm petrel only breeds in Chile and Peru.

MARMORA

Marmora's Warbler *Sylvia sarda* (**Temminck** 1820)

Alberto Ferrero Della Marmora (1789–1863) [or Alessandro or Alexander – depending on the source] was an Italian general and naturalist who had a distinguished career in the Napoleonic wars and was personally decorated by Napoleon I with the Légion d'Honneur. He was later employed by the King of Sardinia. He wrote *Viaggio in Sardegna (Travel in Sardinia)* in 1860. He has a mountain in Sardinia named after him too. Marmora stands accused of having massacred those who revolted against the reign of the Savoys in Genoa by using his newly formed cadre of uniformed soldiers, all carrying a 'carbine' which he invented. He is credited with having named **Eleonora**'s Falcon *Falco eleonorae* and with rediscovering **Cetti**'s Warbler *Cettia cetti*.

MARPLES

> Marples' Penguin *Palaeeudyptes marplesi* (Brodkorb 1953) [Extinct]

Brian John Marples (1907–1997) was Professor of Zoology at Otago University, New Zealand, from 1937 until 1966, and helped to form the Ornithological Society of New Zealand, in 1939. He was born in Yorkshire, England. His father was Principal of Liverpool City School of Art and a keen ornithologist who, with his wife, wrote *Sea Terns and Sea Swallows*, in 1934. In 1990 Marples wrote about his arrival in New Zealand '...*it was an incredible experience, especially for a biologist, to arrive at the other side of the world in a country where both the geology and the ecosystem were unfamiliar, except, surprisingly enough, for some very familiar garden birds*'. His ornithological activities included establishing a netting and banding scheme for Silver-eyes *Zosterops lateralis*, and carrying out an extensive study of the introduced Little Owl *Athene noctua*. He wrote *Vertebrate Palaeontology in New Zealand*, in 1949 and has a very long publications list of books and articles spanning the years 1925 to 1972, on many topics including anatomy, taxonomy, behaviour and ecology; covering freshwater invertebrates, fish, birds and fossil vertebrates. He is remembered most for his work as an avian palaeontologist but he also studied spiders and published a great deal on them. In 1960 he described '*A fossil penguin from the Late Tertiary of North Canterbury*', in the records of the Canterbury Museum. He is also honoured in the genus *Marplesornis* of fossil penguins.

MARSHALL

> Marshall's Fig Parrot *Opopsitta diophthalma marshalli* (Iredale 1946)
> (Alt. Double-eyed/Northern/Blue-faced/Red-faced Fig Parrot)
> Marshall's Iora *Aegithina nigrolutea* (Marshall 1876)
> (Alt. White-tailed Iora)

Captain George Frederick Leycester Marshall (1843–1934) and his brother Colonel Charles Henry Tilson Marshall (1841–1927) wrote on ornithology together. G F L Marshall also wrote *Butterflies Of India, Burmah & Ceylon* with L De Niceville, which was published in three volumes between 1882 and 1890. C H T Marshall served chiefly in the Punjab, where he collected, as well as in the Himalayas. He sent specimens to Hume with whom he wrote *The Game Birds of India, Burmah and Ceylon*, which was published between 1879 and 1881.

MASSENA

> Massena's Lory *Trichoglossus haematodus massena* (**Bonaparte** 1854)
> (Alt. Massena's Lory, Rainbow Lory/Lorikeet)
> Massena's Parrot *Pionus senilis* (**Spix** 1824)

Francois Victor Masséna, Prince D'Essling and Duc de Rivoli (1795–1863). See **Rivoli**.

MATON

> Maton's Parakeet *Trichoglossus chlorolepidotus* (**Kuhl** 1820)
> (Alt. Scaly-breasted/Green and Gold Lorikeet)

Dr William George Maton MD (1774–1835) was a British physician and botanist. In 1794 he became a Fellow of the Linnean Society; later becoming its Vice-President. The members showed their regard for him by naming a woodpecker, a shellfish and a genus of plants after him. He wrote *Observations relative chiefly to the Natural History, Picturesque Scenery, and Antiquities of the Western Counties of England, made chiefly in the Years 1794 and 1796,* which was published in 1797. He was also a Fellow of the London College of Physicians and he was appointed Physician-Extraordinary to Queen Charlotte.

MATSUDAIRA

Matsudaira's Storm Petrel *Oceanodroma matsudairae* (Kuroda 1922)
(Alt. Black Storm Petrel)

Viscount Yorikatsu Matsudaira (1876–1945) was a Japanese ornithologist. He wrote *A Hand-list of the Japanese Birds,* in 1922. The petrels only breed on a few rocky islets off the shore of Japan.

MATTHEWS

Matthews' Panoplites *Panoplites matthewsi* (**Bourcier** 1847)*

Andrew Matthews (?–1841) was an English botanist who collected in Peru and Chile between 1830 and 1841. This is another bird we can only find mention of as a Gould engraving. An A Matthews collected another hummingbird, the Chestnut-breasted Coronet *Trochilus* (*Boissonneaua*) *matthewsii* and the two specimens found their way into the **Loddiges** Collection. **Bourcier** described it using the manuscript name that Loddiges had used. We are not only convinced that this was the same A Matthews, but also that the very same bird was either mistakenly named in parallel when painted by Gould, or was deliberately so named in an attempt to usurp the bird for **Gould**. The fact that there is no subsequent description by Gould rather supports the former theory, and we have come across several examples of genuine mistakes at the height of the first collecting of the very many hummingbird species.

MATHEWS

Mathews' Pink Cockatoo *Cacatua leadbeateri mollis* (Mathews 1920)
(Alt. Little Major Mitchell's Cockatoo)
Mathews' Cockatoo *Cacatua galerita fitzroyi* (Mathews 1912)
(Alt. Fitzroy's Cockatoo)
Mathews' Red-tailed Black Cockatoo *Calyptorhynchus banksii samueli*
(Mathews 1917)
Mathews' [Little] Short-billed Corella *Cacatua sanguinea normantoni*
(Mathews 1917)

Gregory Macalister Mathews (1876–1949) was an Australian ornithologist who moved to England around 1900, after having made a fortune in mining shares and marrying an Englishwoman. He wrote *A Manual of the Birds of Australia,* the first volume of which appeared in 1910 and the 12th and last in 1927. In 1939 he donated his collection of books, pamphlets, reprints, manuscripts and pictorial material to the Australian National Library, comprising what is now known as the Mathews ornithological library. The result of nearly 20 years work, Gregory Mathews' gift to the library is considered to be the finest collection of material relating to the study of Australian birds. Among the pictorial items are works by John Gould, J W Lewin and Lilian Medland, together with manuscripts by Mathews, John Gould and Sylvester Diggles.

MATTHIAS

Matthias Fantail *Rhipidura matthiae* (**Heinroth** 1902)
(Alt. St Matthias Fantail/Rufous Fantail)

This is not named for a person but for the Island of St Matthias in Papua New Guinea. Saint Matthias was the person chosen by the disciples of Jesus to replace Judas.

MAUGE

Mauge's Conure *Aratinga chloroptera maugei* (**Souancé** 1856)
(Alt. Puerto Rican Conure)
Mauge's Flowerpecker *Dicaeum maugei* (**Lesson** 1830)
(Alt. Red-chested/Blue-cheeked/Timor/Lesser Sunda Flowerpecker)

Rene Mauge [de Cely] (?–1802) was a French zoologist who accompanied his friend **Baudin** on his great scientific voyage of 1800 to 1803. He collected in the West Indies between 1796 and 1798 and in the Pacific between 1800 and 1802. Unfortunately, he fell ill in Timor and died when the expedition arrived in Tasmania.

MAXIMILIAN

Maximilian's Jay *Gymnorhinus cyanocephalus* (Maximilian 1841)
(Alt. Pinyon/Cassin's Jay, Maximilian's Nutcracker)
Maximilian's Parrot *Pionus maximiliani maximiliani* (**Kuhl** 1820)
(Alt. Scaly-headed Parrot)

Maximilian Alexander Philip, Prince zu Wied-Neuwied (1782–1867) was an aristocratic German explorer who collected in Brazil between 1815 and 1817, in Guyana in 1921 and in North America from 1832 until 1834. In 1833 he made his famous journey of some 5,000 miles, principally up the Missouri River, on the second voyage of the steamer *Yellowstone*. Artists and scientists from Europe went with him, gathering specimens and painting scenes of the mostly uninhabited countryside. He wrote *Reise nach Brasilien in den Jahren 1815 bis 1817* (Journey to Brazil) in 1820, *Beiträge zur Naturalgeschichte von Brasilien* in 1825 and *Reise in das Innere Nord-Amerika in den Jahren 1832 bis 1834* (Journey to the Interior of North America) in 1840, on his return to Europe. The best-known species named in his honour is the Margay *Leopardus wiedii*. Among other species first described or named by him are the Red-eared Slider Turtle *Chrysemys scripta elegans,* the Western Chorus Frog *Pseudacris triseriata* and the Spring Peeper Frog *Hyla crucifer.* The jay was first discovered and informally described in 1805 on the **Lewis** & **Clark** expedition, but it was not scientifically named until 1841, when Maximilian himself wrote the description, presumably after he collected it again. See **Wied** for several other species attributed to this man.

MAXWELL

Maxwell's Black Weaver *Ploceus albinucha maxwelli* (**Alexander** 1903)
(Alt. White-naped Black Weaver)

Sir Herbert Eustace Maxwell (1845–1937), seventh baronet, hailed from one of the oldest families in Scotland. He became a Knight of the Thistle and Member of Parliament for Wigtownshire, Lord of the Treasury, Secretary of State for Scotland, and Lord Lieutenant of the County of Wigtownshire. His garden at Monreith House became renowned for its many introduced trees from around the world. He himself wrote an account of *Gardens of Scotland.* His grandson was the naturalist and author Gavin Maxwell, famous for his books *Ring of Bright Water* and *Harpoon at a Venture*, among mant others. Boyd **Alexander** first described the weaver in 1903, based on his own collections on the island of Fernando Pó (now Bioko) the previous year, when he obtained 500 specimens of a range of species.

MAYNARD

Maynard's Cuckoo *Coccyzus minor maynardi* (J.F Gmelin 1788)
(Alt. Mangrove Cuckoo)

Professor Charles Johnson Maynard (1845–1929) was an American ornithologist and all-round naturalist who has often been described as 'Newtonville's [Massachusetts] enigmatic naturalist'. Maynard is a legendary name as he was the discoverer, in 1868, of the Ipswich Sparrow *Passerculus sandwichensis princeps*, a highly localised subspecies of the Savannah Sparrow which is considered by some to be a full species, as originally supposed. He was a well-known observer of birds, particularly in Florida and the Bahamas. For example, in 1896, he wrote '*The eagle hovers over a bunch of coots and endeavors by diving down towards the flock to make them scatter. The eagle will never attack a coot when surrounded by its fellows, but the instant one is separated from the flock his life is in jeopardy, for, no matter how expertly he dives, his untiring enemy is above him whenever he comes to the surface, and drives him further and further from his friends, who will never attempt to protect him, but who swim away as fast as their lobated toes would propel them...The reason why the eagle tries to separate one coot from its fellows must be that he can then chase that particular bird, and by chasing it until it is exhausted, effect its capture, whereas it would quite easily elude him if it kept among its fellows. Among coots, their safety lies in numbers, even if all be cowards, but the wonder is, not that the eagles know this, but that the coots themselves do.*' **Batchelder** wrote a catalogue of Maynard's publications. Among other books and articles he wrote *The Naturalist's Guide in Collecting and Preserving Objects of Natural History*, in 1870, *The Birds of Eastern North America* in 1881, *A Manual of North American Butterflies* in 1891, *The Butterflies of New England*, in 1886 and *Birds of Washington and Vicinity* in 1898. Many of these works were published by his own company and he illustrated many of them himself, competently but not brilliantly. The species was described by Gmelin in 1788; *maynardi* was described from Florida by Maynard himself, but most authorities do not now recognise any subspecies.

MAYR

Mayr's Forest Rail *Rallina mayri* (**Hartert** 1930)
(Alt. Mayr's Chestnut Rail)
Mayr's Painted Parrot *Psittacella picta excelsa* (Mayr & Gilliard 1951)
(Alt. Painted Tiger Parrot)
Mayr's Parrot *Psittacella brehmii harterti* (Mayr 1931)
(Alt. Brehm's Tiger Parrot)
Mayr's Pygmy Parrot *Micropsitta pusio harterti* (Mayr 1937)
(Alt. Buff-faced Pygmy Parrot)
Mayr's Red-flanked Lorikeet *Charmosyna placentis ornata* (Mayr 1940)
Mayr's Streaked Honeyeater *Ptiloprora mayri* (Hartert 1930)
(Alt. Mayr's/Red-backed Honeyeater)
Mayr's Munia *Lonchura spectabilis mayri* (Hartert 1930)
(Alt. New Britain/Hooded Mannikin/Munia)
Mayr's Swiftlet *Aerodramus orientalis* (Mayr 1935)
(Alt. Guadalcanal Swiftlet)

Dr Ernst Mayr (1904–) is a German ornithologist and zoologist who started his serious studies of birds in the South Pacific. He is best known as an eminent writer on evolution; it has even been said of him '*he is, without a doubt the most influential evolution theoretician of the twentieth century*'. As a ten-year-old boy he could recognise all the local birds on sight and by their song. In 1928 he led ornithological expeditions to New Guinea, an experience which he said "*fulfilled the greatest ambition of my youth.*" He collected 7,000 skins in 2.5 years. He later joined an expedition to the Solomon Islands, before returning to his academic career at the Berlin museum. In 1931 Mayr was employed by the Department of Ornithology of the American Museum of Natural History, at first for only one year as a visiting curator, to catalogue the collection of South Sea birds obtained by the Whitney Expedition, in which Mayr had participated. He wrote 12 research papers, describing 12 new species and 68 new subspecies, during his first year there. He went on to become the Alexander Agassiz Emeritus Professor of Zoology at Harvard University. He is the originator of the 'founder effect' idea of speciation and is a leading proponent of the Biological Species Concept. His many important books include *Systemics and the origin of species*, 1942, *Animal species and evolution*, 1963 and, with Diamond, *The birds of Melanesia: speciation, ecology and biogeography*, 2001.

MCCALL

McCall's Screech Owl *Otus asio mccalli* (**Cassin** 1854)
(Alt. Eastern Screech Owl)

Brigadier-General George Archibald McCall (1802–1868) was a military man but also an amateur naturalist and collector. He graduated from West Point military academy in 1822 and fought in the Seminole wars and the Mexican war. In May 1861 he was appointed Brigadier-General of Volunteers on the Union side of the American Civil War, where he commanded the Pennsylvania Reserves division. He was captured on 30 June 1862 at Fraser's Farm and exchanged two months later for the Confederate General Simon Bolivar Buckner. He was then on sick leave until his resignation in March 1863. Cassin mentioned him in connection with **Gambel**'s Quail, when McCall was still a Colonel. He wrote a brief paper in 1851; *Some remarks on the habits &c., of birds met with in western Texas, between San Antonio and the Rio Grande and in New Mexico*, which he sent to John **Audubon**. Eastern Screech Owls live in eastern North America and have at least six allopatric subspecies, most of them named after people.

MCCLELLAND

McClelland's [Mountain] Bulbul *Hypsipetes virescens* (**Temminck** 1825)
    (Alt. Sunda Streaked/Streaked[Mountain]/Green-winged/Green-backed Bulbul)
McClelland's Laughing-thrush *Garrulax gularis* (McClelland 1840)
    (Alt. Rufous-vented/Yellow-browed Laughing-thrush)

John McClelland (1805–1875) was a British geologist and zoologist. In 1836, a Coal Committee was set up, with John McClelland as the Secretary, for advising the government on the best means of procuring coal for extending steam navigation. He later served with the East India Company.

MCCONNELL

McConnell's Flycatcher *Mionectes macconnelli* (**Chubb** 1919)
McConnell's Spinetail *Synallaxis macconnelli* (Chubb 1919)

Frederick Vavasour McConnell (1868–1914) was an English traveller and collector. He made some of his collections with a J J Quelch (who wrote *Animal Life in British Guiana*, in 1901) between 1894 and 1898. His collections inspired a book by C H Chubb; *The Birds of British Guiana* written between 1916 and 1921, to which McConnell's wife wrote the foreword. He presented his specimens to the British Museum (Natural History). They comprised collections of mammals and spiders as well as birds, all obtained in British Guiana (now Guyana).

MCCORMICK

McCormick's Skua *Stercorarius maccormicki* (**Saunders** 1893)
(Alt. South Polar Skua)

Robert M McCormick (1800–1890) was a British naval surgeon, explorer and naturalist, who was described as a '*conscientious physician and zoological technician*'. He was assistant surgeon on the *Hecla*, in 1827, during Parry's Arctic expedition. McCormick was also the ship's surgeon on the voyage of what he described as '*a small surveying ten gun brig*', the *Beagle*, in 1832. In 1832 McCormick wrote: '*We anchored off Porta Praya, in the island of St. Jago, Cape de Verde Islands, and I landed there… I paid a visit to the remarkable old baobab-tree… growing in an open space to the westward of the town…as a memento I cut my initials, with the date of the year, high up the main stem…and on measuring the baobab-tree, I found it 36 $^1/_2$ feet in circumference.*' It was the tradition of the time that the ship's surgeon also collected specimens, especially zoological ones, on such trips. The fact that this was done instead by **Darwin** irritated him, and he resigned once the ship returned from Salvador in Brazil, sailing back to England on the *Tyne*. In 1839 he was the surgeon on Sir James Clark **Ross**'s Antarctic expedition on the ships *Erebus* and *Terror*, remaining until 1843. In 1839, on the Ross voyage, he visited the Cape Verde Islands again and recorded in his journal: '*…I made a visit to my old friend the baobab-tree, in the middle of the valley, and a mile to the eastward of the town…On reaching the baobab-tree, I ascended it, and looked for my own initials, which I cut, with the year 1832, in the main stem, about two-thirds up the tree, when here last in that year. Time had impressed them deeper, and they appeared larger, more marked and distinct from the contraction of the bark around. I now added the present year, 1839, beneath the former one…*' When it was realised that **Franklin**'s Northwest Passage expedition had vanished, McCormick led an unsuccessful search party. However, he did chart the Wellington Channel from his ship, appropriately named the *Forlorn Hope*. He wrote *Voyages of Discovery in the Arctic and Antarctic Seas, and Round the World: Being Personal Narratives of Attempts to Reach the North and South Poles*; and also an account of an *Open-Boat Expedition up the Wellington Channel in Search of Sir John Franklin and Her Majesty's Ships Erebus and Terror, in Her Majesty's Boat Forlorn Hope, under the Command of the Author*.

MCCOWN

McCown's Longspur *Calcarius mccownii* (**Lawrence** 1851)

John Porter McCown (1815–1879) was an American soldier who attained the rank of Major-General. During the American Civil War he fought for the Confederacy and, after hostilities were over, he worked as a farmer and teacher. He collected the bird when he fired on a group of Horned Larks *Eremophila alpestris*. His friend George Newbold **Lawrence** named the bird after him whilst working on the collections at the Smithsonian Institution.

MCGREGOR

McGregor's Cuckoo-shrike *Coracina mcgregori* (**Mearns** 1907)
(Alt. Sharp-tailed Greybird)
McGregor's House Finch *Carpodacus mexicanus mcgregori* (**Anthony** 1897)
[Extinct]

Richard Crittenden McGregor (1871–1936) was an Australian who first went to the United

States, and then was appointed as ornithologist to the Manila Bureau of Science in the Philippines. He published several articles on the birds of Santa Cruz County, California. He also wrote *A Manual of Philippine Birds*, in 1909, the first book on the avifauna of the islands.

MCKAY

McKay's Bunting *Plectrophenax hyperboreus* (**Ridgway** 1884)
(Alt. McKay's Snow Bunting)

Charles McKay (1855–1883) was in the United States signal corps and he was also an arctic explorer, who unfortunately drowned whilst on an expedition. McKay collected more than 400 birds, including the one that bears his name, for the United States National Museum.

MEADE-WALDO

Meade-Waldo's Chat *Saxicola dacotiae* (Meade-Waldo 1889)
(Alt. Fuerteventura/Canary Islands Chat)
Meade-Waldo's Oystercatcher *Haematopus meadewaldoi* (**Bannerman** 1913)
(Alt. Canary Island/Canarian Black Oystercatcher)

Edmund Gustavus Bloomfield Meade-Waldo (1855–1934) was an English explorer and ornithologist. He collected around the world including in the Canary Islands and wrote a definitive checklist for that archipelago. In 1896 he was the first to record seeing a Pin-tailed Sandgrouse *Pterocles alchata* taking up water in its breast feathers to take a drink to its chicks. The claim that this behaviour existed was ridiculed right up until the 1960s, although it has since featured in a number of TV documentaries. He owned Hever Castle between 1896 and 1905. He is also famed for having seen an unidentified 'sea serpent' in 1903. He discovered the chat in 1888 and wrote the formal description in 1889. The oystercatcher was last definitely recorded in 1913 and is probably extinct, although doubts are attached to its validity as a separate species.

MEARNS

Mearn's Golden Flicker *Colaptes chrysoides mearnsi* (**Ridgway** 1911)
(Alt. Gilded Flicker)
Mearn's Quail *Cyrtonyx montezuma* (**Vigors** 1830)
(Alt. Montezuma Quail)
Mearn's Thrasher *Toxostoma cinereum mearnsi* (**Anthony** 1895)
(Alt. Grey Thrasher)
Mearn's Woodpecker *Melanerpes formicivorus bairdii* (Ridgway 1881)
(Alt. Acorn/California Woodpecker)

Lieutenant-Colonel Edgar Alexander Mearns (1856–1916) was a surgeon in the United States Army. He was stationed first in Mexico, from 1892 until 1894, then in the Philippines, from 1903 to 1907, and later in Africa, between 1909 and 1911. He published a great deal on natural history during the last decade of his life, including many descriptions of African birds. Among his finds in the Phillippines was the rare Bagobo Babbler. He called it *Leonardia* (now *Trichastoma*) *woodi* after the commanding general of the American forces in Mindanao and Sulu, who was also President, in 1903, of the Philippine Scientific Society and was later to become Governor General of the islands. Mearns was also a friend of Theodore Roosevelt's and accompanied him on his trip to East Africa in 1909. Childs **Frick** approached the Smithsonian Institution in 1911, looking for a scientist to accompany him on his collecting trip to Africa, and Mearns was chosen. Frick agreed to pay Mearns' salary and expenses and to donate all bird collections to the United States National Museum. This was to be Mearns' last expedition. His life was beset with illness including a '*nervous breakdown complicated by malaria*' and various parasitic conditions. Eventually he developed diabetes and, as this was before the development of insulin treatment, nothing could be done for him.

MECHOW

Mechow's Long-tailed Cuckoo *Cercococcyx mechowi* (**Cabanis** 1882)
(Alt. Dusky [Long-tailed] Cuckoo)

Major Alexander D von Mechow was an Austrian explorer and naturalist who led several expeditions to explore and collect in Angola, between 1878 and 1900. He explored the middle Kwango River, in Angola, in 1880 and there collected reptiles (such as *Xenocalamus mechowi*) and amphibians. He is commemorated in the scientific name of the Giant Mole Rat *Cryptomys mechowi* and a number of insects, such as the beetle *Eudicella gralli mechowi* and the Central African butterflies *Hypolymnas mechowi* and *Papilio mechowi,* among many others. The southern subspecies of the Dark Chanting Goshawk *Melierax metabates mechowi* bears his name in the trinomial.

MEEK

Meek's Hawk-Owl *Ninox meeki* (**Rothschild** & **Hartert** 1914)
Meek's Lorikeet *Charmosyna meeki* (Rothschild & Hartert 1901)
Meek's Pigeon *Microgoura meeki* (Rothschild 1904) [Extinct]
(Alt. Solomon Islands Crowned[Ground] Pigeon, Choiseul Pigeon)
Meek's Pygmy Parrot *Micropsitta meeki* (Rothschild & Hartert 1914)
Meek's Streaked Honeyeater *Ptiloprora meekiana* (Rothschild & Hartert 1907)
(Alt. Olive-streaked Honeyeater)
Meek's White-eye *Zosterops meeki* (Hartert 1898)

Albert Stewart Meek (1871–1943) was an English explorer who collected in New Guinea, Australia and the Solomon Islands, where he spent 18 years exploring, only returning to England in 1911. During his long absence in Melanesia he made nine expeditions to New Guinea and three to the Solomon Islands. He wrote *A Naturalist in Cannibal Land* in 1913.

MEES

Mees' Monarch *Monarcha sacerdotum* (Mees 1973)
(Alt. Flores Monarch)

Dr Gerlof Fokko Mees was born in Holland, grew up in the East Indies and is now living in Australia. The monarch was described as recently as 1973, by Mees, who first discovered it on Flores, Indonesia, in 1971. It was not seen again for more than 20 years, although an expedition by the British Ornithologists' Union in 1998 found it to be slightly more widespread than thought but endangered by a road-building programme on Flores. Mees was Curator of Vertebrates (birds and fish) at the Western Australian Museum from 1958 until 1963, and then Curator of Birds at Leiden Museum, from 1963 until his retirement. He returned to Australia in 1991. He has a particular interest in *Zosterops* (Silver-eyes) and has visited Norfolk Island twice to study them there. His many articles and books include *The Birds of Suriname,* with François Haverschmidt.

MEINERTZHAGEN

Meinertzhagen's Snowfinch *Montifringilla theresae* (Meinertzhagen 1937)
(Alt. Theresa's/Afghan Snowfinch)
Meinertzhagen's Warbler *Sylvia* (*deserticola*) *ticehursti* (Meinertzhagen 1939)
(Alt. Tristram's Warbler)

Richard Meinertzhagen (1878–1967) was a soldier, a hunter, an ornithologist, a writer, a spy, an advocate of Zionism and, according to the preface to a second edition of his *Kenya Diary* at least, a killer. He was an empire builder in the *Boys Own* mould, although he lived in an era when the British Empire was in its final decline. He is truly one of the most remarkable characters to appear in this list. He was born to wealth and position. Although he was one of ten children he was still pampered, even to the extent of being bought an elephant by an eccentric uncle as a christening gift. The family had several homes and was well connected; family friends included Florence Nightingale. As a soldier, Meinertzhagen served in India, East Africa (during the First World War) and Palestine. His primary role was intelligence-gathering but he was also known as a hardened killer. He was at the one time xenophobic and a passionate advocate of Zionism, so much so that he met Hitler twice in the late thirties to plead for the Jews. There is a tale, apocryphal or otherwise, about these meetings which is too irresistible to leave out. He reports that, on one of these occasions, when Hitler saluted with *Heil Hitler* he responded with *Heil Meinertzhagen* and was treated to a 40-minute rant from Hitler and Ribbentrop. He told people that, since he had a gun in his pocket at the time, he ever afterwards regretted not shooting the pair of them on the spot!

His Zionism was traceable to an incident when he was serving in Odessa, Russia, in 1910, where he rescued a young Jewish girl from one of the pogroms. He became a proponent of a Jewish state in Palestine since he was, according to his diary, impressed by the Biblical promise that '*the Holy Land forever remains Israel's inheritance*'. He vowed that he would help the Jews whenever and however he could. He was still prepared to help even in 1948 when his ship docked in Haifa, as he was returning to England from a field trip to Saudi Arabia. This was in the middle of the Israeli War for Independence, and there were still three weeks before the British Mandate expired. Meinertzhagen, although 70 years old, saw the opportunity to help the Jewish cause in an intensely personal way. He borrowed the uniform and equipment of one of the Coldstream Guards, who were assigned to protecting government stores, who was sick. Alone he found some of the Haganah in a firefight with some Arabs so he joined in. After an hour of fighting he was caught by one of the Coldstream officers, who ordered him back to the ship. '*It mattered little*', he wrote in his diary, '*as by then I had fired all my 200 rounds*'. Meinertzhagen retired from the army in 1925, after serving as Britain's chief political officer in Palestine and Syria. He indulged his twin hobbies of promoting a Jewish state and ornithology. He travelled widely, gathering material for books, which became standard references, but also frequently acting in support of British intelligence.

Meinertzhagen's most famous exploit happened during the First World War, when the British Army targeted Beersheba in the build-up to attacking Turkish-occupied Jerusalem. Meinertzhagen's task was to confuse the Turks about the real target. His tactics included regularly air-dropping cigarettes to the Turkish troops, who came to expect them; he planned to lace them with opium the night before the attack to impair their defensive capability. The result is not known. He also rode out towards the enemy hoping to be discovered by a patrol. Putting on an act he convinced the Turkish patrol that the papers which he dropped for them to find were authentic. His ruse worked and the focus of their defence shifted to Gaza and away from Beersheba. This subterfuge was portrayed in the Australian film *The Light-horsemen*.

Meinertzhagen wrote *Nicoll's Birds of Egypt* in 1930, *The Birds of Arabia* in 1954, *Kenya Diary* in 1957, *Pirates and Predators* in 1959, *Middle East Diary* in 1959, *Army Diary* in 1960 and *The Diary of a Black Sheep* in 1964.

In his will, he left his collection of over 25,000 bird specimens, recognised as one of the best of its kind in the world, to the British Museum (Natural History). However some suspicions about his ornithological materials were expressed, although it was not until 1993 that a serious investigation of his collection began. The outcome is revealed in *Richard Meinertzhagen – A Case of Fraud Examined* by Alan Knox in The Ibis 135:320–325. According to Pamela Rasmussen, an ornithologist at the Smithsonian Institution and something of a scientific Sherlock Holmes, this respected soldier, war hero, and expert ornithologist is alleged to have systematically engaged in the theft of bird specimens from a variety of museums, re-stuffed them and added them to his own collection. Three subspecies have been removed from the British List as a result of the investigation reported in the article. The warbler is now considered to be synonymous with Tristram's Warbler. The snowfinch was first described by him in 1937 and is named for **Theresa** Clay, his companion and niece!

MELBA

Melba Finch *Pytilia melba* (Linnaeus 1758)
(Alt. Green-winged Pytilia, Crimson-faced Waxbill)

We do not believe that this bird was named after a person. The name goes back as far as 1758 when Linnaeus described it, so if it is named after a person, it certainly is not Dame Nellie Melba, the well-known soprano!

MELL

Mell's Oriole *Oriolus mellianus* (**Stresemann** 1922)
(Alt. Silver/Mell's Maroon/Stresemann's Maroon Oriole)

R E Mell (1878–?) was a German naturalist who collected in China. His descriptions included plants, reptiles and insects, as well as birds. He made trips to a number of different areas including Ding Wu in southern China, north of Guangzhou, in 1922. He wrote two publications on Lepidoptera; *Beiträge zur Fauna Sinica (II). Biologie und Systematik der Süd-chinesischen Sphingiden. Zugleich ein Versuch einer Biologie tropischer Lepidopteren überhaupt*, in 1922, and *Inventur und ökologisches Material zu einer Biologie der südchinesischen Pieriden*, in 1943.

MELLER

Meller's Duck *Anas melleri* (**Sclater** 1864)

Charles James Meller (1836–1869) was a botanist who worked in Nyasaland (now Malawi) in 1861 and on Mauritius in 1865. He was also a surgeon who worked with David **Livingstone**.

MENBEK

Menbek's Coucal *Centropus menbeki* (**Lesson** & Garnot 1828)
(Alt. Greater [Black]/Jungle Coucal)

This is not a person at all. Menebiki is the local, New Guinean, name for the bird, which has been poorly transcribed at some stage.

MENCKE

Mencke's Monarch *Monarcha menckei* (**Heinroth** 1902)
(Alt. White-breasted/Massqu/Mussau Island/St Matthias Monarch [Flycatcher])

Bruno Mencke (?–1901) was a German zoologist who led the first German South Seas Expedition of 1900–1901.

MÉNÉTRIES

Ménétries's Antwren *Myrmotherula menetriesii* (**d'Orbigny** 1837)
(Alt. Grey Antwren)
Ménétries's Warbler *Sylvia mystacea* (Ménétries 1832)

Edouard P Ménétries (1802–1861) was a French zoologist who collected in Brazil, from 1822 to 1824, and in Russia, from 1829 until 1830. At one stage he was a Conservator of the collections of the Russian Academy of Sciences. He wrote *Catalogue Raisonée des Objects de Zoologie Recueillis dans un Voyage au Caucase et Jusqu'aux Frontiers Actuelles de la Perse*, in 1832.

MENZBIER

Menzbier's Pipit *Anthus gustavi menzbieri* (Shulpin 1928)
(Alt. Pechora Pipit)

Mikhail Aleksandrovich Menzbier (1855–1935) was a Russian zoologist from Moscow. He described species across Russia, the eastern Soviet Union and northern China. Menzbier was one of the founding members of Russia's first ornithological society and he has a number of such societies named after him. He was among the first to posit that birds are related to reptiles. His major work was on the taxonomy of birds of prey and he was responsible for much of their modern classification. He wrote *Oritnologicheskaya geografiia evropeiskoi Rossii*, in 1882, and *Ornithologie du Turkestan et des pays adjacents*, in 1888. He is particularly remembered for Menzbier's Marmot *Marmota menzbieri*. Some authorities accord *menzbieri* species status.

MERRIAM

Merriam's Turkey *Meleagris gallopavo merriamii* (**Nelson** 1900)
(Alt. Common/Wild Turkey)

Clinton Hart Merriam (1855–1942) was an American naturalist and physician, and the brother of Florence Augusta **Bailey**. His father was a Congressman and, through him, he met **Baird** of the Smithsonian, in 1871, which led to his being invited to work as a naturalist the following year in Yellowstone, Wyoming, as a member of the Hayden Geological Survey. This experience sparked his interest and guided his choice of further education; he studied biology and anatomy at Yale, and finally graduated as a physician in 1879. His interest in natural history continued as a hobby whilst he practised medicine. In 1883, he forsook his profession for full-time scientific work. He became Chairman of the Bird Migration Committee of the American Ornithologists' Union. Under his chairmanship, they applied to Congress for funds to study birds on the grounds that such work would benefit farmers. With the help of Senator Warner Miller, of New York, Merriam's cousin and family friend, their application was successful and Congress granted them sufficient funds. Merriam became the first chief of the United States Biological Survey's (USBS) Division of Economic Ornithology and Mammalogy. He is most famed for his 'life zone' theory, which hypothesised that '*temperature extremes were the principal desiderata in determining the geographic distribution of organisms.*' He also wrote a *Review of the Birds of Connecticut, with Remarks on their Habits*. Dr E W **Nelson** named this Turkey subspecies honouring Merriam as the first chief of the USBS.

MERRILL, E

Merrill's Fruit Dove *Ptilinopus merrilli* (**McGregor** 1916)
(Alt. Cream-bellied Fruit Dove)

Elmer Drew Merrill (1876–1956) was an American botanist who collected in the

Philippines between 1902 and 1929. He worked for a total of 22 years in the Philippines, during which he became Director of the Bureau of Sciences, as well as Professor of Botany at the University of the Philippines. He wrote *Flora of Manila* in 1912 and *Enumeration of Philippine Flowering Plants*, which was published in sections between 1922 and 1926. His expertise on the Philippines was put into service during the Second World War when he compiled a handbook of *Emergency Food Plants and Poisonous Plants of the Islands of the Pacific*. In 1923 he became Dean of the California College of Agriculture and during his time there he added over 110,000 mounted specimens to the university herbarium and also published work on China, Borneo, and the Philippines. He was the Director of the New York Botanical Garden from 1929 to 1935 and also served Harvard University as Administrator of Botanical Collections. Merrill described a total of over 3,000 new species of plants from the Philippines, Polynesia, China, the Moluccas and Borneo. At least seven plant genera are dedicated to him and some 220 binomials honour his name.

MERRILL, J

Merrill's Horned Lark *Eremophila alpestris merrilli* (Dwight 1890)
Merrill's Pauraque *Nyctidromus albicollis merrilli* (**Sennett** 1888)
  (Alt. Pauraque)
Merrill's Song Sparrow *Melospiza melodia merrilli* (Sennett 1888)

James Cushing Merrill (1853–1902) was a naturalist who served as a surgeon in the United States army. His second posting was to Fort Brown, Texas, where he made observations and collected the local birds, from 1876 to 1878. He published *Notes on the ornithology of southern Texas*, in 1878, on the 252 species he noted. He recorded twelve species and subspecies of birds which he believed were new to the United States. He gave many of the bird skins he collected to his friend William **Brewster** at the Museum of Comparative Zoology, at Cambridge, Massachusetts. His various postings led to further study and publications including *Notes on the birds of Fort Klamath, Oregon*, in 1883 and *Notes on the birds of Fort Sherman, Idaho*, in 1897. Dwight described and named at least three subspecies of birds in his honour including the lark.

METCALFE

Metcalfe's White-eye *Zosterops metcalfii* (**Tristram** 1894)
  (Alt. Bukida/Yellow-throated White-eye)

P H Metcalfe (?–1913) was a British naturalist who collected in the Solomon Islands.

MEVES

Meves' Long-tailed Glossy Starling *Lamprotornis mevesii* (**Wahlberg** 1856)
  (Alt. Southern Long-tailed Glossy Starling)

Friederich Wilhelm Meves (1814–1891) was a German ornithologist and teacher who worked for the Zoological Museum in Stockholm for much of his life. In 1840, before moving to Sweden, he worked in the Anatomical/Zoological Museum at Kiel where he made contact with the ornithologist Fr Boie. Boie had Swedish connections; he taught at Uppsala. Through him, Meves became a curator at the Riksmuseet's Zoological Department in 1841, and remained in that job until 1877. During those 36 years he took part in many expeditions, both in Sweden and abroad, and made many valuable additions to the museum's collections. He published several ornithological works including *Overview of Royal Science Academy Collections*, in 1854, *Contribution to Swedish Ornithology*, in 1868, *Ornithological Observations in Northwest Russia 1869*, in 1871, and *Uber den Schnurrlaut der Bekassine*, in 1876.

MEYER, A B

Meyer's Black-capped Lory *Lorius lory salvadorii* (Meyer 1891)
Meyer's Bronze Cuckoo *Chrysococcyx meyeri* (**Salvadori** 1874)
(Alt. White-eared/Narrow-billed Bronze Cuckoo, Horsfield's Cuckoo)
Meyer's Friarbird *Philemon meyeri* (Salvadori 1878)
Meyer's Goshawk *Accipiter meyerianus* (**Sharpe** 1878)
(Alt. Papuan Goshawk)
Meyer's Lorikeet *Trichoglossus flavoviridis meyeri* (Wallace 1871)
(Alt. Yellow-and-green/Sula Lorikeet)
Meyer's Koklass *Pucrasia macrolopha meyeri* (**Madarász** 1886)
(Alt. Koklass Pheasant)
Meyer's Sicklebill *Epimachus meyeri* (**Finsch** 1885)
(Alt. Brown Sicklebill, Brown Sickle-billed Bird-of-Paradise)
Meyer's Whistler *Pachycephala meyeri* (Salvadori 1889)
(Alt. Vogelkop/Grey-crowned Whistler)

Dr Adolf Bernard Meyer (1840–1911) was a German anthropologist and ornithologist who collected in the East Indies at around the turn of the 19th century. He was a professor at the Anthropological and Ethnographic Museum of Dresden. He wrote *The Birds of the Celebes and Neighbouring Islands*, in 1898, and he is cited as having made the first description of a number of bird species from the East Indies. It was he who first recognised that the red male and green female of the sexually dimorphic Australian King Parrot *Alisterus scapularis* were members of one species not two. He was very interested in the evolution debate and corresponded with **Wallace**.

MEYER, B

Meyer's Parrot *Poicephalus meyeri* (**Cretzschmar** 1827)
(Alt. Brown Parrot)

Dr Bernhard Meyer (1767–1836) was a physician who is noted for his contributions to German ornithology. He wrote *Naturgeschichte der Vogel Deutschlands*, in 1805, and *Tashenbuch der Deutschen Vogelkunde*, in 1810. The parrot is native to Africa and Meyer is not known to have travelled there.

MIDDENDORFF

Middendorff's Bean Goose *Anser fabalis middendorffi* (**Severtzov** 1873)
Middendorff's Grasshopper Warbler *Locustella ochotensis* (Middendorff 1853)
Middendorff's Stint *Calidris subminuta* (Middendorff 1853)
(Alt. Long-toed Stint)

Alexander Theodor [Aleksandr Fedorovitsh] von Middendorf (1815–1894) was a German-Russian traveller and naturalist, who was a member of the St Petersburg Academy of Sciences. From 1842 until 1845, he journeyed throughout Siberia and the surrounding regions. His accounts of the Amur River and other remote regions of Russia were the fullest by a naturalist and anthropologist of what was then a little-explored area. As a naturalist he wrote on the spread of permafrost and how this affected the distribution of plants and animals. His experiences were recorded in *A Journey to the North and East of Siberia*, in 1877. Apart from the birds and some plants and invertebrates, a cape on the island of Novaya Zemlya and a bay on the Taimyr Peninsula are named after him. Amongst his observations of the people of northern Siberia he wrote that no one would remove anything from an unattended sleigh, even if it contained much needed food. '*It is well known that the inhabitants of the far North are frequently on the verge of starvation, but to use any of the supplies left behind would be what we call a crime, and such a crime might bring all sorts of evil upon the tribe*'.

MIKADO

Mikado Pheasant *Syrmaticus mikado* (**Ogilvie-Grant** 1906)

This bird is named after the title of the Japenese emperors and not after any individual person.

MILLER

Miller's Emerald *Thaumatias milleri* (**Gould***)

This is another name which only appears in **Gould**'s works. The notes of the collector **Loddiges**, in 1847, refer to a bird which he meant to carry the name *milleri*. His manuscript name was, however, *Oreotrochilus leucopleurus*, and he intended to send the specimen to Gould. **Bourcier** named a bird *Trochilus milleri* in that year, but this is not the emerald as far as we can tell. There is another hummingbird with this suffix, the Tepui Goldenthroat *Polytmus milleri*, which was named after Waldron de Witt Miller (1879–1929), when described by **Chapman** in 1929. The scientific suffix *milleri* has also been used to refer to two other people, both of whom were not alive when Gould made his drawings, and who could only have been infants when **Sharpe** may have assigned a name for Gould's drawing. The species could be an invention but, given all the above, it seems more likely to have resulted from some confusion.

MILLER

Miller's Crake *Gallirallus milleri* [Extinct]
(Alt. Sooty/Tahiti Crake, Miller's Rail)

The crake may have been named after Waldron de Witt Miller (1879–1929), who was the curator of the American Museum of Natural History, New York for 26 years and a co-founder of the New Jersey Audubon Society. He co-wrote, with A Wetmore the revised classification for the fourth edition of the *AOU Check-list*, in 1926. Miller was injured in a motorcycle accident, on 4 August 1929, when he hit a bus, and died three days later. The crake, which is also known as *Porzana nigra*, was a native of Polynesia. An extinct bat from the same region, which was described by **Elliot** in 1903, is named *Myotis milleri*.

MILLET

Millet's Laughing-thrush *Garrulax milleti* (**Robinson** & Kloss 1919)
(Alt. Black-hooded/Vietnam Laughing-thrush)

F Millet was the superintendent of forests in Annam, in French colonial Vietnam.

MILNE-EDWARDS

Milne-Edwards' Willow Warbler *Phylloscopus armandii* (A Milne-Edwards 1865)
(Alt. Yellow-streaked Warbler)

Henri Milne-Edwards (1800–1885) was born in Belgium, the 27th son of a reproductively prolific Englishman, and became a renowned French naturalist. He took up a professorship at the Sorbonne in 1843. He was also a Professor at the Museum of Natural History in Paris, from 1841, and its Director from 1864. He wrote works on crustaceans, molluscs, corals and a textbook on general zoology, in 1834, as well as *Lessons d'Anatomy et de Physiologie*. In 1859, when Pasteur and Pouchet were debating the notion of spontaneous generation which was losing scientific support, he supported Pasteur saying ''*brute matter cannot organize itself in such a way as to form an animal or plant...life force has been passed on successively through an uninterrupted chain of being since creation.*' He had '*often had the desire to descend in a diving helmet and to be able to examine at leisure the submarine rocks inhabited by those whom I would like to make the object of my researches'*. A friend, Colonel Paulin, Commandant of the Paris fire brigade, had devised and constructed a helmet to allow firemen to walk through smoke. Milne-Edwards asked him to improve it in such a way for it to be suitable for use in diving. In 1844 he tried it out in the waters off Sicily, in what was the first diving expedition ever undertaken by marine biologists. He descended *'to pursue marine creatures into their most hidden retreats'*, which he did *'in the enjoyment of perfect liberty of action'*, being able to examine *'the fissures of the submarine rocks which thronged with molluscs, worms and zoophytes'*. He stayed at a depth of about 12 feet for half an hour. He went on to say *'it would have been simple to descend to much greater depths had not the inadequacy of the life-saving facilities on the fishing boat made me think that it would have been imprudent to try'*. He thus became the first person to describe living marine life in situ.

His son was the noted palaeontologist, Sir Alphonse Milne-Edwards (1835–1900) who wrote *Histoire Naturelle de l'Oiseaux*, as well as a book on the natural history of Madagascar, in 1876. Alphonse corresponded with **Darwin**. He had a close working relationship with Prince Albert I of Monaco and may have been influential in encouraging the prince to establish the Oceanographic Museum in Monte Carlo. He was sent specimens from China by Père **David** – the most notable of which were the Giant Panda and a gerbil *Gerbillus*. He was also the first person to recognise that the Giant Panda was not a bear but belonged in a distinct family; in 1870 he named it *Ailuropoda melanoleuca*, which apparently means 'cat-footed black and white animal'. The warbler's scientific suffix *armandii* refers to Pere David and so the bird is most likely to have been Alphonse's rather than Henri's. The Prix Alphonse Milne-Edwards was created in 1903 in his memory.

MINISTERS, MISSIONARIES & MONKS

The clergy have a tradition of science, as demonstrated by Father Francesco **Cetti** who was a very fine Italian zoologist as well as a monk, and studied birds in Sardinia. Reverend Lansdown **Guilding** was a cleric who lived and died on St Vincent, only leaving home to be educated. However, from the earliest days of European exploration of the rest of the world, Christian ministers of many denominations tagged along to carry 'the word of God' to 'heathen' lands. Particularly in the 19th century, many were missionaries in remote and little-explored areas, making them ideally placed to record new birds for Western science. For example, Brother **Apolinar** Maria was a missionary Colombian monk and a fine ornithologist. Monsignor Felix **Biet** was a French missionary in China, as was Father Jean Pierre Armand **David**, who was certainly one of the greatest zoologists ever to work there. This French tradition in China is also represented by the Reverend F **Courtois**, Father J A **Soulie** and Pierre Marie **Heude,** who was a French naturalist (conchologist) and Jesuit missionary, and Father J N **Renauld** was a French missionary in neighbouring Vietnam. Reverend George **Brown** was a Methodist missionary to Melanesia and Reverend Henry James **Bruce** an American missionary in India. James **Hepburn** was the first Presbyterian missionary to Japan. Brother Matthias **Newell** was a missionary to Hawaii. Reverend William George **Lawes** was a British missionary in New Guinea and an all-round naturalist and linguist. Reverend Robert D S **Woodward** and his brother, John B Woodward, were both Anglican missionaries in Natal, South Africa. Charles Walter **De Vis** was a cleric who actually renounced the Church to concentrate on being an ornithologist in Australia. Brother **Niceforo** Maria was a herpetologist who became a missionary in Colombia. However, the most famous missionary of them all, the Scottish doctor and explorer David **Livingstone**, had no particular interest in natural history. The tradition persists to this day, as Reverend Father O **Appert** is a German missionary in Madagascar, who still pursues his interests as an amateur naturalist.

MIRANDOLLE

Mirandolle's Forest Falcon *Micrastur mirandollei* (**Schlegel** 1862)
(Alt. Slaty-backed Forest Falcon)

Charles François Mirandolle (1789–1841) was Resident of Surinam. **Schlegel**'s original entry reads: '*Adulte, Surinam, présenté par Mr. Mirandolle: individu type, figure dans l'ouvrage cité*'.

MITCHELL

Major Mitchell's Cockatoo *Cacatua leadbeateri* (**Vigors** 1831)
(Alt. Leadbeater's/Pink Cockatoo)
Mitchell's Lorikeet *Trichoglossus haematodus mitchellii* (G R **Gray** 1859)
(Alt. Rainbow Lorikeet/Lory)

Lieutenant-Colonel Sir Thomas Livingstone Mitchell (1792–1855) was a Scottish army surveyor and explorer. He was the Surveyor-General of New South Wales from 1828 until 1855, and led various expeditions into eastern Australia, between 1831 and 1836 and to tropical Australia, from 1845 to 1846. A very life-like coloured plate of his cockatoo appears in Mitchell's *Three Expeditions into the Interior of Eastern Australia*, published in 1838. A town in Queensland is also named after him. **Vigors** described the cockatoo in 1831. This subspecies of the lorikeet is restricted to Bali and Lombok, in Indonesia.

MITCHELL

Mitchell's Plover *Phegornis mitchellii* (**Fraser** 1845)
(Alt. Diademed Sandpiper-plover)

David William Mitchell (1814–1859) was an English zoologist who was secretary of the Zoological Society of London from 1847 until 1859. He was also a fine bird illustrator and illustrated *The Genera of Birds*, by George Robert **Gray**. Other illustrators of the same work included Edward **Lear**.

MLLE THURA

Mlle Thura's Rosefinch *Carpodacus thura* (**Bonaparte** & **Schlegel** 1850)
(Alt. White-browed/Thura's Rosefinch)

See **Thura**.

MOISLEY

Moisley's Penguin *Tereingaornis moisleyi* (**Scarlett** 1984) [Extinct]

William L Moisley is a New Zealand palaeontologist. He published, jointly with Joan Wiffen, in 1986, *Late Cretaceous reptiles (Families Elasmosauridae and Pliosauridae) from the Mangahouanga Stream, North Island, New Zealand* in the New Zealand Journal of Geology and Geophysics.

MOLESWORTH

Molesworth's Tragopan *Tragopan blythii molesworthi* (E C S **Baker** 1914)
(Alt. Blyth's Tragopan)

Probably after Dr B D Molesworth, who was a British physician. In 1937 he was instrumental in setting up a workshop near Kuala Lumpur, Malaysia, to make artificial limbs for victims of leprosy. In 1947, G C Madoc published *An Introduction to Malayan Birds*, and Molesworth provided the illustrations, both photographs and line drawings.

MOLONEY

Moloney's Illadopsis *Illadopsis fulvescens moloneyana* (**Sharpe** 1892)
(Alt. Brown Illadopsis)

Sir Cornelius Alfred Moloney (1848–1913) was a British civil servant. He was Administrator of The Gambia from 1884 until 1886, and Governor of Lagos, Nigeria, from 1886 until 1889 and from 1890 until 1891. From 1891 until 1897 he was Lieutenant-Governor of British Honduras (now Belize). From 1900 to 1904, he was Governor of Trinidad. He wrote *Forest in West Africa*, which initiated a forestry policy in Nigeria. **Sharpe** also commemorates him in another bird, *Turdinus moloneyanus*, which he described in 1892 from a specimen Moloney collected in Ghana; we have been unable to trace the present identity of the latter bird.

MOLTONI

Moltoni's Warbler *Sylvia cantillans moltonii* (Orlando 1937)
(Alt. Subalpine Warbler)

Professor Dr Edgardo Moltoni (1896–1980), the most eminent of Italian ornithologists, was Director of the Museo Civico di Storia Naturale, in Milan. He travelled widely and wrote many papers, including a checklist of Italian birds. The subspecies was first described in 1937 by Orlando but not recognised by subsequent authors, until Gabriel Gargallo redefined its characters, in 1994.

MONDETOUR

Mondetour's Dove *Claravis mondetoura* (**Bonaparte** 1856)
(Alt. Maroon-chested Ground Dove)

Pauline Brière de Mondetour was the widow of the French zoologist Étienne **Geoffroy Saint-Hilaire** (1772–1844). They married in 1804.

MONTAGU

Montagu's Harrier *Circus pygargus* (Linnaeus 1758)

Colonel George Montagu (1751–1815) was a soldier and natural history writer. He attained the rank of captain in the British army at a young age and later served in the American Revolution as a lieutenant-colonel in the English militia. His military career was curtailed when he was court-martialled and cashiered for causing trouble among his brother officers by what was described as '*provocative marital skirmishing*'. Montagu then devoted himself to science, particularly biology. In his own words; '*I have delighted in being an ornithologist from infancy, and, was I not bound by conjugal attachment, should like to ride my hobby to distant parts.*' Montagu was among the first members of the Linnean Society. He was an expert on shells and he maintained a large collection of coins and animals, which was purchased by the British Museum. He wrote many papers on the birds of southern England, but his greatest work was the *Ornithological Dictionary or Alphabetical Synopsis of British Birds*, in 1802. He was renowned for his meticulous work and observations that bordered on the clinical. Such observations led to a better understanding of phenomena which had previously been romanticised. For example, he said of bird song: "*…males of song-birds and of many others do not in general search for the female, but, on the contrary, their business in the*

spring is to perch on some conspicuous spot, breathing out their full and amorous notes, which, by instinct, the female knows, and repairs to the spot to choose her mate." He died of lockjaw (tetanus) after stepping on a rusty nail.

MONTANO

Montano's Hornbill *Anthracoceros montani* (**Oustalet** 1880)
  (Alt. Sulu Hornbill)

Dr Joseph Montano (1844–?) was a French anthropologist who spent some time in the Philippines, between 1879 and 1881, whilst undertaking a scientific survey of the Philippines and Malaysia. He accompanied Don Joaquin Rajal, the governor of Davo, on an expedition to Mt Apo, in 1880, which was the first ascent of the peak. He wrote *Voyages aux Philippines et en Malaisie*, in 1886.

MONTEIRO

Monteiro's Bush Shrike *Malaconotus monteiri* (**Sharpe** 1870)
Monteiro's Golden Weaver *Ploceus xanthops* (**Hartlaub** 1862)
  (Alt. Holub's Golden Weaver)
Monteiro's Hornbill *Tockus monteiri* (Hartlaub 1865)
Monteiro's Twinspot *Clytospiza monteiri* (Hartlaub 1860)
  (Alt. Brown Twinspot)

Joachim João Monteiro (1833–1878) was a Portuguese mining engineer who collected natural history specimens in Angola from 1860 until 1875. In 1875 he wrote *Angola and the River Congo*.

MONTEZUMA

Montezuma Quail *Cyrtonyx montezuma* (**Vigors** 1830)
  (Alt. Mearn's Quail)

Montezuma (1480–1520) was Emperor of the Aztecs, in Mexico, at the time of the Spanish conquest.

MORCOM

Morcom's Hummingbird *Atthis heloisa* (*morcomi*) (**Lesson** & **DeLattre** 1839)
  (Alt. Bumblebee/Heloise's Hummingbird)
Morcom's Yellow Warbler *Dendroica petechia morcomi* (H K Coale 1887)

George Frean Morcom (1845–1932) was a British-born American amateur ornithologist, who settled in Chicago, and later collected and recorded in California and Arizona at the turn of the 19th century. He took work as a book-keeper and progressed in the company, becoming a partner and, eventually, sole proprietor. His free time was spent hunting and shooting, but also in collecting natural history specimens and observing wildlife, particularly birds. His first love was palaeontology, but his interest in ornithology had been inspired by a friendship in England with John Gatcombe who was a first-class painter of birds. Morcom became very involved in the Ridgway Ornithological Club, in Chicago, when it was first organised in 1873. In addition to his own collecting, he did, on occasion, commission others to make collecting expeditions. He corresponded with **Ridgway** and sent a number of his prize specimens to the National Museum because of his liking for the man. These included the type specimen of the hummingbird, which Ridgway first described as *Atthis morcomi* and then *Atthis heloisa morcomi* before his further research, in 1927, established that it was not a valid race, and it was reabsorbed into *Atthis heloisa*. He sent many specimens back home to the British Museum too. There are letters and notes of his in the California Academy of Sciences, together with the G F Morcom collection, which contains most of the specimens he had collected and kept during his lifetime. The collection was already in existence in 1929 and includes letters written in 1918. H K Coale, who prepared many specimens for Morcom and wrote articles with him, wrote the first description of the warbler, a form of the Yellow Warbler from the Rocky Mountains, in 1887.

MORDEN

Morden's Scops Owl *Otus ireneae* (**Ripley** 1966)
(Alt. Sokoke Scops Owl)

Irene Morden was an American sponsor of expeditions and a collector in Kenya in 1965. William and Irene Morden undertook two collecting expeditions in Kenya, in 1953 and 1956, on behalf of the American Museum of Natural History, in New York. With her husband she co-wrote *Our African Adventure*, in 1954 and a couple of articles, *Cattle people of the desert Veld*, in 1954 and *The last four Strandlopers*, in 1955.

MOREAU

Moreau's Sunbird *Nectarinia moreaui* (**W L Sclater** 1933)
Moreau's Tailorbird *Apalis moreaui* (W L Sclater 1931)
(Alt. Moreau's/Long-billed Apalis, Long-billed Tailorbird)

Reginald E Moreau (1897–1970) was a British ornithologist and collector. He wrote *The Bird Fauna of Africa and its Islands*, in 1966, *The Palaearctic–African Bird Migration Systems* in 1972 and, with B P **Hall**, *An Atlas of Speciation in African Passerine Birds*, in 1970, as well as numerous papers, especially on African fauna and its evolution, distribution and migration.

MORELLET

Morellet's Seedeater *Sporophila torqueola morelleti* (**Bonaparte** 1850)
(Alt. White-collared/Sharpe's Seedeater)

P M A Morellet (1809–1892) was a Spanish zoologist who collected in the Canaries and Guatemala. **Bonaparte** named the seedeater, which is sometimes accorded species status. Morellet also had a crocodile *Crocodilus morelleti* named in his honour.

MORENO

Moreno's Bare-faced Ground Dove *Metriopelia morenoi* (**Sharpe** 1902)
(Alt. Bare-eyed Ground Dove)

Francisco Josue Pascasio Moreno (1852–1919) was an Argentine naturalist, geographer, anthropologist and explorer who founded La Plata Museum in 1884, and was its first Director. He began collecting as a child, so much so that his parents set aside a room for his collection of specimens. He started exploring in Patagonia in 1873 and, by 1875 he had crossed that rugged promontory from sea to sea, achieving a long-held ambition. He wrote *Viaje a la Patagonia Austral* about his journey of 1876, which explored unknown territory and mapped it for the first time. In 1879 he donated over 15,000 specimens to the Anthropological and Ethnographic Museum of Buenos Aires, which created a whole new department. He donated books and drew in many overseas scientists, as well as raising money for buildings, all of which culminated in his being appointed Director for life. As an anthropologist he was among the first to plead for attempts to 'civilise' native peoples to cease. In 1879 he was briefly held prisoner by one of the tribes he went to study and after escaping decided to go to Europe to study further. On his return some years later he found those same people imprisoned and did everything he could to have them released and rehabilitated. In the 1880s he was instrumental in establishing the border with Chile. Moreno's last collecting trip, in 1912, was made with American ex-president Theodore Roosevelt. He also wrote the definitive work on his favourite area: *Patagonia, Rest of a Missing Continent*. He was granted territory which he had explored by the government but he donated it back to create the Nahuel Huapi National Park. He is also honoured in the name of a large glacier.

MOSELEY

Moseley's Rockhopper Penguin *Eudyptes chrysocome moseleyi* (**Mathews & Iredale 1921**)
(Alt. Northern Rockhopper Penguin)

Professor Henry Nottidge Moseley (1844–1891) was Head of the Department of Zoology and Comparative Anatomy of the Pitt Rivers Museum, at the University of Oxford. He wrote *Notes by a Naturalist on HMS Challenger*, in 1879, and collected many specimens on that expedition, which was a voyage around the world from 1872 until 1876, providing study materials for many years. He also took part in expeditions to Ceylon (now Sri Lanka) in 1871 and to California and Oregon in 1877. He has many species and even genera named after him, particularly of marine animals such as starfish and corals.

MOSZKOWSKI

Moszkowski's Green-winged King Parrot *Alisterus chloropterus moszkowskii* (**Reichenow** 1911)
(Alt. Papuan/Moczkowski's/Mozskowski's Green-winged King Parrot)

M Moszkowski undertook an expedition to New Guinea around 1910. He published an article *Expedition zur Erforschung des Mamberamo in Hollandish Neu-Guinea*, and *Wirtschaftsleben der primitiven Völker*, which was published in Berlin, in 1911.

MOTHER CAREY

Mother Carey's Chickens
Mother Carey's Goose *Macronectes halli/giganteus*
(Alt. Northern and Southern Giant Petrels)

This name is probably a corruption of the Latin 'Mater cara', which means 'Dear Mother' and is a reference to the Virgin Mary. 'Mother Carey's Chickens' is a traditional seamens' term for storm petrels in general. The term petrel may itself derive from St Peter and relate to these birds' habit of 'walking on the water'. An old name used by sailors for the giant petrels was Mother Carey's Geese.

MOUSSIER

Moussier's Redstart *Phoenicurus moussieri* (Olphe-Galliard 1852)

Jean Moussier (1795–1850) was a surgeon in the French army during the Napoleonic Wars and an amateur naturalist.

MRS BAILEY

Mrs Bailey's Chickadee *Parus gambeli baileyae* (Grinnell 1908)
(Alt. Mountain Chickadee)

See **Bailey**.

MRS BENSON

Mrs Benson's Warbler *Nesillas mariae* (**Benson** 1960)
(Alt. Moheli/Comoro Tsikirity, Moheli Brush-warbler)

Florence Mary Benson was the wife of Constantine (Con) Walter **Benson** (1909–1982) who named the warbler after her. There is no record of whether, like her husband, she ate the specimen!

MRS BOULTON

Mrs Boulton's Woodland Warbler *Phylloscopus laurae* (**Boulton** 1931)
(Alt. Laura's Woodland Warbler, Laura's Warbler)

Laura Boulton (1899–1980) was a famous musicologist, or musical anthropologist, who in her lifetime collected over 30,000 examples of music from around the world. She was also the wife of Wolfrid Rudyerd **Boulton** (1901–1983). Boulton described the warbler, which was collected by her on the **Straus** Central African expedition, and named it after his wife. (See also **Laura**.)

MRS FORBES-WATSON

Mrs Forbes-Watson's Black Flycatcher *Melaenornis annamarulae* (**Forbes-Watson** 1970)
(Alt. Nimba Flycatcher, Liberian/West African Black Flycatcher)

Mrs Anna Forbes-Watson is the wife of A D **Forbes-Watson**. The second part of the binomial also refers to her.

MRS GOULD

Mrs Gould's Sunbird *Aethopyga gouldiae* (**Vigors** 1831)
(Alt. Gould's Sunbird, Blue-throated/Simla Yellow-backed Sunbird)

Elizabeth Gould (1804–1841) was the artist wife of John **Gould** (1804–1881) (See also **Lady Gould**).

MRS HALL

Mrs Hall's Greenbul *Pycnonotus hallae* (**Prigogine** 1972)
(Alt. Hall's Greenbul)

See **Hall**.

MRS HUME

Mrs Hume's Pheasant *Syrmaticus humiae* (**Hume** 1881)
(Alt. Hume's Pheasant)

Mary Hume (?–1890) was the wife of British ornithologist Allan Octavian **Hume** (1829–1912) who named the pheasant after his wife.

MRS MOREAU

Mrs Moreau's Warbler *Scepomycter winifredae* (**Moreau** 1938)

Winifred Moreau (1891–?) was the wife of Reginald E **Moreau** who described the warbler and named it after his wife.

MRS SAGE

Mrs Sage's Blood Pheasant *Ithaginis cruentus annae* (**Mayr** & Birckhead 1937)
(Alt. Blood Pheasant)

The bird might just possibly be named after Anna Sage, the 'woman in red' who delivered the notorious gangster John Dillinger to the FBI; she was with him when he was shot in 1934. The association of Anna Sage with blood is too tempting to ignore! She was an immigrant into the United States from the Balkans around 1914. She worked as a prostitute and a brothel-keeper, and agreed with J Edgar Hoover to betray Dillinger for $10,000. In the event the FBI only paid her $5,000, stripped of her US citizenship on the grounds that a woman of such ill-repute was not fit to be an American, and had her deported!

MRS SWINHOE

Mrs Swinhoe's Sunbird *Aethopyga christinae* (**Swinhoe** 1869)
(Alt. Fork-tailed Sunbird)

See **Christina**

MRS VERNAY

Mrs Vernay's Blood Pheasant *Ithaginis cruentus marionae* (**Mayr** 1941)

Mrs Marion Vernay was the wife of Arthur S Vernay, an English businessman who had a shop in Manhattan and specialised in the sale of English antiques. He was also a naturalist, who both funded and went on expeditions himself. He was a friend of Theodore and Kermit Roosevelt and, especially, of an American millionaire named Suydam Cutting, with whom he travelled quite often; notably they journeyed to Lhasa in 1935 and met the 13th Dalai Lama.

MÜLLER

Müller's Barbet *Megalaima oorti* (Müller 1835)
(Alt. Black-browed/Malayan Barbet)
Müller's Bush Warbler *Cettia vulcania* (**Blyth** 1871)
(Alt. Sunda Bush Warbler)
Müller's Fruit Pigeon *Ducula mullerii* (**Temminck** 1835)
(Alt. Collared/Black-collared Imperial Pigeon)
Müller's Greybird *Coracina morio* (Muller 1843)
(Alt. Celebes/Sulawesi/Black-shouldered Cicadabird/Greybird)
Müller's Parrot *Tanygnathus sumatranus* (**Raffles** 1822)
(Alt. Azure-rumped/Blue-backed Parrot)
Müller's Rail *Lewinia muelleri* (**Rothschild** 1893)
(Alt. Auckland Island Rail)
Müller's Wren-Babbler *Napothera marmorata* (**Ramsay** 1880)
(Alt. Marbled Wren-Babbler)

Dr Salomon Müller (1804–1864) was a Dutch naturalist who collected in Indonesia in 1826, where he worked assisting members of the Netherlands Natural Sciences Commission as a taxidermist. He went on to New Guinea and Timor in 1828 and he explored the interior of Timor in 1829. In 1831 he collected in Java and between 1833 and 1835 he explored western Sumatra.

MULSANT

Mulsant's Woodstar *Acestrura mulsant* (**Bourcier** 1842)
(Alt. White-bellied Woodstar)

Martial Etienne Mulsant (1797–1880) was a French collector and general naturalist, but, was most famous as an entomologist. The best known of his works was one on flea-beetles, *Histoire Naturelle des Coléoptères de France*. He also wrote *Lettres à Julie sur l'Ornithologie*, in 1868, and *Histoire Naturelle des Oiseaux-Mouches ou Colibris*, in 1874.

MURDER

Whether or not Captain Meriwether **Lewis** was murdered it is certain that several of our other 'birdmen' were. It may not be entirely fair to call their deaths murder in this more enlightened age, as they all died at the hands of indigenous peoples whilst 'exploring' their lands. The most famous demise was the earliest; Captain **Cook**, who was killed in 1779 in what was described as a 'skirmish with natives in Hawaii'. John **Gilbert**, another Englishman on an expedition, was speared to death, in June 1845, by Aborigines (native Australians) at the Gulf of Carpentaria in northern Australia. Amazonian Indians killed the very much less well-known Mr **D'Osery** probably in 1847. On yet another continent Baron Carl Claus **von der Decken** met his end in 1865, in Somalia. He had sailed upriver where his ship the *Welf* foundered in the rapids above Bardera. There the Somalis killed him, along with three other Europeans. Captain Boyd **Alexander** was part of a team undertaking the exploration of Africa, between 1908 and 1910, when, it is said, local people in Kenya murdered him. **Emin Pasha** (real name Eduard Schnitzer) was beheaded in the region of Lake Tanganyika.

MURIEL

Muriel's Chat *Saxicola dacotiae murielae* (**Bannerman** 1913) [Extinct]
(Alt. Canary Islands Chat)

Dr David Armitage **Bannerman** (1886–1979) named Muriel's Chat after his first wife, who accompanied him on an expedition to the Canaries, in 1913. The bird, a subspecies of the Fuerteventura Chat, was last seen alive during that 1913 trip, on Allegranza Island, and probably disappeared due to desertification. The species was first discovered on Montaña Clara, although it was only seen later on Allegranza, both small islands north of Lanzarote.

MURPHY

Murphy's Petrel *Pterodroma ultima* (Murphy 1949)
Murphy's White-eye *Zosterops murphyi* (**Hartert** 1929)
(Alt. Hermit/Kulambangra [Mountain] White-eye)

Robert Cushman Murphy (1887–1973) was an American naturalist who worked at the American Museum of Natural History and became a world authority on marine birds. He is also famed for persuading Rachel Carson to write *Silent Spring*, after he was unable to persuade the United States Government to stop spraying DDT. His 1936 masterpiece, *Oceanic Birds of South America* was awarded the John Burroughs Medal for excellence in natural history and the Brewster Medal of the American Ornithologists' Union. Murphy also spent time excavating the extinct moa in New Zealand. On Bermuda, in 1951, he '*slipped a noose onto a pole, slid it down a tunnel between some ocean side rocks, and pulled out a sea bird called a cahow*', the first live member of that species (Bermuda Petrel *Pterodroma cahow*) seen since the early 17th century. A country park and a school in New York State are named after him. According to his obituary in The New York Times, there are also two mountains, a fish, a spider, a lizard and a louse named in his honour. "*As a scientist*," he once said, "*I'd as soon have a louse named for me as a mountain.*"

MUSSCHENBROEK

Musschenbroek's Lorikeet *Neopsittacus musschenbroekii* (**Schlegel** 1871)
(Alt. Yellow-billed Lorikeet)

Samuel Cornelius Jan Willem van Musschenbroek (1827–1883) graduated as a lawyer and trained as a seaman, passing his first mate's examination. He then became a Dutch colonial administrator in the East Indies from 1855 to 1876. He was Resident of Ternate in 1873 and of Meando in 1875. He travelled extensively in the Moluccas with **Beccari**. In 1879 he was in Leiden and was appointed to be the first Director of the Museum der Koloniale Vereniging (Colonial Museum). Many bird skins which he had collected in Indonesia were exhibited here before they were transferred by Voous to the Zoological Museum of Amsterdam. He died shortly after his appointment. Musschenbroek was regarded as an expert on large parts of the Dutch East Indies, as is shown by his pioneering maps of Minahassa and the northern parts of the Moluccas. He also has a spiny rat named for him. The Artis Library, University of Amsterdam, advised us that he wrote *Iets over de fauna van Noord-Celebes*, in 1867, and *Kaart van de bocht van Tomini*, in 1880.

MYTHS

A number of birds' names, both vernacular and scientific, are associated with myths. We have included several eponymous but mythical figures, because those looking up the names may not realise that these birds are not named after real people. For example, the **Calliope** Hummingbird *Stellula calliope* is named after Calliope, the Muse of Epic Poetry in Greek mythology; whilst she was 'fair voiced' we do not think that the hummingbird can make this claim. However, **Orpheus**, the son of Calliope and Apollo, was presented with a lyre by his father and taught to play upon it, which he did to such perfection that nothing could withstand the charm of his music. So the Orphean Warbler *Sylvia hortensis* was probably named for its attractive song. Circe's Hummingbird *Cynanthus latirostris* was named after **Circe** of Greek legend, who, while singing beautifully (which hummers do not), wove delicate and dazzling fabrics, which might be a reference to the bird's nest-making abilities or to its dazzling colours. Incidentally, Circe also turned Picus into a woodpecker. **Cyclops**' Lorikeet is a subspecies of Josephine's Lory *Charmosyna josefinae*, which can appear to have one eye in the middle of its head, as did the Cyclops; the one-eyed giant in Homer's Odyssey. **Goliath** was a Philistine warrior of giant size who succumbed to a slingshot. He was killed by David, later King of the Jews .The Goliath Heron *Ardea goliath* is the largest in that family. The **Horus** Swift *Apus horus* is named after Horus, who was one of the Gods of ancient Egypt, a falcon deity representing the sky. Whilst swifts may not be birds of prey, no birds can claim equal mastery of the sky with the swifts, which may stay on the wing continuously from fledging until first nesting two years later. **Lucifer**'s Hummingbird was named, we presume, for the fallen angel Lucifer of the Judeo-Christian tradition. The **Andromeda** Thrush *Zoothera andromedae* was named after the daughter of Cepheus and Cassiopeia in Greek myth who was exposed to a sea-monster – but we can see no connection.

NAHAN

Nahan's Forest Francolin *Francolinus nahani* (**Dubois** 1905)

Commandant P F Nahan (1867–1930) was a Belgian travelled who explored in tropical Africa.

NAPOLEON

Napoleon's Peacock-Pheasant *Polyplectron emphanum* (**Temminck** 1831)
(Alt. Palawan Peacock-Pheasant)

Napoleon Bonaparte (1769–1821) was Emperor of France. Far more famous among ornithologists, of course, was his nephew Prince Charles Lucien Bonaparte, originally Jules Laurent Lucien (1803–1857), who may well have instigated this honour for his illustrious uncle.

NARINA

Narina's Trogon *Apaloderma narina* (Stephens 1815)

Narina was a beautiful Khoi Khoi (Hottentot) girl. The bird was named by **Le Vaillant**, whose mistress she probably was, according to **Lesson**. Le Vaillant said: '*I found her name difficult to be pronounced, disagreeable to the ear, and very insignificant according to my ideas; I therefore gave her a new one and called her Narina, which in the Hottentot language signifies a flower.*' Stephens described the trogon in 1815.

NAROSKY

Narosky's Seedeater *Sporophila zelichi* (Narosky 1977)
(Alt. Entre Rios Seedeater)

Tito Narosky is an expert on Argentine birds and molluscs. He wrote *Guia de Aves de Patagonia y Tierra del Fuego*, which was published in 2001, *Manual del Observador de Aves* in 1996 and, with the late Dario Yzurieta, *Birds of Argentina and Uruguay: A Field Guide*, whose latest edition was in 1993. The person referred to in the scientific name was an Argentine naturalist, Mateo Ricardo Zelich.

NATALIE

Natalie's Sapsucker *Sphyrapicus thyroideus nataliae* (**Malherbe** 1854)
(Alt. Williamson's Sapsucker)

The name 'Natalie's Sapsucker' is obsolete, but it is sometimes used to distinguish this eastern race from the nominate race of **Williamson**'s Sapsucker.

NATIONALITIES

The number of people of various nationalities who have birds named after them is quite interesting. As the 19th century, in particular, was an era of great exploration and scientific enquiry, and was also the age of empires, the citizens of the colonial powers (Great Britain, France, Germany and the Netherlands, in particular) all had wonderful opportunities to visit their countries' overseas territories on the most favourable terms, and so the numbers of bird names are a good reflection of the sizes and spreads of the various European powers' areas of influence. The United States of America may not have been a colonial power but it occupies an area equivalent to an empire and had influence over surrounding areas. American ornithologists, botanists, entomologists and others had their work cut out keeping up with all the new species that were collected.

The actual numbers of people per nationality are as follows:

1 person Armenia, Cuba, Estonia, Finland, Luxembourg, Norway, Peru, Samoa, Trinidad, Turkey, Venezuela and Vietnam; **2** Ecuador and Kenya; **3** Czech (Republic); **4** Canada, Costa Rica, Hungary and Japan; **5** Ireland, Mexico and Spain; **6** Colombia; **7** Argentina, Denmark and Portugal; **8** Belgium; **9** Brazil; **10** Poland; **11** Switzerland; **12** South Africa; **14** Austria; **15** Sweden; **16** New Zealand and Russia; **21** Australia; **29** Italy; **45** The Netherlands; **137** Germany; **161** France; **201** United States of America; and with **331** persons, Great Britain.

NATTERER

Natterer's Amazon *Amazona ochrocephala nattereri* (**Finsch** 1865)
(Alt. Yellow-crowned Parrot)
Natterer's Cotinga *Cotinga nattererii* (A Boissonneau 1840)
(Alt. Blue Continga)
Natterer's Emerald *Ptochoptera iolaima*
Natterer's Nighthawk *Lurocalis semitorquatus nattereri* (**Temminck** 1822)
(Alt. Semi-collared/Short-tailed/Chestnut-banded Nighthawk)
Natterer's Piculet *Picumnus fuscus* (**Pelzeln** 1870)
(Alt. Rusty-necked Piculet)
Natterer's Piping Guan *Pipile cujibi nattereri* (**Reichenbach** 1862)
(Alt. Natterer's/Bare-faced Curassow)
Natterer's Slaty Antshrike *Thamnophilus stictocephalus* (Pelzeln 1868)
(Alt. Eastern Slaty Antshrike)
Natterer's Tanager *Tachyphonus cristatus nattereri* (Pelzeln 1870)
(Alt. Flame-crested Tanager)
Natterer's Visorbearer *Augastes scutatus* (Temminck 1824)
(Alt. Hyacinth Visorbearer)

Dr Johann Natterer (1787–1843) was an Austrian naturalist and collector. In 1817 he took part as a zoologist, with **Spix** and others, in an expedition to Brazil which started on the occasion of the Austrian Archduchess Leopoldina's wedding to Dom Pedro, the Brazilian Crown Prince. During 1818 and 1819 he explored a potential river route to Paraguay. He continued to explore until 1835, when he returned to Vienna. Natterer accumulated a huge collection of specimens which he deposited with the Vienna museum. He ended his career at the Austrian Imperial Museum of Natural History. He died of a lung ailment. He did not publish an account of his travels and, unfortunately for posterity, his notebooks and diary were destroyed by fire in 1848. Natterer's Bat *Myotis nattereri* is also named after him, along with a number of other birds that commemorate him only in their scientific names eg. Ochre-breasted Pipit *Anthus nattereri*.

NAUMANN

Naumann's Thrush *Turdus naumanni* (**Temminck** 1820)
(Alt. Dusky Thrush)

Johann Andreas Naumann (1744–1826) was a German farmer and an amateur naturalist. He wrote a definitive book on the birds of Germany, *Naturgeschichte der Vogel Deutschlands* in 1804. His son was Johann Friederich Naumann (1780–1857) the German artist and editor who was widely regarded as the founder of scientific ornithology in Europe, and who wrote *Die Eier der Vogel Deutschlands*, in 1818. The elder Naumann's name is also honoured in the scientific name of the Lesser Kestrel *Falco naumanni*.

NAVA

Nava's Wren *Hylorchilus navai* (Crossin & Ely 1973)

Juan Nava Solario was a Mexican ornithologist who worked with Richard S Crossin – they collected the type specimen in of the wren in 1971 in Chiapas, 26 km north of Ocozocoautla, Mexico. They described it as a subspecies of *Hylorchilus sumichrasti*. An American called Adam Kent made recordings in southern Mexico, which led Howell & Webb (1995) to elevate it to a full species based on song as well as plumage. "*I painted a colour plate for the description*" says John O'Neill, who supplied the above information. In The Condor 75:137–139 it says: '*…named for Juan Nava Solario, who, through his devotion to learning the birds of his native Mexico, has earned the admiration and respect of numerous American ornithologists*'. Adam Kent told us how it was realised to be a different species: "*I was in El Ocote in western Chiapas near the border with Oaxaca helping two English biologists, Mark Whittingham and Phil Atkinson, and Ruth Maier, a German, look for the wren. Héctor Gómez de Silva, a Mexican ornithologist, was also with us. Steve Howell was the first person (after J. W. Hardy at the Florida Museum of Natural History) to become 'officially convinced' that Nava's Wren is a full species. Several other people remained doubtful for a while, but the elevated status is widely accepted now. The recording was significant because we had been in the area for 10 days and still not seen the bird until I taped one singing. With that recording we were able to call in wrens in different locations. And, of course, the big significance is that the song of Nava's and Sumicrast's Wrens are very different. Neither wren responds to the other's song*". He went on to say "*My most current knowledge about Juan Nava is from Héctor. He says that in 1993 he heard that Nava was working in Quintana Roo as a wildlife technician, but no news since then. Sounds like there's a good chance he's still alive. I never did meet him*". Héctor and the others went on to conduct further studies of the two wrens (Nava's and Sumichrast's) and publish several articles on the potential split.

NAVAL PERSONNEL

Much exploration of the world started or was conducted at sea. New seabirds were often first spotted from naval vessels and their shore parties found many new landbirds too. On some of the early exploratory vessels, the ship's surgeons often doubled as collectors of specimens, because of their scientific knowledge, access to preservative techniques or just personal interest. Examples of such surgeons, who were instrumental in bird naming, are Lieutenant Dr Alexander **Collie**, Dr Charles **Coquerel**, Emile **Deplanche**, Joseph Paul **Gaimard**, Dr Jacques Bernard **Hombron**, C R A **Leclancher**, Robert M **McCormick**, Sir John **Richardson**, Alexandre **Ricord**, Dr Sir Andrew **Smith** and F L A **Souleyet**. Sir Richard **Owen** started out as a midshipman but became a surgeon, and Charles **Gaudichaud-**Beaupré was a pharmacist. Others who have lent their names to birds were the naval officers in charge of ships or of whole expeditions, and they may or may not have had an interest in such things as new birds. They included Rear-Admiral William **Allen**, Nicolas-Thomas **Baudin**, Admiral Sir Edward **Belcher** CB, J E P **Boyer**, Admiral A M F de **Cande**, James **Cook**, L J **Ducorps**, Sir John **Franklin**, Lieutenant Andreas Leopold **Goffin**, Admiral Sir Geoffrey Phipps **Hornby**, Count Otto Von **Kotzebue**, Vice-Admiral Pierre P de **Lagrandiere**, Sir Clements Robert **Markham**, Commander R **Powell**, Rear-Admiral John **Rodgers** and Captain Charles **Wilkes**. Some sailors, such as the ornithologist Rear-Admiral Hubert **Lynes**, the botanist Chevalier J A **Bernier**, Admiral Prince Heinrich Wilhelm **Adalbert** of Prussia and Carl Peter **Holboell** were clearly interested in birds and Rear-Admiral George Edward **Richards** and Captain H **Storm** may well have had ornithological leanings too.

NEERGAARD

Neergaard's Sunbird *Nectarinia neergaardi* (**C H B Grant** 1908)
(Alt. Neergaard's Double-collared Sunbird)

P Neergaard was a recruiting official for the Witwatersrand mines in southern Africa, in 1907. He assisted C H B **Grant** on his expedition.

NEHRKORN

Nehrkorn's Flowerpecker *Dicaeum nehrkorni* (**Blasius** 1886)
(Alt. Crimson-crowned/Red-headed/Celebes Flowerpecker)
Nehrkorn's Sylph (hybrid of *Aglaiocerus kingi* x *Ramphomicrom micorhynchum*, or *A. kingi* x *Thalurania*) (**Berlepsch** 1887)

Adolf Nehrkorn (1841–1916) was a German oologist. He published *Katalog der Eiersammlung, nebst Beschreibungeh der aussereuropäischen Eier*, in 1910.

NELICOURVI

Nelicourvi's Weaver *Ploceus nelicourvi* (**Scopoli** 1786)
Nelicourvi's Weaver *Ploceus* (*Foudia*) *sakalava* (**Hartlaub** 1861)
(Alt. Sakalava Fody/Weaver)

Another bird's name which originates from a mistranscription as it is not named after anyone or anything. The name comes from a corruption of a Sri Lankan word, *nellukuruvi*, which is a general name for finches. For all that, both the species are Malagasy. The second bird, the fody, is sometimes mistakenly called Nelicourvi's Weaver in error for the other one. Confused? So are we!

NELSON

Nelson's Gull (hybrid of *Larus hyperboreus* x *L.argentatus*)
Nelson's Oriole *Icterus cucullatus nelsoni* (**Ridgway** 1864)
(Alt. Hooded Oriole)
Nelson's Ptarmigan *Lagopus mutus nelsoni* (**Stejneger** 1884)
(Alt. Rock Ptarmigan)
Nelson's Sharp-tailed Sparrow *Ammodramus caudacutus nelsoni* (**Allen** 1875)
Nelson's Shrike *Lanius ludovicianus nelsoni* (**Miller** 1930)
(Alt. Grinell's/Loggerhead Shrike)
Nelson's Vireo *Vireo nelsoni* (Bond 1936)
(Alt. Dwarf Vireo)

Edward William Nelson (1855–1934) was the Chief of the United States Biological Survey

and the founding President of the American Ornithologists' Union. He was only 17 when he travelled to the Rockies. He also collected in Alaska and Mexico. His greatest contribution was the creation of the Migratory Bird Treaty, which is still in force today. **Allen** described the race of the Sharp-tailed Sparrow in 1875 and Bond described the vireo in 1936. **Ridgway** described the race of the oriole in 1964. Miller described a race of the Logger-head Shrike as *nelsoni* in the 1930s but only some authorities recognise this as distinct from *mexicanus*. The Rock Ptarmigan has many aliases appearing in this volume, since it has many races most of which are named after someone.

NEUMANN

Neumann's Coucal *Centropus (leucogaster) neumanni* (**Alexander** 1908)
Neumann's Duyvenbode's Lory *Chalcopsitta duivenbodei syringanuchalis* (Neumann 1915)
   (Alt. Brown Lory)
Neumann's Macaw *Ara nobilis longipennis* (Neumann 1931)
   (Alt. Red-shouldered Macaw)
Neumann's Orange-breasted Fig Parrot *Cyclopsitta gulielmitertii ramuensis* (Neumann 1915)
Neumann's Pearly Conure *Pyrrhura perlata anerythra* (Neumann 1927)
   (Alt. Pearly Parakeet)
Neumann's Red-cheeked Parrot *Geoffroyus geoffroyi minor* (Neumann 1922)
Neumann's Ring-necked Parakeet *Psittacula krameri borealis* (Neumann 1915)
Neumann's Short-tailed Warbler *Hemitesia neumanni* (**Rothschild** 1908)
   (Alt. Short-tailed Warbler)
Neumann's Starling *Onychognathus (morio) neumanni* (Alexander 1908)
Neumann's Waxbill *Estrilda thomensis* (**Sousa** 1888)
   (Alt. Cinderella/São Tomé/Red-flanked Lavender Waxbill)

Left to right: Neumann with Ernst Hartert and Erwin Stresemann

Oskar Rudolph Neumann (1867–1946) was a German ornithologist who collected in Africa between 1892 and 1894. He seems to have ranged very widely from West Africa, to Arabia (Aden), to East Africa and maybe even to South Africa. For example, he described and named a race of the Black-winged Lovebird *Agapornis taranta nana* from Eritrea, in 1931. The coucal was given species status, by Michel Louette in 1986, but is otherwise treated as a race of the Black-throated Coucal *Centropus leucogaster*, which is found in West Africa from Guinea-Bissau to Gabon. **Sousa** described the waxbill in 1888 and his name took precedence over Neumann, who named it *E.cinderella* in 1908. Neumann's Duyvenbode's Lory is the only example which we know of a vernacular name, simultaneously honouring two persons.

NEUMAYER

Neumayer's Rock Nuthatch *Sitta neumayer* (Michahelles 1830)
   (Alt. Western Rock Nuthatch)

Franz Neumayer (?–1840) was an Austrian botanist who collected in Dalmatia.

NEW ZEALANDERS – THE ARCHAEOZOOLOGISTS

Whilst New Zealand is a small nation where sheep outnumber people by 15 to one, it does have a unique avifauna with many endemic birds and even more recently lost or historically extirpated species. This has resulted in a disproportionately large number of ornithologists after whom birds have been named, although just two have living birds to their names; Sir Walter Lawry **Buller** and Arthur T **Pycroft**. Nine others are immortalised in the names of extinct birds: J R **Eyles**, Dr Jack A **Grant-Mackie**, Dr Sir Johann Franz Julius von **Haast** KCMG, William L **Moisley**, Dr Walter Reginald Brook **Oliver**, R J **Scarlett**, Sir Edgar Fraser **Stead** (albeit an amateur), Henry H **Travers** and Dr John C **Yaldwyn** were (or are) all ornithologists or archaeozoologists (this last being a new name coined by Yaldwyn for the study of recently extirpated animals found in historical excavations). Only Peter **Tyree** and Alan **Ridgen**, who found bird fossils on a beach when they were still children, and the amateur Sir Frank Crossley **Mappin**, were not ornithologists.

NEWELL

Newell's Shearwater *Puffinus newelli* (Henshaw 1900)

Brother Matthias Newell (1854–1939) was a missionary to Hawaii between 1886 and 1924. The bird is considered by some to be conspecific with **Townsend**'s Shearwater *P. auricularis* or is regarded as a race of Manx Shearwater *Puffinus puffinus newelli*.

NEWON

Newon's Scrub Warbler *Bradypterus alfredi* (**Hartlaub** 1890)

This name is a transcription error which appears in some books – see **Newton** below

NEWSPAPERMEN

Only two of our 'birdmen' were, so far as we know, newspapermen. Griffing **Bancroft** Jr was an American ornithologist and journalist. Robert Paine **Scripps** was an American newspaper baron who died mysteriously aboard his yacht, at the age of 42, of a 'throat hemorrhage' – causing much speculation as to whether this was a euphemism for murder- just 12 years after his father, also a newspaperman died in mysterious circumstances aboard *his* yacht.

NEWTON, A

Newton's Golden Bowerbird *Prionodura newtoniana* (**De Vis** 1883)
  (Alt. Golden Bowerbird)
Newton's Owl *Strix newtoni* (Lawrence 1860) [Extinct]
  (Alt. Mauritius Owl *Mascarenotus sauzieri*)
Newton's Parakeet *Psittacula exsul* (Newton 1872) [Extinct]
Newton's Scrub Warbler *Bradypterus alfredi* (**Hartlaub** 1890)
  (Alt. Bamboo [Scrub] Warbler)

Professor Alfred Newton FRS (1829–1907) was a British zoologist who was born in Geneva.

He was a co-founder of the British Ornithologists' Union in 1858. Between 1854 and 1865 he studied birds in Lapland, Iceland, the West Indies and North America. He became Professor of Zoology and Comparative Anatomy at Cambridge in 1866 and retained that post until his death. He was a winner of both the Royal Medal of the Royal Society and the Gold Medal of the Linnean Society. Newton edited *The Ibis* from 1865 until 1870. He wrote *Zoology of Ancient Europe* in 1862 and, a landmark publication, *A Dictionary of Birds* with Hans **Gadow** in 1893. Although it is seldom acknowledged, he was instrumental in launching the bird protection movement in England and the rest of the world. Newton studied the vanishing birds of the Mascarenes, a task made all the easier by the fact that his brother was appointed Assistant Colonial Secretary on Mauritius in 1859. The *alfredi* in the binomial of the scrub warbler refers to his own first name. This may be the only example of a surname in the vernacular and a forename in the binomial. **Lawrence** described the owl from a specimen collected for A & E Newton in the Virgin Islands.

NEWTON, E

Newton's Kestrel *Falco newtoni* (**Gurney** 1863)
(Alt. Madagascar Kestrel)

Sir Edward Newton (1832–1897) was, according to **Hartlaub**, in 1862, '...*a gentleman who has recently visited Madagascar, and whose zealous efforts have very materially forwarded our knowledge of the ornithology of the east African archipelago*'. Edward's brother Alfred (above) was Professor of Zoology and Comparative Anatomy at Cambridge, between 1866 and 1907, whilst Edward was a colonial administrator, in Mauritius between 1859 and 1877. Edward sent many specimens to his brother, including the type specimens of the Dodo *Raphus cucullatus* from Mauritius and the Solitaire *Pezophaps solitaria* from Rodrigues. Edward wrote an article, *On a collection of birds from the Island of Anjuan,* which was published in the Proceedings of the Zoological Society of London. The brothers jointly published *On the Osteology of the Solitaire,* in 1869, in the Philosophical Transactions of the Royal Society of London. **Gurney** first described the kestrel from a specimen presented to him by Edward Newton.

NEWTON, F

Newton's Fiscal Shrike *Lanius newtoni* (**Bocage** 1891)
(Alt. São Tomé Fiscal Shrike, Newton's Fiscal)
Newton's [Yellow-breasted] Sunbird *Nectarinia newtonii* (Bocage 1887)
(Alt. Yellow-breasted Sunbird)

Colonel Francesco Newton (1864–1909) was a Portuguese botanist who collected in São Tomé, in 1888, as well as in Timor, in 1896. He wrote accounts of his travels and findings, and was especially meticulous in recording detailed information on the localities and ecology of the specimens in his collection, to a standard exceptional for his time. **Bocage** wrote the first description of the shrike in 1891 and the sunbird in 1887.

NICEFORO

Niceforo's Pintail *Anas georgica nicefori* (Wetmore & Borrero 1946) [Extinct]
Niceforo's Wren *Thryothorus nicefori* (Meyer de Schauensee 1946)

Brother Niceforo Maria (1880–?) was a herpetologist who became a missionary in Colombia. Niceforo's Marsupial Frog *Gastrotheca nicefori* is also named after him.

NICHOLSON

Nicholson's [Rock] Pipit *Anthus similis* (**Jerdon** 1840)
(Alt. Long-billed Pipit)

Francis Nicholson (1843–1925) was a cotton merchant and an active member of the Zoological Society of London. He wrote on African species, as well as those of the English Lake District, but never visited Africa.

NICOLL

Nicoll's Weaver *Ploceus nicolli* (**W L Sclater** 1931)
(Alt. Usambara Weaver/Tanzanian Mountain Weaver)

Michael John Nicoll was an assistant to the more famous R E **Moreau** when the latter was working in Egypt. He wrote *The Water Pipit as a visitor to England* in The Zoologist, in 1906, and two books, *Three Voyages of a Naturalist*, in 1908, and *Handlist of the Birds of Egypt*, in 1919. He started work on *Birds of Egypt*, which was completed by R **Meinertzhagen** and published in 1930. '*Nicoll is also famed for a description of a sea monster whilst on one of his voyages in 1905 whilst cruising off the coast of Brazil, aboard the Earl of Crawford's yacht Valhalla. A fellow voyager, Meade-Waldo, noticed a large, six-foot-long 'fin or frill' in the water about a hundred yards from the boat. Looking more closely, he could see a large body beneath the surface. Just as he got out his binoculars, the scientist reported, a huge head and neck rose up out of the water which was seven to eight feet long and as thick as 'a slight man's body'; the head was about the same thickness and resembled a turtle's, as did the eye. Both head and neck were dark brown on top, whitish underneath. Nicoll's account of the beast was similar to Meade-Waldo's with one important addition: His general impression was of a mammal, not a reptile, although he admitted that he could not be absolutely certain.*' **W L Sclater** described the weaver in 1931.

NIEUWENHUIS

Nieuwenhuis's Bulbul *Pycnonotus nieuwenhuisii* (**Finsch** 1901)
(Alt. Blue/Malaysian Wattled Bulbul)

Anton Willem Nieuwenhuis (1864–1953) was a Dutch collector, especially of tribal items, in Borneo from 1893 until 1900. He wrote *In Central Borneo*, in 1900.

NKWOCHA

Gilbert's Mountain Babbler *Kupeornis gilberti* (**Serle** 1949)
(Alt. White-throated Mountain Babbler)

Gilbert Nkwocha is an African collector of skins.

NOGUCHI

Noguchi's Woodpecker *Sapheopipo noguchii* (**Seebohm** 1887)
(Alt. Okinawa/Pryer's Woodpecker)

T Noguchi was a Japanese collector. There are a number of species of different phyla possibly named after him, including three gastropod molluscs; the species *Fulgoraria noguchii* and the races *Fusinus f. noguchii* and *Buccinum epistomium noguchii*, a pathogenic bacterium *Leptospira noguchii* and at least one plant *Forsstroemia noguchii*. Although there are a number of men with this surname who have become famous, including a poet, an artist and more recently other scientists, we think we have the right man. The woodpecker, a Japanese endemic confined to Okinawa, is considered severely endangered, with a population of fewer than 600 birds, including only 90 breeding pairs.

NORDMANN

Nordmann's Greenshank *Tringa guttifer* (Nordmann 1835)
(Alt. Spotted Greenshank)

Alexander von Nordmann (1803–1866) was a Finnish-born zoologist who collected extensively in southern Russia. He went to Berlin in 1827 and in 1832 became a professor at Odessa, finally becoming Professor of Zoology at Helsinki University, in 1849. A Silver Fir *Abies nordmanni* is also named after him.

NORTH

North's Crake *Porzana atra* (North 1908)
(Alt. Henderson Island Crake/Rail)

Alfred John North (1855–1917) was an Australian ornithologist. He wrote a *List of the Insectivorous Birds of New South Wales*, in 1897 and a *Descriptive Catalogue of the Nests and Eggs of Birds Found Breeding in Australia and Tasmania*, in 1889. The Australian parakeet genus *Northiella* is also named after him.

NORTHROP

Northrop's Oriole *Icterus dominicensis northropi* (J A **Allen** 1890)
(Alt. Black-cowled Oriole)

Alice (Rich) Northrop (1864–1922) was married (in 1889) to John Isiah Northrop (?– 1891) who taught botany and zoology at Columbia University. In 1890 they spent six months in the Bahamas collecting animal, plant and mineral specimens, which was then the most extensive survey ever undertaken of the Bahamas' natural history. When she finished her analysis of the botanical material, ten years later, she found she had discovered 18 new species. John was killed in a laboratory explosion, in 1892, a week before the birth of their only child, a son. Alice raised her son alone, suspending her travels until he was six years old but then taking him with her. She travelled widely in the North American West and Northwest, in Central America and the Caribbean. After her travels she became a Professor at Hunter College, where she had graduated. Throughout her life she looked for ways to make the '*joys of nature*' available to ordinary people. In pursuit of this aim she founded the School Nature League in 1917 and then spent her remaining years establishing the Northrop Memorial Nature Camp. The camp was eventually opened at her property in Mt Washington, Massachusetts, the day after she was killed when her car stalled on a level crossing and was hit by a train. She wrote *A Naturalist in the Bahamas*, with her husband, which was not published until 1910, and *Through Field and Woodland, A Guide to Upland Flora in New England*, in 1925. The bird may be named after either partner but is most likely to have been for Alice.

NOVAES

Novaes's Foliage-gleaner *Philydor novaesi* (Teixeira & Gonzaga 1983)
(Alt. Alagoas Foliage-gleaner)

Dr Fernando Capocchi Novaes (1927–) is a lawyer and an amateur ornithologist based in Santos, São Paulo, Brazil. He was one of the first to discover **Brigida**'s Woodcreeper *Hylexetastes brigidai*. Novaes has written several books on the avifauna of various areas of Brazil. The foliage-gleaner was discovered in 1979.

NUTTALL

Nuttall's Poorwill *Phalaenoptilus nuttallii* (**Audubon** 1844)
(Alt. Common Poorwill)
Nuttall's Sparrow *Zonotrichia leucophrys nuttalli* (**Ridgway** 1889)
(Alt. White-crowned Sparrow)
Nuttall's Woodpecker *Picoides nuttallii* (**Gambel** 1843)
Nuttall's Lesser Marsh Wren *Cistothorus platensis* (Audubon 1831)
(Alt. Marsh Wren)

Thomas Nuttall (1786–1859) was an English botanist and zoologist who collected for Pennsylvania University. He originally went to the United States, aged 22, when he had to leave his home to fulfil the legal requirements of the estate which he inherited. He was the basis for the character 'old curious', the naturalist in Richard Henry Dana's *Two Years Before the Mast*. He was the first to publish a small, inexpensive field guide to US and Canadian birds. He also wrote *Manual of the Ornithology of the United States and Canada*, in 1832. Some of the 'new' birds collected by Nuttall included the American Black Oystercatcher *Haematopus bachmani*, Western Gull *Larus occidentalis*, **Townsend**'s Solitaire *Myadestes townsendii*, Green-tailed Towhee *Pipilio chlorurus*, **Harris**'s Sparrow *Zonotrichia querula*, Common Poorwill, **Anna**'s Hummingbird *Calypte anna*, Tricoloured Blackbird *Agelaius tricolor* and Yellow-billed Magpie. **Audubon** also commemorated him in the scientific name of the latter, *Pica nuttalli*. His friend William **Gambel** named the woodpecker after him.

NUTTING

Nutting's Flycatcher *Myiarchus nuttingi* (**Ridgway** 1883)
(Alt. Pale-throated Flycatcher)

Nutting top left.

Charles Cleveland Nutting (1858–1927) was an American naturalist and collector. In 1886 he became curator of the University of Iowa Natural History Museum. Hornaday donated his collection of birds and mammals to the museum that same year and in 1887 Talbot also gave his collection, of thousands of bird skins. Nutting worked on these specimens and tried to build up the collection further when he became Professor of Systematic Zoology, in 1888. He generated public and private support to finance several expeditions. His journeys to the Bay of Fundy and the Bahamas added many more specimens, including seabirds, to the collection, as did his trips to Nicaragua and Costa Rica. On these trips he was said to be an '*energetic, forceful character, his organizing abilities and his enthusiasm for collecting helped to ensure the success of his trips.*' **Ridgway** named the flycatcher after him in his description.

OATES

Oates' Kalij *Lophura leucomalana oatesi* (**Ogilvie-Grant** 1898)
(Alt. Kalij Pheasant)
Oates' Leaf Warbler *Phylloscopus davisoni* (Oates 1889)
(Alt. White-tailed Willow/White-tailed Leaf Warbler)

Eugene William Oates (1845–1911) was a civil servant in British Colonial India (in the

Public Works Department) and Burma (now Myanmar), and an amateur naturalist. When he moved back to England, he was secretary of the British Ornithologists' Union from 1898 until 1901. He wrote *The Fauna of British India*, in 1889.

OBERHOLSER

Oberholser's Fruit Dove *Ptilinopus subgularis epia* (**Oberholser** 1918)
(Alt. Maroon/Dark-chinned Fruit Dove)

Dr Harry Church Oberholser (1870–1963) was an American ornithologist who worked for the United States Bureau of Biological Survey (now the US Fish and Wildlife Service), from 1895 to 1941. Thereafter, he worked as Curator of Ornithology at the Cleveland Museum of Natural History. Oberholser made extensive ornithological explorations in the United States and Canada. He wrote *Birds of Mt Kilimanjaro*, in 1905, *Birds of the Anamba Islands*, in 1917, and *The Bird Life of Louisiana*, in 1938. He also wrote the massive two-volume work, *The Bird Life of Texas*, which was published posthumously in 1974. Louis Agassiz **Fuertes**, who went with him on his collecting trip to Texas, illustrated the book.

OBERLAENDER

Oberlaender's Rock Thrush *Zoothera oberlaenderi* (**Sassi** 1914)
(Alt. Oberlaender's/Forest Ground Thrush)

P Oberlaender (?–1911) was an Austrian naturalist who collected in Africa.

OGILVIE-GRANT

Ogilvie-Grant's Warbler *Phylloscopus subaffinis* (Ogilvie-Grant 1900)
(Alt. Buff-throated Leaf Warbler)

William Robert Ogilvie-Grant (1863–1924) was a Scottish ornithologist. He was Curator of Birds at the British Museum (Natural History) from 1909 until 1918, having started work there at the age of 19. He enlisted with the First Battalion of the County of London Regiment at the beginning of the First World War and suffered a stroke whilst helping to build fortifications near London in 1916. He is famed for describing of a number of well-known species, such as the huge Philippine Eagle *Pithecophaga jeffreyi*. He wrote *A Hand-book to the Game Birds*, in 1895.

OGLE

Ogle's Laughing-thrush *Garrulax nuchalis* (**Godwin-Austen** 1876)
(Alt. Chestnut-backed Laughing-thrush)
Ogle's Spotted Babbler *Stachyris oglei* (Godwin-Austen 1877)
(Alt. Snowy-throated Babbler, Austen's Spotted [Tree-] Babbler)

M J Ogle (1842–1892) was a British surveyor and collector in Assam, India. He sent his specimens to **Godwin-Austen**, who described both species.

OLALLA

Olalla's (Blue-winged) Parrotlet *Forpus xanthopterygius olallae* (Glydenstope 1941)

Alfonso M Olalla was an Ecuadorian professional collector, in Brazil, from the mid-1930s until the early 1970s. In 1930 he was with Spillman, collecting birds in Ecuador. He sent many of his specimens, particularly of New World monkeys and squirrels, to the Museum of Zoology, in Brazil, but also to United States and European institutions. One monkey,

Olalla's Titi *Callecubus olallae* is named after him. He also discovered the first specimen of the Masked Antpitta *Hylopezus auricularis*, in 1937. Collecting ran in the Olalla family; his brother also collected, as did the sons of both men.

OLDEAN

Oldean's Thrush *Turdus olivaceus oldeani* (**W L Sclater** & **Moreau** 1934)
(Alt. Olive Thrush)

We do not think this subspecies was named after a person. It was described from a specimen taken in Tanganyika (now Tanzania) and Oldeani was a district of Northern Tanganika. We assume that someone assumed that *oldeani* was an honorific for someone called Oldean and mis-transcribed it as Oldean's Thrush, rather than the Oldeani Thrush.

OLIVE

Olive's Quail *Turnix oliveii* (**Robinson** 1900)
(Alt. Buff-breasted/-backed/Robinson's Buttonquail)

Edmund Abraham Cumberbatch Olive (1844–1921) was born in England and emigrated to Australia in the 1870s. He arrived in Cooktown, north Queensland, around 1875, at the peak of the Palmer gold rush. He became an auctioneer and commission agent there in 1875 and remained in that work until his death in 1921. He developed his interest in natural history from his home, Mt Olive, outside Cooktown, with the help of an Aboriginal man known as Billy Olive. Located on a ridge of Mt Cook (431 m) and close to the Annan and Endeavour Rivers, Mt Olive was a good starting point for their excursions to nearby areas of dense vegetation with undisturbed flora and fauna. Olive accumulated impressive collections of various native fauna at his home. He also sent many specimens to Australian, European and American taxonomists, collectors and museums. He collected not only in Cooktown but also in Bellenden Ker and in New Guinea, taking reptiles, bird skins, nests and eggs, fish, insects and other arthropods, molluscs and marsupials. Several species were named in his honour including a gecko, *Gymnodactylus olivii*. Olive's Quail is one of Australia's rarest birds; since Olive collected the first specimen in 1899, it has been recorded at only eight sites, all between Iron Range and Mareeba, and it has never been photographed. Lloyd Nielsen recently (2000) investigated the status of this rare bird with a grant from the Queensland Ornithological Society and has stated that *Turnix oliveii* is even rarer than previously thought and should be considered an Endangered species. (E A C Olive should not be confused with any of his children; Edmund Olive (1874–1923), Carlton Chaloner Olive (1881–1958), Herbert Lawrence Olive (1885–?) and John Henry Olive (1890–?), all of whom also pursued interests in natural history and sent specimens to Australian museums and to private collectors.)

OLIVER

Oliver's Penguin *Korora oliveri* Marples 1952 [Extinct]

Dr Walter Reginald Brook Oliver (1883–1957) was a New Zealand ornithologist and avian palaeontologist. He wrote the definitive *New Zealand Birds*, in 1930, and revised it several times into the 1950s. He also wrote *The Moas of New Zealand and Australia*, in 1949. His research notes for *New Zealand Birds*, from 1920 until 1960, and his collected works, from 1910 until 1957, are in the archives of the Te Papa Tongarewa, the Museum of New Zealand at Canterbury, where he was Director from 1928 until his retirement in 1947. He was described as '*our last true biologist equally authoritative about animals or plants…*' in an article by Professor G T S Baylis.

OLIVIER

Olivier's Rail *Amaurornis olivieri* (Grandidier & **Berlioz** 1929)
(Alt. Sakalava Rail)

G Olivier was a French zoologist who collected in Madagascar. He wrote *Monographie des pies-grieches du genre Lanius*, in 1944. There is another possibility. It might be that the rail was named after Marcel Achille Olivier (1879–1945), who was the Governor-General of Madagascar, from 1924 to 1929, in which latter year Grandidier and **Berlioz** described the bird.

OLROG

Olrog's Cinclodes *Cinclodes olrogi* (Nores & Yzurieta 1979)
Olrog's Gull *Larus atlanticus* (Olrog 1958)
(Alt. Atlantic Gull)

Claes Christian Olrog (1912–1985) was a Swedish ornithologist who lived in Argentina and wrote widely on South American birds. He published *Las Aves Argentinas*, in 1959, as well as an annotated Peruvian checklist and many articles on distribution and other topics. The Institute for the Administration of Protected Areas in Buenos Aires is named after 'Dr Claes C Olrog'. He also wrote *Destination Eldslandet* (*Destination Tierra del Fuego*), in 1943.

OLSON

Olson's Shearwater *Puffinus olsoni* (McMinn, Jaume & Alcover 1990) [Extinct]

 Storrs L Olson (1944–) is currently Curator of the Division of Birds in the Department of Vertebrate Zoology of the Smithsonian Institution, a post which he has held since 1975. The museum houses the third-largest collection of bird skins in the world. Olson's main specialisation is fossil birds and he is also *de facto* curator of the fossil bird collection in the Department of Paleobiology, which is doubtless the largest in the world by far. He graduated in 1966, from the Florida State University, and went on to achieve his doctorate in 1972. He is the author of well over 300 publications in a variety of scientific journals. His interests are primarily in avian palaeontology and systematics, avifaunas of oceanic islands prior to human-caused extinction events, and biogeography and systematics of Neotropical birds, especially those of the Panamanian isthmus. Olson has received many honours from ornithological institutions. This extinct shearwater was described from bones found in Fuerteventura, in the Canary Islands, the bird itself having apparently been eaten by the indigenous people.

OOLOGISTS

Oology is the study of eggs and there was a time when collecting eggs was not considered in any way a danger to conservation. Nowadays some people remain fascinated and are prepared to push species to extinction or local extirpation by selfishly taking eggs from nests. Just two of those who are honoured in the common names of birds described themselves as oologists, although many more collected and/or studied birds' eggs. They were a Briton, Charles **Dixon** and a German, Adolf **Nehrkorn**.

OORT

See **Van Oort**.

ORPHEUS

Orphean Warbler *Sylvia hortensis* (Gmelin 1789)

Orpheus was the son of Apollo and the Muse **Calliope**. He was presented with a lyre by his father and taught to play upon it, which he did to such perfection that nothing could withstand the charm of his music. **Temminck** originally named the bird *Sylvia orphea* in his *Manuel d'Ornithologie*, as a tribute to its song. **Gould** included it in his *Birds of Europe*, deriving the English name from the scientific one and calling it the Orpheus Warbler.

ORTON

Orton's Guan *Penelope ortoni* (**Salvin** 1874)
(Alt. Baudó Guan)

Professor James Orton (1830–1877) was an American zoologist who collected in Latin America in the 1860s. From 1866 until his death he taught at Vassar College, New York. He wrote *The Andes and the Amazon* in 1876 and numerous articles, such as *Notes on Some Birds in the Museum of Vassar College*, in the American Naturalist, in 1871.

OSGOOD

Osgood's Jay *Cyanocitta stelleri* (Gmelin 1788)
(Alt. Steller's/Grinnell's/Queen Charlotte's Jay)

Wilfred Hudson Osgood (1875–1947) was an American zoologist who collected in North America, Chile and elsewhere. The United States Biological Survey employed him in Alaska. He was Curator of Zoology at The Field Museum, in Chicago, from 1909 to 1941, and gave them his personal collection of books on mammalogy and ornithology, which contained many important works, including numerous editions of the works of Linnaeus and other 18th century authors. Whilst at the museum he encouraged **Conover** to develop '*from a wealthy young sportsman to a scientific ornithologist*'. He wrote *The Mammals of Chile*, in 1923. He made an expedition with Louis Agassiz **Fuertes** to Ethiopia in the 1920s and, with him, co-wrote *Artist and Naturalist in Ethiopia*, in 1936.

OUSTALET

Oustalet's Bustard *Lophotis gindiana* (Oustalet 1881)
(Alt. Buff-crested Bustard)
Oustalet's Duck *Anas platyrhynchos oustaleti* (**Salvadori** 1894)
(Alt. Mariana Mallard)
Oustalet's Greenfinch *Carduelis ambigua* (Oustalet 1896)
(Alt. Tibetan/Yunnan/Black-headed Greenfinch)
Oustalet's Sunbird *Nectarinia oustaleti* (**Bocage** 1878)
(Alt. Oustalet's/Angola White-bellied Sunbird)
Oustalet's Swiftlet *Aerodramus germani* (Oustalet 1876)
(Alt. German's Swiftlet)
Oustalet's Tyrannulet *Phylloscartes oustaleti* (P L **Sclater** 1887)

Emile Oustalet (1844–1905) was a French zoologist who worked in the Far East. He wrote *Les Oiseaux de la Chine*, in 1877, with Père Armand **David** as co-author, and *Les Oiseaux du Cambodge*, in 1899. In 1873, he succeeded Jules **Verreaux** at the Paris Natural History Museum and in 1900 succeeded Alphonse **Milne-Edwards** (on his death), with whom he had co-authored a number of works.

OWEN

Owen's Sabrewing *Phaethornis roberti* (**Gould***)

Robert Owen was a collector in Guatemala who supplied specimens to both **Salvin** and **Gould**. Salvin wrote a description of a sabrewing *Aphantochroa roberti* in 1861, which he said was collected by R Owen at Vera Paz, in Guatemala. A Mr Robert Owen is noted as procuring the first eggs of the Resplendent Trogon (now known as the Resplendent Quetzal *Pharomachrus mocinno*) in the same place. The generic name *Phaethornis* seems only to have been used by Gould, however; elsewhere he uses *Campylopterus roberti* for what was presumably the same bird, since it is called Owen's Sabrewing.

OWSTON

Owston's Varied Tit *Parus varius owstoni* (Ijima 1893)
Owston's Fork-tailed Petrel *Oceanodroma tristrami owstoni*
  (Alt. Tristram's Storm Petrel)
Owston's Woodpecker *Dendrocopos leucotos owstoni* (Ogawa 1905)
  (Alt. White-backed Woodpecker)

Alan Owston (1853–1915) was an English collector of Asian wildlife, as well as a business-man and yachtsman. He left for the Orient when still quite young. He married Shimada Rei Jkao, in about 1880, in Japan and they had one child; Susie. He later married Kame (Edith) Miyahara, in about 1893, and had eight children by that marriage. Owston's most active collecting period seems to have been in the early 20th century. He died of lung cancer in Yokohama, Japan. He is also commemorated in the names of several mammals, including the endangered Owston's Palm Civet *Chrotogale owstoni*, which was discovered by his collector, Orii, in 1911 and Owston's Banded Civet *Hemigalus owstoni*. He is honoured too in the scientific names of other birds, such as the Guam Rail *Gallirallus owstoni* and Narcissus Flycatcher *Ficedula narcissina owstoni*, and of several species of fish including the Goblin Shark *Mitsukurina owstoni*, a dogfish *Centroscymnus owstoni* and several other sharks, such as *Etmopterus frontimaculatus, E. lucifer and E. pusillus.* He also described various insects, including the butterfly *Bibasis owstoni*, and at least one amphibian.

PABST

Pabst's Cinclodes *Cinclodes pabsti* (Sick 1969)
  (Alt. Long-tailed Cinclodes)

Dr Guido Frederico João Pabst (1914–1980) was a Brazilian botanist and taxonomist who is famed for his work on orchids. The orchid genus *Pabstia* is named after him. In

1958 he was the founder of the Herbarium Bradeanum, in Rio de Janeiro. He wrote the two-volume *Orchidaceae Brasiliensis*, with F Dungs, in 1975. **Sick**, who also worked at the National Museum in Rio de Janeiro, first described the cinclodes, a Brazilian endemic.

PALLAS

Pallas's Cormorant *Phalacrocorax perspicillatus* (Pallas 1811)
Pallas's Crake *Porzana pusilla* (Pallas 1776)
  (Alt. Baillon's Crake)
Pallas's Dipper *Cinclus pallasii* (**Temminck** 1820)
  (Alt. Brown/Asian/Asiatic Dipper)
Pallas's Eared Pheasant *Crossoptilon auritum* (Pallas 1811)
  (Alt. Blue/Mongolian Eared Pheasant)
Pallas's Fish Eagle *Haliaeetus leucoryphus* (Pallas 1771)
  (Alt. White-bellied/Pallas's Sea Eagle)
Pallas's Grasshopper Warbler *Locustella certhiola* (Pallas 1811)
Pallas's Great Rosefinch *Carpodacus roseus* (Pallas 1776)
  (Alt. Pallas's Rosefinch)
Pallas's Gull *Larus ichthyaetus* (Pallas 1773)
  (Alt. Great Black-headed Gull)
Pallas's Murre *Uria lomvia* (Pallas 1811)
  (Alt. Brünnich's Guillemot, Brunnich's/Thick-billed Murre)
Pallas's Reed Bunting *Emberiza pallasi* (**Cabanis** 1851)
  (Alt. Pallas's Bunting)
Pallas's Ring-necked Pheasant *Phasianus colchicus pallasi* (**Rothschild** 1903)
Pallas's Sandgrouse *Syrrhaptes paradoxus* (Pallas 1773)
Pallas's Leaf Warbler *Phylloscopus proregulus* (Pallas 1811)

Peter Simon Pallas (1741–1811) was a German zoologist and one of greatest of the 18th-century naturalists. He was obviously very intelligent as he earned his doctorate at the age of just 19 years! He was also a geographer and traveller, and he explored widely in the lesser known areas of Russia. He became a member of the St Petersburg Academy of Sciences, and, between 1768 and 1774, he headed an academy expedition which studied many regions of Russia, including southern Siberia especially Lake Baikal and the region to the east of the lake, and also the Altai mountains in Mongolia. He described many new species of mammals, birds, fish and insects. His works include *A Journey Through Various Provinces of the Russian State*, in 1771, *A History of the Mongolian People* and *Asian-Russian Fauna* in 1811. A volcano on the Kurile Islands and a reef off New Guinea are also named in his honour.

The cormorant is now extinct '*The last known individuals of this species were either given away or sold in 1840–1850 from the Commander Islands of Russia; it was extinct by 1852*' (Fuller 2000).

PALLISER

Palliser's Warbler *Bradypterus palliseri* (**Blyth** 1851)
  (Alt. Sri Lanka/Palliser's Bush Warbler)

Captain Edward Palliser (1826–1907) and his brother F H Palliser (1826–?) were travellers who collected together in Sri Lanka between 1845 and 1851. Given their birth date it seems probable that they were twins. (F H Palliser is mentioned in *Eight Years' Wanderings in Ceylon* by Samuel White Baker where the author describes himself and Palliser shooting rogue elephants together – a dangerous occupation considering the propensity of ornithologists to get themselves killed by these beasts! See **Elephants' Revenge**)

PALMER

Palmer's Thrasher *Toxostoma curvirostre* (**Swainson** 1827)
(Alt. Curve-billed Thrasher)

Mervyn George Palmer (1882–1954) was an indefatigable English traveller and collector. After graduating he became an analytical chemist in the cement industry before he decided upon a career as a freelance collecting naturalist. He collected mammals, birds, reptiles, fish, butterflies and shells for the British Museum, and other institutions in Colombia, Ecuador and Nicaragua from 1904 until 1910. He found over 60 species new to science, 11 of which now have the specific name *palmeri*, for example, *Coryphantha palmeri*, a plant with narcotic qualities and the Lycopsid *Isoëtes palmeri*. During this time he also learnt to speak Spanish as well as two South American Indian languages, married a South American woman, undertook archaeo-logical digs, and explored and mapped the Río Segovia between Nicaragua and Honduras. He became a Fellow of the Royal Geographical Society by virtue of his explorations in Central and South America, which were all on foot or by canoe, and was made a Freeman of the City of London. He was also at one time the Editor of the Natural Science Gazette. From 1910 until 1918 he worked for commercial concerns in Ecuador before moving to London with the same company. He was declared unfit for overseas army service during the First World War, having had yellow fever and malaria but he used his commercial skills for his regiment's benefit. From 1919 until 1921 he worked in Venezuela. Later, and until retirement, he was based in England but he travelled widely in South and Central America and the Caribbean, visiting every South American country except Paraguay. He wrote *Through Unknown Nicaragua – The Adventures of a Naturalist on a Wild-Goose Chase*, in 1945. He retired to Ilfracombe in Devon, England where he established a library, museum and field club for the town, in 1932, as he '*wanted something to do*'. He was curator there until his death in 1954. He wrote *The Homeland Guide to North Devon*, which was published posthumously in 1960.

PAMELA

Pamela's Sunbeam *Aglaeactis pamela* (**d'Orbigny** 1838)
(Alt. Black-hooded Sunbeam)

This is another example of someone (probably **Gould**, who was not very careful about names) wrongly assuming that an adjective was a person's name. The name Pamela here is derived from a Greek word which means 'all black' and reflects the general appearance of the bird, as is indicated in the alternative name, Black-hooded Sunbeam.

PANDER

Pander's Ground Jay *Podoces panderi* (Fischer von Waldheim 1821)
(Alt. Turkestan Ground Jay)

Christian Heinrich Pander (1794–1865) was an affluent Latvian of German descent – Latvia then being part of the Romanov Empire. He was a palaeontologist, biologist and evolutionist who joined the Academy of Sciences in St Petersburg. He was described as *the first student of conodonts*, which are extinct primitive vertebrates, relatives of the hagfish.

One of his most notable scientific achievements was to identify the three vertebrate germ layers; ectoderm, mesoderm, and endoderm, in chick embryos, in 1817.

PANTCHENKO

Pantchenko's Conure *Pyrrhura picta pantchenkoi* (Phelps 1977)
(Alt. Painted Parakeet)

We believe this is Georges Pantchenko, a Venezuelan who was a member of the joint Venezuelan/Brazilian team responsible for establishing the border between the two countries. They did this by descending from helicopters into the jungle and literally hacking 'landmarks' to delimit the boundary. He was asked at a conference in Brasília about his surname and is reported to have replied in humorous vein *'My parents are Russian, I was born in Bulgaria, grew up in France, have Venezuelan nationality but my heart is Brazilian!'* William Henry Phelps Jr (1902–1988) described the conure, a native of the Colombian-Venezuelan border region. The type specimen is in the Academy of Natural Science Philadelphia.

PARKER

Parker's Antbird *Cercomacra parkeri* (Davis & O'Neill 1986)
Parker's Spinetail *Cranioleuca vulpecula* (P L **Sclater** & **Salvin** 1866)

Theodor (Ted) A Parker III (1953–1993) was a professional American ornithologist and a former member of the Cornell Laboratory's Administrative Board. He has been described as a *'great Neotropical conservationist and recordist'* and also as the *'world's leading authority on Neotropical bird identification and distribution'*. He was the single largest contributor to the Library of Natural Sounds at Cornell University, providing more than 10,000 recordings of bird sounds. He revolutionised bird surveying methods by employing a tape recorder in the field. There was a less serious side to Ted; in 1971, at the age of 18, he set a then record of 626 species seen in one year in the United States. Parker died tragically in a plane crash in Ecuador in 1993. The book *A Parrot Without a Name: The Search for the Last Unknown Birds on Earth* by Don Stap, was written about Parker's discoveries, and those of John O'Neill, of new bird species in Peru. Davis and O'Neill described the antwren in 1986 but it was not split from Willis's Antbird until 1997 with the name honouring Parker. In the same year Kevin Zimmer raised the spinetail to species status and suggested that it should be named after Parker as a memorial to him.

PARKINSON

Parkinson's Petrel *Procellaria parkinsoni* (**G R Gray** 1862)
(Alt. Black Petrel)

Sydney Parkinson (1745–1771) was an English explorer and collector, who worked as a natural history artist on **Cook**'s voyage on *HMS Endeavour*, in the company of **Banks** and **Solander.** He drew the large collection of plants and seabirds obtained from along the Australian east coast. The young artist had a hard time of it in the cramped quarters, suffering sea-sickness and other tribulations. Joseph Banks recorded that *'at one point a swarm of flies was eating the paint off his* (Parkinson's) *paper as fast as he could lay it on'*. He died at sea from malaria and dysentery contracted in Jakarta, whilst on the way to Cape Town. (There were two artists at the start of the voyage and the other, Alexander Buchan, had earlier also died, of an epileptic seizure, when the voyage reached Tahiti). Parkinson's brother, Stanfield, published the former's *Journal of a Voyage to the South Seas* before the official account, which had been entrusted to Dr John Hawksworth. Hawksworth had a contract from the Earl of Sandwich, who was First Lord of the Admiralty at the time, to edit all journals of exploration of anywhere by anyone. Hawksworth apparently enjoyed a good story and embellished his accounts without due regard for the truth. Cook, apparently, was very irritated by Hawksworth's account. Stanfield's premature publication resulted in a court injunction to prevent any further editions as it was held that Hawksworth's rights had been infringed. It was clear there was much animosity as Hawksworth failed to mention Parkinson at all, despite using some of his papers and drawings, which were of a pleasing quality. Parkinson's account, with extra material, was finally re-issued in 1784.

PARODI

Parodi's Hemispingus *Hemispingus parodii* (Weske & Terborgh 1974)
(Alt. Parodi's Tanager)

Jose Parodi Vargas (Pepe) was a Peruvian landowner and a congressman during the first Belaunde government. Pepe and his father were pioneers. who opened the road from Ayacucho to their Hacienda Luisiana on the Río Apurímac. Parodi also liked to travel to unexplored areas of Peru such as the Cutivineri Falls.

PARZUDAKI

Parzudaki's Starfrontlet *Heliotrypha parzudakii* (**Gould***)

Emile (or according to other sources, Charles) Parzudaki was a French traveller who collected in Colombia between 1841 and 1845. However, the starfrontlet is only found as a **Gould** engraving. Nevertheless, there is another bird, the Flame-faced Tanager *Tangara parzudakii* named in the scientific binomial by **Lafresnaye**, in 1843, after Parzudaki, and Emile Parzudaki described the White-collared Manakin *Manacus candei*, in 1841. So the man was real, he did collect in Latin America, he had at least one bird named after him, and he described at least one other species.

PASSERINI

Passerini's Tanager *Ramphocelus passerinii* (**Bonaparte** 1831)
(Alt. Scarlet-rumped Tanager)

Professor Carlo(s) Passerini (1793–1857) was an Italian entomologist whose collection and papers are now at the Natural History Museum of the University of Pisa. He was an early enthusiast of scientific photography.

PAYNTER

Paynter's Brush Finch *Atlapetes leucopterus paynteri* (Fitzpatrick 1980)
(Alt. White-winged Brush Finch)

Dr Raymond A Paynter Jr (1925–2003) was an American ornithologist who was curator of the Museum of Comparative Zoology, at Harvard University, from 1961. He wrote *Avian Energetics*, in 1974, and *Nearctic Passerine Migrants in South America*, in 1995, as well as a whole series of *Ornithological Gazetteers*. He received the **Elliott Coues** Award in 2001. He revised Ernest A Choate's *The Dictionary of American Bird Names*. His son is a wildlife artist and photographer.

PEALE

Peale's Falcon *Falco peregrinus pealei* (**Ridgway** 1873)
(Alt. Peregrine Falcon)
Peale's Parrotfinch *Erythrura pealii* (**Hartlaub** 1852)
(Alt. Fiji Parrotfinch)
Peale's Petrel *Pterodroma inexpectata* (J R **Forster** 1844)
(Alt. Mottled Petrel)
Peale's [Imperial]Pigeon *Ducula latrans* (Peale 1848)
(Alt. Fijian/Barking [Imperial] Pigeon)

Titian Ramsay Peale (1799–1885) was an American naturalist and artist who collected in the Pacific; in Tahiti, Fiji and Samoa, between 1838 and 1842, on the **Wilkes** expedition. He was also noted for his pen and ink sketches of North American Indians and buffalo, made during a extensive expedition, in 1820, under Major Long, which followed the Lewis and Clark route. Peale was assistant naturalist on this journey. He first accompanied an expedition in 1818, to Florida, where he also recorded the flora and fauna. Many of the birds which he obtained from around the world contributed to the original collections of the Smithsonian Institution. Peale Islet, near Wake Island in the Pacific Ocean, is also named after him. The Peregrine race *pealei* is the largest and darkest of the North American subspecies.

PEARSON

Pearson's Cisticola *Cisticola melanurus* (**Cabanis** 1882)
(Alt. Slender-tailed/Black-tailed Cisticola)

There are two people after whom this cisticola may have been named. The first is Dr Arthur Pearson (1870–1947), who was in the right region; Tanganyika (now Tanzania) and North and South Rhodesia (now Zambia and Zimbabwe respectively), at the time when the bird was found. The second, and far more likely contender, is Dr Edward Pearson Ramsay (1842–1916), who was Curator of the Australian Museum in Sydney from 1874 to 1894 and had a worldwide reputation. Edward Pearson was educated at the University of Sydney, where he studied medicine from 1863 to 1865. He took part in only one collecting expedition, to the Clarence and Richmond rivers in 1866. He owned a new plant and seed nursery and the Iindah sugar plantation in Queensland from 1868 for several years. During his time at the Australian Museum he added 17,600 skins, including the Dobroyd Collection made by himself and his brothers. He also published a *Catalogue of the Australian Birds in the Australian Museum at Sydney* in four parts, from 1876 to 1894, and began publishing the Records of the Museum in 1890. He was the consulting ornithologist to the museum from 1895 until his death in 1916. Edward Pearson was honoured all over the world. He was a corresponding member of the Zoological Society of London, a member of the Italian Anthropological Society and a Knight of the Crown of Italy, a life member of the Royal Society of Edinburgh, a member of the Royal Irish Academy and a founder of the Linnean Society of New South Wales in 1874. He was a medallist for his exhibits at the Colonial and Indian Exhibition in London. He also received a gold medal and a diploma of honour, 'Mitglied', from the Imperial Zoological and Botanical Society of Vienna, in 1883, close to the time when Cabanis described the warbler. As well as ornithology Pearson worked in ichthyology, herpetology, mammalogy and botany. He never visited Africa but then neither did Cabanis. On balance, because of the chronology the cisticola is more likely to be named to honour the latter Pearson than the former.

PEL

Pel's Fishing Owl *Scotopelia peli* (**Bonaparte** 1850)

Hendrik Severinus Pel (1818–1876) was the Dutch Governor of the Gold Coast (now

Ghana) between 1840 and 1850. He was an amateur naturalist but also a trained taxidermist, and acted as such for the Dutch State Museum of Natural History. He first described the bird around 1851. In 1851 he published *Over de jagt aan de Goudkust, volgens eene tienjarige eigene ondervinding.*

PELZELN

Pelzeln's Finch *Sicalis flaveola pelzelni* (**Sclater** 1872)
(Alt. Saffron Finch)
Pelzeln's Flycatcher *Myiarchus swainsoni* (**Cabanis** & **Heine** 1859)
(Alt. Whiteley's/Swainsons's Flycatcher)
Pelzeln's Grebe *Tachybaptus pelzelnii* (**Hartlaub** 1861)
(Alt. Madagascar [Little] Grebe/Dabchick)
Pelzeln's Tody-Tyrant *Hemitriccus inornatus* (Pelzeln 1868)

August von Pelzeln (1825–1891) was an Austrian ornithologist. He was in charge of the mammal and bird collections at the Imperial Museum of Vienna for 40 years, where he worked on the 343 species of birds which **Natterer**, a fellow Austrian, collected in Brazil in 1822. He wrote *Ornithologie Brasileiras*, in 1871, and *Beitrage zur Ornithologie Sud Afrikas*, in 1882.

PENNANT

Pennant's Parakeet *Platycercus elegans elegans* (Gmelin 1788)
(Alt. Crimson Rosella)
Pennant's Parakeet *Platycercus elegans adelaidae* (**Des Murs** & **Provost** 1849)
(Alt. Blue-cheeked/Adelaide/Pennant's Rosella, Yellow Parakeet)
Pennant's Rosella *Platycercus eximius* (Shaw 1792)
(Alt. Eastern/Red-headed/White-cheeked Rosella)

Thomas Pennant (1726–1798) was an extremely highly regarded British naturalist and traveller. His early work, *Tour in Scotland*, in 1771, was instrumental in encouraging tourism in the Highlands. Gilbert White published his *Natural History of Selbourne* in the form of letters to Thomas Pennant and Daines Barrington. Pennant published on the Arctic, Britain and India, and wrote about quadrupeds as well as on birds. His other publications included *British Zoology*, published between 1761 and 1766, with the second volume being devoted to birds, *Genera of Birds*, published in 1777, and *Arctic Zoology*, in 1785. He was said to make '*dry and technical material interesting*'. *Platycercus elegans* and *P. eximius* are distinct species but *P. adelaidae* is a natural hybrid of the crimson and the yellow subspecies of *P. elegans.*

PERCIVAL

Percival's Oriole *Oriolus percivali* (**Ogilvie-Grant** 1903)
(Alt. Montane/Black-tailed Oriole)

Arthur Blayney Percival (1874–1940) was a British game warden in East Africa from 1901 until 1928 and retired there, dying in Kenya in 1940. With the taxidermist W **Dodson** he took part in a Royal Society expedition to Arabia in 1899 which collected many specimens. He was known as one of the most knowledgeable wildlife experts and hunters in East Africa. Percival wrote *A Game Ranger's Notebook* in 1924 and *A Game Ranger on Safari* in 1928. He is commemorated in the trinomials of the Arabian subspecies of both the Black-headed Bush Shrike *Tchagra senegala percivali* (originally named as *Telephorus percivali)* and of the Golden-winged Grosbeak *Rynchostruthos socotranus percivali.*

PÈRE DAVID

See **David**.

PERKINS

Perkins' Mamo *Drepanis funerea* (A **Newton** 1894) [Extinct]
(Alt. Molokai/Black Mamo)

Robert Cyril Layton Perkins (1866–1955) was an English naturalist and collector, primarily an entomologist, who moved to Hawaii in 1892, where he was director of the entomology division at the Hawaiian Sugar Planters' Experimental Station. Here he discovered the Mamo, in 1893, in Pelekunu Valley on Molokai. The last sightings of the bird were in 1907. Perkins virtually lived in the field, only occasionally returning to Honolulu for provisions. Much of his collecting was sponsored by the Bishop Museum, where he became Assistant Superintendent of Entomology. Between 1896 and 1938 he wrote dozens of scientific papers. He returned to England in 1912, settled in Devon and worked mainly on taxonomy. He was elected a Fellow of the Royal Society in 1920 and was awarded the Linnean Medal, the Linnean Society's top award.

PERON

Peron's Ground Thrush *Zoothera peronii* (**Vieillot** 1818)
(Alt. Orange-sided/Orange-banded Thrush)

François Péron (1775–1810) was a French voyager and naturalist. He was a member of the Nicolas **Baudin** scientific expedition to southern and western Australia from 1800 until 1804, which visited New Holland, Maria Island and Van Diemen's Land (now Tasmania) and to Timor in Indonesia. There is a national park in Western Australia named after him, at the north end of the Peron Peninsula. He died of tuberculosis. **Vieillot** wrote the description, presumably from specimens collected by Péron.

PERRIN

Perrin's Bush Shrike *Telophorus viridis* (**Vieillot** 1817)
(Alt. Gorgeous Bush Shrike)

Jean Perrein (1750–1805) was a French naturalist who travelled and collected in northern Africa, Arabia, Persia and India. He presented his specimens to the Academy of Sciences of Bordeaux, where he was elected an associate member. In 1794 he went to North America where he visited Hudson Bay, the Rockies, Quebec, Ontario and all of the New England states. He died of malaria on his return journey to France. **Buffon** used many of his manuscripts in his own works. In 1809, Perrin's *Voyage chez les Indiens de l'Amerique du Nord, avec un aperçu des usages et du caractère de ces peuples* was published in Paris. **Chapin** (1954) does not give English names but, rather intriguingly, he mentions Perrein's Bush Shrike. We believe Perrin is therefore an anglicised version of Perrein. However, the bird's vernacular name has changed many times, as the species has undergone a number of splits and lumps. **Vieillot**, who described the bird, could also have coined the vernacular name after his then recently deceased countryman.

PESQUET

Pesquet's Parrot *Psittrichas fulgidus* (**Lesson** 1830)

This is yet another bird illustrated by **Gould**. The English name could also have come from him as he used *Dasyptilus pesqueti* for the binomial on his engraving.

PETERS

Peters's Finfoot *Podica senegalensis petersii* (**Hartlaub** 1852)
(Alt. African Finfoot)
Peters's Twinspot *Hypargos niveoguttatus* (Peters 1868)
(Alt. Red-throated Twinspot)

Wilhelm Karl Hartwig Peters (1815–1883) was a German zoologist and traveller who made some very important collections in Mozambique. Most of his published works are on herpetology. For many years he was the Head of the Berlin Zoology Museum. In 1876 he was elected as a corresponding member of the Russian Academy of Sciences. Peters' Epauletted Fruit Bat *Epomophorus crypturus* also commemorates him. Peters wrote the first description of the twinspot in 1868.

PETERS

Peters's Apalis *Apalis rufogularis argentea* (**Moreau** 1941)
(Alt. Buff-throated/Kungwe Apalis)
Peters's Conure *Aratinga wagleri transilis* (J L Peters 1927)
(Alt. Scarlet-fronted Conure/Parakeet)

James Lee Peters (1889–1952) was an American ornithologist, who was Curator of Birds at the Museum of Comparative Zoology, at Harvard University. He is the renowned author of the authoritative *Check-list of Birds of the World*, which was published in seven volumes by Harvard University Press, between 1931 and 1952. From 1931 he was a member of the Committee on Classification and Nomenclature of the American Ornithologists' Union. Peters himself described the conure in 1927. The apalis is considered conspecific with the Buff-throated Apalis *Apalis rufogularis*.

PETIT

Petit's Cuckoo-shrike *Campephaga petiti* (**Oustalet** 1884)
Petit's Saw-wing *Psalidoprocne petiti* (**Sharpe** & **Bouvier** 1876)

Louis Petit (1856–1943) was a French naturalist who collected in Angola between 1876 and 1884.

PETZ

Petz's Conure *Aratinga canicularis canicularis* (Linneaus 1758)
(Alt. Orange-fronted Conure/Parakeet)

Linnaeus described the nominate race of the conure in 1758. According to some sources it is the nominate race that is known as Petz's. However, others divide the species into the Eastern Mexican Petz's Conure *Aratinga c. eburnirostrum*, described by **Lesson** in 1842, and the Western Mexican Petz's Conure *Aratinga c. clarae*, described by Moore in 1937.

PFRIMER

Pfrimer's Conure *Pyrrhura* (*leucotis*) *pfrimeri* (Kuhl 1820)
(Alt. Maroon-faced/White-eared Conure/Parakeet)

Rudolph Pfrimer (?–1933?) was a geologist and professional bird collector, who was active in Brazil in about 1910. In the mid-1920s he acquired a farm, Fazenda São Bento, to support his rock crystal explorations. The farm subsequently became a centre for crystal extraction for several decades and was operated by his nephew, Walter Pfrimer. We also find records of frogs which he collected in the same area. Carlos A Bianchi, Bird Curator of the Brasilia Zoological Garden, in Brasilia, Brazil, has recently rediscovered the bird, which is restricted to a tiny area of Goiás state and had not been seen for many years. It has previously been considered a subspecies of the White-eared (Maroon-faced) Conure but is increasingly assigned species status.

PHARAOH

Pharaoh's Eagle Owl *Bubo ascalaphus* (**Savigny** 1809)
(Alt. Desert/Savigny's Eagle Owl)

The bird occurs in Egypt, and across North Africa and parts of the Middel East, and is illustrated on ancient glyphs. There is no evidence of it being named after any particular pharaoh.

PHAYRE

Phayre's Pitta *Pitta phayrei* (**Blyth** 1863)
(Alt. Eared Pitta)

Lieutenant-General Sir Arthur Purves Phayre (1812–1885) was Commissioner in Burma (now Myanmar), between 1862 and 1867, and Governor of Mauritius, from 1871 until 1878. He wrote a *History of Burmah*, in 1883. He also has a monkey, Phayre's Leaf Macaque *Trachypitheaus phayrei*, named after him.

PHELPS

Phelps' Swift *Streptoprocne phelpsi* (Collins 1972)
(Alt. Tepui Swift)

William H Phelps (1875–1965) was an American-born Venezuelan ornithologist. He first visited Venezuela as a Harvard student in 1896. He wrote *Lista de las Aves de Venezuela* in 1958. His son William 'Billy' H Phelps Jr (1902–1988) wrote *A Guide to the Birds of Venezuela* in 1978, with Rodolphe Meyer de Schauenesee. The Colección Ornitológica Phelps in Caracas consists of over 75,000 skins, mostly of Venezuelan origin. It was built up by William, Billy and Billy's wife, Kathleen. The Phelps family had their own, specially-equipped yacht, '*Ornis*', in which they made 49 trips to the Caribbean islands, in addition to about 44 trips to the hinterland of Venezuela. It seems likely that the son suggested that the bird be named after his father. The swift is virtually endemic to Venezuela.

PHILBY

Philby's (Rock) Partridge *Alectoris philbyi* (**Lowe** 1934)

Harry St John Bridger Philby (1885–1960) was a noted Arabist and a British explorer, who was among the first Europeans to travel in the southern Arabian provinces. He became dissatisfied with British policy towards the Middle East and resigned from the Foreign Service in 1925. He was then an advisor for 30 years to King ibn Saud of Saudi Arabia. Philby became a Muslim, re-naming himself Hajj Abdullah. He wrote several works including *Heart of Arabia* in 1923, *Saudi Arabia* in 1955 and *Forty Years in the Wilderness* in 1957. His son was Kim Philby, who spied for the Soviet Union in Britain. The Arabian Woodpecker *Dendrocopos dorae* was so-named for Philby's wife.

PHILIPPA

Philippa's Crombec *Sylvietta philippae* (**Williams** 1955)
(Alt. Short-billed/Philippa's Short-billed/Somali Crombec)

Philippa Williams was the wife of the the British ornithologist, John G **Williams** (1913–1997) who wrote *A Field Guide to the Birds of East and Central Africa*. He named the crombec after his wife in his description of a specimen which he collected in Somalia, in 1954.

PHILIPPI

Philippi's Hermit *Phaethornis philippii* (**Bourcier** 1847)
(Alt. Needle-billed Hermit)

Filippo de' Filippi (1814-1867) was an Italian doctor, traveller and zoologist. He visited, among other places, Alaska, Mongolia and Turkestan. He succeeded Bonelli as professor of zoology at the Museum of Natural History in Turin. His efforts to disseminate knowledge of Darwin's evolutionary theory included the presentation of a seminal lecture in 1864 – L'uomo e le scimmie (Man and the Apes). He died of cholera in Hong Kong. See also DeFillipi.

PHILLIPS

Phillips' Wheatear *Oenanthe phillipsi* (**Shelley** 1885)
(Alt. Somali Wheatear)

E Lort Phillips (1857–1944) was a British big-game hunter in East Africa between 1884 and 1895. He also collected natural history specimens. **Shelley** described the wheatear from a specimen which Phillips collected at the summit of the mountains near Berbera in Somaliland.

PHYSICIANS

No fewer than 63 (and probably more as we do not know everyone's profession) of our subjects had medicine as their primary profession, and this excludes all those ship's surgeons analysed elsewhere. In total, at least 89 of the people mentioned in this book practised some form of medicine. This is by far the most well-represented profession here that is not directly related to the study, classification or collection of biological specimens (i.e. zoologists, botanists, ornithologists and the like). This is perhaps not surprising when one considers that the great expansion in knowledge and classification of the natural world was undertaken by middle-class Europeans and Americans during the 19th century, a time when physicians were likely to be well off and to have the time to indulge their other interests and pastimes.

PICKERING

Pickering's Imperial Pigeon *Ducula pickeringii* (**Cassin** 1854)
(Alt. Grey/Malaysian Imperial Pigeon, Grey Island Pigeon)

Dr Charles F Pickering (1805–1878) was an American ornithologist who was a friend of **Audubon**. He took part in the 1841 United States Exploring Expedition as naturalist.

PINTO

Pinto's Spinetail *Synallaxis infuscata* (Pinto 1950)
(Alt. Plain Spinetail)
Pinto's Sunbird *Nectarinia manoensis pintoi* (Wolters 1965)
(Alt. Miombo Double-collared Sunbird)

Olivério Mario de Oliveira de Pinto (1896–1981) was a Brazilian ornithologist. In the 1940s he was the Head of the Zoological Museum of the University of São Paulo and he led expeditions under its auspices. He wrote on several national parks and their avifauna, as well as standard work on the ornithology of Angola, and a catalogue of all Brazilian birds.

PLATEN

Platen's Babbler *Stachyris plateni* (**Blasius** 1890)
(Alt. Pygmy [Tree]Babbler)
Platen's Celebes Rail *Aramidopsis plateni* (Blasius 1886)
(Alt. Snoring Rail/Crake)
Platen's Flowerpecker *Prionochilus plateni* (Blasius 1888)
(Alt. Palawan [Yellow-rumped] Flowerpecker)

Carl Constantin Platen (1843–1899) was a German doctor who collected in the East Indies between 1878 and 1894. He has butterflies named after him and also seems to have imported live birds in 1879. There are also number of birds whose scientific names honour his wife.

PLESCHANKA

Pleschanka's Pied Chat *Oenanthe pleschanka* (Lepechin 1770)
(Alt. Pied Wheatear)

This is not named after a person at all but is another transcription error. Pleschanka is simply the Russian name for the Pied Wheatear.

PLESKE

Pleske's Grasshopper Warbler *Locustella pleskei* (**Taczanowski** 1890)
(Alt. Styan's Grasshopper Warbler)
Pleske's Ground Jay *Podoces pleskei* (**Zarudny** 1896)
(Alt. Iranian Ground Jay)

Theodor Dimitrievich Pleske (1858–1932) was a Russian zoologist, geographer and ethnographer. He was a Fellow of the Russian Imperial Academy of Science in St Petersburg, from 1886, and Director, from 1890 to 1897, of the Zoological Museum in St Petersburg. He wrote *Ornithological Fauna of Imperial Russia*, in 1891, and *Ornithographia Rossica*, in 1898.

POETS

Only two people in these annals can be described as poets – those who would have put this in their passports as their profession as they had such a document in their time. However, it would be churlish not to give a special mention to Edward **Lear**, who is probably better known for his limericks and nonsense verse than for his scientific or artistic acumen. **Adelbert** von Chamisso was a remarkable man who served as a page at the court of William II of Prussia and who, after army service and travels, became keeper of the royal botanical gardens. His claim to be a poet is born out by the fact that his poetic cycle *Frauenliebe und Leben* was set to music by Schumann. Furthermore, his tale of a man who sold his shadow to the devil (*Peter Schlemihls wundersame Geschichte*) became legend. He also wrote plays as well as diaries of his travels. Allan Octavian **Hume** CB is also mentioned more fully in the section on politicians, and is best described as a poet and political philosopher, although our research turned up little about his poetry and much about his philosophy. There are more tenuous connections with poetry; both Captain George Ernest **Shelley** and Sir Edward **Shelley** were nephews of the famous poet Percy Bysshe Shelley.

POLITICIANS

Some politicians have birds named after them. Of these, some were themselves naturalists but others had birds named for them because of their fame. Firmly in this latter category was Pedro Alcantara **Herran,** who was a Colombian general, a politician and President of New Granada [now Colombia] from 1841 until 1844. A similar person, from another continent, General Louis **Botha,** who was the first Prime Minister of the Union of South Africa from 1910 until 1919. Sir Herbert Eustace **Maxwell**, seventh baronet, was a Knight of the Thistle and MP for Wigtownshire, Lord of the Treasury, Secretary of State for Scotland and Lord Lieutenant of the County. Maxwell was a famed horticulturalist who collected many botanical specimens and transplanted them on his estate, so he rather bridges the merely famous politicians and the politician-naturalists. Heinrich Wolfgang Ludwig **Dohrn** was a German politician who was famed as an entomologist. On the other hand, Allan Octavian **Hume** CB wrote a number of books on Indian birds and was first describer of several taxa, as well as being a political philosopher who co-founded the Congress Party which has governed India ever since independence. We have not included the Polish ornithologists who were exiled for political activities.

POLLEN

> Pollen's Vanga *Xenopirostris polleni* (**Schlegel** 1868)

François P L Pollen (1842–1866) was a French naturalist who collected in Madagascar from 1863 until his death in 1866. He wrote *Récherches sur la Faune de Madagascar et de ses Dépendances – d'après les déscouvertes de F.P.L. Pollen et D.C. van Dam*, in 1868.

POORTMAN

> Poortman's Emerald *Chlorostilbon poortmani* (**Bourcier** 1843)
> (Alt. Short-tailed/Cabini's/Berlepsch's Emerald)

Willem Poortman (1819–1891) was a Dutch ornithologist who collected in Colombia in the 1840s.

POPELAIRE

> Popelaire's Coquette *Popelairia popelairii* (Du Bus de Gisignies 1846)
> (Alt. Wire-crested Thorntail)

Baron Popelaire de Terloo was a Belgian naturalist who collected in Peru. He has a hefty snail named after him too; Popelaire's Giant Snail *Strophocheilus popelarianus* can grow up to six inches! The coquette is a member of the thorntail genus which commemorates the Baron in the generic name. Bernard-Aimé Leonard, Vicomte Du Bus de Gisignies (1808–1874), to whom Popelaire sent all his specimens, first described the bird and named both this species and the genus.

POWELL

> Powell's Buttonquail *Turnix suscitator powelli* (Guillemard 1885)
> (Alt. Barred Buttonquail)

Commander R Powell RN (1851–1938) visited the East Indies in 1885.

PRÊTRE

Prêtre's Hermit *Phaethornis pretrei* (**Lesson** & **Delattre** 1839)
(Alt. Planalto Hermit)
Prêtre's Hermit *Phaethornis longuemareus* (Lesson & Delattre 1832)
(Alt. Little/Longuemare's Hermit)
Prêtre's Parrot *Amazona pretrei* (**Temminck** 1830)
(Alt. Red-spectacled Amazon/Parrot)

Jean Gabriel Prêtre (1800–1840) was a French artist who was employed by the Natural History Museum in Paris. He illustrated Louis **Vieillot**'s classic work *Histoire Naturelle des plus Beaux Oiseaux de la Zone Torride* (Songbirds of the Torrid Zone), which was published in 12 parts, from 1805 through to 1809. He also illustrated *Animal Kingdom*, which was published posthumously in 1850. **Gould** was the first to use the name Planalto Hermit for Prêtre's Hermit, but Planalto Hermit is now standard.

PREUSS

Preuss's Cliff Swallow *Hirundo* (*Petrochelidon*) *preussi* (**Reichenow** 1898)
(Alt. Preuss' Swallow)
Preuss's [Golden] Weaver *Ploceus preussi* (Reichenow 1892)
(Alt. Golden-backed Weaver)
Preuss's Double-collared Sunbird *Nectarinia preussi* (Reichenow 1892)
(Alt. Montane Double-collared Sunbird)

Paul Preuss (1861–1926) was a Polish-born German naturalist. He was known to have collected in West Africa between 1886 and 1898, in New Guinea around 1903 and again in West Africa in 1910. He constructed the botanical gardens of Victoria (today Limbe), in Cameroon, in 1901, and was in the employ of the colonial government there.

PREVOST

Prevost's Ground Sparrow *Melozone biarcuatum* (Prevost & **Des Murs** 1846)
Prevost's Mango *Anthracothorax prevostii* (**Lesson** 1832)
(Alt. Green-breasted Mango)

Florent Prévost [or Prevot] (?–1870) was a French artist and writer who worked on museum collections. He wrote *Iconographie Ornithologique* in 1845 and *Histoire Naturelle des Oiseaux d'Europe* in 1864. He also illustrated works by **Temminck**, **Bonaparte** and **Buffon**.

PRIGOGINE

Prigogine's Alseonax *Muscicapa itombwensis* (Prigogine 1957)
(Alt. Itombwe Flycatcher)
Prigogine's Apalis *Apalis kaboboensis* (Prigogine 1955)
(Syn.Kabobo Apalis)
Prigogine's Bay Owl *Philodus prigoginei* (Schouteden 1952)
(Alt. Congo[Bay] Owl, Tanzanian Bay Owl, Itombwe Owl)
Prigogine's Double-collared Sunbird *Nectarinia prigoginei* (Macdonald 1958)
(Alt. Marunga Sunbird)
Prigogine's Golden Thrush *Zoothera kibalensis* (Prigogine 1958)
(Alt. Prigogine's/Kibale Ground Thrush)
Prigogine's Greenbul *Chlorocichla prigoginei* (De Roo 1967)
Prigogine's Nightjar *Caprimulgus prigoginei* (Louette 1990)
(Alt. Itombwe Nightjar)
Prigogine's Owlet *Glaucidium albertinum* (Prigogine 1983)
(Alt. Albertine Owlet)

Alexandre Prigogine (1913–1989) was a Russian-born Belgian naturalist, whose brother

Ilya (1917–2003) won the Nobel Prize for Chemistry in 1977. The family left Moscow after the Revolution and settled in Belgium. Ilya mentioned Alexandre by name in his Nobel Prize acceptance speech as also having studied chemistry. Alexandre has written extensively on birds and certainly sponsored a number of expeditions to West Africa, especially the area known before as the Belgian Congo. He wrote *Les Oiseaux de l'Itombwe et de son Hinterland*, in three volumes, between 1971 and 1984.

PRIMOLI

Primoli's Hummingbird *Metallura williami primolinus* (**Bourcier** 1853)
(Alt. Ecuadonian/Viridian Metaltail)

Count Joseph Napoleon Primoli (1851–1927) was a scholar and photographer who founded the Napoleonic Museum in Rome. His mother was Contessa Charlotte Honorine Josephine Pauline Primoli di Foglia (1832–1901), daughter of Prince Charles Lucien **Bonaparte**. The macaw genus *Primolius*, namedly Bonaparte in 1857, also commemorates Primoli.

PRINCE ALBERT

Prince Albert's Curassow *Crax alberti* (**Fraser** 1852)
(Alt. Blue-billed/Blue-knobbed/Colombian Curassow)

See **Albert**.

PRINCE HENRY

Prince Henry's Laughing-thrush *Garrulax henrici* (**Oustalet** 1892)
(Alt. Brown-cheeked Laughing-thrush)

Henri Prince d'Orléans (1867–1901) was born in Richmond, England, but was a French Bourbon prince of the Royal House. He was an explorer and geographer who collected in China and Tibet, from 1889 until 1890, in southeast Africa, in 1892, and in Indochina, in 1895. He also discovered the source of the Irrawaddy River. He wrote *Around Tonkin and Siam*, in 1894 and *From Tonkin to India*, in 1897. He died in Saigon (now Ho Chi Minh city), Vietnam.

PRINCE LUCIAN

Prince Lucian's Conure *Pyrrhura picta lucianii* (**Deville** 1851)
(Alt. Painted Parakeet)

Prince Lucian Bonaparte – see **Bonaparte**.

PRINCE OF WALES

Prince of Wales's Pheasant *Phasianus colchicus principalis* (P L **Sclater** 1855)

The Prince of Wales, in 1885, when P L **Sclater** described the bird, became King Edward VII, who was born in 1841, succeeded to the throne on the death of Queen Victoria in 1901, and died in 1910. There is a vast amount of biographical details about him and an excellent official biography, so we would add nothing to this account by trying to précis it.

PRINCE RUDOLPH

Prince Rudolph's Bird-of-Paradise *Paradisaea rudolphi* (**Finsch** 1885)
(Alt. Blue Bird-of-Paradise)

Archduke Rudolf, Crown Prince of Austria-Hungary (1857–1889). His fate is well known and has been the subject of many studies and films. He and his mistress were found dead in mysterious circumstances. It is generally supposed that they were involved in a suicide pact, but this has never been proven, and there are advocates of the theory that they were murdered.

PRINCE RUSPOLI

Prince Ruspoli's Turaco *Tauraco ruspolii* (**Salvadori** 1896)

Prince Eugenio Ruspoli (1866–1893) was an aristocratic explorer. His family were eminent Roman aristocrats who intermarried with the Bonaparte dynasty in the 19th century. An ancestor had been both Scarlatti's and Handel's patron before the latter moved to England. Ruspoli was an Italian explorer, who was in Ethiopia from 1891 until 1893, when he was killed in an '*encounter with an elephant*' which he had wounded! Prince Ruspoli collected the turaco in either 1892 or 1893; he left no note of the locality or date of its collection before his meeting with elephantine fate. **Salvadori** named it after him.

PRINCE

Prince's Hawk *Leucopternis princeps* (P L **Sclater** 1865)
(Alt. Barred Hawk)

Not named for a person but as the prince of birds.

PRINCESS HELENA

Princess Helena's Coquette *Lophornis helenae* (**DeLattre** 1843)
(Alt. Black-crested Coquette)

Princess Helene d'Orléans (1814–1858) was the wife of the Duc d'Orléans, who was a patron of natural history expeditions.

PRINCESS ALEXANDRA

Princess Alexandra's Parrot *Polytelis alexandrae* (**Gould** 1863)
(Alt. Alexandra's/Princess's Parrot)

See **Alexandra**.

PRINCESS STEPHANIE

Princess Stephanie's Astrapia *Astrapia stephaniae* (**Finsch** 1885)
(Alt. Princess Stephanie's Bird-of-Paradise, Stephanie's Astrapia)

See **Stephanie**.

PRINGLE

Pringle's Puffback *Dryoscopus pringlii* (**Jackson** 1893)

Colonel Sir John Wallace Pringle (1863–1938) was the Chief Inspector of Railways in Uganda from 1891 until 1892. He subsequently became an Inspector of Railways for the Board of Trade, in England and is known to have written reports as late as 1924, when he must have been close to retirement.

PRITCHARD

Pritchard's Scrubfowl *Megapodius pritchardii* (**G R Gray** 1864)
(Alt. Polynesian/Niaufoou/Tongan Scrubfowl/Scrubhen/Megapode)

William Thomas Pritchard (1829–1909) was a British Consular Agent in Samoa, in 1856, and then the British Consul in Fiji, between 1857 and 1862, having been instrumental in the addition of Fiji to the Empire. Ratu Seru Cakobau, leader of the most powerful clan, virtually sold Fiji to Queen Victoria. Cakobau had money problems; he had run up huge debts to an American (John B Williams). He made an offer to the Consul, Pritchard, to cede Fiji to Britain if that nation would cover his debts to Williams. The deal did not go through at first but, in 1874, Britain took over. Pritchard wrote *Polynesian Reminiscences*, in 1866.

PRUNELLE

Prunelle's Coeligene *Coeligena prunellei* (**Bourcier** 1843)
(Alt. Black Inca)

Clement François Victor Gabriel Prunelle (1777–1853) was a French scientist.

PRYER

Pryer's Woodpecker *Sapheopipo noguchii* (**Seebohm** 1887)
(Alt. Okinawa Woodpecker)

Henry J S Pryer (1850–1888) was a British lepidopterist who collected in Japan in the late 19th century. He wrote *Rhopalocera Niponica* in 1886. His collection was later donated to the British Museum. The woodpecker, which is endemic to Okinawa, is dedicated in Japan as a 'National Monument'. It is considered severely endangered, with a population of fewer than 600 birds, including only 90 breeding pairs. The scientific name is for T **Noguchi** a Japanese collector. Pryer also has a snake named after him.

PRJEVALSKY

Przewalski's Lark *Eremophila alpestris teleschowi* (Przewalski 1886)
(Alt. Horned/Shore Lark)
Przewalski's Nuthatch *Sitta leucopsis przewalskii* (**Berezowski** & **Bianchi** 1891)
(Alt. White-cheeked Nuthatch)
Przewalski's Parrotbill *Paradoxornis przewalskii* (Berezowski & Bianchi 1891)
(Alt. Grey-crowned/Rusty-throated Parrotbill)
Przewalski's Redstart *Phoenicurus alaschanicus* (Przewalski 1876)
(Alt. Ala Shan Redstart)
Przewalski's Rock Partridge *Alectoris magna* (Przewalski 1876)
(Alt. Rusty-necklaced Partridge)
Przewalski's Rosefinch *Urocynchramus pylzowi* (Przewalski 1876)
(Alt. Pink-tailed Rosefinch)
Przewalski's Thrush *Turdus kessleri* (Przewalski 1876)
(Alt. Kessler's/White-backed Thrush)

General Nikolai Mikhailovitch Prjevalsky (1839–1888) was a Russian Cossack naturalist who explored Central Asia. He was undoubtedly one of the greatest explorers the world has ever seen, and made five major expeditions, one to the Russian Far East and the others to Mongolia. He wrote *Mongolia, and the Tangut Country*, in 1875, and *From Kulja, Across the Tian Shan to Lob-Nor*, in 1879. He is best known for having the horse *Equus przewalskii*, which he discovered, named after him but he is also commemorated by a gerbil *Gerbillus przewalskii*, and even an antpitta, *Grallaria przewalskii*. The Russian Academy of Sciences instituted the Prjevalsky Gold Medal in 1946. There are a least half-a-dozen different spellings of his name but he signed himself as Prjevalsky, and that is pronounced 'She-val-ski'. He died of typhus at the age of 49 whilst preparing for a fifth expedition. Tsar Alexander II decreed that the town where he died, Karakol, should immediately have its name changed to Prjevalsk.

PRZEWALSKI

See **Prjevalsky** above.

PUCHERAN

Pucheran's Emerald *Chlorostilbon aureoventris pucherani* (**Bourcier** &
Mulsant 1848)
(Alt. Glittering-bellied Emerald)
Pucheran's Red-cheeked Parrot *Geoffroyus geoffroyi pucherani* (**Souancé** 1856)
(Alt. Red-cheeked Parrot)
Pucheran's Woodpecker *Melanerpes pucherani* (**Malherbe** 1849)
(Alt. Black-cheeked Woodpecker)

Jacques Pucheran (1817–1894) was a French zoologist who went on the expedition of
the *Astrolabe* with Dumont d'Urville, **Gaimard** and Jacquinot. He wrote *Voyage au Pole Sud
et dans l'Oceanie sur les Corvettes l'Astrolabe et la Zelée*, in 1842.

PULITZER

Pulitzer's Longbill *Macrosphenus pulitzeri* (**Boulton** 1931)

Ralph Pulitzer (1879–1939) was a publisher and a sponsor of speed flying, among other
enterprises. He was the son of Joseph Pulitzer who is commemorated by the 'Pulitzer
Prize', a prestigious award for American journalism, literature or music.

PUVEL

Puvel's Illadopsis *Illadopsis puveli* (**Salvadori** 1901)
(Alt. Puvel's Thrush Babbler/Akalat; *Malacocincla puveli, Trichastoma
puveli*)

Pierre Puvel was a Frenchman who immigrated to Guinea-Bissau.

PYCROFT

Pycroft's Petrel *Pterodroma pycrofti* (Falla 1933)

Arthur T Pycroft (1875–1971) was a New Zealander. He published an article *Santa Cruz
Red Feather Money – its manufacture and use* in the Journal of the Polynesian Society.

QUEEN ALEXANDRA

Queen Alexandra's Parrot *Polytelis alexandrae* (**Gould** 1863)

See **Alexandra**

QUEEN CAROLA

Queen Carola's Parotia *Parotia carolae* (**A B Meyer** 1894)
(Alt. Carola's Parotia, Queen Carola of Saxony's Six-wired Bird-of-Paradise)

Queen Carola of Saxony (1833–1907) was the wife of **King** Albert **of Saxony** (1828–1902).

QUEEN CHARLOTTE

Queen Charlotte Jay *Cyanocitta stelleri carlottae* (**Osgood** 1901)
(Alt. Steller's/Osgood's/Grinnell's Jay Jay)
Queen Charlotte Woodpecker *Picoides villosus picoideus* (Osgood 1901)
(Alt. Hairy/Harris's/Cabanis's Woodpecker)
Queen Charlotte Owl *Aegolius acadicus brooksi* (**Fleming** 1916)
(Alt. Northern Saw-whet Owl)

This is another example of birds being named after places rather than people, in this case the Queen Charlotte Islands (locally known as Haida Gwaii) off British Columbia, in Canada. The islands were named after Sophie Charlotte, Princess of Mecklenburg-Strelitz (1744–1818), who was the Queen and Consort of George III, King of Great Britain, Ireland and Hanover. The birds were not named directly after her but after the islands.

QUEEN OF BAVARIA

Queen of Bavaria's Conure *Aratinga guarouba* (Gmelin 1788)
(Alt. Golden Conure/Parakeet)

Marie Wilhelmine Auguste of Hessen-Darmstadt (1765–1796) was married to Maximilian I, King of Bavaria, in 1785.

QUEEN VICTORIA

See **Victoria**

QUEENS AND OTHER ROYALTY

It is difficult to separate royalty from aristocrats in general, but we drew the line at Dukes and above. Royalty is rather over-represented in the list of those who have had birds named after them. This is a reflection of the peak of discovery of new species coinciding with nationalist expansion in Victorian times – indeed **Victoria** herself was so honoured. Most were honoured for their position rather than their contribution to ornithology. Such persons included Princess **Alexandra**, Queen **Charlotte** wife of King George III, **Louise** Margaret of Prussia, HRH the **Princess** of Connaught, the **Emperor of Germany** Kaiser Wilhelm I, as well as his wife **Empress** Marie Luise Augusta Katharina, Princess of Saxe-Weimar and Eisenach, Empress **Eugenie**, wife of **Napoleon** III, the Duc de Guise (whose brother was an ornithologist), **King** Albert **of Saxony** and his wife **Queen Carola**, Napoleon **Bonaparte** (although his nephew was an ornithologist), Archduke **Rudolf,** Crown **Prince** of Austria-Hungary, Princess Maximiliane Wilhelmine Auguste **Sophie** Marie, wife of Tsar Alexander II, Princess **Stephanie** of Belgium, and **Willem** III of Holland. These individuals were all honoured for being the sovereign or wife thereof, of the person describing the bird, rather than for any ornithological acumen. **Montezuma**, Emperor of the Aztecs in Mexico also fits here, although he was reputed to have very splendid feather cloaks and so has a slightly less tenuous connection to birds. On the other hand, a number of Royal personages were themselves keen ornithologists and collectors. **Adalbert**, Prince **Albert, Henri** Prince d'Orleans and Eugenio, **Prince Ruspoli** were all involved in study or collecting and were at least interested in birds. **Eleonora** of Arborea also fits this category; she was the warrior princess of Sardinia who passed enlightened legislation protecting birds of prey. Princess **Helene** d'Orleans and her husband were great patrons of collecting expeditions. **Herbrand** Arthur Russell, the 11th Duke of Bedford, Prince Charles Lucien Bonaparte (whose wife Princess **Zenaide** Charlotte Bonaparte was also honoured), Edward Smith **Stanley**, the 13th Earl of Derby, Viscount Yorikatsu **Matsudaira**, Maximilian Alexander Philip Prince zu **Wied-Neuwied**, and the Duc de **Rivoli** (Princess **Anna** d' Essling was his wife although not an ornithologist like him) were very good ornithologists in their own right. Sir Charles Johnson **Brooke** fits the latter category, but is a bit of a cheat in as much as his royalty was not in the blood – he styled himself **Rajah** of Sarawak.

RABIER

Rabier's Woodpecker *Picus rabieri* (**Oustalet** 1898)
(Alt. Red-collared Woodpecker)

Lieutenant Colonel Paul Rabier was a French army officer who served in Indochina from 1897 until 1904. He may have been the same person as the Gustave Marie Paul Rabier, a French officer from Indochina who was killed in the First World War and who, along with others, described as French Shanghai patriots, has a street named after him in Shanghai.

RABOR

Rabor's Wren-Babbler *Napothera rabori* (**Rand** 1960)
(Alt. Luzon Wren-Babbler)

Dr Dioscoro S Rabor (1911–1996), known as Joe, was a Filipino ornithologist, conservationist and collector. He also worked in a variety of other fields including ichthyology, fisheries, mammalogy, herpetology and ecology. He founded a museum in Los Baños, Laguna, which houses his collections and concentrated on the flora and fauna of Mindanao, Sulu and Palawan. He collected the babbler in 1960. He wrote *Philippine Birds and Mammals* and *Birds of the Philippine Islands: Siquijor, Mount Malindang, Bohol and Samar*. He was a Fellow of the John Simon Guggenheim Memorial Foundation. Rabor wrote at least one scientific paper with **Rand**, who described the bird.

RACHEL

Rachel's Malimbe *Malimbus racheliae* (**Cassin** 1857)

Rachel Cassin was the daughter of the American ornithologist John **Cassin** (1813–1869).

Rachel was also his mother's name. Cassin married the widow of his lithographer, J T Bowen (1801–1856) at around the time that he wrote the description so his daughter may have been born by then. We think it more likely that he named the bird after his daughter than after his mother.

RADDE

Radde's Accentor *Prunella ocularis* (Radde 1884)
Radde's Warbler *Phylloscopus schwarzi* (Radde 1863)

Gustav Ferdinand Richard Radde (1831–1903) was originally trained as an apothecary. On 22 September 1856, the Prussian naturalist and explorer came across a '*skulking warbler in a kitchen garden in the heart of Central Asia*'. He 'collected' it and, finding it to be a hitherto undiscovered species, apparently named it after himself. He also founded the Caucasian museum in Tiflis, Georgia, in 1867. He wrote *Die Vogelwelt des Kaukasus, systematisch und biologisch-geographisch beschrieben*, in 1888, and *Reisen im Süden von Ost-Sibirien in den Jahren 1855–1859*, in two volumes, published in 1862 and 1863.

RAFFLES

Raffles' Malkoha *Phaenicophaeus chlorophaea* (Raffles 1822)

Sir Thomas Stamford Bingley Raffles (1781–1826) was a colonial officer who was Lieutenant-Governor of Java, from 1811 until 1815, and Lieutenant-Governor of an area of Sumatra, from 1818 until 1924. He actually founded the city-state of Singapore in 1819. He was noted for his '*liberal attitude toward peoples under colonial rule, his rigorous suppression of the slave trade, and his zeal in collecting historical and scientific information*'. He was also the first President of the Zoological Society of London, and he wrote a *History of Java*, in 1817. He employed zoologists and botanists to collect specimens, paying them out of his own pocket. On his return journey to England in 1824 on *HMS Fame*, he lost a huge collection of specimens, notes and drawings to a fire. His wife, Lady Sophia Raffles, mentioned his zoological collection in her memoirs of him.

RAIMONDI

Raimondi's Yellow Finch *Sicalis raimondii* (**Taczanowski** 1874)

Antonio Raimondi (1822–1890) was an Italian explorer and naturalist who collected in Peru between 1850 and 1890. He made numerous journeys of investigation all over the country in the 40 years in which he lived there. He was dedicated to the study of Peru's geography, mineralogy, botany, zoology and ethnography. It seems his motto was 'lose not an instant'. He is perhaps most famed for the bromeliad *Puya raimondii*, which is named after him; this can have 8,000 individual florets on a spike 35 feet tall, the tallest inflorescence in the world, and it also holds the record for lengthy flowering intervals, which can be as much as 150 years apart! Raimondi wrote about encountering this living fossil relative of the pineapple thus: '*The travelling botanist who has the thrill to surprise these strange and admirable plants while they are in flower can do nothing but stop and contemplate ecstatically for some time such a beautiful spectacle.*' What is more the spiky rosette offers protection to a variety of birds which may nest within the leaves of one plant. Another bird, the Peruvian Plantcutter *Phytotoma raimondii* is also named after him in the binomial. The Museo Raimondi in Lima also commemorates his name.

RAJAH

> Rajah's Lory *Chalcopsitta atra insignis* (**Oustalet** 1878)
> (Alt. Black/Raja/Rajah Lory)
> Rajah's Scops Owl *Otus brookii* (**Sharpe** 1892)
> (Alt. Brooke's Scops Owl)

Sir Charles Johnson Brooke (1829–1917), styled as the second Rajah of Sarawak. See **Brooke**.

RAMSAY

> Ramsay's Barwing *Actinodura ramsayi* (Walden 1875)
> (Alt. [White-]Spectacled Barwing)
> Ramsay's Blue Flycatcher *Cyornis lemprieri* (**Sharpe** 1884)
> (Alt. Palawan Niltava)
> Ramsay's Woodpecker *Picoides maculatus ramsayi* (Hargitt 1881)
> (Alt. Sulu/Philippine Woodpecker)

Colonel Robert George Wardlaw Ramsay (1852–1921) was a British ornithologist who spent time in India and Burma (now Myanmar) between 1872 and 1882. He was a President of the British Ornithologists' Union from 1913 until 1918. He was also a nephew of Arthur Hay, Lord Walden, Marquis of **Tweeddale** and sent him the specimens he collected. **Walden** first described the barwing from a specimen collected by Ramsay in Karen-nee, Burma, in 1874. The woodpecker is a strong candidate for elevation to species status.

RAND

> Rand's Modest Parrot *Psittacella modesta subcollaris* (Rand 1941)
> (Alt. Modest Tiger Parrot)
> Rand's Red-billed Helmet-shrike *Prionops gabela* (Rand 1957)
> (Alt. Gabela/Angola Helmet-shrike)
> Rand's Robin-Chat *Cossypha heinrichi* (Rand 1955)
> (Alt. White-headed Robin-Chat)
> Rand's Warbler *Randia pseudozosterops* (**Delacour** & **Berlioz** 1931)
> (Alt. Marvantsetra Warbler)

Austen L Rand (1905–?) was an American ornithologist who collected in several countries. He was Curator of Birds at the Field Museum in Chicago from 1947 until 1955, when he became Chief Curator of Zoology, a post which he held until 1970. He wrote *The Distribution and Habits of Madagascar Birds*, in 1936, and *Handbook of New Guinea Birds*, in 1967. He also named a number of birds after **Archbold**, having written papers on the *Results of the Archbold Expeditions*.

RAVEN

> Raven's Whistler *Pachycephala* (*Coracornis*) *raveni* (Riley 1918)
> (Alt. Maroon-backed Whistler)

Henry Cushier Raven (1889–1944) was an American explorer who collected in Borneo and Sulawesi between 1912 and 1917, when he led an expedition on behalf of the Smithsonian Institution. William L **Abbott** sponsored the trip although he was too ill to go himself. Raven's 178-page field journal is held at the Smithsonian.

REEVE

> Reeve's Thrush *Turdus reevei* (**Lawrence** 1869)
> (Alt. Plumbeous-backed Thrush)

J P Reeve was an American who collected in Ecuador.

REEVES

Reeves' Pheasant *Syrmaticus reevesii* (J E **Gray** 1829)

John R Reeves (1774–1856) was an English amateur naturalist and collector who served in China, chiefly Macao, as a civil servant between 1812 and 1831. He sent the first specimens of the Muntjac Deer *Muntjacius reevei* back to England, where escapes from collections have established it as a by no means uncommon feral species. He also introduced many plants into Britain, including the Wisteria *Wisteria sinensis*. Reeves collected the type specimens of the lark *Alauda sinensis* and the bunting *Emberiza lathami* and ten non-passerines. Neither of the two passerines' names is current. J E **Gray** named the pheasant to honour him as the man who first brought the live birds to Europe.

REICHARD

Reichard's Seedeater *Serinus reichardi* (**Reichenow** 1882)
(Alt. Stripe-breasted Serin/Canary)

Paul Reichard (1845–1938) was a German geographer and engineer. He collected in East Africa between 1880 and 1884, and sent ethnographical specimens to the museum in Berlin. He wrote a number of papers including *Deutsch-Ostafrika Das Land und seine Bewohner*, in 1882, and *Das Afrikanische Eisenbahn und sein Handel*, in 1899.

REICHENBACH

Reichenbach's Sunbird *Nectarinia reichenbachii* (**Hartlaub** 1857)

Dr Heinrich Gottlieb Ludwig Reichenbach (1793–1879) was a German zoologist and botanist. From 1810 he studied medicine and natural science at Leipzig and practised there as a doctor after he graduated. He then also qualified as a private tutor in medicine and natural science, but in 1820 he was appointed Professor of Natural History at the Surgical/Medical Academy in Dresden, and he also became responsible for the Natural History Museum. He founded the Dresden Botanical gardens which can still be seen. He researched very extensively and his legacy included over 6,000 drawings, most of them his own work. Reichenbach devised his own unique method of botanical classification, under which there are eight categories depending upon the plants' organs. He wrote *Praktische Naturgeschichte der Vogel*, in 1845, and *Avium Systema Naturale, das Naturliche System der Vogel*, in 1849. He retired from his posts in 1862.

REICHENOW

Reichenow's Batis *Batis reichenowi* (Grote 1911)
(Alt. Reichenow's Puffback/Flycatcher)
Reichenow's Blue-headed Parrot *Pionus menstruus reichenowi* (**Heine** 1884)
Reichenow's Cape Parrot *Poicephalus robustus suahelicus* (Reichenow 1898)
Reichenow's Crimsonwing *Cryptospiza reichenowi* (**Hartlaub** 1874)
(Alt. Red-faced/Nyasa Crimsonwing)
Reichenow's Dove *Streptopelia reichenowi* (**Erlanger** 1901)
(Alt. White-winged Collared/Ringed Dove)
Reichenow's Firefinch *Lagonosticta umbrinodorsalis* (Reichenow 1910)
(Alt. Chad/Pink-backed Firefinch)
Reichenow's Guineafowl *Numida meleagris reichenowi* (**Ogilvie-Grant** 1894)
(Alt. Helmeted Guineafowl)

Reichenow's Melidectes *Melidectes rufocrissalis* (Reichenow 1915)
(Alt. Yellow-browed Honeyeater)
Reichenow's Nightjar *Caprimulgus clarus* (Reichenow 1892)
(Alt. Slender-tailed Nightjar)
Reichenow's Orange-bellied Parrot *Poicephalus senegalus mesotypus* (Reichenow 1910)
Reichenow's Orange-breasted Fig Parrot *Cyclopsitta gulielmiterti amabilis* (Reichenow 1891)
Reichenow's Reed Warbler *Bradypterus cinnamomeus mildbreadi* Reichenow 1908
(Alt. Cinnamon Bracken Warbler)
Reichenow's Serin *Serinus reichenowi* (**Salvadori** 1888)
(Alt. Yellow-rumped Canary/Seedeater)
Reichenow's Swift *Tachymarptis aequatorialis* (Von Muller 1851)
(Alt. Mottled Swift)
Reichenow's Turaco *Tauraco livingstonii* (G R **Gray** 1864)
(Alt. Livingstone's Turaco)
Reichenow's Wattle-eye *Platysteira chalybea* (Reichenow 1897)
(Alt. Black-necked Wattle-eye)
Reichenow's Weaver *Ploceus baglafecht reichenowi* (**Fischer** 1884)
(Alt. Emin's/Stuhlmann's Weaver)
Reichenow's Woodpecker *Campethera bennettii scriptoricauda* (Reichenow 1896)
(Alt. Bennett's Woodpecker)

Dr Anton Reichenow (1847–1941) was the German son-in-law of **Cabanis**. He dominated German ornithology for many years and was widely regarded as the leading expert of his time on African birds, although he only visited Africa once, on a collecting expedition, to West Africa from 1872 through 1873. He published a three-volume handbook on the birds of Africa, *Die Vogel Africas*, from 1900 to 1905. In 1899 he published *Die Vögel der Bismarckinseln*. He also named a number of species after their collectors; **Stierling, Reichenbach**, **Reichard** and **Fülleborn** and others. Müller described the swift in 1851 and we assume that a form of it was, for a short time, thought to be a separate species and named for Reichenow.

REINHARDT

Reinhardt's Ptarmigan *Lagopus mutus rupestris* (J F Gmelin 1789)
(Alt. Rock Ptarmigan)

Professor Johannes Theodor Reinhardt (1816–1882) was a Dutch zoologist. In 1861 he published a *List of birds hitherto observed in Greenland*, which included the Eskimo Curlew *Numenius borealis* and the Great Auk *Alca impennis*. The latter inclusion has been questioned but does not seem entirely implausible, given that the species' main colonies were in Iceland and Newfoundland. The Rock Ptarmigan subspecies is the Greenland race.

REINWARDT

Reinwardt's Blue-tailed Trogon *Harpactes reinwardtii* (**Temminck** 1822)
(Alt. Javan/Blue-tailed Trogon)
Reinwardt's Long-tailed Pigeon *Reinwardtoena reinwardtii* (Temminck 1824)
(Alt. Great Cuckoo-Dove)
Reinwardt's Scrubfowl *Megapodius reinwardt* (**Dumont** 1823)
(Alt. Orange-footed Scrubfowl/Megapode)

Caspar Georg Carl Reinwardt (1773–1854) was a Dutch ornithologist who collected in

Java from 1817 until 1822. At the age of 14, he went to study botany and chemistry in Amsterdam, where he also studied mathematics, classical and modern languages and history. He gained a doctorate in Natural Philosophy and Medical Science in 1801. That year he also became Professor of Chemistry and Natural History at the University of Harderwijk, where he was responsible for the University's botanical garden. Louis Napoleon made him director of his menagerie, which was in Amsterdam, and he became Professor of Natural History there. In 1816 he was made responsible for all matters concerning agriculture, arts and sciences in Java, where he remained for the next five years. He contributed greatly to education and public health on Java. He founded the Botanical Gardens of Buitenzorg (Bogor) and travelled extensively. He laid the foundation for two important museum collections in Leiden: the National Museum of Natural History and the National Museum of Ethnography. While collecting he was meticulous and detailed in the documentation of his specimens. He was very concerned with the systematic development of collections and their documentation, and he was always pleased to extend opportunities for research to others. It was through this that he was honoured by many fellow naturalists, who named many plants (29) and birds after him. Reinwardt is also honoured in a number of birds' scientific names including those of the Orange-backed Woodpecker *Reinwardtipicus validus*, the Pied Cuckoo-Dove *Reinwardtoena browni*, the Crested Cuckoo-Dove *Reinwardtoena crassirostris*, the Golden-collared Toucanet *Selenidera reinwardtii* and the Blackcap Babbler *Turdoides reinwardtii*.

REISER

Reiser's Recurvebill *Megaxenops parnaguae* (Reiser 1905)
(Alt. Great Xenops)
Reiser's Spinetail *Synallaxis* [*Gyalophylax*] *hellmayri* (Reiser 1905)
(Alt. Red-shouldered/White-browed Spinetail)
Reiser's Tyrannulet *Phyllomyias reiseri* (**Hellmayr** 1905)

Othmar Reiser (1861–1936) was an Austrian oologist and collector who collected in northeastern Brazil with the expedition of the Austrian Academy of Sciences in 1903. He published an account of this enterprise; *Die Ergebnisse der Zool. Expedition der Syn.d. der Wissenschaften nach Nordostbrasilien im Jahre 1903*. Reiser became curator of the museum in Sarajevo, in present-day Bosnia, and published a four-volume series; *Materialen zu einer Ornis Balcanica*, the second volume of which was devoted entirely to the birds of Bulgaria.

RENAULD

Renauld's Ground Cuckoo *Carpococcyx renauldi* (**Oustalet** 1896)
(Alt. Coral-/Red-billed Ground Cuckoo)

Father J N Renauld (1839–1898) was a French missionary in Vietnam. He collected many specimens of Vietnamese fauna and flora in Quang Tri province, between 1869 and 1896, and this collection was used, in 1896, to found the Vietnamese Natural History Museum. Oustalet described **Edward**'s Pheasant *Lophura edwardsi*, in 1896, from four skins which Renauld sent to the Natural History Museum in Paris.

RETZ

Retz's [Red-billed] Helmet-shrike *Prionops retzii* (**Wahlberg** 1856)
(Alt. Red-billed Helmet-shrike)

Anders Jahan Retzius (1742–1821) was a Swedish naturalist and Professor of Natural History, Economy and Chemistry in Lund. The shrike may have been named after one of his sons; Anders Adolph Retzius (1796–1860), who was Professor in Anatomy and Physiology at the Karolinska Institute or Carl Gustaf Retzius (1798–1833), who was a veterinary professor in Stockholm. Other sources say it was named after A J Retzius himself.

RHEINHARD

Rheinhard's Pheasant *Rheinardia ocellata* (**Elliot** 1871)
(Alt. Crested Argus)

Pierre-Paul Rheinhard (1840–1902) was an officer in the French army and an administrator in Vietnam. He was Chargé d'Affaires in Annam from 1879 until 1889 and Résident-Générale in Annam-Tonkin in 1889. He sent the first specimen of the pheasant to Paris.

RIBEIRO

Ribeiro's Scaly-headed Parrot *Pionus maximiliani melanoblepharus* (Ribeiro 1920)

Alipio de Miranda Ribeiro (1874–1939) was a Brazilian ichthyologist who worked for the National Museum, in Rio de Janeiro. Ribeiro started to describe new fish species but he had competition from **Goeldi** who would go to a market and buy the fish from the same ship, the *Annie*, and would then describe them and send them to the British Museum. In 1929 he became Professor of the Department of Zoology, a post which he held until his death. Ribeiro explored the Amazon and organized the *Inspectoria de Pesca*, the first official fisheries department in Brazil. He published *Fauna Brasiliensis-Peixes* in 1911.

RICHARD

Richard's Pipit *Anthus richardi* (Vieillot 1818)

Monsieur Richard of Luneville was a French naturalist and collector. The pipit was named after him and described by **Vieillot**.

RICHARDS

Richards' Fruit Dove *Ptilinopus richardsii* (E P Ramsay 1882)
(Alt. Silver-capped/Pink-capped Fruit Dove)
Richards' Monarch *Monarcha richardsii* (E P Ramsay 1881)
(Alt. White-capped Monarch)

Rear-Admiral George Edward Richards (1852–1927) was an English geographer who collected in the East Indies.

RICHARDSON

Richardson's Goose *Branta canadensis hutchinsii* (Richardson 1831)
(Alt. Hutchins'/Canada Goose)
Richardson's Grouse *Dendragapus obscurus richardsonii* (Douglas 1829)
(Alt. Blue/Fleming's Grouse)
Richardson's Owl *Aegolius funereus richardsoni* (**Say** 1831)
(Alt. Boreal/Tengmalm's Owl)
Richardson's Skua *Stercorarius parasiticus* (Linnaeus 1758)
(Alt. Parasitic/Arctic Skua [Jaeger])
Richardson's Warbler *Basileuterus luteoviridis richardsoni* (Chapman 1912)
(Alt. Citrine Warbler)

Sir John Richardson (1787–1865) was a Scottish naval surgeon and arctic explorer, knighted in 1846, who assisted **Swainson**. He was a friend of Sir John **Franklin**, to whom he was also related by marriage, and he took part in Franklin's expeditions of 1819 to 1822 and 1825 to 1827. He also participated from 1847 in the vain search for Franklin and his colleagues; their fate was not discovered until Rae's expedition of 1853–1854. The Richardson Mts in Canada are also named after him.

RICKETT

Rickett's Parrotbill *Paradoxornis (brunneus) ricketti* (**Rothschild** 1922)
    (Alt. Brown-winged/Yunnan Parrotbill)
Rickett's Hill Partridge *Arborophila gingica* (**Ogilvie-Grant** 1899)
    (Alt. White-necklaced Partridge)
Rickett's Willow Warbler *Phylloscopus ricketti* (**Slater** 1897)
    (Alt. Sulphur-breasted Warbler)

Charles Boughey Rickett (1851–1943) was a British banker and an amateur ornithologist. He left records of his observations in Scotland and Cornwall, from 1901 through to 1907. He later collected in China and various other parts of Asia including Japan, the Straits Settlements (now in Malaysia), Java and India. Throughout his 33-year career in Asia he worked for the same bank, the Hong Kong & Shanghai Banking Corporation.

RICORD

Ricords' Hummingbird *Sporadinus ricordii* (**Lawrence** 1877)
    (Alt. Brace's Emerald *Chlorostilbon bracei* [*ricordii*])

Alexandre Ricord (1798–1876) was a French naval surgeon who qualified as a physician in Paris, in 1824, and became a Corresponding Member of the French Academy of Medicine, in 1838. He collected in Latin America between 1826 and 1834.

RIDGEN

Ridgen's Penguin *Aptenodytes ridgeni* (Simpson 1972) [Extinct]

Ian Ridgen (1957–) collected the type specimen of the fossil penguin which is named after him near Montunau Beach, North Canterbury, New Zealand. Like Peter **Tyree** he was 11 years old at the time! We assume that Ridgen and Tyree may well have been school friends. George Gaylord Simpson (1902–1984) described the bird 1972. His paper states: '*At Christmas 1967, Peter Tyree, then aged 11, found another unusually complete fossil penguin skeleton at Motunau Beach. In July of the following year Alan Ridgen, then also 11 found still another specimen at a nearby locality, less complete than the first two but including a number of well-preserved associated bones from one individual. These young men appreciated the exceptional scientific value of their finds and therefore submitted them for technical study and presented them for permanent preservation to the Canterbury Museum, Christchurch, which is also the repository of the first Motunau specimen.*' (Records of the Canterbury Museum 9:159–160).

RIDGWAY

Ridgway's Cotinga *Cotinga ridgwayi* (Ridgway 1887)
    (Alt. Turquoise Cotinga)
Ridgway's Hawk *Buteo ridgwayi* (**Cory** 1883)
    (Alt. Hispaniolan Hawk)
Ridgway's Junco *Junco hyemalis aikeni* (Ridgway 1873)
    (Alt. Dark-eyed/White-winged Junco)
Ridgway's Nightjar *Caprimulgus ridgwayi* (**Nelson** 1897)
    (Alt. Buff-collared Nightjar, Ridgway's Whip-poor-will)
Ridgway's Pygmy Owl *Glaucidium brasilianum ridgwayi* (**Sharpe** 1875)
    (Alt. Ferruginous Pygmy Owl)
Ridgway's Rough-winged Swallow *Stelgidopteryx ruficollis ridgwayi* (Nelson 1901)
    (Alt. Southern Rough-winged Swallow)
Ridgway's Titmouse *Parus inornatus ridgwayi* (Richmond 1902)
    (Alt. Plain Titmouse)

Robert Ridgway (1850–1929) was a professional zoologist and curator. At the remarkably young age of 17 he was appointed zoologist on a geological survey of the 40th parallel. He was the Curator of Birds at the United States National Museum, the Smithsonian Institution, in Washington D.C., between 1880 and 1929. He also became the Founder President of American Ornithologists' Union. Ridgway co-wrote *A History of North American Birds* with **Baird** and **Brewer** in 1901, and *The Birds of Middle and North America*, with Herbert **Friedmann** in 11 volumes, from 1901 to 1950. He was also a fine illustrator and is famed for having sketched and collected birds around his home in Richland county, Illinois. Because he encountered an almost infinite number of colours and needed accuracy for a scientific description he realised that this would only be possible through some form of standardisation. He therefore proposed a colour system, which was published in 1912 under the title Colour Standards and Nomenclature. Ridgway's system exploits the possibilities of additive colour mixing. The basis for the required systematic order of colours is a circle subdivided into 36 pure, solid colours (full colours) which are numbered 1–71. Ridgway's method (through a series of other steps) gives 1,115 colour standards intended for use in the identification of the colours of birds. He developed an 18-acre area near his home as a bird sanctuary which he called Bird Haven. He also established an experimental plot for the cultivation of trees and plants native to his area and it remains as a memorial.

RIEDEL

Riedel's Parrot *Eclectus roratus riedeli* (A B **Meyer** 1882)
(Alt. Eclectus Parrot)

Johan Gerard Friederich Riedel (1832–1911) was a Dutch administrator in the colonial Dutch East Indies (now mainly Indonesia) between 1853 and 1883. He was also an amateur naturalist who collected in Timor. The Australian website 'Birds down under' relates *'This interesting bird was sent first from Timor Laut by Mr Riedel, recently Dutch resident at Amboina, to Dr Meyer at Dresden, by whom it was named after the discoverer. Like all the green and red parrots, the usual differences of the sexes are observed, the male being green and the female red'*.

RIEFFER

Rieffer's Hummingbird *Amazilia tzacatl* (de la Llave 1833)
(Alt. Rufous-tailed Hummingbird)
Rieffer's Tanager *Chlorornis riefferii* (A Boissonneau 1840)
(Alt. Grass-green Tanager)

All we know is that Rieffer was a collector in South America in the 1830s and 1840s, and the attribution for the hummingbird merely states that he was an otherwise unknown collector of this name. He is also commemorated in the binomial of a cotinga; the Green-and-black Fruiteater *Pipreola riefferii*, which was also described by Boissonneau in 1840, together with the tanager. Both birds are native to Ecuador and Colombia. The Mexican naturalist and politician Pablo de la Llave described the hummingbird.

RIPLEY

Ripley's Fruit Dove *Ptilinopus arcanus* (Ripley & **Rabor** 1955)
(Alt. Negros Fruit Dove)

S Dillon Ripley (1913–2001) was was an eminent American ornithologist who was awarded the Presidential Medal of Freedom, the highest civilian honour of the United States. He was privately educated and travelled widely in both Europe and India. He graduated in history at Yale but then studied zoology at Columbia University, where he specialised in ornithology. Aged only 23 he joined an expedition to New Guinea, where he spent 18 months collecting bird specimens. Birds were his first love; at 17, he built a pond to attract waterfowl. His service during the Second World War was with the Office of Strategic Services, coordinating United States and British intelligence efforts in Southeast Asia. After the war he taught at Yale, and was then Director of the Peabody Museum of Natural History, until he was asked to go to the Smithsonian, where he was Secretary from 1964 until 1984. On his retirement he was reported to have said: '*I shall enjoy my freedom from the tyranny of the In and Out boxes*'. He travelled '*around the world from Patagonia to Pakistan*'. Ripley was instrumental in the founding of the Charles **Darwin** Foundation for the Galápagos Islands in 1959. He is also widely recognised as one of the giants of Indian ornithology. Among his many publications, he wrote *Handbook of the Birds of India* (with the late Salim Ali) and *Rails of the World*. He described the fruit dove with his friend **Rabor**.

RIPPON

Rippon's Silver Pheasant *Lophura nycthemera ripponi* (**Sharpe** 1902)
(Alt. Jones's Silver Pheasant)

Lieutenant-Colonel G C Rippon (1861–1927) served in the British army in Burma (now Myanmar) and India between 1880 and 1914. There is a Rippon who was an entomologist in the 1890s, and who described a number of Far Eastern birdwing butterflies, e.g. *Troides dohertyi,* and is perhaps the same person. The butterfly genus *Ripponia* is named after him.

RIVOLI

Rivoli's Hummingbird *Eugenes fulgens* (**Swainson** 1827)
(Alt. Magnificent Hummingbird)

François Victor Masséna Prince d'Essling, Duc de Rivoli (1798–1863), was the son of one of Napoleon's marshals and an amateur ornithologist. He amassed a huge collection of hummingbirds. This species was named after him by **Lesson**. His wife **Anna** is commemorated in the eponymous hummingbird; they may be the only husband and wife to have birds of the same family named after them.

ROBERT

Robert's Hummingbird *Phaeochroa (cuvierii) roberti* (**Salvin** 1861)
(Alt. Scaly-breasted Hummingbird)

Alphonse Robert was a French collector in Latin America, particularly Brazil. This northeast Middle American race of the Scaly-breasted Hummingbird has at times been treated as a species.

ROBERTS

Robert's Parakeet *Bolborhynchus aurifrons robertsi* (**Carriker** 1933)
(Alt. Mountain Parakeet)
Roberts' Prinia *Prinia robertsi* (Benson 1946)
(Alt. Forest Prinia, Briar Warbler)

J Austin Roberts (1883–1948) was a South African zoologist. He was born in Pretoria, South Africa, in 1883 and died in a traffic accident in 1948. During the first half of the 20th century he was the most prominent ornithologist in southern Africa. He worked at the Transvaal Museum for 38 years studying birds. Although he did not have formal academic training, he received several high academic awards and an honorary doctorate. Roberts is best remembered for his *Birds of South Africa*, a landmark publication in African ornithology, which first appeared in 1940, and was a best seller in its numerous subsequent editions. **Benson** named the prinia after him.

ROBINSON

Robinson's Buttonquail *Turnix oliveii* (Robinson 1900)
(Alt. Buff-breasted/Buff-backed Buttonquail, Olive's Quail)
Robinson's Whistling Thrush *Myophonus robinsoni* (**Ogilvie-Grant** 1905)
(Alt. Malaysian Whistling Thrush)

Herbert Christopher Robinson (1874–1929) was a British zoologist and ornithologist. In 1894, after education at Marlborough College, he went to Switzerland because of ill health. In 1896 he made a trip to Queensland and when he returned to England he worked as assistant to Dr H O **Forbes** at the Liverpool Museum, from 1897 until 1900. After 1900 he spent 30 years in the tropics, initially with Dr Annandale in the Malay Peninsula. In 1903 he became Curator of the Federated Malay States Museum, at Selangor, and held that post until 1926. In 1908 he joined Cecil Boden Kloss in exploring the Indo-Malay region. He sent many of the specimens which he collected to Liverpool and to the British Natural History Museum. He wrote *The Birds of Singapore* and *The Birds of the Malay Peninsular*, in 1927, and many articles, which were mostly published in the Journal of the Federated Malay States Museum. In addition to the quail and thrush he was honoured in the scientific names of another six birds; a bulbul *Pycnonotus robinsoni*, woodpecker *Gecinulus viridis robinsoni*, the green magpie *Cissa chinensis robinsoni*, *Gecinus robinsoni*, *Sphenocercus robinsoni* and a swiftlet *Collocalia lowi robinsoni*. Not all of these names are in current use. Robinson is also honoured in the names of ten mammals including goats and rats, two amphibians, *Kalophrynus robinsoni* and *Rhacophorus robinsoni*, and two reptiles, *Gonocephalus robinsoni* and *Tropido robinsoni*.

ROBOROVSKI

Roborovski's Rosefinch *Koslowi roborowskii* (**Prjevalsky** 1887)

Captain Vladimir I Roborovski (1856–1910) was a Russian explorer of parts of China and Tibet. He accompanied **Prjevalsky** on his third and fourth expeditions. He wrote *Ekspeditisii v storonu ot pugey Tibetskoy ekspeditsii*, in 1896, and *Otchet nachalnika ekspeditskii*, in 1900. He also had a Dwarf Hamster *Phodopus roborovskii* named after him.

ROCK

Rock's Blood Pheasant *Ithaginis cruentus rocki* (**Riley** 1925)
(Alt. Greenway's Blood Pheasant)

Dr Joseph Francis Charles Rock (1884–1962) was a naturalised American who originally came from Austria. He started off as a self-taught botanist in Hawaii and from 1920 to 1949 collected plant specimens for a number of American institutions including Harvard University, the National Geographic Society and the United States National Museum. He was also an anthropologist and ornithologist and spent 27 years living in Yunnan province, in the Tibetan area of China. He became the leading authority on the Naxi people, who live in that area. Bangs and Peters published *Birds collected by Doctor Joseph F. Rock in Western Kansu & Eastern Tibet* in 1928 and J H Riley in 1931 published *A Second Collection of Birds from the Provinces of Yunnan and Szechwan, China, Made for the National Geographic Society*. Rock led the National Geographic Society's Expedition to Yunan-Sichuan (1927 to 1930). He was the author of a number of books and articles including *Seeking the Mountains of Mystery*, *Life among the Lamas of Choni* and *Through the Great River Trenches of Asia*. In his career in China he collected 60,000 plant specimens and 1,600 bird specimens, which were sent to American ornithologists. The blood pheasant occurs in northwest Yunnan, China, where Rock lived.

ROCKEFELLER

Rockefeller's Sunbird *Nectarinia rockefelleri* (**Chapin** 1932)

John Sterling Rockefeller (1904–1944) was an American who collected in the Congo between 1928 and 1929, and also sponsored other collecting expeditions. He was an enthusiastic conservationist; for example, he purchased Kent Island in Maine, USA, in 1930 and made it a bird sanctuary. Earlier, Allan Moses, who accompanied Rockefeller on the African expedition had described the problems in the Grand Manan Archipelago, which led to his decision to purchase this island.

RODGERS

Rodgers' Fulmar *Fulmarus glacialis rodgersii* (**Cassin** 1862)
(Alt. Northern Fulmar)

Commander (later Rear-Admiral) John Rodgers (1812–1882) of the United States navy led various expeditions to Kamchatka between 1853 and 1856, and elsewhere. We presume that the fulmar was named after him, as this race is confined to that area and **Cassin** wrote the first description in 1862, which chronology also supports our assumption.

RODRIGUES

Rodrigues Starling *Necrospar rodericianus* (Slater 1879) [Extinct]
(Alt. Leguat's/Rodriguez's Starling)

This bird is named after the island of Rodrigues, rather than directly after the Portuguese navigator, Diego Rodrigues, who discovered the island in 1528.

RODRIGUEZ

See **Rodrigues**.

ROEHL

Roehl's Thrush *Turdus olivaceus roehli* (**Reichenow** 1905)
(Alt. Olive Thrush)
Roehl's Swamp Warbler *Bradypterus lopeszi usambarae* (Reichenow 1917)
(Alt. Evergreen-forest Warbler)

Possibly named after Karl Roehl (1870–1951), who was a missionary at Usambara in Tanganyika Territory (now Tanzania), from 1896 until 1908 and in Rwanda, from 1908 until 1916, when he was taken prisoner. He returned to Tanganyika from 1926 until at least 1934. He is most famous for having translated the Bible into Swahili. This effort was recognised by the award of the Leibniz Citizens Medal, of the Berlin Academy of Sciences, and by an honorary doctorate from the philosophical faculty of the University of Hamburg. He wrote *Versuch einer systematischen Grammatik der Schambala-Sprache,* in 1911, *Ostafrikas Heldenkampf,* in 1918, and *The Linguistic Stuation in East Africa,* in 1930. He is also commemorated in the trinomials of a race of the African Black Swift *Apus barbatus roehli* and of Shelley's Greenbul *Andropadus masukuensis roehli.* **Reichenow** described the swift, which was collected at Usambara, in 1906. Both the thrush and warbler are natives of the Usambaras.

ROGERS

Rogers' Fairy-wren *Malurus lamberti rogersi* Matthews 1912
(Alt. Variegated Fairy-wren)

The Reverend H M C Rogers (1879–1926) was a missionary to Tristan da Cunha in 1922.

ROLLAND

Rolland's Grebe *Rollandia rolland* (Quoy & **Gaimard** 1824)
(Alt. White-tufted Grebe)

Rolland was a master gunner in the French Navy. He was on board the corvette *Uranie* under the command of Louis Freycinet, whose account of the voyage was later published, during her circumnavigation of the globe between 1817 and 1820. The vessel suffered severe weather damage when rounding Cape Horn and had to be beached in the Falkland Islands, at what is now called Uranie Bay, where the nominate race of this species is found. The vessel was abandoned as a shipwreck but the expedition's notes and collections were saved. Quoy and **Gaimard**, who described the bird, were also both on board the *Uranie*.

ROSENBERG, C

Rosenberg's Myzomela *Myzomela rosenbergii* (**Schlegel** 1871)
(Alt. Red-collared Myzomela)
Rosenberg's Owl *Tyto rosenbergi* (**Hartert** 1895)
(Alt. Sulawesi/Celebes [Masked] Owl)
Rosenberg's Rail *Gymnocrex rosenbergi* (Schlegel 1866)
(Alt. Bald/Blue/Bare-faced Rail)
Rosenberg's Woodcock *Scolopax saturata rosenbergi* (Schlegel 1871)
(Alt. Dusky Woodcock)

Baron Carl Benjamin Hermann von Rosenberg (1817–1888) was a German naturalist and geographer who collected in the East Indies. He served in the Dutch colonial army in the Malay archipelago for 30 years, the first 16 as topographic draughtsman on the island of Sumatra and then as a civil servant in the Moluccas and around New Guinea. He took part in mapping the outlying districts of the Indonesian archipelago and all the while he pursued his interest in ornithology, including publishing a series of articles in the journals. He published *Reistochten naar de Geelvinkbaai op Nieuw-Guinea in de jaren 1869 en 1870,* which is an important zoological and ethnographical study on New Guinea and west Irian Jaya. The subspecies of the woodcock may be elevated to a species.

ROSENBERG, W

Rosenberg's Lorikeet *Trichoglossus haematodus rosenbergii* (**Schlegel** 1873)
(Alt. Rainbow Lorikeet/Lory)

W F H Rosenberg was a British dealer in natural history specimens who collected in Latin America around 1898. Boulenger wrote *An account of the reptiles and batrachians collected by Mr. W F H Rosenberg in western Ecuador,* in the Proceedings of the Zoological Society of London, in 1898. He seems to have supplied specimens to museums all over Europe. The lorikeet subspecies occurs on the island of Biak, Indonesia.

ROSITA

Rosita's Bunting *Passerina rositae* (**Lawrence** 1874)
(Alt. Rose-bellied Bunting)

Rosita Sumichrast was the wife of the Mexican naturalist Francis E **Sumichrast** (1828–1882).

ROSS

Ross's Goose *Anser rossii* (**Cassin** 1861)

Bernard Rogan Ross (1827–1874) was an Irish trader and administrator who was employed as a chief factor in the Hudson's Bay Company. He may have obtained his position largely as a result of marrying his boss's daughter, but nonetheless, he apparently proved to be a very able administrator. The goose was named after Ross by **Cassin** with **Kennicott**'s encouragement, in appreciation for the cooperation which Ross showed Kennicott in arranging transportation of the latter's specimens to the Smithsonian Institution. Ross was himself an associate of the Smithsonian.

ROSS

Ross's Gull *Rhodostethia rosea* (**MacGillivray** 1824)

Rear-Admiral Sir James Clark Ross (1802–1862) discovered the Ross Sea and the Ross Ice Shelf. He discovered an island in January 1841 which Scott, on his first expedition, named Ross Island in his honour. Ross joined the Royal Navy at the age of 12. He was also a member of several important expeditions to the Arctic. He commanded *Erebus* and *Terror* during the Antarctic expedition of 1839–1843. It was while close to the Magnetic South Pole that he broke through a wide expanse of pack ice and into a large and clear sea that later bore his name.

ROTHSCHILD

Rothschild's Amazon *Amazona barbadensis rothschildi* (**Hartert** 1892)
   (Alt. Yellow-shouldered Amazon/Parrot)
Rothschild's Astrapia *Astrapia rothschildi* (**Foerster** 1906)
   (Alt. Huon Bird-of-Paradise/Astrapia)
Rothschild's Canary *Serinus rothschildi* (**Ogilvie-Grant** 1902)
   (Alt. Arabian Serin)
Rothschild's Fairy Lorikeet *Charmosyna pulchella rothschildi* (Hartert 1930)
   (Alt. Fairy Lorikeet)
Rothschild's Fody *Foudia omissa* (Rothschild 1912)
   (Alt. [Red] Forest Fody)
Rothschild's Myna *Leucopsar rothschildi* (**Stresemann** 1912)
   (Alt. Bali Starling, Rothschild's Grackle)
Rothschild's Parakeet *Psittacula intermedia* (Rothschild 1895)
   (Alt. Intermediate Parakeet)
Rothschild's Peacock-Pheasant *Polyplectron inopinatum* (Rothschild 1903)
   (Alt. Mountain Peacock-Pheasant)
Rothschild's Pheasant *Phasianus colchicus rothschildi* (**La Touche** 1922)
   (Alt. Ring-necked Pheasant)
Rothschild's Red Lory *Eos bornea rothschildi* (Stresemann 1912)
   (Alt. [Bernstein's] Red Lory)
Rothschild's Seedcracker *Pyrenestes ostrinus rothschildi*
Rothschild's Swift *Cypseloides rothschildi* (**Zimmer** 1945)
   (Alt. Giant Swift)

Lord Lionel Walter Rothschild (1868–1937) was the Founder of the Tring Museum. It is now known as *The Walter Rothschild Zoological Museum* and comprises the Natural History Museum's ornithology section. According to the history of the museum: '*As a child Walter Rothschild knew exactly what he was going to do when he grew up, announcing at the age of seven, 'Mama, Papa, I am going to make a museum....'. He had already started collecting insects and stuffed animals by then, and a year later started setting his own collection of butterflies. By the time he was 10, Walter had enough natural history objects to start his first museum – in a garden shed! Before long Walter's insect and bird collections were so large that they had to be stored in rented rooms and sheds around Tring. Then in 1889, when Walter Rothschild was 21, his father gave him some land on the outskirts of Tring Park. Two small cottages were built, one to house his books and insect collection, the other for a*

caretaker. Behind these was a much larger building, which would contain Lord Rothschild's collection of mounted specimens. This was the beginning of the zoological museum which opened to the public in 1892 and the beginning of Lord Rothschild's life long passion for natural history.' He amassed the largest bird collection in the world; 300,000 bird skins, 200,000 birds eggs and 30,000 books. Ernst **Hartert,** who described and named the lorikeet, was one of his curators. The museum still houses hand-coloured lithographs of some of the original paintings by John **Gould** and Edward **Lear.** Rothschild lived in Tring and was Member of Parliament for Aylesbury, a major in the Buckinghamshire Yeomanry, a Justice of the Peace and a Deputy Lieutenant for the County of Buckinghamshire. Rothschild's own pictures of extinct birds have been used in posters.

ROUGET

Rouget's Rail *Rougetius rougetii* (**Guerin-Meneville** 1843)

J Rouget (?–1840) was a French explorer who collected in Ethiopia between 1839 and 1840.

ROWLEY

Rowley's Flycatcher *Eutrichomyias rowleyi* (**A B Meyer** 1878)
(Alt. Cerulean Paradise-flycatcher/Flycatcher)

George Dawson Rowley (1822–1878) was an English amateur ornithologist. He wrote *Ornithological Miscellany* in 1875. He was also a skilled artist at both drawing and painting and his pictures of extinct birds have been used in posters. The Flycatcher was discovered in 1874 but was feared to be extinct until it was rediscovered in 1998, on its native island of Sangihe, Indonesia.

RTAS

In the United Kingdom, at least, RTA is police-speak for a Road Traffic Accident. Here we are liberally interpreting the term to include calamities affecting all forms of motorised transport, as a number of our personalities met their ends in a diversity of such accidents. Maria **Koepcke**, Ted **Parker** and Charles Francis Massy **Swynnerton** all died in plane crashes. Little is known about the latter, but Maria Koepcke, 'The Mother of Peruvian Ornithology' was killed in an air crash in Amazonia on Christmas Eve 1971, a crash which will shortly be covered in a feature film about one of the other passengers. Louis Agassiz **Fuertes**, Alice (Rich) **Northrop** and J Austin **Roberts** were all killed in road accidents, although since Alice Northrop was killed when her car stalled on a level crossing and was hit by a train it is hard to say whether hers was a road or rail accident. The case of Hugh Edwin **Strickland** is unambiguous as there were no motorised road vehicles at the time; he was killed when a passenger train struck him as he was making a pencil sketch of the strata in a railway cutting, in pursuit of his geological interests.

RUCKER

Rucker's Hermit *Threnetes ruckeri* (**Bourcier** 1847)
(Alt. Band-tailed Barbthroat, Rucker's/Blue Fan-tailed Barbthroat)

S Rucker (1815–1890) was a British naturalist who collected in Ecuador in 1846. A number of plants, including orchids, have *ruckeri* in their scientific names.

RÜCK

Rück's Blue Flycatcher *Cyornis rueckii* (**Oustalet** 1881)
(Alt. Rück's Niltava, Rueck's Blue Flycatcher)

M Rück was a French traveller who collected in Malaya (now Malaysia).

RUDD

Rudd's Apalis *Apalis ruddi* (**Grant** 1908)
Rudd's [Long-clawed] Lark *Mirafra ruddi* (Grant 1908)

Charles Dunnel Rudd (1844–1916) was an associate of Cecil Rhodes and attended to their mining business while Rhodes got himself into politics, obtained the concession, in 1883, to go into Mashonaland to establish mining, and founded Rhodesia. He collected in southeast Africa between 1860 and his death. Rudd financed Captain C H B **Grant** who described and perhaps found both the apalis and the lark.

RÜPPELL

Rüppell's Bustard *Eupodotis rueppellii* (**Wahlberg** 1856)
  (Alt. Rüppell's Korhaan)
Rüppell's Griffon Vulture *Gyps rueppellii* (A E **Brehm** 1852)
  (Alt. Rüppell's Vulture/Griffon)
Rüppell's Long-tailed Glossy Starling *Lamprotornis purpuropterus* (J & E **Verreaux** 1851)
Rüppell's Parrot *Poicephalus rueppellii* (G R **Gray** 1848)
Rüppell's [Black] Robin-Chat *Cossypha semirufa* (Rüppell 1837)
  (Alt. Black-tailed Robin-Chat)
Rüppell's Shrike *Eurocephalus rueppelli* (**Bonaparte** 1853)
  (Alt. White-rumped Shrike)
Rüppell's Warbler *Sylvia rueppellii* (**Temminck** 1820)
Rüppell's Weaver *Ploceus galbula* (Rüppell 1837)

Wilhelm Peter Eduard Simon Rüppell (1794–1884) was a German collector. He made two extended expeditions to northern and eastern Africa in the first quarter of the 19th century, the first from 1822 until 1827, and the second between 1830 and 1833. **Abdim** Bey helped him in Egypt. Although he brought back large zoological and ethnographical collections, his expeditions impoverished him. **Kittlitz** accompanied him on his second expedition. Rüppell wrote *Reisen in Nubien, Kordofan und dem Petraischen Arabien*, in 1929, and *Systematische Übersicht der Vogel Nordost-Afrikas*, in 1845. He was also a collector in the broadest sense of the word and presented his collection of coins and rare manuscripts to the Historical Museum in Frankfurt, his home town.

RUSPOLI

Ruspoli's Turaco *Tauraco ruspolii* (Salvadori 1896)
  (Alt. Prince Ruspoli's Turaco)

See **Prince Ruspoli**.

RUSSIANS

At least a dozen Russians have the common names of birds named after them and there may be more. Alexander Eduard Friedrich **Eversmann**, was a Professor of Zoology who travelled in remote areas of the Russian Empire; he described several birds, and others were named after him by admirers. General Pyotr Kuzmich **Kozlov** was an explorer in Central Asia and had a bird of that area named after him because of his fame. Count Otto Von **Kotzebue** travelled widely too and the bird named after him *may* have been collected on one of his voyages. Mikhail Aleksandrovich **Menzbier** was a zoologist who described species across Russia, the Far East and northern China. He was one of the founder members of Russia's first ornithological society and has a number of such societies named after him as well as birds. Theodor Dimitrievich **Pleske** was also a Russian zoologist, but he seems to have been museum-based. Alexandre **Prigogine** was a Russian-born Belgian naturalist and a professional ornithologist, whose brother Ilya won the Nobel Prize for Chemistry. Perhaps the most famous was General Nikolai Mikhailovitch **Prjevalsky**, who made five major expeditions to the Russian Far East and Mongolia during which he discovered many new animals including a horse, a gerbil and several birds. Captain Vladimir **Roborovski** was also an explorer, who had a hamster named after him as well as a bird, as was Nikolai Alekseevich **Severzov**. We know of no ornithological or zoological acumen ascribed to Princess Maximiliane Wilhelmine Auguste **Sophie** Marie (1824–1880), the wife of Tsar Alexander II. L S **Stepanyan** was a Russian ornithologist, taxonomist and member of the Severtzov Institute of Ecology and Evolution of the Russian Academy of Sciences. V P **Sukatschev** was a Russian trader and explorer who collected specimens in China.

RUWET

Ruwet's Masked Weaver *Ploceus ruweti* (Louette & **Benson** 1982)
    (Alt. Lake Lufira Masked Weaver)

Professor J C Ruwet is a Belgian zoologist. He has published extensively, mostly in the Belgian Journal of Zoology. He has worked on the Black Grouse *Tetrao tetrix* and presented a paper in 2000 entitled *Compared modelling of the climate's influence on the dynamics of six European Black Grouse populations*, with M Loneux and J K Lindsey. Louette and **Benson** described the weaver as *Ploceus reichardi ruweti*.

SABINE, E

Sabine's Gull *Xema sabini* (J **Sabine** 1819)
Sabine's Puffback *Dryoscopus sabini* (J E **Gray** 1831)
    (Alt. Large-billed Puffback)
Sabine's Snipe *Scolopax sabini* (J Sabine 1818)

General Sir Edward Sabine (1788–1883) combined a successful military career with notable achievements in physics and astronomy, as well as being an explorer. He was elected a Fellow of the Royal Society in 1818 and was the Royal Society's Treasurer from 1850 until 1861, and its President between 1862 and 1871. The gull was discovered by Edward's brother Joseph, who named it after his famous sibling, on the expedition in search of the Northwest Passage led by John Ross in 1818. (John Ross was the uncle of **James Clark Ross** of Ross's Gull fame). Sir Edward was the expedition's astronomer and

geologist but as a keen ornithologist he was also expected to write up the expedition's zoological findings. Ross and Edward quarrelled, however, and the task fell to the ship's surgeon and assistant surgeon. It was then edited and corrected by William **Leach**. Following the dispute Joseph Sabine was quick to publish *A Memoir of the birds of Greenland* in the Transactions of the Linnean Society in 1819 before the official report could appear and also wrote the official description of the Gull himself. J E **Gray** described the puffback; presumably a specimen was sent to the museum he worked in and he decided to honour the Royal Society luminary. The snipe has been found to be a melanisitc form of Common Snipe *Gallinago gallinago*.

SABINE, J

> Sabine's Spinetail *Rhaphidura sabini* (J E **Gray** 1829)
> (Alt. Sabine's Spine-tailed Swift)

Joseph Sabine (1770–1837) was the English zoologist whose younger brother was Sir **Edward Sabine** (see above for details of Joseph Sabine's explorations with his brother). He was also a co-founder of the Linnean Society and was the first Secretary of the Royal Horticultural Society, which was founded in 1803.

SALLÉ

> Sallé's Hermit *Phaethornis augusti* (**Bourcier** 1847)
> (Alt. Sooty-capped Hermit)
> Sallé's Quail *Cyrtonyx montezumae sallaei* (**Verreaux** 1859)
> (Alt. Montezuma's Quail)

Auguste Sallé (1820–1896) was a French taxonomist and entomologist who collected in tropical America between 1846 and 1856. Many insects, shellfish and other animals have *sallaei* included in their binomial. **Sclater** used *sallaei* in the binomial for birds collected by him, such as the Grey-throated Chat *Granatellus sallaei*.

SALMON

> Salmon's Jacamar *Brachygalba salmoni* (**P L Sclater** & **Salvin** 1879)
> (Alt. Dusky-backed Jacamar)
> Salmon's Tiger Heron *Tigrisoma fasciatum salmoni* (P L Sclater & Salvin 1875)
> (Alt. Fasciated Tiger Heron)

Colonel Thomas K Salmon (1841–1878) was a Colombian engineer who worked for the state between 1870 and 1877, during which time he collected as part of his hobby of natural history. He also wrote vividly about his experiences, for example; '*I once went to see the breeding place of the Cock-of-the-Rock and a darker or wilder place I have never been in. Following up a mountain stream the gorge became gradually more enclosed and more rocky, till I arrived at the mouth of a cave with high rock on each side, and overshadowed by high trees, into which the sun never penetrated. All was wet and dark, and the only sound heard was the rushing of the water over the rocks. We had hardly become accustomed to the gloom when a nest was found, a dark bird stealing away from what seemed to be a lump of mud upon the face of the rock. This was a nest of the Cock-of-the-Rock, containing two eggs; it was built upon a projecting piece, the body being made of mud or clay, then a few sticks, and on the top lined with green moss. It was about five feet from the water. I did not see the male bird, and, indeed, I have rarely ever seen the male and female birds together, though I have seen both sexes in separate flocks.*'

SALOMONSEN

Salomonsen's Blue-naped Parrot *Tanygnathus lucionensis hybridus*
(Salomonsen 1952)
Salomonsen's Racket-tailed Parrot *Prioniturus discurus whiteheadi*
(Salomonsen 1953)
(Alt. Blue-crowned Racquet-tail)

Finn Salomonsen (1909–1983) was a Danish ornithologist and artist. He led a natural history expedition to northwest Greenland in 1936 and assembled much of the ornithology collection of the Zoological Museum at the University of Copenhagen, which covers Denmark and the North Atlantic Dependencies. In 1952 he co-wrote and illustrated *Birds of Greenland*. He also wrote *Øversigt øver Danmarks fugle*, in 1963.

SALVADORI

Salvadori's Antwren *Myrmotherula minor* (Salvadori 1867)
Salvadori's Blue-winged Parrotlet *Forpus xanthopterygius flavescens*
(Salvadori 1891)
Salvadori's Crimsonwing *Cryptospiza salvadorii* (**Reichenow** 1892)
(Alt. Ethiopian/Abyssinian Crimsonwing, Crimson-backed Forest Finch)
Salvadori's Duck *Salvadorina waigiuensis* (**Rothschild** & **Hartert** 1894)
(Alt. Salvadori's Teal)
Salvadori's Eremomela *Eremomela salvadorii* (Reichenow 1891)
Salvadori's Fig Parrot *Psittaculirostris salvadorii* (**Oustalet** 1880)
Salvadori's Green-winged King Parrot *Alisterus chloropterus callopterus*
(Salvadori & **D'Albertis** 1879)
(Alt. Papuan King Parrot)
Salvadori's Nightjar *Caprimulgus pulchellus* (Salvadori 1879)
Salvadori's Orange-breasted Fig Parrot *Cyclopsitta gulielmitertii fuscifrons*
(Salvadori 1876)
Salvadori's Pheasant *Lophura inornata* (Salvadori 1879)
Salvadori's Seedeater *Serinus xantholaema* (Salvadori 1896)
(Alt. Salvadori's Serin)
Salvadori's Weaver *Ploceus dicrocephalus* (Salvadori 1896)
(Alt. Somali Yellow-backed/Jubaland/Juba Weaver)

Conte Adelardo Tommaso Paleotti Salvadori (1835–1923) was an eminent Italian physician, author, educator and ornithologist. He was Vice-Director of the Museum of Zoology at the University of Turin, from 1879 until 1923. He was also medical officer in Garibaldi's battalion during his second 'expedition' in Sicily. His collection was donated to the Natural Science Museum of Villa Vitali. He wrote *Catalogo Sistimatico Degli Uccelli di Borneo*, in 1874, and *Ornitologia della Papuasia e delle Molucche*, in 1880.

SALVIN

Salvin's Albatross *Diomedea cauta salvini* (**Rothschild** 1893)
(Alt. Shy Albatross, Salvin's Mollyawk)
Salvin's Amazon *Amazona autumnalis salvini* (Salvin 1891)
(Alt. Red-lored Parrot/Amazon)
Salvin's Antbird *Myrmeciza laemosticta* (Salvin 1865)
(Alt. Dull-mantled Antbird)
Salvin's Ant Tanager *Habia fuscicauda salvini* (**Berlepsch** 1883)
(Alt. Red-throated Ant Tanager)

Salvin's Chuckwill *Caprimulgus salvini* (**Hartert** 1892)
    (Alt. Tawny-collared Nightjar)
Salvin's [Razor-billed] Curassow *Mitu salvini* (**Reinhardt** 1879)
Salvin's Emerald *Chlorostilbon salvini* (**Cabanis** & **Heine** 1860)
    (Alt. Fork-tailed/Canivet's/Golden-crowned/Cozumel Emerald)
Salvin's Negrito *Manacus aurantiacus* (Salvin 1870)
    (Alt. Salvin's/Orange-collared Manakin)
Salvin's Petrel *Pterodroma hypoleuca* (Salvin 1888)
    (Alt. Bonin Petrel)
Salvin's Pigeon *Columba oenops* (Salvin 1895)
    (Alt. Peruvian Pigeon)
Salvin's Prion *Pachyptila* (*vittata*) *salvini* (**Mathews** 1912)
    (Alt. Medium-billed Prion)
Salvin's Rusty-faced Parrot *Hapalopsittaca pyrrhops* (Salvin 1876)
Salvin's Screech Owl *Otus ingens* (Salvin 1897)
    (Alt. Rufescent Screech Owl)
Salvin's Silky Flycatcher *Phainopepla melanoxantha* (Salvin 1877)
    (Alt. Black-and-yellow Silky Flycatcher/Phainoptila)
Salvin's Wren *Thryothorus semibadius* (Salvin 1870)
    (Alt. Riverside Wren)

Osbert Salvin (1835–1898) was an English naturalist who became a Fellow of the Royal Society. He was a life-long friend of **Godman**, whom he met when both were at Cambridge University, where Salvin studied mathematics. In 1861, he wrote that he was '*determined, rain or no rain, to be off to the mountain forests in search of quetzals, to see and shoot which has been a daydream for me ever since I set foot in Central America.*' He was the first European to record observing a Resplendent Quetzal *Pharomachrus mocinno*, pronounced it '*unequalled for splendour among the birds of the New World*', and promptly shot it. During the course of the next three decades, thousands of quetzal plumes crossed the Atlantic to fill the specimen cabinets of European collectors and adorn the fashionable milliners' shops of Paris, Amsterdam and London. Salvin redeemed himself by co-authoring with Godman the incredible 40-volume *Biologia Centrali Americana*, in 1879, which provided a near-complete catalogue of Middle American species. Earlier he had written *Exotic Ornithology*, in 1866, *Nomenclatur Avium Neotropicalium*, in 1873 and *Biologia Centrali Americana*, in 1879. Salvin and Godman combined their bird collections and over a 15-year period from 1885 presented them to the British Natural History Museum. The Godman-Salvin Medal, a prestigious award of the British Ornithologists' Union, is named after him and Frederick Godman.

SANDFORD

Sometimes used in error for **Sanford**. See below.

SANFORD

Sanford's Bowerbird *Archboldia sanfordi* (**Mayr** & Gilliard 1950)
    (Alt. Tomba Bowerbird)
Sanford's Niltava *Cyornis sanfordi* (**Stresemann** 1931)
    (Alt. Matinan Flycatcher)
Sanford's Ptarmigan *Lagopus mutus sanfordi* (**Bent** 1912)
    (Alt. Rock Ptarmigan)
Sanford's Sea Eagle *Haliaeetus sanfordi* (Mayr 1935)
    (Alt. Sandford's Eagle/Fish Eagle)

Sanford's White-eye *Woodfordia lacertosa* (**Murphy** & **Mathews** 1929)

Leyland Cutler Sanford (1868–1950) was an American zoologist. He wrote *The Waterfowl family*, in 1924, with L B Bishop and T S van Dyke. The scientific name of many species of animals as diverse as dinosaurs and butterflies include *sanfordi*, e.g. the Northern Royal Albatross *Diomedea (epomophora) sanfordi*.

SASSI

Sassi's Olive Greenbul *Phyllastrephus lorenzi* (Sassi 1914)
(Alt. Sassi's Greenbul, Lorenz's Bulbul)

Luigi Sassi was an Italian ornithologist. He is credited with the first description of the Olive Long-tailed Cuckoo *Cercococcyx olivinus*, in 1912, as well as that of the greenbul. The scientific honorific of the latter is for Ludwig Ritter Lorenz von Liburnau (1856–1943). Sassi appears to have been in Costa Rica in 1929 and 1938. He wrote an ornithological dictionary of the birds of Italy in 1921, the *Dizionario Ornitologico, con la nomenclatura Latina, Italiana, Francese, Inglese e tedesca degli Uccelli d'Italia*. He was interested in photography and took pictures using a 'stenopeica technique', which seems to be an adaptation of the camera obscura method.

SAUNDERS

Saunders's Gull *Larus saundersi* (**Swinhoe** 1871)
(Alt. Chinese Black-headed Gull)
Saunders's Little Tern *Sterna saundersi* (**Hume** 1877)
(Alt. Saunders'/Black-shafted Tern)

 Howard Saunders (1835–1907) was a British ornithologist who worked at the British Museum. He was known as the 19th century's foremost expert on gulls and terns, and wrote books entitled *Sternæ* and *An Illustrated Manual of British Birds*, in 1889. In 1896, jointly with Salvin, he published *Catalogue of the Gaviae and Tubinares in the Collection of the British Museum*, His contemporary **Swinhoe**, named the gull when Saunders was completing a study of that family. Saunders clearly applied strict standards to sight records, at a time when field identification was in its relative infancy and optical aids were much inferior to modern equipment. He rejected his own sighting of a Masked Shrike *Lanius nubicus* near Gibraltar in May 1863, writing *as I am frequently sceptical of other people's identifications…I do not want anyone to accept mine until the bird can be produced as proof*.

SAVI

Savi's Warbler *Locustella luscinioides* (Savi 1824)

Paolo Savi (1798–1871) was an Italian naturalist, zoologist, palaeontologist and geologist. He studied physics and natural science at Pisa University, becoming Professor of Natural History there, and also director of the museum. He became an Italian senator in 1862. His greatest work was *Ornitologia Italiana*, which was published posthumously between 1873 and 1876. There are several mammals, such as a bat and a shrew, named after him too.

SAVIGNY

Savigny's Eagle Owl *Bubo ascalaphus* (Savigny 1809)
(Alt. Desert/Pharaoh's Eagle Owl)

Marie Jules Cesar Lelorgne de Savigny (1777–1851) was a French zoologist and artist.

He started a medical education but was influenced by **Geoffroy Saint-Hilaire** and turned to zoology. From 1798 until at least 1800 he was in Egypt and undertook several expeditions, including one to Lake Manzala, where he studied the birds, sending specimens to Saint-Hilaire. He gave the Osprey its scientific name *Pandion haliaetus*, but got the spelling wrong by poorly translating from the Greek. *Haliaetus* is Greek for sea eagle but Savigny's error was to assume the 'e' was a short 'e' (an epsilon) when in fact it was a long 'e' (an eeta), as witnessed in the scientific name of the Bald Eagle *Haliaeetus leucocephalus*. Savigny's error has never been corrected; the name should be *Pandion haliaeetus*. He wrote *Description d'Egypte; ou Recueil des observations et des recherches qui ont été faites en Egypte pendant l'expédition de l'armée française*, 1798–1801, *Histoire naturelle et mythologique de l'ibis*, in 1805, and *Système des oiseaux de l'Égypte et de la Syrie*, in 1810, derived from research conducted during Napoleon's occupation of Egypt during the 1790s. He illustrated most of the birds in his works himself, although some are by **Barraband.** Savigny fell out with Saint-Hilaire, who blocked him from becoming professor at the Natural History Museum. From 1823 he became ill and he seems to have spent all his latter years in poor health.

SAVILE

Savile's Bustard *Lophotis savilei* (**Lynes** 1920)
(Alt. Lyne's Pygmy Bustard)

Lieutenant-Colonel Robert Vesey Savile (1873–1947) was a British soldier and diplomat who served in the Sudan from 1901, becoming a provincial governor from 1917 until 1923. **Lynes** described the bird as *Eupodotis savilei.*

SAWTELL

Sawtell's Swiftlet *Collocalia sawtelli* (Holyoak 1974)
(Alt. Atiu/Cook Islands Swiftlet)

Gordon Henry Sawtell (1929–) was a British-born civil servant who was educated in Britain and New Zealand. Following military service, he was a civil servant, who worked in New Zealand and the Cook Islands, before attaining the post of Secretary to the Prime Minister of the latter. He was instrumental in the swiftlet's discovery, in 1973, in Annatake-take cave. The cave is also inhabited by quantities of land crabs which despatch any nestlings that fall from their nests. Sawtell told us in August 2002 "*I use the name Kopeka on my personalised motor vehicle registration plate, Kopeka being the Polynesian name for 'my' bird*". Sawtell knew of the swiftlets and told Holyoak about them when he visited the islands in 1973. He made arrangements for him to visit all of the islands and to visit the caves. He was surprised when he found out that Holyoak had named the swiftlet after him in his type description.

SAY

Say's Phoebe *Sayornis saya* (**Bonaparte** 1825)
(Alt. Eastern Phoebe)

Thomas Say (1787–1843) was a self-taught American naturalist and zoologist whose primary interest was entomology. He described over 1,000 new species of beetles and over 400 new insects of other orders. He was the grandson of John **Bartram** and a friend of **Wilson**. He was appointed chief zoologist with Major S H Long's expeditions, and explored the Rocky Mountains with him. There he discovered several new bird species including the phoebe in 1820, as well as the Long-billed Dowitcher *Limnodromus scolopaceus* and the Blue Grouse *Dendragapus obscurus*. During the 1819–20 expedition, Say also first described the Coyote *Canis latrans*, the Swift Fox *Vulpes velox*, the Western Kingbird *Tyrannus verticalis*, the Band-tailed Pigeon *Columba fasciata*, the Rock Wren *Salpinctes* *obsoletus,* the Lesser Goldfinch *Carduelis saltria,* the Lark Sparrow *Chondestes grammacus,* the Lazuli Bunting *Passerina amoena* and the Orange-crowned Warbler *Vermivora celata.* He lived at the utopian village of 'New Harmony' until his death. Say wrote *American Entomology* in 1824, *American Entomology, or Descriptions of the Insects of North America* published between 1817 and 1828, and *American Conchology* in 1830. His friend **Bonaparte** described and named the phoebe after him.

SCARLETT

Scarlett's Duck *Malacorhynchus scarletti* (Olson 1977) [Extinct]

Ronald J Scarlett is a New Zealand archaeologist with a strong interest in birds and philately. He is the Patron of the Christchurch Philatelic Society. A recent nomination for the Meritorious Service Award of the Ornithological Society of New Zealand read *'Ron Scarlett has made a major contribution to New Zealand ornithology, maintaining single-handedly the field of palaeornithology here for 30 years. He collected and catalogued bird fossils from throughout New Zealand, and described several species, including Eyles's Harrier, Hodgens' Waterhen, and the New Zealand Owlet-nightjar. Many papers on fossil and living birds, and a book on bone identification, brought the extinct avifauna into the lives of others. The large, carefully catalogued, skeleton collection he built up in Canterbury Museum is now the basis of much research on the history of the New Zealand avifauna.'* Together with J Kear he published a paper in 1970, on The extinct Auckland Islands Merganser *Mergus australis.* In 1984, he wrote, jointly with R E Molnar, *Terrestrial bird or dinosaur phalanx from the New Zealand Cretaceous.* He also published *Bones for the New Zealand Archaeologist* in the New Zealand Journal of Zoology, in 1972. The New Zealand Archaeological Association published a monograph, *Avifaunal Composition of Skeletal Material Collected From Skua Middens and Beaches at Some Australasian Sub-Antarctic Islands* in *Birds of A Feather. Osteological and Archaeological Papers From the South Pacific in Honour of R J Scarlett.*

SCHALOW

Schalow's Turaco *Turaco schalowi* (**Reichenow** 1891)
Schalow's Wheatear *Oenanthe lugubris* (**Rüppell** 1837)
(Alt. Abyssinian Black Wheatear)

Hermann Schalow (1852–1925) was a German banker in Berlin. He was also an amateur ornithologist who worked with both **Cabanis** and **Reichenow**. He wrote *Die Muso-phagidae* in 1886 and *Beitrage zur Vogelfauna der Mark Brandenburg* in 1919. The Berlin Natural History Museum library is named the Schalow Library in his honour. In 1990 the wheatear was split from the Mourning Wheatear *Oenanthe lugens,* of which it had formerly been considered a subspecies.

SCHEEPMAKER

Scheepmaker's Crowned Pigeon *Goura scheepmakeri* (**Finsch** 1876)
(Alt. Southern Crowned Pigeon)

C Scheepmaker was a Dutch civil servant and collector in New Guinea who was active around 1875. In addition to the pigeon, two gastropods, *Azorinus scheepmakeri* and *Fasciolaria scheepmakeri,* appear to have been named after him.

SCHEFFLER

Scheffler's Owlet *Glaucidium (capense) scheffleri* (**Neumann** 1911)
(Alt. African Barred Owlet)

Georg Scheffler was a German collector in various parts of Africa, including Tanganyika (now Tanzania), in the last decade of the 19th century and the first two decades of the 20th century. A number of African shrubs and trees, such as *Isoberlinia scheffleri* and *Euphorbia scheffleri*, and the genus *Schefflerodendron* were named after him, as was Scheffler's Dwarf Gecko *Lygodactylus scheffleri*. **Neumann** first described the owlet as a separate species, but most authorities consider it to be a race of the African Barred Owlet, which was named by Sir Andrew **Smith** in 1834.

SCHINZ

Schinz's Sandpiper *Calidris alpina schinzii* (**Brehm** 1822)
(Alt. Dunlin)

Heinrich Rudolph Schinz (1777–1861) was a Swiss zoologist. In 1815 he published *Die Vögel des Schweiz* with F Meisner. He also wrote *Naturgeschichte und Abbildungen der Saugethiere* in 1824.

SCHLEGEL

Schlegel's Asity *Philepitta schlegeli* (Schlegel 1867)
Schlegel's Chat *Cercomela schlegelii* (**Wahlberg** 1855)
(Alt. Karoo/Grey-rumped Chat)
Schlegel's Francolin *Peliperdrix schlegelii* (**Heuglin** 1863)
Schlegel's Fruit Dove *Ptilinopus insolitus* (Schlegel 1863)
(Alt. Knob-billed/Orange-bellied/Red-knobbed Fruit Dove/Pigeon)
Schlegel's Myna *Streptocitta albertinae* (Schlegel 1866)
(Alt. Bare-eyed Myna, Sula Starling/Magpie)
Schlegel's Parrotlet *Forpus passerinus cyanochlorus* (Schlegel 1864)
(Alt. Green-rumped Parrotlet)
Schlegel's Petrel *Pterodroma incerta* (Schlegel 1863)
(Alt. Atlantic Petrel)
Schlegel's Twinspot *Mandingoa nitidula* (**Hartlaub** 1865)
(Alt. Green-backed/-eyed Twinspot)
Schlegel's Whistler *Pachycephala schlegelii* (Schlegel 1871)
(Alt. Regent Whistler)

Hermann Schlegel (1804–1884) was a German zoologist and the first person to use trinomials to describe separate races. In 1860 he became Director of the Rijksmuseum van Natuurlijke Historie in Leiden. He wrote both *Fauna Japonica – Aves* and *Kritische Ubersicht der Europaischen Vogel*, in 1844. The specific name of the myna is after his wife Albertina.

SCHNEIDER

Schneider's Pitta *Pitta schneideri* (**Hartert** 1909)

Gustav Schneider (1867–?) was a Swiss zoologist who collected in Sumatra in 1897. Werner published *Reptilien und Batrachier aus Sumatra gesammelt von Hern Gustav Schneider im Jahre 1897/1898*, in 1900. Schneider also commented on the distribution and diet of the Rough-necked Monitor lizard *Varanus rudicollis*.

SCHOMBURGK

Schomburgk's Parrotlet *Forpus sclateri eidos* (**Peters** 1937)
(Alt. Dusky-billed Parrotlet)

Sir Robert Hermann Schomburgk (1804–1865) was a German-born English traveller and an explorer for the Royal Geographical Society. He made a botanical and geographical exploration of British Guiana (now Guyana) in 1835. He later surveyed the colony for the British government, from 1841 until 1843. During the survey he outlined the 'Schomburgk Line', a boundary which played a prominent part in subsequent border disputes with Venezuela. He was knighted in 1844 and was appointed British Consul at Santo Domingo in 1848 and in Bangkok in 1857. He wrote books on British Guiana and Barbados, and edited Walter Raleigh's journal of his second voyage to Guiana in 1848.

SCHOUTEDEN

Schouteden's Swift *Schoutedenapus schoutedeni* (**Prigogine** 1960)

Henri Eugene Alphonse Hubert Schouteden (1881–1972) was a Belgian zoologist who undertook many expeditions to the Congo. He was an expert on swifts and published on both ornithology and entomology. He wrote *De Vogels van Belgisch-Congo en van Ruanda-Urundi*.

SCHREIBERS

Schreibers' Hummingbird *Heliodoxa schreibersii* (**Bourcier** 1847)
(Alt. Black-throated Brilliant)

Dr Karl Franz Anton von Schreibers (1775–1852) was an Austrian zoologist who was originally trained as a physician and became a University Professor in Vienna in 1806. He was one of the directors of the Vienna Natural History Museum, where he was the 'Keeper of the Imperial-Royal Repository of Natural Specimens'. He turned the Repository from merely a collection of curiosities into a scientific research institute. He researched and published widely, but unfortunately nearly all his specimens, papers and personal possessions were destroyed by a fire at the museum in 1848, after it was bombarded by Imperial troops. That year was, of course, one of upheaval and revolutions in Europe. Also lost were all of **Natterer**'s papers and the diary of the 1817 Austrian expedition to Brazil. It is not entirely clear whether or not Schreibers himself took part in this expedition, but there are reports that he was collecting in Brazil in 1817. Greatly upset by the loss of so much material, he retired in 1851 and died shortly thereafter. His major interest seems to have been reptiles and amphibians and a number of such fauna have Schreiber in their scientific names, including Schreiber's Green Lizard *Lacerta schreiberi*, which might be named after him.

SCHRENCK

Schrenck's Little Bittern *Ixobrychus eurhythmus*
(**Swinhoe** 1873)
(Alt. Schrenck's Bittern)
Schrenck's Reed Warbler *Acrocephalus bistrigiceps*
(Swinhoe 1860)
(Alt. Black-browed Reed Warbler)

Leopold Ivanovich von Schrenck (1826–1894) was a Russo-German zoologist, geographer and ethnographer who was a Fellow of the Imperial Academy of Sciences at St Petersburg. He eventually became a Member of the Council and, from 1879, the director of that institution. He explored the Amur region from 1854 to 1856 and published his findings in *Reisen und Forschungen im Amur-Lande in den Jahren 1854–1856 im Auftrage des Kaiserl*, in 1860. He was associated with several branches of natural science and a considerable variety of animals have been named after him including Shrenck's Limpet *Notoacmea schrenckii*, the Amur Sturgeon *Acipenser schrenckii*, the Manchurian Black Water Snake *Elaphe schrenckii* and a butterfly *Amuriana schrenckii*. (His name is occasionally mistranscribed as Schenk or Shrenk.)

SCHWARTZ

Schwartz's Ant-thrush *Chamaeza turdina* (**Cabanis** & **Heine** 1859)
(Alt. Scalloped Ant-thrush)

Ludwig Schwartz (1822–1894) was a German astronomer who accompanied on the Trans-Baykal expedition of 1855 to 1858.

SCLATER, P L

Sclater's Antbird *Cercomacra cinerascens sclateri* (**Hellmayr** 1905)
(Alt. Gray Antbird)
Sclater's Antwren *Myrmotherula sclateri* (**Snethlage** 1912)
Sclater's Bare-eyed Corella *Cacatua sanguinea gymnops* (P L Sclater 1871)
(Alt. Little Cockatoo/Corella)
Sclater's Crowned Pigeon *Goura scheepmakeri* (**Finsch** 1876)
(Alt. Southern Crowned Pigeon)
Sclater's Curassow *Crax sclateri* (G R **Gray** 1867)
(Alt. Bare-faced/Banded/Fasciated Curassow)
Sclater's Forest Falcon *Micrastur plumbeus* (W L Sclater 1918)
(Alt. Plumbeous Forest Falcon)
Sclater's Hanging Parrot *Loriculus sclateri* (**Wallace** 1863)
(Alt. Sula Hanging Parrot)
Sclater's Lark *Spizocorys sclateri* (**Shelley** 1902)
Sclater's Mannikin *Munia* (*Lonchura*) *melaena* (P L Sclater 1880)
(Alt. Sclater's/New Britain Munia)
Sclater's Monal Pheasant *Lophophorus sclateri* (**Jerdon** 1870)
(Alt. Sclater's Monal)
Sclater's Myzomela *Myzomela cineracea* (P L Sclater 1879)
(Alt. Umboi/Bizmark/Ashy Myzomela/Honeyeater)
Sclater's Myzomela *Myzomela sclateri* (Forbes 1879)
(Alt. Red-bibbed/Scarlet-throated Myzomela/Honeyeater)
Sclater's Parrotlet *Forpus sclateri* (G R Gray 1859)
(Alt. Dusky-billed Parrotlet)
*Sclater's Pleasing Lorikeet *Charmosyna placentis* (**Temminck** 1834)
(Alt. Red-flanked Lorikeet)
Sclater's Penguin *Eudyptes sclateri* (**Buller** 1888)
(Alt. Erect-crested Penguin)
Sclater's Pygmy Parrot *Micropsitta pusio* (P L Sclater 1865)
(Alt. Buff-faced Pygmy Parrot)
Sclater's Rail *Gallirallus insignis* (P L Sclater 1880)
(Alt. Bismarck/New Britain Rail)
Sclater's Tanager *Tangara arthus sclateri* (Lafresnaye 1854)
(Alt. Golden Tanager)
Sclater's Tyrannulet *Phyllomyias sclateri* (**Berlepsch** 1901)
Sclater's Whistler *Pachycephala soror* (P L Sclater 1874)
Sclater's Woodswallow *Artamus insignis* (P L Sclater 1877)
(Alt. Bismarck/New Britain/White-backed Woodswallow)
Sclater's Wren *Campylorhynchus rufinucha humilis* (P L Sclater 1856)
(Alt. Rufous-naped Wren)

The birds are named after two Sclaters, father and son, and it is not always clear which species was named after whom. Between them they described no fewer than 913 species; 189 non-passerines and 724 passerines! Thirteen passerines and eight non-passerines have *sclateri* in their binomials. The father wrote more descriptions and one can safely assume that most of the vernacular names are after him. Sclater's Monal Pheasant, at least, was named for the father, as was the scientific name of the Mexican Chickadee *Parus sclateri*. It is likely too that all of the South American species were named for the father. Twenty-six birds were recorded as collected by P L Sclater, or as coming from the Sclater collection, some of which may have been presented to him.

Dr Philip Lutley Sclater (1829–1913) was a graduate of Oxford and practiced law for many years. In 1858 he was the founder and first Editor of The Ibis, the Journal of the British Ornithologists' Union. He edited it from 1858 to 1865 and again from 1877 until 1912. He was also Secretary of the Zoological Society of London from 1860 until 1903. Sclater's study of bird distribution resulted in the classification of the biogeographical regions of the world into six major categories. He later adapted his scheme for mammals and it is still the basis for work in biogeography. He wrote *A Monograph of the Birds Forming the Tanagrine Genus Calliste*, in 1857, *Exotic Ornithology*, in 1866, *The Curassows*, in 1875, *A Monograph of the Jacamars and Puffbirds*, in 1879, *Birds of the Challenger Expedition*, in 1881 and *Argentine Ornithology*, in 1888.

SCLATER, W L

William Lutley Sclater (1863–1944) was the son of Philip Lutley **Sclater** and the brother of **Lilian** Sclater. Like his father, he too was educated at Oxford, obtaining a first-class honours degree in Natural Science in 1885. He was President of the British Ornithologists' Union from 1928 to 1933. For a few years he was Deputy-Superintendent of the Indian Museum in Calcutta and in 1896 he was appointed as the first Director of the South African Museum, in Cape Town. He was also a one-time president of the South African Ornithologists' Union. Sclater resigned from the South African Museum in 1906 and for the following 30 years he worked at the British Museum (Natural History). He succeeded his father as Editor of The Ibis from 1913 until 1930. In July 1944 he was killed by a V1 flying bomb in London. He wrote *Systema Avium Aethiopicarum* in 1924. **Shelley** described the lark from a specimen collected by C J Andersson, in 1862, and presented by R B Sharpe to the British Museum.

SCOPOLI

Scopoli's Shearwater *Calonectris* (*diomedea*) *diomedea* (Scopoli 1769)
(Alt. Cory's Shearwater)

Johannes Antonius Scopoli (1723–1788) was an Italian-Austrian who studied medicine and became Professor of Mineralogy and Metallurgy in Schemnitz and then Professor of Chemistry and Botany at the University of Pavia. His most famous publication was *Flora Carniolica* in 1760. He was first to describe a number of plant species and one genus. He corresponded with Linnaeus and adopted his system of classification. The drug Scopalamine, an alkaloid of henbane which is a sedative and is one of the so-called 'truth drugs' is named after him. The above name has recently (1998) been proposed for the nominate Mediterranean race of Cory's Shearwater to distinguish it from the Atlantic race *borealis*, which was described by **Cory** and would continue to be known as Cory's Shearwater if the species is split. Scopoli himself described the shearwater.

SCORESBY

Scoresby's Gull *Larus scoresbii* (**Traill** 1823)
(Alt. Dolphin Gull)

William Scoresby (1789–1857) was an English captain of a whaling ship and an explorer of the Arctic. William Scoresby's own father was taken out of school at the age of nine by his father to work on the family farm. When hired out to another farm he was ill treated and decided not to follow the family trade but to seek a life at sea and he signed up at the age of ten. By the 1790s he had worked his way up to second officer, mostly aboard whalers; around 1780 he invented the 'crow's nest'. In 1803 William Scoresby was apprenticed aboard his father's ship *Resolution*, a Greenland whaler in which his father owned a one-eighth share. At 17 he became mate and by the age of 21 became captain. In 1806 he left the sea to study at Edinburgh University, which sparked his interest in science. Nevertheless, Scoresby returned to sea in the Royal Navy without completing his studies, although he later met Sir Joseph **Banks** who persuaded him to do so. From 1813 he commanded the *Esk*, which undertook scientific studies at sea, and he developed scientific instruments with Banks. In 1819 he commanded the *Baffin*, which was built to his specification and began his exploration of Arctic waters. He wrote *The Arctic regions* in 1820. Scoresby continued to explore and collect over the next few years and went on inventing scientific instruments. Many of his original instruments and much of his written work may be seen at the Whitby Museum. Later in life he took holy orders.

SCOTT

Scott's Oriole *Icterus parisorum* (**Bonaparte** 1838)
Scott's Sparrow *Aimophila ruficeps* (**Cassin** 1852)
(Alt. Boucard's Summer Sparrow, Rufous-crowned/Rusty Sparrow)

Winfield Scott (1786–1866) was a commander in the United States forces during the Mexican War. Lieutenant **Couch** who was under his command found the sparrow and named it after the hero Scott, mistakenly thinking it was new to science. Scott stood as a Whig for the Presidency in 1852 and was defeated by Pierce. Although a Southerner, he remained loyal to the Union throughout the American Civil War and died at West Point.

SCRIPPS

Scripps' Murrelet *Synthliboramphus hypoleucus scrippsi* (Green & Arnold 1939)
(Alt. Xantus's Murrelet)

Robert Paine Scripps (1895–1938) was an American newspaper baron who died mysteriously at the age of 42. He joined the company, which his father had set up, when he was 16, and by 1917 he was editorial director of the chain. He became president and chief stockholder in the 1920s. He made many donations to an institution set up by his aunt, the Scripps Institution of Oceanography (formerly the San Diego Marine Biological Institution). He died unexpectedly aboard his yacht off Baja California, the cause of death being recorded as a 'throat hemorrhage'. To deepen the mystery, 12 years previously, his father had also died whilst aboard *his* yacht off the African coast.

SEEBOHM

Seebohm's Courser *Rhinoptilus cinctus seebohmi* (**Sharpe** 1893)
(Alt. Three-/Treble-banded Courser)
Seebohm's Feather-tailed Warbler *Dromaeocercus seebohmi* (**Sharpe** 1879)
(Alt. Grey Emu-tail)
Seebohm's Wheatear *Oenanthe* (*oenanthe*) *seebohmi* (**Dixon** 1882)
(Alt. [North African] Northern Wheatear)

Henry Seebohm (1832–1895) was a British businessman and an amateur ornithologist, oologist and traveller, who explored the Yenisey tundra of Siberia. **Blakiston** sent skins to England, which were the subject of a series of papers by Robert **Swinhoe** and Henry Seebohm. Seebohm also employed Charles **Dixon** as a collector. **Meinhertzhagen** recorded in his diary that he used to visit Seebohm to examine his collection, that Seebohm died of influenza. He wrote *A History of British Birds*, in 1883, *The Geographical Distribution of the Family Charadriidae*, in 1887, *The Birds of the Japanese Empire* in 1890, *A Monograph of the Turdidae*, in 1898, and *The Birds of Siberia*, in 1901.

SEIMUND

Seimund's Green Pigeon *Treron seimundi* (**Robinson** 1910)
  (Alt. Yellow-vented Green Pigeon)
Seimund's Sunbird *Nectarinia seimundi* (**Ogilvie-Grant** 1908)
  (Alt. Little Green Sunbird)

E C H Seimund was a British taxidermist who collected in South Africa from 1899 until 1903, in Fernando Pó in 1904, in Thailand in 1913 and in Malaya (now Malaysia) in 1916. Specimens from the last expedition are held in the Raffles Museum in Singapore. He collected the pigeon which he presented to the Kuala Lumpur Museum and was described by Robinson, in 1910, as *Sphenocercus seimundi*. Sharpe earlier described another dove from a specimen collected by Seimund as *Haplopelia seimundi*. They may be the same species. Seimund and Robinson were on the British Natural History Museum Expedition to Fernando Pó in 1904. There is also a race of a monkey *Presbytis obscurus seimundi* with an honorific for Seimund in the trinomial.

SEMPER

Semper's Warbler *Leucopeza semperi* (P L **Sclater** 1877) [Extinct]

The Reverend John E Semper was a parish priest and amateur ornithologist who was resident in St Lucia. The bird was last definitely seen in 1961, although there are unconfirmed sightings from as recently as 1995, and so is likely to be extinct. P L **Sclater**, who wrote the description, collected it on St Lucia, with Semper, around 1872.

SENNETT

Sennett's Nighthawk *Chordeiles minor sennetti* (**Coues** 1888)
  (Alt. Common Nighthawk)
Sennett's Olive-backed Parula *Parula pitiayumi* (**Vieillot** 1817)
  (Alt. Tropical Parula)
Sennett's Oriole *Icterus cucullatus* (**Swainson** 1827)
  (Alt. Nelson's/Hooded Oriole)
Sennett's Thrasher *Toxostoma longirostre* (**Lafresnaye** 1838)
  (Alt. Long-billed Thrasher)
Sennett's Titmouse *Parus bicolor sennetti* (**Ridgway** 1904)
  (Alt. Tufted Titmouse)
Sennett's White-tailed Hawk *Buteo albicaudatus* (Vieillot 1816)
  (Alt. White-tailed Hawk)

George Burritt Sennett (1840–1900) was a businessman and naturalist from New York. After schooling, he spent four years travelling in Europe and then managed the family iron foundry. He is best known for his studies of Texan birds, particularly those of the Lower Rio Grande Valley. He made collecting trips to Texas in 1877, 1878 and 1882, and then paid collectors, including **Frazar,** to send specimens from Texas and Mexico to him. His collection is now in the American Museum of Natural History, in New York. In spring 1877 Sennett collected at Galveston, Corpus Christi, and Brownsville, and Hidalgo.

The account of that expedition was an annotated list of 150 species, including the description of Sennett's Olive-backed Warbler. His 1878 trip along the coast recorded 168 species including Sennett's White-tailed Hawk. He was one of the original members of the American Ornithologists' Union and from 1886 until 1893 he was Chairman of the Committee on the Protection of North American Birds. Sennett described two new species and eight new subspecies of Texan birds. He is honoured in the names of four subspecies of Texas birds, a species of rodent and a moth.

SERLE

> Serle's Bush Shrike *Telophorus kupeensis* (Serle 1952)
> (Alt. Mount Kupe Bush Shrike)

Dr William Serle OBE (1912–1992) was a Scottish ornithologist who co-wrote *A Field Guide to the Birds of West Africa*.

SEVERTZOV

See **Severzov** below.

SEVERZOV

> Severzov's Hazel Grouse *Bonasa sewerzowi* (**Prjevalsky** 1876)
> (Alt. Chinese Grouse)
> Severzov's Rosefinch *Carpodacus rubicilla* (**Güldenstadt** 1775)
> (Alt. Spot-crowned Rosefinch, Caucasian Great Rosefinch)
> Severzov's Tit-Warbler *Leptopoecile sophiae* (Severzov 1873)
> (Alt. Stoliczka's/White-browed Tit-Warbler)

Nikolai Alekseevich Severzov (1827–1885) was a Russian zoologist who explored Central Asia. He has a number of fishes named after him in their binomials and a great number of plants.

SEVERTZOW

See **Severtzov** above.

SEXAGENARIANS, SEPTUAGENARIANS AND BEYOND...

Does ornithology make you live longer? It looks like it! We know the life spans of 838 of the people we have studied. Some died tragically young; 15 before their 30th birthday and another 45 before reaching 40. Sixty-seven died in their forties, 111 in their fifties, 178 in their sixties, 209 in their seventies, 164 in their eighties and 50 in their ninties, of whom three (**Leguat**, **Batchelder**, and **Steere**) all reached 98! Considering that most of them lived during a time of shorter life expectancy and that many travelled widely in unexplored areas, the survival rates are impressive. As far we know, no one has made it into a second century, but Dr Ernst **Mayr** is 99 (as we write in June 2003) and we look forward to drinking his health in 2004 as our first centenarian.

SHARPE, A

> Sharpe's Pied Babbler *Turdoides sharpei* (**Reichenow** 1891)
> (Alt. Black-lored Babbler)

Sir Alfred Sharpe KCMG, CB, LL.D. (1853–1935) was His Majesty's Commissioner and

Consul-General for the British Central Africa Protectorate, Governor of Nyasaland (now Malawi) and an amateur naturalist.

SHARPE, R

Sharpe's Akalat *Sheppardia sharpei* (**Shelley** 1903)
Sharpe's Apalis *Apalis sharpii* (Shelley 1884)
Sharpe's Drongo *Dicrurus ludwigii sharpei* (Oustalet 1879)
    (Alt. Square-tailed Drongo)
Sharpe's Frogmouth *Batrachostomus mixtus* (Sharpe 1892)
    (Alt. Bornean Frogmouth)
Sharpe's Greenbul *Phyllastrephus alfredi* (Sharpe 1876)
    (Alt. Malawi Greenbul)
Sharpe's Longclaw *Macronyx sharpei* (**Jackson** 1904)
Sharpe's Pipit *Anthus sharpei* (Jackson 1904)
Sharpe's Rail *Gallirallus sharpei* (**Büttikofer** 1893) [Extinct]
Sharpe's Rosefinch *Carpodacus rodopeplus verreauxii* (David & Oustalet 1877)
    (Alt. Spot-winged Rosefinch)
Sharpe's Seedeater *Sporophila torqueola sharpei* (**Lawrence** 1889)
    (Alt. White-collared Seedeater)
Sharpe's Starling *Cinnyricinclus sharpii* (Jackson 1898)
Sharpe's Wren *Cinnycerthia olivascens* (Sharpe 1882)

Richard Bowdler Sharpe (1847–1909) was a British zoologist. He was the Assistant Keeper of the Vertebrate Section of the British Museum's Zoology Department from 1895 until his death from pneumonia in 1909. He had a particular interest in classification and phylogeny and its relation to evolution. He wrote descriptions of over 200 bird species. He was also Librarian to the Royal Society of London from 1867 until 1872. He was co-author of the series *Birds of Europe*. When he joined the British Museum in 1872 as a Senior Assistant in the Department of Zoology, he commenced his massive *Catalogue of the Birds in the British Museum*, which appeared in 27 volumes between 1874 and 1898. Sharpe founded the British Ornithologists' Club in 1892 and edited its Bulletin for many years. The Western Negrofinch *Nigrita* (*canicapilla*) *emiliae* was originally named after his wife Emily. They had many children, judging by the title of C E Jackson's book, published in 1994, *Richard Bowdler Sharpe and His Ten Daughters!* We would love to have found a picture of Mr and Mrs Sharpe *en famille*! The greenbul is sometimes considered conspecific with the Yellow-streaked Greenbul *Phyllastrephus flavostriatus*. Throughout this volume you will find references to the relationship between Sharpe and John **Gould** and this is dealt with in some detail in the Preface.

SHELLEY, E

Shelley's Crimsonwing *Cryptospiza shelleyi* (**Alexander** 1899)
    (Alt. Red-billed Crimsonwing)
Shelley's Francolin *Francolinus shelleyi* (**Ogilvie-Grant** 1890)

Sir Edward Shelley (1827–1890) was an English traveller. Like Captain George Ernest **Shelley**, he too was a nephew of the poet. As a young man he was an army officer but resigned his commission to travel in Africa, where he lived for a number of years with the indigenous people. **Livingstone** records meeting him in his correspondence. He was in San Francisco quite shortly after the end of the American Civil War and from there sailed to Honolulu.

SHELLEY, G

Shelley's Eagle Owl*Bubo shelleyi* (**Sharpe** & **Ussher** 1872)
　(Alt. Banded Eagle Owl)
Shelley's Greenbul *Andropadus masukuensis* (G Shelley 1897)
Shelley's Oliveback *Nesocharis shelleyi* (**Alexander** 1903)
　(Alt. Fernando Pó Oliveback, Little Olive Weaver/Waxbill)
Shelley's Red-throated Sunbird *Anthreptes rhodolaema* (G Shelley 1878)
　(Alt. Red/Rufous-shouldered/Rufous-throated Sunbird, Shelley's
　[Eastern] Sunbird)
Shelley's Rufous Sparrow *Passer motitensis shelleyi* (Sharpe 1891)
　(Alt. Kenya Rufous Sparrow)
Shelley's Starling *Lamprotornis shelleyi* (Sharpe 1890)
Shelley's Sunbird *Nectarinia shelleyi* (Alexander 1899)
　(Alt. Shelley's African/Double-collared Sunbird)

Captain George Ernest Shelley (1840–1910), a nephew of the famous poet, was a geologist who became interested in ornithology. He was educated in England and at the Lycée de Versailles, after which he joined the Grenadier Guards in 1863, retiring a few years later with the rank of captain. The government of South Africa sent him on a geological survey. He wrote books on the birds of Egypt and a review of sunbirds; *A Monograph of the Nectariniidae*, in 1880. He collected in Africa, Australia and Burma but suffered a paralysing stroke in 1906, which prevented him travelling further.

SHOT

No fewer than five (or six if you count Goliath dying by sling-shot) of our 'birdmen' are known to have died from gunshots – although there may well have been more who met their ends in this way during the two world wars. What is even more remarkable is that at least three, and possible all four did so at their own hands, albeit, supposedly, by accident. The famous American explorer Captain Meriwether **Lewis** met his death in 1809 from two gunshot wounds to the head and chest – it still is not known whether this was murder or suicide. The German herpetologist Johann Georg **Wagler** died from an accidental, self-inflicted, gunshot wound whilst collecting in 1832. Captain John Hanning **Speke**, the famous British explorer, was killed by his own shotgun in 1864 when he stumbled crossing a stile whilst out shooting in England, although some people still believe he committed suicide. Walter Beick committed suicide by shooting himself and John Simpson **Cairns**, an American collector, accidentally shot and killed himself while collecting birds in 1895. 'What's hit is history' as they say!

SHUFELDT

Shufeldt's Junco *Junco hyemalis shufeldti* (Coale 1887)
　(Alt. Dark-eyed Junco)

Professor Dr Robert Wilson Shufeldt (1850–1934) was an expert on bird bones both of extant species and fossils. He made a number of expeditions to Africa. He was most prolific between 1885 and 1925.He also seems to have been profoundly racist! '*Dr Shufeldt is a Northern man, a former member of the medical corps of the United States Army and a naturalist of profound learning. His experience with the Negro has extended to all the southern States and to the West Indies. During the fifty years of his scientific observation of the Negro, he has accumulated knowledge of that race second to none other. His publication,* America's Greatest Problem: The Negro *(1915) contains the epitome of the results of his years of investigation. He makes it clear to us that if the Negro remains in the United States the future American is to be a mongrel and the future civilization reduced to the level of the mongrel.*' This is a quote from *The American Racial Problem as Seen in a Worldwide Perspective* by Earnest Sevier Cox. Shufeldt served as a major in the medical corps in the First World War.

SICK

Sick's Manakin *Pipra vilasboasi* (Sick 1957)
(Alt. Golden-crowned Manakin)

Helmut Sick (1910–1991) was a German-born Brazilian ornithologist who worked for the National Museum in Rio de Janeiro for many years. He is particularly famed for being the man who rediscovered, in 1978, one of the few surviving populations of the Critically Endangered Indigo (Lear's) Macaw *Anodorhynchus leari*. His particular interest was macaws and he was also responsible for re-ordering of some genera in the taxonomic sequence. It has been said that he '*was one of the most dedicated and active ornithologists ever to work in South America*'. He wrote *Ornitologia Brasileira, uma Introdução* in 1984. This great work was translated into English, in 1993, as *Birds in Brazil – A Natural History*. Sick discovered the manakin in 1957 but it was not seen again until its rediscovery in 2002. He is also commemorated in the binomial of the Orange-bellied (Sick's) Antwren *Terenura sicki*.

SIEBER

Sieber's Jay *Aphelocoma ultramarina* (**Bonaparte** 1825)
(Alt. Grey-breasted Jay)

Possibly named after Friedrich Wilhelm Sieber (1789–1844), who was a botanist from Prague, which is nowadays the capital of the Czech Republic, but in his day was in the Austro-Hungarian Empire. He travelled very extensively. He was in Paraguay around 1812 and in 1818 he visited Jerusalem and produced the first geodesic map of the city. During the same trip he visited Crete and produced an early plan of the Labyrinth. Between 1822 and 1825 he circumnavigated the world and made an important collection of botanical specimens in Australia. He described the Sumba Myzomela *Myzomela dammermani*, a type of honeyeater, in Treubia, a journal on zoology and hydrobiology of the Indo-Australian archipelago. The jay has an indeterminate number of races and there are some unresolved questions concerning their taxonomic status.

SIEBOLD

Siebold's Green Pigeon *Treron sieboldii* (**Temminck** 1835)
(Alt. White-bellied Green Pigeon)

Dr Philipp Franz Balthazar von Siebold (1796–1866) was a German physician and naturalist. He served as medical officer to the Dutch East Indian Army in Batavia (now Jakarta, Indonesia) and then in Japan. He collected in Japan, sending local collectors into the interior, from 1823 until 1830, when he was expelled from the country for having prepared a map. On his return to Holland he was promoted to major and then colonel. He wrote *Fauna Japonica – Aves*, in 1844, as well as a number of other books on Japan, its natural history, language and ethnography. In 1859 he returned to Japan and was invited to Court by the Emperor. By 1861 he was the chief negotiator for all the European nations who were trying to establish trade links with the Japanese. He returned home, via Java, in 1862, and continued to write scientific papers until his death. His ethnographical collections were bought by the Bavarian government and exhibited in Munich.

SILLEM

Sillem's Rosy Finch *Leucosticte sillemi* (Roselaar 1992)
(Alt. Sillem's Mountain Finch)

Jérome Alexander 'Lex' Sillem (1902–1986) was a Dutch banker, who eventually became the Director of the Bank Mees & Hope in The Hague. He was also an amateur ornithologist. Together with two of his own brothers and with two other brothers (his nephews) of the Van Marle family he founded the Sillem-Van Marle Society for the advancement of knowledge of ornithological science. The society attempted to assemble a large collection of study skins to study geographical variation in Palearctic birds, mostly by buying skins from dealers, but occasionally by funding collecting expeditions, for example to Romania and Portugal. In 1979 the collection of about 10,000 bird skins was acquired by the Bird Department of the Zoological Museum at the University of Amsterdam. Of the four brothers, only Lex Sillem and John G van Marle were active field birdwatchers; the other two had a more marginal interest (but were still good for the money). Shortly after obtaining his Bachelor's degree at the Economic University of Rotterdam, Lex Sillem participated as a zoological collector in the Third Netherlands Karakoram Expedition, under the leadership of the geologist P C Visser. This expedition left Srinagar (Kashmir) on 2 May 1929 and returned there 12 August 1930, after traversing unexplored parts of the western Tibetan Plateau and overwintering in western Xinjiang. In Kashgar, where the expedition spent the winter as guests at the British Consulate-General, Sillem met Frank **Ludlow**, a professional bird collector working for the British Natural History Museum. Ludlow and Sillem both travelled during the winter to explore the western fringes of the Takla Maklan desert, during which Sillem's bird-skinning abilities strongly improved. The finch is still only known from the two specimens, which were collected in September 1929, during the Karakoram Expedition. Sillem originally thought that they were Brandt's Mountain Finches *Leucosticte brandti*. There is also a giant spider *Sillemia clavifemur* collected by and named after him. Kees Roselaar, who described the finch in 1992, contributed much of this entry, with additional material from the Artis Library, University of Amsterdam.

SIMEON

Simeon's Gull *Larus belcheri* (**Vigors** 1829)
(Alt. Belcher's/Band-tailed Gull)
Simeon's Gull *Larus atlanticus* (**Olrog** 1958)
(Alt. Olrog's Gull)

Our opinion is that this is NOT named after a person but is a transcription error. We believe that the original was the Simeon Gull, possibly referring to an area where it occurred rather than to a person who found it. The fact that the name also refers to two closely related species is due to Olrog's Gull having originally been treated as a subspecies of Belcher's Gull.

SIMON

Simon's Emerald *Chlorostilbon* (*mellisugus*) *vitticeps*
(Alt. Blue-tailed Emerald)

Eugene Louis Simon (1848–1924) was a French ornithologist who was an expert on hummingbirds. He wrote *Histoire Naturelle des Trochilidae* in 1921. The subspecies *vitticeps* has been absorbed into the subspecies *phoeopygus* (**Tschudi** 1844).

SIMONS

Simons' Brush Finch *Atlapetes seebohmi simonsi* (**Sharpe** 1900)

P O Simons (1869–1901) was an American citizen who collected in South America. Around 1900 he collected for herpetologists in Peru and he collected birds in Bolivia in 1901. His name is honoured in a number of species from a spiny mouse to a catfish. He is also commemorated in the recently split Andean Tapaculo *Scytalopus* (*magellanicus*) *simonsi*, which was originally described by **Chubb**, who seems to have studied Simons' collections extensively in the second decade of the 20th century. There are more than a dozen type-specimens in the British Museum (Natural History) which he collected. A certain F A A Simons was collecting in Colombia a decade earlier and we would love to know if they were related.

SJÖSTEDT

Sjöstedt's [Barred] Owlet *Glaucidium sjostedti* (**Reichenow** 1893)
Sjöstedt's Honeyguide Greenbul *Baeopogon clamans* (Sjostedt 1893)
(Alt. White-tailed Greenbul)
Sjöstedt's Pigeon *Columba sjostedti* (Reichenow 1901)
(Alt. Cameroon Olive/Rameron Pigeon)

Bror Yngve Sjöstedt (1866–1948) was a Swedish entomologist and ornithologist. Between 1890 and 1891 he was in Cameroon collecting for the Uppsala University Zoological Department and for the State Natural History Museum. In 1897 he joined the entomology section of the National Natural History Museum and in 1898 went on an expedition to the United States and Canada to visit entomological stations and to study their methods. He was part of the 1905–06 Swedish Zoological Expedition to Mount Kilimanjaro. He published extensively, including *Zur ornithologie Kameruns, Wissenschaftliche ergenbisse der schwedischen expedition nach dem Kilimanjaro.*

SLADEN

Sladen's Barbet *Gymnobucco sladeni* (**Ogilvie-Grant** 1907)

Major A G Sladen (1880–1960) was a British collector in the Congo. Sladen's Hatchet Fish *Argyropelecus sladeni* is also named after him.

SLATER

Slater's Leaf Warbler *Phylloscopus ricketti* (Slater 1897)
(Alt. Sulphur-breasted Warbler)

The Reverend Henry Horrocks Slater (1851–1934) was a Northamptonshire clergyman. In 1902 he wrote *The Victoria History of the Counties of England.* C B Rickett collected a specimen of a warbler in China in 1896, which was described a year later by Sclater as *Cryptolopha ricketti.* We thought it too much of a coincidence for it to be any0thing other than the bird above, and assumed it to be a transcription error of 'Sclater's Warbler' but we were wrong! We have been unable to discover to which species Rickett's bird now belongs.

SMITH, A

Smith's Chestnut-vented Sandgrouse *Pterocles gutturalis* (A **Smith** 1836)
(Alt. Yellow-throated Sandgrouse)

Smith's Francolin *Francolinus archeri* (Smith 1836)
  (Alt. Archer's Francolin)
Smith's Helmet-shrike *Prionops plumatus* (Shaw 1809)
  (Alt. White-crested/White-crowned Helmet-shrike)
Smith's Bare-eyed Pigeon *Geophaps smithii* (**Jardine** & Selby 1830)
  (Alt. Partridge/Bare-eyed/Squatter/Naked-eyed Bronzewing Pigeon)
Smith's Shoveler *Anas smithii* (**Hartert** 1891)
  (Alt. Cape/South African Shoveler)

Dr Sir Andrew Smith (1797–1872) was a Scotsman who started his professional life as a ship's surgeon. He was a zoologist whose first love was reptiles and he was famed for his scrupulous accuracy. Smith was Director-General of the British Medical Services during the Crimean War. He was in the Cape Colony, South Africa, from 1820 until 1837, and led the first scientific expedition into the South African interior, from 1834 until 1836. He wrote *Illustrations of the Zoology of South Africa*. However, he stopped his natural history collecting and study after returning to Britain. Later in life he became a British Member of Parliament. Much of his private collection was given to Edinburgh University and is now in the Royal Museum of Scotland.

SMITH, G

Smith's Longspur *Calcarius pictus* (**Swainson** 1832)

Dr Gideon Smith MD (1793–1867) was an editor and a friend of **Audubon**, who named the bird after him. Audubon's friends E **Harris** and J G **Bell** first discovered the Longspur. A man of the same name (and it may be our man) patented the first fake gold coin detector in 1853.

SNETHLAGE

Snethlage's Tody-Tyrant *Hemitriccus minor* (Snethlage 1907)
Snethlage's Woodcreeper *Xiphocolaptes* (*falcirostris*) *franciscanus* (Snethlage 1927)

Maria Emilie Snethlage (1868–1929) was a German ornithologist (Doctor of Natural Philosophy and Assistant in Zoology at the Berlin Museum) who collected in the Brazilian Amazon and elsewhere in the country from 1905 until her death. She published *Catalogo das Aves Amazonicas*, in 1914, and also wrote on local languages. The collections of the Goeldi Museum in Brazil comprise five sections. The zoology section is known as the Emilie Snethage collection because she was the Museum Director between 1914 and 1922. She was formerly an assistant of Zoology at the Museum of Berlin, specialising in ornithology, and was the first woman scientist to direct a museum in Brazil and to work in Amazonia.

SNOW

Snow's (Alagoas) Antwren *Myrmotherula snowi* (Teixeira & Gonzaga 1985)
Snow's Cotinga *Tijuca condita* (Snow 1980)
  (Alt. Grey-winged/Órgãos Cotinga)

Dr David W Snow (1924–) was a Demonstrator at the Edward Grey Institute of Field Ornithology at Oxford University, from 1949 to 1956. He then served as Resident Naturalist for the New York Zoological Society at its tropical field station in Trinidad from 1957 until 1961, and as Director of the Charles Darwin Research Station in the Galápagos from 1963 to 1964. Thereafter, he was then Director of Research for the

British Trust for Ornithology from 1964 until 1968 before becoming Senior Principal Scientific Officer at the British Natural History Museum from 1968 until his retirement in 1984. He wrote *A Study of Blackbirds* in 1958, *The Web of Adaptation* in 1976, *The Cotingas* in 1982 and *Birds and Berries* (with Barbara Snow) in 1988. He was also an editor of the *Handbook of the Birds of the Western Palearctic*, and has written many scientific papers. We might add that no one (least of all Snow himself) seems to know how the bird became 'Snow's Cotinga', as it came as complete news to him, until we approached him about it!

SOEDERSTROM

Soederstrom's Puffleg *Eriocnemis soederstromi* (**Lönnberg** & Rendahl 1922)

L Söderström (1843–1927) was the Swedish Consul-General in Ecuador in 1896. His name is also commemorated in the scientific name of the Ecuadorian Cougar *Felis concolor soederstroemi*. The bird is now regarded as conspecific with the Turquoise-throated or **Godin**'s Puffleg *Eriocnemis godini* or simply as an aberrant form of it. On the other hand, it may be a hybrid of the Black-breasted Puffleg *E. nigrivestris* and the Sapphire-vented Puffleg *E. luciani*.

SOEMMERRING

Soemmerring's Pheasant *Syrmaticus soemmerringii* (**Temminck** 1830)

Samuel Thomas von Soemmerring (1755–1830) was a German anatomist and a noted freemason. He was the author of a large number of anatomical works who took an interest in many aspects of science and philosophy, and was a correspondent of Goethe's.

SOLANDER

Solander's Petrel *Pterodroma solandri* (**Gould** 1844)
(Alt. Providence Petrel)

Daniel Carl [Karl] Solander (1733–1782) was a Swedish naturalist and explorer. He was one of Linnaeus's pupils at Uppsala. In 1756 he undertook an expedition to the extreme north of the Scandinavian peninsula. In 1760, on Linnaeus' recommendation, he went to England to continue his natural history studies. In London he associated with J Ellis and P Collinson and through whom he met Sir Joseph **Banks**. It was Banks' influence which resulted in him sailing on **Cook**'s first expedition on *HMS Endeavour* to the Southern Ocean, together with Banks and **Parkinson**. The expedition lasted from 1768 until 1771. The botanical observations of Banks and Solander were published under the aegis of the British Museum, between 1900 and 1905, under the title *Illustrations of the Botany of Captain Cook's Voyage Round the World*. In 1772 Solander accompanied Banks on an expedition to Iceland. He is credited with an unpublished manuscript *Descriptions of plants from various parts of the world*, which was written in 1767. A monument was erected at Botany Bay, New South Wales, in 1914, to mark the spot where Cook, Banks and Solander landed in Australia, on 28 April 1770. He died in London and was buried in the Swedish Church there although his remains were removed, in 1913, to the Swedish Cemetery in Woking.

SOLDIERS

Over 60 of the fellows mentioned in this tome served as professional soldiers in various armies in the world, that is quite apart from the very many who served their countries in this way during times of war. They are too many to summarise here so we merely list the majority. James William **Abert**, Captain Boyd **Alexander**, Lieutenant-Colonel Henry Haversham Godwin-**Austen**, Félix Manuel de **Azara**, Major Charles Emil **Bendire**, Captain **Bertrand** L Sclater, Thomas Wright **Blakiston**, General Louis **Botha**, Dr Henry **Bryant**, Colonel Charles **Buckley**, Colonel Francis O **Cave**, Captain William **Clark**, Brigadier-General Goland **Clarke**, Henry Boardman **Conover**, General Darius Nash **Couch**, Dr Elliott B **Coues**, Lieutenant-Colonel Dixon **Denham**, Colonel Henry Nason **Dunn**, Louis Rodolphe **Germain**, General George Washington **Goethals**, Major Edward Alphonso **Goldman**, Captain G B **Gosling**, Captain Claude Henry Baxter **Grant**, Sir George **Grey**, Surgeon-General Dr William Alexander **Hammond**, Major-General Thomas **Hardwicke**, Colonel Herbert Hasting **Harington**, Major R W E **Kenrick**, General Pyotr Kuzmich **Kozlov**, Marie Joseph Paul Yves Roch Gilbert du Mothier Marquis de **Lafayette**, Commandant William Vincent **Legge**, Captain Meriwether **Lewis**, Major-General Sir John **Malcolm**, General Alberto Ferrero Della **Marmora**, Brigadier-General George Archibald **McCall**, Major-General John Porter **McCown**, Charles **McKay**, Major Edgar Alexander **Mearns**, Major Alexander D von **Mechow**, Richard **Meinertzhagen**, James Cushing **Merrill**, Lieutenant-Colonel Sir Thomas Livingstone **Mitchell**, Colonel George **Montagu**, Jean **Moussier**, Colonel Francesco **Newton**, Captain Edward **Palliser**, Lieutenant-General Sir Arthur Purves **Phayre**, General Nikolai Mikhailovitch **Prjevalsky**, Lieutenant-Colonel Paul **Rabier**, Colonel Robert George Wardlaw **Ramsay**, Pierre-Paul **Rheinhard**, General Sir Edward **Sabine**, Lieutenant-Colonel Robert Vesey **Savile**, Winfield **Scott**, Major A G **Sladen**, Captain John Hanning **Speke**, Major C G J **Teerink**, Colonel Samuel Richard **Tickell**, Colonel R C **Tytler**, General Sir James **Willcocks**, Lieutenant Robert Stockton **Williamson** and Captain Malcolm **Wilson**. Many, like Bendire, Bryant, Coues, Dunn, Hammond, Mearns, Merrill and Moussier, were army surgeons and Germain was an army veterinarian. By our reckoning that makes one lieutenant, nine captains, five majors, five lieutenant-colonels, nine colonels, two brigadiers, two major-generals, one lieutenant-general and seven full generals, in addition to the medical men.

SOLOMON

Solomon's Thicketbird *Megalurulus whitneyi* (**Mayr** 1933)
(Alt. Guadalcanal Thicketbird, Whitney's Thicket Warbler)

In view of the fact that Guadalcanal is in the Solomon Islands, we believe that this bird is named after the islands rather than the biblical king.

SONNERAT

Sonnerat's Junglefowl *Gallus sonnerati* (**Temminck** 1813)
(Alt. Grey Junglefowl)

Pierre Sonnerat (1748–1814) was a French explorer, naturalist and collector. He wrote *Voyage a la Nouvelle Guinee*, in 1776, although, despite the title, he actually only landed on nearby islands. He also wrote *Voyage aux Indes orientales et à la Chine*, in 1782, both books being illustrated with engravings taken from his own drawings. He bought back many natural history specimens and other curiosities, which were exhibited by the Crown. He also recognised that India and China were the seats of ancient civilisations writing about the former: '*We find among the Indians the vestiges of the most remote antiquity...We know that all peoples came there to draw the elements of their knowledge...India, in her splendour, gave religions and laws to all the other peoples; Egypt and Greece owed to her both their fables and their wisdom...*'. The junglefowl was discovered by Sonnerat on his voyage to the Far East, from 1774 to 1781, and was named after him by **Temminck**.

SOPHIA

Sophia's Erythronota *Erythronota sophiae* (**Gould***)

Severzov wrote that the scientific name *sophiae* was for the Tsarina, formerly Princess Maximiliane Wilhelmine Auguste Sophie Marie (1824–1880), wife of Tsar Alexander II. We only know the bird from one of **Gould**'s engravings. However, there is a *Saucerottia sophiae*, which is an old name for a subspecies of the Steely-vented Hummingbird *Saucerottia saucerottei hoffmanni*, which could be the same bird.

SOUANCÉ

Souancé's Maroon-tailed Conure *Pyrrhura melanura souancei* (J **Verreaux** 1858)
(Alt. Maroon-tailed Parakeet)

Baron Charles de Souancé (1823–1896) was a French ornithologist, naval commissary, and author.

SOULE

Soule's Barwing *Actinodura souliei* (**Oustalet** 1897)
(Alt. Streaked Barwing)

Père (Father) Jean André Soulie (1858–1905) was a French missionary to China. He discovered a shrub which is now very widespread in Europe, the buddleia or butterfly bush, whose naming was a very clerical affair. The vernacular name honours the Reverend Adam Buddle, a Church of England rector of an Essex parish who wrote a *Herbarium of British Plants* in 1708. The scientific name *Buddleia davidii* honours the much more famous Lazarite missionary, Père Andre **David**. Père Soulie also has a rhododendron named for him.

SOULEYET

Souleyet's Woodcreeper *Lepidocolaptes souleyetii* (**Des Murs** 1849)
(Alt. Streak-headed Woodcreeper)

F L A Souleyet (1811–1852) was a French naval surgeon and naturalist in the Pacific, from 1836 to 1837. He was on board the *Bonite* which undertook a circumnavigation of the globe. Eydoux and **Vaillant** were also scientists aboard, as was Charles **Gaudichaud-Beaupré**.

SOUMAGNE

Soumagne's Owl *Tyto soumagnei* (Grandidier 1878)
(Alt. Madagascar Grass Owl/Red Owl)

M Soumagne was French Consul in Madagascar in 1863. This rare owl has recently been reported from six sites in Madagascar and may yet prove to be less uncommon than currently believed.

SOUZA

Souza's Shrike *Lanius souzae* (**Bocage** 1878)
Souza's Tchagra *Tchagra australis souzae* (Bocage 1892)
(Alt. Brown-headed Tchagra/Bush Shrike)

José Augusto de Souza (1837–1889) was a Portuguese ornithologist who was the Director of Ornithology at the Museum of Lisbon. He wrote numerous articles on African birds although he never visited Africa.

SOWERBY

Sowerby's Barbet *Stactolaema whytii sowerbyi* (**Sharpe** 1897)
(Alt. Whyte's Barbet)

J W Sowerby was a trooper in the British South African Mounted Police as well as a natural history collector. He collected this race of **Whyte**'s Barbet near Fort Chiquaqua in August 1897. **Hartert** described Whyte's Barbet in 1898 and **Sharpe** described this form in 1897, originally as a full species.

SPALDING

Spalding's Logrunner *Orthonyx spaldingii* (R G W **Ramsay** 1868)
(Alt. Chowchilla)

Edward Spalding (?–1894) was an Australian entomologist and taxidermist. He also collected aboriginal artefacts, many of which are now part of the Macleay Museum Ethnographic Collection. He was employed by **Macleay** as a collector in the 1870s and went with him in 1875 on his expedition to Papua New Guinea.

SPEKE

Speke's Weaver *Ploceus spekei* (**Heuglin** 1861)

Captain John Hanning Speke (1827–1864) was a British explorer. He was the first European to see Lake Victoria (Lake Nyanza) and it was he who proved it to be the source of the Nile. Speke joined Burton's expedition to discover the source not because he was particularly interested in finding it but more because he wanted the chance to hunt big game. By the time he parted from Burton, who went on to Lake Tanganyika, Speke too had caught the source-location obsession. Speke hunted to supply the expedition but he also observed the behaviour and ecology of birds, one of which was named after him. His own shotgun killed him when he stumbled over a stile whilst out shooting in England, although some believe that he committed suicide.

SPENCE

Spence's Sunangel *Heliangelus spencei* (**Bourcier** 1847)
(Alt. Mérida Sunangel)

William Spence (1783–1860) was an English entomologist. He was a close friend of the Reverend W Kirby, a fellow entomologist, with whom he wrote and published *Introduction to Entomology* in four volumes, between 1815 and 1826.

SPENGEL

Spengel's Parrotlet *Forpus xanthopterygius spengeli* (**Hartlaub** 1885)
(Alt. Turquoise-rumped Parrotlet)

Johann Wilhelm Spengel (1852–1921) was a German zoologist. He wrote *Die Fortschritte des Darwinismus* in 1874. He founded the journal Zoology, originally as Zoologische Jahrbücher, in 1886.

SPILLMANN

Spillmann's Tapaculo *Scytalopus spillmanni* (**Stresemann** 1937)

Professor Dr Franz Spillmann was an Austrian zoologist who lived in Ecuador. His collection of fossils and other specimens was donated to the National Polytechnic School in Quito, Ecuador around 1946. He became a curator at the Upper Austria Federal Museum in 1946, staying in that post until 1948.

SPIX

Spix's Guan *Penelope jacquacu* (Spix 1825)
Spix's Macaw *Cyanopsitta spixii* (**Wagler** 1832)
  (Alt. Little Blue Macaw)
Spix's Sawbill *Grypus spixi* (**Gould*** 1860)
Spix's Spinetail *Synallaxis spixi* (P L **Sclater** 1856)
  (Alt. Chicli Spinetail)
Spix's Woodcreeper *Xiphorhynchus spixii* (**Lesson** 1830)

Johann Baptist Von Spix (1781–1826) was a German naturalist who is best known for his work in Brazil, from 1817 until 1820. He studied theology for three years in Würzburg, then medicine and the natural sciences, qualifying as a physician in 1806. He had already gained his PhD at the age of 19! In 1808 he was awarded a scholarship by the King of Bavaria and went to Paris to study zoology. At that time Paris was *the* centre for the natural sciences with renowned scientists such as **Cuvier, Buffon, Lamarck** and Etienne **Geoffroy** de **Saint-Hilaire** at the heights of their reputations. In 1810 the King appointed him assistant to the Bavarian Royal Academy of Sciences with special responsibility for the natural history exhibits. When, in 1816, a group of academicians was invited to travel to Brazil, King Maximilian I agreed that two members of the Bavarian Academy of Sciences should accompany them. Hence Spix went to South America in 1817. He returned in 1820 with specimens of 85 mammals, 350 birds, 130 amphibians, 116 fish and 2,700 insects as well as 6,500 botanical items. The expedition also brought back 57 species of living animals, mainly monkeys, parrots and curassows. The collections were to form the basis for the Natural History Museum in Munich. The King awarded him a knighthood and a pension for life. After his return from Brazil, Spix catalogued and published his findings despite extremely poor health caused by his stay there. The report on the expedition was published in three volumes, in 1823, 1828 and 1831. In 1824 he also published *Avium Brasiliensium Species Novae*, which included a description of the Hyacinth Macaw *Anodorhynchus maximiliani*, which he dedicated to his royal sponsor. (It is now called *A.hyacinthinus*.) It was he who first classified blue macaws under the generic name of *Anodorhynchus*, which refers to the lack of a notch in the upper mandible. **Wagler** decribed the macaw in 1832 after Spix's death, when he realised it was not a subspecies of the Hyacinth Macaw but a distinct species.

SPRAGUE

Sprague's Pipit *Anthus spragueii* (**Jackson** 1904)
  (Alt. Sprague's Lark)

Isaac S Sprague (1811–1895) was an artist who accompanied **Audubon** on his Missouri trip of 1843, during which Edward **Harris** and John **Bell** shot a small brown bird near the mouth of the Yellowstone River. Audubon recognised it as a new species and named it 'Sprague's Missouri Lark'. Apparently, a few days later, whilst sitting drawing specimens, Sprague put down his drawing tools and found his namesake's nest and eggs in a mound of prairie grass. Sprague became America's best-known botanical illustrator and was chosen to illustrate Asa Gray's classics, the *Botanical Textbook* and *Flora*. He also worked with the ornithologist Henry Henshaw, who named **Allen**'s Hummingbird.

ST ANDREW

St Andrew Vireo *Vireo caribaeus* (Bond & **Meyer de Schauensee** 1942)
(Alt. San Andrés Vireo)

There seems to be a transcription or translation error involved in this bird's name. San Andrés (St Andrew) is a Colombian island in the Caribbean, where the bird occurs and after which it was named.

ST JOHN

St John's Black Hawk *Buteo lagopus sanctijohannis* (Gmelin 1788)
(Alt. Rough-legged Buzzard, Rough-legged/American Rough-legged Hawk)

This is an obsolete English name for an American bird. It is probably named after St John's in Newfoundland, where the species certainly occurs. We assume that the St John honoured is either St John the Evangelist or St John the Divine, but there are other candidates for the honour.

ST THOMAS

St Thomas's Mango *Lampornis virginalis* (**Gould***)
St Thomas's Canary *Neospiza concolor* (Barboza du Bocage 1888)
(Alt. São Tomé Grosbeak)

The mango appears to be another bird only found in Gould's engravings. St Thomas is an island in the American Virgin Islands and the Latin *virginalis* causes us to think that someone may have named it after the islands rather, than directly after the Christian saint. St Thomas is also the English translation of São Tomé, the island where the grosbeak occurs and after which it is named.

STAGER

Stager's Piculet *Picumnus subtilis* (Stager 1968)
(Alt. Fine-barred Piculet)

Kenneth E Stager is a Fellow of the American Ornithologists' Union. He has, with others, written a number of booklets on the results of various collecting expeditions in East Africa. Among his other claims to fame he demonstrated that the Turkey Vulture *Cathartes aura* relies upon a keen sense of smell to find carrion and that some other birds, such as the honeyguides (Indicatoridae), have well-developed olfactory lobes of the brain.

STANLEY

Stanley's Bustard *Neotis denhami stanleyi* (J E **Gray** 1831)
(Alt. Denham's/Jackson's Bustard)
Stanley's Crane *Grus paradiseus* (**Lichtenstein** 1793)
(Alt. Blue Crane)

Stanley's Parakeet *Platycercus icterotis* (**Kuhl** 1820)
  (Alt. Western/Yellow-cheeked Rosella)
Stanley's Thornbill *Chalcostigma stanleyi* (**Bourcier** 1851)
  (Alt. Blue-mantled Thornbill)

The Hon Edward Smith Stanley (1775–1851), 13th Earl of Derby, was a zoologist and collector. He founded the Derby Museum, which was formed from his specimen collection and from material derived from the live animals, including 318 bird species, which he kept at Knowsley Park, near Liverpool. He was President of the Linnean Society and of the Zoological Society of London for over 20 years. He was first elected Member of Parliament for Preston, in Lancashire, in 1796, when he was just 21, and served until 1812. In 1826 he met **Audubon** who gave him a few Passenger Pigeons *Ectopistes migratorius*. These started breeding in 1832 but they quickly became a nuisance-sized flock of 70 and Stanley allowed them to fly free. If only he had built up the flock he might have saved the bird from extinction, just as he contributed to saving the Hawaiian Goose or Néné *Branta sandvicensis*, which was first bred in captivity at Knowsley, in 1824. He employed Edward **Lear**, between 1832 and 1837, to draw the plates for the *Knowsley Menagerie*, which was published in 1846. (Lear also invented the *Book of Nonsense* for Stanley's grandchildren, published in the same year.) Stanley purchased **Bartram**'s original work, some of which is still in the present Earl of Derby's library. He also employed **MacGillivray** as a collector. His father gave his name to the world-famous horse race and his son, the 14th Earl, was three times Prime Minister of Great Britain.

STARK

Stark's Lark *Eremalauda starki* (**Shelley** 1902)

Arthur Cowell Stark (1846–1899) was a British physician and naturalist who travelled widely to collect birds. He was co-author, with W L **Sclater**, of *Fauna of South Africa*. He was killed by shellfire during the Boer War at the siege of Ladysmith.

STEAD

Stead's Bush Wren *Xenicus longipes variabilis* (Stead 1936) [Extinct]

Sir Edgar Fraser Stead (1882–1949) was a New Zealand electrical engineer, plant breeder, ornithologist and marksman. He first began birdwatching at his parents' home at Strowan, now the site of St Andrew's College. He trained as an electrical engineer and worked for a time in America. His father was a grain merchant who, on his death in 1908, left a fortune to Edgar. When he inherited this he '*angled in summer, shot animals and birds in winter and was a world-class marksman*', according to the inscription on his gravestone. When he returned to New Zealand he bought a property at Ilam, which is now the University of Canterbury staff club. There he developed extensive aviaries and treated injured native birds. There, too, he became famous for his work in hybridising rhododendrons, importing the seeds from **Rothschilds**' gardens in England. He once painstakingly reconstructed a Moa egg from 230 pieces. The Robert McDougall Art Gallery in Canterbury, New Zealand has the Edgar Stead Hall of New Zealand Birds. He wrote *Life Histories of New Zealand Birds* in 1932.

STEERE

Steere's Broadbill *Eurylaimus steerii* (**Sharpe** 1876)
  (Alt. Mindanao/Wattled Broadbill)
Steere's Coucal *Centropus steerii* (Bourns & **Worcester** 1894)
  (Alt. Black-hooded Coucal)
Steere's Liocichla *Liocichla steerii* (**Swinhoe** 1877)

Steere's Pitta *Pitta steerii* (Sharpe 1876)
(Alt. Azure-breasted Pitta)

Professor Dr Joseph Beal Steere (1842–1940) was an American ornithologist who collected in the Philippines between 1874 and 1875 and again between 1887 and 1888. *A list of the birds and mammals collected by the Steere Expedition to the Philippines* was published at Ann Arbor in 1890. He was Curator of the Smithsonian Institution, from 1876 to 1894, and expanded the collections by adding more than 2,500 specimens, including over 50 previously undescribed species, which he collected during his explorations in the Amazon, Peru, Malacca, Formosa (now Taiwan), the Celebes and especially in the Philippines. His travels included a trip around the world, which lasted from 1870 to 1875.

STEINBACH

Steinbach's Canastero *Asthenes steinbachi* (**Hartert** 1909)
(Alt. Chestnut Canastero)

Dr Jose Steinbach (1856–1929) was a collector for the Chicago Field Museum of Natural History, in Argentina and Bolivia. His collection is in the Carnegie Museum of Natural History and many of the plants are held at the Darwin Institute, at San Isidro in Argentina.

STEJNEGER

Stejneger's Petrel *Pterodroma longirostris* (Stejneger 1893)

Dr Leonhard Hess Stejneger (1851–1943) was a Norwegian ornithologist and herpetologist who settled in the United States, where he became the Smithsonian Institution's vertebrate expert. He was the first full-time curator of the herpetology division and held the position of Curator of the Department of Reptiles and Batrachians from 1889 until his death in 1943. He wrote the *Aves* volume in the series, *Standard Natural History*, in 1885 and *Birds of the Commander Islands and Kamtschatka*. He had a lifelong fascination with **Steller** and retraced many of his journeys, discovering the petrel during one of them. He published a biography of Steller in 1936.

STELLA

Stella's Lorikeet *Charmosyna* (*papou*) *stellae* (A B **Meyer** 1886)
(Alt. Papuan Lorikeet)

Baroness Stella Erggelet was the wife of Alex Fuhr von Salzburg. *C. stellae* is usually regarded as conspecific with the Papuan Lorikeet *C. papou*.

STELLER

Steller's Albatross *Diomedea albatrus* (**Pallas** 1769)
(Alt. Short-tailed Albatross)
Steller's Eider *Polysticta stelleri* (Pallas 1769)
Steller's Jay *Cyanocitta stelleri* (Gmelin 1788)
Steller's Sea Eagle *Haliaeetus pelagicus* (Pallas 1811)

Georg Wilhelm Steller (1709–1746) was a German naturalist and explorer in Russian service. He studied medicine at Halle, between 1731 and 1734, and was a physician in the Russian army in 1734. He became an assistant at the Academy of Sciences in St Petersburg in 1737 and accompanied Vitus Bering on his second expedition (1738–

1742) to Alaska and Kamchatka. Between 1742 and 1744 he worked in Petropavlovsk but died on the return journey to St Petersburg. John Latham, the English naturalist, first described the Steller's Jay in 1781 based on Steller's detailed journals and on a skin from Vancouver Island collected by **Cook**'s expedition. Steller published a *Journal of a Voyage with Bering 1741–1742*, in 1743. Johann Gmelin (1748–1804) named the jay in his honour in his description. Steller himself discovered the eagle and eider.

STEPANYAN

Stepanyan's Grasshopper Warbler *Locustella fasciolata amnicola* (Stepanyan 1972)
(Alt. Sakhalin Grasshopper Warbler)

Leo Surenovich Stepanyan (1931–2002) was a Moscow-based Armenian ornithologist and taxonomist, who was a member of the **Severtzov** Institute of Ecology and Evolution of the Russian Academy of Sciences. He wrote *Composition and Distribution of the Fauna of Birds of the USSR*, in 1990 and *Birds of Vietnam*, in 1950. The former was based on his investigations between 1978 and 1990 and on extensive published material in the Russian Journal of Zoology. Much of his work was on taxonomy, based on studies of existing collections of skins, and he described many bird subspecies.

STEPHANIE

Stephanie's Astrapia *Astrapia stephaniae* (**Finsch** 1885)
(Alt. Princess Stephanie's Bird-of-Paradise)

Princess Stephanie of Belgium (1864–1945) was the wife of Crown **Prince Rudolf** of Austria-Hungary. It was an arranged marriage and Stephanie was not yet 17. Her husband '*wandered the streets of Vienna in search of licentious enjoyments*'. After his untimely mysterious death (he probably shot himself in a suicide pact with his lover) she married Count Lonyay.

STEPHAN

Stephan's Dove *Chalcophaps stephani* (Pucheran 1853)
(Alt. Stephan's/Brown-backed Emerald Dove, Stephan's Ground Dove)

Étienne Stephan Jacquinot was the father of the French explorer Vice-Admiral Charles Hector Jacquinot (1796–1879) who was ensign on the *Coquille* (1822–25) and second in command to Dumont d'Urville on the *Astrolabe*. He served with him between 1837 and 1840. His brother Honoré Jacquinot (1815–1887) was a ship's surgeon on the same expeditions. '*Honoré Jacquinot, the captain of the Zelée, relates that when he brought a bird down with a shot from his musket, the initial fright of his native companions turned to shocked amazement as they saw the creature lying lifeless on the ground*'. Honoré collaborated closely with **Pucheran** in preparing descriptions of specimens. We believe that Honoré asked Pucheran to name it after his father.

STEPHEN

Stephen's Lory *Vini stepheni* (A J **North** 1908)
(Alt. Stephen's/Henderson Lorikeet)

Alfred Ernest Stephen (1879–1961) was an Australian civil servant, businessman and collector. The lory is endemic to Henderson Island, in the Pitcairn group. The Records of the Australian Museum include a 1903 paper entitled *Notes on the zoology of Paanopa or Ocean Island and Nauru or Pleasant Island, Gilbert group*, by A J North, F Danvers Power and A E Stephen.

STEPHENS

Stephens' Sparrow *Passerella iliaca stephensi* (A W Anthony 1895)
(Alt. Fox Sparrow)
Stephen's Vireo *Vireo huttoni stephensi* (**Cassin** 1851)
(Alt. Hutton's/Anthony's/Frazar's Vireo)
Stephens' Whip-poor-will *Caprimulgus vociferus* (Cassin 1851)
(Alt. Whip-poor-will)

James Francis Stephens (1792–1853) was an amateur British entomologist. From 1818 he assisted **Leach** with the insect collection at the British Museum. In 1829 he wrote *Systematic Catalogue of British Insects, and Forming a Guide to their Classification*. The three names are obsolete English names for American birds which have been superseded long ago.

STEVENS

Stevens' Honeyeater *Meliphaga gracilis stevensi* (**Rand** 1936)
(Alt. Graceful Honeyeater)

Samuel Stevens was a natural history dealer in Covent Garden, London, where his auction rooms sold birds' eggs, mounted specimens of birds and insects, and other material. He acted as general agent for Alfred Russell **Wallace** while the latter was away in Brazil and the Far East. He kept the best specimens in storage and sold off duplicates at the best price he could get. Wallace wrote of him in the preface to his book *The Malay Archipelago* thus: '*I am also greatly indebted to Mr. Samuel Stevens (who acted as my agent), both for the care he took of my collections, and for the untiring assiduity with which he kept me supplied, both with useful information and with whatever necessaries I required*'. Apparently when Wallace returned from Brazil after being shipwrecked, Stevens gave him his first proper meal in weeks, bought him new clothes and urged him to go on collecting, despite his traumatic losses. There are at least 80 bird specimens in the Natural History Museum, Tring, marked '*purchased of S Stevens*'. These were collected by a variety of professional collectors and scientists, and it is likely that he financed some expeditions. Stevens was well respected and worked with many naturalists with interests as varied as beetles and birds. The nominate race of the honeyeater was described by **Gould** in 1866.

STEWART

Stewart's Bunting *Emberiza stewarti* (**Blyth** 1884)
(Alt. White-capped Bunting)

Surgeon-General L C Stewart (1819–1888) was an officer in the British army in India. A predatory Indian snakehead fish *Channa stewarti*, described when he was probably still serving in India, may well have been named after him too.

STIERLING

Stierling's Barred Warbler *Calamonastes* [*Camaroptera*] *stierlingi*
(**Reichenow** 1901)
(Alt. Stierling's/Barred/Miombo Wren-Warbler, Barred Bush Warbler)
Stierling's Woodpecker *Dendropicos stierlingi* (Reichenow 1901)

Dr N Stierling was a German naturalist who collected in Nyasaland (now Malawi) and Tanganyika (now Tanzania) between 1887 and 1901. **Reichenow** named both birds after Dr Stierling.

STIRTON

Stirton's False-toothed Pelican *Pseudodontornis stirtoni* (Howard & Warner 1972) [Extinct]

Ruben Arthur Stirton (1901–1966) was an American palaeontologist who specialised in mammals, and a Professor at the University of California, Berkeley. His earlier work was on extant North American mammals. He conducted fieldwork in South America in the 1940s and turned his attention to Neogene mammalian fauna from Australia in the 1950s.

STOKES

Stokes' Hummingbird *Sephanoides fernandensis* (King 1831)
(Alt. Juan Fernandez Firecrown)

We believe this hummingbird is named after Captain John Lort Stokes (1811–1855). It was collected by Captain Phillip Parker King on Juan Fernández Island, Chile, and described by him. It also appears in a monograph by **Gould**, in 1861. Captain Phillip Parker King was the son of the third Governor of New South Wales and one of the Royal Navy's most senior navigators. He established his reputation during a series of four surveying voyages in Australian waters from 1817 to 1822. He also collected widely, especially on the voyage of *HMS Adventure* in 1828. Stokes also collected with Fitzroy, the Captain of *HMS Beagle*. Gould described many species which were collected by Charles **Darwin** on the *Beagle* voyage. Stokes was first mate on the *Beagle* in 1838 and succeeded Fitzroy as captain in 1846. Captain Stokes of the survey ship *HMS Acheron* surveyed in New Zealand and spent much of his time exploring in Australasia. He wrote *Discoveries in Australia* in 1846. It was said of him '*Stokes, in the course of his voyages around both the Australian mainland and Tasmania, had taken the trouble to get to know some Aboriginal people personally, and the fact that he had once been speared did not affect his opinion that actions of the colonists, some of which he had himself witnessed, were atrocious in the extreme.*' In view of the, albeit convoluted, connections it seems likely that he is the Stokes honoured in the hummingbird's name.

STOLICZKA

Stoliczka's Bushchat *Saxicola macrorhyncha* (Stoliczka 1872)
(Alt. White-browed Bushchat)
Stoliczka's Tit-Warbler *Leptopoecile sophiae* (**Severzov** 1873)
(Alt. White-browed/Severtzov's Tit-Warbler)
Stoliczka's Treecreeper *Certhia nipalensis* (**Blyth** 1845)
(Alt. Rusty-flanked Treecreeper)

Dr Ferdinand Stoliczka (1838–1874) was an Austrian palaeontologist and zoologist who was born in Moravia. He was educated at Prague and at the University of Vienna, where he obtained his doctorate. He collected during travels throughout India, from 1864 to 1874, as an assistant superintendent of the Geological Survey of India. He wrote some scientific papers, such as *Contribution towards the knowledge of Indian Arachnoidea*, in the Journal of the Asiatic Society. During the last ten years of his life he published geological memoirs on the western Himalayas and Tibet, and many papers on Indian zoology, from mammals to insects and corals. He took part in the Second Yarkand Mission, 1873–1874 but collapsed and died of spinal meningitis when '*returning loaded with the spoils and notes of nearly a year's research in one of the least-known parts of Central Asia*', according to his obituary in Nature. He is commemorated in species, from many phyla.

STONE

Stone's Catbird *Ailuroedus (buccoides) stonii* (**Sharpe** 1881)
(Alt. White-eared Catbird)
Stone's Pheasant *Phasianus colchicus elegans* (**Elliot** 1870)
(Alt. Ring-necked Pheasant)

Octavius C Stone was a collector who took the specimen of the catbird near the Laloki River, in southeastern New Guinea, around 1877. He supplied a number of specimens from New Guinea to Sharpe, from 1875 until 1878, but we can find no record of him having supplied anyone else. He wrote for the Royal Geographical Society's Journal a *Description of the country and catives of Port Moresby and neighbourhood, New Guinea*, in 1876, noting of certain indigenous people '*They paint the face with streaks by means of a rose-coloured lime*'. This account may well have been upstaged by **Stanley**'s report of his meeting with **Livingstone**, which appeared in the same issue. **Gould** made a lithograph of the catbird in his birds-of-paradise series. It is now generally regarded as a subspecies of the White-eared Catbird *A. buccoides.*

STORM

Storm's Stork *Ciconia stormi* (**Blasius** 1896)

Captain Hugo Storm was a German seaman from Lübeck who was captain of the steamship *Lübeck*, from 1887 until the mid-1890s. He collected in those parts of the Far East where his vessel traded; Sumatra, Singapore, Borneo, the Moluccas and Java, and visited areas where few Europeans had been before. He resigned his command in 1896 and settled in a town called Tower in North America. Storm sent zoological specimens, including Orang-utans *Pongo pygmaeus*, from the Far East to the museum in Lübeck, and he continued sending specimens there from North America. The museum's magazine, in 1901, named him as a donor and a life-sized portrait was placed in the collection room. Unfortunately this picture has been lost. The stork has been treated as a subspecies of the Woolly-necked Stork *C. episcopus*, but is now generally regarded as a separate species.

STRAUCH

Strauch's Pheasant *Phasianus colchicus strauchi* (**Prjevalsk**y 1876)
(Alt. Ring-necked Pheasant)

Probably after Professor Dr Alexander A Strauch (1832–1893), a Russian-German, who was Russian Consul, in Persia (Iran), in the later years of the 19th century. He was a physician and also a naturalist, mainly interested in reptiles and amphibians. A number of creatures are named after him in the vernacular and scientific forms, e.g. Strauch's Spotted Newt *Neurergus strauchii strauchii* and Strauch's Toad Agama *Phrynocephalus strauchii*. He described a number of reptiles, e.g. a tortoise *Testudo campanulata*, in 1862 and there are several fish named after him in their binomials in the 1870s. He was an academician of the Imperial Academy of Sciences in St Petersburg, through whom he published, in 1862, *Essai d'une exploration de L'Algérie*. He died in St Petersburg and is buried in the Lutheran cemetery there.

STRAUS

Straus's Apalis *Apalis chapini strausae* (**Boulton** 1931)
(Alt. Chapin's/Chestnut-headed Apalis)

Mrs Oscar Straus was the wife of the American collector and explorer Oscar Straus. Together and with others (such as **Mrs Laura Boulton**) they organised and made the Straus Central African Expedition under the auspices of the American Museum of Natural History, in New York, which collected botanical and ornithological specimens between 1920 and 1931.

STRESEMANN

Stresemann's Bristlefront *Merulaxis stresemanni* (**Sick** 1960) [Extinct]
Stresemann's Bush Crow *Zavattariornis stresemanni* (**Moltoni** 1938)
(Alt. Ethiopian Bush Crow)
Stresemann's Lorikeet *Trichoglossus forsteni stresemanni* (Meise 1929)
(Alt. Scarlet-breasted Lorikeet)
Stresemann's Lory *Lorius amabilis* (Stresemann 1931)
Stresemann's Maroon Oriole *Oriolus mellianus* (Stresemann 1922)
(Alt. Silver/Mell's [Maroon]Oriole)

Stresemann's Orange-fronted Hanging Parrot *Loriculus aurantiifrons batavorum* (Stresemann 1913)
Stresemann's Pygmy Parrot *Micropsitta pusio stresemanni* (**Hartert** 1926)
(Alt Buff-faced Pygmy Parrot)
Stresemann's Rosefinch *Carpodacus eos* (Stresemann 1930)
(Alt. Pink-rumped Rosefinch)
Stresemann's Scops Owl *Otus spilocephalus stresemanni* (**Robinson** 1927)
(Alt. Sumatran/Spotted [Mountain]/Vanderwater's Scops Owl)

Professor Erwin Friedrich Theodor Stresemann (1889–1972) was a German ornithologist and collector in the Far East. He wrote *Aves* in 1927 and *Die Entwicklung der Ornithologie von Aristoteles biz zur Gegenwart* in 1951. He was chairman of the Standing Committee on Ornithological Nomenclature of the International Ornithological Congress in 1954 and Curator of Birds at the Berlin Natural History Museum. He was the editor of the highly authorative *Journal für Ornithologie* for many years. The lory is now generally regarded as an aberrant specimen of the Purple-bellied Lory *L. hypoinchrous*. **Blyth** described the nominate race of the scops owl in 1846; the form *stresemanni* has been considered a subspecies of three different *Otus* species, a morph of *O. s. vandewateri* or even a separate species in its own right. The bristlefront is known from only two specimens and is perhaps extinct.

STRICKLAND

Strickland's Babbler *Trichastoma celebense* (Strickland 1849)
(Alt. Sulawesi/Celebes [Jungle]Babbler)
Strickland's Jay *Cyanolyca pumilo* (Strickland 1849)
(Alt. Black-throated [Dwarf] Jay)
Strickland's Shama *Copsychus stricklandii* (Motley & Dillwyn 1855)
(Alt. White-crowned Shama)
Strickland's Snipe *Gallinago stricklandii* (**G R Gray** 1845)
(Alt. Fuegian Snipe)
Strickland's Woodpecker *Picoides stricklandi* (**Malherbe** 1845)
(Alt. [Mexican] Brown-backed Woodpecker)

Hugh Edwin Strickland (1811–1853) was a geologist and naturalist who travelled quite widely after graduating from Oxford. In 1845 he married Catherine, daughter of Sir William **Jardine**. After their marriage they went on a European tour though Holland, Copenhagen, Berlin, Switzerland, Frankfurt and Brussels, visiting most of the museums on the way. Strickland was a well-liked and respected naturalist who corresponded with all the giants of his day including **Darwin**. He eventually became the Deputy Reader of Geology at Oxford. Strickland collected both fossils and birds; his home was described as '*quite a museum of ornithology*'. Most of Strickland's fossil collection is now in the Sedgwick Museum, Cambridge. The birds assembled by Strickland formed the original nucleus of the skin collection of the University Museum of Zoology also at Cambridge, which houses many of the specimens collected by Darwin. His book on *Ornithological Synonyms* was edited by his wife and Sir William Jardine, after his death, and published in 1855. He is most remembered for creating the 'Strickland Code' in

1842, which tried (in vain) to standardise zoological nomenclature for all time. He was killed in an accident in a railway cutting near Hull when making a pencil sketch of the strata in pursuit of his geological interests. The passenger train struck him – killing him instantly – at 29 minutes past four, according to his gold watch, which was broken in the impact.

STUHLMANN

> Stuhlmann's [Double-collared] Sunbird *Nectarinia* (*Cinnyris*) *stuhlmanni* (**Reichenow** 1893)
> Stuhlmann's Starling *Poeoptera stuhlmanni* (Reichenow 1893)
> Stuhlmann's Weaver *Ploceus baglafecht stuhlmanni* (Reichenow 1893)
> (Alt. Baglafecht Weaver)

Professor Dr Franz Stuhlmann (1863–1928) was a German zoologist and naturalist who collected in East Africa from 1888 until 1900. He did not confine himself to zoological specimens, as a number of the artefacts he collected in Africa from anthropological exhibits in museums. Stuhlmann travelled with **Emin** Pasha and after Emin's murder the German government published a monograph by Stuhlmann *Dr Franz Stuhlmann: Mit Emin Pasha ins Herz von Africa.*

STYAN

> Styan's Bulbul *Pycnonotus taivanus* (Styan 1893)
> (Alt. Taiwan/Formosan Bulbul)
> Styan's Grasshopper Warbler *Locustella pleskei* (**Taczanowski** 1889)
> (Alt. Pleske's Grasshopper Warbler)

Frederick William Styan was a tea trader and collector in China for 27 years who corresponded from Kiukiang. He was a Fellow of the Zoological Society and was elected as a Member of the British Ornithologists' Union in 1887. Styan's Red Panda *Panda fulgens styani* is also named after him.

SUCH

> Such's Ant-thrush *Chamaeza meruloides* (**Jardine** & Selby 1826)
> (Alt. Cryptic Ant-thrush)

Dr George Such (1798–1879) was the original collector of this ant-thrush, a southeastern Brazilian endemic that bears his name, which was given by **Vigors** in 1825. **Jardine** and Selby described the type, stating it to have been obtained by Dr Such in the 'Brazils'.

SUEUR

> Sueur's Triller *Lalage sueurii* (**Vieillot** 1818)
> (Alt. White-winged/-shouldered Triller)

Charles Alexandre Lesueur (1778–1846) was a French naturalist, artist and explorer. At the age of 23 he set sail for Australia and Tasmania. During the next four years he and fellow naturalist François **Péron** collected more than 100,000 zoological specimens, representing 2,500 new species, and Lesueur made 1,500 drawings. From 1815 until he returned to France, in 1837, he lived in the southern United States and undertook some local travel and collecting. In 1845, Lesueur was appointed Curator of the Musée d'Histoire Naturelle du Havre, which was created to house his drawings and paintings.

SUKATSCHEV

Sukatschev's Laughing-thrush *Garrulax sukatschewi* (**Berezowski** & **Bianchi** 1891)
(Alt. Snowy-cheeked/Black-fronted Laughing-thrush)

V P Sukatschev was a Russian trader and explorer, who collected in China from 1884 until 1887.

SUMICHRAST

Sumichrast's Blackbird *Dives dives* (**Deppe** 1830)
(Alt. Melodious Blackbird)
Sumichrast's Jay *Aphelocoma californica sumichrasti* (**Baird** & **Ridgway** 1874)
Sumichrast's Sparrow *Aimophila sumichrasti* (**Lawrence** 1871)
(Alt. Cinnamon-tailed Sparrow)
Sumichrast's Wren *Hylorchilus sumichrasti* (Lawrence 1871)
(Alt. Slender-billed Wren)

Francis E Sumichrast (1828–1882) was a Mexican naturalist. In 1863 he undertook an expedition in Mexico for the Smithsonian Institute, and their records refer to him as Professor Sumicrast. A number of other animals are named after him, e.g. Sumichrast's Vesper Rat *Nyctomys sumichrasti* and Sumichrast's Skink *Eumeces sumichrasti*.

SUNDEVALL

Sundevall's Waxbill *Estrilda rhodopyga* (Sundevall 1850)
(Alt. Crimson-rumped/Rosy-rumped/Red-eared/Rosy-winged Waxbill)

Carl Jakob Sundevall [sometimes written Sundewall] (1801–1875) was a Swedish zoologist and ornithologist, who had a strong interest in spiders as well as birds. He wrote *Svenska fåglarna*, in 1856, and *Tentamen (Methodi naturalis avium disponendarum tentamen)* in 1889.

SUTTON

Sutton's Screech Owl *Otus kennicottii suttoni* (Moore 1944)
(Alt. Western/Guadeloupe Screech Owl)
Sutton's Sharp-shinned Hawk *Accipiter striatus suttoni* (**Van Rossem** 1939)
Sutton's Warbler *Dendroica potomac*

George Miksch 'Doc' Sutton (1898–1982) was an American ornithologist and bird artist. When he was 17 he spent some weeks with Louis **Agassiz** with whom he had corresponded for a year. He began his professional life as keeper of the egg collection at the Carnegie Museum. In 1925 he became State Ornithologist for Pennsylvania and spent his time trying to persuade hunters that raptors should not be shot. He completed his doctorate at Cornell, where he remained for some years as Curator of Birds, which enabled him to undertake a number of trips and expeditions in the United States, Canada and Mexico. He was Curator of Birds at the Stovall Museum, in the University of Oklahoma, from 1952 and stayed on after retiring, in 1968, as George Lynn Cross Research Professor Emeritus of Zoology. The George Miksch Sutton Avian Research Centre (GMSARC) of Bartlesville, Oklahoma is named after him. According to the center 'A *recently-published bibliography of his works lists 13 books, 18 monographs and museum publications, 201 journal articles, 12 book reviews, four obituaries, 18 popular articles and eight essays. He also illustrated at least another 18 books*'. His books included *Iceland Summer: Adventures of a Bird Painter, Portraits of Mexican Birds, Fifty Selected Paintings* and *Bird Student*, his autobiography, in 1980. 'Who's Who' described him as '*the most prominent ornithologist of his time*'. **Van Rossem** described the large Mexican race of the hawk. Moore originally described the owl as a race of the Eastern Screech Owl *O. asio* but today it is considered a race of the Western Screech Owl. Sutton's Warbler proved to be a hybrid between the Northern Parula *Parula americana* and the Yellow-throated Warbler *Dendroica dominica*.

SWAINSON

Swainson's Antbird *Myrmeciza longipes* (Swainson 1825)
   (Alt. White-bellied Antbird)
Swainson's Fire-eye *Pyriglena atra* (Swainson 1825)
   (Alt. Fringe-backed Fire-eye)
Swainson's Flycatcher *Myiarchus swainsoni* (**Cabanis** & **Heine** 1859)
Swainson's Francolin *Francolinus swainsonii* (A **Smith** 1836)
   (Alt. Swainson's Spurfowl)
Swainson's Fruit Pigeon *Ptilinopus regina* (Swainson 1825)
   (Alt. Ewing's Fruit Pigeon, Rosy-crowned Fruit Dove)
Swainson's Glossy Starling *Lamprotornis* (*chalybeus*) *elisabeth*
(Stresemann 1924)
   (Alt. Miombo/Southern/Lesser Blue-eared Glossy Starling)
Swainson's Hawk *Buteo swainsonii* (**Bonaparte** 1838)
Swainson's Hummingbird *Avocettula recurvirostris* (Swainson 1822)
   (Alt. Fiery-tailed Awlbill)
Swainson's Lorikeet *Trichoglossus haematodus moluccanus* (J F Gmelin 1788)
   (Alt. Rainbow Lorikeet/Lory)
Swainson's Royal Flycatcher *Onychorhynchus coronatus swainsoni*
(Pelzeln 1858)
   (Alt. Atlantic Royal Flycatcher)
Swainson's Sparrow *Passer griseus swainsonii* (**Rüppell** 1838)
   (Alt. Northern Grey-headed Sparrow)
Swainson's Tanager *Piranga bidentata* (Swainson 1827)
   (Alt. Flame-coloured Tanager)
Swainson's Thrush *Catharus ustulatus* (**Nuttall** 1840)
   (Alt. Olive-backed Thrush)
Swainson's Toucan *Ramphastos swainsonii* (**Gould** 1843)
   (Alt. Chestnut-mandibled Toucan)
Swainson's Vireo *Vireo gilvus* (**Vieillot** 1808)
   (Alt. Eastern Warbling Vireo, Warbling Vireo)
Swainson's Warbler *Limnothlypis swainsonii* (Audubon 1834)
Swainson's Weaver *Ploceus nigricollis brachypterus* (Swainson 1837)
   (Alt. Black-necked Weaver)

William Swainson (1789–1855) was a naturalist and bird illustrator. He was born in Liverpool, the son of a collector of customs duty. After elementary education, he worked as a junior clerk and then in the army commissariat, in Malta and Sicily. Before going abroad he drew up, at the request of the Liverpool Museum, the *Instructions for Collecting and Preserving Subjects of Natural History*, which was privately printed in Liverpool in 1808. He served for eight years from 1807 to 1815 with the army commissariat and amassed a very large collection of zoological specimens. At the end of the Napoleonic wars he retired on half-pay. In 1816 he left for Brazil and travelled, collecting specimens, through Pernambuco to the Rio São Francisco and then on to Rio de Janeiro. On his return, in 1818, he published a sketch of his journey in the Edinburgh Philosophical Journal, in 1819, very briefly describing the voyage without any scientific detail.

He then endeavoured to sort his zoological specimens. He learned the new technique of lithography and produced *Zoological Illustration* in three volumes, from 1820 to 1823, the *Naturalists Guide*, in 1822 and *Exotic Conchology*. In 1828 he visited museums in Paris under the guidance of **Cuvier** and **St Hilaire**, meeting the other great French naturalists. In the same year he moved to the English countryside and worked as a full-time artist and author. In 1840 he left for New Zealand and became the country's first Attorney General. Unfortunately most of his specimen collection was lost on the voyage. He remained in New Zealand for the rest of his life. Swainson was a Fellow of the Linnean Society and of the Royal Society, as well as of numerous foreign academies. He published many papers, as well as *Birds of Brazil*, which appeared in five parts between 1834 and 1835. He wrote the bird section of Sir John **Richardson**'s *Fauna Boreali-Americana* and contributed to the 11 volumes of Lardner's *Cabinet Encyclopaedia*, from 1834 until 1840 and the three volumes of **Jardine**'s *Naturalist's Library*, from 1833 to 1846. Andrew **Smith** named the francolin after him and **Bonaparte** named the hawk in his honour. **Audubon** named the warbler after him and **Nuttal** the thrush. **Stresemann** described the glossy starling, *elisabeth* being named after his wife. The subspecies of the Rainbow Lorikeet is native to the islands of the Torres Strait and northeastern Australia.

SWIERSTRA

Swierstra's Francolin *Francolinus swierstrai* (**Roberts** 1929)

C J Swierstra (1874–1952) was a Dutch-South African entomologist who was born in Groningen and died in Pretoria. He became a Deputy Director of the Transvaal Museum, under J W B **Gunning**, around the beginning of the 20th century and eventually succeeded him as Director, a post he held from 1922 to 1946. He started his career in the museum in 1897 as a general assistant. He was an accomplished collector of butterflies, who described many type specimens, including *Lepidochrysops jefferyi* and *Lycaena jefferyi* in 1909, and *Leptoneura jansei* in 1911. He managed the ethnology collection, having conducted some field studies among the Hananwa people in 1912. A South African sucker-mouth fish *Chiloglanis swierstrai* is also named after him, as are a number of African beetles such as *Heterochelus swierstrai* and *Agraptocorixa swierstra*.

SWINDEREN

Swinderen's Parakeet *Agapornis swinderniana* (**Kuhl** 1820)
(Alt. Black-collared Lovebird)

Professor Dr Theodorus van Swinderen (1784–1851) was a Dutch naturalist, who was also a Doctor of Linguistics and of Law and was a school inspector for 40 years.

SWINHOE

Swinhoe's Bush Warbler *Cettia acanthizoides* (**Verreaux** 1871)
(Alt. Verreaux's/Yellowish-bellied Bush Warbler)
Swinhoe's Egret *Egretta eulophotes* (Swinhoe 1860)
(Alt. Chinese Egret)
Swinhoe's Finch-billed Bulbul *Spizixos semitorques* (Swinhoe 1861)
(Alt. Collared/Black-headed Finchbill)
Swinhoe's Minivet *Pericrocotus* (*roseus*) *cantonensis* (Swinhoe 1861)
(Alt. Brown-rumped Minivet)
Swinhoe's Pheasant *Lophura swinhoii* (**Gould** 1863)
Swinhoe's Pitta *Pitta nympha* (**Temminck** & **Schlegel** 1850)
(Alt. Fairy/Lesser Blue-winged/Chinese Pitta)
Swinhoe's Rail *Coturnicops exquisitus* (Swinhoe 1873)
(Alt. Siberian/Yellow Crake)

Swinhoe's Red-tailed Robin *Luscinia sibilans* (Swinhoe 1863)
(Alt. Rufous-tailed Robin/Pseudo Robin, Whistling Nightingale)
Swinhoe's Rock Thrush *Monticola gularis* (Swinhoe 1863)
(Alt. White-throated/breasted Rock Thrush)
Swinhoe's Snipe *Gallinago megala* (Swinhoe 1861)
Swinhoe's Storm Petrel *Oceanodroma monorhis* (Swinhoe 1867)
Swinhoe's Wagtail *Motacilla alba ocularis* (Swinhoe 1860)
(Alt. Pied/White Wagtail)
Swinhoe's Wagtail *Motacilla alba baicalensis* (Swinhoe 1861)
(Alt. Pied/White Wagtail)

Robert Swinhoe (1836–1877) was born in Calcutta, India but in 1852 he was sent to London to be educated. While at the University of London, in 1854, he was recruited into the China consular corps by the Foreign Office. Before he left for Hong Kong he deposited a small collection of British birds' nests and eggs with the British Museum. His time in China as a diplomat gave him a terrific opportunity as a naturalist; he explored a vast area which had not been open previously to any other collector. As a result he discovered new species at the rate of about one per month throughout the more than 19 years he was there. He was primarily an ornithologist and so the majority of his discoveries were birds, but his name is also associated with dozens of Chinese mammals, fish and insects. He first returned to London in late 1862. He brought part of his vast collection of specimens to meetings of the Zoological Society, as well as to their counterparts in France and Holland. He was somewhat taken aback by having to allow someone else to name the 200-plus new bird species which he had discovered, as he himself related; '*I have been blamed by some naturalists for allowing Mr. Gould to reap the fruits of my labours, in having the privilege of describing most of my novelties. I must briefly state, in explanation, that I returned to England elated with the fine new species I had discovered, and was particularly anxious that they should comprise one entire part of Mr. Gould's fine work on the Birds of Asia, still in progress. On an interview with Mr. Gould, I found that the only way to achieve this was to consent to his describing the entire series to be figured, as he would include none in the part but novelties, which he should himself name and describe. I somewhat reluctantly complied; but as he has done me the honour to name the most important species after me, I suppose I have no right to complain...*'.

SWYNNERTON

Swynnerton's Robin *Swynnertonia swynnertoni* (**Shelley** 1906)
(Alt. Swynnerton's Forest Robin)
Swynnerton's Thrush *Turdus olivaceus swynnertoni* (**Bannerman** 1913)
(Alt. Olive Thrush)

Charles Francis Massy Swynnerton (1877–1938) was principally an entomologist. He was born in India and worked in Africa, becoming the first game warden in Tanganyika (now Tanzania) between 1919 and 1929. He then spent ten years between 1929 and 1938 as head of tsetse research in East Africa. He published papers on many aspects of natural history, including *On the birds of Gazaland, Southern Rhodesia* in 1907. He was killed in an air-crash.

SYKES

Sykes' Crested Lark *Galerida deva* (Sykes 1832)
(Alt. Tawny Lark)
Sykes' Nightjar *Caprimulgus mahrattensis* (Sykes 1832)
Sykes' Warbler *Hippolais rama* (Sykes 1832)

Colonel William Henry Sykes (1790–1872) saw plenty of action in the 20 years after he joined the Bombay army, a part of the armed forces of the Honourable East India Company, at the age of 14. In 1824 he was appointed a statistician's position and later his statistical researches involved him in natural history. In 1832 he published *Catalogue of Birds of the Rapotorial and Incessorial Orders Observed in the Dukkan*. He retired from the military in 1837 and became a director of the East India Company, Rector of Aberdeen University and Member of Parliament for Aberdeen. The warbler is sometimes treated as a race of the Booted Warbler *Hippolais caligata* but authorities now accord it species status.

SYMONS

> Symons' Siskin *Serinus symonsi* (**Roberts** 1916)
> (Alt. Drakensberg Siskin)

Roden E Symons (1884–?) was a South African game warden and collector. The siskin is endemic to the Drakensberg Mountains of South Africa and Lesotho.

SZÉCHENYI

> Széchenyi's Monal Partridge *Tetraophasis szechenyii* (**Madárasz** 1885)
> (Alt. Buff-throated Partridge, Széchenyi's Pheasant Partridge)

Graf Bela Széchenyi (1837–1918) was a Hungarian explorer of Central Asia, Tibet, India, China and Japan. In 1877 he financed a three-year expedition to these regions, whose results were published by Kreitner, in 1881, in Vienna and attracted great attention among scientists throughout Europe. His father employed **Xantus**'s father on his estate.

TACZANOWSKI

> Taczanowski's Brush Finch *Atlapetes schistaceus taczanowskii* (P L **Sclater** & **Salvin** 1875)
> (Alt. Slaty Brush Finch)
> Taczanowski's Cinclodes *Cinclodes taczanowskii* (**Berlepsch** & Stolzmann 1892)
> (Alt. Surf Cinclodes)
> Taczanowski's Emerald *Agyrtia taczanowskii** (P L Sclater 1879)
> Taczanowski's Finch *Pyrgilauda taczanowskii* (**Prjevalsky** 1876)
> (Alt. White-rumped/Mandeili's Snowfinch)
> Taczanowski's Finch *Sicalis taczanowskii* (**Sharpe** 1888)
> Taczanowski's Grebe *Podiceps taczanowskii* (Berlepsch & Stolzmann 1894)
> (Alt. Junín Flightless Grebe)
> Taczanowski's Nightjar *Lurocalis rufiventris* (Taczanowski 1884)
> (Alt. Rufous-bellied Nighthawk)
> Taczanowski's Tinamou *Nothoprocta taczanowskii* (P L Sclater & Salvin 1875)

Wladyslaw Taczanowski (1819–1890) was a Curator for the Zoological Cabinet of the Royal University of Warsaw, later the Branicki Museum, which he transformed from a teaching institution into a scientific centre. An outstanding zoologist and ornithologist, he took part in collecting expeditions in North Africa with A S Waga, in 1866 to 1867, and with **Kalinowski** in South America. He wrote *Ornithologie du Peru* which was published in French, in three volumes, between 1884 and 1886. This was the first handbook of the birds of a Neotropical country and is still considered an important benchmark for South American ornithology. There is also a fish, Taczanowski's Gudgeon *Ladislavia taczanowskii*, named after him.

TALLMAN

Tallman's Fruiteater *Pipreola riefferii tallmanorum* (O'Neill & **Parker** 1981)
(Alt. Green-and-black Fruiteater)

Professor Dan A Tallman (1947–) and Dr Erika J Tallman (1949–) are a married couple of American ornithologists. Erika is Chief Information Officer for the Northern State University, Aberdeen, South Dakota. Dan is currently working there as a Professor of Biology, having taught at this institution since 1979. That year he was awarded a PhD by Louisiana State University, Baton Rouge, where he was a Graduate Research and Teaching Assistant from 1971. He is associated with the Patuxent Wildlife Research Centre's Bird Banding Program and is editor of South Dakota Bird Notes, the journal of the South Dakota Ornithologists' Union. He also co-authored *The Birds of South Dakota* in 1991. The couple have published a great many articles, both jointly and separately, in national and international journals and in South Dakota Birds. Dan and Erika discovered a new taxon whilst Dan was undertaking fieldwork in Peru for his PhD, which was entitled *Colonization of a Semi-isolated Temperate Cloud Forest: Preliminary Interpretation of Distributional Patterns of Birds in the Carpish Region of the Department of Huanuco, Peru.*

TAVERNER

Taverner's Goose *Branta canadensis taverneri* (**Delacour** 1951)
(Alt. Richardson's/Todd's/Hutchins'/Canada Goose)

Sir Percy Algernon Taverner (1875–1947) was a Canadian ornithologist employed at the National Museum of Natural Sciences, in Ottawa, from 1911 until 1942. He was a leading advocate of conservation and wild bird protection and his recommendations, based on his own research, played a major part in designating Point Pelee National Park and in establishing other bird sanctuaries along the north shore of the Gulf of St Lawrence and on Bonaventure Island. He was an active member of the Council of the Ottawa Field-Naturalists' Club and an associate editor and frequent contributor to The Canadian Field-Naturalist. He wrote *Birds of Eastern Canada, Birds of Western Canada* and *Birds of Canada.* A special issue of *The Canadian Field-Naturalist*, written by John L Cranmer-Byng, is devoted to his life and work. The Taverner Cup, a 24-hour bird race in Canada, is named after him.

TAXIDERMISTS

Taxidermy, is on the one hand, a necessary scientific endeavour: it involves not just mounting specimens in realistic poses for display purposes, but also the production of the thousands of cabinet skins which form museum reference collections. On the other hand, taxidermy has sometimes been seen as a rather dubious artistic pursuit. Skilled practioners have identified fake specimens, produced by amalgamating material from various sources, in order to fool the unwary. As a result its reputation sometimes fell so low that a number of creatures (including the Duck-billed Platypus *Ornithorhynchus anatinus* and the Dodo *Raphus cucullatus*) were once assumed, mistakenly, to be attempts to defraud a credulous public. No fewer than 12 people who described themselves as taxidermists have birds named after them. Charles Andrew **Allen**, who also invented a bird-call device, Abraham Dee **Bartlett**, who was more famed as a zoologist, and John Graham **Bell**, who was a companion to **Audubon** and C **Constant** head the list. Pierre Antoine **Delalande** was another who used his skills for a museum. Theodor **Erckel** stuffed the specimens he collected himself as did Bruno **Geisler** with his brother. Leonard **Harwood** also stuffed what he collected, but as a hobby. Benjamin **Leadbeater** was a dealer who sold his work, as did George **Loddiges**, who was also an artist. H C **Macklot** was so accomplished that he was appointed to assist members of the Dutch Natural Science Commission on a New Guinean expedition. Many of E C H **Seimund**'s mounted birds are on display in the Raffles Museum. There were others who were not primarily taxidermists but had the necessary skill and experience to prepare skins of the specimens which they handled.

TEERINK

Teerink's Munia *Lonchura teerinki* (**Rand** 1940)
(Alt. Black-breasted Mannikin)

C G J Teerink (1897–1942) was a major in the Dutch army in the East Indies. As a captain in 1938, he commanded a Dutch army contingent of 56 officers and men that accompanied the third **Archbold** Expedition to New Guinea. In the early days of March 1942 he commanded the fifth Battalion of Regular Infantry and was involved in heavy fighting in Java against Japanese invaders. His demise in 1942 suggests that he either died in action or in captivity.

TEIJSMANN

Teijsmann's Fantail *Rhipidura teysmanni* (**Büttikofer** 1892)
(Alt. Rusty-bellied/Rusty-flanked/Sulawesi/Celebes [Rusty] Fantail)

Johannes Elias Teijsmann [or Teysmann] (1808–1882) was a Dutch botanist who was the Curator of the Buitenzorg Gardens, in Java, from 1830 until his death. The gardens were subsequently renamed in his honour. He also collected in Sumatra and was an occasional visitor to Timor. Other people collected living botanical specimens for him.

TEMMINCK

Temminck's Cormorant *Phalacrocorax capillatus* (Temminck & **Schlegel** 1850)
(Alt. Japanese Cormorant)
Temminck's Courser *Cursorius temminckii* (**Swainson** 1822)
Temminck's Crowned Willow Warbler *Phylloscopus coronatus* (Temminck & Schlegel 1847)
(Alt. Eastern Crowned Warbler)
Temminck's Cuckoo-shrike *Coracina temminckii* (**Müller** 1843)
(Alt. Cerulean Cuckoo-shrike)
Temminck's Gull *Larus crassirostris* (**Vieillot** 1818)
(Alt. Black-tailed Gull)
Temminck's Hornbill *Penelopides exarhatus* (Temminck 1823)
(Alt. Sulawesi Hornbill)
Temminck's Jungle Babbler *Trichastoma pyrrogenys* (**Blyth** 1859)

Temminck's Kingfisher *Cittura cyanotis* (Temminck 1824)
(Alt. Lilac-cheeked/Lilac-marked Kingfisher, Sulawesi/Celebes Blue-eared Kingfisher)
Temminck's Lark *Eremophila bilopha* (Temminck 1823)
(Alt. Temminck's Horned Lark)
Temminck's Pygmy Woodpecker *Picoides temminckii* (**Malherbe** 1849)
(Alt. Sulawesi/Celebes Pygmy Woodpecker)
Temminck's Robin *Erithacus komadori* (Temminck 1835)
(Alt. Riukiu/Ryukyu Robin)
Temminck's Roller *Coracias temminckii* (Vieillot 1819)
(Alt. Purple-winged/Celebes/Sulawesi Roller)
Temminck's Sapphirewing *Pterophanes cyanopterus* (*temminckii*) (**Fraser** 1839)
(Alt. Great Sapphirewing)
Temminck's Seedeater *Sporophila falcirostris* (Temminck 1820)
Temminck's Stint *Calidris temminckii* (Leisler 1812)
Temminck's Sunbird *Aethopyga temminckii* (Müller 1843)
Temminck's Tragopan *Tragopan temminckii* (J E **Gray** 1831)

Coenraad Jacob Temminck (1778–1858) was a Dutch ornithologist, illustrator and collector. He was the first Director of the Rijksmuseum van Natuurlijke Historie, in Leiden, in 1820 and held that post until he died. He was a wealthy man who had a very large collection of specimens and live birds. His first task as an ornithologist was to catalogue his father's very extensive collection and he may have named some birds after his father. (His father was Jacob Temminck, for whom **Le Vaillant** collected specimens). In 1815 he issued his *Manuel d'ornithologie, ou Tableau Systematique des Oiseaux qui se Trouvent en Europe* and he wrote *Nouveau Recueil de Planches Coloriees d'Oiseaux* in 1820.

TENGMALM

Tengmalm's Owl *Aegolius funereus* (Linnaeus 1758)
(Alt. Boreal/Richardson's Owl)

Peter Gustaf Tengmalm (1754–1803) was a doctor and naturalist. He qualified at Uppsala and practised as a family doctor in Uppsala, Västerås and Eskilstuna. When he died he left comprehensive medical and ornithological notes. The owl was first classified as *Strix funerea* by Linnaeus but later was named after Dr Tengmalm, initially as *S. tengmalmi*. Subsequently this was changed to the present-day *Aegolius funereus*.

TESSMAN

Tessman's Flycatcher *Muscicapa tessmanni* (**Reichenow** 1907)

Gunter Tessman (1889–1971) was a German botanist and anthropologist who collected in Guinea and Cameroon from 1904 until 1914, and in Peru in 1923. He contributed to the translation and understanding of at least one Andean language. In 1921 he reported on homosexuality, amongst different ethnic groups in Cameroon. He was later based in Curitiba in Paraná state, Brazil and worked at the Museu Paraná. He wrote *Die Indianer Nordost-perus*, in 1930, and *Die Volker und Sprachen Kamerun*, in 1932.

THAYER

Thayer's Gull *Larus thayeri* (W S Brooks 1915)

Colonel John Eliot Thayer (1862–1933) was an American ornithologist and collector who amassed a very large collection of specimens and an ornithological library. His bird skins are still at Harvard University, who bought his collection in 1904. His father and brother were merchant bankers.

THEKLA

Thekla Lark *Galerida theklae* (Brehm 1858)

Thekla Brehm (1832–1858) was the daughter of the German ornithologist Christian Ludwig Brehm. Brehm wrote the description of the lark in 1858, the year in which his daughter died of heart disease.

THERESA

Theresa's Snowfinch *Montifringilla theresae* (**Meinertzhagen** 1937)
(Alt. Meinertzhagen's/Afghan Snowfinch)

Theresa Clay was a British parasitologist and ornithologist and a companion to her uncle Richard **Meinertzhagen**. She wrote *Fleas, Flukes and Cuckoos – A Study of Bird Parasites* with Miriam Rothschild in 1952. Her uncle described and named the snowfinch after her. He also described a number of other subspecies which he named after her in their trinomials, including a no-longer recognised race of the Red-rumped Wheatear *Oenanthe moesta theresae*.

THOLLON

Thollon's Moorchat *Myrmecocichla tholloni* (**Oustalet** 1886)
(Alt. Congo Moorchat)

F-R Thollon (?–1896) was a French collector in the Congo and a member of the de Brazza Mission, in Gabon, which was noted for its fish collection, in 1884. (The Congolese city of Brazzaville was named after the Mission.) He is also celebrated in the names of a wide range of animals including Thollon's Red Colobus *Procolobus tholloni*, several fish, such as *Tilapia tholloni, Alestes tholloni* and *Brycinus tholloni*, the velvet worm *Mesoperipatus tholloni*, the elephant tick *Amblyomma tholloni* (which carries the cattle disease 'Heartwater') and a number of plants, such as *Peperomia tholloni*, from Gabon.

THOMSON

Thomson's Flycatcher *Erythrocercus livingstonei thomsoni* (**Shelley** 1882)
(Alt. Livingstone's Flycatcher)

Joseph Thomson (1858–1895) was a Scot who has been described as '*one of the most colourful and prudent of 19th century African explorers*'. At only 20 years old he was placed as second in charge on his very first exploration for the Royal Geographic Society, in 1879. The leader, the Scottish cartographer Keith Johnson, succumbed to dysentery, at the age of 34, very early in the expedition. Thomson buried him under a tree on which he carved Johnston's initials and the date of his death (28 June 1879), just outside the village of Behobeho, near the Rufiji River, in southern Tanzania. He said that because of his inexperience he asked himself, "*should we simply turn back?*" and answered, "*I feel I must go forward, whatever might be my destiny.*" He carried on and successfully led the expedition to Lake Nyasa (now Lake Malawi) and Lake Tanganyika. Thereafter, he made many more safe and successful explorations on behalf of the Royal Geographic Society. He explored routes through Kenya and Tanzania, from 1878 until 1884, Nigeria, in 1885 and Morocco, in 1888. He was the first to explore Maasai land successfully, simply because he was not confrontational. He said: "*in my opinion the travellers strength would lie more in his manner towards and treatment of the natives than in his guns and revolvers.*" Despite his relaxed 'fun' style of leadership he always put the safety of the party first and his motto was '*He who goes slowly, goes safely; he who goes safely, goes far.*'He is most famous for having Thomson's Gazelle *Gazella rufifrons thomsoni*, which he was first to find, named in his honour. In 1885 he wrote *Through Masai Land: A Journey Of Exploration Among The Snowclad Volcanic Mountains And Strange Tribes Of Eastern Equatorial Africa, Being The Narrative Of The Royal Geographical Society's Expedition To Mount Kenya And Lake Victoria Nyanza, 1883–1884.* The diseases he caught in tropical Africa led to his early death from pneumonia. He is buried at Morton Cemetery in Thornhill, Dumfries & Galloway, Scotland.

THUNBERG

Thunberg's Swiftlet *Aerodramus fuciphagus* (Thunberg 1812)
(Alt. Edible-nest Swiftlet)

Karl Peter Thunberg (1743–1828) was a Swedish student of Linnaeus. In August 1770 he journeyed through the Low Countries to Paris, where he stayed for six months to study medicine and natural history. Between 1772 and 1775 he travelled to South Africa, Japan, Java for the Dutch East India Company and later to Ceylon in 1778, before returning to Europe in 1779. His major publications include *Flora Japonica*, in 1784, *Flora Capensis* and *Prodromus Plantarum Capensium*, in 1794. He was subject to much ridicule during his life for his 'Thunbergisms'. For example: '*Water is the element which makes sea journeys both outside and inside of the Netherlands so nimble and comfortable*'. Or, on first going to France: '*To me it could not but seem both strange and ridiculous to hear Burghers and Farmers all speak that, in other places so noble, language.*'

THURA

Thura's Rosefinch *Carpodacus thura* (**Bonaparte** & **Schlegel** 1850)
(Alt. White-browed Rosefinch)

Thura Nilsson was the daughter of the Swedish ornithologist, geologist, palaeontologist and ethnologist Svenn Nilsson (1787–1883).

THURBER

Thurber's Junco *Junco hyemalis thurberi* (A W **Anthony** 1893)
(Alt. Dark-eyed/Oregon Junco)

Dr George Thurber (1821–1890) was a self-educated chemist and botanist. He is often called the most accomplished horticulturist in America, but he first worked as a pharmacist. He served as botanist of the United States Boundary Commission, which surveyed the boundary between the United States and Mexico, from 1850 until 1854. He took a master's degree in chemistry at Brown University and then went through a succession of different jobs until he became editor of American Agriculturist, a position which he held for 22 years. He was an expert on grasses, and many species such as Thurber's Fescue *Festuca therberi* are named after him. He left an uncompleted manuscript on American grasses at his death. **Anthony** described the junco.

TICKELL

Tickell's Blue Flycatcher *Cyornis tickelliae* (**Blyth** 1843)
(Alt. Tickell's Niltava)

Tickell's Flowerpecker *Dicaeum erythrorhynchos* (**Latham** 1790)
(Alt. Pale-billed Flowerpecker)
Tickell's Hornbill *Anorrhinus tickelli* (Blyth 1855)
(Alt. Brown Hornbill)
Tickell's Jungle Babbler *Pellorneum tickelli* (Blyth 1859)
(Alt. Tickell's/Buff-breasted/Buettikofer's Babbler, Mountain Brown Babbler)
Tickell's Laughing-thrush *Garrulax strepitans* (Blyth 1855)
(Alt. White-necked Laughing-thrush)
Tickell's Leaf Warbler *Phylloscopus affinis* (Tickell 1833)
(Alt. Tickell's Willow Warbler)
Tickell's Sibia *Heterophasia melanoleuca* (Blyth 1859)
(Alt. Black-headed/Black-capped/Black-eared Sibia)
Tickell's Thrush *Turdus unicolor* (Tickell 1833)

Colonel Samuel Richard Tickell (1811–1875) was a British army officer, artist and ornithologist in India and Burma (now Myanmar). He has been described by Sir Norman B Kinnear, as '*one of the best field naturalists India has known*'. He made important early contributions to Indian ornithology and mammalogy through field observations and the collection of specimens, while he was stationed in several localities in the 1830s and 1840s. He planned to publish a book on the birds and mammals of India but he never did. However, his manuscript notes and illustrations are preserved in the library of the Zoological Society of London. These notes contain many references to observations of birds in Bihar, Orissa, Darjeeling and Tenasserim. He also published studies about the structure and vocabulary of the Ho language. The flycatcher was probably named for his wife and was described by **Blyth**.

TODD

Todd's Antwren *Herpsilochmus stictocephalus* (Todd 1927)
Todd's Scrub Flycatcher *Sublegatus obscurior* (Todd 1920)
(Alt. Amazonian Scrub Flycatcher)
Todd's Goose *Branta canadensis interior* (Todd 1927)
(Alt. Canada Goose)

Walter Edmond Clyde Todd (1874–1969) was a US ornithologist who first described **Willis**'s Antbird *Cercomacra (tyrannina) laeta*, in 1920. He wrote *Birds of the Labrador Peninsula* and *Birds of Western Pennsylvania*. Todd was a prolific ornithologist on South American avifauna, cooperating with many of the seminal contributors of his day, including Frank **Chapman** and co-authoring the classic *The Birds of the Santa Marta Region of Colombia: A Study of Altitudinal Distribution* with Meb **Carriker**.

TOWNSEND

Townsend's Shearwater *Puffinus auricularis* (C H Townsend 1890)

Charles Haskins Townsend (1859–1944) was an American who spent much of his life working for the US Fish Commission and later became the Director of the New York Aquarium. During 1883 and 1884 he explored northern California and, in 1885, the Kobuk River in Alaska. He published *Field Notes on the Mammals, Birds, and Reptiles of Northern California* in Proceedings of the U.S. National Museum, Washington, D.C, 1887. He discovered the bird in 1889 and described it himself the next year.

TOWNSEND

Townsend's Bunting *Spiza townsendi*
(Alt. Townsend's Finch)
Townsend's Cormorant *Phalacrocorax penicillatus* (**Brandt** 1837)

(Alt. Brandt's Cormorant)
Townsend's Junco *Junco hyemalis oreganus* (Townsend 1837)
(Alt. Dark-eyed Junco)
Townsend's Petrel *Oceanodroma melania* (**Bonaparte** 1854)
(Alt. Black Storm Petrel)
Townsend's Ptarmigan *Lagopus mutus townsendi* (**Elliot** 1896)
(Alt. Rock Ptarmigan)
Townsend's Solitaire *Myadestes townsendi* (Audubon 1833)
Townsend's Sparrow *Passerella iliaca townsendi* (Audubon 1838)
(Alt. Fox Sparrow)
Townsend's Warbler *Dendroica townsendi* (Townsend 1837)

John Kirk Townsend (1809–1851) was an American naturalist, ornithologist and collector. He sent many specimens to **Audubon** who gave him free reign in naming anything which he found. These specimens included the solitaire and the bunting, which Audubon named after him. Apparently Townsend was going to name the warbler that he found but learned that **Nuttall** had provisionally named it for him already, so he acknowledged the latter's precedence. However, the accepted citation has remained with Townsend. He wrote *Narrative of A Journey across the Rocky Mountains*, which tells the story of Wyeth's expedition across the Rockies to the Pacific Ocean, between 1834 and 1835. Ironically, Townsend died of arsenic poisoning, which was the 'secret' ingredient of the powder he had formulated to use in his taxidermy. **Ridgway** named a subspecies of the Snow Bunting *Plectrophenax nivalis townsendi* in his honour. Townsend's Bunting is only known from a single specimen, which is now regarded as a freak individual of the Dickcissel *S. americana*, lacking the normal carotenoid pigments.

TOULSON

Toulson's Swift *Apus horus toulsoni* (**Bocage** 1871)
(Alt. Horus Swift)

A Toulson was a collector in Angola around 1870. **Bocage** described him as '*an amateur…former trader with Loanda*'. He is also commemorated in the names of at least one mammal *Cephalopus toulsoni* and an amphibian *Hyperolius parallelus toulsonii*, both described by Bocage. The swift may be a distinct subspecies, but is often regarded as a dark local colour morph of the Horus Swift *A.horus*.

TRADERS/TRAVELLERS

Quite a few of the people honoured eponymously were travellers who happened upon new species serendipitously rather than through zoological endeavour. Thomas C **Bridges**, W **Dodson**, M **Rück** and Sir E **Shelley** were cases in point, whereas Alcide Dessalines **d'Orbigny**, Xander Theodor von **Middendorf**, Francois **Peron** and Karl Peter **Thunberg** were travellers who also saw themselves as naturalists. Frederick P **Drowne** was a traveller, who like many in his day, was an amateur collector of curiosities. Some, like Frederick Vavasour **McConnell**, later presented their collections to museums. Others, like Mervyn George **Palmer** and Emile **Parzudaki**, were sent on collecting expeditions by museums because they were seasoned travellers. A number of travellers did so to trade; Roderick Ross **MacFarlane** and Bernard Rogan **Ross** being examples, as was V P **Sukatschev**, who also explored during the same period. A few travellers, such as Baron Dr Johann Jacob von **Tschudi**, Pieter van den **Broecke** and Johan Frederik **Victorin,** had birds named after them purely because of their fame.

TRAILL

Traill's Flycatcher *Empidonax traillii* (**Audubon** 1828)
(Alt. Willow Flycatcher)

Dr Thomas Stewart Trail (1781–1862) was a Scottish zoologist, physician and philosopher. He was a founder of the Royal Institution of Liverpool and was appointed Professor of Medical Jurisprudence at Edinburgh University, in 1832. He edited the eighth edition of the *Encyclopaedia Britannica*. He was also influential in the separation of the Natural History Museum from the British Museum and in the latter's reconstitution in South Kensington, London. **Audubon** visited Traill in Liverpool and described the Flycatcher, writing '*I have named this species after my learned friend, Doctor Thomas Stewart Traill, of Edinburgh, in evidence of the gratitude which I cherish toward that gentleman for all his kind attention to me*'.

TRAVERS

Travers's Wren *Traversia lyalli* (Travers 1894) [Extinct]
(Alt. Stephens/Stephens Island Wren)

Henry H Travers (1844–1928) was a New Zealand ornithologist who sold **Buller** two specimens of the wren, which he had himself described, although **Rothschild** had earlier obtained nine specimens. The construction of a lighthouse on Stephens Island in 1894 was accompanied by wholesale deforestation there, and the lighthouse keeper's cat is credited with exterminating the wren, which was possibly the only truly flightless passerine. The scientific honorific commemorates Lyall, the lighthouse keeper, who was an amateur ornithologist.

TRAYLOR

Traylor's Forest Falcon *Micrastur buckleyi* (Swann 1919)
(Alt. Lesser Collared/Buckley's Forest Falcon)
Traylor's Tinamou *Crypturellus obsoletus traylori* (**Blake** 1961)
(Alt. Brown Tinamou)

Major Melvin Alvah Traylor Jr (1915–) is an American ornithologist and collector, and son of a man of the same name, who was an unsuccessful candidate for the Democratic nomination for President and created the First National Bank of Chicago. Traylor became Assistant Curator of Birds at the Chicago Field Museum in recognition of his contributions to the ornithology division since 1937 as an expedition collector and unpaid associate. Since his retirement, in 1980, Traylor has continued his work as Curator Emeritus. He wrote *Birds of Angola*, in 1960 and, together with J V Remsen, *An Annotated List of the Birds of Bolivia*, in 1989. He also collaborated in the production of a number of *Ornithological Gazetteers*; with Lorain Stephens on Peru (1983) and on the Guianas (1985) and with Raymond A Paynter Jr, on Brazil, in 1991. Traylor and Paynter were joint recipients of the Elliot **Coues** Award in 2001. Swann described the falcon in 1919 as a race of the Collared Forest Falcon, but Traylor established it as a full species in 1948. He was also recently honoured in the name *Tolmomyias traylori*, the Orange-eyed Flycatcher, in 1997.

TREGANZA

Treganza's Heron *Ardea herodias treganzai* (Court 1908)
(Alt. Great Blue Heron)

Alberto Owen Treganza was an architect, an able artist and a well-known amateur ornithologist. As a Californian architect he was influenced by Craftsman architecture and the Midwest's Prairie School style. Among the buildings he designed was the original

police station in San Diego. His homestead was purchased for $5 in 1906, by his parents, who arrived in San Diego County, in 1890, by wagon from Salt Lake City, Utah. His wife Antoinette Treganza (née Kaufman) was a writer and also an ornithologist. We do not know which of the two the heron was named for; it could have been for both of them. However, the subspecies *treganzai* is not currently recognised. In 1928, the Lemon Grove Chamber of Commerce commissioned Alberto to design a float for the Fourth of July parade in San Diego. Alberto designed a seven-by-twelve-foot plaster lemon mounted on a wooden platform adorned with lemons, oranges, and grapefruit from local orchards and borne on a truck from the Lemon Grove Fruit Packing House. His daughter Amorita rode on the float as 'Miss Lemon Grove'. (She went on to greater things, becoming an actress at the Old Globe in the 1930s and 1940s, San Diego Woman of the Year in 1964, and a pioneer in paediatric optometrics.) In 1929 Antoinette began a regular column, Walks and Talks with Mother Nature. Alberto passed on his interest in natural history to his son Professor Adaan Eduardo Treganza, known as 'Don' or 'Trig' (1916–1968), who was primarily an anthropologist and archaeologist. The Adaan E Treganza Anthropological Museum is named after him as he established it at the San Francisco State College, where he was head of the then-new anthropology department.

The Treganzas studied 'snowy herons' (presumably Snowy Egrets *Egretta thula*) in the Tule marshes around Great Salt Lake around 1914; to quote from their notes of 2 May 1914: '*This date found us in the marsh country destined for the rookeries. Within half a mile we noted a number of snowy herons rise at our right, whereupon we immediately secured a boat and set out to make investigation. We nosed into the dense Tule growth to moor our boat, and had just started to break our way. With the first crackle of the reeds, head after head was seen to rise, long crane like necks stretched up for inquiry, pure white birds, and in close proximity an iridescent black one; the ibis with their curved bills looking for all the world like quaint old Jews, lacking but spectacles and a skull cap. Another breaking of reeds and the whole colony rose en masse, a worrying confusion of wings and squawks and dangling legs; and for once we were actually convinced that white was black and black was white, so confounded were heron and ibis. This colony covered an area 20 yards wide by 100 yards long, and contained no less than 150 pairs of snowy herons, and about 100 pairs of white-faced glossy ibis. All of the ibis nests and many of the herons' were under construction, while some of the latter contained four to five fresh eggs. Having traversed this portion of the marsh at least once annually, we were surprised to find this new and larger colony, for previous years it contained only ducks and a very small colony of black-crowned night heron. All the nests were constructed of the growing reeds and rushes. Though quite dense, there was little matted down growth of years previous, thus much resembling the site of Black Sloughs, Salt Lake County.*'

TRINIDADIAN

Friederich William **Urich** was a Trinidadian Naturalist. He was a founder member of the Trinidad Field Naturalists Club and, so far as we know, the only Trinidadian ever to have a common bird name honouring him.

TRISTRAM

Tristram's Bunting *Emberiza tristrami* (**Swinhoe** 1870)
Tristram's Flowerpecker *Dicaeum tristrami* (**Sharpe** 1884)
(Alt. Mottled Flowerpecker)

Tristram's Grackle *Onychognathus tristramii* (**P L Sclater** 1858)
(Alt. Tristram's Starling)
Tristram's Honeyeater *Myzomela tristrami* (E P Ramsay 1881)
(Alt. Sooty Myzomela)
Tristram's Pygmy Parrot *Micropsitta finschii tristrami* (**Rothschild** & **Hartert** 1902)
(Alt. Green Pygmy Parrot)
Tristram's Scrubfowl *Megapodius layardi* (Tristram 1879)
(Alt. New Hebrides/Banks Island/Vanuatu Scrubfowl)
Tristram's Serin *Serinus syriacus* (**Bonaparte** 1850)
(Alt. Syrian Serin)
Tristram's Storm Petrel *Oceanodroma tristrami* (Salvin 1896)
(Alt. Stejneger's Storm Petrel)
Tristram's Warbler *Sylvia deserticola* (Tristram 1859)
Tristram's Wheatear *Oenanthe moesta* (**Lichtenstein** 1823)
(Alt. Red-rumped Wheatear)
Tristram's Woodpecker *Dryocopus javensis richardsi* (Tristram 1879)
(Alt. White-bellied Woodpecker)

The Reverend Henry Baker Tristram FRS (1822–1906) was canon of Durham cathedral and a traveller, archaeologist, naturalist and antiquarian, who asembled a large collection. Despite being a churchman he was an early supporter of **Darwin**. He wrote a number of accounts of his explorations including *A Journal of Travels in Palestine* and *The Great Sahara: Wanderings South of the Atlas Mountains*, in 1860. In the latter he describes how he penetrated far into the desert and made an ornithological collection in the course of gathering material for his work. He writes extremely interestingly on the indigenous peoples and their customs, as well as on the natural history of the region, including references to mammals, reptiles, molluscs and plants, as well as birds. He actually originally went there because of ill health. **Salvin**, who described the Petrel, was Tristram's cousin by marriage.

TRITON

Triton's Cockatoo *Cacatua galerita triton* (**Temminck** 1849)
(Alt. Sulphur-crested Cockatoo)

The correct name is actually the Triton Cockatoo, not Triton's and as far as we can ascertain it is not named after a person.

TRUDEAU

Trudeau's Tern *Sterna trudeaui* (**Audubon** 1838)
(Alt. Snowy-crowned Tern)

James de Berty Trudeau (1817–1887) was at various times a physician, a surgeon, a painter, an explorer, a collector and a General in the artillery of the Confederacy in the American Civil War. He was severely wounded at Shiloh and was later captured by forces of the Union. He was another friend of **Audubon**'s and may have accompanied him over the Rockies in 1842. He procured the tern which Audubon named after him.

TSCHUDI

Tschudi's Parrot *Pionus tumultuosus* (Tschudi 1844)
(Alt. Speckle-faced/Plum-crowned Parrot)
Tschudi's Woodnymph *Thalurania tschudii* (**P L Sclater & Salvin** 1858)
Tschudi's Tyrannulet *Zimmerius viridiflavus* (Tschudi 1844)
(Alt. Golden-faced Tyrannulet)

Baron Dr Johann Jacob von Tschudi (1818–1889) was a Swiss explorer, who travelled in

Peru, Brazil, Argentina and Chile. He was also a physician, a diplomat, a naturalist, a student of South America, a zoologist, a hunter, an anthropologist, a cultural historian, a language researcher and a statesman, who collected in Peru between 1838 and 1842. He wrote *Untersuchungen uber die Fauna Peruana Ornithologie*, in 1844. P L **Sclater** and **Salvin** described the hummingbird, using a name coined for it by **Gould**, but we are unable to ascertain to which species the name appertains..

TULLBERG

Tullberg's Woodpecker *Campethera tullbergi* (**Sjöstedt** 1892)
(Alt. Fine-banded Woodpecker)

Tycho Fredrik Hugo Tullberg (1842–1920) was a Swedish zoologist. He gained a doctorate in philosophy at Uppsala in 1869 and became a lecturer there in 1871. He was instrumental in the development of modern zoological veterinary medicine in Sweden. Between 1882 and 1907 he was Professor of Zoology at Uppsala and after 1902 he was the Chairman of the Linnean Society at Hammarby. As far as we can ascertain he was an academic as opposed to someone active in the field. He published in Swedish, English and German (which was the preferred learned language for Swedes of his day). His works included *Neomeni, a new genus of invertebrate animals* in 1875 and *Djurriket* (Animals of the Kingdom) in 1885.

TURATI

Turati's Boubou *Laniarius turatii* (J **Verreaux** 1858)
(Alt. Turati's Bush Shrike)

Conte Ercole Turati (1829–1881) was a Milanese banker as well as a naturalist and collector. Although he accumulated an enormous collection of over 20,000 skins, he had no time to study them, but instead made the specimens available for others to so do. A palace which was constructed for him in Milan in 1880 is now the Chamber of Commerce. Giacinto Martorelli wrote a book about him, *Commemorazione scientifica del Conte Ercole Turati*, in 1898.

TURNER

Turner's Eremomela *Eremomela turneri* (**Van Someren** 1920)

H V Allan Turner (1876–1953) lived in Kenya from 1909 until his death.

TURNER

Turner's Ptarmigan *Lagopus mutus atkhensis* (Turner 1882)
(Alt. Rock Ptarmigan)

Lucien M Turner (1848–1909) was a member of the Army Signal Corps who collected natural history and ethnological specimens for the Smithsonian Institution. From 1874 to 1877, he was a meteorological observer for the Signal Service at St Michael, Alaska, and then trained voluntary observers in the Aleutians from 1878 to 1881. In 1882 he was sent to Fort Chimo, Labrador, as an observer and remained there for two years before returning to Washington. Everywhere he went, Turner made extensive collections and sent them to the Smithsonian. He also had a rapport with the local people, the Innu and Inuit, and spent his free time studying and recording their culture; noting everything from their clothing, dwellings and weapons to their tools. He also observed their routines, language and stories. His pictures of them and their camps are among the earliest photographs of the arctic. He wrote a number of books including *Contributions to the Natural History of Alaska*, in 1886, and *Ethnology of the Ungava District, Hudson Bay Territory* in 1894. The Rock Ptarmigan has many subspecies, most of them named eponymously.

TWEEDDALE

Tweeddale's Babbler *Stachyris speciosa* (Tweeddale 1878)
(Alt. Flame-templed Babbler)
Tweeddale's Hawk-Owl *Ninox philippensis spilocephalas* (Tweeddale 1879)
(Alt. Philippine Hawk-Owl)
Tweeddale's Woodpecker *Mulleripicus funebris fuliginosus* (Tweeddale 1877)
(Alt. Sooty Woodpecker)

Arthur Hay (1824–1878) was the ninth Marquis of Tweeddale, Viscount Walden, although he only succeeded to the title in 1876. He was President of the Zoological Society of London and an amateur ornithologist, who had a large collection of birds, insects, reptiles and mammals. He appointed Carl Bock to complete his collection with species from the Malay Archipelago. Bock collected more than 130 specimens, which are now in the Natural History Museum, Tring and he described around 40 of them.

TYREE

Tyree's Penguin *Pygoscelis tyreei* (G G Simpson 1972) [Extinct]

Peter Tyree (1956–) collected the type specimen of this fossil penguin, which is named after him, on Montunau Beach, North Canterbury, New Zealand. Like Alan **Ridgen** he was 11 years old at the time! We assume that Ridgen and Tyree may well have been school friends. George Gaylord Simpson (1902–1984) described the extinct bird in 1972 in the Records of the Canterbury Museum, stating: '*At Christmas 1967, Peter Tyree, then aged 11, found another unusually complete fossil penguin skeleton at Motunau Beach. In July of the following year Alan Ridgen, then also 11 found still another specimen at a nearby locality, less complete than the first two but including a number of well-preserved associated bones from one individual. These young men appreciated the exceptional scientific value of their finds and therefore submitted them for technical study and presented them for permanent preservation to the Canterbury Museum, Christchurch, which is also the repository of the first Motunau specimen.*'

TYTLER

Tytler's Willow/Leaf Warbler *Phylloscopus tytleri* (W E **Brooks** 1872)

Colonel Robert Christopher Tytler (1818–1872) was a naturalist, a photographer and a collector. He served very actively in the British army throughout India and even in Kabul and other parts of Afghanistan, from 1835 until his death on 10 September 1872. This service was only broken by a return to England for two years in the 1850s due to ill health. He was the third superintendent of the convict settlement at Port Blair, part of the Andaman Islands administration. He spent the last six months of his life in charge of the museum at Simla. He was a very keen photographer and took some 500 large-format calotype negatives of scenes associated with the Indian Mutiny of 1857. He is also remembered in the scientific names of several other species, such as the Long-tailed Parakeet *Psittacula longicauda tytleri*.

UNKNOWN

As we stated in the Preface there are five birds for which we have heard, come across or accidentally invented common names, but for which as yet we have been unable to find corresponding scientific names. In our nightmares, we wonder if they are not figments of our own imaginations! However, it is right that they should be mentioned, in case some reader may be able to identify them. They are: Cabanis's Batis, Harris's Hornbill, Heuglin's Starling, Moreau's Bustard and Reichenow's Reed Warbler.

UPCHER

Upcher's Warbler *Hippolais languida* (Ehrenberg 1833)

Sir Henry Morris Upcher JP (1839–1921), Deputy-Lieutenant of the County of Norfolk, was a close friend and travelling companion of H B **Tristram**. He was born at Sheringham Hall, near Cley, Norfolk, and was apparently the owner of the only private lifeboat in England, in 1911. According to a report '*In January, 1876, a male specimen of the Great Bustard appeared in a Fen near Feltwell, the property of Mr. H. M. Upcher.*' Ehrenberg described the warbler in 1833 but his original description is 'rather vague' and Tristram redescribed it in 1864, calling it Upcher's Warbler *Hippolais upcheri* after his friend. The binomial reverted to Ehrenberg's original but the newer common name has endured.

URICH

Urich's Tyrannulet *Phyllomyias urichi* (**Chapman** 1899)

Friederich William Urich (1872–1936) was a Trinidadian Naturalist. He was a founder member of the Trinidad Field Naturalists Club, in about 1891, and is most famous for discovering an eyeless cave-dwelling catfish *Caecorhamdia urichi*, which is endemic to the island. He published his finding in an article in the Field Naturalists Club Journal in 1895 as *A visit to the Guacharo Cave of Oropuche*. In 1915 we find him described as Adjutant, with the rank of captain, to the Military Department of the Government of Trinidad, presumably a temporary job during the First World War. **Chapman** described the tyrannulet in 1899.

URSULA

Ursula's Sunbird *Nectarinia* [*Cinnyris*] *ursulae* (**Alexander** 1903)
(Alt. Fernando Pó Sunbird)

Ursula Davies was the niece of the British explorer Captain Boyd **Alexander**, who described and named the sunbird.

USSHER

Ussher's Dusky Flycatcher *Muscicapa ussheri* (**Sharpe** 1871)
(Alt. Ussher's Flycatcher)
Ussher's Spinetail *Telacanthura ussheri* (Sharpe 1870)
(Alt. Mottled Spinetail)

Herbert Taylor Ussher CMG (1836–1880) was, at various times, the Governor of the Gold coast (now Ghana), the Governor of Tobago and Consul-General in Borneo. He sent many specimens back to the British Museum. His African specimens were collected for him by Aubinn, a local man. He seems to have been highly regarded by his contemporaries since he is honoured in the binomials of various fish, butterflies and other animals, as well as in those of the Rufous Fishing Owl *Scotopelia ussheri* and the Garnet Pitta *Pitta granatina ussheri*. He wrote *Notes on the Ornithology of the Gold Coast*, which was published in 1874, and was a co-author on another work with **Sharpe**, who described both species.

VAN DAM

Van Dam's Vanga *Xenopirostris damii* (**Schlegel** 1865)

D C Van Dam was a Dutch naturalist who collected in Madagascar, particularly in Cacamba and Pasandava, in the 1860s to 1880s, initially in the company of François P L **Pollen** until the latter's death in 1866. He also collected in Réunion in 1862 and 1863. His work was the subject of a book by Bleeker in 1875; *Recherches sur la Faune de Madagascar et de ses Dépendances d'après les Découvertes de François P. L. Pollen et D. C. van Dam*. Many of Van Dam's and Pollen's specimens were sent to **Milne-Edwards** and Grandidier, at the British Museum (Natural History) or the Royal Museum of Natural History, in Holland. Van Dam is also remembered in many other scientific names including those of the butterfly *Acraea damii* and of the Damba, a Madagascan endemic freshwater fish *Paretroplus damii*.

VAN DEN BROECKE

Van den Broecke's Rail *Aphanapteryx bonasia* (Sélys Longchamps 1848)
[Extinct]
(Alt. Mauritius Red Rail)

Pieter van den Broecke (1585–1640) was a Dutch traveller, who was first a merchant commander in West Africa and subsequently served the Dutch East India Company in Java, Arabia, Persia and India. He also took part in the battle of Jakarta. He wrote a journal of his voyages to Cape Verde, Guinea and Angola, between 1605 and 1612. In 1630 he brought home a fleet from India and was rewarded by the company for 17 years of service with a gold chain worth 1,200 guilders. It is just visible in his portrait. Van den Broecke knew Frans Hals well, and was a witness at the baptism of Hals's daughter, Susanna, in 1634. The rail was last seen in the wild in 1638 by Peter Mundy, an English traveller, by which time it appears already to have been rare.

VAN HASSELT

Van Hasselt's Sunbird *Nectarinia [Leptocoma] sperata hasseltii* (**Temminck** 1825)
(Alt. Purple-throated Sunbird)

Dr Johan Coenraad van Hasselt (1797–1823) came to fame as the first person to climb Mt Pangrango in Java. In August 1821, **Kuhl** and van Hasselt, two young biologists working for The Netherlands Commission for Natural Sciences made the first ascent. Van Hasselt qualified as a physician. However, he was more interested in natural history, as was his fellow student and close friend Heinrich Kuhl. They made various excursions in Europe, visiting some natural history museums where they met de Lamarck, **Cuvier** and other famous zoologists of the time, and they published several papers on zoological subjects. In 1820 they were sent to western Java to study natural history. They started their work on the way, studying the pelagic fauna, as well as that of Madeira, the Cape of Good Hope and the Cocos Islands. When Kuhl died after less than a year in Java, van Hasselt spent his time working still harder until he himself died two years later. It is confusing that A W M Van Hasselt was also a zoologist who worked in Java in the 1820s and later. We believe that a large number of arachnids, fish and other animals are named for him and not for J C van Hasslet, although some of these may have been collected by J C van Hasselt and studied later by other zoologists. They include Hasselt's Spiny Spider *Gasteracantha hasseltii*, Hasselt's Catfish *Silurichthys hasseltii*, Hasselt's Goby *Callogobius hasseltii*, Hasselt's Goatfish *Osteochilus hasseltii* and Van Hasselt's Sprat *Dussumieria elopsoides*. **Temminck**, who Kuhl assisted, described this race of the sunbird, which is no longer recognised.

VAN OORT

Van Oort's Black Lory *Chalcopsitta atra spectabilis*
(Alt. Black Lory)
Van Oort's Fantail *Rhipidura dedemi* (Van Oort 1911)
(Alt. Seram/Ceram [Rufous]/Streaky-breasted Fantail)
Van Oort's Fig Parrot *Psittaculirostris desmarestii intermedia* (Van Oort 1909)
(Alt. Large Fig Parrot)
Van Oort's Palm Cockatoo *Probosciger aterrimus stenolophus* (Van Oort 1911)
(Alt. Great Black/Great Palm Cockatoo)

Eduard Daniel Van Oort (1876–1933) was a Dutch zoologist who collected in the East Indies. He wrote *Ornithologia Neerlandica. De Vogels van Nederland* in 1918. The race of Black Lory is known from just one specimen, which represents a hybrid with the Yellow-streaked Lory *C. scintillata*.

VAN ROSSEM

Van Rossem's Grosbeak *Pheucticus chrysopeplus*
(**Vigors** 1832)
(Alt. Vigor's/Yellow Grosbeak)
Van Rossem's Gull-billed Tern *Gelochelidon nilotica vanrossemi* (**Bancroft** 1929)

Adriaan Joseph Van Rossem was an American ornithologist who published most prolifically in the 1920s and 1930s. He collected for the University of Arizona and made a number of expeditions, including one to El Salvador in 1925. Together with Miller he produced a study on Laughing Gulls *Larus atricilla* in 1929 and *Two new races of the Black Chachalaca from Central America* in 1934. He worked as an ornithologist at the California Institute of Technology and was co-author of a number of books and articles with Donald

R **Dickey**, including *The Birds of El Salvador* in 1938. He also wrote *A Distributional Survey of the Birds of Sonora, Mexico*, which was published in 1945. A number of other birds have *vanrossemi* in their scientific name, including the Russet-crowned Motmot *Momotus mexicanus vanrossemi*.

VAN SOMEREN

Van Someren's Canary *Serinus koliensis* (**Grant** & Mackworth-Praed 1952)
(Alt. Papyrus Canary)

Victor Gurney Logan Van Someren (1886–1976) was a naturalist who worked in East Africa. He certainly worked on both butterflies and weavers (Ploceidae) in Kenya since he wrote scientific papers on both. His collection of butterflies and other insects is in the Natural History Museum Tring, and his collection of African birds is in The Field Museum, Chicago. We also came across a reference to *Birds of East Africa: A Collection of Lithographs Prepared from the Originals Drawn from Nature by VGL van Someren Between the Years 1909 and 1937*. He published *Days with Birds – Studies of Habits of some East African Species*, in 1956 and also *Revisional Notes on African Charaxes (Lepidoptera: Nymphalidae)*, in 1963. There are several other birds commemorating him, such as a race of the African Finfoot *Podica senegalensis somereni* and a race of the Black-throated Canary *Serinus atrogularis somereni*.

VANDERBILT

Vanderbilt's Babbler *Malacocincla vanderbilti* (Meyer de Schauense & **Ripley** 1940)
(Alt. Vanderbilt's Jungle Babbler)

George Washington Vanderbilt (1862–1914) was a famously rich American philanthropist who sponsored collecting expeditions. He was also a conservationist as evidenced by the existence of what has been called '*The Cradle of Forestry in America (a National Historic Site… an outdoor museum and monument to the birthplace of scientific forestry in the United States – formerly a part of George Washington Vanderbilt's estate called 'Pisgah Forest'. Here, Dr Carl Alwin Schenck, hired by Vanderbilt to oversee his vast private forestlands, established the Biltmore Forest School in 1898.*' Meyer de Schauensee and **Ripley** described the babbler from a single specimen taken in northern Sumatra. It has at times been regarded as a species but alternatively as conspecific with either Horsfield's Babbler *M. sepiaria* or the Black-browed Babbler *M. perpiciliata*.

VANDEWATER

Vandewater's Scops Owl *Otus spilocephalus vandewateri* (**Robinson** & Kloss 1916)
(Alt. Spotted/Mountain/Stresemann's Scops Owl)

The origin of this name is a mystery. There were a number of Dutch people called Van der Watter living in Sumatra around the time when the bird was first collected, but we have been entirely unsuccessful in connecting the bird with any particular individual. There is also a plant, *Parahebe vandewateri*, honouring the name. **Robinson** and Kloss originally collected the type specimen of the owl from Korinchi Peak, in west Sumatra in 1914, and named it *Pisorhina vandewateri*.

VAURIE

Vaurie's Flycatcher *Ficedula crypta* (Vaurie 1951)
(Alt. Cryptic Flycatcher)
Vaurie's Nightjar *Caprimulgus centralasicus* (Vaurie 1960)

Dr Charles J Vaurie (1906–1975) was a French ornithologist and systematist, who published many definitive articles between the 1940s and 1960s, including, for example, *A Genetic*

Revision of Flycatchers of the Tribe Muscicapini in the Bulletin of the American Museum of Natural History. He is best known for his *Birds of the Palearctic Fauna*, which was published between 1959 and 1965 and *Tibet and Its Birds*, in 1972. He seems to have been a keen stamp collector too.

VAUX

Vaux's Swift *Chaetura vauxi* (**Townsend** 1839)

William Sansom Vaux (1811–1882) was a Philadelphian mineralogist and archaeologist, who served as President of the United States Zoological Society and Vice-President of the Academy of Natural Sciences, Philadelphia. During his life Vaux acquired an extensive mineralogical and archaeological collection, which he bequeathed to the Academy of Natural Sciences, together with a handsome endowment for their preservation. His friend John Kirk **Townsend** discovered the swift in 1835 and named it in Vaux's honour.

VELEZ

Velez's Rusty-faced Parrot *Hapalopsittaca amazonina velezi* (Graves & Uribe Restrepo 1989)
(Alt. Rusty-faced Parrot)

We do not believe that the bird is named after a person at all but instead after Velez, a location in the Central Andes of Colombia where this parrot is found. The parrot is more commonly (and we believe more correctly) referred to as the Velez Rusty-faced Parrot.

VERAGUA

Veragua's Parakeet *Aratinga pertinax ocularis* (P L **Sclater** & **Salvin** 1864)
(Alt. Brown-throated Conure)

This should more properly be called the Veraguas Parakeet since it is named after a geographical region and not a person It is found in the western state of Veraguas, on the border with Colombia.

VERREAUX, J B

Verreaux's Eagle *Aquila verreauxii* (**Lesson** 1831)
(Alt. Black Eagle)

Jean Baptiste Edouard Verreaux (1810–1868) was brother to Jules (see below) and was also a French naturalist, collector and dealer. They both worked in China and in South Africa's Cape Colony. There was a third brother, Joseph Alexis Verreaux, yet another naturalist, who lived in Cape Town and also died in 1868. The Verreaux family traded in Paris from a huge emporium for stuffed birds and feathers, which they called the Maison Verreaux. They were clearly ambitious taxidermists and gained notoriety on account of having once attended the funeral of a tribal chief, whose body they then disinterred, took to Cape Town and stuffed! The Catalán veterinarian Francisco Darder, then curator of the zoo of Barcelona, purchased the 'specimen' from one of the brothers' sons, Edouard Verreaux, in 1888. This controversial exhibit was on show in Barcelona until the end of the 20th century, when the man's descendants demanded that it should be returned for a decent burial.

VERREAUX, J P

Verreaux's Batis *Batis minima* (J & J Verreaux 1855)
(Alt. Gabon Batis)
Verreaux's Bush Warbler *Cettia acanthizoides* (Jules Verreaux 1871)

(Alt. Yellowish-bellied Bush Warbler)
Verreaux's Coua *Coua verreauxi* (Grandidier 1867)
Verreaux's Fulvetta *Alcippe ruficapilla* (J Verreaux 1870)
    (Alt. Spectacled/Rufous-headed Fulvetta/Tit-Babbler)
Verreaux's Monal Partridge *Tetraophasis obscurus* (J Verreaux 1869)
    (Alt. Chestnut-throated Partridge)
Verreaux's Eagle Owl *Bubo lacteus* (**Temminck** 1820)
Verreaux's Song Thrush *Turdus mupinensis* (Laubmann 1920)
    (Alt. Chinese Song Thrush)
Verreaux's Turaco *Tauraco macrorhynchus* (**Fraser** 1839)
    (Alt. Yellow-billed Turaco)
Verreaux's Twinspot *Hypargos margaritatus* (**Strickland** 1844)
    (Alt. Rosy/Pink-throated Twinspot)

Jules Pierre Verreaux (1807–1873) was a French natural historian, a nephew of **Delalande** and married to the latter's sister. He was employed as an ornithologist and plant collector for the Musée d'Histoire Naturelle, in Paris, which sent him to Australia in 1842. He made collections of plants around Hobart, Tasmania, between December and April 1844 and around Sydney, New South Wales from April 1844 to November 1846. His servant, Émile, collected plants for him near Port Macquarie and Camden Haven, New South Wales, and also from the Moreton Bay district and Durundur, Queensland. He returned to France, around 1851, with a collection of natural history specimens, reported to number 115,000 items! He also assisted Andrew **Smith** in founding the South African National Museum at Cape Town. **Bonaparte** (1855) named the White-tipped Dove *Leptotila verreauxi* after him and his brother Jean (see above).

VERSTER

Verster's Berrypecker *Melanocharis versteri* (**Finsch** 1876)
    (Alt. Fan-tailed Berrypecker)

Florentius Abraham Verster van Wulverhorst (1826–1923) was a Dutch professional zoologist. He was the full-time administrator of the Rijksmuseum van Natuurlijke Historie in Leiden, from 1860 to 1920. His son Floris Hendrik Verster (1861–1926) became a very well known 'dark' impressionist painter.

VICTORIA

Victoria Crowned Pigeon *Goura victoria* (**Fraser** 1844)
    (Alt. Queen Victoria Crowned Pigeon)
Victoria Nuthatch *Sitta victoriae* (Rippon 1904)
    (Alt. White-browed Nuthatch)
Victoria's Riflebird *Ptiloris victoriae* (**Gould** 1849)
    (Alt. Queen Victoria Riflebird)

Queen Victoria (1819–1901) was Queen of Great Britain and Empress of India from 1837. **Gould** named the pigeon in 1850. The riflebird was collected by J **MacGillivray** and presented to the British Museum by Captain Stanley, following the voyage of *HMS Rattlesnake*.

VICTORIN

Victorin's Warbler *Bradypterus victorini* (**Sundevall** 1860)
    (Alt. Victorin's Scrub Warbler)

Johan Frederik Victorin (1831–1855) was a Swedish traveller who visited South Africa's Cape Colony, between 1853 and 1855, where he died of tuberculosis. He wrote *Resa I kaplandet åren 1853–1855* (Journey to the Cape Land in the Years 1853–1855) *and Jakt och naturbilder* (Hunting and Nature Scenes), which was published in 1863. **Sundevall** named the warbler in Victorin's honour after his early death.

VIEILLOT

Vieillot's Barbet *Lybius vieilloti* (**Leach** 1815)
Vieillot's [Black] Weaver *Ploceus nigerrimus* (Vieillot 1819)
Vieillott's Crested Fireback *Lophura ignita rufa* (**Raffles** 1822)
(Alt. Crested Fireback)
Vieillot's Starling *Streptocitta albicollis* (Vieillot 1818)
(Alt. White-necked/Celebes/Sulawesi/Buton Myna/Starling)
Vieillot's Storm Petrel *Fregetta grallaria* (Vieillot 1817)
(Alt. White-bellied Storm Petrel)

Louis Jean Pierre Vieillot (1748–1831) was a French ornithologist and businessman who was in Haiti for some time. He and his family eventually fled to the United States during the French Revolution but he returned to France later where he died in poverty. His fellow Frenchmen **Buffon** and **Cuvier** have largely overshadowed him but his contributions to ornithology are very significant and **Lesson** described him as a genius. In Vieillot's time a number of ornithologists mistook juveniles, females or moulting individuals of *known* birds for new species. Vieillot was the first to study these plumage changes, which was in itself a major development in accurate classification. He was also an early proponent of studying *living* birds and not only the *dead* skins in museum collections. Nevertheless, he described a great many species and his name appears in the scientific name of many more, such as that of the Puerto Rican Lizard-Cuckoo *Saurothera vieilloti*. He wrote *Oiseaux Dorés ou a Reflets Metalliques*, in 1800, *Histoire Naturele des plus Beaux Oiseaux Chanteurs de la Zone Torride*, in 1805, and *La Galerie des Oiseaux*, in 1820.

VIGORS

Vigors's Bustard *Eupodotis vigorsii vigorsii* (A **Smith** 1831)
(Alt. Karoo/Vaal Korhaan, Karoo/Black-throated Bustard)
Vigors's Crested Tit *Parus melanolophus* (Vigors 1831)
(Alt. Black-crested/Spot-winged Tit)
Vigors's Grosbeak *Pheucticus chrysopeplus* (Vigors 1832)
(Alt. Van Rossem's/Yellow Grosbeak)
Vigors's Warbler *Dendroica pinus* (**Wilson** 1811)
(Alt. Pine Warbler)
Vigors's Wren *Thryomanes bewickii spilurus* (Vigors 1830)
(Alt. Bewick's Wren)

Nicholas Aylward Vigors (1785–1840) was the Irish-born Secretary of the Zoological Society of London, in 1826, and edited their journal from 1827 until 1834. He served in the Peninsular War from 1809 to 1811. He went to Oxford and took his MA in 1818. He was elected a Fellow of the Royal Society in 1826. Vigors contributed a chapter on ornithology in *Zoology of Captain Beechey's Voyage, 1839*, based on coloured drawings and notes made by **Collie** during an expedition to the western coasts of the Americas. Vigors named several species, including some collected by Collie in California, for instance the Black Turnstone *Arenaria melanocephala*, Pygmy Nuthatch *Sitta pygmaea*, Bewick's Wren *Thryomanes bewickii*, California Towhee *Pipilo crissalis*, Band-tailed Pigeon *Columba fasciata*, Western Bluebird *Sialia mexicana*, Black Phoebe *Sayornis nigricans* and American Avocet *Recurvirostra americana*. **Audubon** was a friend and he named Vigors' Warbler in his honour, but the name disappeared when the type specimen proved to be an immature Pine Warbler.

VILLAVISCENSIO

Villaviscensio Sabrewing *Campylopterus villaviscensio* (**Bourcier** 1851)
(Alt. Napo Sabrewing)

Manuel Villaviscensio was an Ecuadorian geographer who collected in his native country from 1850 until 1865. In 1858 he produced a street plan of the capital, Quito. That same year he wrote the first description of a beverage most widely known as ayahuasca and related its use in sorcery and divination among the peoples of the Upper Río Napo. He described his own self-intoxication when using it, an experience which made him feel that he was 'flying' to most marvellous places. He reported that '*natives using this drink were able to foresee and answer accurately in difficult cases, be it to reply opportunely to ambassadors from other tribes in a question of war; to decipher plans of the enemy through the medium of this magic drink and take proper steps for attack and defence; to ascertain, when a relative is sick, what sorcerer has put on the hex; to carry out a friendly visit to other tribes; to welcome foreign travellers or, at least to make sure of the love of their womenfolk*'. In 1888 he reported 'tar' on the surface of the Río Hollin. This turned out to be a natural surface-seepage of crude oil, which is now commercially produced in Ecuador. His son, also Manuel Villaviscensio (1840–1925) became a rear-admiral, war hero, senator and government minister.

VIOSCA

Viosca's Pigeon *Columba fasciata vioscae* (**Brewster** 1888)
(Alt. Band-tailed Pigeon)

Paul Percy Viosca Sr was the United States consul at La Paz in Baja California, Mexico. According to **Bent**, in his *Life Histories of North American Gallinaceous Birds*, in 1932, the bird was named in Viosca's honour at the request of Marston Abbott **Frazar** because he (Viosca) '*has been most kind and helpful in furthering the success of Mr. Frazar's explorations.*' Paul Percy Viosca Sr married Wilhelmine A Bischoff in 1890. Their son Paul Percy Viosca Jr (1892–1961) was a notable professional biologist, who worked as Curator of Reptiles and Amphibians and Curator of Fishes at the Los Angeles State Museum, and as Director of Fisheries, Los Angeles, among other posts. Among Viosca Jr's claims to fame was discovering the importance of fire in the ecology of the Louisiana marshes. He wrote *Louisiana Out-of-Doors* in 1933 and *Pondfish Culture* in 1937. He is commemorated in the scientific name of a salamander, the Gulf Coast Waterdog *Necturus beyeri viosca*. We can find no further information about the father, after whom we assume the bird was named. The pigeon was originally described by **Say** in 1823, who wrote '*A beautiful species of pigeon was shot near the mountain…along a small tributary of the Platte River near the Rockies, July 9, 1819. It may be distinguished by the name of band-tailed pigeon.*' **Brewster** described this race.

VIRGINIA

Virginia's Warbler *Vermivora virginiae* (**Baird** 1860)

Named for Mary Virginia Anderson (1833–1912), whose husband was a United States army surgeon and who discovered the species, around 1858.

VO QUY

Vo Quy's Pheasant *Lophura* (*edwardsi*) *hatinhensis* (Vo Quy 1975)
(Alt. Vietnamese Pheasant)

Professor Vo Quy (1929–) is a Vietnamese ornithologist. In 1951, during the Vietnamese uprising against French colonial rule, he walked to China, where he and his colleagues set up a temporary university. In 1956 Vo Quy, amongst others, founded the University of Hanoi and established the Department of Zoology, which he later headed. For years he was Dean of the Faculty of Biology. He has a PhD in ornithology from the University of Moscow, which was awarded in 1966. Vo Quy has inspired and trained several generations of conservationists. He led the first team of environmental scientists south of the 17th parallel to investigate the environmental damage caused during the Vietnam war. Now almost every school student in Vietnam plants 1–3 trees per year as part of the school curriculum. In 1985 he founded the country's first conservation and management training institution, the Centre for Natural Resources and Environmental Studies (CRES). He ran the conservation centre on a shoestring and undertook activities which the government did not have money for when it was recovering from the ravages of war. The Vietnamese government declared the forests near Ho Ke Go as a nature reserve but had no money to protect them. These forests are the home of the Ha Tinh or Vo Quy's Pheasant as it is fondly called after this 'son of Ha Tinh province', who discovered the bird in 1964. During the Vietnam war it was thought that the pheasant and several other species of birds and mammals had become extinct, as the region along the Ho Chi Minh trail was one of the most heavily bombed and deforested during the many years of uninterrupted warfare. However, in 1990 villagers in the Ho Ke Go area caught some Ha Tinh pheasants. Those that managed to escape the local dinner plates were taken to the Hanoi Zoo, where a successful captive breeding programme is underway. In 1996 Vo Quy was awarded the World Wide Fund for Nature's highest honour, the Gold Medal, in recognition of his pioneering environmental conservation and education in Indochina. He was the architect of an agreement between Laos, Cambodia and Vietnam for international cooperation in protecting rare and endangered migratory species, and in establishing trans-frontier reserves, or 'Peace Parks', on their shared borders. Today Vo Quy is recognised by practically everyone as the 'star' conservationist of one of Vietnam's favourite television programmes. Twice a week he explains in simple language the mysteries of nature and why people should protect it. Vo Quy's Pheasant was con-sidered a full species until recently but is now classed by some as a subspecies of Edward's Pheasant *L. edwardsi*. Vo Quy himself described the pheasant as a new species in 1975.

VON DER DECKEN

Von der Decken's Hornbill *Tockus deckeni* (**Cabanis** 1869)

Baron Carl Claus von der Decken (1833–1865) was a German explorer. He visited the region of Lake Nyasa (now Lake Malawi) on his first expedition in 1860. He later explored East Africa and was the first European to try to climb Mt Kilimanjaro. In 1861, together with a geologist, he visited the Kilimanjaro massif. A year later, he ascended the mountain to 13,780 feet, approaching its permanent snowcap and mapping the area. He also established its height to be about 20,000 feet. His 1863 expedition took him to Madagascar and the Mascarene Islands. His final journey was in Somalia, in 1865, when he sailed up the River Jubba until his ship, the *Welf*, foundered in the rapids above Bardera (Baardheere). There he and three other Europeans were killed by Somalis. He sent a considerable quantity of specimens from Somalia to the museum in Hamburg. After his death his letters were edited and published in book form, in 1869, under the title *Reisen in ost-Afrika*.

VON SCHRENCK

See **Schrenck**

VUILLEUMIER

Vuilleumier's Flowerpiercer *Diglossa brunneiventris vuilleumieri* (G R Graves)
(Alt. Black-throated Flowerpiercer)

Dr François Vuilleumier (1938–) was awarded his PhD in biology from Harvard University, in 1967, under Professor Ernst **Mayr**. He has been Curator of Birds in the Department of Ornithology of the American Museum of Natural History since 1974 and chaired that department from 1987 to 1992. He is also Adjunct Professor of Biology at the City University of New York. He has taught at the University of Paris, in France, the University of Lausanne, in Switzerland, the University of the Andes, in Merida, Venezuela, and the College of the Atlantic in Bar Harbor, Maine, USA. Between 1964 and 1986 he carried out research on the evolution and systematics of Andean birds. During that period he wrote a monograph on the genus *Diglossa*, as well as numerous other papers and monographs. Since 1985 he has undertaken research on the evolution and systematics of birds elsewhere in southern South America, especially in Patagonia, and published many papers on this topic. He has written about 260 articles, mostly scientific but including two in Birding Magazine. He has also been a host lecturer and study leader on about 18 cruises with the Discovery Tours Program of the American Museum, to destinations such as the North Pole, Antarctica, Kenya, Irian Jaya and Amazonia. He is a President of the Neotropical Ornithological Society. Vuilleumier's Flowerpiercer was originally described by Gary R Graves as a subspecies of the Black-throated Flowerpiercer, *Diglossa brunneiventris vuilleumieri*, in an article entitled *A new subspecies of Diglossa (carbonaria) brunneiventris*, published in the Bulletin of the British Ornithologists' Club. Graves's paper gives detailed information concerning the geographical distribution, habitat and morphological differences between the taxon *vuilleumieri* and other taxa of the *Diglossa brunneiventris–carbonaria* complex. The type specimen of *vuilleumieri* is deposited at the United States National Museum and was collected by M A Carriker Jr at Páramo Frontino, Antioquia, Colombia, on 21 August 1951 at an altitude of 11,880 feet. The new taxon was named *vuilleumieri* by Graves who said: "*I take pleasure in naming this new form for François Vuilleumier in recognition of his contributions to Andean evolutionary biology.*" A discussion of geographical variation in the *Diglossa carbonaria–brunneiventris* complex was later published by Graves in an article entitled: *Bergmann's rule near the equator: latitudinal clines in body size of an Andean passerine bird*, published in the Proceedings of the National Academy of Sciences, in 1991. *Vuilleumieri* continues to be considered a subspecies of *Diglossa brunneiventris*, although political problems in northern Colombia have prevented any recent study or collecting of those populations since Carriker.

WAGLER

Wagler's Chachalaca *Ortalis wagleri* (G R **Gray** 1867)
(Alt. Rufous-bellied Chachalaca)
Wagler's Macaw *Ara glaucogularis* (**Dabbene** 1921)

(Alt. Blue-throated Macaw)
Wagler's Oropendola *Psarocolius wagleri* (G R Gray 1845)
(Alt. Chestnut-headed Oropendola)
Wagler's Oriole *Icterus wagleri* (P L **Sclater** 1857)
(Alt. Black-vented Oriole)
Wagler's Pearly Conure *Pyrrhura perlata lepida* (Wagler 1832)
(Alt. Pearly Parakeet)
Wagler's Woodnymph *Thalurania wagleri* (**Gould***)
Wagler's Woodpecker *Melanerpes rubricapillus* (**Cabanis** 1862)
(Alt. Red-crowned Woodpecker)

Johann Georg Wagler (1800–1832) was a German herpetologist. He was **Spix**'s assistant and upon the former's death, in 1826, he became the Director of the Zoological Museum of the University of Munich, and worked there to continue the treatment of the extensive collections from Brazil. In addition he worked on systematics of amphibians and reptiles in the museum. He wrote the highly regarded *Monographia Psittacorum,* which includes various descriptions of the blue macaws, in 1832. Wagler died accidentally from a self-inflicted gunshot wound whilst out collecting. The woodnymph appears to be another **Gould** original!

WAHLBERG

Wahlberg's Eagle *Aquila wahlbergi* (**Sundevall** 1851)
Wahlberg's Honeyguide *Prodotiscus regulus* (Sundevall 1850)
(Alt. Brown-backed Honeybird, Sharp-billed Honeyguide)

Johan August Wahlberg (1810–1856) was a Swedish naturalist and collector. He studied chemistry and pharmacy at Uppsala in 1829 and worked in a chemist's shop in Stockholm whilst studying at the Skogsinstitutet (Forestry Institute). He travelled and collected widely in southern Africa between 1838 and 1856, sending thousands of specimens home to Sweden. He returned briefly to Sweden in 1853 but was soon back in Africa where he was in Walvis Bay until 1854. He was exploring the headwaters of the Limpopo when a wounded elephant killed him.

WAHNES

Wahnes's Lorikeet *Charmosyna papou wahnesi* (**Rothschild** 1906)
(Alt. Papuan Lorikeet)
Wahnes's Parotia *Parotia wahnesi* (Rothschild 1906)

Carl Wahnes (1835–1910) was a German naturalist who collected in New Guinea.

WALDEN

Walden's Barwing *Actinodura waldeni* (**Godwin-Austen** 1874)
(Alt. Streak-throated/Austen's Barwing)

Arthur Hay, Viscount Walden, later ninth Marquis of Tweeddale (1824–1878). See **Tweeddale.**

WALLACE

Wallace's Bird-of-Paradise *Semioptera wallacii* (G R **Gray** 1859)
(Alt. [Wallace's] Standardwing Bird-of-Paradise, Standardwing)
Wallace's Fairy-wren *Sipodotus wallacei* (G R Gray 1862)
(Alt. Wallace's Wren-Warbler)
Wallace's [Green] Fruit Dove *Ptilinopus wallacii* (G R Gray 1858)
(Alt. Gold[en]-shouldered/Crimson-capped Fruit Dove)
Wallace's Fig Parrot *Psittaculirostris desmarestii* (**Desmarest** 1826)
(Alt. Desmarest's Fig Parrot)
Wallace's Hanging Parrot *Loriculus flosculus* (Wallace 1863)
Wallace's Hawk-Eagle *Spizaetus nanus* (Wallace 1868)
Wallace's Violet-necked Lory *Eos squamata wallacei* (**Salvadori** 1877)
(Alt. Moluccan Red/Violet-headed/Violet-naped Lory)
Wallace's Owlet-Nightjar *Aegotheles wallacii* (G R Gray 1859)
(Alt. Wallace's Frogmouth)
Wallace's Rail *Habroptila wallacii* (G R Gray 1860)
(Alt. Invisible/Drummer Rail)
Wallace's Scops Owl *Otus silvicola* (Wallace 1864)
(Alt. Lesser Sunda Scops Owl)
Wallace's Scrubfowl *Megapodius wallacei* (G R Gray 1861)
(Alt. Moluccan Scrubhen/Scrubfowl/Megapode)
Wallace's White-eye *Zosterops wallacei* (**Finsch** 1901)
(Alt. Yellow-spectacled White-eye)

Alfred Russell Wallace (1823–1913) was an English naturalist, evolutionary scientist, geographer and anthropologist. He has claims to be regarded as the father of zoogeography. He was also a social critic and theorist, a follower of the utopian socialist Robert Owen. His interest in natural history began whilst working as an apprentice surveyor, at which time he also attended public lectures. He went to Brazil, in 1848, on a self-sustaining natural history collecting expedition. Even on his first expedition he was very interested in how geography limited or facilitated the extension of species's ranges. He not only collected but also mapped, using his surveying skills. His return to England was a near disaster; his ship caught fire and sank with all his specimens, and he was lucky to be rescued by a passing vessel. He spent the next two years writing *Palm Trees of the Amazon and Their Uses* and *A Narrative of Travels on the Amazon and Rio Negro*, and organising another collecting expedition to the Indonesian archipelago. He managed to get a grant from the Royal Geographical Society covering his passage to the East Indies, in 1854. He spent nearly eight years there, during which he undertook about 70 different expeditions involving a total of around 14,000 miles of travel. He visited every important island in the archipelago at least once, some many times. He collected a remarkable 125,660 specimens, including more than 1,000 new 'species'. He wrote *The Malay Archipelago*, in 1869, which is the most celebrated of all writings on Indonesia and ranks as one of the 19th-century's best scientific travel books. He also published *Contributions to the History of Natural Selection*, in 1870, and *Island Life*, in 1880. His essay *On the law which has regulated the introduction of new species,* which encapsulated his most profound theories on evolution, was sent to **Darwin**. He later sent Darwin his essay *On the tendency of varieties to depart indefinitely from the original type,* presenting the theory of 'survival of the fittest'. Darwin and Lyell presented this essay, together with Darwin's own work to the Linnean Society. Wallace's thinking spurred Darwin to encapsulate these ideas in *The Origin of Species;* the rest is history. Wallace developed the theory of natural selection, based on the differential survival of variable individuals, halfway through his stay in Indonesia. He remained for four more years, during which he continued his systematic exploration and recording of the region's fauna, flora and people. For the rest of his life he was known as the greatest living authority on the region and its zoogeography, including his discovery and description of the faunal discontinuity that now bears his name, Wallace's Line. This natural boundary runs between the islands of Bali and Lombok in the south and Bor.neo and Sulawesi in the north, and separates the Oriental and Australasian faunal regions. The fig parrot was first described by Desmarest and it is unusual that the binomial carries his own name, unless of course he named it for a relative.

WALLER

Waller's Chestnut-winged Starling *Onychognathus walleri* (**Shelley** 1880)
(Alt. Waller's [Red-winged] Starling)

Gerald Waller was an English naturalist who collected in East Africa. In about 1888 the British East Africa Association became known as the Imperial British East Africa Company and two members of the company submitted a Draft of Concession to His Highness the Sultan of Zanzibar, by which he ceded to Britain his land on the African mainland. The two officials were the Reverend G P Badger and Mr Gerald Waller. We think that the latter was the same man. The other individual, George Percy Badger, in addition to being Chaplain to the East India Company, in Bombay, and a missionary, was also a noted explorer and cartographer, who published a map of Oman and the Persian Gulf in 1871. The Gerenuk or Giraffe Gazelle *Litocranius walleri* also commemorates Waller in the binomial.

WALLICH

Wallich's Pheasant *Catreus wallichi* (**Hardwicke** 1827)
(Alt. Cheer Pheasant)

Dr Nathaniel Wallich (1786–1854) was a Danish physician and botanist. In 1806 he graduated from the Royal Academy of Surgeons, in Copenhagen, and the same year was appointed surgeon to the Danish settlement at Serampore, in Bengal, then known as Frederischnagor, taking up the post in 1807. By the time he arrived the British had annexed the area and he was interned, but he was later paroled into the service of the East India Company. He was instrumental in establishing a museum in Calcutta, which was established in 1814 with many of his own botanical specimens. He supervised the gardens belonging to the East India Company, in Calcutta, between 1815 and 1846, giving up his museum post around 1819. He prepared a catalogue of more than 20,000 specimens, in addition to publishing *Tentamen flora nepalensis illustratae*, in 1824 and *Plantae asiaticae Rariories*, in 1830. He also collected in Nepal from 1820 to 1822. Hardwicke sent seeds which he collected to Wallich at the gardens. The present authorities of the Indian Botanical Garden have honoured him by naming an avenue after him.

WARD

Ward's Flycatcher *Pseudobias wardi* (**Sharpe** 1870)
(Alt. Ward's Shrike-Flycatcher)

Christopher Ward FLS was an English naturalist whose chief interest was entomology. He was also a collector, who obtained the type specimen of the flycatcher. He wrote *African Lepidoptera, Being Descriptions of New Species*, which was published in three parts from 1873 to 1875 and which contained descriptions of at least 55 new species. The extinct Seychelles Parakeet *Psittacula wardi* also honours his name. **Sharpe** described the flycatcher from the specimen, which he bought from the collector A **Crossley**.

WARD

Ward's Heron *Ardea herodias wardi* (**Ridgway** 1882)
(Alt. Great Blue Heron)

Charles W Ward was an amateur American naturalist. The Charles W Ward reserve in Massachusetts is named after him.

WARD

Ward's Trogon *Harpactes wardi* (**Kinnear** 1927)

Captain Francis Kingdon-Ward (1885–1958) was an English botanist, collector and explorer. He wrote *The Land of the Blue Poppy*, in 1913, and *Plant Collecting on the Edge of the World*, in 1930. He was one of those intrepid late Victorians who went everywhere, surviving the most enormous perils; in his case storms, torrents and an earthquake measuring over 9.5 on the Richter scale! In practice, his stamping ground was Asia, where he travelled repeatedly, exploring in Assam, Burma (now Myanmar), China, India and Tibet. He served in the Indian Army in the First World War, and went on to teach jungle survival techniques to Allied Forces in the Second World War, after previously avoiding capture by Japanese forces and having made his way alone through the Burmese jungle to India. He was awarded the Founders' Gold Medal of the Royal Geographical Society, in 1930. Ward died of a stroke. Kinnear wrote the description of the trogon, as *Pyrotrogon wardi* from a specimen '*collected* [in Burma] *by a native for F. Kingdon-Ward and presented by the latter*'.

WARSZEWISCZ

Warszewiscz's Rainbow *Coeligena iris aurora* (**Gould** 1854)
(Alt. Rainbow Starfrontlet)

Joseph Ritter von Rawicz Warszewiscz (1812–1866) was a Lithuanian Polish botanist who collected in Peru in 1860. He is regarded as one of the greatest orchid collectors of all time. **Gould** originally described the bird as the race *warszewizii* (*sic.*) of *Coeligena iris* but the race *aurora*, also attributed to Gould, has superseded it. He is also honoured in the trinomial of the Steely-vented Hummingbird *Saucerottia saucerottii warscewiczi* (*sic*).

WATERS

Waters's Crake *Sarothrura watersi* (**Bartlett** 1880)
(Alt. Slender-billed Flufftail)

Thomas Waters (or Watters) (1840–1904) was in the British Consular Service in East Africa and collected specimens in central and southeastern Madagascar. Bartlett presented three papers to the Zoological Society of London on the *Mammals and birds collected by Mr Waters in Madagascar*, between 1875 and 1879.

WATERSTRADT

Waterstradt's Racket-tailed Parrot *Prioniturus waterstradt* (**Rothschild** 1904)
(Alt. Mindanao Racquet-tail)

Johannes Waterstradt (1869–1932) was a Danish botanist, ornithologist and entomologist, who conducted extensive expeditions in Ceylon (now Sri Lanka), Borneo, the Malay Peninsula, the Moluccas and Palawan, especially in the first two decades of the 20th century. In 1903 he roamed the area of Mt Apo (an extinct volcano whose summit is the highest point in the Philippines) and discovered two new birds, the above-mentioned parrot and a race of the Green-backed Flowerpecker *Dicaeum ignipectus apo*. In addition many plants and insects are named after him.

WATERTON

Waterton's Woodnymph *Thalurania watertonii* (**Bourcier** 1847)
(Alt. Long-tailed Woodnymph)

Charles Waterton (1782–1865) was a highly idiosyncratic English naturalist and collector, whose activities are revealed in Richard Aldington's *The Strange Life of Charles Waterton* published in 1949, which we recommend and from which we quote here. He has been called '*the type specimen of the British eccentric naturalist*' and was known to everyone as '*the Squire of Walton Hall*'. He was one of the first to convert land to the sole purpose of a wildlife sanctuary. '*He hated scientific names, John James Audubon (whom he called a charlatan), Protestants, Hanoverians, Hanoverian Protestants, rats and Charles Darwin; he loved the natural world, birds, taxidermy, climbing, and practical jokes*'. He travelled and collected in South America, in 1825, when he wrote *Wanderings*, which included an account of riding a Cayman and trying deliberately to get bitten by a vampire bat (without success). He thought bloodletting was the best way to treat all ills. The Rev Wood describes his self-medication as consisting solely of '*the lancet and calomel*' and suggests that Waterton had drunk so much claret that only a starving vampire bat would be interested. His most long-lasting practical jokes were his many taxidermy mounts of imaginary (fake) animals which he enjoyed foisting on the general public. He was extraordinary to the end; a Dr Hobson wrote 'W*hen Mr. Waterton was seventy-seven years of age, I was witness to his scratching the back part of his head with the big toe of his right foot*'. In 1858, Thomas **Blakiston** named Waterton Lakes, now a national park in western Canada, after him.

WATERY GRAVES

Alfred Edmund **Brehm** was famed as a German traveller, collector and zoologist. It is unclear whether the bird named apparently in his honour was in fact named for his elder brother, Oskar, who joined him in Africa but was drowned in 1850 when he got out of his depth whilst bathing in a river. Perhaps the only other 'birdman' who found a watery grave was Charles **McKay**, who collected more than 400 birds for the United States National Museum. He was also an arctic explorer and drowned whilst on an expedition there. Several of our chaps were shipwrecked and lost collections but saved their lives. Finally, the ill-fated Sir John **Franklin** may qualify for inclusion, even though his grave seems to have involved solid water.

WATKINS

Watkins's Antpitta *Grallaria watkinsi* (**Chapman** 1919)
(Alt. Scrub Antpitta)

Henry George Watkins was an English collector in Peru between 1910 and 1912, who also seems to have mapped the area. A number of other objects, including a fossil, have *watkinsi* in their scientific names. **Chapman** described the antpitta and he also described the Little Inca Finch *Incaspiza watkinsi*, in 1925, but in this case the binomial name is after H G Watkins' brother, C Watkins, with whom he clearly travelled, as both the antpitta and the inca finch are found in Peru. [He should not be confused with the Arctic explorer Henry George Watkins (1907–1932).]

WATSON

[Forbes-]Watson's Swift *Apus berliozi* (Ripley 1965)

See **Forbes-Watson**.

WAYNE

Wayne's Warbler *Dendroica virens waynei* (**Bangs** 1918)
(Alt. Black-throated Green Warbler)

Arthur Trezevant Wayne (1863–1930) was an American who collected between 1880 and 1910, in particular in South Carolina. He gave his name to the Arthur T Wayne Society, which is open to anyone who has seen over 200 bird species of bird in South Carolina. In 1910 he co-edited, with Paul M Rea, *Birds of South Carolina*, an annotated list of birds from the state. In 1910 Wayne recorded having encountered more than 200 Ivory-billed Woodpeckers *Campephilus principalis* in Florida during the years 1892–94, a species now believed to be extinct. The warbler is a poorly marked race of the Black-throated Green Warbler confined to wet woodland in the southeast United States.

WEBB

Webb's Parrotbill *Paradoxornis webbianus* (**Gould** 1852)
(Alt. Rufous-headed/Vinous-throated Parrotbill)

Philip Barker Webb (1793–1858) was originally an English barrister, but also a botanist, mapmaker and collector. He travelled in Italy and Greece, from 1817 to 1818, and collected in Spain in 1826, Portugal and Morocco in 1827, the Canary Islands from 1820 to 1830, in Italy again from 1848 to 1850 and in the west of Ireland in 1851. In 1854 he made a financial bequest to the Museum of Physics and Natural History of Florence, and also bequeathed them his correspondence and writings. He also donated his enormous collection of about 320,000 specimens. Some of these he had collected himself, but he had acquired others from the early collectors in Africa and also from the first collectors in Australia. He was on his way to Brazil when he stopped at Tenerife and so appreciated the Canarian archipelago that abandoned his South American project. Webb published in English, French and Italian. His works included the ten-volume *Natural History of the Canary Islands*, which he wrote with Sabin **Berthelot** over 20 years.

WEBER

Weber's Lorikeet *Trichoglossus haematodus weberi* (**Hartert** 1898)
(Alt. Rainbow Lorikeet/Lory)

Max Wilhelm Carl Weber van Bosse (1852–1937) was a German-Dutch zoologist who became Director of the Zoological Museum in Amsterdam. He co-authored the authoritative account of *The Fishes of the Indo-Australian Archipelago*, with **De Beaufort**. He dedicated this great work to his wife **Anna** '*who has been always a joyful and helpful travelling-companion to me, in the extreme North, in South Africa, in the Indo-Australian Archipelago and also during the Siboga Expedition*'. He also defined Weber's Line, an important zoo-geographical boundary between Sulawesi and the Moluccas, which is occasionally preferred over **Wallace**'s line, which runs between Sulawesi and Borneo, as the separator of the Oriental and Australo-Papuan faunal regions. This race of the lorikeet is native to the island of Flores in the Lesser Sundas, Indonesia.

WEDDELL

Weddell's Conure *Aratinga weddellii* (**Deville** 1851)
(Alt. Dusky-headed Conure)

Hugh Algernon Weddell (1819–1877) was a French botanist who explored Latin America from 1843 to 1847. He wrote *Voyage Dans le Nord de la Bolivie et Dans les Parties Voisines du Peror*, in 1853, and *Chloris Andina – Essai d'une Flore de la Région Alpine des Cordillières de l'Amerique du Sud*, in 1855. He was *not* related to the sealer Captain James Weddell (1787–1834), after whom the Weddell Sea and the Weddell Seal *Leptonychotes weddellii* are named.

WEID

Weid's Crested Flycatcher *Myiarchus tyrannulus* (Muller 1776)
(Alt. Brown-crested Flycatcher)

We are convinced that this is a transcription error. See **Wied**.

WEIGALL

Weigall's Roller *Coracias spatulatus weigalli* (Dresser 1890)
(Alt. Racquet-tailed Roller)

This subspecies is possibly named after Sir Arthur Edward Pearse Weigall (1880–1934) the English Egyptologist who was very famous in his time for having worked with Carter in the Valley of the Kings. He is noted as one of the most colourful writers of his time. His works included *The Life and Times of Akhnaton, Pharoah of Egypt*, in 1922, and *Personalities of Antiquity*, in 1928. He also wrote on religious issues.

WELCH

Welch's Ptarmigan *Lagopus mutus welchi* (**Hartert** 1921)
(Alt. Rock Ptarmigan)

George O Welch (1912–1986) was an American missionary in Africa. His *Memories of a Sky Pilot – the Autobiography of a Missionary* was published in 1997. He collected the type specimen of this race.

WELLS, J

Wells' Dove *Leptotila wellsi* (**Lawrence** 1884)
(Alt. Grenada Dove)

John G Wells was an ornithologist who was active in the West Indies in general and in Grenada in particular. He wrote *A catalogue of the birds of Grenada, West Indies, with observations thereon*, which appeared in the Proceedings of the US National Museum, in 1886, and *Birds of the Island of Carriacou*, in 1902. Wells is honoured in a number of scientific names such as that of the Lesser Yellow-naped Woodpecker *Picus chlorolophus wellsi*.

WELLS, T

Wells' Wagtail *Motacilla capensis wellsi* (**Grant** 1911)
(Alt. Cape Wagtail)

Thomas (Jimmy) Wells (1868–1939) worked at the British Museum (Natural History), where he started as a Boy Attendant in 1883. During his early days there he assisted in moving the cabinets containing the bird collection from the old building at Bloomsbury to South Kensington. By the time he retired in 1930, after 47 years service, he was a higher grade clerk in the Bird Section. He is mentioned in **Bannerman**'s *Birds of Tropical West Africa* as having compiled the indexes. '*Much unobtrusive work was done by him in assisting authors with their systematic contributions and his name is perpetuated in ornithological literature by many species named in his honour; as an indexer and proof-reader he had few equals and was the possessor of beautifully clear handwriting as hundreds of bird labels can testify.*' He is also mentioned in C Frost's *History of British Taxidermy*.

WESTERMANN

Westerman's Eclectus Parrot *Eclectus roratus westermani* (**Bonaparte** 1850)
Westerman's Flycatcher *Ficedula westermanni* (**Sharpe** 1888)
   (Alt. Little Pied Flycatcher)

Gerald Frederick Westermann (1807–1890) was a Dutch zoologist. With Werlemann and Weismuller he founded the zoological society Natura Artis Magistra'in May 1838, a body which later evolved into the Zoological Museum of Amsterdam. He wrote *De Toerakos* (The Turacos) in 1860.

WETMORE

Wetmore's Rail *Rallus wetmorei* (**Zimmer** & **Phelps** 1944)
   (Alt. Plain-flanked Rail)
Wetmore's Tanager *Wetmorethraupis sterrhopteron* (Lowery & O'Neill 1964)
   (Alt. Orange-throated Tanager)

Frank Alexander Wetmore (1886–1978), always known as Alexander, was an American ornithologist and avian palaeontologist who conducted extensive fieldwork in Latin America. His first job was as a bird taxidermist at the Denver Museum of Natural History, Colorado, in 1909. He spent 1911 in Puerto Rico studying birdlife. Later he travelled throughout South America for two years, investigating bird migration between continents, whilst working for the United States Bureau of Biological Survey. In 1925 he was appointed Assistant Secretary of the Smithsonian Institution, the United States National Museum, where he worked for 20 years. He was President of the American Ornithologists' Union, from 1926 to 1929, and he became the Smithsonian's sixth secretary, from 1945 until 1952. Wetmore made a number of short trips to Haiti, the Dominican Republic, Guatemala, Mexico, Costa Rica, and Colombia He also conducted a research programme in Panama every year from 1946 to 1966, during which he made an exhaustive survey of the birds of the isthmus. A canopy bridge in the Río Bayano Basin, in Panama, was named in his honour in 1973. He wrote *A Systematic Classification for the Birds of the World*, in 1930, which he revised in 1951 and again in 1960. Therein he devised the Wetmore Order, a sequence of bird classification which had widespread acceptance until very recently, and is still in use. His other publications included *Birds of Haiti and the Dominican Republic* in 1931 and *The Birds of the Republic of Panamá* in 1965. Numerous taxa, comprising 56 new genera, species, and subspecies of birds (both recent and fossil), mammals, amphibians, insects, molluscs and plants, a named in his honour. He wrote the first descriptions of 189 species and subspecies of living birds, mostly from central and northern South America.

WEYNS

Weyns's Weaver *Ploceus weynsi* (A J C Dubois 1900)

Lieutenant Colonel Auguste F G Weyns (1854–1944) was a Belgian explorer who collected in Central Africa from 1888 until 1903. He was also the governor, from 1900 to 1903, of the semi-autonomous state of Katanga within the Congo, as 'representative' of the Comité Spécial du Katanga.

WHISTLER

Whistler's Warbler *Seicercus* (*burkii*) *whistleri* (Ticehurst 1925)
   (Alt. Golden-spectacled Warbler)

Hugh Whistler (?–1942) was a British ornithologist attached to the British Museum (Natural History) and was a Fellow of the Zoological Society. He lived at Battle in Sussex, England, where he was a Justice of the Peace. The Whistler Prize of Sussex University, which is awarded to the best essay on natural history or archaeology, is named after him. He worked very closely with C B Ticehurst in Spain, Albania, India and Ceylon (now Sri Lanka). He spent much time in India and undertook a number of surveys there, such as one in Rajasthan, in 1938, which listed 300 species. Whistler and Ticehurst published a number of articles in The Ibis, including *On the Avifauna of Galicia*, in 1928, and *On the ornithology of Albania*, in 1932. They wrote a monograph, *Birds of India*, which appears to exist only in manuscript in the Smithsonian archives in Washington. Whistler alone wrote *Migration notes from a passenger steamer*, in 1916, and *In The High Himalayas – Sport and Travel in the Rhotang and Baralacha, With Some Notes on the Natural History of that Area*. He published his *Popular Handbook of Indian Birds* in 1928. The latter has been updated many times by others and has been regarded as *the* book which popularised birdwatching as a hobby among the Indian elite. Salim Ali, the grand master of Indian ornithology, included Whistler's notes in *The Birds of Mysore*, which Ali published in 1942. Whistler is also commemorated in races of the Meadow Pipit *Anthus pratensis whistleri*, the Red-whiskered Bulbul *Pycnonotus jocosus whistleri* and the White-throated Laughing-thrush *Garrulax albogularis whistleri*. He named the Sri Lankan form of the White-browed Bulbul *Pluteolus insulae*. Ticehurst first described the warbler as a subspecies of Golden-spectacled Warbler, but more recently it has been proposed as a full species.

WHITE

White's Thrush *Zoothera dauma* (**Latham** 1790)
(Alt. Scaly Thrush)

The Reverend Gilbert White (1720–1793) was a country parson at Selbourne in Hampshire, England. He was a keen amateur naturalist famed for his meticulous observations; for example he played a major part in recognising that the *Phylloscopus* warblers which nest in Britain belong to three different species. He is also noted for his correspondence with other enthusiasts of his day. His letter to Daines Barrington of 12 February 1772, at a time when there was much speculation regarding whether birds migrated or hibernated, provided his recognition of the former; he wrote '*We must not, I think, deny migration in general; because migration certainly does subsist in some places, as my brother* [Reverend John White] *in Andalusia has fully informed me. Of the motions of these birds he has ocular demonstration, for many weeks together, both spring and fall, during which periods myriads* [sic] *of the swallow kind traverse the Straits* [sic] *from north to south and from south to north, according to the season..*'. He published his observations and letters in 1789 as *The Natural History and Antiquities of Selbourne*, one of the most delightful books ever written and still in print over 200 years later. **Latham** described the thrush in 1790 perhaps in response to that volume. It is likely that the two men met.

WHITEHEAD

Whitehead's Broadbill *Calyptomena whiteheadi* (**Sharpe** 1888)
Whitehead's Stubtail *Urosphena whiteheadi* (Sharpe 1888)
(Alt. Bornean Stubtail, Short-tailed Bush Warbler)
Whitehead's Magpie *Urocissa whiteheadi* (**Ogilvie-Grant** 1899)
(Alt. White-winged Blue Magpie)

Whitehead's Scops Owl *Otus megalotis* (**Walden** 1875)
(Alt. Philippine Scops Owl)
Whitehead's Spiderhunter *Arachnothera juliae* (Sharpe 1887)
Whitehead's [Mountain] Swiftlet *Aerodramus whiteheadi* (Ogilvie-Grant 1895)
Whitehead's Tree Babbler *Stachyris whiteheadi* (Ogilvie-Grant 1894)
(Alt. Chestnut-faced Babbler)
Whitehead's Trogon *Harpactes whiteheadi* (Sharpe 1888)

John Whitehead (1860–1899) was a British explorer who collected in Borneo between 1885 and 1888, in the Philippines between 1893 and 1896, and in Hainan in 1899. He wrote *Explorations of Mount Kina Balu, North Borneo*, in 1893, and he may have been the first European to reach the summit of the mountain. The owl was formerly known as *O. whiteheadi*. The *juliae* in the scientific name of the spiderhunter is after Julia, Marchioness of Tweeddale (1846–1937), wife of Arthur, ninth Marquess of **Tweeddale**.

WHITELY

Whitely's Flycatcher *Myiarchus swainsoni phaeonotus* (**Salvin** & **Godman** 1883)
(Alt. Swainson's Flycatcher)
Whitely's Hummingbird *Iololaema whitelyana* (**Gould***)
Whitely's (Roraiman) Nightjar *caprimulgus whitelyi* (Salvin 1885)
Whitely's Tanager *Tangara cyanoptera whitelyi* (Salvin & Godman 1884)
(Alt. Black-headed Tanager)

Henry Whitely Jr (1844–1892) was an Englishman who collected in parts of Brazil, British Guiana (now Guyana) and Peru between 1879 and 1884. He also collected in Japan. The hummingbird is another we can only find in **Gould**'s work.

WHITLOCK

Whitlock's Thornbill *Acanthiza apicalis whitlocki* (North 1909)
(Alt. Inland Thornbill)

Frederick Bulstrode Lawson Whitlock (1860–1953) was a British-born Australian ornithologist who emigrated to Australia in 1901. He collected more extensively than any other single ornithologist in Western Australia. He also visited the Hermannsburg Range, in central Australia, in search of the Night Parrot *Geopsittacus occidentalis*. As well as being the first to collect the eggs and nests of many species, in 1909 he collected the last 'new' bird to be discovered in Western Australia, the Grey Honeyeater *Lacustroica whitei*. His bird skins are in the Western Australian Museum, in Perth, and in the H L White Collection in the National Museum, in Melbourne, along with most of the eggs that he collected. His research and travels were recorded in numerous articles in The Emu. He was made an Honorary Life Member of the Royal Australian Ornithologists Union and the Western Australian Naturalists' Club. A genus and a number of species of birds were named after him between 1909 and 1915, mainly by G M **Mathews**, but we have been unable to trace them. He is also commemorated in the trinomials of at least two other Australian birds, the western race of the Shy Heathwren *Hylacola cauta whitlocki* and the Australian Crested Dove *Ocyphaps lophotes whitlocki*.

WHITNEY, H

Whitney's Thicket Warbler *Megalurulus whitneyi* (**Mayr** 1933)
(Alt. Guadalcanal Thicketbird)

Harry Payne Whitney (1872–1930) was an American banker who was the heir to a tobacco and oil empire. He was a philanthropist who co-sponsored a number of expeditions to the Pacific, notably the Sanford-Whitney Expeditions, in 1921 and 1929. In 1896 he married the banker's daughter and artist Gertrude Vanderbilt (1875–1942) and there are a number of birds with *gertrudae* in their binomial named after her. Whitney was a passionate racehorse owner who captained the United States polo team in 1910. The thicket warbler was collected on the Whitney expedition to the South Seas.

WHITNEY, J

Whitney's Elf Owl *Micrathene whitneyi* (**Cooper** 1861)

Josiah Dwight Whitney (1819–1896) was a Californian state geologist who founded the Harvard School of Mining. Mt Whitney in California is named for him too. He published *The Yosemite Book; A Description of the Yosemite Valley and the Adjacent Region of the Sierra Nevada, and of the Big Trees of California* in 1868. A member of his staff, James Cooper, the son of W C **Cooper**, found and described the bird in 1861.

WHYTE

Whyte's Barbet *Stactolaema whytii* (**Shelley** 1893)

Alexander Whyte FLS (1834–1905) was a government naturalist in Nyasaland (now Malawi), where he collected extensively under the patronage of Sir Harry **Johnston**, between 1891 and 1897. Britten wrote *The Plants of Milanji, Nyasa-land, Collected by Mr. Alexander Whyte*, in 1894, and Thomas Oldfield wrote *On the mammals obtained by Mr. A Whyte in Nyasaland, and presented to the British Museum by Sir HH Johnston*m in 1897, in the Proceedings of the Zoological Society of London.

WIED

Wied's Crested Flycatcher *Myiarchus tyrannulus* (**Müller** 1776)
(Alt. Brown-crested Flycatcher)
Wied's Crested Flycatcher *Myiarchus oberi* (**Lawrence** 1877)
(Alt. Lesser Antillean Flycatcher)
Wied's Tinamou *Crypturellus noctivagus* (Wied-Neuwied 1820)
(Alt. Yellow-legged Tinamou)
Wied's Tyrant-Manakin *Neopelma aurifrons* (Wied-Neuwied 1831)

Prince Alexander Philipp Maximilian II of Wied-Neuwied (1782–1867) was a German explorer and naturalist. See **Maximilian**. There is much confusion over the two crested flycatchers which are apparently attributed to two people with very similar names. We are convinced that all references to Weid are transcription errors. **Müller** first described Wied's Crested Flycatcher *Myiarchus tyrannulus* in 1776. **Lawrence** described Wied's Crested Flycatcher *Myiarchus oberi* in 1877. Somehow both seem to have been known, at different times, after our man. Currently most ornithologists describe the former as the Brown-crested Flycatcher and the latter as the Lesser Antillean Flycatcher. Our view is that the latter was known as Wied's Flycatcher first and that people seeing the other bird may have confused the two, since the descriptions are similar and they are closely related.

WILKES

Wilkes' Pigeon *Ducula aurorae* (**Peale** 1848)
(Alt. Society Island/Polynesian/Tahitian [Imperial] Pigeon)

Charles Wilkes (1798–1877) was a pioneering navy captain who led the United States Exploring Expedition, of 1838 to 1842, which was a milestone in American science. The expedition comprised four naval vessels, the flagship *Vincennes*; a sloop of war of 780 tons, the *Peacock*, the *Porpoise* and the store ship *Relief*. Two New York pilot boats, the *Sea Gull* and the *Flying Fish*, were used as survey vessels close to shore. They visited Brazil, Tierra del Fuego, Antarctica, Chile, Australia, New Zealand, the west coast of North America, the Philippines and the East Indies. The two penetrations into Antarctic waters sighted land and provided the first proof of an Antarctic continent. Wilkes was a strict disciplinarian who was disliked by many of the crew. He took with him 82 officers, nine naturalists, scientists and artists, and 342 sailors. Of the latter, only 223 returned. During the voyage, 62 were discharged as unsuitable, 42 deserted and 15 died of disease, injury or drowning. However, he brought back a wealth of geological, botanical, zoological, anthropological and other material, which was to be the foundation for much of American science. Titian Ramsay **Peale** (1800–1885), one of the expedition scientists and its official illustrator, described the pigeon.

WILHELMINA

Wilhelmina's Lorikeet *Charmosyna wilhelminae* (A B **Meyer** 1874)
(Alt. Pygmy Lorikeet)

Wilhelmina Meyer who was the wife of Adolph B **Meyer**, the German zoologist, who described the Lorikeet and named it after her in 1874.

WILKINS

Wilkins's Bunting *Nesospiza wilkinsi* (**Lowe** 1923)
(Alt. Wilkins's Finch, Thick-billed/Grosbeak Bunting)

Captain Sir George Hubert Wilkins (1888–1958) was an Australian polar explorer and ornithologist. He explored both the Arctic, between 1913 and 1917, and the Antarctic, between 1920 and 1922. He was the 13th child born to a South Australian sheep-farming family. An official biography lists his career as war correspondent, polar explorer, naturalist, geographer, climatologist, aviator, author, balloonist, war hero, reporter, secret agent, submariner and navigator! His twin loves were aviation (he always carried a miniature Australian flag in his cockpit) and cinematography. However, his exploits were legion and we recommend further reading on this extraordinary man (see for example Grierson 1960 or Lowell 1961). Between 1928 and 1930 his adventures included the purchase of a surplus First World War submarine for $1. He renamed it *Nautilus* and attempted to cruise beneath the ice to the North Pole. Unfortunately, the old ship broke down and the expedition failed. In 1922, Shackleton's ship *Quest* called briefly at Tristan da Cunha, where Wilkins, who was the ship's cameraman/naturalist discovered the bunting which now bears his name. He published *No Foxes Seen, A Log of Arctic Flying Adventures*, in 1928. His last expedition was to Antarctica at the age of 69, as a guest of Operation Deepfreeze. He died of a heart attack in the United States and his ashes were taken to the North Pole and scattered there.

WILLCOCKS

Willcocks's Honeyguide *Indicator willcocksi* (**Alexander** 1901)

General Sir James Willcocks (1847–1926) commanded the Ashanti expedition of 1900, which was to assist in the suppression of the Ashanti Rebellion led by Yaa Asantewa, a woman. The then Colonel Wilcocks led 1,400 soldiers to Kumasi in the Gold Coast (now Ghana) from Nigeria. He wrote *From Kabul to Kumassi – Twenty-Four Years of Soldiering and Sport*, in 1904. In 1914 he commanded the Indian Army Corps in the British Expeditionary Force in France during the First World War. However, he resigned in 1915, following differences with the Commander, Sir Douglas (later Earl) Haig. He became Governor of Bermuda from 1917 to 1922. He died in India, at Bharatpur.

WILLIAM

William's Fig Parrot *Cyclopsitta gulielmitertii* (**Schlegel** 1866)
(Alt. Orange-breasted Fig Parrot)
William's Khalij *Lophura leucomelanos williamsi* (**Oates** 1896)
(Alt. Kalij Pheasant)

Willem III (1817–1890) was King of the Netherlands from 1849 until his death.

WILLIAMS

Williams's (Bush) Lark *Mirafra williamsi* (Macdonald 1956)
(Alt. Marsabit Lark)

John George Williams (1913–1997) was a British ornithologist, taxidermist and illustrator who was Curator of the Coryndon Museum, now the National Museum, in Nairobi, Kenya from 1946 to 1966. He was regarded as the world authority on the sunbirds *Nectariniidae*. He wrote *A Field Guide to the Birds of East Africa* in 1980, illustrated by Norman Arlott, which was an expanded version of his pioneering similar work of 1963. He was also the author of *A Field Guide to the National Parks of East Africa* in 1967. His obituary in Ibis in 1999 notes that '*Early on, he saw the need for conservation. The establishment of a National Park at Lake Nakuru, famous for its flamingos, was in large part due to his efforts.*' He and his wife returned to England in 1978 but he never fully retired. Just before his death he prepared superb specimens of birds for the Royal Scottish Museum in Edinburgh.

WILLIAMSON

Williamson's Flycatcher *Muscicapa cassini* (**Heine** 1860)
(Alt. Chocolate/Brown-streaked Flycatcher)
Williamson's Sapsucker *Sphyrapicus thyroideus* (**Cassin** 1852)
(Alt. Natalie's Sapsucker)

Lieutenant Robert Stockton Williamson (1825–1882) led the United States Army survey of Northern California and was a member of the team which discovered the eponymous Sapsucker. John Strong Newberry (1822–1892) an army surgeon and geologist and himself named the species after Williamson. It is a curious fact that Williamson's collection in 1857 only obtained males whereas Cassin had named it six years earlier from a collection of female specimens. Hence the common name is Williamson's and scientific name is Cassin's. Mount Williamson in California was perhaps also named after him in 1864. [or may be not... *In an interview, Don McLain told John Robinson that he had named this peak for Will Williamson, a friend of his. When reminded of Lt. Williamson, McLain added, 'Well, yes, I named* [it] *for him too'. Angeles N.F. historian Don Hedly reported that this same Williamson story was told him by McLain's widow*]. In 1870, by which time his rank was Lieutenant-Colonel; he was put in charge of the construction of the Cape Blanco Lighthouse on behalf of the United States Lighthouse Board.

WILLIS

Willis's Antbird *Cercomacra* (*tyrannina*) *laeta* (**Todd** 1920)
(Alt. Dusky Antbird)

Dr Edwin O'Neill Willis (1935–) is an American ornithologist who lives in Brazil and is Professor of Zoology at the Universidade Estadual Paulista in Rio Claro, São Paulo. He has done a great deal of work on antbird ecology and systematics, chiefly in Brazil but also in Panama. He is a great pioneer of field studies of Neotropical birds and the world's recognised expert on Neotropical ant-following birds. Many of his papers deal with what might be called 'applied avian biogeography'. His publications include *The Behaviour of Ocellated Antbirds*, in 1973, and *The composition of avian communities in remanescent woodlots in southern Brazil*, in 1979. He was instrumental in the division of the southeastern Brazilian ant-thrushes of the genus *Chamaeza* into three species; the original Brazilian Ant-thrush *C. ruficauda*, Such's Ant-thrush *C. merloides* and the Short-tailed Ant-thrush *C. turdina* (Condor 94 [1992]: 110–116). In reply to our inquiry about the discovery of Willis's Antbird Dr Willis wrote: '*I was the first person to note that the bird had a different voice from the ordinary species, both at Belém and Manaus. So, Rob Bierregaard named it for me. Also, I have been working on antbirds since the 1960s.*' **Todd** first described the antbird as a subspecies of the Dusky Antbird *C. tyrannina*.

WILSON, A

Wilson's Bird-of-Paradise *Cicinnurus respublica* (**Bonaparte** 1850)
Wilson's Phalarope *Phalaropus tricolor* (**Vieillot** 1819)
Wilson's Plover *Charadrius wilsonia* (**Ord** 1814)
 (Alt. Belding's Plover)
Wilson's Storm Petrel *Oceanites oceanicus* (**Kuhl** 1820)
 (Alt. Wilson's Petrel)
Wilson's Snipe *Gallinago (gallinago) delicata* (Ord 1825)
 (Alt. Common Snipe)
Wilson's Thrush *Catharus fuscescens* (**Stephens** 1817)
 (Alt. Veery)
Wilson's Warbler *Wilsonia pusilla* (Wilson 1811)

Alexander Wilson (1766–1813) was a pioneering American ornithologist, and the first to study American birds in their native habitats. As such he is often called the Father of American Ornithology. Wilson was born in Paisley, Scotland where he earned a meagre livelihood as an itinerant poet and peddler of muslin. His narrative poem *Watty and Meg* was published anonymously in 1792, attaining great popularity, but was ascribed to the Scottish poet Robert Burns. Subsequently, during a labour dispute in Paisley, Wilson wrote satiric verses lampooning the manufacturers and was imprisoned for libel. Following his release, in 1794, he emigrated to the United States, where **Bartram** befriended him. While working as a village schoolmaster in Pennsylvania, Wilson began to collect material for a comprehensive work, illustrated with his own drawings, on the birds of America. From 1808 through 1813 he published seven volumes of his *American Ornithology;* an additional two volumes were edited and published posthumously. Wilson is noted for the accuracy of his descriptions and for his superior illustrations. **Ord** named the plover after him, **Vieillot** named the phalarope, **Kuhl** the storm petrel and **Bonaparte** named the bird-of-paradise. Wilson himself described the warbler, giving his own name to the genus!

WILSON, M

Wilson's Widow Finch *Vidua wilsoni* (**Hartert** 1901)
 (Alt. Wilson's Indigobird)

Captain Malcolm Wilson (1869–1900) served in Africa and collected birds along the Niger River.

WILSON, T

Wilson's Coeligene *Coeligena wilsoni* (**DeLattre** & **Bourcier** 1846)
 (Alt. Brown Inca)

Thomas B Wilson (1807–1865) was an American amateur ornithologist. He was a Trustee of the Academy of Natural Sciences Philadelphia and he bought the John Gould Collection of Australian Birds on their behalf in 1848. He was largely responsible for accumulating their enormous collection of birds and his patronage was recognised when he was eventually elected the academy's president. **Cassin** catalogued the collection and served for a while as vice-president.

WINCHELL

Winchell's Kingfisher *Todirhamphus winchelli* (**Sharpe** 1877)
(Alt. Rufous-lored Kingfisher)

Newton Horace Winchell (1839–1914) was an American archaeologist and geologist, who took part in the expedition which led to the discovery of gold in the Black Hills of Dakota. The expedition was led by Lieutenant-Colonel George Armstrong Custer, who as General Custer later gained notoriety when he and his entire company were killed by Sioux Indians at the Battle of the Little Bighorn, in Montana. Winchell was state geologist of Minnesota. He published a classic study of the post-glacial retreat of St Anthony Falls, which carved the Mississippi River gorge in Minneapolis. The Winchell Trail, a path through the gorge, commemorates him, as does the Newton Horace Winchell School of Earth Sciences at the University of Minnesota. He wrote *The Aborigines of Minnesota* in 1910.

WITHERBY

Witherby's Lark *Alaemon hamertoni* (Witherby 1905)
(Alt. Lesser Hoopoe Lark)

Henry Forbes (Harry F) Witherby MBE (1873–1943) was an English ornithologist who was an expert on British and Spanish birds. His varied activities had an enduring influence in most fields of British ornithology. The family firm of H F & G Witherby & Co. began specialising in bird books in the early 20th century. They were merely printers until Harry published his own works. He edited the *Handbook of British Birds*, which was published in five volumes between 1938 and 1941. He started the first bird ringing scheme in Britain in 1909; a second scheme which began at around the same time amalgamated with his at the outbreak of the First World War. In 1937 Witherby transferred the control of his scheme to the British Trust for Ornithology (BTO), which still administers it. He was an early Vice-Chairman of the BTO and his donations were vital to it. They included a capital endowment derived from the proceeds of the sale of his collection of skins to the British Museum. From 1924 until 1927 he was Chairman of the British Ornithologists' Club. He also chaired the Council of the British Ornithologists' Union (BOU). He was awarded the **Godman-Salvin** Medal of the BOU in 1938, a signal honour for distinguished ornithological work. He founded British Birds in 1907, a monthly journal that has become an institution.

WOODFORD, C

Woodford's Rail *Nesoclopeus woodfordi* (**Ogilvie-Grant** 1889)
Woodford's White-eye *Woodfordia superciliosa* (North 1906)
(Alt. Bare-eyed White-eye)

Charles Morris Woodford (1852–1927) was the Resident Commissioner in the Solomon Islands Protectorate between 1896 and 1914. He was an adventurer, a naturalist and also a philatelist. He established the first postal service in the islands and issued their first stamps, personally franking the envelopes. He wrote *A Naturalist Among the Headhunters* in 1890 (which is referred to in a letter by his friend, the novelist Jack London) and *Notes on the Solomon Islands* in 1926.

WOODFORD, E

Woodford's Owl *Strix woodfordi* (A **Smith** 1834)

Colonel E J A Woodford (1761–1835) served in the British army in Europe between 1794 and 1817. He may well have been the Colonel Woodford of the Guards who fought with distinction at the Battle of Salamanca, in 1812, and who was specifically mentioned by Wellington in his despatch after the battle. The same Woodford probably fought at Waterloo in 1815 and is known to have commanded a battalion of the Coldstream Guards as part of the garrison at Cambrai around 1816, whilst allied troops were still based in immediate post-Napoleonic France. Woodford was also a natural history collector who subsequently also dealt in bird art in London.

WOODHOUSE

Woodhouse's Antpecker *Parmoptila woodhousei* (**Cassin** 1859)
(Alt. Red-headed Antpecker)
Woodhouse's Jay *Aphelocoma coerulescens woodhousei* (S F Baird 1858)
(Alt. Western Scrub Jay)

Samuel Washington Woodhouse (1821–1904) was an American surgeon, explorer and naturalist who collected in the United States. He first described **Cassin**'s Sparrow *Aimophila cassinii* in 1852. He was on the 1852 Sitgreaves exploration of the Colorado and Zuni Rivers, in the joint capacities of doctor and naturalist. This expedition was the first to find the Petrified Forest of Arizona. He published his journals under the title of *A Naturalist in Indian Territory: The Journal of S.W.Woodhouse, 1849–50*. Woodhouse's Toad *Bufo woodhousei*, a large species up to 12.5 cm long, is also named for him.

WOODWARD

Woodwards' Barbet *Stactolaema* (*olivacea*) *woodwardi* (**Shelley** 1895)
Woodwards' Batis *Batis fratrum* (Shelley 1900)
(Alt. Zululand Puffback Flycatcher)

The Reverend Robert B Woodward (1848–1899) and his brother John D S Woodward (1849–1899) were Anglican missionaries in Natal, South Africa, between 1881 and 1899. They were both deeply interested in ornithology and sent many specimens to **Sharpe** at the British Museum. They were co-authors of *Natal Birds*, which was published just before their deaths. The barbet has recently been proposed as a full species; it had hitherto been regarded as a subspecies of the Green Barbet *S. olivacea*.

WORCESTER

Worcester's Buttonquail *Turnix worcesteri* (**McGregor** 1904)
Worcester's Hanging Parrot *Loriculus philippensis worcesteri* (**Steere** 1890)
(Alt. Colasisi/Philippine/Luzon Hanging Parrot)

Dean Conant Worcester (1866–1924) was an American ornithologist, zoologist and collector, who was Professor of Zoology at the University of Michigan. He served as a member of the Philippine Commission from 1899 to 1913, as Secretary of the Interior. He first went to the Philippines with the Steere Expedition of 1887 to 1889 along with Frank Swift **Bourns**, after whom another race of the parrot is named.

WORTHEN

Worthen's Sparrow *Spizella wortheni* (**Ridgway** 1884)

Charles K Worthen (1850–1909) was an American collector. He presented his collection of birds to the Museum of Science at Buffalo, New York. The sparrow is occasionally regarded as being conspecific with the Field Sparrow *S. pusilla.*

WRIGHT

Wright's Flycatcher *Empidonax wrightii* (S F Baird 1858)
(Alt. Grey Flycatcher)

Charles Wright (1811–1885) was an American botanist, teacher and collector who explored the western USA for the Pacific Railroad Company. He supported himself by surveying and teaching, whilst pursuing botany in his spare time. In 1844 he sent a collection of plants to Asa Gray. He collected in Texas whilst working for the Boundary Survey Commission. Wright was botanist on the United States North Pacific Exploring Expedition, from 1853 to 1855, which visited Madeira, Cape Verde, the Cape of Good Hope, Sydney, Hong Kong, several Japanese islands and the Bering Strait. They returned to San Francisco where Wright was asked to leave the expedition, which was due to continue around Cape Horn and on to New York. He proceeded to Nicaragua, where he collected for some months before making his own way to New York. From 1856 to 1867 he explored in Cuba. In 1871 he went with a United States Commission to Santo Domingo. Between collecting trips, Wright spent time at his Connecticut home and at the Gray Herbarium in Cambridge, Massachusetts. He also served as librarian of the Bussey Institution for a few months.

WURDEMANN

Wurdemann's Heron *Ardea herodias wurdemannii* (**Baird** 1858)
(Alt. Great Blue Heron)

Gustavus (sometimes called William) Wurdemann was a master mechanic for the United States Coastal Survey, and surveyed Texas, Louisiana and Florida from 1854 to 1858. He seems also to have been interested in astronomy, since he created several telescopes, including his 'zenith' telescope of 1855, as well as a survey theodolite in the 1840s. He later set up a company making astronomic and geodetic instruments. He made a study of *Tidal Observations on the Hudson between Albany and New York City* and it was for this skill in observing and recording tides and weather that he was employed by the survey. The survey's leader also invited Louis Agassiz to join the survey at various times and records him being '*quite absorbed by the specimens of shell-fishes we dredged or brought up in mud'*. The Peppermint Shrimp *Lysmata wurdemanni* is found off the Florida coast. **Baird** initially described the heron as a separate species and named it Wurdemann's Heron after Gustavus, in 1858. It is now considered a hybrid between two races of the Great Blue Heron, the white form *occidentalis* and a typical form *wardi.*

WYMAN

Wyman's Gull *Larus occidentalis wymani* (**Dickey** & **Van Rossem** 1925)
(Alt. Western Gull)

Luther Everet Wyman (1870–1928) was Curator of Birds at the Los Angeles Museum of History, Science and Art. He was always interested in natural history and made a collection of mounted birds whilst still at school. He first earned his living as a businessman, being a member of the Board of Trade in Chicago for 15 years. It was there that he met a fellow natural history enthusiast and together they spent much time collecting and studying the birds in the woods and fields around Chicago. The stress of business led to a nervous

breakdown and he left the board and bought an apple ranch. He became an amateur member of the Biological Survey and sent his specimens to Washington. His friend from the Board of Trade became Director of the Museum in Los Angeles, and Wyman moved there to supervise palaeontological excavations, later becoming Curator of Birds. He wrote *Field Book of the Birds of the Southwestern United States*, with Elizabeth F Burnel, in 1925. **Dickey** and **van Rossem** described this race of the Western Gull, naming it after Wyman in recognition of his work on birds and his special study of the species.

WYNAAD

Wynaad's Laughing-thrush *Garrulax delesserti* (**Jerdon** 1839)
(Alt. Rufous-vented Laughing-thrush)

Wynaad is a region in Kerala state in India, forming part of the Malabar district. We believe that the bird was named after it, rather than for a person.

X TO XXIV

Just 26 chaps have made it into double figures when it comes to the number of birds named after them. As one might expect, given the nations who were undertaking expeditions in the heyday of species discovery, one was Dutch, one was Italian, two were French, three were American, four were German and the rest were British. **Everett, Bonaparte**, and **Townsend** tie for 24th place with ten birds each. **Tristram, David** and **Hartlaub**, with 11 birds each are joint 21st. Four people, **Sharpe, Swinhoe, Wallace** and **Salvadori** with 12 birds each tie for 17th, **Jerdon, Rothschild, Pallas, Cassin** and **Chapman** come in at 12th equal with 13 birds. **Hume** and **Salvin**, with 14 birds, are tenth equal and **Hodgson** with 15 is ninth. Seventh equal, with 16 birds, are **Blyth** and **Finsch** and fourth equal with 17 birds each are **Swainson, Temminck** and **Reichenow**. And in the medal positions?

Bronze Medal   (19 birds)   **Sclater** P L
Silver Medal   (21 birds)   **Darwin**
Gold Medal   (24 birds)   **Gould** – it's that man again!

XANTUS

Xantus's Becard *Pachyramphus aglaiae* (**Lafresnaye** 1839)
(Alt. Rose-throated Becard)
Xantus's Gnatcatcher *Polioptila californica* (**Brewster** 1881)
(Alt. Californian Gnatcatcher)

Xantus's Hummingbird *Basilinna* [*Hylocharis*] *xantusii* (**Lawrence** 1860)
Xantus's Jay *Aphelocoma coerulescens* (Bosc 1795)
  (Alt. Florida Scrub Jay)
Xantus's Murrelet *Synthliboramphus hypoleucus* (Xantus 1860)
  (Alt. Scripps' Murrelet)
Xantus's Screech Owl *Otus kennicottii xantusii* (**Brewster** 1902)
  (Alt. Western Screech Owl)

Louis Janos (John) Xantus de Vesey (1825–1894) was a Hungarian who was on the staff of William **Hammond**, the collector. Between 1855 and 1861, whilst living in the United States, he sent the Smithsonian 10,000 specimens; his name is associated with many species. He is also renowned as a pathological liar (a kind of 19th-century Walter Mitty)! '*Xantus fled his native Hungary after taking part in the unsuccessful revolt against the Austrian Empire in 1848. A poor but educated and ambitious man, he wrote grandiose accounts of his American exploits. They were published in Hungary where he became famous. His letters make Private Xantus sound like he was in charge. Despite the fact that he* plagiarized other travel accounts of the American West, lied about himself, and always claimed to be superior to those around him, Xantus did great work for **Baird** and the Smithsonian. Xantus once had a photo taken of himself as a US Navy captain, which was published in Hungary. Xantus never even served in the Navy' (Schoenman & Benedek 1976).

XAVIER

Xavier's Greenbul *Phyllastrephus xavieri* (**Oustalet** 1892)
  (Alt. Dybowski's Astrild)

Xavier Dybowski was a French explorer who collected plants and animals in the Congo, between 1891 and 1892, presumably as part of a military-aided French survey mission headed by Jan [Jean-Thadée] Dybowski (1856–1928) which took place during those years. [See also Jan **Dybowski** who we speculate may have been Xavier's brother or even, according to one source, the same person.] He wrote an article *Tremblement de terre de Turqui observe a Adapazari*, in 1894, published in La Nature.

YALDWYN

Yaldwyn's Wren *Pachyplichas yaldwyni* (Millener 1988) [Extinct]

Doctor John C Yaldwyn is a New Zealand zoologist who specialises in crustaceans and he has published extensively on these and other subjects. In 1975, the Department of Land and Surveys in Wellington published *Preliminary Results of the Auckland Island Expedition 1972–1973*, which he edited. This detailed report on the distribution of the flora and fauna there formed the basis for a programme to rid the islands of non-native mammals including rodents, which was completed in the early 1990s. He was Director of the

National Museum of New Zealand, and he is still an Honorary Research Associate there. During his tenure he founded a department to deal specifically with archaeozoology. In 1971 he wrote *Australian Crustaceans in Colour*, with Anthony Healy. In 1981 he published *The bird fauna of Niue Island, southwest Pacific, with special notes on the White-tailed Tropicbird and Golden Plover* with F C Kinsky. In 1998 he wrote a paper on a new species of crab with **Ken-Ichi Hayashi**. There is also a fish, Yaldwyn's Triplefin *Nontclinops yaldwyni* named after him. Dr Jack **Grant-Mackie** was Phil Millener's thesis supervisor and arranged for Yaldwyn to be the latter's PhD examiner. Millener wrote the description of the wren, a New Zealand bird which became extinct at some time between the arrivals of the Polynesians and the Europeans.

YARRELL

Yarrell's Curassow *Crax globulosa* (**Spix** 1825)
   (Alt. Wattled Curassow)
Yarrell's Goldfinch *Carduelis yarrellii* (**Audubon** 1839)
   (Alt. Yellow-faced Siskin)
Yarrell's Woodstar *Eulidia yarrellii* (**Bourcier** 1847)
   (Alt. Chilean Woodstar)

William Yarrell (1784–1856) was an English bookseller, zoologist and amateur ornithologist. He wrote *History of British Birds*, in 1843, and *History of British Fishes*, which was published in 1859. He once sent a letter to Jenyns as he was '*most excited about a new species of swan*' which he '*knew was different from the Hooper*'. He apparently haunted the London markets to purchase any novel animal specimens. Yarrell found enough of the new birds to enable him to publish internal and external descriptions of the swan in a paper for the Linnean Society. Yarrell wrote to Jenyns '*I am almost afraid you have missed another new swan ...the North Americans have a species which they call the Great Grey headed Swan, both the Hooper and the new one are common at Hudson's Bay, and why may not their Great Grey headed Swan occasionally visit us, as well as the others*'. The swan in question is Bewick's Swan *Cygnus (columbianus) bewickii* (Yarrell 1830). He mentioned to his friend that he intended to add to the Philosophical Society's Collection '*one or more of every British Bird's egg that I possess beyond a pair, which I keep for my own drawers*'. He also has a fish, Yarrell's Blenny *Chirolophis ascanii*, named for him.

YEN

Yen's Fulvetta *Alcippe variegaticeps* (Yen 1932)
   (Alt. Gold-fronted Fulvetta)

Yen wrote the first description of a subspecies of the Silver-eared Mesia *Mesia argentauris tahanensis*, in 1934, according the annals of the University of Sun Yatsen, Canton, China. That specimen was collected in Malaya in 1905 and was lodged in the Selangore State Museum by H C **Robinson** who became the curator there. Yen adopted Robinson's draft name at that time. Yen himself wrote the description of the fulvetta in the Bulletin du Musée d'Histoire Naturelle de Marseilles. The bird is an endangered Chinese endemic.

YERSIN

Yersin's Laughing-thrush *Garrulax yersini* (**Robinson** & Kloss 1919)
   (Alt. Collared Laughing-thrush)

Alexandre Yersin (1863–1943) was a Swiss bacteriologist. Around 1882 and shortly after graduating in Paris, he joined Dr Louis Pasteur's team and took French citizenship in 1889. Later, in 1919, he was the Director of the Pasteur Institute in French Indochina

(now Vietnam), which he established. He was responsible for introducing the Brazilian rubber tree to Vietnam and for the first quinine plantations there. Yersin discovered the Plague bacillus *Yersina pestis*, which is named after him, and developed an antiserum. He also had a hand in the development of a vaccine for diphtheria. He took an interest in everything around him, which led him to explore in the Vietnamese highlands. He died at Nha Trang, in Annam.

YOUTH

Extreme youth is seldom a likely characteristic of those honoured in any capacity. The youngest people appearing among the eponymous were almost all children of ornithologists, their friends, relatives or sponsors. However, the three youngest people to have made it into these annals through their scientific endeavour are Thomas Henry Bowyer-**Bower,** who was Curator of Ornithology at the Western Australian Museum, Francois P L **Pollen,** the French naturalist and collector and Johan Frederik **Victorin,** who was a Swedish traveller and naturalist that visited South Africa. All three died at the age of 24. The only other persons worthy of mention in this category are Peter **Tyree** and Alan **Ridgen** who each found a fossil penguin on a beach when they were still children.

ZAPPEY

Zappey's Parrotbill *Paradoxornis zappeyi* (**Thayer** & **Bangs** 1912)
(Alt. Grey-hooded Parrotbill)

W R Zappey (1878–1914) was a collector for Harvard University. In 1905 he wrote *Birds of the Isle of Pines*, with Outram **Bangs.** His name is also associated with a race of a rodent, the Tibetan Mountain Pika *Ochotona thibetana zappeyi*.

ZARUDNY

Zarudny's Pheasant *Phasianus colchicus zarudnyi* (**Buturlin** 1904)
(Alt. Ring-necked Pheasant)

Nicolai Alekseyivich Zarudny (?–1919) was a Russian zoologist, traveller and ornithologist. He published *Third Excursion over Eastern Persia (Horassan, Seistan and Persian Baluchistan) in 1900–1901,* in 1916. He made an extensive collection of reptiles, amphibians and fishes in Iran, between 1895 and 1904, and in 1903 he published *Les Reptiles, Amphibiens, et Poissons de la Perse Orientale.* The Asian Desert Sparrow *Passer simplex zarudnyi,* Zarudny's Gerbil *Meriones zarudnyi,* Zarudny's Shrew *Crocidura zarudnyi* and Zarudny's Skink *Eumenes schn234234iderii zarudnyi* are all named after him.

ZELEDÓN

Zeledón's Manakin *Pipra pipra anthracina* (**Ridgway** 1906)
   (Alt. White-crowned Manakin)
Zeledón's Bush Tanager *Chlorospingus pileatus* (*zeledoni*) (**Lawrence** 1869)
Zeledón's Tyrannulet *Phyllomyias burmeisteri zeledoni* (Lawrence 1868)
   (Alt. Rough-legged Tyrannulet)

José Cástulo Zeledón (1846–1923) was a Costa Rican ornithologist. He had humble beginnings as an apprentice, but later became an internationally known ornithologist as well as co-administrator of the drugstore 'Botica Francesa', which is currently one of the largest private companies in that country. Advertisements in the press of the time said that the drugstore was '*managed by naturalists Frantzius and Zeledón*'. He studied under **Frantzius**, and under **Baird** and **Ridgway** at the Smithsonian. In 1871 he returned to Costa Rica as part of a scientific expedition, organised by Dr William Gabb, to explore the forest of Talamanca, where Zeledón made a very important collection of birds. The Smithsonian published his *Catalogue of the Birds of Costa Rica*, in 1885. His collection of 1,500 birds is in the National Museum of Costa Rica, which he co-founded. His name is also associated with the Wren-thrush *Zeledonia coronata*, the sole member of that eponymous genus, as well as several other subspecies. His tanager, however, has been proven to be a colour phase.

ZENAIDE

Zenaida Dove *Zenaida aurita* (**Bonaparte** 1838)

Princess Zénaide Charlotte Bonaparte (1801–1854) was the daughter of Joseph Bonaparte, the elder brother of Napoleon I. She married her cousin, Prince Charles Lucien **Bonaparte**, the famed ornithologist, who named the dove and the genus *Zenaida* of seven species after his wife.

ZENKER

Zenker's Honeyguide *Melignomon zenkeri* (**Reichenow** 1898)
Zenker's Lovebird *Agapornis swindernianus zenkeri* (Reichenow 1895)
   (Alt. Black-collared Lovebird)

Georg Zenker (1855–1922) was a German botanist who collected in Central Africa. He had very significant land holdings around Bipindi and it is possible that the type specimens were collected there.

ZENO

See **Zino**.

ZIMMER

Zimmer's Flatbill *Tolmomyias assimilis* (**Pelzeln** 1868)
   (Alt. Yellow-margined Flycatcher)
Zimmer's Tapaculo *Scytalopus zimmeri* (**Bond** & Meyer de Schauensee 1940)
Zimmer's Swift *Cypseloides cryptus* (Zimmer 1945)
   (Alt. White-chinned Swift)

Zimmer's Tody-Tyrant *Hemitriccus minimus* (**Todd** 1925)
Zimmer's Woodcreeper *Xiphorhynchus* (*picus*) *keinerii* (Zimmer 1934)
(Alt. Straight-billed Woodcreeper)

Dr John Todd Zimmer (1889–1957) was an American ornithologist who was Curator of Birds at The Field Museum of Natural History, Chicago from 1921 to 1930. He wrote *Birds of the Marshall Field Peruvian Expedition*, in 1930, and *Studies of Peruvian Birds* from 1931. He also wrote a catalogue of the Edward E Ayer Ornithological Library, a part of The Field Museum, in 1926. He was co-author of the *Check-list of Birds of the World, Volume 8* which was published in 1979. Bond and Meyer de Schauensee described the tapaculo as a subspecies of the Andean Tapaculo *S. magellanicus*, a group whihc has been subject to extensive revision in recent years.

ZINO

Zino's Petrel *Pterodroma madeira* (**Mathews** 1934)
(Alt. Freira, Madeira Petrel)

The petrel is not so much named after a person but after a whole family! Paul Alexander Zino, universally known as 'Alec' and his son Dr Francis Zino, are amateur ornithologists. Alec ran the family business and Francis is a general practitioner. The ancestral family originally moved from Genoa to Gibraltar and became British. Later, in about 1830, the family business, which involved Madeira, was moved to Funchal. Father Ernest Schmitz, who thought the bird was a **Fea**'s Petrel *Pterodroma feae* first recorded it in 1903. (The latter species was thought in the middle of the 20th century to have become extinct, but it was rediscovered in the Cape Verde Islands and also on Bugio in the Selvagem Islands off Madeira.) In 1963, Alec and Francis Zino accompanied Christian **Jouanin** and Francis Roux from the Paris Museum of Natural History on an expedition to the Selvagems. Christian Jouanin wakened their interest in ornithology. The bird was re-discovered in 1969, by Alec, and a protection strategy, the Freira Conservation Project, was set up, with Francis as the co-ordinator. Dr Bill Bourne was responsible for naming the bird after the Zino family. Alec Zino has virtually single-handedly turned the Selvagems into a strict nature reserve, to which Jouanin and Roux have returned regularly over about 30 years. Alec and Francis Zino in 1986 contributed to the *Study of petrels of the Pterodroma taxa in the archipelago of Madeira* (Biol. Mus. Mun. Funchal 38: 141–165).

ZÖE

Zöe's Imperial Pigeon *Ducula zoeae* (**Lesson** 1826)
(Alt. Bar-breasted/Banded Imperial Pigeon/Fruit Pigeon)

Zöe Lesson was the first wife of the French ornithologist René **Lesson** (1794–1849) who described the pigeon.

ZOOLOGISTS

All ornithologists are zoologists, but not all zoologists are ornithologists. However, no fewer than 80 general zoologists have been honoured in the common name of a bird. Among those who described themselves as zoologists, perhaps the man of greatest stature was René Primevère **Lesson**, who was a naturalist of enormous influence and importance. Still, if you have read all the way through this book, rather than skipped to this point in an attempt to see 'who done it', you will have made up your own mind who the giants of scientific endeavour in this field really were.

BIBLIOGRAPHY

Aldington, R. 1949. *The Strange Life of Charles Waterton.* Duell, New York.

American Ornithologists' Union. 1983. Checklist of Birds. (and 1985, 1987, and 1989 Supplements).

Banks, R. C. *Obsolete English Names of North American Birds and their Modern Equivalents.* http://www.pwrc.usgs.gov/research/pubs/banks/obsall.htm. National Museum of Natural History, Washington.

Bannerman, David Armitage, 1931-1951. *The birds of tropical west Africa: with special reference to those of the Gambia, Sierra Leone, the Gold Coast and Nigeria.* The Crown Agents for the Colonies, London.

Baylis, G. T. S. 1997. *The New Zealand Garden Journal* (Journal of the Royal New Zealand Institute of Horticulture). 2:1.

Beebe, W 1918-1922. *A Monograph of the Pheasants.* 4 vols. Witherby, London.

Bennett, G. 1860. *Gatherings of a Naturalist in Australasia: Being Observations principally on the animal and vegetable productions of New South Wales, New Zealand, and some of the Austral Islands.* John van Voorst, London.

Bishop, N. H. 1878. *Voyage of the Paper Canoe.* Lee & Shepard, New York.

Blyth, E. 1835. An Attempt to Classify the 'Varieties' of Animals with Observations on the Marked Seasonal and Other Changes Which Naturally Take Place in Various British Species, and Which Do Not Constitute Varieties. *The Magazine of Natural History* 8:40-53.

Bresse, F. 1708. *Voyage et Aventures en Deux Iles Desertes des Indes Orientales.*

de Castelnau, F. 1850-1855. *Expédition dans les parties centrales de l'Amérique du Sud, de Rio de Janeiro à Lima, et de Lima au Para: exécuté par ordre du gouvernement Français pendant les années 1843 à 1847.* P. Bertrand, Paris.

Chapin, J. P. 1954. The Birds of the Belgian Congo. *Bulletin American Museum of Natural History* Part 4. 758:37.

Choate, E. A. 1985. *The Dictionary of American Bird Names.* Harvard Common Press, Boston.

Clements, J.F. 1991. *Birds of the World: a Checklist.* Ibis Publishing Company, California.

Clinning, C. 1989. *Southern African Bird Names Explained.* Southern African Ornithological Society, Johannesburg.

Coates, B. J. 1990. *The birds of Papua New Guinea.* Vol.2. Passerines. Dove Publications, Alderley.

Cobb, A. F. 1910. *Wild Life in the Falklands.* Gowan's Nature Books, London.

Cobb, A. F. 1933. *Birds of the Falkland Islands.* Witherby, London.

Columbia University Press. 2001. *Columbia Encyclopedia* 6th Edition.

Cox, E. S. 1937. *The American Racial Problem as Seen in a Worldwide Perspective.* The Noontide Press, California.

Craig, A. (Rhodes University ?) 1989 & 1990. *Whose Name for the Bird?* Vol 41 (4) & Vol 41 (1) Birding in South Africa.

Darwin, C. 1859. *On the Origin of Species.* John Murray, London.

Darwin, C. 1871. *The Descent of Man and Selection in relation to Sex.* John Murray, London.

Delacour, J. 1977. *The Pheasants of the World.* Spur Publications, Reading.

Devlin, J. C. & Naismith, G. 1977. *The World of Roger Tory Peterson.* Times Books, New York.

Oxford University Press. In prep. *Dictionary of National Biography.* Oxford University Press, Oxford.

Dumont d'Urville, J.S.C. 1853, *Voyage au Pole Sud et dans l'Oceanie sur les Corvettes l'Astrolabe et la Zelee [execute par ordre du roi] pendant les annees 1837-1838-1839-1840 sous le commandent de M. Dumont-d'Urville Captaine de Vaisseau.*

Emmett, E. T. 1954. *Tasmania by Road and Track.* Melbourne University Press, Melbourne.

Frost, C. 1987. *History of British Taxidermy.* The Lavenham Press, Suffolk.

Fuller, E. 2000. *Extinct Birds.* Oxford University Press, Oxford.

Gebhardt, L. 1964. *Die Ornithologen Mitteleuropas I.* Giessen und Berlin.

Gebhardt, L. 1970. *Die Ornithologen Mitteleuropas II.* Giessen und Berlin.

Gill, B. & Martinson, P. 1991. *New Zealand's Extinct Birds.* Random Century, New Zealand.

Grant, P. J. 1982. *Gulls: A Guide to Identification.* T & A D Poyser, Calton.

Grierson, J. 1960. *Sir Hubert Wilkins: Enigma of Exploration.* Robert Hale, London.

Grote, A. 1875. Catalogue of Mammals and Birds of Burma, by the late E. Blyth. *Journal of the Asiatic Society of Bengal* Part II.

Hall, B.P & Moreau, R.E. 1970. *An Atlas of Speciation in African Passerine Birds.* British Museum (Natural History), London.

Hanson, H. G. *Biographical Etymology of Marine Organism Names.* University of Stockholm, Stockholm.

Henwood, C. 2001. The Discovery of the Syrian (Golden) Hamster. *British Hamster Association Magazine* 39.

Hoffman, M. (Ed.) 1983. *Tibet: The Sacred Realm:* Aperture Books, New York.

Howman, K. C. R. 1996. *Introduction to Ornamental Pheasants.* Hancock House Publishing, Washington.

Jaeger, E. C. 1955. *A Source-book of Biological Names and Terms.* Charles C. Thomas, Springfield.

James, E. 1823. *Account of an Expedition from Pittsburgh to the Rocky Mountains, Performed in the Years 1819 and 1820, By Order of The Hon. J. C. Calhoun, Sec'y of War: Under the Command of Major Stephen H. Long, from the Notes of Major Long, Mr. T. Say, and Other Gentlemen of the Exploring Party.* Philadelphia.

Jobling, J. A. 1991. *A Dictionary of Scientific Bird Names.* Oxford University Press, Oxford.

Kastner, J. 1986. *A World of Watchers.* Sierra Club Books, San Francisco.

Kropotkin, P. 1924. *Ethics: Origins and Development.* George E. Harrap, London

Lagden, G. 1910. *The Basutos: the mountaineers and their country; being a narrative of events relating to the tribe from its formation early in the nineteenth century to the present day.* Constable & Co, London.

Le Vaillant, F. 1790. *Travels into the Interior Parts of Africa.*

Low, R. 1998. Duyvenbode's, *Chalcopsitta duyvenbodei*: a uniquely beautiful Lori. *Lori Journaal Internationaal* No. 1.

Lowell, T. 1961. *Sir Hubert Wilkins: His World of Adventure.* McGraw-Hill, London.

MacGillivray, W., ed. Ralph, R. 1998. *A Walk to London.*, Acair, Stornoway.

Maclean, G. L. 1993. Roberts' *Birds of South Africa.* 5th edition. New Holland, London.

McCormick, R. 1884. *Voyages of Discovery in the Arctic and Antarctic Seas, and Round the World: Being Personal Narratives of Attempts to Reach the North and South Poles.*

McDaniel, L. 1998. *The Longstreet Highroad Guide to the Mountains of North Carolina.* Longstreet Press, Atlanta.

Mearns, B. & Mearns, R. 1988. *Biographies for Bird Watchers - The Lives of Those Commemorated in Western Palearctic Bird Names.* Academic Press, London.

Mearns, B. & Mearns, R. 1992. *Audubon to Xantus: The Lives of Those Commemorated in North American Bird Names.* Academic Press, London.

Mearns, B. & Mearns, R. 1998. *The Bird Collectors.* Academic Press, London.

Muir, J. 1917. *The Cruise of the Corwin.* Houghton Mifflin, Cambridge.

Olrog, C. C. 1943. *Destination Eldslandet.* Bonniers, Stockholm.

Potter, P. E. 1996. *Biography of Samuel M. Klages.*

Ridgway, R. 1912. *Colour Standards and Nomenclature.* Ridgway, Washington.

Roosevelt, T. 1914. *Through the Brazilian Wilderness.* Charles Scribner's Sons, New York.

Schoenman, T. & Benedek, H. (eds & translators). 1976. Xantus, John. *Travels in Southern California.* Wayne State University Press, Detroit.

Sibley, C. G. & Monroe, B. L. 1990. *Disrtibution and Taxonomy of the Birds of the World.* Yale University Press, New Haven.

Simpson, G. G. 1972. Pliocene penguins from North Canterbury, New Zealand. *Records of the Canterbury Museum 9:* 159 - 182.

Smith, T. 1998. The Names of Pheasants. *Heart of America Game Breeders' Association Newsletter,* Oct. 1, 1998.

Swinhoe, R. 1872. Descriptions of two new Pheasants and a new Garrulax from Ningpo, China. *Proceedings of the Zoological Society of London* (April 16 meeting), pp550-554.

Wallace, A. A. 1863. *The Malay Archipelago.* Linnaean Society, London.

Walters, M. 1980. *The Complete Birds of the World.* David & Charles, London.

Weber, M & De Beaufort, L. F. 1931. *The Fishes of the Indo-Australian Archipelago.* E. Brill, Leiden.

Weintraub, J. D. *Western Bird Names - A Supplement For Your Western Peterson Field Guide And Other Guides.* Dept. of Biological Science, California State University, California.

Wells, M. G. 1998. *World Bird Species Checklist.* Worldlist.

White, J. A. 1999. *Ornithology Collections in the Libraries at Cornell University: A Descriptive Guide.* Ithaca, New York.

Wynne O. E., 1969. *Biographical Key - Names of Birds of the World - to Authors and those Commemorated.* Fordingbridge, Hants.

Zimmer, K. J. 1985. *The Western Bird Watcher.* Prentice-Hall, New Jersey.

APPENDIX
List of birds by scientific name in alphabetical order

Scientific name	Common name
Abeillia abeillei	Abeille's Hummingbird
Acanthiza murina	De Vis's Tree Warbler
Acanthiza pusilla whitlocki	Whitlocks Hornbill
Accipiter (Megatriorchis) doriae	Doria's Hawk
Accipiter cooperii	Cooper's Hawk
Accipiter francesii	Frances's Goshawk
Accipiter gundlachii	Gundlach's Hawk
Accipiter henicogrammus	Gray's Goshawk
Accipiter henstii	Henst's Goshawk
Accipiter meyerianus	Meyer's Goshawk
Accipiter soloensis	Horsfield's Goshawk/ Sparrowhawk
Accipiter striatus suttoni	Sutton's Sharp-shinned Hawk
Aceros everetti	Everett's Hornbill
Aceros subruficollis	Blyth's Hornbill
Acestrura harterti	Hartert's Woodstar
Acestrura mulsant	Mulsant's Wood Star
Acrocephalus bistrigiceps	Schrenck's Reed Warbler
Acrocephalus brevipennis	Dohrn's Warbler
Acrocephalus dumetorum	Blyth's Reed Warbler
Acrocephalus orinus	Hume's [Large-billed] Reed Warbler
Acrocephalus rehsei	Finsch's Reed Warbler
Acrocephalus stentoreus celebensis	Heinroth's Reed Warbler
Actenoides hombroni	Hombron's Kingfisher
Actinodura ramsayi	Ramsay's Barwing
Actinodura soulei	Soule's Barwing
Actinodura waldeni	Austen's Barwing (Godwin-Austen's)
Actinodura waldeni	Walden's Barwing (Tweeddale's)
Aechmophorus clarkii (occidentalis)	Clark's Grebe
Aegithalos iouschistos	Blyth's Long-tailed Tit
Aegithina nigrolutea	Marshall's Iora
Aegolius acadicus	Kirtland's Saw-whet Owl
Aegolius acadicus brooksi	Queen Charlotte Owl
Aegolius funereus	Tengmalm's Owl
Aegolius funereus richardsoni	Richardson's Owl
Aegotheles archboldi	Archbold's Mountain Owlet-Nightjar
Aegotheles wallacii	Wallace's Owlet-Nightjar
Aeluroedus geislerorum	Geisler's Catbird
Aeluroedus stonii	Stone's Catbird
Aepypodius bruijnii	Bruijn's Brush Turkey
Aerodramus ficiphagus	Thunberg's Swiflet
Aerodramus germani	Oustalet's Swiftlet
Aerodramus maximus	Hume's Swiftlet
Aerodramus orientalis	Mayr's Swiftlet
Aerodramus whiteheadi	Whitehead's Swiftlet
Aethopyga christinae	Mrs Swinhoe's Sunbird (Christina's)
Aethopyga duyvenbodei	Duyvenbode's Sunbird
Aethopyga eximia	Kuhl's Sunbird
Aethopyga gouldiae	Gould's Sunbird
Aethopyga gouldiae	Mrs Gould's Sunbird (Lady Gould's)
Aethopyga linaraborae	Lina's Sunbird (Lind's)
Aethopyga linaraborae	Lind's Sunbird (Lina's)
Aethopyga primigenius	Hachisuka's Sunbird
Aethopyga temminckii	Temminck's Sunbird
Agapornis fischeri	Fischer's Lovebird
Agapornis lilianae	Lilian's Lovebird
Agapornis swindernianus	Swinderen's Parrakeet
Agapornis swindernianus zenkeri	Zenker's Lovebird
Aglaeactis pamela	Pamela's Sunbeam
Agyrtia taczanowskii	Taczanowski's Emerald
Aimophila aestivalis	Bachman's Sparrow
Aimophila botterii	Botteri's Sparrow
Aimophila carpalis	Bendire's Summer Sparrow
Aimophila cassinii	Cassin's Sparrow
Aimophila ruficeps	Boucard's Summer Sparrow
Aimophila ruficeps	Scott's Sparrow
Aimophola sumichrasti	Sumichrast's Sparrow
Alaemon hamertoni	Witherby's Lark
Alcedo hercules	Blyth's Kingfisher
Alcippe brunnea	Gould's Fulvetta
Alcippe ludlowi	Ludlow's Fulvetta
Alcippe ruficapilla	Verreaux's Fulvetta
Alcippe variegaticeps	Yen's Fulvetta
Alcippe vinipectus	Hodgson's Fulvetta
Alectoris magna	Prjevalsky's Rock Partridge
Alectoris philbyi	Philby's Rock Partridge
Alectura lathami	Barnard's Brush Turkey
Aleptes leucopterus paynteri	Paynter's Brushfinch
Alethe fuelleborni	Fülleborn's Alethe
Alisterus chloropterus callopterus	Salvadori's Green-winged King Parrot
Alisterus chloropterus moczkowskii	Moczkowski's Green-winged King Parrot
Alisterus chloropterus moszkowskii	Moszkowski's Green-wing King Parrot
Alophoixus finschii	Finsch's Bearded Bulbul
Amaurocichia bocagei	Bocage's Longbill
Amaurornis bicolor	Elwes' Crake
Amaurornis olivieri	Olivier's Rail
Amazilia boucardi	Boucard's Hummingbird
Amazilia edward	Edwards' Hummingbird
Amazilia (Argyrtia) franciae	Francia's Azure Crown
Amazilia lactea bartletti	Bartlett's Emerald
Amazilia luciae	Lucy's Emerald
Amazilia tzacatl	Rieffer's Hummingbird
Amazona autumnalis salvini	Salvin's Amazon
Amazona barbadensis rothschildi	Rothschild's Amazon
Amazona brasiliensi dufresniana	Dufresne's Amazon
Amazona farinosa chapmani	Chapman's Mealy Amazon
Amazona festiva bodini	Bodin's Amazon (Bodinus's)
Amazona finschi	Finsch's Amazon
Amazona guildingi	Guilding's Amazon
Amazona kawalli	Kawall's Parrot
Amazona ochrocephala nattereri	Natterer's Amazon
Amazona pretrei	Prêtre's Parrot
Amblycercus holosericeus australis	Chapman's Cacique
Amblyornis macgregoriae	Gardener Bowerbird
Amblyornis macgregoriae	Lady MacGregor Bowerbird
Amblyornis macgregoriae	MacGregor's Bowerbird
Ammodramus bairdii	Baird's Sparrow
Ammodramus caudacutus nelsoni	Nelson's Sharp-tailed Sparrow
Ammodramus henslowii	Henslow's Sparrow
Ammodramus leconteii	Le Conte's Sparrow
Ammomanes grayi	Gray's Lark
Amphispiza belli	Bell's Sparrow

Scientific name	Common name
Amphispiza bilineata bangsi	Bangs' Sparrow
Amytornis dorotheae	Dorothy's Grasswren
Anairetes fernandezianus	Juan Fernández Tit-Tyrant
Anas bernieri	Bernier's Teal
Anas breweri	Brewer's Duck
Anas cyanoptera borreroi	Borrero's Cinnamon Teal
Anas (acuta) eatoni	Eaton's Pintail
Anas georgica nicefori	Nicefero's Pintail (Extinct)
Anas melleri	Meller's Duck
Anas platyrhynchos oustaleti	Oustalet's Duck
Anas smithii	Smith's Shoveller
Anas strepera couesi	Coue's Gadwall (Extinct)
Andropadus (Pycnonotus) ansorgei	Ansorge's Greenbul
Andropadus hallae	Hall's Greenbul
Andropadus importunus fricki	Frick's Sombre Greenbul
Andropadus masukuensis	Shelley's Greenbul
Anodorhynchus leari	Lear's Macaw
Anorrhinus (tickelli) austeni	Austen's Brown Hornbill (Godwin-Austen's)
Anorrhinus tickelli	Tickell's Hornbill
Anser fabalis middendorffi	Middendorff's Bean Goose
Anser rossi	Ross's Goose
Anthracothorax prevosti	Prevost's Mango
Anthracoceros montani	Montano's Hornbill
Anthreptes anchietae	Anchieta's Sunbird
Anthreptes fraseri	Fraser's Sunbird
Anthreptes rectirostris	Berlioz' Sunbird
Anthreptes rhodolaema	Shelley's Red-throated Sunbird
Anthus bannermani	Bannerman's Pipit
Anthus berthelotii	Berthelot's Pipit
Anthus godlewski	Blyth's Pipit
Anthus godlewski	Godlewski's Pipit
Anthus gustavi menzbieri	Menzbier's Pipit
Anthus hellmayri	Hellmayr's Pipit
Anthus (cinnamomeus) latistriatus	Jackson's Pipit
Anthus leucophrys goodsoni	Goodson's Pipit
Anthus nyassae	Chaplin's Pipit
Anthus richardi	Richards' Pipit
Anthus roseatus	Hodgson's Pipit
Anthus sharpei	Sharpe's Pipit
Anthus similis	Nicholson's (Rock) Pipit
Anthus spragueii	Sprague's Pipit
Apalis chapini strausae	Straus's Apalis
Apalis goslingi	Gosling's Apalis
Apalis kaboboensis	Prigogine's Apalis
Apalis moreaui	Moreau's Tailorbird
Apalis ruddi	Rudd's Apalis
Apalis rufogularis argentea	Peters's Apalis
Apalis sharpii	Sharpe's Apalis
Apalis sharpii chapini	Chapin's Apalis
Apaloderma narina	Narina Trogan
Aphanapterix bonasia	Van den Broecke's Rail (Extinct)
Aphanapterix leguati	Leguat's Gelinote (Extinct)
Aphelocoma californica sumichrasti	Sumichrast's Jay
Aphelocoma coerulescens	Belding's Jay
Aphelocoma coerulescens	Xantus's Jay
Aphelocoma coerulescens woodhousei	Woodhouse's Jay
Aphelocoma ultramarina	Sieber's Jay
Aphelocoma ultramarina couchii	Couch's Jay
Aplonis corvina	Kittlitz's Starling
Aplonis mystacea	Grant's Starling
Aptenodytes ridgeni	Ridgen's Penguin (Extinct)
Apus alexandri	Alexander's Swift
Apus batesi	Bates' (Black) Swift
Apus berliozi	Berlioz's Swift
Apus berliozi	Forbes-Watson's Swift
Apus bradfieldi	Bradfield's Swift
Apus horus toulsoni	Horus Swift
Aquila adalberti	Adalbert's Eagle
Aquila gurneyi	Gurney's Eagle
Aquila verreauxii	Verreaux's Eagle
Aquila wahlbergi	Wahlberg's Eagle
Ara ambigua	Buffon's Macaw
Ara glaucogularis	Wagler's Macaw
Ara gossei	Gosse's Macaw
Ara nobilis cumanensis	Lichtenstein's Noble Macaw
Ara nobilis longpennis	Neumann's Macaw
Arachnothera everetti	Everett's Spiderhunter
Arachnothera juliae	Whitehead's Spiderhunter
Aramidopsis plateni	Platen's Celebese Rail (Extinct)
Aratinga canicularis canicularis	Petz's Conure
Aratinga chloroptera maugei	Mauge's Conure
Aratinga finschi	Finsch's Conure
Aratinga guarouba	Queen of Bavaria's Conure
Aratinga holochlora brewsteri	Brewster's Green Conure
Aratinga labati	Labat's Conure (Extinct)
Aratinga mitrata alticola	Chapman's Mitred Conure
Aratinga pertinax ocularis	Veragua's Parakeet
Aratinga wagleri minor	Carriker's Conure
Aratinga wagleri transilis	Peters's Conure
Aratinga weddellii	Weddell's Conure
Arborophila (orientalis) campbelli	Campbell's Hill Partridge
Arborophila charltonii	Eyton's Hill Partridge
Arborophila davidi	David's Tree Partridge
Arborophila gingica	Ricket's Tree Partridge
Arborophila orientalis	Horsfield's Hill Partridge
Arborophila rufipectus	Boulton's Hill Partridge
Archaeosphenicus lopdelli	Lopdell's Penguin (Extinct)
Archaeosphenicus lowei	Lowe's Penguin (Extinct)
Archboldia papuensis	Archbold's Bowerbird
Archboldia sanfordi	Sanford's Bowerbird
Archilochus alexandri	Alexander Hummingbird
Archilochus alexandri	Alexandre's Hummingbird
Ardea goliath	Goliath Heron
Ardea herodias	Treganza's Heron
Ardea herodias fannini	Fannin's Heron
Ardea herodias wardi	Ward's Heron
Ardea herodias wurdemannii	Wurdemann's Heron
Ardea humbloti	Humblot's Heron
Artamus insignis	Sclater's Woodswallow
Asthenes berlepschi	Berlepsch's Canastero
Asthenes hudsoni	Hudson's Canastero
Asthenes sclateri lilloi	Lillo's Canastero
Asthenes steinbachi	Steinbach's Canastero
Astrapia rothschildi	Rothchild's Astrapia
Astrapia stephaniae	Princess Stephanie's (Stephanie's)
Astrapia stephaniae	Princess Stephanie's Astrapia (Stephanie's)
Atelornis crossleyi	Crossley's Ground Roller
Athene blewitti	Blewitt's Owl
Atlatpetes schistaceus taczanowski	Taczanowski's Brush-Finch
Atlatpetes seebohmi simonsi	Simons's Brush Finch
Atthis heloisa	Heloise's Hummingbird
Atthis heloisa (morcomi)	Morcom's Hummingbird
Augasma cyaneo-beryllina	Berlioz's Woodnymph
Augastes geoffroyi	Geoffroy's Wedgebill

Augastes scutatus	Natterer's Vizor-bearer
Aulacorhynchus derbianus	Lord Derby's Aracari (Stanley's)
Aviceda jerdoni	Jerdon's Baza
Aviceda jerdoni (ceylonensis)	Legge's Baza
Avocettula recurvirostris	Swainson's Hummingbird
Aythya baeri	Baer's Pochard
Babax koslowi	Kozlow's Babax
Baeopogon clamans	Sjostedt's Honeyguide Greenbul
Bambusicola fytchii	Anderson's Bamboo Partridge
Barnardius barnardi	Barnard's Parrakeet
Barnardius zonarius	Bauer's Parakeet
Bartramia longicauda	Bartramian Tattler
Bartramia longicauda	Bartram's Sandpiper
Basileuterus belli	Bell's Warbler
Basileuterus culicivorus	Brasher's Warbler
Basileuterus fraseri	Fraser's Warbler
Basileuterus luteoviridis richardsoni	Richardson's Warbler
Basilinna (Hylocharis) xantusii	Xantus's Hummingbird
Batis fratrum	Woodwards' Batis
Batis (minima) iturensis	Chapin's Puff-backed Flycatcher
Batis margaritae	Boulton's Puff-back Flycatcher
Batis margaritae	Margaret's Batis
Batis minima	Verreaux's Grey-headed Puffback Flycatcher
Batis occulta	Lawson's Batis
Batis reichenowi	Reichenow's Batis
Batrachostomus affinis	Blyth's Frogmouth
Batrachostomus hodgsoni	Hodgson's Frogmouth
Batrachostomus mixtus	Sharpe's Frogmouth
Batrachostomus stellatus	Gould's Frogmouth
Biziura delautouri	De Lautour's Duck (Extinct)
Boissonneaua jardini	Jardine's Hummingbird
Bolborhynchus aurifrons margaritae	Margarit's Parakeet
Bolborhynchus aurifrons robertsi	Roberts's Parakeet
Bonasa sewerzowi	Severtzov's Hazel Grouse
Bourceria conradi	Conrad's Inca
Brachygalba salmoni	Salmon's Jacamar
Brachypteryx leucophrys carolinae	Caroline's Shortwing
Brachypteryx stellata	Gould's Shortwing
Brachyramphus brevirostris	Kittlitz's Murrelet
Brachyramphus (Synthliboramphus) craveri	Craveris's Murrelet
Bradypterus alfredi	Newton's Scrub-warbler
Bradypterus barratti	Barratt's Warbler
Bradypterus davidi	David's Bush Warbler
Bradypterus davidi	Père David's Bush Warbler (David's)
Bradypterus gruaeri	Grauer's Rush Warbler
Bradypterus lopezi	Lopez's Warbler
Bradypterus lopezi usambarae (roehli)	Roehl's Swamp Warbler
Bradypterus palliseri	Palliser's Warbler
Bradypterus victorini	Victorin's Warbler
Branta canadensis	Richardson's Goose
Branta canadensis (hutchinsi)	Hutchin's Goose
Branta canadensis interior	Todd's Goose
Branta canadensis taverneri	Taverner's Goose
Brotogeris cyanoptera cyanoptera	Deville's Parakeet
Brotogeris cyanoptera gustavi	Gustav's Parakeet
Brotogeris chiriri behni	Behn's Parakeet
Bubo ascalaphus	Pharoh's Eagle Owl
Bubo ascalaphus	Savigny's Eagle Owl
Bubo bubo aharonii	Aharoni's Eagle Owl
Bubo capensis mackinderi	MacKinder's Eagle Owl
Bubo lacteus	Verreaux's Owl
Bubo leguati	Leguat's Owl (Extinct)
Bubo poensis	Fraser's Eagle Owl
Bubo shelleyi	Shelley's Eagle Owl
Buccanodon duchaillui	Duchaillu's Yellow-spotted Barbet
Bucephala islandica	Barrow's Goldeneye
Buettikoferella bivittata	Büttikofer's Warbler
Bulweria bulwerii	Bulwer's Petrel
Bulweria fallax	Jouanin's Petrel
Buteo albicaudatus	Sennett's White-tailed Hawk
Buteo augur	Archer's Buzzard
Buteo jamaicensis	Cooper's Buzzard
Buteo jamaicensis fuertesi	Fuertes's Hawk
Buteo jamaicensis harlani	Harlan's Hawk
Buteo jamaicensis krideri	Krider's Hawk
Buteo lagopus sanctijohannis	St John's Black Hawk
Buteo poecilochrous	Gurney's Buzzard
Buteo ridgwayi	Ridgway's Hawk
Buteo solitarius	Gruber's Hawk
Buteo swainsonii	Swainson's Hawk
Buthraupis arcaei	Arce's Tanager
Butorides striatus anthonyi	Anthony's Green Heron
Butorides striatus frazari	Frazar's Green Heron
Cacatua ducorpsii	Ducorp's Cockatoo
Cacatua galerita eleonora	Eleanora's Cockatoo
Cacatua galerita fitzroyi	Fitzroy's Cockatoo
Cacatua galerita fitzroyi	Mathews' Cockatoo
Cacatua galerita tritoni	Triton's Cockatoo
Cacatua goffini	Goffin's Cockatoo
Cacatua leadbeateri	Leadbeater's Cockatoo
Cacatua leadbeateri	Major Mitchell's Cockatoo
Cacatua leadbeateri mollis	Mathews' Pink Cockatoo
Cacatua sanguinea gymnopis	Sclater's Bare-eyed Corella
Cacatua sanguinea normantoni	Mathews' Short-billed Corella
Cacatua sulphurea abbotti	Abbott's Lesser Sulphur-crested Cockatoo
Cacicus koepckeae	Koepcke's Cacique
Cacomantis heinrichi	Heinrich's Brush Cuckoo
Calamonastes [Camaroptera] stierlingi	Stierling's Barred Warbler
Calandrella acutirostris	Hume's Short-toed Lark
Calandrella blanfordi	Blanford's Lark
Calandrella cinerea erlangeri	Erlanger's Lark
Calcarius mccownii	McCown's Longspur
Calcarius pictus	Smith's Longspur
Calidris alpina schinzii	Schinz's Sandpiper
Calidris bairdii	Baird's Sandpiper
Calidris fuscicollis	Bonaparte's Sandpiper
Calidris paramelanotos	Cox's Sandpiper
Calidris subminuta	Middendorff's Stint
Calidris temminckii	Temminck's Stint
Callipepla californica cranfieldae	Canfield's Quail
Callipepla gambelii	Gambel's Quail
Calocitta colliei	Collie's Magpie-Jay
Calonectris diomedea	Cory's Shearwater
Calonectris (diomedea) diomedea	Scopoli's Shearwater
Calothorax fanny	Fanny's Woodstar
Calothorax heliodori	Heliodore's Woodstar
Calothorax lucifer	Lucifer's Hummingbird
Calypte anna	Anna's Hummingbird

383

Calypte costae	Costa's Calypte	*Carpodacus rubescens*	Blanford's Rosefinch
Calyptomena hosii	Hose's Broadbill	*Carpodacus rubicilla*	Severzov's Rosefinch
Calyptomena whiteheadi	Whitehead's Broadbill	*Carpodacus thura*	Mlle. Thura's Rosefinch
Calyptorhynchus banksii	Banksian Cockatoo		(Thura's)
Calyptorhynchus banksii	Latham's Cockatoo	*Carpodacus thura*	Thura's Rosefinch
Calyptorhynchus banksii	Leach's Red-tailed	*Carpodectes antoniae*	Antonia's Cotinga
	Cockatoo	*Carpodectes hopkei*	Hopke's Cotinga
Calyptorhynchus banksii	Mathews' Red-tailed Black	*Casuarius bennetti*	Bennett's Cassowary
samueli	Cockatoo	*Catharacta lonnbergi*	Lonnberg's Skua
Calyptorhynchus baudini	Baudin's Cockatoo	*Catharacta maccormicki*	McCormick's Skua
Calyptorhynchus funereus	Carnaby's White-tailed	*Catharus bicknelli*	Bicknell's Thrush
latirostris	Black Cockatoo	*Catharus frantzii*	Frantzius' Nightingale-
Calyptorhynchus latirostris	Carnaby's Black Cockatoo		Thrush
Calyptorhynchus	Gould's Red-tailed Black	*Catharus fuscescens*	Wilson's Thrush
macrorhynchus	Cockatoo	*Catharus ustulatus*	Swainson's Thrush
Camarhynchus crassirostris	Darwin's Vegetarian Finch	*Catharus ustulatus almae*	Alma's Thrush
Camarhynchus heliobates	Darwin's Mangrove Finch	*Catreus wallichi*	Wallich's Pheasant
Camarhyunchus pallidus	Darwin's Woodpecker Finch	*Centrocercus minimus*	Gunnison's Sage Grouse
Camarhynchus parvulus	Darwin's Small Tree Finch	*Centropus bernsteini*	Bernstein's Coucal
Camarhynchus pauper	Darwin's Medium Tree Finch	*Centropus burchelli*	Burchell's Coucal
Camarhynchus pauper	Charles' Tree-finch	*Centropus goliath*	Goliath Coucal
	(Darwin's)	*Centropus menbeki*	Menbek's Coucal
Camarhynchus psittacula	Darwin's Large Tree Finch	*Centropus (leucogaster)*	
Camaroptera harterti	Hartert's Camaroptera	*neumanni*	Neumann's Coucal
Campephaga petiti	Petit's Cuckoo-shrike	*Centropus senegalensis flecki*	Fleck's Coucal
Campethera bennetti	Bennett's Woodpecker	*Centropus steerii*	Steere's Coucal
Campethera bennetti		*Cephalepsis loddigesi*	Loddiges' Plovercrest
scriptoricauda	Reichenow's Woodpecker	*Cepphus grylle mandtii*	Mandt's Guillemot
Campethera tullbergi	Tullberg's Woodpecker	*Cercococcyx mechowi*	Mechow's Long-tailed
Campylopterus delattrei	De Lattre's Sabrewing		Cuckoo
	(Henry De Lattre's)	*Cercomacra cinerascens*	
Campylopterus villavicencio	Villavicencio's Sabrewing	*sclateri*	Sclater's Antbird
Campylorhynchus jocosus	Boucard's Wren	*Cercomacra laeta*	Willis's Antbird
Campylorhynchus rufinucha		*Cercomela schlegelii*	Schlegel's Chat
humilis	Sclater's Wren	*Cercomela tractrac*	Layard's Chat
Caprimulgus atripennis	Jerdon's Nightjar	*Cercotrichas leucosticta collsi*	Colls' Forest Robin
Caprimulgus batesi	Bates' Nightjar	*Certhia nipalensis*	Stolizcka's Treecreeper
Caprimulgus centralasicus	Vaurie's Nightjar	*Certhidea olivacea*	Darwin's Warbler Finch
Caprimulgus clarus	Reichenow's Nightjar	*Certhilauda barlowi*	Barlow's Lark
Caprimulgus concretus	Bonaparte's Nightjar	*Cettia acanthizoides*	Swinhoe's Bush Warbler
Caprimulgus donaldsoni	Donaldson-Smith's Nightjar	*Cettia acanthizoides*	Verreaux's Bush Warbler
Caprimulgus inornatus		*Cettia cetti*	Cetti's Warbler
ludovicianus	Ludovic's Nightjar	*Cettia vulcania*	Muller's Bush Warbler
Caprimulgus mahrattensis	Sykes' Nightjar	*Ceyx goodfellowi*	Goodfellow's Kingfisher
Caprimulgus monticolus	Franklin's Nightjar	*Chaetocercus jourdanii*	Jourdan's Woodstar
Caprimulgus prigoginei	Prigogine's Nightjar	*Chaetura andrei*	Andre's Swift
Caprimulgus pulchellus	Salvadori's Nightjar	*Chaetura chapmani*	Chapman's Swift
Caprimulgus ridgwayi	Ridgway's Nightjar	*Chaetura vauxi*	Vaux's Swift
Caprimulgus rufus	Chuck Will's Widow	*Chalcophaps stephani*	Stephan's Dove
Caprimulgus salvini	Salvin's Chuckwill	*Chalcopsitta atra bernsteinii*	Bernstein's Black Lory
Caprimulgus vociferus	Stephen's Whip-poor-will	*Chalcopsitta atra insignis*	Rajah's Lory
Caracara polyborus auduboni	Audubon's Caracara	*Chalcopsitta atra spectabilis*	Van Oort's Black Lori
Carduelis ambigua	Oustalet's Greenfinch	*Chalcopsitta duyvenbodei*	Duyvenbode's Lory
Carduelis flammea holboelli	Holboell's Redpoll	*Chalcopsitta duyvenbodei*	Neumann's Duyvenbode's
Carduelis hornemanni	Hornemann's Redpoll	*syringanuchalis*	Lory
Carduelis hornemanni		*Chalcostigma herrani*	Herran's Thornbill
exilipes	Coues' Redpoll	*Chalcostigma stanleyi*	Stanley's Thornbill
Carduelis lawrencei	Lawrence's Goldfinch	*Chalybura buffoni*	Buffon's Plumeleteer
Carduelis yarrellii	Yarrell's Goldfinch	*Chalybura urochrysia*	Gould's Dusky Plumeleteer
Carpoccyx renauldi	Renauld's Ground Cuckoo	*Chamaepetes goudotii*	Goudot's Guan
Carpodacus cassinii	Cassin's Finch	*Chamaeza meruloides*	Such's Ant-thrush
Carpodacus edwardsii	Edwards' Rosefinch (Milne-	*Chamaeza turdina*	Schwartz's Ant-thrush
	Edwards')	*Charadrius collaris*	Azara's Sandplover
Carpodacus eos	Stresemann's Rosefinch	*Charadrius forbesi (trocollaris)*	Forbes' Plover
Carpodacus mexicanus	McGregor's House Finch	*Charadrius leschenaultii*	Geoffroy's Dotterel
mcgregori	(Extinct)	*Charadrius pecuarius*	Kittlitz's Plover
Carpodacus rhodoclamys	Blyth's Rosefinch	*Charadrius wilsonia*	Wilson's Plover
Carpodacus rodopeplus		*Charadrius wilsonia beldingi*	Belding's Plover
verreauxii	Sharpe's Rosefinch	*Charmosyna (papou) stellae*	Stella's Lorikeet
Carpodacus roseus	Pallas's Great Rosefinch	*Charmosyna josefinae*	Josephine's Lory

Charmosyna josefinae cyclopum	Cyclops Lorikeet
Charmosyna margaritae	Duchess of Connaught's Parakeet (Connaught's)
Charmosyna meeki	Meek's Lorikeet
Charmosyna papou wahnesi	Wahnes's Lorikeet
Charmosyna placentis	Sclater's Pleasing Lorikeet
Charmosyna placentis ornata	Mayr's Red-flanked Lorikeet
Charmosyna pulchella rothschildi	Hartert's Fairy Lorikeet
Charmosyna pulchella rothschildi	Rothschild's Fairy Lorikeet
Charmosyna wilhelminae	Wilhelmina's Lorikeet
Chersophilus duponti	Dupont's Lark
Chionis minor	Hartlaub's Sheathbill
Chlamydera lauterbachi	Lauterbach's Bowerbird
Chlamydotis undulata macqueenii	MacQueen's Bustard
Chloebia gouldiae	Lady Gouldian Finch (Mrs Gould's)
Chlorestes notatus	Audebert's Hummingbird
Chlorocichla falkensteini	Falkenstein's Greenbul
Chlorocichla prigoginei	Prigogine's Greenbul
Chloropsis cochinchinensis jerdoni	Jerdon's Leafbird
Chloropssis hardwickii	Hardwicke's Leafbird
Chlorornis riefferii	Rieffer's Tanager
Chlorospingus zeledoni	Zeledon's Tanager
Chlorostilbon (mellisugus) vitticeps	Simon's Emerald
Chlorostilbon alice	Alice's Emerald
Chlorostilbon atala	Atala's Emerald
Chlorostilbon aureoventris pucherani	Pucheran's Emerald
Chlorostilbon bracei (ricordii)	Brace's Emerald (Extinct)
Chlorostilbon canivetii	Canivet's Emerald
Chlorostilbon elegans	Gould's Emerald (Extinct)
Chlorostilbon poortmani	Berlepsch's Emerald
Chlorostilbon poortmani	Cabini's Emerald
Chlorostilbon poortmani	Poortman's Emerald
Chlorostilbon salvini	Salvin's Emerald
Chlorothraupis carmioli	Carmiol's Tanager
Chlorstilbon bracei (ricordii)	Ricords' Hummingbird
Chlorusa chlorusa	Blanding's Finch
Chordeiles minor assariensis	Cherrie's Nighthawk
Chordeiles minor howelli	Howell's Nighthawk
Chordeiles minor sennetti	Sennett's Nighthawk
Chrysococcyx basalis	Horsfield's Bronze Cuckoo
Chrysococcyx basalis	Meyer's Bronze Cuckoo
Chrysococcyx klaas	Klaas's Cuckoo
Chrysococcyx lucidus	Gould's Bronze Cuckoo
Chrysocolaptes indicus	Malherbe's Golden-backed Woodpecker
Chrysolophus amherstiae	Lady Amherst's Pheasant
Chrysomma altirostre	Jerdon's Babbler
Chunga burmeisteri	Burmeister's Seriema
Cichlornis whitneyi	Solomon's Thicketbird
Cicinnurus respublica	Wilson's Bird-of-Paradise
Ciconia abdimii	Abdim's Stork
Ciconia stormi	Storm's Stork
Cinclodes olrogi	Olrog's Cinclodes
Cinclodes pabsti	Pabst's Cinclodes
Cinclodes taczanowskii	Taczanowski's Cinclodes
Cinclus pallasii	Pallas's Dipper
Cinnycerthia olivascens	Sharpe's Wren
Cinnyricinclus femoralis	Abbott's Starling
Cinnyricinclus sharpei	Sharpe's Starling
Circaetus beaudouini	Beaudouin's Snake Eagle
Circus approximans gouldi	Gould's Harrier
Circus assimilis	Jardine's Harrier
Circus eylesi	Eyles' Harrier (Extinct)
Circus pygargus	Montagu's Harrier
Cissilopha melanocyaneus	Hartlaub's Jay
Cisticola ayresii	Ayres' Cisticola
Cisticola carruthersi	Carruthers's Cisticola
Cisticola chubbi	Chubb's Cisticola
Cisticola distinctus	Lynes's Cisticola
Cisticola dorsti	Dorst's Cisticola
Cisticola hunteri	Hunter's Cisticola
Cisticola melanurus	Pearson's Cisticola
Cisticola tinniens	Levaillant's Cisticola
Cistothorus apolinari	Apolinar's Marsh Wren
Cittura cyanotis	Temminck's Kingfisher
Clamator levaillantii	Levaillant's Cuckoo
Claravis godefrida	Geoffroy's Dove
Claravis montedoura	Mondetour's Dove
Clytospiza monteiri	Monteiro's Twinspot
Cnemophilus loriae	Loria's Bird-of-Paradise
Coccyzus minor maynardi	Maynard's Cuckoo
Coeligena bonapartei	Bonaparte's Starfrontlet
Coeligena inca	Gould's Inca
Coeligena iris	King Louis's Starfront (Louis XVI)
Coeligena iris aurora	Warszewiscz's Rainbow
Coeligena lutetiae	Conte de Paris' Starfrontlet
Coeligena prunelli	Prunelle's Coeligene
Coeligena wilsoni	Wilson's Coeligene
Colaptes auratus	Malherbe's Flicker
Colaptes chrysoides mearnsi	Mearns' Golden Flicker
Colaptes fernandinae	Fernandina's Flicker
Colibri coruscans	Gould's Violetear
Collocalia germani	German's Swiftlet
Collocalia maxima	Lowe's Swiftlet
Collocalia sawtelli	Sawtell's Swiftlet
Colluricincia boweri	Bower's Shrike-Thrush
Columba bolli	Bolle's Pigeon
Columba delegorguei	Delegorgue's Pigeon
Columba elphinstonii	Elphinstone's Pigeon
Columba eversmannii	Eversmann's Pigeon
Columba fasciata vioscae	Viosca's Pigeon
Columba goodsoni	Goodson's Pigeon
Columba hogsonii	Hodgson's Pigeon
Columba jouyi	Jouy's Woodpigeon
Columba oenops	Salvin's Pigeon
Columba sjostedti	Sjostedt's Pigeon
Columba subvinacea	Berlepsch's Pigeon
Columba versicolor	Kittlitz's Woodpigeon
Columbina buckleyi	Buckley's Ground Dove
Contopus pertinax	Coues' Flycatcher
Copsychus stricklandii	Strickland's Shama
Coracias spatulatus weigalli	Weigall's Roller
Coracias temminckii	Temminck's Roller
Coracina abbotti	Abbott's Cuckoo-shrike
Coracina boyeri	Boyer's Cuckoo-shrike
Coracina dohertyi	Doherty's Greybird
Coracina graueri	Grauer's Cuckoo-shrike
Coracina mcgregori	McGregor's Cuckoo-shrike
Coracina morio	Muller's Greybird
Coracina schisticeps	Gray's Greybird
Coracina temminckii	Temminck's Cuckoo-shrike
Coracopsis nigra libs	Bangs' Black Parrot
Corvus kubaryi	Kubary's Crow
Corythopis delalandi	Delalande's Antpipit
Cossypha anomala macclounii	MacClounie's Robin-Chat
Cossypha (Xenocopsychus) ansorgei	Ansorge's Robin-Chat
Cossypha archeri	Archer's Robin-Chat
Cossypha heinrichi	Heinrich's Robin[Chat]
Cossypha heinrichi	Rand's Robin-Chat
Cossypha heuglini	Heuglin's Robin-Chat

Cossypha semirufa	Rüppell's Robin-Chat
Cotinga nattererii	Natterer's Cotinga
Cotinga ridgwayi	Ridgway's Cotinga
Coturnicops exquisitus	Swinhoe's Rail
Coturnicops notatus	Darwin's Rail (Extinct)
Coua coquereli	Coquerel's Madagascar Coucal
Coua delalandei	Delalande's Coua (Extinct)
Coua verreauxi	Verreaux's Coua
Cranioleuca antisiensis	Fraser's Spinetail
Cranioleuca baroni	Baron's Spinetail
Cranioleuca vulpecula	Parker's Spinetail
Craspedophora alberti	Prince Albert's Riflebird (Albert's)
Crax alberti	Prince Albert's Curassow (Albert's)
Crax blumenbachii	Blumenbach's Crassow
Crax daubentoni	Daubenton's Curassow
Crax globulosa	Yarrell's Curassow
Crax sclateri	Sclater's Curassow
Crossoptilon auritum	Pallas's Eared Pheasant
Crossoptilon crossoptilon dolani	Dolan's Eared Pheasant
Crossoptilon harmani	Elwes' Eared Pheasant
Crossoptilon harmani	Harman's Eared Pheasant
Cryptospiza jacksoni	Jackson's Crimsonwing
Cryptospiza reichenovii	Reichenow's Crimsonwing
Cryptospiza salvadorii	Salvadori's Crimsonwing
Cryptospiza shelleyi	Shelley's Crimsonwing
Crypturellus (atrocapillus) garleppi	Garlepp's Tinamou
Crypturellus bartletti	Bartlett's Tinamou
Crypturellus berlepschi	Berlepsch's Tinamou
Crypturellus boucardi	Boucard's Tinamou
Crypturellus noctivagus	Wied's Tinamou
Crypturellus obsoletus traylori	Traylor's Tinamou
Cuculus fugax	Hodgson's Hawk-Cuckoo
Cuculus saturatus	Blyth's Cuckoo
Curaeus forbesi	Forbes's Blackbird
Cursorius (Rhinoptilus) bitorquatus	Jerdon's Courser
Cursorius rufus	Burchell's Courser
Cursorius temminckii	Temminck's Courser
Cyanocitta stelleri	Osgood's Jay
Cyanocitta stelleri carbonacea	Grinell's Jay
Cyanocitta stelleri carlottae	Queen Charlotte Jay
Cyanocitta stelleri	Steller's Jay
Cyanocorax beecheii	Beechey's Jay
Cyanocorax dickeyi	Dickey's Jay
Cyanocorax heilprini	Heilprin's Jay
Cyanolimnas cerverai	Cervera's Rail
Cyanolyca pumilo	Strickland's Jay
Cyanophaia doubledayi	Doubleday's Hummingbird
Cyanopsitta spixii	Spix's Macaw
Cyanoramphus auriceps forbesi	Forbes' Parakeet (Extinct)
Cyanoramphus malherbi	Malherbe's Parakeet
Cyanthus latirostris	Circe Hummingbird
Cyclopsitta diophthalma coxeni	Coxen's Double-eyed Fig Parrot
Cyclopsitta diophthalma virago	Hartert's Double-eyed Fig Parrot
Cyclopsitta gulielmiterti amabilis	Reichenow's Orange-breasted Fig Parrot
Cyclopsitta gulielmiterti fuscifrons	Salvadori's Orange-breasted Fig Parrot
Cyclopsitta gulielmiterti ramuensis	Neumann's Orange-breasted Fig Parrot
Cyclopsitta gulielmiterti suavissima	D'Albertis' Orange-breasted Fig Parrot
Cyclopsitta gulielmitertii	William's Fig Parrot
Cygnus columbianus	Bewick's Swan
Cygnus columbianus jankowskii	Jankowski's Swan
Cygnus davidi	David's Swan
Cygnus davidi	Père David's Swan (David's) (Extinct)
Cyornis hainanus	Grant's Niltava
Cyornis hoevelli	Hoevell's Flycatcher
Cyornis lemprieri	Ramsay's Blue Flycatcher
Cyornis poliogenys	Brooks's Niltava
Cyornis rueckii	Rück's Blue Flycatcher
Cyornis sanfordi	Sanford's Niltava
Cyornis tickelliae	Tickell's Blue Flycatcher
Cypseloides cherriei	Cherrie's Swift
Cypseloides cryptus	Zimmer's Swift
Cypseloides rothschildi	Rothschild's Swift
Cyrtonyx montezuma	Mearns' Quail
Cyrtonyx montezuma	Montezuma Quail
Cyrtonyx (montezuma) sallei	Salle's Quail
Dacelo gaudichaudi	Gaudichaud's Kingfisher
Dacelo leachii	Leach's Kingfisher
Damophila julie	Julie's Hummingbird
Delattria henrici	Henry de Lattre's Cacique (De Lattre's)
Dendragapus obscurus richardsoni	Fleming's Grouse
Dendragapus obscurus richardsoni	Richardson's Grouse
Dendragapus obscurus howardi	Howard's Grouse
Dendrcincla fuliginosa atrirostris	D'Orbigny's Woodcreeper
Dendrocolaptes hoffmannsi	Hoffmanns' Woodcreeper
Dendrocops leucotos lilfordi	Lilford's Woodpecker
Dendrocops leucostos owstoni	Owston's Woodpecker
Dendrocygna eytoni	Eyton's Whistling Duck
Dendroica adelaidae adelaidae	Adelaide's Warbler
Dendroica auduboni (coronata)	Audubon's Warbler
Dendroica caerulescens cairnsi	Cairns' Warbler
Dendroica coronata goldmani	Goldman's Warbler
Dendroica fusca	Blackburnian Warbler
Dendroica graciae	Grace's Warbler
Dendroica kirtlandii	Kirtland's Warbler
Dendroica magnolia	Magnolia Warbler
Dendroica petechia morcomi	Morcom's Yellow Warbler
Dendroica pinus	Vigors's Warbler
Dendroica potomac	Sutton's Warbler
Dendroica townsendi	Townsend's Warbler
Dendroica virens waynei	Wayne's Warbler
Dendropicos elliotii	Elliot's Woodpecker
Dendropicos stierlingi	Stierling's Woodpecker
Depranornis albertisi cervinicauda	Bennett's Bird-of-Paradise
Dicaeum annae	Anna's Flowerpecker
Dicaeum anthonyi	Anthony's Flowerpecker
Dicaeum erythrorhynchos	Tickell's Flowerpecker
Dicaeum everetti	Everett's Flowerpecker
Dicaeum maugei	Mauge's Flowerpecker
Dicaeum nehrkorni	Nehrkorn's Flowerpecker
Dicaeum tristrami	Tristram's Flowerpecker
Dicaeum vincens	Legge's Flowerpecker
Dicrurus ludwigii sharpei	Sharpe's Drongo
Diglossa brunneiventris vuilleumieri	Vuilleumier's Flowerpecker
Diomedea albatrus	Steller's Albatross
Diomedea bulleri	Buller's Albatross
Diomedea cauta salvini	Salvin's Albatross
Diomedea gibsoni	Gibson's Albatross

Diphyllodes saleucides	Lesson's Bird-of-Paradise
Diopsittaca nobilis nobilis	Hahn's Macaw
Dives dives	Sumichrast's Blackbird
Drepanis funerea	Perkins' Mamo (Extinct)
Drepanornis albertisi	D'Albertis' Bird-of-Paradise
Drepanornis bruijnii	Bruijn's Bird-of-Paradise
Dromaeocercus seebohmi	Seebohm's Feather-tailed Warbler
Drymophila rubricollis	Bertoni's Antwren
Drymornis bridgesii	Bridges's Woodhewer
Dryocopus javensis richardsi	Tristram's Woodpecker (Extinct)
Dryolimnas cuvieri	Cuvier's Rail
Dryoscopus pringlii	Pringle's Puffback
Dryoscopus sabini	Sabine's Puffback
Dubusia taeniata carrikeri	Carriker's Mountain Tanager
Ducula aurorae	Wilkes' Pigeon
Ducula badia	Hodgson's Imperial Pigeon
Ducula badia	Jerdon's Imperial Pigeon
Ducula bakeri	Baker's Pigeon
Ducula finschii	Finch's Imperial Pigeon
Ducula latrans	Peale's Pigeon
Ducula mullerii	Muller's Fruit Pigeon
Ducula pickeringii	Pickering's Imperial Pigeon
Ducula zoeae	Zoe's Imperial Pigeon
Eclectus roratus cornelia	Cornelia's Eclectus Parrot
Eclectus roratus riedel	Riedel's Parrot
Eclectus roratus westermani	Westerman's Eclectus Parrot
Egretta eulophotes	Swinhoe's Egret
Egretta rufescens dickeyi	Dickey's Egret
Egretta thula	Brewster's Egret
Emberiza buchanani	Buchanan's Bunting
Emberiza cabanisi	Cabanis's Bunting
Emberiza caesia	Cretzschmar's Bunting
Emberiza godlewskii	Godlewski's Bunting
Emberiza jankowskii	Jankowski's Bunting
Emberiza koslowi	Kozlow's Bunting
Emberiza pallasi	Pallas's Reed Bunting
Emberiza stewarti	Stewart's Bunting
Emberiza tristami	Tristram's Bunting
Empidonax hammondii	Hammond's Flycatcher
Empidonax wrightii	Wright's Flycatcher
Empidonax traillii	Traill's Flycatcher
Enicurus leschenaulti	Leschenault's Forktail
Eos bornea bernsteini	Bernstein's Red Lory
Eos bornea goodfellowi	Goodfellow's Lory
Eos bornea rothschildi	Rothschild's Red Lory
Eos histrio challengeri	Challenger's Lory
Eos squamata riciniata	Bechstein's Violet-necked Lory
Eos squamata wallacei	Wallace's Violet-necked Lory
Epimachus meyeri	Meyer's Sicklebill
Eremalauda dunni	Dunn's Lark
Eremalauda starki	Stark's Lark
Eremiornis carteri	Carter's Desert-Bird
Eremomela salvadori	Salvadori's Eremomela
Eremomela turneri	Turner's Eremomela
Eremophila alpestris merrilli	Merrill's Horned Lark
Eremophila alpestris teleschowi	Prjevalksy's Lark
Eremophila bilopha	Temminck's Lark
Eremopterix leucopareia	Fischer's Finch-Lark
Eriocnemis derbyi	Derby's Puffleg (Stanley's)
Eriocnemis d'orbignyi	D'Orbigny's Puffleg
Eriocnemis godini	Godin's Puffleg
Eriocnemis godini isaacsonii	Isaacson's Puffleg
Eriocnemis luciani	Buquet's Puffleg
Eriocnemis soederstroemi	Soderstrom's Puffleg
Erithacus komodori	Temminck's Robin
Erythrocercus livingstonei	Livingstone's Flycatcher
Erythrocercus livingstonei thomsoni	Thomson's Flycatcher
Erythronata sophiae	Sophia's Erythronote
Erythrotriorchis (Accipiter) buergersi	Bürger's Hawk
Erythrura gouldiae	Gouldian Finch
Erythrura pealii	Peale's Parrotfinch
Estrilda kandti	Kandt's Waxbill
Estrilda melanotis	Dufresne's Waxbill
Estrilda quartinia bocagei	Bocage's Waxbill
Estrilda rhodopyga	Sundevall's Waxbill
Estrilda thomensis	Neumann's Waxbill
Eudoptis (senegalensis) barrowii	Barrow's Bustard
Eudyptes chrysocome moseleyi	Moseley's Rockhopper Penguin
Eudyptes sclateri	Sclater's Penguin
Eugenes fulgens	Rivoli's Hummingbird
Eulidia yarellii	Yarrell's Woodstar
Euphagus cyanocephalus	Brewer's Blackbird
Euphagus cyanocephalus	Finsch's Blackbird
Euphonia affinis	Lesson's Euphonia
Euphonia gouldi	Gould's Euphonia
Euphonia hirundinacea	Bonaparte's Euphonia
Euplectes gierowii	Gierow's Bishop
Euplectes hartlaubi	Hartlaub's Marsh Widow
Euplectes jacksoni	Jackson's Widow
Eupodotis rueppellii	Rüppell's Bustard
Eupodotis rueppellii	Rüppell's Korhaan
Eupodotis vigorsii vigorsii	Vigors's Bustard
Eurocephalus rueppelli	Rüppell's Shrike
Eurostopodus archboldi	Archbold's Nightjar
Eurostopodus diabolicus	Heinrich's Eared Nightjar
Euryanas finschii	Finsch's Duck (Extinct)
Eurylaimus steerii	Steere's Broadbill
Euschistospiza dybowskii	Dybowski's Dusky Twinspot
Eustephanus stokesi	Stokes' Hummingbird
Eutrichomyias rowleyi	Rowley's Flycatcher
Falcipennis canadensis franklini	Franklin's Grouse
Falco alexandri	Alexander's Kestrel
Falco dickinsoni	Dickinson's Kestrel
Falco eleonorae	Eleonora's Falcon
Falco kreyenborgi	Kleinschmidts's Falcon
Falco newtoni	Newton's Kestrel
Falco peregrinus pealei	Peale's Falcon
Ferminia cerverai	Cervera's Wren
Ficedula crypta	Vaurie's Flycatcher
Ficedula harterti	Hartert's Flycatcher
Ficedula westermanni	Westermann's Flycatcher
Formicarius analis hoffmanni	Hoffmann's Ant-thrush
Forpus cyanopygius insularis	Grayson's Parrotlet
Forpus passerinus cyanochlorus	Schlegel's Parrotlet
Forpus sclateri	Sclater's Parrotlet
Forpus sclateri eidos	Schomburgk's Parrotlet
Forpus xanthopterygius flavescens	Salvadori's Blue-winged Parrotlet
Forpus xanthopterygius olallae	Olalla's Blue-winged Parrotlet
Forpus xanthopterygius spengeli	Spengel's Parrotlet
Foudia omissa	Rothschild's Fody
Francolinus (Pternistis) clappertoni	Clapperton's Francolin
Francolinus (Pternistis) hartlaubi	Hartlaub's Francolin
Francolinus (Scleroptila) finschi	Finsch's Francolin

Francolinus afer cranchii	Cranch's Francolin
Francolinus archeri	Archer's Francolin
Francolinus archeri	Smith's Francolin
Francolinus coqui	Coqui Francolin
Francolinus erckelii	Erckel's Francolin
Francolinus hildebrandti	Hildebrandt's Francolin
Francolinus icterorhynchos	Heuglin's Francolin
Francolinus jacksoni	Jackson's Francolin
Francolinus lathani	Lathan's Forest Francolin
Francolinus nahani	Nahan's Forest Francolin
Francolinus sephaena rovuma	Kirk's Francolin
Francolinus shelleyi	Shelley's Francolin
Francolinus swainsonii	Swainson's Francolin
Francolinus swierstrai	Swierstra's Francolin
Fraseria ocreata	Fraser's Flycatcher
Fregata andrewsi	Andrew's Frigatebird
Fregata grallaria	Vieillot's Storm Petrel
Fulmaris glacialis rodgersii	Rodgers' Fulmar
Galerida deva	Sykes' Crested Lark
Galerida theklae	Thekla Lark
Gallicolumba beccarii	Beccari's Ground Dove
Gallicolumba criniger	Bartlett's Bleeding-heart
Gallicolumba ferruginea	Forster's Dove of Tanna (Extinct)
Gallicolumba keayi	Keay's Bleeding-heart
Gallinago gallinago delicata	Wilson's Snipe
Gallinago hardwicki	Latham's Snipe
Gallinago jamesoni	Jameson's Snipe
Gallinago megala	Swinhoe's Snipe
Gallinago stricklandii	Strickland's Snipe
Gallinula hogdeni	Hogden's Rail (Extinct)
Gallirallus dieffenbachii	Dieffenbach's Rail (Extinct)
Gallirallus insignis	Sclater's Rail
Gallirallus milleri	Miller's Crake (Extinct)
Gallirallus sharpei	Sharpe's Rail (Extinct)
Gallirallus sylvestris	Lord Howe's Rail
Gallus lafayetti	Lafayette's Junglefowl
Gallus sonnerati	Sonnerat's Junglefowl
Garrulax austeni	Austen's Laughing-thrush (Godwin-Austen's)
Garrulax austeni	Godwin-Austen's Laughing-thrush (Austen's)
Garrulax bieti	Biet's Laughing-thrush
Garrulax davidi	David's Laughing-thrush
Garrulax davidi	Père David's Laughing Thrush (David's)
Garrulax delesserti	Wynaad's Laughing-thrush
Garrulax elliotii	Elliot's Laughing-thrush
Garrulax galbanus	Courtois' Laughing-thrush
Garrulax gularis	McClelland's Laughing-thrush
Garrulax henrici	Henry's Laughing-thrush (Prince Henry's)
Garrulax henrici	Prince Henry's Laughing-thrush
Garrulax jerdoni	Jerdon's Laughing-thrush
Garrulax maesi	Maes' Laughing-thrush
Garrulax milleti	Millet's Laughing-thrush
Garrulax nuchalis	Ogle's Laughing-thrush
Garrulax strepitans	Tickell's Laughing-thrush
Garrulax sukatschewi	Sukatschev's Laughing-thrush
Garrulax yersini	Yersin's Laughing-thrush
Garrulus glandarius brandtii	Brandt's Jay
Garrulus lidthi	Lidth's Jay
Gelochelidon nilotica vanrossemi	Van Rossem's Gull-billed Tern
Geoffroyus geoffroyi	Geoffroy's Parrot
Geoffroyus geoffroyi minor	Neumann's Red-cheeked Parrot
Geoffroyus geoffroyi pucherani	Pucheran's Red-cheeked Parrot
Geoffroyus simplex buergersi	Bürger's Blue-collared Parrot
Geomalia heinrichi	Heinrich's [Whistling] Thrush
Geopelia placida	Gould's Zebra Dove
Geophaps smithii	Smith's Bare-eyed Pigeon
Geospiza conirostris	Darwin's Large Cactus Ground Finch
Geospiza difficilis	Darwin's Sharp-beaked Ground Finch
Geospiza fortis	Darwin's Medium Ground Finch
Geospiza fuliginosa	Darwin's Small Ground Finch
Geospiza magnirostris	Darwin's Large Ground Finch
Geospiza scandens	Darwin's Cactus Ground Finch
Geothlypis beldingi	Belding's Yellowthroat
Geothlypis trichas	Goldman's Yellowthroat
Geotrygon frenata	Bourcier's Quail-Dove
Geotrygon goldmani	Goldman's Quail-Dove
Geotrygon lawrencii	Lawrence's Quail-Dove
Glaucidium albertinum	Prigogine's Owlet
Glaucidium brasilianum ridgwayi	Ridgway's Pygmy Owl
Glaucidium hardyi	Hardy's Pygmy Owl
Glaucidium (gnoma) hoskinsii	Hoskins' Pygmy Owl
Glaucidium jardinii	Jardine's Pygmy Owl
Glaucidium (capense) scheffleri	Scheffler's Owlet
Glaucidium sjostedti	Sjostedt's Barred Owlet
Glaucis [Ramphodon] dohrnii	Dohrn's Hermit
Glaucis fraseri	Fraser's Hermit
Goethalsia bella	Goethal's Hummingbird
Goldmania violiceps	Goldman's Hummingbird
Gouldia laetitiae	Letitiaa's Hummingbird
Goura scheepmakeri	Scheepmaker's Crowned Pigeon
Goura scheepmakeri	Sclater's Crowned-Pigeon
Goura victoria	Victoria Crowned Pigeon
Grallaria kaestneri	Kaestner's Antpitta
Grallaria watkinsi	Watkins's Antpitta
Grandala coelicolor	Hodgson's Grandala
Graueria vittata	Grauer's Warbler
Grus paradiseus	Stanley's Crane
Grypus spixi	Spix's Sawbill
Gymnobucco bonapartei	Bonaparte's Barbet
Gymnobucco sladeni	Sladen's Barbet
Gymnocrex rosenbergii	Rosenberg's Rail
Gymnophaps albertisii	D'Albertis' Mountain Pigeon
Gymnorhinus cyanocepalus	Cassin's Jay
Gymnorhinus cyanocepalus	Maximilian's Jay
Gyps coprotheres	Kolbe's Vulture
Gyps ruppellii	Rüppell's Griffon Vulture
Habia fuscicauda salvini	Salvin's Ant Tanager
Habroptila wallacei	Wallace's Rail
Haematopus meadewaldoi	Meade-Waldo's Oystercatcher
Haematopus palliatus	Frazar's Oystercatcher
Halcyon macleayi	Macleay's Forest Kingfisher
Haliaeetus leucoryphus	Pallas's Fish Eagle
Haliaeetus pelagicus	Steller's Sea Eagle
Haliaeetus sanfordi	Sanford's Sea Eagle
Hapalopsittaca amazonina theresae	Hellmayr's Rusty-faced Parrot

Hapalopsittaca amazonina velezi	Velez's Rusty-faced Parrot
Hapalopsittaca fuertesi	Fuertes's Parrot
Hapalopsittaca pyrrhops	Salvin's Rusty-faced Parrot
Haplophaedia aureliae	Aurelia's Puffleg
Harpactes diardii	Diard's Trogon
Harpactes (reinwardtii) mackloti	Macklot's Trogon
Harpactes reinwardtii	Reinwardt's Blue-tailed Trogon
Harpactes wardi	Ward's Trogon
Harpactes whiteheadi	Whitehead's Trogon
Harpagornis moorei	Haast's Eagle (Extinct)
Heliangelus amethysticollis clarisse	Longuemare's Sunangel
Heliangelus micrastur	Gould's Sunangel
Heliangelus spencei	Spence's Sunangel
Heliodoxa aurescens	Gould's Jewelfront
Heliodoxa branickii	Branicki's Hummingbird
Heliodoxa branickii	Count Branicki's Hummingbird (Branicki's)
Heliodoxa imperatrix	Empress Hummingbird
Heliodoxa jamesoni jamesoni	Jameson's Brilliant
Heliodoxa leadbeateri	Leadbeater's Brilliant
Heliodoxa schreibersii	Schreiber's Hummingbird
Heliomaster angelae	Angela Starthroat
Heliomaster constantii	Constant's Starthroat
Heliothryx barroti	Barrot's Fairy
Heliotrypha parzudakii	Parzudaki's Starfrontlet
Hemispingus parodii	Parodi's Hemispingus
Hemitisia neumanni	Neumann's Short-tailed Warbler
Hemitriccus inornatus	Pelzeln's Tody-Tyrant
Hemitriccus iohannis	Johannis's Tody-Tyrant
Hemitriccus kaempferi	Kaempfer's Tody-Tyrant
Hemitriccus minima	Zimmer's Tody-Tyrant
Hemitriccus minor	Snethlage's Tody-Tyrant
Herpsilochmus dugandi	Dugand's Antwren
Herpsilochmus stictocephalus	Todd's Antwren
Hesperiphona abeillei	Abeille's Grosbeak
Heterophasia melanoleuca	Tickell's Sibia
Hieraaetus (Spizaetus) africanus	Cassin's Hawk-Eagle
Hieraaetus ayresii (dubius)	Ayres' Hawk-Eagle
Hieraaetus fasciatus	Bonelli's Eagle
Hippolais caligata	Eversmann's Booted Warbler
Hippolais languida	Upcher's Warbler
Hippolais rama	Sykes' Warbler
Hirundo (Petrochelidon) preussi	Preuss's Cliff Swallow
Horizorhinus dohrni	Dohrn's Flycatcher
Humblotia flavirostris	Humblot's Flycatcher
Hydrobatidae	Mother Carey's Chickens
Hylexetastes brigadai	Brigida's Woodcreeper
Hylocharis eliciae	Elicia's Goldentail
Hylocharis grayi	Gray's Sapphire
Hylophylax punctulata	Des Mur's Antbird
Hylorchilus navai	Nava's Wren
Hylorchilus sumichrasti	Sumichrast's Wren
Hyolocharis humboldtii	Humboldt's Sapphire
Hypargos margaritatus	Verreaux's Twinspot
Hypargos niveoguttatus	Peters's Twinspot
Hypsipetes charlottae	Charlotte's Bulbul (Queen Charlotte's)
Hypsipetes thompsoni	Bingham's Bulbul
Hypsipetes virescens	Blyth's Olive Bulbul
Hypsipetes virescens	McClelland's (Mountain) Bulbul
Ianthothorex bensbachii	Bensbach's Bird-of-Paradise
Icterus bullocki	Bullock's Oriole
Icterus chrysater	Lesson's Oriole
Icterus cucullatus	Sennett's Oriole
Icterus cucullatus nelsoni	Nelson's Oriole
Icterus dominicensis northropi	Northrop's Oriole
Icterus galbula abeillei	Abeille's Oriole
Icterus graduacauda	Audubon's Oriole
Icterus gularis	Lichtenstein's Oriole
Icterus parisorum	Scott's Oriole
Icterus spurius fuertesi	Fuertes's Oriole
Icterus wagleri	Wagler's Oriole
Illadopsis fulvescens moloneyanum	Moloney's Illadopsis
Illadopsis puveli	Puvel's Illadopsis
Indicator exilis	Chapin's Least Honeyguide
Indicator willcocksi	Willcocks's Honeyguide
Iole olivacea	Finsch's Olive-brown Bulbul
Iololaema whitelyana	Whitely's Hummingbird
Ithaginis cruentus annae	Mrs Sage's Blood Pheasant
Ithaginis cruentus beicki	Beick's Blood Pheasant
Ithaginis cruentus berezowskii	Berezowski's Blood Pheasant
Ithaginis cruentus clarkei	Clarke's Blood Pheasant
Ithaginis cruentus geoffroyi	Geoffroy's Blood Pheasant
Ithaginis cruentus holoptilus	Greenway's Blood Pheasant
Ithaginis cruentus kuseri	Kuser's Blood Pheasant
Ithaginis cruentus marionae	Mrs Vernay's Blood Pheasant
Ithaginis cruentus michaelis	Bianchi's Blood Pheasant
Ithaginis cruentus rocki	Rock's Blood Pheasant
Ithaginis cruentus sinensis	David's Blood Pheasant
Ixobrychus eurythmus	Schrenck's Little Bittern
Ixobrychus involucris	Azara's Bittern
Ixobrychus neoxenus	Cory's Bittern
Ixos everetti	Everett's Bulbul
Jabouilleia danjoui	Danjou's Babbler
Junco phaenotis bairdii	Baird's Junco
Junco hyemalis aikeni	Ridgway's Junco
Junco hyemalis oreganus	Townsend's Junco
Junco hyemalis shufeldti	Shufeldt's Junco
Junco hyemalis thurberi	Thurber's Junco
Ketupa blakistoni	Blackiston's Fish Owl
Klais guimeti	Guimet's Flutterer
Knipolegus hudsoni	Hudson's Black Tyrant
Knipolegus signatus	Jelski's Bush Tyrant
Knipolegus subflammulatus	Berlioz's' Tyrant
Korora oliveri	Oliver's Penguin (Extinct)
Koslowia roborowskii	Roborovski's Rosefinch
Kupeornis gilberti	Gilbert's Mountain Babbler (Nkwocha's)
Lagonosticta rhodopareia	Jameson's Firefinch
Lagonosticta umbrinodorsalis	Reichenbach's Firefinch
Lagopus lagopus alexandrae	Alexander's Ptarmigan
Lagopus lagopus alleni	Allen's Ptarmigan
Lagopus mutus atkhensis	Turner's Ptarmigan
Lagopus mutus chamberlaini	Chamberlain's Ptarmigan
Lagopus mutus dixoni	Dixon's Ptarmigan
Lagopus mutus eversmanni	Eversmann's Ptarmigan
Lagopus mutus kellogae	Kellogg's Ptarmigan
Lagopus mutus nelsoni	Nelson's Ptarmigan
Lagopus mutus reinhardti	Reinhardt's Ptarmigan
Lagopus mutus sanfordi	Sanford's Ptarmigan
Lagopus mutus townsendi	Townsend's Ptarmigan
Lagopus mutus welchi	Welch's Ptarmigan
Lalage sueurii	Sueur's Triller
Lampornis margaritae	Margaret's Hummingbird
Lampornis virginalis	St Thomas's Mango
Lamprolaima rhami	De Rham's Garnet
Lamprotornis australis	Burchell's Starling
Lamprotornis elisabeth	Swainson's Glossy Starling
Lamprotornis hildebrandti	Hildebrandt's Starling

Lamprotornis mevesii	Meves' Long-tailed Glossy Starling
Lamprotornis purpuropterus	Rüppell's Long-tailed Glossy Starling
Lamprotornis shelleyi	Shelley's Starling
Laniarius atrococcineus	Burchell's Gonolek
Laniarius brauni	Braun's Bushshrike
Laniarius fulleborni	Fülleborn's Boubou
Laniarius luehderi	Lühder's Bush Shrike
Laniarius turati	Turati's Boubou
Laniisoma elegans buckleyi	Buckley's Cotinga
Lanius gubernator	Emin's Shrike
Lanius ludovicianus gambeli	Gambel's Shrike
Lanius ludovicianus grinnelli	Grinell's Shrike
Lanius ludovicianus nelsoni	Nelson's Shrike
Lanius mackinnoni	Mackinnon's Grey Shrike
Lanius newtoni	Newton's Fiscal Shrike
Lanius souzae	Souza's Shrike
Larus atlanticus	Olrog's Gull
Larus atlanticus	Simeon's Gull
Larus audouinii	Audouin's Gull
Larus belcheri	Simeon's Gull
Larus bridgesii	Bridges' Gull
Larus bulleri	Buller's Gull
Larus crassirostris	Temminck's Gull
Larus glaucoides kumlieni	Kumlien's Iceland Gull
Larus hartlaubii (novaeholandiae)	Hartlaub's Gull
Larus heermanni	Heermann's Gull
Larus hemprichii	Hemprich's Gull
Larus (argentatus) heuglini	Heuglin's Gull
Larus hyperboreus x argentatus	Nelson's Hybrid Gull
Larus ichthyaetus	Pallas's Gull
Larus occidentalis wymani	Wyman's Gull
Larus philadelphia	Bonaparte's Gull
Larus pipixcan	Franklin's Gull
Larus saundersi	Saunders's Gull
Larus scoresbii	Scoresby's Gull
Larus thayeri	Thayer's Gull
Lathrotriccus euleri lawrencei	Lawrence's Flycatcher
Leiothrix lutea	Astley's Leiothrix
Lepidocolaptes souleyetii	Souleyet's Woodcreeper
Lepidopyga coeruleogularis	Duchassain's Hummingbird
Leptocoma sperata henkei	Henke's Sunbird
Leptopoecile sophiae	Severtzov's Tit-Warbler
Leptopoecile sophiae	Stoliczka's Tit-Warbler
Leptopterus chabert	Chabert's Vanga
Leptosittica branickii	Branicki's Conure
Leptotila cassini	Cassin's Dove
Leptotila conoveri	Conover's Dove
Leptotila wellsi	Wells' Dove
Leucopeza semperi	Semper's Warbler (Extinct)
Leucopternis princeps	Prince's Hawk
Leucospar rothschildi	Rothschild's Mynah
Leucosticte brandti	Brandt's Rosy Finch
Leucosticte (tephrocotis) littoralis	Hepburn's Finch
Leucosticte nemoricola	Hodgson's Rosy Finch
Leucosticte sillemi	Sillem's Mountain Finch
Lewinia muelleri	Muller's Rail
Lewinia pectoralis clelandi	Lewin's (Western Water) Rail
Lewinia pectoralis pectoralis	Lewin's (Eastern Water) Rail
Lichmera notabilis	Finsch's Honeyeater
Limnothlypsis swainsonii	Swainson's Warbler
Liocichla steeri	Steere's Liocichla
Lioptilus chapini	Chapin's Flycatcher-Babbler
Lissotis hartlaubi	Hartlaub's Bustard
Locustella certhiola	Pallas's Grasshopper Warbler
Locustella fasciolata	Gray's Grasshopper Warbler
Locustella fasciolata amnicola	Stepanyan's Grasshopper Warbler
Locustella luscinoides	Savi's Warbler
Locustella ochotensis	Middendorff's Grasshopper Warbler
Locustella pleskei	Pleske's Grasshopper Warbler
Locustella pleskei	Styan's Grasshopper-warbler
Loddigesia mirabilis	Loddiges Spatuletail
Lonchura hunsteini	Forbes' Mannikin
Lonchura hunsteini	Hunstein's Mannikin
Lonchura kelaarti jerdoni	Jerdon's Mannikin
Lonchura spectabilis mayri	Mayr's Munia
Lonchura striata	Hodgson's Munia
Lonchura teerinki	Teerink's Munia
Lophophorus sclateri	Sclater's Monal Pheasant
Lophornis delattrei	De Lattre's Coquette (Henry De Lattre's)
Lophornis gouldii	Gould's Coquette
Lophornis helenae	Princess Helena's Coquette
Lophotis gindiana	Oustalet's Bustard
Lophotis savilei	Savile's Bustard
Lophozosterops dohertyi	Doherty's White-eye
Lophozosterops goodfellowi	Goodfellow's White-eye
Lophura berliozi	Berlioz's' Pheasant
Lophura bulweri	Bulwer's Pheasant
Lophura diardi	Diard's Fireback
Lophura edwardsi	Edwards' Pheasant (Milne-Edwards')
Lophura (edwardsi) hatinhensis	Vo Quy's Pheasant
Lophura (inornata) hoogerwerfi	Hoogerwerf's Pheasant
Lophura ignita macartneyi	Delacour's Crested Fireback Pheasant
Lophura ignita rufa	Viellot's Crested Fireback Pheasant
Lophura inornata	Salvadori's Pheasant
Lophura leucomelanos moffiti	Horsfields Kalij
Lophura leucomelanos oatesi	Oates' Kalij
Lophura leucomelanos williamsi	William's Khalij
Lophura nycthemera beli	Bel's Silver Pheasant
Lophura nycthemera crawfurdi	Crawfurd's Khalij
Lophura nycthemera engelbachi	Engelbach's Silver Pheasant
Lophura nycthemera jonesi	Jones's Silver Pheasant
Lophura nycthemera lewisi	Lewis's Silver Pheasant
Lophura nycthemera ripponi	Rippon's Silver Pheasant
Lophura swinhoii	Swinhoe's Pheasant
Loriculus aurantiifrons batavorum	Stresemann's Orange-fronted Hanging Parrot
Loriculus aurantiifrons meeki	Hartert's Orange-fronted Hanging Parrot
Loriculus aurantiifrons tener	Bismarck Hanging Parrot
Loriculus flosculus	Wallace's Hanging Parrot (Extinct)
Loriculus philippensis bonapartei	Bonaparte's Hanging Parrot
Loriculus philippensis bournsi	Bourn's Hanging Parrot
Loriculus philippensis dohertyi	Doherty's Hanging Parrot
Loriculus philippensis worcesteri	Worcester's Hanging Parrot
Loriculus sclateri	Sclater's Hanging Parrot
Lorius amabilis	Stresemann's Lory (Extinct)
Lorius lory salvadorii	Meyer's Black-capped Lory
Lorius lory viridicrissalis	Beaufort's Black-capped Lory
Loxia curvirostra bendire	Bendire's Crossbill
Loxia curvirostra benti	Bent's Crossbill
Loxia curvirostra grinelli	Grinell's Crossbill
Lurocalis rufiventris	Taczanowski's Nightjar

Scientific name	Common name
Lurocalis semitorquatus nattereri	Natterer's Nighthawk
Luscinia johnstoniae	Johnstone's Bush Robin
Luscinia obscura	La Touche's Shortwing
Luscinia (Erithacus) pectardens	David's Rubythroat
Luscinia pectardens	Père David's Rubythroat (David's)
Luscinia sibilans	Swinhoe's Red-tailed Robin
Lybius chaplini	Chaplin's Barbet
Lybius minor macclounii	MacClounie's Barbet
Lybius vieilloti	Vieillot's Barbet
Macgregoria pulchra	MacGregor's Bird-of-Paradise
Macrocephalon maleo	Gray's Brush Turkey
Macronectes halli	Hall's Giant Petrel
Macronectes halli/giganteus	Mother Carey's Goose
Macronous kelleyi	Kelley's Tit-Babbler
Macronyx fuelleborni	Fülleborn's Longclaw
Macronyx grimwoodi	Grimwood's Longclaw
Macronyx sharpei	Sharpe's Longclaw
Macropygia mackinlayi	Mackinlay's Cuckoo-Dove
Macrosphenus kempi	Kemp's Longbill
Macrosphenus kretschmeri	Kretschmer's Longbill
Macrosphenus pulitzeri	Pulitzer's Longbill
Malacocincla abbotti	Abbot's Babbler
Malacocincla vanderbilti	Vanderbilt's Babbler
Malaconotus bocagei	Bocage's Bush Shrike
Malaconotus lagdeni	Lagden's Bush Shrike
Malaconotus monteiri	Monteiro's Bush Shrike
Malacorhynchus scarletti	Scarlett's Duck (Extinct)
Malimbus ballmanni	Ballmann's Malimbe
Malimbus cassini	Cassin's Malimbe
Malimbus nitens	Gray's Malimbe
Malimbus racheliae	Rachel's Malimbe
Malurus cambelli	Campbell's Fairy-wren
Malurus coronatus macgillivrayi	MacGillivray's Fairy-wren
Malurus lamberti rogersi	Roger's Fairy-wren
Manacus aurantiacus	Salvin's Negrito
Manacus candei	Cande's Manakin
Mandingoa nitidula	Schlegel's Twinspot
Mandingoa nitidula chubbi	Chubb's Twinspot
Manucodia keraudrenii	Keraudren's Manucode
Marplesornis novaezealandiae	Harris's Penguin (Extinct)
Megalaima incognita	Hume's Blue-throated Barbet
Megalaima lagrandieri	Lagrandier's Barbet
Megalaima oorti	Muller's Barbet
Megalurulus whitneyi	Whitney's Thicket Warbler
Megalurus albolimbatus	D'Albertis' Grassbird
Megapodius cumingi	Cuming's Scrubfowl
Megapodius forstenii	Forsten's Scrubfowl
Megapodius layardi	Tristram's Scrubfowl
Megapodius pritchardii	Pritchard's Scrubfowl
Megapodius reinwardt	Reinwardt's Scrubfowl
Megapodius wallacei	Wallace's Scrubfowl
Megaxenops parnaguae	Reiser's Recurvebill
Melaenornis annamarulae	Mrs Forbes-Watson's Black Flycatcher
Melaenornis ardesiacus	Berlioz's' Black Flycatcher
Melanerpes formicivorus bairdii	Mearns' Woodpecker
Melanerpes hoffmannii	Hoffmann's Woodpecker
Melanerpes lewis	Lewis's Woodpecker
Melanerpes pucherani	Pucheran's Woodpecker
Melanerpes rubricapillus	Wagler's Woodpecker
Melanerpes uropygialis	Brewster's Woodpecker
Melanitta deglandi	Degland's Scoter
Melanocharis versteri	Verster's Berrypecker
Melazone biarcuatum	Cabanis's Ground Sparrow
Meleagris gallopavo merriamii	Merriam's Turkey
Meleagris gallopavo mexicana	Gould's Turkey
Melidectes belfordi	Belford's (Melidectes) Honeyeater
Melidectes foersteri	Foerster's Honeyeater
Melidectes rufocrissalis	Reichenow's Melidectes
Melidectes whitemanensis	Gilliard's Honeyeater
Melignomon eisentrauti	Coe's Honeyguide
Melignomon eisentrauti	Eisentraut's Honeyguide
Melignomon zenkeri	Zenker's Honeyguide
Meliphaga gracilis stevensi	Steven's Hornbill
Meliphaga lewinii	Lewin's Honeyeater
Meliphaga macleayana	Macleay's Honeyeater
Meliphaga notata	Lewin's Lesser Honeyeater
Melitograis gilolensis	Bonaparte's Friarbird
Mellisuga helenae	Helena's Calypte
Melospiza lincolnii	Forbush's Sparrow
Melospiza lincolnii	Lincoln's Sparrow
Melospiza melodia merrilli	Merrill's Song Sparrow
Melozone biarcuatum	Prevost's Ground Sparrow
Menura alberti	Albert's Lyrebird (v. Prince Albert)
Menura alberti	Prince Albert's Lyrebird (Albert's)
Merops boehmi	Böhm's Bee-eater
Merulaxis stresemanni	Stresemann's Bristlefront (Extinct)
Metallura heterocerca	Jelski's Coppertail
Metallura wiliami primolinus	Primoli's Hummingbird
Metriopelia ceciliae	Cecilia's Dove
Metriopelia morenoi	Moreno's Bare-faced Ground Dove
Micrastur buckleyi	Buckley's Forest Falcon
Micrastur buckleyi	Traylor's Forest Falcon
Micrastur mirandollei	Mirandolle's Forest Falcon
Micrastur plumbeus	Sclater's Forest Falcon
Micrathene whitneyi	Whitney's Elf Owl
Microgoura meeki	Meek's Pigeon (Extinct)
Micropsitta bruijnii bruijnii	Bruijn's Pygmy Parrot
Micropsitta bruijnii necopinata	Hartert's Pygmy Parrot
Micropsitta finschii	Finsch's Pygmy Parrot
Micropsitta finschii tristami	Tristam's Pygmy Parrot
Micropsitta meeki	Meek's Pygmy Parrot
Micropsitta pusio	Sclater's Pygmy Parrot
Micropsitta pusio beccari	Beccari's Pygmy Parrot
Micropsitta pusio harterti	Mayr's Pygmy Parrot
Micropsitta pusio stresemanni	Stresemann's Pygmy Parrot
Microrhopias quixensis boucardi	Boucard's Antwren
Mimus gundlachii	Gundlach's Mockingbird
Mino dumontii	Dumont's Mynah
Mionectes macconnelli	McConnell's Flycatcher
Mirafra affinis	Jerdon's Bush Lark
Mirafra archeri	Archer's Lark
Mirafra ashi	Ash's Lark
Mirafra barlowi cavei	Cave's Lark
Mirafra degodiensis eradi	Erard's Lark
Mirafra gilletti	Gillett's Lark
Mirafra javanica	Horsfield's Lark
Mirafra naevia (sabota)	Bradfield's Lark
Mirafra pulpa	Friedmann's Bush Lark
Mirafra ruddi	Rudd's Lark
Mirafra ruficinnamomea buckleyi	Buckley's Lark
Mirafra williamsi	Williams's Lark
Mitu salvini	Salvin's Curassow
Moho bishopi	Bishop's Oo
Momotus momota lessonii	Lesson's Motmot

Monarcha browni	Brown's Monarch
Monarcha everetti	Everett's Monarch
Monarcha menckei	Mencke's Monarch
Monarcha richardsii	Richards' Monarch
Monarcha sacerdotum	Mees' Monarch
Monias benschi	Bensch's Monia
Monticola gularis	Swinhoe's Rock Thrush
Montifringilla davidiana	Père David's Snowfinch (David's)
Montifringilla theresae	Meinertzhagen's Snowfinch
Montifringilla theresae	Theresa's Snowfinch
Montifringillia adamsi	Adams' Snowfinch
Montifringillia davidiana	David's Snowfinch
Montifringillia taczanowskii	Mandelli's Snowfinch
Motacilla alba alboides	Hodgson's Pied Wagtail
Motacilla alba baicalensis	Swinhoe's Wagtail 2
Motacilla alba ocularis	Swinhoe's Wagtail 1
Motacilla capensis wellsi	Wells' Wagtail
Mulleripicus funebris fuliginosus	Tweeddale's Woodpecker
Munia (Lonchura) melaena	Sclater's Mannikin
Muscicapa cassinii	Cassin's Grey Flycatcher
Muscicapa cooperi	Cooper's Flycatcher
Muscicapa itombwensis	Prigogine's Alseonax
Muscicapa lendu	Chapin's Flycatcher
Musciscapa muttui	Layard's Flycatcher
Muscicapa tessmanni	Tessman's Flycatcher
Muscicapa ussheri	Ussher's Dusky Flycatcher
Muscicapa williamsoni	Williamson's Flycatcher
Musophaga johnstoni	Johnston's Turaco
Musophaga rossae	Ross's Turaco (Lady Ross's)
Myadestes townsendi	Townsend's Solitaire
Myiabeillia typica	Abeille's Flutterer
Myiarchus nuttingi	Nutting's Flycatcher
Myiarchus oberi	
Myiarchus sagrae	La Sagra's Flycatcher
Myiarchus swainsoni	Pelzeln's Flycatcher
Myiarchus swainsoni	Swainson's Flycatcher
Myiarchus swainsoni phaenotus	Whitely's Flycatcher
Myiarchus tuberculifer lawrencei	Lawrence's Crested Flycatcher
Myiarchus tyrannulus	Weid's Crested Flycatcher
Myiarchus tyrannulus	Wied's Crested Flycatcher (1)
Myiodynastes bairdii	Baird's Flycatcher
Myiornis boehmi	Böhm's Flycatcher
Myophonus blighi	Bligh's Whistling Thrush
Myophonus robinsoni	Robinson's Whistling Thrush
Myrmeciza goeldii	Goeldi's Antbird
Myrmeciza laemosticta	Salvin's Antbird
Myrmeciza longipes	Swainson's Antbird
Myrmecocichla tholloni	Thollon's Moorchat
Myrmotherula (brachyura) ignota	Griscom's Antwren
Myrmotherula cherriei	Cherrie's Antwren
Myrmotherula iheringi	Ihering's Antwren
Myrmotherula klagesi	Klage's Antwren
Myrmotherula longipennis garbei	Garbe's Antwren
Myrmotherula menetriesii	Ménétries's Antwren
Myrmotherula minor	Salvadori's Antwren
Myrmotherula sclateri	Sclater's Antwren
Mystacornis crossleyi	Crossley's Babbler
Myzomela adolphinae	Adolphina's Myzomela
Myzomela cineracea	Sclater's Myzomela 1
Myzomela kuehni	Kuhn's Myzomela
Myzomela rosenbergi	Rosenberg's Myzomela
Myzomela sclateri	Sclater's Myzomela 2

Myzomela tristrami	Tristram's Honeyeater
Napothera marmorata	Muller's Wren-Babbler
Napothera rabori	Rabor's Wren-Babbler
Neafrapus boehmi	Böhm's Spine-tailed Swift
Neafrapus cassini	Cassin's Spinetail
Necarinia bouvieri	Bouvier's Sunbird
Necrospar rodericanus	Leguat's Starling (Extinct)
Necrospar rodericanus	Rodrigues Starling (Extinct)
Nectarinia bannermani	Bannerman's Sunbird
Nectarinia batesi	Bates' (Olive) Sunbird
Nectarinia bocagei	Bocage's Sunbird
Nectarinia calcostella	Macklot's Sunbird
Nectarinia hartlaubi	Hartlaub's Sunbird
Nectarinia humbloti	Humblot's Sunbird
Nectarinia hunteri	Hunter's Sunbird
Nectarinia johannae	Johanna's Sunbird
Nectarinia johannae	Madame Verreaux's Sunbird (Johanna's)
Nectarinia kilimensis gadowi	Gadow's Sunbird
Nectarinia lotenia	Loten's Sunbird
Nectarinia loveridgei	Loveridge's Sunbird
Nectarinia monoensis pintoi	Pinto's Sunbird
Nectarinia moreaui	Moreau's Sunbird
Nectarinia neergaardi	Neergaard's Sunbird
Nectarinia newtonii	Newton's Yellow-breasted Sunbird
Nectarinia oustaleti	Oustalet's Sunbird
Nectarinia preussi	Preuss's Double-collared Sunbird
Nectarinia prigoginei	Prigogine's Double-collared Sunbird
Nectarinia reichenbachii	Reichenbach's Sunbird
Nectarinia rockefelleri	Rockefeller's Sunbird
Nectarinia seimundi	Seimund's Sunbird
Nectarinia shelleyi	Shelley's Sunbird
Nectarinia [Leptocoma] sperata hasseltii	Van Hasselt's Sunbird
Nectarinia stuhlmanni	Stuhlmann's Double-collared Sunbird
Nectarinia (cinnyris) ursulae	Ursula's Sunbird
Neocossyphus finschii	Finsch's Flycatcher-Thrush
Neocossyphus fraseri	Fraser's Ant-thrush
Neocossyphus rufus	Fraser's Rusty Thrush
Neolesbia nehrkorni	Nehrkorn Hummingbird
Neomorphus rufipennis	Chapman's Ground Cuckoo
Neopelma aurifrons	Wied's Tyrant-Manakin
Neophema (Neopsephotus) bourkii	Bourke's Parrot
Neopsittacus musschenbroekii	Musschenbroek's Lorikeet
Neospiza concolor	St Thomas's Canary
Neospiza wilkinsi	Wilkins' Bunting
Neotis denhami burchellii	Burchell's Bustard
Neotis denhami denhami	Denham's Bustard
Neotis denhami jacksoni	Jackson's Bustard
Neotis denhami stanleyi	Stanley's Bustard
Neotis heuglinii	Heuglin's Bustard
Neotis ludwigii	Ludwig's Bustard
Neotis savilei	Lynes's Pigmy Bustard
Nesillas mariae	Mrs Benson's Warbler (Laura's)
Nesocharis shelleyi	Shelley's Oliveback
Nesoclopeus woodfordi	Woodford's Rail
Nesominus trifasciatus	Charles's Mockingbird (Darwin's)
Nesospiza wilkinsi	Wilkins's Finch
Newtonia archboldi	Archbold's Newtonia
Niltava davidi	David's Niltava
Niltava davidi	Père David's Niltava (David's)
Ninox meeki	Meek's Hawk-Owl

Ninox scutulata obscura	Hume's Brown Hawk-Owl
Ninox spilocephala	Tweeddale's Hawk-Owl (Walden's)
Nothocercus bonapartei	Bonaparte's Tinamou
Nothoprocta kalinowskii	Kalinowski's Tinamou
Nothoprocta kalinowskii	Taczanowski's Tinamou
Nothura darwinii	Darwin's Nothura
Nucifraga columbiana	Clark's Nutcracker
Numidea meleagris reichenowi	Reichenow's Guineafowl
Nycticorax violaceus bancrofti	Bancroft's Night Heron
Nyctidromus albicollis merrilli	Merrill's Paraque
Oceanites gracilis	Elliot's Storm Petrel
Oceanites oceanicus	Wilson's Storm Petrel
Oceanodroma (Hydrobates) castro	Harcourt's Storm Petrel
Oceanodroma hornbyi	Hornby's Storm Petrel
Oceanodroma (leucorhoa) kaedingi	Kaeding's Storm Petrel
Oceanodroma leucoptera beali	Beal's Storm Petrel
Oceanodroma leucorhoa	Leach's Storm Petrel
Oceanodroma leucorhoa chapmani	Chapman's Petrel
Oceanodroma leucorhoa owstoni	Owston's Fork-tailed Petrel
Oceanodroma markhami	Markham's Storm Petrel
Oceanodroma matsudairae	Matsudaira's Storm Petrel
Oceanodroma melania	Townsend Petrel
Oceanodroma monorhis	Swinhoe's Storm Petrel
Oceanodroma tristrami	Tristram's Storm Petrel
Ochthoeca jelskii	Jelski's Chat Tyrant
Ochthoeca oenanthoides	D'Orbigny's Chat Tyrant
Oenanthe alboniger	Hume's Wheatear
Oenanthe bottae	Botta's Wheatear
Oenanthe finschii	Finsch's Wheatear
Oenanthe finschii barnesi	Barnes' Wheatear
Oenanthe heuglini	Heuglin's Wheatear
Oenanthe lugubris	Schalow's Wheatear
Oenanthe moesta	Tristram's Wheatear
Oenanthe phillipsi	Phillips' Wheatear
Oenanthe pleschanka	Pleschanka's Pied Chat
Oenanthe (oenanthe) seebohmi	Seebohm's Wheatear
Onychognathus neumanni	Neumann's Starling
Onychognathus tristramii	Tristram's Grackle
Onychognathus walleri	Waller's Chestnut-winged Starling
Onychorhynchus coronatus swainsoni	Swainson's Royal Flycatcher
Opopsitta diophthalma marshalli	Marshall's Fig Parrot
Oporornis tolmei	MacGillivray's Warbler
Oreomystis bairdi	Baird's Creeper
Oreophasis derbianus	Derby's Guan (Stanley's)
Oreotrochilus adelae	Adela's Hillstar
Oreotrochilus estella	Estella's Hillstar
Oriolia bernieri	Bernier's Vanga
Oriolus forsteni	Forsten's Oriole
Oriolus isabellae	Isabella Oriole
Oriolus mellianus	Mell's Oriole
Oriolus mellianus	Stresemann's Maroon Oriole
Oriolus percivali	Percival's Oriole
Oriolus phaeochromus	Gray's Oriole
Oroaetus isidori	Isidor's Eagle
Ortalis wagleri	Wagler's Chachalaca
Orthonyx spaldingi	Spalding's Logrunner
Otus alfredi	Everett's Owl
Otus angelinae	Angelina's Scops Owl
Otus asio hasbroucki	Hasbrouck's Screech Owl
Otus asio mccallii	McCall's Screech Owl
Otus beccarii	Beccari's Scops Owl

Otus brookii	Brooke's Scops Owl (Rajah's)
Otus brookii	Rajah's Scops Owl (Brooke's)
Otus brucei	Bruce's Scops Owl
Otus commersoni	Commerson's Scops Owl
Otus hoyi	Hoy's Screech Owl
Otus ingens	Salvin's Screech Owl
Otus ireneae	Morden's Scops Owl
Otus kennicottii	Bancroft's Screech Owl
Otus kennicottii	Grinell's Screech Owl
Otus kennicottii	Kennicott's Screech Owl
Otus kennicottii aikeni	Aiken's Screech Owl
Otus kennicottii brewsteri	Brewster's Screech Owl
Otus kennicottii gilmani	Gilman's Screech Owl
Otus kennicottii macfarlanei	MacFarlane's Screech Owl
Otus kennicottii suttoni	Sutton's Screech Owl
Otus kennicottii xantusii	Xantus's Screech Owl
Otus koepckeae	Koepcke's Owl
Otus koepckeae	Maria Koepcke's Screech Owl
Otus megalotis	Whitehead's Scops Owl
Otus silvicola	Wallace's Scops Owl
Otus spilocephalus stresemanni	Stresemann's Scops Owl
Otus spilocephalus vandewateri	Vandewater's Scops Owl
Oxypogon guerinii lindenii	Linden's Helmetcrest
Pachycephala (Coracornis) raveni	Raven's Whistler
Pachycephala inornata	Gilbert's Whistler
Pachycephala lorentzi	Lorentz's Whistler
Pachycephala meyeri	Meyer's Whistler
Pachycephala schlegelii	Schlegel's Whistler
Pachycephala soror	Sclater's Whistler
Pachyplichas jagmi	Grant-Mackie's Wren (Extinct)
Pachyplichas yaldwyni	Yaldwyn's Wren (Extinct)
Pachyptila desolata	Banks' Dove Petrel
Pachyptila salvini macgillivrayi	MacGillivray's Prion
Pachyptila salvini (vittata)	Salvin's Prion
Pachyramphus (Platypsaris) aglaiae	Xantus's Becard
Pacyornis (elephantopus) mappini	Mappin's Moa (Extinct)
Palaeeudyptus marplesi	Marples' Penguin (Extinct)
Pamphocelus passerinii	Passerini's Tanager
Panoplites matthewsi	Matthews' Panoplites
Papasula abbotti	Abbott's Booby
Parabuteo unicinctus	Harris's Hawk
Paradisaea decora	Goldie's Bird-of-Paradise
Paradisaea guilielmi	Emperor-of-Germany Bird of Paradise
Paradisaea intermedia	De Vis's Bird-of-Paradise
Paradisaea raggiana	Count Raggi's Bird of Paradise
Paradisaea rudolphi	Prince Rudolph's Bird of Paradise
Paradoxornis davidianus	David's Parrotbill
Paradoxornis davidianus	Père David's Parrotbill (David's)
Paradoxornis flavirostris	Gould's Parrotbill
Paradoxornis heudi	Heude's Parrotbill
Paradoxornis nipalensis	Blyth's Parrotbill
Paradoxornis przewalskii	Prjevalsky's Parrotbill
Paradoxornis (brunneus) ricketti	Rickett's Parrotbill
Paradoxornis webbianus	Webb's Parrotbill
Paradoxornis zappeyi	Zappey's Parrotbill
Parisoma layardi	Layard's Titbabbler
Parmoptila rubrifrons	Jameson's Antpecker
Parmoptila woodhousei	Woodhouse's Antpecker

Parotia carolae	Carola Parotia (Queen Carola's)
Parotia carolae	Queen Carola's Parotia
Parotia lawesii	Lawe's Parotia
Parotia wahnesi	Wahnes's Parotia
Parula pitiayumi	Sennett's Olive-backed Parula
Parula superciliosa	Hartlaub's Warbler
Parus bicolor sennetti	Sennett's Titmouse
Parus carpi (leucomelas)	Carp's Black Tit
Parus davidi	David's Tit
Parus davidi	Père David's Tit (David's)
Parus gambeli	Gambel's Chickadee
Parus gambeli abbreviatus	Grinell's Chickadee
Parus gambeli baileyae	Bailey's Chickadee
Parus inornatus ridgwayi	Ridgway's Titmouse
Parus melanolophus	Vigors's Crested Tit
Parus rufuscens barlowi	Barlow's Chickadee
Parus varius owstoni	Owston's Varied Tit
Passer eminbey	Emin Bey's Sparrow
Passer griseus swainsonii	Swainson's Sparrow
Passer motitensis shelleyi	Shelley's Rufous-sparrow
Passerculus sandwichensis	Blyth's Sparrow
Passerculus sandwichensis	Bryant's Sparrow
Passerculus sandwichensis beldingi	Belding's Sparrow
Passerella iliaca stephensi	Stephen's Sparrow
Passerella iliaca townsendi	Townsend's Sparrow
Passerina leclancherii	Lechlancher's Bunting
Passerina rositae	Rosita's Bunting
Peliperdix schlegelii	Schlegel's Francolin
Penelope dabbenei	Dabbene's Guan
Penelope jacquacu	Spix's Guan
Penelope ortoni	Orton's Guan
Penelopides exharhatus	Temminck's Hornbill
Perdix hodgsoniae	Hodgson's Partridge
Pericrocotus cantonensis (roseus)	Swinhoe's Minivet
Pericrocotus erythropygius	Jerdon's Minivet
Phaechroa (cuvierii) roberti	Robert's Hummingbird
Phaenicophaeus chlorophaea	Raffles' Malkoha
Phaeochra cuvieri	Cuvier's Sabrewing
Phaethornis (superciliosus) margarettae	Margaretta's Hermit
Phaethornis adolphi	Adolph's Hermit
Phaethornis adolphi	Boucard's Hermit
Phaethornis augusti	Salle's Hermit
Phaethornis bourceri	Bourcier's Hermit
Phaethornis griseogularis	Gould's Hermit
Phaethornis guy	Guy's Hermit
Phaethornis koepckeae	Koepcke's Hermit
Phaethornis longuemareus	Longuemare's Hermit
Phaethornis longuemareus	Prêtre's Hermit 2
Phaethornis oseryi	D'Osery's Hermit
Phaethornis philippi	Philippi's Hermit
Phaethornis pretrei	Prêtre's Hermit 1
Phaethornis roberti	Owen's Sabrewing
Phaethornis syrmatophorus	Baron Rothschild Hermit (Rothschild)
Phainopepla melanoxantha	Salvin's Silky-flycatcher
Phalacrocorax chalconotus	Gray's Shag
Phalacrocorax gaimardi	Gaimard's Cormorant
Phalacrocorax kenyoni	Kenyon's Shag
Phalacrocorax pelagicus resplendens	Baird's Cormorant
Phalacrocorax penicillatus	Brandt's Cormorant
Phalacrocorax penicillatus	Townsend's Cormorant
Phalacrocrax perspicillatus	Pallas's Cormorant (Extinct)
Phalaenoptilus nuttalli	Nuttall's Poorwill
Phalaropus tricolor	Wilson's Phalarope
Phalcoboenus albogularis	Darwin's Caracara
Phalcoboenus australis	Forster's Caracara
Phalocrocorax capillatus	Temminck's Cormorant
Phasianus colchicus bianchii	Bianchi's Pheasant
Phasianus colchicus elegans	Stone's Pheasant
Phasianus colchicus pallasi	Pallas's Ring-necked Pheasant
Phasianus colchicus principalis	Prince of Wales' Pheasant
Phasianus colchicus rothschildi	Rothschild's Pheasant
Phasianus colchicus strauchi	Strauch's Pheasant
Phasianus colchicus zarudnyi	Zarudny's Pheasant
Phedina brazzae	Brazza's Martin
Phegornis mitchellii	Mitchell's Plover
Pheucticus aureoventris terminalis	Chapman's Grosbeak
Pheuticus chrysopeplus	Van Rossem's Grosbeak
Pheuticus chrysopeplus	Vigors's Grosbeak
Philemon brassi	Brass's Friarbird
Philemon eichorni	Eichhorn's Friarbird
Philemon meyeri	Meyer's Friarbird
Philepitta schlegeli	Schlegel's Asity
Philodus prigoginei	Prigogine's Bay Owl
Philydor dimidiatus baeri	Baer's Foliage-gleaner
Philydor erythropterus	Lichtenstein's Foliage-gleaner 2
Philydor lichtensteini	Lichtenstein's Foliage-gleaner
Philydor novaesi	Novaes's Foliage-gleaner
Phoenicopterus [Phoenicoparrus] jamesi	James's Flamingo
Phoeniculus damarensis	Grant's Woodhoopoe
Phoenicurus alashanicus	Prjevalsky's Redstart
Phoenicurus erythrogaster	Güldenstädt's Redstart
Phoenicurus erythronotus	Eversmann's Redstart
Phoenicurus hodgsoni	Hodgson's Redstart
Phoenicurus moussieri	Moussier's Redstart
Phonygama hunsteini	Hunstein's Bird-of-Paradise
Phonygammus diamondi	Diamond's Paradise-Crow
Phyllastrephus alfredi	Sharpe's Greenbul
Phyllastrephus apperti	Colston's Bulbul
Phyllastrephus apperti	Appert's Greenbul
Phyllastrephus baumanni	Baumann's (Olive) Greenbul
Phyllastrephus cabanisi (fischeri)	Cabanis's Greenbul
Phyllastrephus fischeri	Fischer's Greenbul
Phyllastrephus lorenzi	Lorentz's Bulbul
Phyllastrephus lorenzi	Sassi's Olive Greenbul
Phyllastrephus xavieri	Dybowski's Astrild (v. Xavier)
Phyllastrephus xavieri	Xavier's Greenbul
Phyllomyias reiseri	Reiser's Tyrannulet
Phyllomyias sclateri	Sclater's Tyrannulet
Phyllomyias urichi	Urich's Tyrannulet
Phyllomyias zeledoni	Zeledon's Tyrannulet
Phylloscartes chapmani	Chapman's Tyrannulet
Phylloscartes difficilis	Ihering's Tyrannulet
Phylloscartes oustaleti	Oustalet's Tyrannulet
Phylloscopus affinis	Tickell's Leaf Warbler
Phylloscopus armandii	Milne-Edward's Willow Warbler
Phylloscopus bonelli	Bonelli's Warbler
Phylloscopus borealis	Eversmann's Warbler
Phylloscopus borealis	Kennicott's Willow Warbler
Phylloscopus cebuensis	Dubois' Leaf Warbler
Phylloscopus coronatus	Temminck's Crowned Willow Warbler
Phylloscopus davisoni	Oates' Leaf Warbler
Phylloscopus griseolus	Jerdon's Willow Warbler
Phylloscopus herberti	Herbert's Woodland Warbler
Phylloscopus humei	Hume's Leaf Warbler

Phylloscopus ijimae	Ijima's Willow Warbler
Phylloscopus laurae	Laura's Woodland Warbler (Mrs Boulton's)
Phylloscopus laurae	Mrs Boulton's Woodland Warbler
Phylloscopus proregulus	Pallas's Warbler
Phylloscopus reguloides	Blyth's Crowned Willow Warbler
Phylloscopus ricketti	Rickett's Willow Warbler
Phylloscopus ricketti	Slater's Leaf Warbler
Phylloscopus schwarzi	Radde's Warbler
Phylloscopus subaffinis	Grant's Leaf Warbler
Phylloscopus subaffinis	Ogilvie-Grant's Warbler
Phylloscopus subviridis	Brooks's Willow Warbler
Phylloscopus tytleri	Tytler's Willow Warbler
Pianroloxias inornata	Darwin's Cocos Island Finch
Picoides maculatus ramsayi	Ramsay's Woodpecker
Picoides nuttallii	Nuttall's Woodpecker
Picoides pubescens gairdnerii	Batchelder's Woodpecker
Picoides pubescens gairdnerii	Gairdner's Woodpecker
Picoides stricklandi	Strickland's Woodpecker
Picoides temminckii	Temminck's Pygmy Woodpecker
Picoides villosus hyloscopus	Cabanis's Woodpecker
Picoides villosus picoideus	Queen Charlotte Woodpecker
Picoides villosus harrisi	Harris's Woodpecker
Picoides villosus audubonii	Audubon's Woodpecker
Picumnus fuscus	Natterer's Piculet
Picumnus lafresnayi	Lafresnaye's Piculet
Picumnus subtilis	Stager's Piculet
Picus rabieri	Rabier's Woodpecker
Picus vaillantii	Levaillant's Green Woodpecker
Pinaroloema buckleyi	Buckley's Mountain Hummingbird
Pionopsitta barrabandi	Barraband's Parrot
Pionus maximiliani maximiliani	Maximilian's Parrot
Pionus maximiliani melanoblepharus	Ribeiro's Scaly-headed Parrot
Pionus menstruus reichenowi	Reichenow's Blue-headed Parrot
Pionus senilis	Massena's Parrot (Rivoli's)
Pionus tumultuosus tumultuosus	Tschudi's Parrot
Pipile cujibi nattereri	Natterer's Piping Guan
Pipile cumanensis grayi	Gray's Piping Guan
Pipilo aberti	Abert's Towhee
Pipilo fuscus	Anthony's Towhee
Pipra pipra anthracina	Zeledon's Manakin
Pipra vilasboasi	Sick's Manakin
Pipreola riefferii tallmanorum	Tallman's Fruiteater
Piranga bidentata	Swainson's Tanager
Piranga rubra cooperii	Cooper's Tanager
Piranga rubriceps	Gray's Tanager
Pirinis rufescens	Beavan's Wren Warbler
Pisobia (Tringa) cooperi	Cooper's Sandpiper
Pitangus sulphuratus derbianus	Lord Derby's Kiskadee
Pitta ellioti	Elliot's Pitta
Pitta ellioti	Gurney's Pitta
Pitta erythrogaster	Macklot's Pitta
Pitta kochi	Koch's Pitta
Pitta nympha	Swinhoe's Pitta
Pitta phayrei	Phayre's Pitta
Pitta schneideri	Schneider's Pitta
Pitta steeri	Steere's Pitta
Platycercus brownii	Brown's Parakeet
Platycercus elegans adelaidae	Pennant's Parakeet 2

Platycercus elegans elegans	Pennant's Parakeet 1
Platycercus eximius	Pennant's Parakeet 3
Platycercus eximius ceciliae	Cecilia's Rosella
Platycercus icterotis	Earl of Derby's Parakeet (Stanley's)
Platycercus icterotis	Lord Derby's Parakeet (Stanley's)
Platycercus icterotis	Stanley's Parrakeet
Platydyptes amiesi	Amies' Penguin (Extinct)
Platysteira blissetti	Blissett's Wattle-eye
Platysteira chalybea	Reichenow's Wattle-eye
Platysteira jamesoni	Jameson's Wattle-eye
Plectrophenax hyperboreus	McKay's Bunting
Plocepasser donaldsoni	Donaldson-Smith's Sparrow-Weaver
Ploceus albinucha maxwelli	Maxwell's Black Weaver
Ploceus baglafecht	Emin's Weaver
Ploceus baglafecht reichenowi	Reichenow's Weaver
Ploceus baglafecht stuhlmanni	Stuhlmann's Weaver
Ploceus bannermani	Bannerman's Weaver
Ploceus batesi	Bates' Weaver
Ploceus bertrandi	Bertram's Weaver (Bertrand's)
Ploceus bertrandi	Bertrand's Weaver
Ploceus dichrocephalus	Salvadori's Weaver
Ploceus galbula	Rüppell's Weaver
Ploceus golandi	Clarke's Weaver
Ploceus heuglini	Heuglin's Masked Weaver
Ploceus jacksoni	Jackson's Golden-backed Weaver
Ploceus megarhynchus	Finn's Weaver
Ploceus nelicourvi	Nelicourvi's Weaver 1
Ploceus nicolli	Nicoll's Weaver
Ploceus nigerrimus	Vieillot's Black Weaver
Ploceus nigriceps	Layard's Black-headed Weaver
Ploceus nigricollis brachypterus	Swainson's Weaver
Ploceus preussi	Preuss's Weaver
Ploceus reichardi ruweti	Ruwet's Masked Weaver
Ploceus (Foudia) sakalava	Nelicourvi's Weaver 2
Ploceus spekei	Speke's Weaver
Ploceus spekeoides	Fox's Weaver
Ploceus temporalis	Bocage's Weaver
Ploceus weynsi	Weyns' Weaver
Ploceus xanthops	Holub's Golden Weaver
Ploceus xanthops	Monteiro's Golden Weaver
Podica senegalensis petersii	Peters's Finfoot
Podiceps grisegena holboelli	Holboell's Grebe
Podiceps taczanowskii	Taczanowski's Grebe
Podoces biddulphi	Biddulph's Ground Jay
Podoces hendersoni	Henderson's Ground Jay
Podoces panderi	Pander's Ground Jay
Podoces pleskei	Pleske's Ground Jay
Poecilotriccus luluae	Lulu's Tody-Tyrant
Poeoptera kenricki	Kenrick's Starling
Poeoptera stuhlmanni	Stuhlmann's Starling
Poephila cincta atropygialis	Diggles's Finch
Poephila cincta nigrotecta	Diggles's Chocolate Parson Finch
Poicephalus gulielmi	Jardine's Parrot
Poicephalus meyeri	Meyer's Parrot
Poicephalus robustus	Levaillant's Parrot
Poicephalus robustus fuscicollis	Kuhl's Cape Parrot
Poicephalus robustus suahelicus	Reichenow's Cape Parrot
Poicephalus ruepellii	Rüppell's Parrot
Poicephalus senegalus mesotypus	Reichenow's Orange-bellied Parrot
Polihierax insignis	Fielden's Falconet

Polioptila californica	Xantus's Gnatcatcher
Polioptila dumicola	Berlepsch's Gnatcatcher
Polyonomus caroli	Charlie's Comet
Polyplectron bicalcaratum baileyi	Lowe's Grey Peacock-Pheasant
Polyplectron bicalcaratum ghigii	Ghigi's Grey Peacock-Pheasant
Polyplectron chalcurum	Lesson's Peacock-Pheasant
Polyplectron emphanum	Napoleon's Peacock-Pheasant
Polyplectron germaini	Germain's Peacock-Pheasant
Polyplectron inopinatum	Rothschild's Peacock-Pheasant
Polysticta stelleri	Steller's Eider
Polytelis alexandrae	Alexandra's Parrot
Polytelis alexandrae	Princess Alexandra's Parrot (Alexandra's)
Polytelis alexandrae	Queen Alexandra's Parrot (Alexandra's)
Pomatorhinus ochraceiceps	Lloyd's Scimitar Babbler
Pomatorhinus othraceiceps	Horsfield's Scimitar Babbler
Pomatostomus halli	Hall's Babbler
Pomatostomus isidorei	Isidor's Rufous Babbler
Popelairia conversii	Convers' Thorntail
Popelairia langsdorffi	Langsdorff's Thorntail
Popelairia popelairii	Popelaire's Coquette
Porphyrio alleni	Allen's Gallinule
Porzana atra	North's Crake
Porzana monasa	Kittlitz's Crake
Porzana pusilla	Baillon's Crake
Porzana pusilla	Pallas's Crake
Primolius maracana	Illiger's Macaw
Prinia cinereocapilla	Hodgson's Long-tailed Warbler
Prinia criniger	David's Hill Warbler
Prinia criniger	Père David's Hill Warbler (David's)
Prinia hodgsoni	Franklin's Prinia
Prinia robertsi	Roberts' Prinia
Prioniturus discurus whiteheadi	Salomonsen's Racket-tailed Parrot
Prioniturus waterstradti	Waterstradt's Racket-tailed Parrot
Prionochilus plateni	Platen's Flowerpecker
Prionodura newtoniana	Newton's Golden Bowerbird
Prionops gabela	Rand's Red-billed Helmet-shrike
Prionops plumatus	Smith's Helmet-shrike
Prionops retzii	Retz's Red-billed Helmet-shrike
Probosciger aterrimus stenolophus	Van Oort's Palm Cockatoo
Procellaria parkinsoni	Parkinson's Petrel
Prodotiscus insignis	Cassin's Honeyguide
Prodotiscus regulus	Wahlberg's Honeyguide
Promerops gurneyi	Gurney's Sugarbird
Propyrrhura couloni	Coulon's Macaw
Prosobonia ellisi	Ellis' Sandpiper
Prunella koslowi	Kozlow's Accentor
Prunella ocularis	Radde's Accentor
Psalidoprocne antinorii blanfordi	Blanford's Saw-wing
Psalidoprocne petiti	Petit's Saw-wing
Psaltriparus minimus lloydi	Lloyd's Bushtit
Psarocolius wagleri	Wagler's Oropendola
Pseudibis davisoni	Davison's Ibis
Pseudobias wardi	Ward's Flycatcher
Pseudocalyptomena graueri	Grauer's Green Broadbill
Pseudocolaptes lawrencii	Lawrence's Tuftedcheek
Pseudocolopteryx dinellianus	Dinelli's Doradito
Pseudocossyphus bensoni	Benson's Rock Thrush

Pseudocossyphus bensoni	Farkas' Rock Thrush
Pseudodontornis stirtoni	Stirton's False-toothed Pelican (Extinct)
Pseudopodoces humilis	Hume's Ground Chough
Psittacella brehmii	Brehm's Parrot
Psittacella brehmii harterti	Mayr's Parrot
Psittacella maderaszi	Maderasz's Parrot
Psittacella maderaszi hallstromi	Hallstrom's Parrot
Psittacella modesta subcollaris	Rand's Modest Parrot
Psittacella picta excelsa	Mayr's Painted Parrot
Psittacella picta lorentzi	Lorentz's Painted Parrot
Psittacula alexandri dammermani	Dammerman's Moustached Parakeet
Psittacula calthorpae	Layard's Parakeet
Psittacula caniceps	Blyth's Parakeet
Psittacula eques	Daubenton's Parakeet (Extinct)
Psittacula exsul	Newton's Parakeet (Extinct)
Psittacula finschii	Finsch's Parrot
Psittacula finschii	Hume's Parakeet
Psittacula intermedia	Rothschild's Parakeet
Psittacula krameri borealis	Neumann's Ring-necked Parakeet
Psittaculirostris desmarestii	Desmarest's Fig Parrot
Psittaculirostris desmarestii	Wallace's Fig Parrot
Psittaculirostris desmarestii godmani	Godman's Fig Parrot
Psittaculirostris desmarestii intermedia	Van Oort's Fig Parrot
Psittaculirostris erdwardsii	Edwards' Fig Parrot (Milne-Edwards')
Psittaculirostris salvadorii	Salvadori's Fig Parrot
Psitteuteles goldiei	Goldie's Lorikeet
Psittrichas fulgidus	Pesquet's Parrot
Pteridophora alberti	King of Saxony's Bird of Paradise
Pternistis harwoodi	Harwood's Francolin
Pterocles burchelli	Burchell's Sandgrouse
Pterocles gutturalis	Smith's Chestnut-vented Sandgrouse
Pterocles lichtensteinii	Lichtenstein's Sandgrouse
Pterocnemia pennata	Darwin's Rhea
Pterodroma arminjoniana	Herald's Petrel
Pterodroma atrata	Henderson Petrel
Pterodroma baraui	Barau's Petrel
Pterodroma (rostrata) becki	Beck's Petrel (Extinct)
Pterodroma cookii	Cook's Petrel (Extinct)
Pterodroma defilippiana (cookii)	Defilippe's Petrel
Pterodroma externa	Juan Fernández Petrel
Pterodroma feae	Fea's Petrel
Pterodroma hypoleuca	Salvin's Petrel
Pterodroma incerta	Schlegel's Petrel
Pterodroma inexpectata	Fischer's Petrel
Pterodroma inexpectata	Peale's Petrel
Pterodroma leucoptera	Gould's Petrel
Pterodroma longirostris	Stejneger's Petrel
Pterodroma macgillivrayi	MacGillivray's Petrel
Pterodroma madeira	Zino's Petrel
Pterodroma pycrofti	Pycroft's Petrel
Pterodroma solandri	Solander's Petrel
Pterodroma ultima	Murphy's Petrel
Pteronetta hartlaubi	Hartlaub's Duck
Pterophanes cyanopterus (temmincki)	Temminck's Sapphirewing
Ptilinopus arcanus	Ripley's Fruit Dove
Ptilinopus dohertyi	Doherty's Fruit Dove
Ptilinopus eugeniae	Eugenie's Fruit Dove
Ptilinopus fischeri	Fischer's Fruit Dove

Ptilinopus greyii	Grey's Fruit Dove
Ptilinopus huttoni	Hutton's Fruit Dove
Ptilinopus insolitus	Schlegel's Fruit Dove
Ptilinopus insularis	Henderson Fruit Dove
Ptilinopus leclancheri	Lechlancher's Pigeon
Ptilinopus marchei	Marche's Fruit Dove
Ptilinopus merrilli	Merrill's Fruit Dove
Ptilinopus ornatus	Gestro's Fruit Dove
Ptilinopus regina	Ewing's Fruit Pigeon
Ptilinopus regina	Swainson's Fruit Pigeon
Ptilinopus richardsii	Richards' Fruit Dove
Ptilinopus subgularis epia	Oberholser's Fruit Dove
Ptilinopus wallacii	Wallace's Fruit Dove
Ptilocichla mindanensis	Blasius's Wren-Babbler
Ptiloprora guisei	Guise's Honeyeater
Ptiloprora mayri	Mayr's Streaked Honeyeater
Ptiloprora meekiana	Meek's Streaked Honeyeater
Ptiloris victoriae	Victoria's Riflebird
Ptochoptera iolaima	Natterer's Emerald
Ptychoramphus aleuticus	Cassin's Auklet
Puchrasia macrolopha darwini	Darwin's Pheasant
Pucrasia macrolopha joretiana	Joret's Koklass
Pucrasia macrolopha meyeri	Meyer's Koklass
Puffinus auricularis	Townsend's Shearwater
Puffinus bannermani	Bannerman's Shearwater
Puffinus bulleri	Buller's Shearwater
Puffinus gavia	Forster's Petrel/Shearwater
Puffinus heinrothi	Heinroth's Shearwater
Puffinus huttoni	Hutton's Shearwater
Puffinus lherminieri	Audubon's Shearwater
Puffinus mauretanicus	Hammond's Petrel
Puffinus newelli	Newell's Shearwater
Puffinus olsoni	Olson's Shearwater (Extinct)
Pycnonotus blanfordi	Blanford's Olive Bulbul
Pycnonotus (barbatus) dodsoni	Dodson's Bulbul
Pycnonotus nieuwenhuisii	Nieuwenhuis's Bulbul
Pycnonotus taivanus	Styan's Bulbul
Pycnonotus xanthorrhous andersoni	Anderson's Bulbul
Pygoscelis adeliae	Adelie Penguin
Pygoscelis tyreei	Tyree's Penguin (Extinct)
Pyrenestes ostrinus rothschildi	Rothschild's Seedcracker
Pyrgilauda blanfordi	Blanford's Snowfinch
Pyrgilauda taczanowskii	Taczanowski's Finch
Pyriglena atra	Swainson's Fire-eye
Pyrrhula erythaca	Beavan's Bullfinch
Pyrrhula pyrrhula cassini	Cassin's Bullfinch
Pyrrhura (frontalis) devillei	Deville's Conure
Pyrrhura frontalis chiripepe	Azara's Conure
Pyrrhura hoffmanni	Hoffmann's Conure
Pyrrhura leucotis emma	Emma's White-eared Conure
Pyrrhura melanura	Berlepsch's Parakeet
Pyrrhura melanura chapmani	Chapman's Conure
Pyrrhura melanura souancei	Souancé's Maroon-tailed Conure
Pyrrhura perlata anerythra	Neumann's Pearly Conure
Pyrrhura perlata lepida	Wagler's Pearly Conure
Pyrrhura (leucotis) pfrimeri	Pfrimer's Conure
Pyrrhura picta lucianii	Prince Lucian's Conure
Pyrrhura picta pantchenkoi	Pantchenko's Conure
Pytilia melba	Melba Finch
Rallina forbesi	Forbes' Forest Rail
Rallina mayri	Mayr's Forest Rail
Rallus longirostris beldingi	Belding's Rail
Rallus wetmorei	Wetmore's Rail
Ramphastos swainsoni	Swainson's Toucan
Ramphastos tucanus cuvieri	Cuvier's Toucan
Ramphocelus costricensis	Cherrie's Tanager
Ramphocelus passerinii	Passerini's Tanager

Ramphocorys clotbey	Clot Bey's Lark
Randia pseudozosterops	Rand's Warbler
Raphidura sabini	Sabine's Spinetail
Regulus cuvieri	Cuvier's Kinglet
Reinwardtoena browni	Brown's Long-tailed Pigeon
Reinwardtoena reinwardti	Reinwardt's Long-tailed Pigeon
Rheinardia ocellata	Rheinhard's Pheasant
Rhinomyias goodfellowi	Goodfellow's Jungle Flycatcher
Rhinoptilus cinctus	Heuglin's Courser
Rhinoptilus cinctus seebohmi	Seebohm's Courser
Rhipidura cockerelli	Cockerell's Fantail
Rhipidura dedemi	Van Oort's Fantail
Rhipidura drownei	Drowne's Fantail
Rhipidura matthiae	Heinroth's Fantail
Rhipidura matthiae	Matthias Fantail
Rhipidura teysmanni	Teijsmann's Fantail
Rhodopechys obsoleta	Lichtenstein's Desert Finch
Rhodostethia rossae	Lady Ross's Gull (Ross's)
Rhodostethia rossae	Ross's Gull (Lady Ross's)
Rissa tridactyla	Kotzebue's Kittiwake
Rollandia rolland	Rolland's Grebe
Rougetius rougetii	Rouget's Rail
Salvadorina waigiuensis	Salvadori's Duck
Sapheopipo noguchii	Noguchi's Woodpecker
Sapheopipo noguchii	Pryer's Woodpecker
Sarothrura boehmi	Böhm's Flufftail
Sarothrura lugens lynesi	Lynes's Flufftail
Sarothrura watersi	Waters's Crake
Saucerottia alfaroana	Alfaro's Hummingbird (Extinct)
Saxicola dacotiae	Meade-Waldo's Chat
Saxicola dacotiae murielae	Muriel's Chat (Extinct)
Saxicola insignis	Hodgson's Bush Chat
Saxicola jerdoni	Jerdon's Bush Chat
Saxicola macrorhyncha	Stoliczka's Bush Chat
Sayornis saya	Say's Phoebe
Sceptomycter winifredae	Mrs Moreau's Warbler
Schoutedenapus schoutedeni	Schouteden's Swift
Scissirostrum dubium	Latham's Myna
Scopolax sabini	Sabine's Snipe
Scolopax saturata	Horsfield's Woodcock
Scolopax saturata	Rosenberg's Woodcock
Scotopelia bouvieri	Bouvier's Fishing Owl
Scotopelia peli	Pel's Fishing Owl
Scytalopus magellanicus	Zimmer's Tapaculo
Scytalopus spillmanni	Spillmann's Tapaculo
Seicerus noveboracensis notabilis	Grinell's Waterthrush
Seicercus (burkii) whistleri	Whistler's Warbler
Seicercus (burkii) valentini	Bianchi's Warbler
Selasphorus floresii	Floresi's Flamebearer
Selasphorus sasin	Allen's Hummingbird
Selenidera gouldii	Gould's Toucanet
Selenidera reinwardtii	Langsdorff's Toucanet
Semioptera wallacei	Wallace's Standardwing Bird-of-Paradise
Sephanoides fernandensis	Juan Fernández Firecrown
Sericornis beccarii	Beccari's Scrubwren
Sericulus bakeri	Adelbert's Bowerbird
Sericulus bakeri	Baker's Bowerbird
Sericulus bakeri	Beck's Bowerbird
Serilophus lunatus	Gould's Broadbill
Serilophus lunatus	Hodgson's Broadbill
Serinus koliensis	Van Someren's Canary
Serinus leucopterus	Layard's Seedeater
Serinus reichardi	Reichard's Seedeater
Serinus reichnowi	Reichenow's Serin
Serinus rothschildi	Rothschild's Canary

Serinus symonsi	Symon's Siskin	Stercorarius longicaudus	Buffon's Skua
Serinus syriacus	Tristram's Serin	Stercorarius maccormicki	McCormick's Skua
Serinus xantholaema	Salvadori's Seedeater	Stercorarius parasiticus	Richardson's Skua
Sheppardia aequatorialis	Jackson's Akalat	Sterna antillarum	Brown's Tern
Sheppardia bocagei	Bocage's Akalat	Sterna dougallii	Dougall's Tern
Sheppardia gunningi	Gunning's Robin	Sterna forsteri	Forster's Tern
Sheppardia poensis	Alexander's Akalat	Sterna hirundinacea	Cassin's Tern
Sheppardia sharpei	Sharpe's Akalat	Sterna sandvicensis	
Sialia mexicanus anabelae	Anabel's Bluebird	acuflavidus	Cabot's Tern
Sicalis flaveola pelzelni	Pelzeln's Finch	Sterna saundersii	Saunders's Little Tern
Sicalis raimondii	Raimondi's Yellow Finch	Sterna trudeaui	Trudeau's Tern
Sipodotus wallacei	Wallace's Fairy-wren	Stizoptera (Poephila)	
Sitta cashmirensis	Brooks' Nuthatch	bichenovii	Bicheno's Finch
Sitta krueperi	Krüper's Nuthatch	Streptocitta albertinae	Schlegel's Myna
Sitta leucopsis przewalskii	Prjevalsky's Nuthatch	Streptocitta albicollis	Vieillot's Starling
Sitta neumayer	Neumayer's Nuthatch	Streptopelia reichenowii	Reichenow's Dove
Sitta victoriae	Victoria Nuthatch	Streptoprocne phelpsi	Phelps's Swift
Smithornis capensis delacouri	Delacour's Broadbill	Strix (leptogrammica)	
Somateria fischeri	Fischer's Eider	bartelsi	Bartels' Wood Owl
Spelaeornis chocolatinus	Godwin-Austen's Wren-	Strix butleri	Hume's Owl
	Babbler (Austen's)	Strix davidi	David's Wood Owl
Spenocichla humei	Hume's Wren-Babbler	Strix davidi	Père David's (Wood) Owl
Spermophaga poliogenys	Grant's Bluebill		(David's)
Spheniscus humboldti	Humboldt Penguin	Strix newtoni	Newton's Owl (Extinct)
Sphyrapicus thyroideus	Williamson's Sapsucker	Strix woodfordii	Woodford's Owl
Sphyrapicus thyroideus		Sturnella magna lilianae	Lilian's Meadowlark
nataliae	Natalie's Sapsucker	Sturnella superciliaris	Bonaparte's Blackbird
Spiza townsendi	Townsend's Bunting	Sturnus burmannicus	Jerdon's Starling
Spiza townsendi	Townsend's Finch	Sublegatus obscurior	Todd's Scrub Flycatcher
Spizaetus alboniger	Blyth's Hawk-Eagle	Sula leucogaster	Brewster's Booby
Spizaetus nanus	Wallace's Hawk-Eagle	Swynnertonia swynnertoni	Swynnerton's Forest Robin
Spizaetus nipalensis		Sylvia althaea	Hume's Whitethroat
orientalis	Hodgson's Hawk-Eagle	Sylvia cantillans moltonii	Moltoni's Warbler
Spizella breweri	Brewer's Sparrow	Sylvia deserticola	Tristram's Warbler
Spizella wortheni	Worthen's Sparrow	Sylvia hortensis	Orphean Warbler
Spizixos semitorques	Swinhoe's Finch-billed	Sylvia (sylvia) layardi	Layard's Warbler
	Bulbul	Sylvia leucomelaena	Blandford's Warbler
Spizocorys (Botha)		Sylvia mystacea	Ménétries's Warbler
fringillaris	Botha's Lark	Sylvia ruepelli	Rüppell's Warbler
Spizocorys sclateri	Sclater's Lark	Sylvia sarda	Marmora's Warbler
Sporadinus ricordii	Ricard's Hummingbird	Sylvia (deserticola) ticehursti	Meinertzhagen's Warbler
Sporophila ardesiaca	Dubois' Seedeater	Sylvietta (leucophrys)	
Sporophila bouvronides	Lesson's Seedeater	chapini	Chapin's Crombec
Sporophila falcirostris	Temminck's Seedeater	Sylvietta philippae	Philippa's Crombec
Sporophila torqueola		Sylvietta rufescens ansorgei	Ansorge's Crombec
morelleti	Morellet's Seedeater	Sylviorthorhynchus desmursii	Des Mur's Wiretail
Sporophila torqueola sharpei	Sharpe's Seedeater	Synallaxis azarae	Azara's Spinetail
Sporophila zelichi	Narosky's Seedeater	Synallaxis cabanisi (moesta)	Cabanis's Spinetail
Spreo fischeri	Fischer's Starling	Synallaxis courseni	Blake's Spinetail
Stachyris ambigua		Synallaxis courseni	Coursen's Spinetail
(rufifrons)	Harington's Babbler	Synallaxis (Gyalaphlax)	
Stachyris herberti	Herbert's Babbler	hellmayri	Lafresnaye's Spinetail
Stachyris oglei	Austen's Spotted Babbler	Synallaxis infuscata	Pinto's Spinetail
	(Godwin-Austen's)	Synallaxis macconnelli	McConnell's Spinetail
Stachyris oglei	Ogle's Spotted Babbler	Synallaxis spixi	Spix's Spinetail
Stachyris plateni	Platen's Babbler	Synthliboramphus	
Stachyris rodolphei	Deignan's Babbler	hypoleucus	Xantus's Murrelet
Stachyris rufifrons	Hume's Babbler	Synthliboramphus	
Stachyris speciosa	Tweedale's Babbler	hypoleucus scrippsi	Scripps' Murrelet
	(Walden's)	Syrmaticus ellioti	Elliot's Pheasant
Stachyris whiteheadi	Whitehead's Tree Babbler	Syrmaticus humiae	Mrs Hume's Pheasant
Stactolaema anchietae	Anchieta's Barbet	Syrmaticus humiae humiae	Hume's Bar-tailed Pheasant
Stactolaema whytii	Whyte's Barbet	Syrmaticus mikado	Mikado Pheasant
Stactolaema whytii sowerbyi	Sowerby's Barbet	Syrmaticus reevesi	Reeves' Pheasant
Stactolaema (olivacea)		Syrmaticus soemmerringii	Soemmering's Pheasant
woodwardi	Woodwards' Barbet	Syrmaticus soemmerringii	
Stelgidopteryx (ruficollis)	Ridgway's Rough-winged	ijimae	Ijima's Pheasant
ridgwayi	Swallow	Syrrhaptes paradoxus	Pallas's Sandgrouse
Stellula calliope	Calliope Hummingbird	Tachybaptus pelzelnii	Pelzeln's Grebe
Stephanoxis lalandi	Delalande's Plovercrest	Tachybaptus rufolavatus	Delacour's Little Grebe

Scientific name	Common name
Tachymarptis aequatorialis	Reichenow's Swift
Tachyphonus cristatus nattereri	Natterer's Tanager
Tangara arthus sclateri	Sclater's Tanager
Tangara cabanisi	Cabanis's Tanager
Tangara cyanoptera whitelyi	Whitely's Tanager
Tangara dowii	Dow Tanager
Tangara lavinia	Lavinia's Tanager
Tanygnathus lucionensis hybridus	Salomonsen's Blue-naped Parrot
Tanygnathus sumatranus	Muller's Parrot
Tanygnathus sumatranus burbidgii	Burbidge's Blue-backed Parrot
Tanygnathus sumatranus duponti	Du Pont's Blue-backed Parrot
Tanygnathus sumatranus duponti	Du Pont's Blue-backed Parrot
Tanygnathus sumatranus everetti	Everett's Blue-backed Parrot
Tanygnathus sumatranus freeri	Freer's Blue-backed Parrot
Tauraco bannermani	Bannerman's Turaco
Tauraco fischeri	Fischer's Turaco
Tauraco hartlaubi	Hartlaub's Turaco
Tauraco livingstonii	Reichenow's Turaco
Tauraco livingstonii	Livingstone's Lourie
Tauraco macrorhynchus	Verreaux's Turaco
Tauraco ruspolii	Prince Ruspoli's Turaco
Tauraco schalowi	Schalow's Turaco
Tchagra australis souzae	Souza's Tchagra
Tchagra jamesi	James's Tchagra
Tchagra minuta anchietae	Anchieta's Tchagra
Tchagra tchagra	Levaillant's Bush Shrike
Telecanthura melanopygia	Chapin's Spinetail
Telecanthura ussheri	Ussher's Spinetail
Telophorus (malaconotus) dohertyi	Doherty's Bush Shrike
Telophorus kupeensis	Serle's Bush Shrike
Telophorus viridis	Perrin's Bush Shrike
Tereingaornis moisleyi	Moisley's Penguin (Extinct)
Terpsiphone batesi	Bates' Paradise-flycatcher
Terpsiphone bedfordi	Bedford's Paradise flycatcher
Terpsiphone rufocinerea bannermani	Bannerman's Paradise-flycatcher
Tetraophasis obscurus	Verreaux's Monal Partridge
Tetraophasis szechenyii	Szechenyi's Monal Partridge
Thalassarche carteri	Carter's Albatross
Thalassarche chrysostoma	Gould's Albatross
Thalurania jelskii	Jelski's Woodnymph
Thalurania lerchi	Lerch's Woodnymph
Thalurania tschudi	Tschudi's Woodnymph
Thalurania wagleri	Wagler's Woodnymph
Thalurania watertoni	Waterton's Woodnymph
Thamnolaea (Myrmecocichla) arnoti	Arnott's Chat
Thamnomanes zarumae	Chapman's Antshrike
Thamnophilus bridgesi	Bridges' Antshrike
Thamnophilus cryptoleucus	Castelnau's Antshrike
Thamnophilus stictocephalus	Natterer's Slaty Antshrike
Thaumastura cora	Cora's Shear-tail
Thaumatias milleri	Miller's Emerald
Theristicus branickii	Branicki's Ibis
Thinocorus orbignyianus	D'Orbigny's Seedsnipe
Thraupis abbas	Abbott's Tanager
Thraupis bonariensis darwinii	Darwin's Tanager
Threnetes niger cristinae	Christina's Barbthroat
Threnetes ruckeri	Rucker's Hermit
Thryomanes bewickii	Bewick's Wren
Thryomanes bewickii erimophilus	Baird's Wren
Thryomanes bewickii spiluris	Vigors's Wren
Thryothorus nicefori	Nicefero's Wren
Thryothorus semibadius	Salvin's Wren
Tiaris olivacea	Bryant's Grassquit
Tigrisoma fasciatum salmoni	Salmon's Tiger Heron
Tigrisoma mexicanum	Caboni's Tiger Heron
Tijuca condita	Snow's Cotinga
Tilmatura dupontii	Dupont's Hummingbird
Timolia lerchii	Lerch's Sapphire
Tockus bradfieldi	Bradfield's Hornbill
Tockus deckeni	Von der Decken's Hornbill
Tockus hemprichii	Hemprich's Hornbill
Tockus jacksoni	Jackson's Hornbill
Tockus monteiri	Monteiro's Hornbill
Todiramphus winchelli	Winchell's Kingfisher
Touit purpurata viridiceps	Chapman's Sapphire-rumped Parrotlet
Touit surda ruficauda	Berla's Golden-tailed Parrotlet
Toxostoma bendirei	Bendire's Thrasher
Toxostoma cinereum mearnsii	Mearns' Thrasher
Toxostoma curvirostre	Palmer's Thrasher
Toxostoma lecontei	Le Conte's Thrasher
Toxostoma longirostre	Sennett's Thrasher
Trachyphonus darnaudii	D'Arnaud's Barbet
Trachyphonus vaillantii	Levaillant's Barbet
Tragopan blythii	Blyth's Tragopan
Tragopan blythii molesworthi	Molesworth's Tragopan
Tragopan caboti	Cabot's Tragopan
Tragopan temminckii	Temminck's Tragopan
Travesia lyalli	Travers's Wren
Treron seimundi	Seimund's Green Pigeon
Treron sieboldii	Siebold's Green Pigeon
Treron sphenura korthalsi	Korthals's Green Pigeon
Treron waalia	Bruce's Green Pigeon
Trichastoma (Pellorneum) tickelli	Tickell's Jungle Babbler
Trichastoma buettikoferi	Büttikofer's Babbler
Trichastoma celebense	Strickland's Babbler
Trichastoma pyrrogenys	Temminck's Jungle Babbler
Trichastoma rostratum	Blyth's Jungle Babbler
Trichastoma sepiarium	Horsfield's Babbler
Trichoglossus chlorolepidotus	Maton's Parakeet
Trichoglossus flavoviridis meyeri	Meyer's Lorikeet
Trichoglossus haemotodus brooki	Brook's Lorikeet
Trichoglossus haemotodus capistratus	Edwards' Lorikeet
Trichoglossus haemotodus deplanchii	DePlanche's Lorikeet
Trichoglossus haemotodus forsteni	Forsten's Lorikeet
Trichoglossus haemotodus massena	Massena's Lorikeet (Rivoli's)
Trichoglossus haemotodus mitchellii	Mitchell's Lorikeet
Trichoglossus haemotodus moluccanus	Swainson's Lorikeet
Trichoglossus haemotodus rosenbergi	Rosenberg's Lorikeet
Trichoglossus haemotodus stresemanni	Stresemann' Lorikeet
Trichoglossus haemotodus weberi	Weber's Lorikeet
Trichoglossus johnstoniae	Johnstone's Lorikeet

Tricholimnas lafresnayarus	Lafresnaye's Rail
Tringa guttifer	Armstrong's Sandpiper
Tringa guttifer	Nordmann's Greenshank
Troglodytes cobbi	Cobb's Wren
Trogon bairdii	Baird's Trogon
Trogon massena lessonii	Chapman's Trogon
Turdoides (Argya) earlei	Earle's Babbler
Turdoides hartlaubii	Hartlaub's Babbler
Turdoides hindei	Hinde's Pied Babbler
Turdoides jardineii	Jardine's Babbler
Turdoides leucocephalus	Cretzschmar's Babbler
Turdoides malcolmi	Malcolm's Babbler
Turdoides sharpei	Sharpe's Pied Babbler
Turdus feae	Fea's Thrush
Turdus grayi	Gray's Robin
Turdus graysoni	Grayson's Thrush
Turdus hauxwelli	Hauxwell's Thrush
Turdus kessleri	Kessler's Thrush
Turdus kessleri	Prjevalsky's Thrush
Turdus lawrencii	Lawrence's Thrush
Turdus mupinensis	Verreaux's Song Thrush
Turdus naumanni	Naumann's Thrush
Turdus olivaceus oldeani	Oldean's Thrush
Turdus olivaceus roehli	Roehl's Thrush
Turdus olivaceus swynnertoni	Swynnerton's Thrush
Turdus plebejus	Cabanis's Thrush
Turdus reevei	Reeve's Thrush
Turdus rufopalliatus	Grayson's Robin
Turdus subalaris	Behn's Thrush
Turdus swalesi	La Selle's Thrush
Turdus unicolor	Tickell's Thrush
Turnix everatti	Everett's Buttonquail
Turnix olivei	Olive's Quail
Turnix olivei	Robinson's Buttonquail
Turnix suscitator powelli	Powell's Buttonquail
Turnix worcesteri	Worcester's Buttonquail
Tympanuchus cupido attwateri	Attwater's Prairie Chicken
Tyrannus apolites	Heine's Kingbird
Tyrannus couchii	Couch's Kingbird
Tyrannus melancholicus	Lichtenstein's Kingbird
Tyrannus vociferans	Cassin's Kingbird
Tyto rosenbergi	Rosenberg's Owl
Tyto soumagnei	Soumagne's Owl
Unknown – see note in Section U	Cabanis's Batis
Unknown – see note in Section U	Harris's Hornbill
Unknown – see note in Section U	Heuglin's Starling
Unknown – see note in Section U	Moreau's Bustard
Unknown – see note in Section U	Reichenow's Reed Warbler
Uria lomvia	Brünnich's Guillemot
Uria lomvia	Pallas's Murre
Urocissa whiteheadi	Whitehead's Magpie
Urocynchramus pylzowi	Prjevalsky's Rosefinch
Urosphena whiteheadi	Whitehead's Stubtail
Vermivora bachmanii	Bachman's Warbler (Extinct)
Vermivora luciae	Lucy's Warbler
Vermivora pinus x Vermivora chrysoptera	Brewster's Warbler
Vermivora pinus x Vermivora chrysoptera	Lawrence's Warbler
Vermivora virginiae	Virginia's Warbler
Vidua codringtoni	Codrington's Indigobird
Vidua fischeri	Fischer's Whydah
Vidua wilsoni	Wilson's Widowfinch
Vini kuhlii	Kuhl's Lorikeet
Vini stepheni	Stephen's Lory
Vireo bellii	Bell's Vireo
Vireo caribaeus	St Andres Vireo
Vireo carmioli	Carmiol's Vireo
Vireo gilvus	Swainson's Vireo
Vireo huttoni	Frazar's Vireo
Vireo huttoni	Hutton's Vireo
Vireo huttoni obscurus	Anthony's Vireo
Vireo huttoni stephensi	Stephen's Vireo
Vireo nelsoni	Nelson's Vireo
Vireo solitarius	Cassin's Vireo
Wetmorethraupis sterrhopteron	Wetmore's Tanager
Wilsonia pusilla	Wilson's Warbler
Woodfordia lacertosa	Sanford's White-eye
Woodfordia superciliosa	Woodford's White-eye
Xanthotis polygramma	Gray's Honeyeater
Xema sabini	Sabine's Gull
Xenicus longipes variabilis	Stead's Bush Wren (Extinct)
Xenoligea montana	Chapman's Warbler
Xenopirostris damii	Van Dam's Vanga
Xenopirostris polleni	Pollen's Vanga
Xenopirostris xenopirostris	Lafresnaye's Vanga
Xiphocolaptes franciscanus	Snethlage's Woodcreeper
Xiphorhynchus erythropygius aequatorialis	Berlepsch's's Woodcreeper
Xiphorhynchus necopinus	Zimmer's Woodcreeper
Xiphorhynchus spixii	Spix's Woodcreeper
Xiphorhynchus spixii insignis	Hellmayr's's Woodcreeper
Xiphorhynchus spixii juruanus	Ihering's Woodcreeper
Yuhina bakeri	Baker's Yuhina
Yuhina bakeri	Blyth's Yuhina
Zavattariornis stresemanni	Stresemann's Bush-Crow
Zenaida aurita	Zenaide Dove
Zimmerius viridiflavus	Tschudi's Tyrannulet
Zonotrichia leucophrys gambeli	Gambel's Sparrow
Zonotrichia leucophrys nuttalli	Nuttall's Sparrow
Zonotrichia querula	Harris's Sparrow
Zoothera andromedae	Andromeda Thrush
Zoothera cameronensis graueri	Grauer's Ground Thrush
Zoothera crossleyi	Crossley's Ground Thrush
Zoothera dauma	White's Thrush
Zoothera everetti	Everett's Thrush
Zoothera gurneyi	Gurney's Ground Thrush
Zoothera heinei	Heine's Ground Thrush
Zoothera horsfieldi	Horsfield's Thrush
Zoothera interpres	Kuhl's Ground Thrush
Zoothera kibalensis	Prigogine's Golden Thrush
Zoothera oberlaenderi	Oberlaender's Rock Thrush
Zoothera peronii	Peroni's Ground Thrush
Zoothera terrestris	Kittlitz's Thrush (Extinct)
Zosterops everetti	Everett's White-eye
Zosterops explorator	Layard's White-eye
Zosterops finschii	Finsch's White-eye
Zosterops fuscicapillus crookshanki	Crookshank's White-eye
Zosterops kirki	Kirk's White-eye
Zosterops kuehni	Kuhn's White-eye
Zosterops luteirostris	Hartert's White-eye
Zosterops meeki	Meek's White-eye
Zosterops metcalfii	Metcalfe's White-eye
Zosterops murphyi	Murphy's White-eye
Zosterops poliogaster	Heuglin's White-eye
Zosterops wallacei	Wallace's White-eye